Lecture Notes in Artificial Intelligence 2504

Subseries of Lecture Notes in Computer Science
Edited by J. G. Carbonell and J. Siekmann

Lecture Notes in Computer Science

Edited by G. Goos, J. Hartmanis, and J. van Leeuwen

Springer
Berlin
Heidelberg
New York
Barcelona
Hong Kong
London
Milan
Paris
Tokyo

M.Teresa Escrig   Francisco Toledo
Elisabet Golobardes (Eds.)

Topics in
Artificial Intelligence

5th Catalonian Conference on AI, CCIA 2002
Castellón, Spain, October 24-25, 2002
Proceedings

Springer

Series Editors

Jaime G. Carbonell, Carnegie Mellon University, Pittsburgh, PA, USA
Jörg Siekmann, University of Saarland, Saarbrücken, Germany

Volume Editors

M. Teresa Escrig
Francisco Toledo
Universitat Jaume 1
Departament d'Enginyeria i Ciència dels Computadors
Campus de Riu Sec, 12071 Castellón, Spain
E-mail:{escrigm/toledo}@icc.uji.es

Elisabet Golobardes
Universitat Ramon Llull
Computer Science Department
Passeig Bonanova, 8, 08022 Barcelona, Catalunya, Spain
E-mail: elisabet@salleURL.edu

Cataloging-in-Publication Data applied for

Bibliograhpic information published by Die Deutsche Bibliothek
Die Deutsche Bibliothek lists this publication in the Deutsche Nationalbibliografie;
detailed bibliographic data is available in the Internet at http://dnb.ddb.de

ISSN 0302-9743
ISBN 3-540-00011-9 Springer-Verlag Berlin Heidelberg New York

Springer-Verlag Berlin Heidelberg New York,
a member of BertelsmannSpringer Science+Business Media GmbH

http://www.springer.de

© Springer-Verlag Berlin Heidelberg 2002
Printed in Germany

Typesetting: Camera-ready by author, data conversion by PTP-Berlin, Stefan Sossna
Printed on acid-free paper   SPIN: 10870839   06/3142   5 4 3 2 1 0

Preface

The papers included in this volume were presented at the Catalonian Conference on Artificial Intelligence, which was held in Castellón, Spain on October 24–25, 2002. The main aim of the 5th Catalonian Conference on Artificial Intelligence (CCIA 2002) was to get the Catalonian Artificial Intelligence community together for a fruitful interchange of ideas, allowing researchers to get a quick overview of the local state of the art. Another important aim of the conference was to promote collaborations among research groups in the community.

Seventy-seven contributed papers were submitted. The program committee selected 48 among them, after considering the reviews provided by at least two referees per paper. Among these 48 accepted papers, 37 were original papers and therefore they were included in this volume. The number of submitted papers and the number of rejected papers had increased with respect to the last conference.

In this volume, final versions of the accepted papers incorporating the reviewers' comments have been included. We have arranged the contents into five subjects: Reasoning Models, Constraint Satisfaction, Machine Learning and Classification, Multi-Agent Systems, and Computer Vision and Robotics.

In the first subject, *Reasoning Models*, six of the 11 papers included deal with qualitative reasoning, four papers deal with case-based reasoning, and the other paper deals with representing dynamic processes.

In the second subject, *Constraint Satisfaction*, three papers were included two of them contain theoretical results and the other one combines Petri Nets with Constraint Satisfaction methodology to represent manufacturing architectures and production logistics.

In the third subject, *Machine Learning and Classification*, six of the eight papers included in the proceedings deal with classification of knowledge, another paper evaluates algorithms which perform feature selection for improving the inductive learner, and the remaining paper evaluates algorithms for record linkage.

The use of the *Multi-Agent System* (MAS) paradigm has increased sharply, and it's now an important field within Artificial Intelligence. In fact, many papers on this subject were received, from which five were included in this volume. The topics of these papers are very different: real-time MAS; the combination of MAS with case-based reasoning for autonomous learning from experience; the combination of MAS with learning and fuzzy logic for robot navigation; the application of MAS for organizing the procurement of organs and tissues for transplantation purposes; and the application of several approaches based on ant colony optimization to solve the resource constraint project scheduling problem.

For the last subject, *Computer Vision and Robotics*, one paper deals with robot path planning, and the other nine papers deal with topics of computer vision, each very different and interesting: 3-D reconstruction; face classification; recognition of textures from different distances; unsupervised approach to image segmentation; the use of panoramic images for motion segmentation; unsupervised parameterization of Gaussian Mixture Models; real-time visual inspection and classification of cork stoppers; the fusion of information from angiograms and intravascular ultrasound images; and an application to seek people wearing specific clothes.

CCIA 2002 was organized by the *Asociació Catalana d'Intel·ligència Artificial* (ACIA) which promotes this conference and the Universitat Jaume I de Castelló, the hosting institution. Support for this event was provided by the Asociació Catalana d'Intel·ligència Artificial, the Departamento de Ingeniería y Ciencia de los Computadores de la Universitat Jaume I, the Fundació Caixa Castelló-Bancaixa, British Petroleum Oil Castellón, Generalitat Valenciana, and the Ministerio de Educación y Ciencia.

We would like to express our sincere gratitude to all the authors for making the conference and this book possible with their contributions and participation. We sincerely thank the members of the organizing and program committees, and the reviewers, for their invaluable efforts in helping with the preparation of this event. We explicitly want mention the invaluable effort of Feliciano Manzano Casas. Thanks also to the invited speakers, Christian Freksa and José del R. Millán.

The global assessment of the contributions contained in this volume is positive. They give a representative sample of the current state of the art in the Catalonian Artificial Intelligence community.

July 2002   Maria Teresa Escrig Monferrer
                                                  Francisco Toledo Lobo

Organization

CCIA 2002 was organized by the Departamento de Ingeniería y Ciencia de los Computadores, Universitat Jaume I and the Asociació Catalana d'Intel·ligència Artificial.

General Chair

Maria Teresa Escrig Monferrer

Program Committee

Elisabet Golobardes (EALS-URL)
Francisco Toledo Lobo (ICC-UJI)

Scientific Committee

Núria Agell (ESADE-URL)
Joseph Aguilar (Tou-UPC)
Isabel Aguilo (UIB)
M. Isabel Alfonso (CCIA-UA)
Cecilio Angulo (GREC-UPC)
Ester Bernardó (URL)
Vicent Botti (UPV)
Nuria Castell (UPC)
Andreu Català (UPC)
Enric Cervera (ICC-UJI)
Ulises Cortés (UPC)
Ana García (UPM)
Luis A. García (ICC-UJI)
Rafael García (UGi)
Elisabet Golobardes (EALS)
Maria Teresa Escrig (ICC-UJI)
César Fernández (UdL)
Pilar Fuster (UIB)
Josep M. Garrell (EALS-URL)
Antoni Grau (ESAI-UPC)

Angeles Lopez (ICC-UJI)
Lluís Marquez (UPC)
Joan Martí (Ugi)
Gregorio Martín (UV)
Mario Martín (UPC)
Andrés Marzal (LSI-UJI)
Joaquim Melendez (Ugi)
Antonio Moreno (URV)
Xavier Parra (GREC-UPC)
Enric Plaza (IIIA-CSIC)
Miguel A. Piera (UAB)
Filiberto Pla (LSI-UJI)
Monique Polit (Uper)
Josep Puyol (IIIA-CSIC)
David Riaño (URV)
Horacio Rodríguez (UPC)
Miquel Sánchez (UPC)
José M. Sanchiz (ICC-UJI)
Carles Sierra (IIIA-CSIC)
Vicenc Torra (IIIA-CSIC)

Organization Committee

José M. Badía

Enrique Cervera

Luis A. García

Angeles López

Feliciano Manzano

Begoña Martínez

Gloria Martínez

Lledo Museros

Julio Pacheco

José M. Sanchiz

Sponsoring Institutions

Asociació Catalana d'Intel·ligència Artificial

British Petroleum Oil Castellón

Depart. de Ingeniería y Ciencia de los Computadores, Universitat Jaume I

Fundació Caixa Castelló-Bancaixa

Generalitat Valenciana

Ministerio de Educación y Ciencia

Table of Contents

Machine Learning and Classification

MultiAgent Systems

Computer Vison and Robotics

Components for Case-Based Reasoning Systems

Chema Abásolo, Enric Plaza, and Josep-Lluís Arcos

IIIA - Artificial Intelligence Research Institute
CSIC - Spanish Council for Scientific Research
Campus UAB, 08193 Bellaterra, Catalonia, Spain.
{abasolo,enric,arcos}@iiia.csic.es
http://www.iiia.csic.es

Abstract. In this paper we present CAT-CBR a component-based platform for developing CBR systems. CAT-CBR uses UPML (Universal Problem-solving Methods Language) for specifying CBR components. A collection of CBR components for retrieval of propositional cases is presented in detail. The CAT-CBR platform guides the engineer using a case-based recommendations system to develop a configuration of components that satisfies the requirements of a CBR system application. We also present how to develop a runtime CBR application from the configuration resultant of the configuring process.

Keywords: CBR, Knowledge modeling.

1 Introduction

Developing a CBR system is a very complex problem, many decisions have to be taken during the development. These decisions concern to the techniques we want to use and how they can be integrated in the CBR system; also a representation model of the cases must be chosen, according to the domain where the CBR system will be applied.

Knowledge modelling aims on solving this kind of problems, developing complex software systems. The approach we take is to model the different techniques or components as Problem-Solving Methods. These Problem-Solving Methods represent reasoning processes or software components that achieve a specific task.

UPML is used to specify these components. UPML is a language that allows us to describe Problem-Solving Methods, Tasks, Domain Models and the Ontologies used by them. UPML also provides, as a software architecture, connectors (Bridges) for these components.

In this paper we present the CAT-CBR platform; a platform for developing CBR systems. CAT-CBR provides to the engineer a library of CBR components that he can combine in an application (a CBR system). The platform provides to the engineer recommendations of which components will fit better to the requirements; these recommendations are given using a case-based recommendation system based on previous applications developed using CAT-CBR. Finally

M.T. Escrig Monferrer and F. Toledo Lobo (Eds.): CCIA 2002, LNAI 2504, pp. 1–16, 2002.

CAT-CBR gives the possibility to the engineer of generating a runtime application from the configuration he has made; this process of generating a runtime application has two parts: one automatic and the other has to be done manually by the engineer.

The paper is divided in the following sections. First, in section 2, the general aspects of the platform are presented. Section 3 presents a brief description of UPML. In section 4 we present the UPML library of CBR components. After this section 5 describes the process of configuring a CBR system using the platform. Section 6 describes how the platform operationalizes a CBR system. Finally section 7 presents some conclusions and future work.

2   The **CAT-CBR** Platform

In this section, we present the general concepts of the CAT-CBR platform. This platform uses a library of CBR components to guide the engineer in the development of CBR systems. These components describe the different tasks that can appear in a CBR system and also the problem-solving methods that can be applied to these tasks. That drives us to work with these components in a problem-solving methods framework. The CAT-CBR platform has been developed on Noos platform [2]. Noos uses *feature terms* as representation language. Noos is a platform used for developing CBR systems.

To describe CBR components, inside this framework, we have used UPML (Universal Problem-solving Methods Language) [5]. UPML is a language for specifying components of knowledge systems. Two levels can be differentiated in a component description: a specification level —where we use UPML— and an operational level; as operational language we use Noos, defining functions that implement the components. Using UPML and feature terms a library of CBR components has been specified.

The goal of CAT-CBR is, given the requirements of an engineer, to develop a CBR application; to achieve this objective two processes has been specified: Configuration Process and Operationalization Process. The configuration process consists in selecting different components and connect them in order to specify an application. The CAT-CBR has an interactive tool where the engineer chooses the components to be included in the application. This tool is built over a CBR system that guides and gives support to the engineer during this configuration process. Section 5 explains in more detail this configuration process.

Finally, the operationalization process takes an application specification (in the form of a configuration of components) and generates an executable application. The approach we have taken to operationalize a configuration is that the platform generates a file that links the Noos methods following the structure of the configuration of components. This operationalization process is described in more detail in section 6.

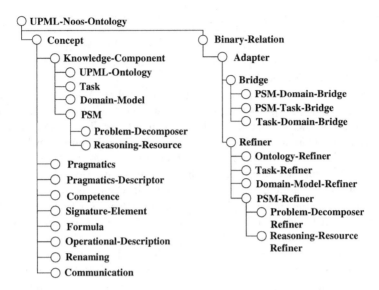

Fig. 1. The UPML hierarchy of elements.

3   The UPML Language

Problem-Solving Methods are reusable components for implementing the reasoning part of knowledge-based systems. The UPML language aims at describing and implementing such architectures and components to facilitate their semiautomatic reuse and adaptation.

UPML provides both a framework and a language to describe libraries of knowledge components and their relationships to form knowledge systems. UPML is a software architecture that defines a set of components and connectors between these components. Figure 1 shows the hierarchy of the different components and connectors defined in UPML.

There are three main entities in the UPML: Tasks, Problem-Solving Methods and Domain Models.

A *Tasks* specifies the goals to be achieved by the Problem Solving Methods of the library. A Task is characterized by its input roles and output roles together with preconditions and postconditions. Input and output roles describe the types of elements used as input and the type of the result of the task. Preconditions describe some properties needed by the task to be achieved; and postconditions describe the properties that we get when a task is achieved.

Problem-Solving Methods (PSM) describe which reasoning steps and which types of knowledge are needed to perform a task. A PSM specifies a particular way to solve a task. The main attributes of a PSM are the input/output roles, plus the preconditions and postconditions to be fulfilled by the input and output roles. These attributes determine when a PSM can solve a task. There are two subclasses of PSM: *Problem Decomposers* and *Reasoning Resources*. Problem Decomposers specify decomposition of tasks into subtasks and the data flow between the different subtasks (*operational description*). Reasoning Resources are the elementary PSMs; they specify how to solve a task using external knowledge described as Domain Models.

A *Domain Model* characterizes domain knowledge. A Domain Model consists of three elements: properties, meta-knowledge, and domain knowledge itself. The meta-knowledge captures the implicit and explicit assumptions made while building a Domain Model of the real world. The domain knowledge is the explicit knowledge of a Domain Model. The domain knowledge is build under the assumption that the meta-knowledge is true. Properties are statements of the domain knowledge and can be directly used in the configuration.

The UPML framework has the notion of *Ontology*. An Ontology defines a vocabulary used to describe the properties of the previous components. In our case we have an ontology for describing CBR concepts (section 4.1).

Finally UPML as a software architecture, defines different connectors between previous entities; these connectors are called bridges, and allow the interaction between two different entities. There are three kind of bridges, depending os which components it connects: PSM-Task Bridges, PSM-Domain Bridges and Task-Domain Bridges.

The different characteristics of the entities described above are defined using an Object Language. UPML leaves open the decision of which Object Language is used to describe the components. This Object Language will be used by the inference process in the configuration of an application. In our case, as the platform has been built over Noos platform, the Object Language is Feature Terms and the inference process is that of term subsumption [2].

The CAT-CBR platform supports in part the UPML software architecture. In particular, some assumptions have been made to focus on the characteristics that we deem more useful for CBR system engineering. Specifically, CAT-CBR does not support automatic use of bridges. In practice this amounts to two effects: first, the PSM-Domain and Task-Domain bridges need be defined manually by the engineer; second, PSM-Task bridges are not need because CAT-CBR uses only one CBR-ontology to describe Tasks and PSMs.

4   CBR Components Library

The main idea of a CBR system is to use past situations (cases) to solve a new problem. A case is composed by a past problem and the solution to this problem. A CBR system entails four phases: Retrieve, Reuse, Revise and Retain [1], as shown in Figure 2. In CAT-CBR we are developing components for three stages: Retrieve, Reuse and Retain. The Revise phase is not incorporated in the library of components, because normally this process is done by an expert externally.

Currently, Retrieve PSMs for propositional cases and relational cases have been analyzed and implemented. In Reuse we have started adding to the library

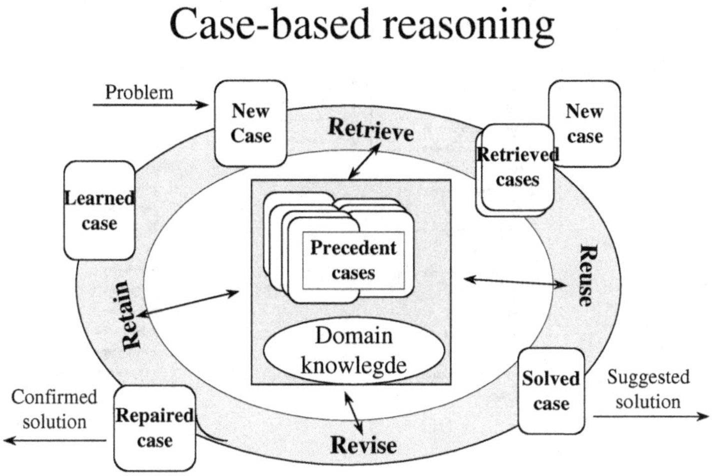

Case-based reasoning

Fig. 2. The CBR cycle [1].

of components for classification, and some components for adaptation, as Constructive Adaptation [12]. We plan to incorporate components for the Retain phase in the future.

First we will present a vocabulary (ontology) used to describe CBR components (section 4.1). Then we will introduce a description of some components for the Retrieve and Reuse stages (section 4.2).

4.1   CBR Components Ontology

As it is presented in section 3, the UPML entities (Tasks and PSMs) are described using an ontology. In this section we present briefly the ontology defined for describing CBR components. This ontology allow us to describe the preconditions and postconditions, the assumptions and the type of the input and output roles of tasks and PSMs. Moreover, these concepts can be used to describe the type of knowledge and its properties used in a Domain Model.

Let us start with the concepts used to characterize preconditions, postconditions and assumptions of the components.

The CBR ontology is organized by different groups of concepts. A first group of concepts characterize performance issues of the components. In this group we have, as example, concepts that describe: the noise tolerance of a component (High Noise Tolerant, Noise Tolerant and Low Noise Tolerant), the accuracy of component (High Accuracy, Medium Accuracy and Low Accuracy), the space and time consumption (Low and High Space Consumption, and Low and High Time Consumption) and tolerance with missing values in the data.

Fig. 3. Hierarchy of concepts defined in the CBR Ontology

Furthermore we need concepts to characterize properties of the inputs and output roles of the components. A retrieval PSM can return only a set of cases with no order, a set of cases partially ordered or a set of cases ranked by similarity. To characterize these properties the ontology has concepts such as: retrieve-similar-cases, retrieve-similar-cases-with-similarity.

Moreover, in this vocabulary there are concepts for describing the types of inputs and outputs used by a task or PSM, and the knowledge of a Domain Model. In this way we have, for example, *Dtree-Model* (that represents a Decision Tree), *Case-Base-Model* and *Case-Language-Model* (that represents the language of attributes used to describe propositional cases). Other models in CAT-CBR include: *Weight-Model* and *Order-Model* (used for aggregation PSMs); and *k-Model* (used in the *k-NN-Retrieval*).

4.2 CBR Components

In this section we will explain in detail part of the library, specifically we will focus on tasks and PSMs for retrieval with propositional cases[1]. Also we describe other Tasks and PSMs for classification (Retrieve and Reuse).

The process to construct this library involves analyzing existing techniques from a task-method decomposition point of view. Once this analysis is made, the different components are specified in UPML. The conclusion is that different components can be used in a same problem decomposition, giving us the notion of families of PSMs for solving a task.

---

[1] PSMs for relational cases include: LAUD, LID and Perspectives, but they are not presented here for lack of space.

The family of PSMs related with k-Nearest Neighbour can be described as a problem decomposer with two subtasks: *Assess-Similarity* and *Select-k*. These PSMs are used with propositional cases and achieves the retrieve stage. Figure 4 shows this decomposition and the different PSMs that can be applied for its subtasks, which are described below.

The *Asses-Similarity* task is achieved for propositional cases by a problem decomposer, called *Feature-Similarity-and-Aggregation*. This component has to subtasks: *Feature-Similarity*, that evaluates the similarity of the attributes one by one, and *Aggregation*, that aggregate the similarities of the attributes in an unique value. The *Feature-Similarity* task can be solved by two reasoning resources, depending if the cases have missing values or not; these two components are: *Feature-Similarity-without-Missing-Values* and *Feature-Similarity-with-Missing-Values*. For the *Aggregation* task the following PSMs can be applied: *City-Block-Aggregation*, *Euclidean-Aggregation*, *Txebitxev-Aggregation*, *Weighted Mean*, *OWA* and *WOWA*. These three first PSMs do not need any additional domain model to aggregate the *Feature Similarity*; while the others need a *Weight Model* of the attributes to achieve *Aggregation* (in *Weighted-Mean* and *WOWA*), and a *Order Model* between the attributes in *OWA* and *WOWA*. For other type of cases, more complex and more expressive, new PSMs will be added to the platform for achieving *Assess-Similarity* task.

For the *Select-k* task different PSMs can be applied depending on the available domain model. These PSMs are reasoning resources that use a model of k. These are the PSMs included in the library:

k-selection: It is a reasoning resource that uses a unique k as model to select the cases. It returns the k nearest neighbors of the problem. The value of k can be learned using techniques like leave-one-out or can be given by the engineer.

k-selection-case: It is a reasoning resource that adaptively selects a value of k for a problem given a *k-case model* (a model characterizing for each case in the Case Base the k values that are better classifying that case).

Group-selection-class: It is a reasoning resource that uses a *k-class model* (this model has a k value for each class). This reasoning resource returns the neighbors grouped by classes (*Grouping Model*).

Group-selection-cluster: It is a reasoning resource that uses k-cluster model (this model has a k value for each cluster). This reasoning resource returns the neighbors grouped by clusters (*Grouping Model*).

The CBR library also includes PSMs for learning this different models of k given a Case Base.

Another family of PSMs for the Retrieve phase use Decision Trees to retrieve similar cases. Retrieval using *Decision-Trees* is a PSM that uses a Decision Tree model indexing cases in a Case Base. This Decision Tree model has cases in its leaves nodes; the cases in a leaf node are those which satisfy all the test nodes in the path from the root to the leaf. There are four reasoning resources that solve Decision Tree Retrieval task:

DT-Retrieval: It is a reasoning resource that assumes no unknown values on the current problem. *DT-Retrieval-Missing-Values*: It is a reasoning resource

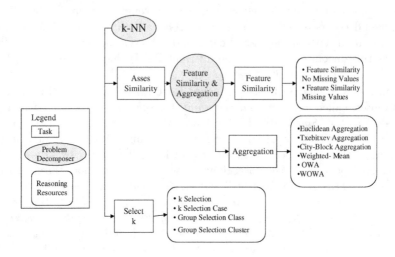

Fig. 4. K Nearest Neighbour decomposition and the different PSMs that can be applied.

that retrieves a set of cases from a decision tree allowing missing values in the current problem. When a missing value is found the PSM returns all the cases found on the leaves under the node where the missing value has been found. *DT-Retrieval-MostFV*: in this reasoning resource when a missing value is found, the PSM evaluates which is the most frequent value and continues the retrieve through this branch. *DT-Retrieval-AllBranch*: in this reasoning resource when a missing value is found, this PSM continues the retrieve process through all the branches (notice that this PSM is different from *DT-Retrieval-Missing-Values* in that it continues the retrieve process while *DT-Retrieval-Missing-Values* stops the retrieve process in the node where a missing value is found).

The library has two PSMs for inducing Decision Trees:

DT-Construction: It is a problem decomposer that has three subtasks: *Stop-Criteria*, *Select-Test* and *Branching*. The PSM evaluates whether a collection of cases satisfies the *Stop-Criteria*. If they do not satisfy it, then *Select-Test* determines the best criteria to split the collection into subcollections. After this, *Branching* generates all the branches for each subcollection. This PSM is applied recursively until all the final branches satisfy the *Stop-Criteria*. *DT-Construction-Pruning*: It is a problem decomposer that works in the same way than the previous one, but after the decision tree is made, a *Pruning* task eliminates branches in the Decision Tree in such a way that the accuracy improves.

The two main subtasks in these two PSMs are *Select-Test* and *Pruning*. For *Select-Test* task the library has several heuristic reasoning resources: *Gain* [13], *Chi-Square* ([6],[11]), *G-Statistic* [11], *GINI-Index* [4], *Gain-Ratio* [8] and *RLM-Distance* [10]. For *Pruning* task the library has the following reasoning resources:

Reasoning-Resource		
Feature	**Range**	**Default**
Name	String	
Pragmatics	Pragmatics	
Ontologies	Upml-Ontology	Empty-Set
Communication	Communication	
Input-Roles	Var	Empty-Set
Output-Roles	Var	Empty-Set
Competence	Competence	
Knowledge-Roles	Signature-Element	Empty-Set
Assumptions	Formula	Empty-Set

Fig. 5. Features of a *reasoning resource* and default values.

Error-Complexity [4], *Critical-Value* [7], *Minimum-Error* [14], *Reduce-Error* [9] and *Pessimistic-Error* [8].

Classification. Classification in CBR can be described as a problem decomposer with two subtasks; a *Retrieve* task and a *Reuse* task. For the retrieve task, the PSMs that can be applied are the ones described above. Reuse is a task that receives a *Similarity Model* (from the retrieve task) holding the cases retrieved that are more similar to current problem. The goal of the *Reuse* task is to determine a class for the current problem based on the information of the similarity model. For the reuse task the following three PSMs are included in the library:

Majority-Classification: This is a reasoning resource that selects the majority class from the set of cases in the similarity model. *Probabilistic-Classification*: This is a reasoning resource that selects a class probabilistically from the set of cases in the similarity model. *Grouping-Classification* is a reasoning resource that selects the most representative class, using a *Grouping-Model* (this is a model obtained from PSMs *Group-Selection-Class* and *Group-Selection-Cluster*). This similarity model has a grouping for each class. The reasoning resource determines the grouping that is best (according to an entropic criterion) and classifies in the class of that grouping.

5   CBR System Configuration

Before explaining the configuration process itself, the representation of the elements used in the CAT-CBR will be introduced. As is presented before, this platform is developed on the Noos platform, and the representation language are feature terms.

CAT-CBR uses feature terms to represent both UPML and the Object Language. That is to say, every element of UPML is represented as a feature term and every type of UPML element is represented as a sort; see, for instance, figure 5 where a sort for *Reasoning Resource* is shown.

User-Consult		
Feature	**Range**	**Default**
Task	Task	Empty-Set
Preconditions	Formula	Empty-Set
Postconditions	Formula	Empty-Set
Inputs	Signature-Element	Empty-Set
Knowledge-Roles	Domain-Model	Empty-Set

Fig. 6. Features and default values of the *Consult* sort.

The configuration process starts with an engineer input, that is what we call a *Consult*. A Consult contains the requirements for the target application, specifying its inputs, preconditions and postconditions, plus the Domain Models available for configuring an application. As preconditions the engineer describes all the properties that he can assure that are true, while the postconditions represents the properties that he wants to be satisfied by the application. Figure 6 shows the Consult sort.

A target application will be a configuration of components of the library that satisfies the consult. A configuration specifies a PSM for each Task. A PSM can be decomposed in new subtasks (problem decomposer) or be elementary (reasoning resource). A configuration also specifies which Domain Models available will be used by each reasoning resource. Figure 7 shows an example of configuration.

The configuration process has been developed as a case-based recommendation. CAT-CBR needs information about past configurations in order of giving the recommendations to the engineer. These past configurations are modeled as *Configuration Case*, and are stored in a Case Base.

Once we have seen the representation of the components and some extra elements, let us start describing the configuring process.

First of all, the engineer has to determine his requirements of the CBR system he wants to develop. For that purpose, CAT-CBR presents a first interface to the engineer (see fig.8) where he can select the goals, assumptions, inputs and domain models (knowledge that is available) for his CBR system and that constitutes the Consult. After this the platform searches, in the configuration-case case base, for a past configuration that satisfies these requirements; if there is one configuration, the CAT-CBR presents to the engineer the possibility of reusing this past configuration as a solution.

During the configuring process, the engineer selects a task as top level task of his CBR system. Then, CAT-CBR presents to the engineer an ordered list of PSMs that can be used to solve that task. The PSMs presented by the system are those which *match* with the task, in the sense of component matching explained presently.

Fig. 7. A Configuration of a CBR application, where balls represent tasks, triangles represents PSMs and containers represents domain models.

Component matching has two parts, signature matching and specification matching. Thus, for two components, a task and a PSM, they match when they have signature matching and specification matching.

Signature matching requires that their input and output signatures match, and in our context this means that a problem-solving method has input and output signatures that are equal or that refine those of a task.

Moreover, specification matching requires that a problem-solving method has weaker preconditions than a task and stronger postconditions than a task.

The PSMs are presented, to the engineer using a case-based recommendation criterion. First it computes the similarity of the new consult with the consults of the configuration-case case base. This similarity measure allows us to derive a ranking of the most similar configurations to the new problem. As similarity function we have used LAUD [3], that evaluates the similarity between two structures of feature terms. The PSMs are ordered using this ranking in such a way, a PSM is better than other one if the configuration where it appears is more similar than the other one.

Once the PSMs are presented, the engineer selects the one that will be used to solve the task. To make this selection easier to the engineer, the interface presents some extra information (see Fig.9). This extra information includes the

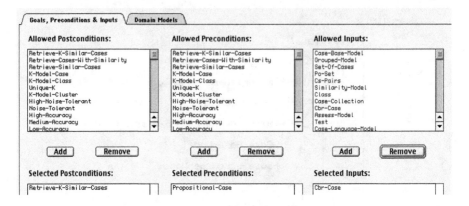

Fig. 8. Interface that shows the options to the engineer to start the configuring process.

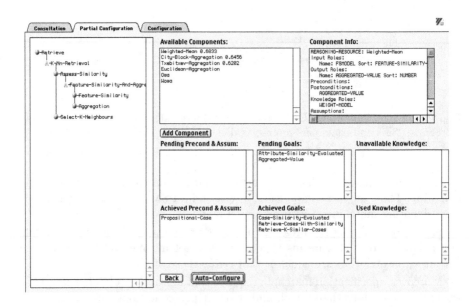

Fig. 9. Interface that shows a partial configuration and all the extra information.

goals and assumptions that are achieved and the ones that are not yet satisfied in the partial configuration. Also the interface shows the specification of the PSMs that match a particular task.

The process of selecting PSMs for each open task continues until the partial configuration is considered a final one. A configuration is final when: a) all the requirements of the engineer are achieved and b) it is complete. A configuration is complete when all the tasks have a PSM to solve them and all the domain models needed by the reasoning resources of a configuration are available.

During the configuration process the engineer can take back his decisions; moreover he can use an auto-configure option, this starts an automatic configuring process starting in the last partial configuration. This automatic process is done using Constructive Adaptation [12]. This automatic process is a best-first search process in the space of legal configurations. Constructive Adaptation uses similarity with past configurations to direct the search process. The search is exhaustive, so cases are used only to order the sequence in which alternatives are considered. Once the process is ended the engineer can store the configuration in the Configuration case base.

6   Operationalization

The configuration process yield a configuration of UPML components (see fig.7). A configuration must be operationalized to get an executable application. As we have seen a configuration is a task-method decomposition. To operationalize a configuration, the different PSMs that solve the tasks and the Domain Models used by the reasoning resources must be linked. CAT-CBR provides support for operationalizing a CBR system. CAT-CBR provides the "glue code" that links the implementations of the different PSMs following the structure of the configuration. CAT-CBR does not generate automatically the connectors between reasoning resources and Domain Models; these connectors must be manually defined by the engineer.

The two kinds of PSMs (problem decomposer and reasoning resource) have different implementation. First, the *problem decomposer* has an operational description; this expresses the control and data flow between the different subtasks of a PSM. In our case the operational description is described in a functional way. Let us see an example, we present, for instance, the operational description of the *k-NN-Retrieval* Problem Decomposer:

```
(use-subtask
        (Select-K-Neighbours
            Problem
            (use-subtask
              (Assess-Similarity Problem))))
```

This Problem Decomposer (PD) has two subtasks (*Assess-Similarity* and *Select-k-Neighbours*) and one input (*Problem* of sort CBR-Problem). The operational description expresses (with the use-subtask construct) that the *Assess-Similarity* subtask has as input Problem (the input of *k-NN-Retrieval*) and that *Select-k-Neighbours* has as inputs the Problem and the result of the Assess-Similarity task.

On the other hand, a Reasoning Resource (RR) solves a Task using input roles and some domain models. For instance, the *K-Selection* reasoning resource will be used to solve the *Select-k-Neighbours* in our example. This reasoning resource has as inputs the problem to be solved (`Problem` of sort CBR-Problem) and the output of the *Assess-Similarity* Task (a Assess-Model). This RR also uses two domain models, a *Case-Language-Model* (that characterizes the kind of attributes used for describing a propositional case) and *k-Model* (model of k). The *resource identifier* in the *pragmatics* feature determines the name of the function (*k-Selection*), that implements the reasoning resource.

The operationalization process generates the "glue code" that calls, at the appropriate places, the operational descriptions of PDs and the code of the "resource identifier" of the RRs. Moreover, the domain models used by a RR, are referenced using an identifier. CAT-CBR provides a Project file where the engineer declares the files or URLs containing each domain model, and determines an identifier for each one.

Let us see an example: consider the PD *k-NN-Retrieval* and assume that for subtask *Assess-Similarity* the PSM *Feature-Similarity-And-Aggregation* is chosen, and for subtask *Select-k-Neighbours* task the PSM *k-Selection* is chosen. CAT-CBR generates the following Noos-method for this PD:

```
(define-method k-NN-Retrieval-Code
                   ((Problem CBR-Problem))
  (k-Selection
     Problem
     (Feature-Similarity-And-Aggregation-Code
                Problem))
     !Case-Language-Model
     !k-Model))
```

The name of the Noos-method is the name of the PD with the -`Code` ending and the input parameter is a `Problem` of sort CBR-Case. The body of this method corresponds with the operational description of the PD, substituting the `use-subtask` calls with the methods that implement the PSMs that solve the tasks. In our example `use-subtask` of *Select-k-Neighbours* is substituted by *k-Selection* with input parameters *Problem* and the result of the *Assess-Similarity* task; moreover, as *k-Selection*, being a RR, uses domain models they are added as parameters (*Case-Language-Model* and *k-Model*). The `use-subtask` of *Assess-Similarity* is substituted by `Feature-Similarity-And-Aggregation-Code` (that is the implementation of the PD selected) with input parameter `Problem`; notice that the result of this method (of sort *Assess-Model*) is the second input parameter of the `k-Selection` method.

All the Noos-methods generated and the functions of the resources identifiers, together with the domain models declared by the engineer, constitutes the runtime application that implements the CBR system configured by the engineer.

7 Conclusions

This paper presents the CAT-CBR platform for rapid and flexible development of CBR systems. The platform uses a library of CBR components described with UPML. UPML is a language for describing problem-solving methods, tasks, domain models and ontologies. In this paper we have described only the relevant aspects of UPML used in our work.

Using UPML we have analyzed in more detail the phases of the CBR cycle as tasks. We have presented, for propositional cases, the retrieval methods more frequently used and have modeled them in a family of components that use a common CBR ontology.

We have also presented how CAT-CBR guides the engineer in the development of a CBR system using a case-based recommendation system. In this configuration process, CAT-CBR only presents to the engineer those PSMs that match with a task and presents them in a ranking recommendation (based on a similarity between past configurations and the current requirements).

CAT-CBR provides the engineer a runtime CBR application for the components configuration. This runtime application is generated automatically, except for the connectors between PSMs and domain models that have to be manually defined by the engineer.

Currently Reuse phase includes components for classification; we plan to incorporate components for design and configuration tasks. Finally, components for the Retain phase of the CBR cycle also will be incorporated.

Acknowledgements. This research has been supported by the Esprit Long Term Research Project 27169: IBROW the TIC Project 2000-1094-C02 Tabasco and FPI TIC2000-1094-C02-02 grant.

References

1. Agnar Aamodt and Enric Plaza. Case-based reasoning: Foundational issues, methodological variations, and system approaches. *Artificial Intelligence Communications*, 7(1):39–59, 1994.
2. Josep Lluís Arcos. *The Noos representation language*. PhD thesis, Universitat Politècnica de Catalunya, 1997.
3. Eva Armengol and Enric Plaza. Similarity assessment for relational cbr. In *Proceedings ICCBR 2001*, LNAI. Springer Verlag, 2001.
4. Breinman L. et al. Classification and regression trees. *Wadsworth International*, 1984.
5. D. Fensel, V. R. Benjamins, M. Gaspari S. Decker, R. Groenboom, W. Grosso, M. Musen, E. Motta, E. Plaza, G. Schreiber, R. Studer, and B. Wielinga. The component model of upml in a nutshell. In *Proceedings of the International Workshop on Knowledge Acquisition KAW'98*, 1998.
6. A. Hart. Experience in the use of an inductive system in knowledge engineering. In M. Bramer, editor, *Research and Developments in expert systems*. Cambridge University Press, 1984.
7. Mingers J. Expert systems-rule induction with statistical data. *Journal of the Operational Research Society*, 1987.
8. Quinlan J.R. Inducing of decision trees. *Machine Learning, 1, 81-106*, 1986.
9. Quinlan J.R. Simplifying decision trees. *International Journal of Man-Machine Studies*, 1987.

10. Ramon López de Mántaras. A distance-based attribute selection measure for decision tree induction. *Machine Learning*, 6:81–92, 1991.
11. J. Mingers. Expert systems-rule induction with statistical data. *Journal of the Operational Research Society*, 1987.
12. E. Plaza and J.L. Arcos. Constructive adaptation: A search-based approach to reuse in cbr. In *Submitted*, 2002.
13. J.R. Quinaln. Learning efficient calssification procedures and their application to chess and games. In J. G. Carbonell R. S. Michalski and T. M. Mitchell, editors, *Machine Learning: An Artificial Intelligence approach*. Morgan-Kaufmann, 1983.
14. Niblett T. Construction decision trees in noisy domains. *Progress in machine Learning*, 1986.

Analysis of Tensions in a Population Based on the Adequacy Concept

J. Aguilar-Martin[1], N. Agell[2], M. Sánchez[3], and F. Prats[3]

[1] LAAS-CNRS (LEA-SICA)
aguilar@laas.fr
[2] ESADE (LEA-SICA)
agell@esade.edu
[3] UPC-GREC (LEA-SICA)
{monicas,prats}@ma2.upc.es

Abstract. The concept of similarity between objects has traditionally been taken as the criterion for recognising their membership of a given class. This paper considers how well an object fits into a class by using the concept of adequacy introduced by the LAMDA learning system [6],[9]. The Global Adequacy Degree (GAD) is a function of the object's class membership. An adequacy threshold is associated with a non-informative class (NIC). Objects falling below this threshold value are not considered to belong to any significant class. In this research, the tensions produced by a classification scheme are defined by means of the adequacy of an object in a class. This allows us to analyse the stability or balance of the scheme. An example is given in the form of the adequacy and the tension of a classification scheme for a group of customers patronising an imaginary shop.

Keywords: classification algorithms, knowledge representation, qualitative reasoning, fuzzy reasoning.

1 Introduction

Summarising the information contained in a set of observations in order to obtain knowledge is of fundamental importance in both scientific and technological endeavour. It is therefore not surprising that there is considerable interest in many fields of finding methods of automated learning which permit one to classify a population according to the criteria chosen [3],[4],[7]. This article analyses the possible classification schemes obtained by such a learning process. The tensions produced by a classification scheme are based on the concept of an object's adequacy in a class. This allows us to analyse the stability or balance of the scheme.

A set of pre-established classes serves as the starting point. The aim is to measure both the tensions between classes and those within each class and in the population as a whole by examining badly-fitting objects (i.e. ones falling below the predetermined threshold value).

M.T. Escrig Monferrer and F. Toledo Lobo (Eds.): CCIA 2002, LNAI 2504, pp. 17–28, 2002.

This work employs a fuzzy logic methodology to capture the ambiguity of the object descriptors. In this case, the methodology employed is LAMDA (Learning Algorithm for Multivariate Data Analysis) [6],[9] which develops a connectivist method of conceptual clustering that allows simultaneous use of qualitative and quantitative descriptors. This algorithm calculates an object's degree of adequacy in a class by summarising all the partial or marginal information available. Objects are placed in the class in which they best fit. This is achieved by calculating the extent to which each object fits in various classes, following the heuristic rule of maximum adequacy.

A basic feature of this algorithm is the use of a non-informative class (NIC) that accepts all objects equally. This class represents the concept of chaos or maximum entropy of the population to be classified.

The concepts of tension in a population and within classes is based on the concept of adequacy and the NIC class.

Section 2 discusses general concepts of marginal adequacy and of the global adequacy of an object in a class. It also sets out the LAMDA method for calculating both measures of adequacy. Section 3 introduces a definition of population tension based on these concepts. Section 4 defines the internal tensions of classes in a classification scheme. Section 5 furnishes a simple example of how tensions are calculated. Section 6 concludes the paper by stating conclusions and suggesting lines for future research.

2   The Concept of Adequacy

The concept of similarity between objects has traditionally been considered essential for deciding whether items are members of a particular class or not. The LAMDA system introduces a more basic idea: that of an object's adequacy in a class. Adequacy is formally expressed as a function of membership or a fuzzy set.

The starting point is the coding of classes and the objects to be classified according to their descriptors. The Marginal Adequacy Degree (MAD) is calculated for each descriptor, class and object and these partial results are then combined using some specific connectives or aggregation functions linked to fuzzy logic operators. This permits calculation of the Global Adequacy Degree (GAD) of an object in a class.

The macro-structure obtained for a set of classes defined using the adequacy concept is clearly influenced by the observer's epistemological attitudes, reflected in his choice of connectors. Fuzzy logic thus provides a mathematical tool for modelling these attitudes, which range from the strictest demand for simultaneous conjunction by all descriptors to the laxest one corresponding to total disjunction. However, people tend to resolve conflicting attitudes by opting for a position somewhere between these two extremes [8].

2.1   Marginal Adequacy

The Marginal Adequacy Degree (MAD) is expressed as a function of marginal membership to class Cl_k:

$$\mu_k^i(x_i) = MAD(x_i \,/\, i \text{ descriptor of class } Cl_k)$$

This function depends on descriptor x_i of object X and descriptor θ_{ki} of class Cl_k:

$$\mu_k^i(x_i) = f_i(x_i, \theta_{ki}).$$

Descriptor θ_{ki} is iteratively calculated based on the i descriptors of all the objects that are members of class Cl_k.

We shall now show how these degrees of marginal adequacy are calculated in the case of a qualitative descriptor. The calculation is then performed for a quantitative descriptor.

In the qualitative case, the possible values of the i descriptor form a set of modes:

$$D_i = \{Q_{i1}, \ldots, Q_{ij}, \ldots, Q_{iM_i}\}$$

Let Φ_{ij} be the probability of Q_{ij} in class Cl_k, estimated by its relative frequency; thus the multinomial probability of x_i is:

$$q_{ij} = \begin{cases} 1 \text{ if } x_i = Q_{ij} \\ 0 \text{ if } x_i \neq Q_{ij} \end{cases}$$

$$\mu_k^i(x_i) = \Phi_{i1}{}^{q_{i1}} \cdot \ldots \cdot \Phi_{iM_i}{}^{q_{iM_i}}$$

In the quantitative case, the values of the i descriptor belong to an $[x_{imin}, x_{imax}]$ interval, where the limits may be either the limits of the data set or independently placed landmarks.

The presence function $\alpha(x_i)$ is first introduced, which is an application of the interval $[x_{imin}, x_{imax}]$ in $\{0,1\}$, corresponding to the presence of a mode in a qualitative case.

For this function, the i quantitative descriptor can be treated as a qualitative one with just two modes: $Q_{i1} = 1$ and $Q_{i2} = 0$.

Writing $\Phi_{i1} = \rho$, yields $\Phi_{i2} = 1 - \rho$, and

$$MAD(x_i \,/\, i \text{ descriptor of class } Cl_k) = \mu_i^k(x_i) = \rho^{\alpha(x_i)}(1-\rho)^{1-\alpha(x_i)} \qquad (*)$$

Note that $\mu_i^k(x_i)$ is the probability of x_i in class Cl_k.

The extension of the formulation $(*)$ of $\{0,1\}$ to interval $[0,1]$ is performed by considering the presence function

$$\alpha(x_i) = (x_i - x_{imin})/(x_{imax} - x_{imin})$$

which corresponds to a normalisation of interval $[x_{imin}, x_{imax}]$ to the unit interval.

For $\rho = 0$ to 1, step $= .1$, and $\alpha(x) = x$, the graph of the function $\mu_k^i(x)$ is shown in Figure 1.

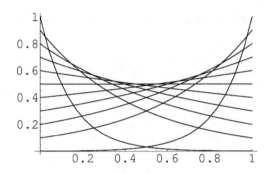

Fig. 1. $MAD(x/\rho) = \rho^x (1 - \rho)^{1-x}$

Other presence functions can also be considered which depend on a single parameter ρ. Figure 2 gives an example of the function

$MAD(x/\rho) = (1 - \rho^*)^{\alpha(x)} (\rho^*)^{1-\alpha(x)}$, with $\rho^* = \max(\rho, 1 - \rho)$, and $\alpha(x) = |x - \rho|$.

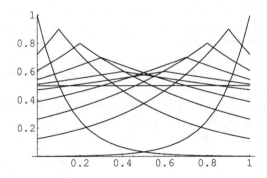

Fig. 2. $MAD(x/\rho) = (1 - \rho^*)^{\alpha(x)} \rho^{*1-\alpha(x)}$

Another family of presence functions can be obtained by using Pseudo-Gaussian functions, shown in Figure 3.

$$MAD(x/\rho) = \exp\left(-\frac{(x-\rho)^2}{2\sigma^2}\right), \quad \sigma^2 = \frac{1}{2\pi}$$

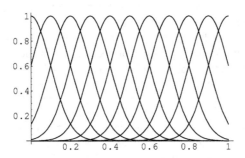

Fig. 3. $MAD(x/\rho)$ Pseudo-Gaussian

Normally parameter ρ is estimated by taking the arithmetic mean of the values for i descriptors of all the elements of the class and parameter σ as its Standard Deviation.

2.2   Global Adequacy

The global adequacy function (GAD) is expressed as a function of membership in class Cl_k, interpreted as a fuzzy set:

$$\mu_k(X) = GAD(\text{object } X/\text{class } Cl_k)$$

This function depends separately on each of n object descriptors; the global adequacy is the result of combining the marginal adequacies using an aggregation function F, i.e., for $X = [x_1, \ldots, x_n]^t$,

$$\mu_k(X) = F(\mu_k^1(x_1), \ldots, \mu_k^n(x_n)),$$

where $\mu_k^i(x_i)$ is the Marginal Adequacy Degree of i descriptor of object X to i descriptor of class Cl_k, whether the descriptor is a qualitative or quantitative one.

In fuzzy logic, the binary aggregation function is an application $F : [0,1] \times [0,1] \rightarrow [0,1]$ which satisfies the following axioms:

- $F(x,0) = F(1,0) \cdot x$
- $F(x,1) = (1 - F(1,0)) \cdot x + F(1,0)$
- $\forall x \leq x', y \leq y' \;\; F(x,y) \leq F(x',y')$
- $\forall x,y \;\; F(x,y) = F(y,x)$

Arithmetic means, Min and Max functions and all the t-norms and t co-norms are examples of binary aggregation functions.

The t-norms and t-conorma are the only associative aggregation functions. The Min function (resp. Max) is the only function where $F(x,x) = x$ and $F(1,0) = 0$ (resp. $F(1,0) = 1$).

The associative aggregation functions give rise to n-ary aggregation functions by direct iteration on n arguments; the notation $F(x_1, \ldots, x_n)$ will be maintained for these functions. Specifically, the aggregation functions used by LAMDA are the so-called lineally balanced hybrid connectives [6], which are obtained using a convex linear combination of a t-norm and its associated t co-norm:

$$F(x_1, \ldots x_n) = \lambda T(x_1, \ldots, x_n) + (1 - \lambda)T^*(x_1, \ldots, x_n),$$

where parameter λ determines the strictness of the classification, given that when $\lambda = 1$ one obtains the t-norm, which represents the concept of intersection in fuzzy logic, while when $\lambda = 0$ one obtains the t co-norm, which represents the concept of union.

One needs to consider the concept of a neutral or non-informative class in order to introduce the concept of tension into a classification scheme. The non-informative class (NIC) is the one which maximises entropy, accepting all objects equally:

$$Cl_0, \text{ so that } \forall X \ GAD(X/NIC) = \mu_0(X) = \mu_0,$$

where value μ_0 is the threshold such that no object is a member of a significant class if its adequacy lies under this value μ_0.

In the case of qualitative descriptors, the neutral marginal adequacy arises in a natural fashion since all M modes have the same parameter, i.e. the following holds true for all modes of the descriptor:

$$\forall j \ \Phi_{0j} = 1/M.$$

Thus for all X object:

$$MAD(x_i/i \text{ descriptor of class } Cl_0) = \mu_0^i(x_i) = 1/M.$$

In the case of quantitative descriptors, it is considered a constant for neutral marginal adequacy.

3   Internal Tension of a Population

Adequacy is a powerful concept for analysing a given population P. It provides a new framework for studying the balance of a group of objects in accordance with their simultaneous assignation to the same class. One considers the laxest classification when needs to define the internal tension of the population (i.e. the classification scheme in which a single class corresponds to the whole population).

The methodology described earlier allows one to calculate the Global Adequacy Degree for each object in this class P.

As indicated earlier, the concept of a non-informative class (NIC) gives a natural threshold $\mu_0 = GAD(X/NIC)$, for any object X, with regard to adequacy.

The objects or individual items X of the population which satisfy $GAD(X/P) \geq GAD(X/NIC)$, are adequate individuals of the population to which they belong. In the opposite case, individuals satisfying $GAD(X/P) < GAD(X/NIC)$, are badly-fitted members of the population and accordingly may create *internal tension* in the population.

Let $P = \{X_1, \ldots, X_n\}$ be the population, let $D = \{d_1, \ldots, d_m\}$ be the set of descriptors, which may be quantitative or qualitative. The **internal tension of the population** can now be defined as:

$$T_P = \frac{\sum_{X_i \in P} \max\{GAD(X_i/NIC) - GAD(X_i/P), 0\}}{\sum_{X_i \in P} GAD(X_i/NIC)}$$

Thus population tension is always a number between 0 and 1; tension is least (0) when all the individuals in the population satisfy:

$$GAD(X_i/NIC) \leq GAD(X_i/P),$$

i.e. when there are no badly-fitting (inadequate) members in the population. By contrast, maximum tension is represented by 1, which applies when all the elements have a GAD of 0 in the population.

4   The Internal Tensions of Classes

Likewise, when the initial population is classified (i.e. subdivided in a given number k of disjointed classes): $P = Cl_1 \cup \ldots \cup Cl_k$, the individual items that can generate internal tension in a class Cl_j are those classified in that class but which are badly-fitting, i.e. $X \in Cl_j$ which satisfy $GAD(X/Cl_j) < GAD(X/NIC)$.

Let $P = \{X_1, \ldots, X_n\}$ be a population or set of objects, let $D = \{d_1, \ldots, d_m\}$ be the set of descriptors, $d_i : P \to \mathbb{R}$, which may be numerical or qualitative, and let $P = Cl_1 \cup \ldots \cup Cl_k$ be a partition of population P. The internal tension of class Cl_j can be defined as:

$$T_{Cl_j} = \frac{\sum_{X_i \in Cl_j} \max\{GAD(X_i/NIC) - GAD(X_i/Cl_j), 0\}}{\sum_{X_i \in Cl_j} GAD(X_i/NIC)}$$

which, as in the case of the internal tension of the population, takes values between 0 and 1.

5   Example

The concept of internal tension in a group of objects or individuals is illustrated in the following example of a population of customers patronising an imaginary shop. Let us consider a population of customers shopping at a given retail outlet. The population is described by 5 attributes (3 quantitative and 2 qualitative). Table 1 shows the values of these attributes: The quantitative ones cover the total spent in the three sections of the shop and the qualitative ones concern the customer's occupation and the language he uses when speaking to the shop assistant.

Table 1. Individuals and Descriptors

Client	food	cleaning	clothes	occupation	language
Juan	150	50	120	employee	Spanish
Ruth	10	210	47	housewife	English
Maria	45	32	56	housewife	Catalan
Ronald	0	120	10	business-man	English
Pere	130	35	0	jobless	Catalan
Núria	160	20	130	house-wife	Catalan
Rocío	170	68	130	employee	Spanish
Ramon	168	70	142	employee	Spanish
Rosa	165	53	132	business-man	Catalan
Teresa	60	0	132	jobless	Catalan

Customers are classified in three pre-determined classes:
$Cl_1 = \{$ Juan, Núria, Rocío, Ramon, Rosa $\}$
$Cl_2 = \{$ Ronald, Pere, Teresa $\}$
$Cl_3 = \{$ Ruth, Maria $\}$
Table 2 shows the values of parameter ρ of the quantitative descriptors of the whole population, of classes $Cl; 1$, Cl_2, Cl_3, and class NIC.

Table 2. ρ of the Quantitative Descriptors

ρ	food	cleaning	clothes
Population	0,6224	0,3133	0,6224
Cl_1	0,6300	0,6440	0,4909
Cl_2	0,4872	0,4305	0,3586
Cl_3	0,5000	0,5000	0,5000
NIC	0,5000	0,5000	0,5000

Tables 3 and 4 show the values of the parameters of the qualitative descriptors for occupation and language, labelled Φ_1 and Φ_2, of the whole population of classes Cl_1, Cl_2, Cl_3, and class NIC.

Table 3. Parameters of the Occupation Descriptor

Φ_1	occupation			
	employee	housewife	Business man	jobless
Pop.	0,3000	0,3000	0,2000	0,2000
Cl_1	0,6000	0,2000	0,2000	0
Cl_2	0	0	0,3333	0,6667
Cl_3	0	1	0	0
NIC	0,2500	0,2500	0,2500	0,2500

Table 4. Parameters of the Language Descriptor

Φ_2	language		
	Spanish	English	Catalan
Pop.	0,3000	0,2000	0,5000
Cl_1	0,6000	0	0,4000
Cl_2	0	0,3333	0,6667
Cl_3	0	0,5000	0,5000
NIC	0,3333	0,3333	0,3333

Tables 5 and 6 show the degrees of global adequacy of each of the individuals in the population class, NIC and the class to which they belong. The shaded individuals are ones whose degree of adequacy lies under the NIC class threshold.

Table 5. Degrees of adequacy in relation to the population and the NIC

CLIENT	Population	NIC
Juan	0,2400	0,3500
Ruth	0,4000	0,3500
Maria	0,4000	0,3500
Ronald	0,4000	0,3500
Pere	0,4000	0,3500
Núria	0,2000	0,3500
Rocío	0,6727	0,3500
Ramon	0,7600	0,3500
Rosa	0,4200	0,3500
Teresa	0,4000	0,3500

Juan and Núria are clearly individuals who generate internal tension in the global group. The internal tension of the population can be calculated by the formula given earlier. In this case it yields:

$$T_P = 0,07428571$$

One can then use Table 6 to calculate the internal tensions of each class.

Table 6. Degrees of adequacy in the classes

CLIENT	Cl_1	NIC
Juan	0,2400	0,3500
Núria	0,2000	0,3500
Rocío	0,6727	0,3500
Ramon	0,7600	0,3500
Rosa	0,4200	0,3500
CLIENT	Cl_2	NIC
Ronald	0,4000	0,3500
Pere	0,4000	0,3500
Teresa	0,4000	0,3500
CLIENT	Cl_3	NIC
Ruth	0,4000	0,3500
Maria	0,4000	0,3500

The only class which contains inadequate elements is Cl_1, the tension values being:

$$T_{Cl_1} = 0,14857143; \qquad T_{Cl_2} = 0; \qquad T_{Cl_3} = 0$$

6   A Classification Based on the Tension Concept

The tension concepts introduced in the previous sections arise from a given classification scheme. We shall now reflect on a new methodology which can be used in learning processes in order to create a classification scheme which minimises tensions.

In the majority of learning schemes, the classification depends largely on the order in which one deals with the elements to be classified (i.e. the first elements take on greater importance than the rest). By contrast, our methodology ensures that all the elements have the same weight.

The idea is to create a partition or classification scheme for a given population in order to minimise tensions. The internal tension of the population is constant, depending as it does on the individuals in the population and the set of descriptors. Accordingly, this tension cannot be reduced.

The internal tensions (or stresses) within classes can be reduced by changing the partition under consideration, i.e. by moving certain elements from one class to another.

Clearly, the partition in unit sets of a population $P = \{X_1\} \cup \ldots \cup \{X_n\}$ satisfies the condition that the internal tensions of all the classes are 0, however the task is to find a coarser population partition that ensures that internal tensions in classes is 0. The following classification algorithm provides a population partition which meets this condition:

Let $P = \{X_1, \ldots, X_n\}$ be a population. The Global Adequacy Degree is calculated for each one of X_i objects as well in population $GAD(X_i/P)$ as in the NIC class $GAD(X_i/NIC)$. The population is sub-divided into two classes, $P = C_1 \cup C_0$; class C_1 of elements fitting well within the population and class C_0 consisting of badly-fitting elements.

The following step consists of sub-dividing C_1 and C_0 into two classes, $C_1 = C_{11} \cup C_{10}$ and $C_0 = C_{01} \cup C_{00}$, C_{i1} being the class of well-fitting elements in C_i and C_{i0} the class of badly-fitting elements in C_i:

$$
\text{Population} \begin{cases} C_1 \begin{cases} C_{11} \begin{cases} C_{111} \\ C_{110} \end{cases} \\ C_{10} \begin{cases} C_{101} \\ C_{100} \end{cases} \end{cases} \\ C_0 \begin{cases} C_{01} \quad C_{01} \\ C_{00} \begin{cases} C_{001} \\ C_{000} \end{cases} \end{cases} \end{cases}
$$

Figure 4: Example of a classification scheme

Depending on the requirements of the problem, one has to strike a compromise between the degrees of tension accepted and the number of classes generated.

7 Conclusions and Future Research

This paper introduced the concept of tension generated by a fuzzy adequacy concept defined by the LAMDA algorithm. This concept does not only allow one to analyse a given classification but also permits more balanced classification schemes to be built (i.e. ones with less tensions).

It is reasonable to expect that one can obtain groups with tensions below the given threshold by iterating the procedure detailed in Section 6. Future research will consider making the whole process converge.

Future research may also study other methods for evaluating internal tensions, such as functions of the differences between the degree of adequacy in an inadequate group and NIC thresholds.

The fuzzy segmentation techniques provided by LAMBA have yielded interesting results in the marketing field [1],[2]. It is hoped that the theoretical formulation of tensions put forward in this paper will help in developing innovative concepts in segmenting markets, particularly in the distribution field (shops, supermarkets, hypermarkets, etc.), thus contributing to optimisation of marketing strategies [5] customer loyalty campaigns.

Acknowledgements. This work has been partly funded by LEA-SICA, European Laboratory on Intelligent Systems and Advanced Control and by project DISCO (TIC2000-0193-P4-02).

References

1. Agell,N., Aguado,J.C. Aplicación del clasificador LAMDA a la predicción de la fidelidad de clientes. CCIA 2000, Vilanova i la Geltrú, pp.186-190
2. Agell,N., Aguado,J.C. A hybrid qualitative-quantitative classification technique applied to aid marketing decisions. ESOMAR Congress and Trade Exhibition 2001 Rome (Italy). September 2001
3. Aguilar-Martin J., J.Waissman, R.Sarrate, F.Nejjari , B.Dahhou On line expert situation assessment of the biological modes in a wastewater plant by means of fuzzy classification CIMCA'2001, Las Vegas (USA), 9-11 July 2001,5p.
4. Aguilar-Martin J., L Haenlein, J. Waissman Knowledge-based signal analysis and case-based condition monitoring of a machine tool 9th IFSA World Congress and 20th NAFIPS International Conference, Vancouver (Canada), 25-28 July 2001, pp.286-291
5. Ezop, P. "Database marketing research". A Marketing Research. Fall 1994, vol. 6, n. 4, p. 34.
6. Piera, N. Connectius de lògiques no estàndard com a operadors d'agregació en classificació multivariable i reconeixement de formes. Ph.D. Thesis. Universitat Politècnica de Catalunya, 1987.
7. Piera N., and J. Aguilar-Martin. (1991). Controlling selectivity in nonstandard pattern recognition algorithms. Trans. in Syst. Man and Cybernetics, 21(1), 71-82.
8. Sarrate, R., J. Aguilar and J. Waissman (1998). On-line event-based supervision of a biotechnological process. In: Preprints for the 3rd Ifac Workshop on On-line Fault Detection and Supervision in the Chemical Process Industries, vol. 2. Solaize, France.
9. Waissman, J., J. Aguilar, B. Dahhou and G. Roux (1998). Généralisation du degré d'adequation marginale dans la méthode de classification LAMDA. 6èmes Rencontres de la Société Francophone de Classification, Montpellier, France.

Qualitative Velocity

M. Teresa Escrig Monferrer and Francisco Toledo Lobo

Universitat Jaume I, Engineering and Computer Science Department,
E-12071 Campus Riu Sec, Castellón (Spain)
{escrigm,toledo}@icc.uji.es

Abstract. The concept of velocity of an object relates an interval of time with the space that this object has travelled in such interval of time. Velocity is always relative: we compare the distance that an object has travelled in a period of time with respect to the position of another object. Although velocity is a quantitative physical concept, we also need a qualitative model of velocity if we want to automatically reason in a human-like way. In this paper, a qualitative model for representing and reasoning with the concept of velocity has been introduced.

1 Introduction

Historically, the effort of scientists has been in measuring and naming everything in nature, in order to understand and classify the physical world. However, human way of thinking is qualitative in nature, when we do not use any measure tool.

In the last years, several qualitative models have been developed for dealing with spatial concepts such as orientation in 2-D [1,2,3,4,5,6], orientation in 3-D [7], named distances [8], [9], [10], [11], compared distances [12], cardinal directions [13], and so on. See [14] for a review of these approaches. Some approaches represent and reason with one or two of the previous mentioned spatial aspects. In [14], all previous spatial aspects have been integrated in the same model, thanks to represent each spatial aspect as an instance of the Constraint Satisfaction Problem (CSP) and to reason using Constraint Logic Programming extended with Constraint Handling Rules (CLP+CHRs) as tool. The concept of qualitative motion has been dealt in [15], [16,17]. In most of these approaches, motion has been modelled as a sequence of changes of positions, taking into account conceptual neighbourhood, but without integrating the concept of time into the same model.

Velocity is the physical concept which relates space travelled by an object and time needed for this movement. The quantitative formula in physics is:

$$\text{Velocity} = \text{Space} / \text{Time}$$

Velocity is always relative (among other things because the earth is moving): we compare the position of an object "a" with respect to the position of another object "b" in two different times. Velocity is the distance travelled in this period of time.

In the rest of the paper we are going to introduce the algebra of a qualitative model for representing and reasoning with velocity.

M.T. Escrig Monferrer and F. Toledo Lobo (Eds.): CCIA 2002, LNAI 2504, pp. 29–39, 2002.

2 Representing Velocity: The Algebra

The information that we are going to represent is the relative velocity of an object b with respect to (wrt) the position of an object a, namely, b wrt a.

The velocity reference system (VRS) has four components, VRS={UD, UT, LAB, INT}, where UD refers to the unit of distance or space travelled by the object; UT is the unit of time, both of which are context dependent; LAB refers to the set of qualitative velocity labels, the amount of which depend on the granularity level; and INT refers to the intervals associated to each velocity label of LAB, which will describe the velocity label in terms of the UD and the UT.

Assuming that in a determined context we fix UD to ud and UT to ut, we are going to define as examples two different VRS at coarse and fine levels of granularity, respectively. The UD and UT values might be changed depending on the context.

For the coarse VRS we define:

LAB_1={zero, slow, normal, quick}, and the corresponding INT_1={[0,0],]0,ud/2ut],]ud/2ut,ud/ut],]ud/ut, ∞[}.

That means that for velocity "zero", there is no space travelled per unit of time. We will say that the velocity label is "slow" if the space travelled by the object in the unit of time is between zero (not included) and half of the unit of distance (included). The velocity label "normal" corresponds to the interval "half of the unit of distance (not included)" to "the unit of distance (included)", travelled per unit of time. The last label corresponds to an open interval from the unit of distance travelled per unit of time, to infinite.

For the fine VRS we define:

LAB_2={zero, very slow, slow, normal, quick, very quick}, and the corresponding INT_2={[0,0],   ]0,ud/4ut],   ]ud/4ut,ud/2ut],   ]ud/2ut,ud/ut],   ]ud/ut,2ud/ut],]2ud/ut, ∞[}, with similar meaning to the coarse VRS.

It is possible to define other VRSs, and it will be possible to reason using velocity information at different levels of granularity, by following the steps introduced in [12].

Velocity information is a binary relationship: b wrt a. Therefore, it can also be expressed by: a wrt b, as result of applying the INVERSE operation. The inverse is an identity operation, in the sense that if an object "b" is travelled at a particular speed from another object "a", which is considered as reference point, the speed at which object "a" is separating from object "b", which is now consider as reference point, is the same.

3 Reasoning with Velocity

We are going to distinguish two parts in the reasoning process: the Basic Step of the Inference Process (BSIP) and the Full Inference Process (FIP). For the concept of velocity, the BSIP can be defined such as: given two velocity relationships: (1) object "b" wrt object "a", and (2) object "c" wrt object "b"; the BSIP consists of obtaining the velocity relationship of object "c" wrt object "a".

When more velocity relationships among several spatial landmarks are provided, then the FIP is necessary. It consists of repeating the BSIP as many times as possible, with the initial information and the information provided by some BSIP, until no more information can be inferred.

3.1 The Basic Step of the Inference Process

In the BSIP we can distinguish two different situations: 1) when the relative movement of the implied objects is in the same direction, and 2) when the relative movement of the implied objects is in any direction. They are both developed in the next sections.

3.1.1 Composition of Velocity in the Same Direction

The BSIP for the concept of velocity, when the relative movement of the implied objects is in the same direction, is given in the composition table of figure 1, for the coarse VRS_1, and in the composition table of figure 2 for the fine VRS_2.

	Z_1	S_1	N_1	Q_1
Z_1	$\{Z_1\}$	$\{S_1\}$	$\{N_1\}$	$\{Q_1\}$
S_1	$\{S_1\}$	$\{S_1,N_1\}$	$\{N_1,Q_1\}$	$\{Q_1\}$
N_1	$\{N_1\}$	$\{N_1,Q_1\}$	$\{N_1,Q_1\}$	$\{Q_1\}$
Q_1	$\{Q_1\}$	$\{Q_1\}$	$\{Q_1\}$	$\{Q_1\}$

Fig. 1. The composition table which solves the BSIP for the coarse VRS1 with LAB1={zero (Z1), slow (S1), normal (N1), quick (Q1)}.

	Z_2	VS_2	S_2	N_2	Q_2	VQ_2
Z_2	$\{Z_2\}$	$\{VS_2\}$	$\{S_2\}$	$\{N_2\}$	$\{Q_2\}$	$\{VQ_2\}$
VS_2	$\{VS_2\}$	$\{VS_2,S_2\}$	$\{S_2,N_2\}$	$\{N_2,Q_2\}$	$\{Q_2,VQ_2\}$	$\{VQ_2\}$
S_2	$\{S_2\}$	$\{S_2,N_2\}$	$\{N_2\}$	$\{N_2,Q_2\}$	$\{Q_2,VQ_2\}$	$\{VQ_2\}$
N_2	$\{N_2\}$	$\{N_2,Q_2\}$	$\{N_2,Q_2\}$	$\{Q_2\}$	$\{Q_2,VQ_2\}$	$\{VQ_2\}$
Q_2	$\{Q_2\}$	$\{Q_2,VQ_2\}$	$\{Q_2,VQ_2\}$	$\{Q_2,VQ_2\}$	$\{VQ_2\}$	$\{VQ_2\}$
VQ_2	$\{VQ_2\}$	$\{VQ_2\}$	$\{VQ_2\}$	$\{VQ_2\}$	$\{VQ_2\}$	$\{VQ_2\}$

Fig. 2. The composition table which solves the BSIP for the fine VRS2 with LAB2={zero (Z2),very slow, (V2S), slow (S2), normal (N2), quick (Q2), very quick (VQ2)}.

The first column of both tables refers to the velocity relationship "b wrt a", and the first raw of both columns refers to the velocity relationship "c wrt b". The rest of the cells of both tables refers to the composition, the velocity relationship "c wrt a", which are included into brackets because sometimes they contain disjunction of relations. The first label in both VRS (zero) are the neutral element, therefore the second column and the second raw of both tables correspond to the original relationship. The last labels of both VRS (quick and very quick, respectively) are the absorbent elements, that is, everything composed with these last relationships provide the last relationships of both VRS, respectively.

Both tables are symmetrical with respect to the main diagonal, therefore it is necessary to represent only the upper or the downer part of both tables.

It is also important to notice that the results in both inference tables maintain conceptual neighbourhood.

3.1.2 Composition of Velocity in Any Direction

The BSIP for the velocity concept when the relative movement of the implied objects is in any direction, is studied by integrating the concept of velocity with the qualitative orientation model of Freksa & Zimmermann [4,5]. The Freksa & Zimmeramnn's coarse orientation reference system contains nine orientation regions, as we can see in figure 3. The reference system per se is represented by the perpendicular lines, whereas the black dots are only included if the corresponding orientation region is referred. For representing the velocity of b wrt a, integrated with this orientation reference system, we consider that the reference object is always on the cross point of both perpendicular lines which defines the coarse reference system. Therefore, a finer reference system is not necessary.

The composition table which solves the BSIP for the integration of the coarse VRS_1 (4 velocity distinctions) with the coarse orientation reference system (9 qualitative regions), has 36×36 entries. One of these entries is shown in figure 4 a).

Fig. 3. The Freksa & Zimmerman's coarse orientation reference system.

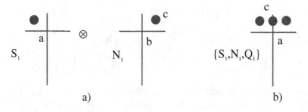

a)   b)

Fig. 4. An example of composition: a) b wrt a ("slow" velocity towards the "left front" orientation) composed with c wrt b ("normal" velocity towards the "right front" orientation), gives as result b) c wrt a ("slow", "normal" or "quick" velocities towards "left front", "straight front" or "right front" orientations).

The composition table which solves the BSIP for the integration of the fine VRS_1 (6 velocity distinctions) with the coarse orientation reference system (9 qualitative regions), has 54×54 entries.

For the management of velocity, we can consider the orientation regions as intervals of orientations as well. Therefore we redefine the Freksa & Zimmermann's orientation reference system (ORS) to ORS={LABo, INTo}, where LABo refers to the set of qualitative orientation labels and INTo refers to the intervals associated to each orientation label of LABo, which will describe the orientation label in terms of ranges of angles. For instance, for the coarse orientation reference system we consider:

LABo={front-left (fl), straight front (sf), front-right (fr), left (l), none (n), right (r), back-left (bl), straight-back (sb), back-right (br)}; and

INTo={]90,180[,[90,90],]0,90[,[180,180],_,[0,0],]180,270[, [270,270],]270,360[}.

In general, those qualitative orientation regions which correspond to a line are close initial and final intervals, which includes a unique angle, and those qualitative orientation regions which corresponds to an area are always open initial and final intervals which includes the range of angles that define the region.

In order to obtain the composition of velocity at any orientation, instead of filling two inference tables for both granularity levels, we are going to implement an algorithm which is based on the idea of reasoning with the extreme points/angles which define the INT part of the velocity/orientation reference systems, respectively. In general, we want to compose a velocity with label V1, at an orientation with label O1, with a velocity with label V2 at an orientation with label O2. Each velocity label V is defined by the interval: open or closed initial velocity to open or closed final velocity (o/c, vi, o/c, vf). Each orientation label O is defined by the interval: open or closed initial orientation to open or closed final orientation, (o/c, oi, o/c, of).

There exists sixteen possible combinations of extreme velocity/orientation for computing each one of the entries of the composition table, which are the following:

$$(o/c, vi1, o/c, oi1) \otimes (o/c, vi2, o/c, oi2);$$
$$(o/c, vi1, o/c, of1) \otimes (o/c, vi2, o/c, oi2);$$
$$(o/c, vf1, o/c, oi1) \otimes (o/c, vi2, o/c, oi2);$$
$$(o/c, vf1, o/c, of1) \otimes (o/c, vi2, o/c, oi2);$$
$$(o/c, vi1, o/c, oi1) \otimes (o/c, vi2, o/c, of2);$$
$$(o/c, vi1, o/c, of1) \otimes (o/c, vi2, o/c, of2);$$
$$(o/c, vf1, o/c, oi1) \otimes (o/c, vi2, o/c, of2);$$
$$(o/c, vf1, o/c, of1) \otimes (o/c, vi2, o/c, of2);$$
$$(o/c, vi1, o/c, oi1) \otimes (o/c, vf2, o/c, oi2);$$
$$(o/c, vi1, o/c, of1) \otimes (o/c, vf2, o/c, oi2);$$
$$(o/c, vf1, o/c, oi1) \otimes (o/c, vf2, o/c, oi2);$$
$$(o/c, vf1, o/c, of1) \otimes (o/c, vf2, o/c, oi2);$$
$$(o/c, vi1, o/c, oi1) \otimes (o/c, vf2, o/c, of2);$$
$$(o/c, vi1, o/c, of1) \otimes (o/c, vf2, o/c, of2);$$
$$(o/c, vf1, o/c, oi1) \otimes (o/c, vf2, o/c, of2);$$
$$(o/c, vf1, o/c, of1) \otimes (o/c, vf2, o/c, of2).$$

The result of each of the previous compositions will have two components: 1) the module of the velocity, which will be a quantitative amount in terms of the unit of distance and the unit of time; and 2) an angle which corresponds to a quantitative orientation.

In general, for the composition of (O/Cv1, V1, O/Co1, O1) ⊗ (O/Cv2, V2, O/Co2, O2) the following algorithm will obtain both result components (velocity and orientation):

1) If one of both velocities is equal to zero, then the module of the velocity and the orientation corresponds to the one which is different from zero. If the resulting orientation corresponds to the beginning of the interval, one degree is added to the result (because the interval is open and the exact orientation is not included in the result); if the resulting orientation corresponds to the end of the interval, one degree is subtracted to the result.

2) If the subtraction of both orientations is zero, then the resulting module of velocity will be the sum of velocities. The orientation will correspond to the higher orientation. If the resulting orientation corresponds to the beginning of the interval, one degree is added to the result; if the resulting orientation corresponds to the end of the interval, one degree is subtracted to the result.

3) If the module of the subtraction of both orientations is 90 degrees, then the Pythagorean theorem is applied in order to obtain the velocity module, that is:
$$V= \sqrt{V1^2 + V2^2 - 2 \times V1 \times V2 \times \cos \alpha}$$
where $\alpha=|O1-O2|/2$.

The orientation will be given by the following sequence:

maxmin(O1,O2,Omax,Omin) {Omax and Omin contain the maximum and minimum of O1 and O2, respectively}
O=Omin+(Omax-Omin)/2

4) If the module of the subtraction of both orientations is 180 degrees, then the resulting module of velocity will be the subtraction of velocities. If the velocity is zero then the orientation is not important. Otherwise, the orientation will correspond to the higher orientation. If the resulting orientation corresponds to the beginning of the interval, one degree is added to the result; if the resulting orientation corresponds to the end of the interval, one degree is subtracted to the result.

The two quantitative components (velocity and orientation) which deliver the previous algorithm are translated into qualitative terms, by using the corresponding reference systems and the following formula:

label=LAB[pos(interval(VorO,INT))]

That is, the label associated with a quantity (label) is obtained by looking at the label set (LAB) for the position of the interval (INT) where the quantity of velocity or orientation (VorO) belongs.

The union of the resulting velocity labels will define the resultant velocity, and the union of the resulting orientation labels will define the resultant orientation. Both results for velocity and orientation might be a disjunction of relations. They have to maintain conceptual neighbourhood.

3.2 The Full Inference Process

In order to define a straightforward algorithm to solve the full inference process, the concept of qualitative velocity is seen in our approach as a Constraint Satisfaction Problem (CSP). The velocity relationships are represented as binary constraints such as ctr_vel(X,Y,V,O), which refers to the velocity relationship V at the orientation O which there exists between objects X and Y. The CSP can be defined for binary constraints such as: given a set of variables $\{X_1,...,X_n\}$, a discrete and finite domain for each variable $\{D_1,...,D_n\}$, and a set of binary constraints $\{c_{ij}(X_i,X_j)\}$, which define the relationship (qualitative velocity) between every pair of variables X_i,X_j ($1 \leq i<j \leq n$); the problem is to find an assignment of values $<v_1,...,v_n>$, $v_i \in D_i$, to variables such that all the constraints are satisfied.

The constraint minimal graph —the graph which contains no implicit constraints— allows us directly the generation of all the solutions of a CSP without backtracking. However, the cost of finding a constraint minimal graph is exponential. Therefore, it is approximated by local consistency techniques, such as path consistency. For complete graphs —those which contain an edge between every pair of nodes— it suffices to compute paths of length two at most, which means that for each group of three nodes (i,j,k) we repeatedly compute the following operation:

$$c_{ij} := c_{ij} \oplus c_{ik} \otimes c_{kj} \tag{1}$$

until a fix point is reached. Although the set of velocity constraints does not form a complete graph, this operation can also be applied for qualitative velocity, with some variations, as it will be explained.

The part ($c_{ik} \otimes c_{kj}$) of the formula computes composition and it obtains the constraint c_{ij}. This result is intersected with previous computed or user-defined constraints (if they exist) which relates the same spatial objects, by means of the part of the formula ($c_{ij} \oplus$). The complexity of such an algorithm is $O(n^3)$, where n is the number of nodes in the network [18]. Formula (1) is implemented in our algorithm by Constraint Logic Programming extended with Constraint Handling Rules (CHRs) [19] which supports a rapid prototyping to define an incremental, flexible and general purpose solver for disjunctive qualitative velocity relationships.

The composition part of the formula ($c_{ik} \otimes c_{kj}$) will be implemented by propagation CHRs, which are of the form:

$$H_1,...,H_i \mathbin{-\!\!>} G_1,...,G_j \mid B_1,...,B_k \qquad (i>0, j \geq 0, k \geq 0)$$

It means that if a set of constraints matches the head of a propagation CHR $(H_1,...,H_i)$ and the guards $(G_1,...,G_j)$ are satisfied, then the set of constraints $(B_1,...,B_k)$ is added to the set of initial constraints $(H_1,...,H_i)$.

The part of the formula which referees to intersection $(c_{ij}\ \oplus)$ will be implemented by simplification CHRs which are of the form:

$$H_1,...,H_i <-> G_1,...,G_j \mid B_1,...,B_k \qquad\qquad (i>0,\ j\geq0,\ k\geq0)$$

It means that if a set of constraints (H') matches the head of a simplification CHR $(H_1,...,H_i)$ and the guards $(G_1,...,G_j)$ are satisfied, then the set of constraints $(B_1,...,B_k)$ is substituted by the set of initial constraints $(H_1,...,H_i)$. The set of constraints $(B_1,...,B_k)$ is simpler than the set of constraints $(H_1,...,H_i)$ and preserves logical equivalence. CHRs are included as a library in ECLiPSe [20].

Algorithm 1 implements the full inference process for qualitative velocity. Predicates ctr_vel/4 and ctr_vel/7 are declared in (1a). Predicate ctr_vel/4 corresponds to the user-defined constraints for qualitative velocity. For example ctr_vel(X,Y,V,O) means that the spatial object Y moves at any velocity, included in the list V, in any orientation, included in the list O, wrt the spatial object X. They are translated into ctr_vel/7 by the simplification CHR (1d), where the length of velocity and orientation lists are added, as well as the length of the shortest path from which the constraint has been derived (length 1 means that the constraint is direct, i.e. it is user-defined). These three arguments are included to increase efficiency. The two first avoid composition between constraints which does not provide more information (simplification CHR (1e) removes the constraints which contain all the velocity labels and CHR (1f) removes the constraints which contain all the orientation labels). The last argument is used to restrict the propagation CHRs to involve at least one direct constraint. In (1c), *member(V1,V)* nondeterministically chooses one primitive qualitative velocity, V1, from the disjunctive relationship, V, and one primitive orientation relationship, O1, from the disjunctive relationship, O, which implements the backtrack search part of the algorithm.

Simplification CHRs (2a), (2b) and (2c) perform the intersection part of the algorithm. When there exist two constraints which relate the same two spatial objects, the intersection of the corresponding relations (V1 and V2) is computed (plain set intersection) and the previous constraints are substituted by the new one. For the case in which the constraint graphs is not complete (i.e. there is not two arcs between each pair or nodes), two simplifications CHRs more have been defined: (2b) and (2c). In CHR (2b), the inverse operation is applied to the first constraint, in order to relate the same spatial objects in the same order. In CHR (2c), the inverse operation is applied to the second constraints, in order to relate the same spatial objects in the same order.

Propagation CHRs (3a), (3b) and (3c) compute composition. (3a) computes composition as it was originally defined by formula (1). For the cases in which the constraint graph is not complete, two propagation CHRs more (3b) and (3c) are included, with the same meaning as for computing the intersection part of formula (1).

% Constraint definitions

(1a)   constraints ctr_vel/4, ctr_vel/7.
(1b)   label_with ctr_vel(Nv,No,X,Y,V,O,I) if Nv>=1 and No>=1.
(1c)   ctr_vel(Nv,No,X,Y,V,O,I):- member(V1,V), member(O1,O),
           ctr_vel(1,1,X,Y,[V1],[O1],I).

% Initializations

(1d)   ctr_vel(X,Y,V,O) <=> length(L,Nv), length(O,No) |
           ctr_vel(Nv,No,X,Y,V,O,1).

% Special cases

(1e)   ctr_vel(Nv,No,X,Y,V,O,I) <=> Nv=9 | true.
(1f)   ctr_vel(Nv,No,X,Y,V,O,I) <=> No=9 | true.
(1g)   ctr_f_o(Nv,No,X,X,V,O,I) <=> true.

% Intersection

(2a)   ctr_vel(Nv1,No1,X,Y,V1,O1,I), ctr_vel(Nv2,No2,X,Y,V2,O2,J) <=>
           inter(V1,V2,V3),length(V3,Nv3), inter(O1,O2,O3),length(O3,No3),
           min(I,J,K) | ctr_vel(Nv3,No2,X,Y,V3,O3,K).

(2b)   ctr_vel(Nv1,No1,Y,X, V1,O1,I),ctr_vel(Nv2,No2,X,Y,V2,O2,J) <=>
           inv(V1,Vi1),inv(O1,Oi1),inter(Vi1,V2,V3),length(V3,Nv3), inter(Oi1,O2,O3),
           length(O3,No3), min(I,J,K) | ctr_vel(Nv3,No2,X,Y,V3,O3,K).

(2c)   ctr_vel(Nv1,No1,X,Y,V1,O1,II),ctr_vel(Nv2,No2,Y,X,V2,O2,J) <=> inv(V2,Vi2),
           inv(O2,Oi2),inter(V1,Vi2,V3),length(V3,Nv3), inter(O1,Oi2,O3),
           length(O3,No3), min(I,J,K) | ctr_vel(Nv3,No2,X,Y,V3,O3,K).

% Composition

(3a)   ctr_vel(Nv1,No1,X,Y, V1,O1,I),ctr_vel(Nv2,No2,Y,Z,V2,O2,J) ==>
           J=1, composition_vel(V1,O1,V2,O2,V3,O3),length(V3,Nv3),
           length(O3,No3), K is I+J | ctr_vel(Nv3,No3,X,Z,V3,O3,K).

(3b)   ctr_vel(Nv1,No1,Y,X, V1,O1,I),ctr_vel(Nv2,No2,Y,Z,V2,O2,J) ==>
           J=1, inv(V1,Vi1), inv(O1,Oi1), composition_vel(Vi1,Oi1,V2,O2,V3,O3),
           length(V3,Nv3), length(O3,No3), K is I+J | ctr_vel(Nv3,No3,X,Z,V3,O3,K).

(3c)   ctr_vel(Nv1,No1,X,Y, V1,O1,I),ctr_vel(Nv2,No2,Z,Y,V2,O2,J) ==>
           J=1, inv(V2,Vi2), inv(O2,Oi2), composition_vel(V1,O1,V2,O2,V3,O3),
           length(V3,Nv3), length(O3,No3), K is I+J | ctr_vel(Nv3,No3,X,Z,V3,O3,K).

Algorithm 1. Path consistency algorithm to propagate compositions of disjunctive qualitative velocity relationships.

Conclusions and Future Work

In this paper the following three aspects are described:
*   The algebra for representing a qualitative model of velocity. The corresponding reference system is defined using the logic of intervals.
*   The basic step of the inference process —BSIP— which solves the reasoning mechanism when two related velocity relationships are involved. It has been necessary to take into account the orientation of the movement of the implied objects. If the movements described by the implied objects are in the same orientation, two straightforward inference tables have been defined for the velocity BSIP at two levels of granularity. When those movements are in any orientation, the coarse Freksa & Zimmermann's orientation reference system [Freksa 92, Freksa & Zimmermann 92] has been redefined using the logic of intervals. The composition of velocity at any orientation has been solved by an algorithm based on the idea of reasoning with the extreme points/angles of the intervals of both velocity and orientation reference systems, respectively. This algorithm has allowed us the automatic construction of the inference tables for the BSIP for the velocity concept at any orientation.
*   The full step of the inference process —FIP— which solves the reasoning mechanism when more than two related velocity relationships are involved. Velocity relationships are dealt as binary constraints, and constraint propagation is implemented by using Constraint Logic Programming extended with Constraint Handling Rules (CLP+CHR) as tool. The use of this tool has provided two very important advantages: (1) the support of a rapid prototype to define an incremental, flexible and general purpose solver for disjunctive qualitative velocity relationships; and (2) the integration of the velocity concept with other spatial concepts such as position, distance, cardinal directions, and so on (as defined in [Escrig & Toledo 98, 01], [Pacheco et al. 01]), based on the idea of a common representation using first order predicate logic.

We are currently working on (1) the definition of the BSIP and the FIP at different levels of granularity; and (2) the use of these qualitative spatial and spatio-temporal models for solving real robot navigation in structured environments.

Acknowledgements. The preliminary ideas described in this paper where discussed with students of a doctoral course given by one of the authors at Santiago de Cuba. We want to specially thank their contribution. This work has been partially supported by CICYT under grant number TAP99-0590-002-02.

References

1.   Guesgen, H.W., "Spatial reasoning based on Allen's temporal logic", Technical Report TR-89-049, International Computer Science Institute, Berkeley, 1989.
2.   Jungert, E., "The Observer's Point of View: An Extension of Symbolic Projections", in International Conference GIS -From Space to Territory: Theories and Methods of Spatio-Temporal Reasoning in Geographic Space. Volume 639 of Lectures Notes in Computer Science. Ed. Springer-Verlag, 1992.

3.   Mukerjee, A., Joe, G., "A Qualitative Model for Space". In 8th-AAAI, pag. 721-727, 1990.
4.   Freksa, C., "Using Orientation Information for Qualitative Reasoning", in A. U. Frank, I. Campari, and U. Formentini (editors). Theories and Methods of Spatio-Temporal Reasoning in Geographic Space. Proceedings of the International Conference on GIS-From Space to Territory, Pisa, volume 639 of Lecture Notes in Computer Science, pag. 162-178, 1992. Springer, Berlin.
5.   Freksa, C., Zimmermann, K., "On the Utilization of Spatial Structures for Cognitively Plausible and Efficient Reasoning", Proceedings of the IEEE International Conference on Systems, Man and Cybernetics, pag. 18-21, 1992.
6.   Hernández, D. Qualitative Representation of Spatial Knowledge. In volume 804 in Lecture Notes in AI. Ed. Springer-Verlag, 1994.
7.   Pacheco, J., Escrig, M.T., Toledo, F., "A model for representing and reasoning with 3-D Qualitative Orientation", in Proceedings of the 9th Conference of Spanish Association of Artificial Intelligence, October 2001.
8.   Zimmermann, K., "Enhancing Qualitative Spatial Reasoning Combining Orientation and Distance", in Frank, A. U. and Campari, I. (eds.). Spatial Information Theory. A Theoretical Basis for GIS. European Conference, COSIT'93, pag. 69-76, Marciana Marina, Italy, Volume 716 of Lecture Notes in Computer Science. Springer, Berlin.
9.   Jong, J. H., "Qualitative Reasoning About Distances and Directions in Geographic Space". Ph.D. thesis. Department of Surveying Engineering. University of Maine, 1994.
10. Clementini, E., Di Felice, P., Hernández, D., "Qualitative Representation of Positional Information", TR FKI-208-95, Technische Universität München, 1995.
11. Escrig, M.T., Toledo, F., "Autonomous Robot Navigation using human spatial concepts". International Journal of Intelligent Systems, Vol.15, No.3, March 2000, pp.165-196, 2000. ISBN 0884-8173.
12. Escrig, M.T., Toledo, F., "Reasoning with compared distances at different levels of granularity", in Proceedings of the 9th Conference of Spanish Association of Artificial Intelligence, October 2001.
13. Frank, A., "Qualitative Spatial Reasoning about Distance and Directions in Geographic Space". In Journal of Visual Languages and Computing 3, pag. 343-373, 1992.
14. Escrig, M.T., Toledo, F., Qualitative Spatial Reasoning: theory and practice. Application to Robot Navigation. IOS Press, Frontiers in Artificial Intelligence and Applications, ISBN 90 5199 4125. 1998.
15. Zimmermann, K., Freksa, C., "Enhancing Spatial Reasoning by the concept of motion", in the Proceedings of the AISB'93 Conference, 1993.
16. Musto, A. et al., "Qualitative and Quantitative representations of Locomotion and their application in robot navigation", in Proceedings of the IJCAI-99, Morgan Kaufman Publishers, 1999.
17. Musto, A. et al., "From motion observation to qualitative representation", in C. Freksa, C. Habel, C. Hendel (eds.), Spatial Cognition II. LNCS-Series, Springer Berlin, Heidelberg, New York, 2000.
18. Mackworth, A.K., Freuder, E.C., "The complexity of some Polynomial networks consistency algorithms for constraint satisfaction problems", Journal of Artificial Intelligence 25: pag. 65-74, 1985.
19. Fruehwirth, T., "Constraint Handling Rules", in A. Podelski (ed.), Constraint Programming: Basic and Trends, volume 910 of Lecture Notes in Computer Science, pag. 90-107, 1994. Springer.
20. P. Brisset et al., ECLiPSe 3.4 Extensions User Manual, European Computer-Industry Research Centre, Munich, Germany, 1994.

Knowledge Representation Model for Dynamic Processes

Gabriel Fiol-Roig

Departamento de Matemáticas e Informática. Universidad de las Islas Baleares.
dmigfr0@ps.uib.es

Abstract. Dynamic Processes are characterized by their evolutionary behaviour over time, defining a sequence of operation states of the System. Ascertaining the causes of a given system situation may become a difficult task, particularly in complex dynamic systems, since not all information required about the system state may be available at the precise moment.

Knowledge-Based Supervision is an outstanding Artificial Intelligence field contributing successfully to the progress of the control and supervion areas. Three essential factors characterize the function of a supervisor system: time constraints demanded from the supervision process, temporal updating of information coming from the dynamic system and generation of qualitative knowledge about the dynamic system.

In this work, an evolutionary data structure model conceived to generate, store and update qualitative information from raw data coming from a dynamic system is presented. This model is based on the concept of abstraction, in such a way an abstraction mechanism to generate qualitative knowledge about the dynamic system which the Knowledge-Based Supervisor is based on, is triggered according to some pre established considerations, among which real time constraints play a special role.

1   Introduction

Computer Science constitutes one of the main basis of the success of the Dynamic Systems progress; Artificial Intelligence contributions being particularly interesting to the advances in fields like Control, Monitoring, Supervision, Diagnosis and Decision of such systems.

Research in these fields is not new, some works concerned are already found in classical literatute, thus Mendel and Zapatac [14], Gibson [13] and Miró and Brousil [15] already considered the application of Artificial Intelligence techniques to Control Systems.

The tasks of Control, Monitoring and Supervision of dynamic processes constitute a guarantee of the quality and safety of the system, and are based on five main stages:

· Acquisition of data and parameters about the dynamic process.

· Generating control actions according to the data and parameters acquired, in order to satisfy some pre-established quality levels of the system function and to guarantee the system safety.

M.T. Escrig Monferrer and F. Toledo Lobo (Eds.): CCIA 2002, LNAI 2504, pp. 40-53, 2002.

· Detecting the existence of disturbances and consequently acting (by activating alarms, calibrating some devices, …and so on…).

· Generating diagnostic information about the quality and causes of the behaviour of the process.

· Generating corrective actions according to the resultant diagnostic information, which may involve the configuration of some control devices, suggesting certain actions on the process, … and so on…. This is the so called Decision Stage.

Control actions are based on premises defining the theoretical behaviour that the dynamic system should exhibit; however, the control device can not satisfy its objectives in some cases, because of several reasons, such as the occurrence of not predicted operation states, or perhaps a strong change of the characteristics of the system, out of the expected range of operation. In such situations, some changes in the own structure of the controllers are required. However, adequate information about the process state must be available to guarantee suitable responses.

Monitoring and Supervision are in charge of performing the three last stages listed above. While the Monitoring System processes quantitative and qualitative knowledge about the system state, a Supervisor System, also called a Knowledge-Based Supervisor, handles qualitative knowledge mostly, which determines the high quality demanded from its actions. Generating qualitative knowledge from raw data coming from the system implies the translation of information about signals, variables and indicators of situations into symbolic values, represented by the corresponding propositions, which take the form of production rules and can be manipulated by inferential mechanism of Artificial Intelligence.

Time constraints constitute another important factor affecting the Monitoring and Supervision tasks, whose corresponding procedures must be able to incorporate pre-established (real) time considerations. A formal model for real time diagnosis of dynamic systems is presented in [2]. This model is based on inductive learning techniques and considers both, the diagnosis of disturbances of a dynamic system, which determines the quality of the actual operation state of the system together with the existence of possible disturbances, and the causal diagnosis of the detected disturbances, determining why a disturbance occurred.

The state of development of such Supervisor Systems is incipient, but characterized by the significant progress of contributed works. In [1] a system prototype for nuclear plant supervision is presented, whose objectives are mainly focused to safety measures. The main modules in this system are: safety objectives, threat monitoring, diagnosis to determine the cause of threats, performing plans to control threats and predicting the consequences in order to synthesize control actions. Bernard et al [11] have implemented a control system prototype capable of diagnosing the operation state of an experimental reactor, with a little set of available control algorithms which may be activated according to the operation state of the reactor. In [17] a supervisor control prototype for a multimodular plant is presented, where a hierarchical multilevel structure for automatic control systems is developed in. Aguilar [8], [9], [10], is a pioneering researcher in the field of Knowledge-Based Supervision of Dynamic Systems, whose research turns on finding adequate ways to generate and formalize qualitative knowledge about a dynamic process.

The components of an Expert System for Control and Supervision of Dynamic Systems are the Monitoring and Supervisor Systems and the Intelligent Data Base (IDB) as knowledge model of the dynamic process.

A common aspect of most control, monitoring and supervision systems is the small generality of their design, limiting the range of application of the methods to particular dynamic systems. This is the case of the diagnostic methods presented in [12] and [18]. These two works consider model based techniques, whose knowledge model depend on the particular structure of the considered dynamic system. Therefore, the Intelligent Data Base should be conceived in a general way, as a knowledge model applicable to any dynamic system, independently of its particular characteristics.

The development of data interfaces such as the IDB, allowing the tasks of the Control, Monitoring and Supervision Systems to cooperate, is fundamental, being a wide research field to be explored. Such a knowledge representation model should be evolutionary over time, with three essential functions incorporated: *storing, updating* and *generating* qualitative knowledge about the system state. In [5] the conceptual aspects of a prototype of Intelligent Data Base for Control and Supervision of Dynamic Processes covering the mentioned aims are introduced.

A formal algebraic specification for such a IDB writen in terms of the formalism of the Abstract Data Type theory exposed in [7], is provided in this work. Also, the essential characteristics to do with the generation and updating of qualitative knowledge are discussed. Practical results were successfully developed within the scope of the TAP96-1114-C03-03 research project of the spanish government.

2   Levels of Information of a Control Process

The final decision about a critical situation of a control process corresponds, generally, to a human operator, which evaluates the variables and indicators representing the state of the process. The knowledge about the process activity of the human operator is expert, allowing a real time response of the operator. However, the complexity of some situations such as determining the causes of a disturbance or finding the best action to be adopted at a given moment, do not allow a real time action from the human operator. Monitoring and Supervisor Systems are designed to carry out, total or partially, such complex tasks, because of which the adequate information (quantitative or qualitative) about the process must be available when required. Table 1 illustrates the levels of information of a control process, according to [8] and [9].

Information in Level 0 or Instrumentation Level come from the sensors and actuators of the process, adopting usually an electrical format. Such information is translated into numerical or digitalized values and sent to Level 1 or Control Level, where the control devices process it in a procedural way (control algorithms). Direct real time control actions with immediate response time are carried out at this level. Level 2 or Monitoring Level stores and processes information about the dynamic process, which is expressed generally in graphic form, through communication protocols or data base format. The main functions associated to this level are the evaluation of situations of the control process and deciding some actions such as activating alarms, triggering special signals, and so on... Time constraints imposed at this level are not so strict as those from level 1, since the information format demands some abstraction procedures to be performed in order to generate the corresponding qualitative knowledge about the system. Level 3 or Supervision Level sees about providing information to complete some human operator tasks besides to assist the human operator in taking complex decisions. Typical tasks at this level are real time causal diagnosis of disturbances and decision taking. Information of this level is generally qualitative, expressed through a symbolic format, which supposes the application of refined abstraction procedures. The supervisor responses demand a reasoning period, which is limited by the time constraints imposed at this level.

Table 1. Levels of information of a control process

HUMAN OPERATORS			Linguistic	Nature of Information
LEVEL 3	SUPERVISION	Artificial Intelligence & Dialogue	Symbolic	
LEVEL 2	MONITORING	Data Base & Display	Visual	
LEVEL 1	CONTROL	PLCs Regul., Optimization	Numerical	
LEVEL 0	INSTRUMENTATION	Sensors & Actuators	Electrical	
PROCESS			Physical	

3   Conceptual Model for Knowledge Representation of Dynamic Systems

Common abstraction processes in the field of dynamic systems are in charge of transforming numerical (quantitative) into symbolic (qualitative) knowledge. These processes, together with the need for having adequate information in an optimal state of processing for each function of the Supervisor and Monitor Systems, require an appropiate arrangement of information about the system. A structured way to organize such information consists of arranging it in a non-decreasing hierarchy of levels, according to the degree of abstraction of the considered information, in such a way that each level contains information about the system state in a certain degree of abstraction.

Under these considerations, the basic design of the knowledge representation model for dynamic systems can be conceived as a device made up of some information layers, in such a way each layer corresponds to a level of abstraction in the hierarchy, whose information is used to carry out some functions of the Supervisor or Monitor Systems in an efficient way. Such a knowledge model must be evolutionary over time, since information from the process has to be updated constantly. Figure 1 shows a graphical illustration of such a knowledge model, with four abstraction layers.

This model has been illustrated as a concentric circle made up of four layers, which are arranged according to their levels of abstraction, in a non-decreasing order from the external layer (layer 1) to the internal one (layer 4), in such a way that layer 1 represents the most specific level of abstraction, whereas layer 4 contains information with a biggest expressive power or semantic intensity. Note that there may exist two adjacent layers, for example, layer i and layer i+1 whose levels of abstraction are identical, the only difference between these two layers being the code to represent the information. When a layer is full, the oldest data may be removed according to the formal specification of the model given in section 4.

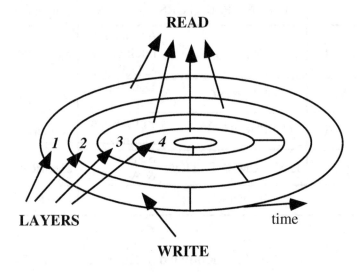

Fig. 1. Evolutionary Knowledge Representation Model

Only layer 1 can be written from raw data coming from the sensor and actuators readings, then all the layers except the first are written by abstraction procedures. When new raw data are written in the first layer, a device called *event detector* is triggered, which will interpret whether an abstraction involving these new raw data has to be carried out. There are two ways to activate the event detector:

· By using a clock generating pre-scheluded times.

· Through the detection of significant circumstances, indicating that the new raw data have enough significance to improve the current information of upper layers. This is a case of asynchronous event detection.

Each layer of the knowledge model of figure 1 has its own event detector associated, which will decide when the corresponding abstraction procedure associated to this layer must be performed. The results of applying an abstraction procedure to the data in a given layer, will be stored in the corresponding upper layer.

All the layers, including the first, can be read from external modules. The suitable number of layers for such a knowledge representation model seems to depend on the particular problem to be solved and on the abstraction model used by the particular Monitoring and Supervision Systems.

Under the above considerations, a knowledge representation model such as that illustrated through figure 1, called an *Evolutionary Knowledge Representation Model* and abbreviated *EKRM*, is evolutionary over time according to two essential factors:

· Information to be updated at the first layer of the model, called *quantitative evolution* of the model. That is, how data in layer 1 is updated over time from the sensor readings?.

· The abstraction mechanism incorporated to generate qualitative knowledge about the system, also called *qualitative evolution* of the model. That is, how qualitative knowledge about the system is generated over time?. Note that qualitative evolution is applied to all layers in the EKRM except layer 1.

To understand how quantitative and qualitative evolution are carried out, some aspects about the arrangement of knowledge in a layer are considered below.

Memory space assigned to a given layer j in an EKRM is broken into n portions, $d_1, d_2,..., d_n$, called *knowledge records*, arranged in sequential order, each one of which containing one *knowledge element*, whose abstraction degree corresponds to that of layer j. Figure 2 illustrates such an arrangement, where knowledge records d_1 and d_2 have been filled with the corresponding knowledge elements, in the specified order, whereas portions $d_3,...,d_n$ are still free, but available to store new knowledge elements coming from the application of an abstraction procedure, or from the plant, if it is the case of layer 1.

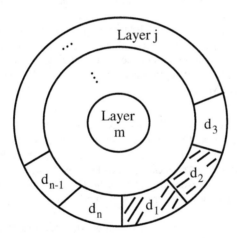

Fig. 2. Quantitative arrangement of knowledge

Once all the n knowledge records have been occuped by the corresponding knowledge elements in a given layer, then the process of storing new knowledge elements in this layer starts again from knowledge record d_1, rewriting so the previously occuped knowledge records.

The number of knowledge records in a given layer seems to depend on the particular characteristics of the monitoring and supervision processes, however, this parameter may be adjusted over time, so that more refined results of the abstraction procedure based on this layer are obtained.

4   Algebraic Specification of an Evolutionary Knowledge Representation Model

According to the description of an EKRM in section 3, such a model is made up of several abstraction layers, arranged in a non decreasing order of their abstraction degrees. The behaviour of an abstraction layer is that of a circular list, in the sense that once an abstraction layer is full, that is, all its knowledge records have been occuped by knowledge elements, then the process of storing new information elements starts again by occuping sequentially the first record, the second, the third, …, and so on.

In this section the formal algebraic specification of the EKRM is exposed, so avoiding any vague interpretation of the concept. Such specifications are used commonly in the field of computer programming, to describe abstract data types, abbreviated ADT, as abstract data structures. An ADT is defined in terms of an algebra, that is, as an x-tuple made up of sets of elements and operations defined on these sets, whose behaviour is defined through equational axioms. Moreover, abstract data types are *generated*, in the sense that any element of the sets in the algebra is generated by operations also in the algebra. Parameterized specifications of ADT's constitute a powerful tool to specify families of ADT's, by allowing to specify an ADT independently of its parameters.

In order to make the concepts understandable by unfamiliar readers, a parameterized specification of the EKRM made up of two steps is presented:

Step 1. The specification of the EKRM without considering the behaviour of the concept of abstraction layer is exposed at this step. Abstraction layers making up an EKRM are considered the parameters of the EKRM, being defined at the second step.

Step 2. The concept of abstraction layer is specified, completing the whole specification of the EKRM.

Parameterized Specification of the EKRM. The *EKRM*, also called the *EKRM abstract data type* and denoted by *ADT(EKRM)* is defined as a 13-tuple as follows:

ADT(EKRM) = (*Ekrm, Ad, Layers, Pos, Boolean,* CREATE_EKRM, INSERT_LAYER, POP_LAYER, LAST_LAYER, LAST_DEGREE, DEGREE, POSITION, BELONGS_TO).

Italic typed elements represent the sets of the EKRM abstract data type, whereas the others are the corresponding operations defined on these sets. Their meanings are as follows:

• *Ekrm* is the set of all Evolutionary Knowledge Representation Models. Each Evolutionary Knowledge Representation Model is made up of abstraction layers, included in set *Layers*.

• *Ad* is the ordered set of all possible abstraction degrees associated with abstraction layers. Note that set *Ad* could be represented as a subrange of integers.

• *Layers* is the set of all possible abstraction layers.

• *Pos* is the set of elements identifying the position of abstraction layers in an EKRM. It is important to identify the position of any abstraction layer in an EKRM, since an EKRM may be interpreted as an ordered list of elements, each element concerning an abstraction layer.

• *Boolean* is the boolean set with values *true* and *false*.

- CREATE_EKRM is an operation initializing any EKRM. It is a function of arity 0, also called a *constant function* since it constitutes in fact the starting point to create any EKRM.
- INSERT_LAYER is a function taking charge of adding a new abstraction layer to a given evolutionary knowledge representation model. Only empty layers, that is, layers with no elements can be added.
- POP_LAYER deletes the layer with a highest abstraction degree in an EKRM. If the considered EKRM contains more than one layer with a highest abstraction degree, then the last layer inserted is removed. Layer deleted corresponds to the most inner layer of figure 1.
- LAST_LAYER retrieves the layer with a highest abstraction degree in an EKRM. If the considered EKRM has more than one layer with a highest abstraction degree, then the last layer inserted is retrieved. Note that layer retrieved corresponds to the most inner layer of figure 1.
- LAST_DEGREE retrieves the abstraction degree of the layer with a higher one in an EKRM.
- DEGREE is the abstraction degree of a given layer n in an EKRM.
- POSITION retrieves the position of a layer n in an EKRM.
- BELONGS_TO is a boolean function, indicating if a given layer belongs to a considered evolutionary knowledge representation model.

Equational axioms defining formally the behaviour of operations of the just described EKRM, are defined below. Operation CREATE_EKRM and INSERT_LAYER are the *builders* also called *generating operations* of the abstract data type EKRM, that is, the operations in terms of which any Evolutionary Knowledge Representation Model in set *Ekrm* may be defined. Defining equational axioms for builders of an abstract data type is not necessary, except for those cases where different sintactic expressions have the same semantic meaning.

Equational Axioms of the abstract data type EKRM.

- INSERT_LAYER*: Ekrm × Layers × Ad → Ekrm*

$\forall N \in$ *Ekrm*, $n \in$ *Layers*, $d \in$ *Ad*:

E1. INSERT_LAYER(N,n,d) =

if N≠CREATE_EKRM then

  if n BELONGS_TO N then 'error'

  else if n is a non empty layer then 'error'

      else if d<LAST_DEGREE(N) then

            INSERT_LAYER(INSERT_LAYER(POP_LAYER(N),n,d), LAST_LAYER(N),

            DEGREE(N,LAST_LAYER(N)))

         end if;

      end if;

  end if;

end if;

- POP_LAYER*: Ekrm → Ekrm*

$\forall N \in$ *Ekrm*, $n \in$ *Layers*, $d \in$ *Ad*:

E2. POP_LAYER (CREATE_EKRM) = 'error';

E3. POP_LAYER(INSERT_LAYER(N,n,d)) =

      if n = LAST_LAYER(INSERT_LAYER(N,n,d)) then N

      else INSERT_LAYER(POP_LAYER(N),n,d)

      end if;

• LAST_LAYER: *Ekrm→ Layers*

$\forall$N $\in$ *Ekrm*, n $\in$ *Layers*, d $\in$ *Ad*:

E4. LAST_LAYER(CREATE_EKRM) = 'error';

E5. LAST_LAYER(INSERT_LAYER(N,n,d)) = if d $\geq$ LAST_DEGREE(N) then n
                                             else LAST_LAYER(N)
                                             end if;

• LAST_DEGREE: *Ekrm→ Ad*

$\forall$N $\in$ *Ekrm*, n $\in$ *Layers*, d $\in$ *Ad*:

E6. LAST_DEGREE(CREATE_EKRM) = 0;

(Note that abstraction degrees of layers are considered greater than 0)

E7. LAST_DEGREE(INSERT_LAYER(N,n,d)) =if d $\geq$ LAST_DEGREE(N) then d
                                             else LAST_DEGREE(N)
                                             end if;

• DEGREE: *Ekrm $\times$ Layers $\rightarrow$ Ad*

$\forall$N $\in$ *Ekrm*, n, n' $\in$ *Layers*, d $\in$ *Ad*:

E8. DEGREE(CREATE_EKRM,n) = 'error';

E9. DEGREE(INSERT_LAYER(N,n,d),n') =   if (n = n') then d
                                             else DEGREE(N,n')
                                             end if;

• POSITION: *Ekrm $\times$ Layers $\rightarrow$ Pos*

$\forall$N $\in$ *Ekrm*, n, n' $\in$ *Layers*, d $\in$ *Ad*:

E10. POSITION(CREATE_ERKM,n) = 'error'

E11. POSITION(INSERT_LAYER(N,n,d),n') =
  if n = n' then
      if n = LAST_LAYER(INSERT_LAYER(N,n,d))
          then POSITION (N,LAST_LAYER(N))+1
      else POSITION(INSERT_LAYER(POP_LAYER(N),n,d),n')
      end if;
  else
    if BELONGS_TO (N,n') then
      if DEGREE(N,n') > DEGREE (N, n) then
                              POSITION(N,n') + 1
      else POSITION(N,n')
      end if;
    else 'error'
    end if;
  end if;

• BELONGS_TO: *Ekrm $\times$ Layers $\rightarrow$ Bool*

$\forall$N $\in$ *Ekrm*, n,n' $\in$ *Layers*, d $\in$ *Ad*:

E12. BELONGS_TO(CREATE_EKRM,n) = false;

E13. BELONGS_TO (INSERT_LAYER(N,n,d),n') =if (n = n') then true
                                            else BELONGS_TO (N,n')
                                           end if;

Specification of the Concept of Abstraction Layer. Abstraction layers constitute the basic component of an EKRM and work as a circular list, such as has been explained in section 3. Figure 2 illustrates the evolutionary behaviour of an abstraction layer.

Once the n knowledge records of a given layer have been filled with the corresponding data, then the process of storing new data starts again at the first record, so only the n most recent elements inserted are considered as the elements of the considered layer.

Consider l to be a sequence of n knowledge records defining a full abstraction layer, then all possible sequences of records having l as the last (right) subsequence of elements added to the sequence, can be represented by $seq_i \bullet l$, $\forall i = 0...\infty$, seq_i representing an arbitrary sequence of i information records, and $seq_i \bullet l$ being the left-to-right concatenation of subsequences seq_i and l respectively.

An equivalence class $[l]$ of sequences of records equivalent to sequence l is now defined through the equivalence relation $\equiv$, as follows: $l \equiv seq_i \bullet l$. This fact indicates that once a layer l with n information records is full, then only the last n information records inserted are considered as the valid elements of this layer. Elements inserted previously to these last n elements are not taken into account, since they do not take part in the actual history of the system.

Abstraction layers with synchronous insertion of elements are specified here, considering an arbitrary time period T as the time interval between two consecutive insertions of elements in a given layer.

The concept of parameterized specification is also used to define the abstract data type abstraction layer, abbreviated *ADT(AL)*, as follows:

ADT(AL) = (*Layers, Elem, Layer_Size, Posit, Layer_Time_Period, Time, Boolean, Nat*, CREATE_LAYER, INSERT_ELEM, DELETE_ELEM, RETRIEVE_ELEM, LENGTH_LAYER, SIZE, TIME_LAST_ELEM, TIME_NEXT_ELEM, LAYER_TIME_PERIOD).

Italic typed elements are also used to represent the sets of the AL abstract data type, whereas the others parameters correspond to the operations, whose meaning is as follows:

• *Layers* is the set of all possible abstraction layers, which appears as a parameters of ADT(EKRM).

• *Elem* is the set of information elements making up abstraction layers. These elements may come directly from a dynamic system, in which case they will be stored in the first layer of an EKRM, or may result of applying an abstraction procedure to elements in other layers, being now stored in inner layers of an EKRM. Note that elements in set *Elem* are considered as parameters of ADT(AL) since they may adopt an arbitrary format.

• *Layer_Size* is the set of possible sizes of abstraction layers in set *Layers* and could be considered as a subrange of integers.

• *Posit* is the set positions of elements in abstraction layers.

• *Layer_Time_Period* is the set of time periods available to carry out a synchronous evolution of a layer. This set could be considered as a subrange of integers.

• *Time* is the set of values generated by a clock. This set may be easily represented through real numbers.

• *Boolean* is the boolean set with values true and false.

• *Nat* is the set of natural numbers.

• CREATE_LAYER is a generating operation of ADT(AL), whose function consist of initializing an abstraction layer. It is also a function of arity 0, like the function CREATE_EKRM.

• INSERT_ELEM adds a new information element to a considered layer. All insertions of information elements are made at the same end, whereas deletions are made at the opposite end, in a similar way than that of a queue abstract data type. This is also a generating operation.

• DELETE_ELEM removes the oldest element in a given full abstraction layer. All deletions take place at the same end of the abstraction layer.

• RETRIEVE_ELEM retrieves the element placed at a given position in a considered layer.

• LENGTH_LAYER returns the length in terms of the number of elements of a given abstraction layer.

• SIZE returns the size of a given abstraction layer. The size of an abstraction layer is defined as the number of elements that an abstraction layer may contain to be considered full, and must be defined when initializing the layer.

• TIME_LAST_ELEM returns the time of the last insertion of an element in a given layer.

• TIME_NEXT_ELEM returns the time at which next insertion of an element in a given abstraction layer will take place.

• LAYER_TIME_PERIOD returns the time period of progress, that is, the time period between two consecutive insertions in an abstraction layer.

Equational Axioms of abstract data type Abstraction Layer.

• INSERT_ELEM: *Layers* × *Elem*→ *Layers*

∀L ∈ *Layers*, e ∈ *Elem*, true ∈ *Bool:*

E14. INSERT_ELEM(L,e) = if LENGTH_LAYER(L) = SIZE(L) then

　　　　　　　　　　　　INSERT_ELEM(DELETE_ELEM(L,SIZE(L),true),e)

　　　　　　　end if;

(Note that condition LENGTH_LAYER(L) = SIZE(L) indicates wether layer L is full)

• DELETE_ELEM: *Layers* × *Layer_Size* × *Bool* → *Layers*

∀L ∈ *Layers*, e ∈ *Elem*, m ∈ *Layer_Size*, full ∈ *Bool:*

E15. DELETE_ELEM(CREATE_LAYER,m,full) = 'error';

E16. DELETE_ELEM(INSERT_ELEM(L,e),m,full) =

　　if (LENGTH_LAYER(INSERT_ELEM(L,e))=(SIZE(INSERT_ELEM(L,e))) or (full = true))

　　　　then

　　　　　　if m = 1 then CREATE_LAYER

　　　　　　else INSERT_ELEM(DELETE_ELEM(L,m-1,true),e)

　　　　　　end if;

　　else 'error'

　　end if;

(Note that function DELETE_ELEM can be applied only to full layers).

• LENGTH_LAYER: *Layers*→ *Nat*

∀L ∈ *Layers*, e ∈ *Elem:*

E17. LENGTH_LAYER(CREATE_LAYER) = 0;

E18. LENGTH_LAYER(INSERT_ELEM(L,e)) = if LENGTH_LAYER(L) < SIZE(L) then

　　　　　　　　　　　　　　　1+LENGTH_LAYER(L)

　　　　　　　　　　　else SIZE(L)

　　　　　　　　　　　end if;

- RETRIEVE_ELEM: *Layers* × *Posit* → *Elem*

∀L ∈ *Layers*, e ∈ *Elem*, p ∈ *Posit*:

E19. retrieve_elem(create_layer,p) = 'error';

E20. retrieve_elem(insert_elem(L,e),p) =

    if LENGTH_LAYER(INSERT_ELEM(L,e)) ≥ p then

                       if p = 1 then e

                       else RETRIEVE_ELEM(L,p-1)

                       end if;

    else 'error'

    end if;

- TIME_NEXT_ELEM: *Layers* → *Time*

∀L ∈ *Layers*, e ∈ *Elem*:

E21. TIME_NEXT_ELEM(create_layer) = starting_time;

E22. TIME_NEXT_ELEM(INSERT_ELEM(L,e)) =

    TIME_LAST_ELEM(INSERT_ELEM(L,e)) + LAYER_TIME_PERIOD(INSERT_ELEM(L,e))

The behaviour of the remaining operations (SIZE, LAYER_TIME_PERIOD and TIME_LAST_ELEM) in terms of equational axioms is omitted, since they can be described in a very simple way. However, algebraic specifications consider only the essential aspects of the EKRM and Abstraction Layer abstract data types.

5   The Abstraction Mechanism

An abstractor is a function taking parameters in the form of data coming from several information layers, whose semantic intensity of its results is higher than that of the corresponding parameters. Note that if parameters and results of a given abstractor belong to the same Evolutionary Knowledge Representation Model, then layers containing the results will occupe more inner places in the EKRM than those containing the parameters.

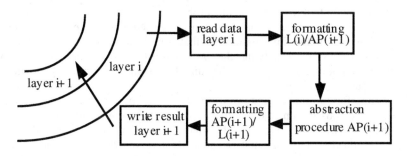

Fig. 3. Abstraction mechanism

An abstractor *abs* adopts the following general feature:

    abs: $l_1 \times a\_e_1 \times l_2 \times a\_e_2 \times ... \times l_p \times a\_e_p \rightarrow elem$

l_1, l_2,...,l_p being the layers from which parameters a_e_1, ..., a_e_p have been taken respectively. These parameters are represented by arrays of elements, each array containing an arbitrary number of them.

The general mechanism taking charge of performing an abstraction is made up of five steps, such as figure 3 illustrates, whose parameters of the abstractor belong to layer i and results are stored in layer i+1.

Step 1. Read data layer i consists of reading the corresponding parameters from layer i in order to be used by the abstraction procedure AP(i+1) of layer i+1.

Step 2. Formatting L(i)/AP(i+1) translates information from layer i into useful information to be accepted by the abstraction procedure AP(i+1).

Step 3. Abstraction procedure AP(i+1) carries out an abstraction on the basis of the formatted information coming from layer i, placing the results into layer i+1. In fact, there may exist several abstraction procedures for each layer, but only one of them is activated at each instant. The selection of the abstraction procedure to be activated depends on the nature of the problem.

Step 4. Formatting AP(i+1)/L(i+1) translates the resultant information coming from the abstraction procedure AP(i+1) into adequate information to be stored in layer i+1.

Step 5. Write result layer i+1 writes the results obtained by the abstraction procedure AP(i+1), already formatted, in layer i+1.

An abstraction of information of layer i may cause events at layer j which may require the corresponding abstraction procedure to be performed; in the extreme case, the need for performing abstractions may be propagated to all layers $k \geq j$.

6   Conclusions

The problem of storing information for real time based supervision of dynamic processes has been stated. Keeping the pre-established constraints about the response time is a difficult task since information about each function of the supervisor and control systems must be available when required, in an optimal state of processing.

In the case of complex dynamic systems the problem is still more evident, since the large amount of raw data coming from the sensors reading may not allow to process the necessary information according to the real time constraints imposed. Abstraction constitutes the main tool to overcome this problem of superabundance of information, in such a way raw data are analysed and processed over time, generating the corresponding qualitative information so that supervision and control tasks are performed satisfactorily, satisfying the pre established real time considerations. However, abstraction procedures must be suitably designed in order to guarantee the considered real time constraints.

Knowledge-Based Supervision is a recent research area based on Artificial Intelligence methods to generate qualitative knowledge from quantitative data in an evolutionary environment. One of the main aspects of these methods is the arrangement and storage of quantitative and qualitative knowledge, since a significant amount of functions are frequently demanded by the control and supervisor systems.

A formal Evolutionary Knowledge Representation Model to store, update and generate qualitative knowledge is proposed in this work. This model constitutes the data interface among the control, the monitoring and the supervisor systems and it is characterized by its evolutionary behaviour over time, allowing to satisfy the pre established real time considerations. The formality of the model is expressed through the corresponding equations of the abstract data type theory, so avoiding any vague interpretation.

Finally, a data base for supervision and control can be conceived as an entity made up of several EKRM's suitably connected, in such a way there is one EKRM for each element of the dynamic system to be controlled or supervised. Lab experiments with successful results have proved the usefulness of this methodology in Real Time Knowledge Based Supervision of dynamic systems.

References

1. Chandrasekaran, B., Bhatnagar, R., Sharna, D.: Real Time Disturbance Control. Communications of the ACM, Vol. 34, No. 8 (1991) 32-47

2. Fiol, G.: Formal Model for Real Time Diagnosis of Dinamic Systems. Proceedings of the International IEEE Joint Symposia on Intelligence and Systems (1998) 218-225

3. Fiol, G., Miró, J.: A Diagnosis Problem Approach Based on Inductive Acquisition of Knowledge from Examples. Heuristics, Vol. 6, No. 3 (1993) 54-65

4. Fiol, G., Miró-Julià, J., Miró-Nicolau, J.: A New Perspective in the Inductive Acquisition of Knowledge from Examples. Lecture Notes in Computer Science, Vol. 682. Springer Verlag, Berlin Heidelberk New York, (1993) 219-228

5. Fiol, G., Ferrer, M.: Data Base for Supervision. Proceedings of the 14th International Congress on Cybernetics (1995) 633-638

6. Fiol, G., Ferrer, M.: Expert System for Supervision of Real Time Control Processes. IEEE Conference on Systems, Man and Cybernetics (1996) 1966-1971

7. Ehrig, H., Mahr, B.: Fundamentals of Algebraic Specification 1. Equations and Initial Semantics, Springer Verlag, Berlin Heidelberg New York (1985)

8. Aguilar-Martín, J.: Knowledge Representation for Real Time Industrial Process Modelization. Invited talk to the 1992 IEEE International Conference on Systems, Man and Cybernetics. Chicago (1992)

9. Aguilar-Martín, J.: Knowledge-Based Systems for the Supervision of Real Time Control Processes. Invited talk to the 4th International Symposium on Knowledge Engineering. Barcelona (1990)

10. Aguilar-Martín, J.: Qualitative Control, Diagnostic and Supervision of Complex Processes. Mathematics and Computers in Simulation Vol. 36 (1994) 115-127

11. Bernard, J.: The Application of Digital Control Technology to the Control of Reactor Power: A Review of the MIT Reactor Experiments. Proceedings of the 6th. Power Plant Dynamics, Control & Testing Symposium (1986)

12. de Kleer, J., Seely, J.: Model-Based Diagnosis in SOPHIE III, Readings in Model-Based Diagnosis, Morgan Kaufman Publishers, San Mateo, Cal. USA (1992) 179-204

13. Gibson, J. E.: Adaptative Learning Systems, ASTIA Alexandria, Virginia, AD292 796 (1963)

14. Mendel, J., Zapalac, J. J.: The Application of Techniques of Artificial Intelligence to Control System Design. Advances in Control Systems, Vol 6 (1968)

15. Miró, J., Brousil, J. K.: Simulation of an Evolutive System. Annals of the Spanish Royal Academy of Physics and Chemistry, Vol. LXIV, No. 5 and 6, (1968), pp. 149

16. Ferrer, M.: UIB-IK, an Inductive Acquisition of Knowledge System. In: Inductive Knowledge Acquisition System Prototype to describe the disease of Ascites. Final project. Computer Science Department, University of the Balearic Islands, SPAIN (1993)

17. Otaduy, P. J., Britain, C. R., Rovere, A.: Supervisory Hierarchical Control for a Multi-modular LMR. Proceedings of the 7th. Power Plant Dynamics, Control & Testing Symposium (1989)

18. Milne, R.: Model-Based Reasoning: The Application GAP. IEEE Expert, Vol. 6, No. 6 (1992) 5-7

A Decision Case-Based System, That Reasons in Uncertainty Conditions

Iliana Gutiérrez Martínez and Rafael E. Bello Pérez

Department of Computer Science
Universidad Central de Las Villas
Carretera a Camajuaní km 5.5
Santa Clara, Cuba
Phone: (53) (42) 281416, 281156, 281515
Fax :(53) (42) 281608
iliana@cei.uclv.edu.cu
rbellop@uclv.edu.cu

Abstract. Generally, most Decision Systems do not consider the uncertainty that might be present in knowledge. On many occasions, this leads to proposed solutions that are sometimes inconsistent with the expected results.

Case-Based Reasoning is one of the techniques of Artificial Intelligence used in the solution of decision-making problems. Consequently, Case-Based Systems, must consider imperfection in the available knowledge about the world.

In this paper, we present a model to make case-based decisions under uncertainty conditions. The model uses Decision Trees and Rough Set Theory to assure an efficient access and an adequate retrieval of cases.

Keywords: Case-Based Systems, Knowledge Representation, Uncertainty, Rough Sets Theory

1. Introduction

The purpose of Information Systems is to model the real world, however, sometimes the information about the world is not certain, complete or precise [10]. Thus, to build useful Information Systems, it is necessary to learn how to represent uncertain information and to reason with it.

Several studies focus the uncertainty problems from various points of view: Probabilistic [13], [9], [5], Fuzzy [1], [2] and even more recently, using the Rough Set Theory [11], [12], [14], [3] Up to now, the question of uncertainty has not been fully studied in Case-Based Systems due to the fact that flexibility in the representation of uncertain information has affected efficiency while searching for new solutions.

In this study we discuss classifications and the sources of uncertainty in Case-Based Systems. Then, starting from a model of a classical case-based system, we propose a new approach to allow the determination and handling of uncertainty in a case-base. The results are showed through the real problem.

M.T. Escrig Monferrer and F. Toledo Lobo (Eds.): CCIA 2002, LNAI 2504, pp. 54–63, 2002.

2. Case-Based Systems as Information Systems

A table can represent a data set where each row represents, for instance, an object, a case, or an event. Every column represents an attribute that is a variable, an observation, or a property that can be measured for each object. This table, more formally called an Information System, is a pair $A = (U, A)$ where U is a none-empty finite set of objects called the universe and A is a none-empty finite set of attributes such that $a : U \rightarrow V_a$ for every $a \in A$. The set V_a is called the value set of a.

A Decision System is any Information System of the type $A = (U, A \cup \{d\})$, where $d \notin A$ is the decision attribute.

There are two types of Case-Based Systems: interpretative and problem solver. A Case-Based System problem solver is a Decision System where the universe represents the case set and where the attributes A are called predictor features and decision d is called the objective feature.

The fundamental components of a Case-Based System are: the Case-Base, the Retrieval Module and the Adaptation Module.

A case-base is described starting from the values that are assigned to the predictor features and to the objective ones. The former determine the value of the latter. A case that has n predictor features and an objective feature is described in the following way:

$$O_t(x_1(O_t),...,x_i(O_t),...,x_n(O_t),y(O_t)) \tag{1}$$

where

$x_i(O_t)$: Value of the predictor feature x_i, $i=1,...,n$ for the case O_t, $t=1,...,m$ of the case-base

$y(O_t)$: Value of the objective feature for the case $O_t, t=1,...,m$ of the case-base

A new problem is represented starting from the predictor features in the following way:

$$O_0(x_1(O_0),...,x_i(O_0),...,x_n(O_0)) \tag{2}$$

Retrieval Module

To solve the new problem the most similar cases are obtained from the retrieval module.

The two key aspects of this phase are the access algorithm to cases and the similarity measure among cases. To determine how similar a case is to another, several techniques have been developed. The simplest one consists of the use of a group of heuristics that allow us to determine which characteristics have greater relevance in order to formulate a similarity function involving the similarity among each feature with relevance in mind. A mathematical model of this technique is the Near-Neighbor Similarity Function:

$$\beta(O_0, O_t) = \frac{\sum\limits_{i=1}^{n} p_i \cdot \delta_i(O_0, O_t)}{\sum\limits_{i=1}^{n} p_i} \tag{3}$$

where:

p_i : Weight or relevance of the feature x_i .

$\delta_i(O_0, O_t)$: Comparison function between the cases O_0 and O_t according to the feature x_i .

Adaptation Module

In this module, starting from the solutions of the retrieval cases, the new problem is solved.

2.1   Uncertainty in the Case-Base Systems

As can be noticed, in this model, the description of a case results from a set of variables that take different values. The consideration of all the potential cases is unlikely and just a subset of sets comprising real cases is taken into account. This brings about uncertainty caused by incomplete data. Besides, the values of the case can be obtained from different sources: exact methods, several experts' criteria and measuring instruments, or in many cases such values must even be made discrete or may be omitted [4].

The fact that there is uncertainty in the values of the feature drives us to resolve the following questions [6]:

- How can a certainty value be estimated considering the different sources of uncertainty?
- How can the similarity function (3) be redefined in order to consider both the values of the features and the value of their certainty?
- How can the certainty value be considered in the process of adaptation?

The solving of these questions leads us to redefine the model previously presented. Next, we present a new approach, capable of solving these questions.

3. Model for the Uncertainty Management on a Case-Base

The proposed model allows for the building of a decision tree starting from the fundamentals of the Rough Set Theory.

The Rough Set Theory

The Rough Set Theory lies on the assumption that some sort of information is associated with every object of the discourse universe. The objects that are characterized by the same information are similar in terms of the information available. Thus they can be represented in the same equivalence class.

Let $A = (U, A)$ be an information system. To each $B \subseteq A$ an equivalence relation $R_A(B)$ is associated as follows:

$$R_A(B) = \{(x, y) \in U^2 | \forall a \in B, a(x) = a(y)\} \qquad (4)$$

In this case, the class of equivalence of an element $x \in U$ is denoted as $[x]_B$.

The Rough Membership Function is defined as $\mu_B^X : U \to [0,1]$

On applying this function to an x object, it quantifies the relative overlapping degree between the X set and the equivalence class to which x belongs. It can be interpreted as an estimate based on the frequency $P(x \in X | x, B)$, which is the probability that the x object might belong to the X set according to the information on hand of x with regards to the attributes of B .

$$\mu_B^X(x) = \frac{\|[x]_B \cap X\|}{\|[x]_B\|} \qquad (5)$$

Using this theory we next present an algorithm to allow the building of a decision tree starting from a case-base.

Decision Tree

We are proposing a decision tree structure in order to represent the case-base. The presented algorithm allows for the building of a decision tree starting from the fundamentals of the Rough Set Theory. Along with the advantages of decision trees as structures that make the access to cases easy, we can also profit from the easy calculations of the uncertainty present in the values.

Algorithm 1. Decision Tree Construction

Let y be the decision (objective feature), which takes values in the set: $N = \{y_1, ..., y_q, ..., y_\theta\}$ where θ is the cardinality of the set of values that this objective feature takes.

Let K be the set of predictor features $x_i, i = 1, n$, which takes the values in the sets $M_i = \{x_{i1}, ..., x_{ip}, ..., x_{i\eta_i}, x_{i\eta_i+1}\}$ where η_i is the cardinality of the group of values that the predictor features x_i take and where $x_{\eta_i+1} = unknown$ represents the missing values.

AD1: Locate one of the equivalence classes associated to the objective feature in the root of each tree.

AD2: Find in set K the predictor feature that according to the experts' criteria is best associated to the objective feature y.

AD3: Determine the classes of equivalence taking into account the objective feature and the selected predictor feature.

AD4: Expand the root of each tree by the corresponding equivalence classes determined in the previous step.

AD5: Delete in K set, the selected predictor feature.

AD6: Find in K set, the predictor feature that according to the experts' criteria is best associated to the predictor feature in the leaves. If there are no other associated features, stop.

AD7: Expand the leaves of the trees whose correspondent equivalence class is not an empty set formed by the intersection of the equivalence class found in that leaf and each one of the equivalence classes associated to the new selected feature. Go to AD5.

As a result of this algorithm, we now have the case-base represented through a set of trees. In these trees, each branch leads to a node where you can find one of the equivalence classes corresponding to the features that have appeared up to this level. These equivalence classes are represented by I_{lb}^q where q indicates that it is in a node of the tree in whose root appears the equivalence class associated to the y_q value of the objective feature, l is the level of the tree where it is found and b is the branch. As a result, the cases have remained arranged in a hierarchical structure where in each level there is an equivalence relationship associated to the predictor features appearing up to that level and to the objective feature. From this structure the certainties of the values of the predictor features and of the objective feature are determined.

Certainty Determination of Predictors and Objectives Values

The certainties $\zeta_i(O_t)$ and $v(O_t)$ of the predictor and objective features is calculated by using the decision tree that describes the dependence relationship between the values of the predictor and the objective features

Algorithm 2. First Certainty

PP1: Certainty associated to the values of the predictor features that do not appear in the decision tree

$\forall O_t \in U$

$$\zeta_i(x_i(O_t) = x_{ip}) = \begin{cases} \dfrac{\left|[O_t]_{x_i}\right|}{m} & if \ x_{ip} = unknown \\ \max\limits_{k=1,m}\left(\dfrac{\left|[O_k]_{x_i}\right|}{m}\right) & else \end{cases} \qquad (6)$$

If $(x_i(O_t) = unknown)$ and $[O_s]_{x_i}$ is the equivalence class for which

$\dfrac{\left\| [O_k]_{x_i} \right\|}{m}, k = 1,...,m$ resulted as the maximum, then $x_i(O_t) = x_i(O_s)$.

PP2: Certainty for the values of the predictor features appearing in the decision trees:

Let l_n be the number of the tree levels and let b_l be the number of nodes of the l level.

For $q = 1,...,\theta$

    For $l = 1,...,l_n$

        For $b = 1,...,b_l$

            $\forall O_t \in I_{lb}^q$

        If the feature x_i appears in the l level and $x_i(O_t) = x_{ip}$

$$\zeta_i\big(x_i(O_t) = x_{ip}\big) = \begin{cases} \dfrac{\left| I_{lb}^q \right|}{\left| I_{l-1\left[\frac{b}{\eta_i+1}\right]}^q \right|} & if\ x_{ip} = unknown \\[4ex] \max_{b=1,b_l} \dfrac{\left| I_{lb}^q \right|}{\left| I_{l-1\left[\frac{b}{\eta_i+1}\right]}^q \right|} & else \end{cases} \tag{7}$$

If $(x_i(O_t) = unknown)$ and I_{lp}^q was the set for which $\dfrac{\left| I_{lb}^q \right|}{\left| I_{l-1\left[\frac{b}{\eta_i+1}\right]} \right|}, b = 1,...,b_l$ resulted as

the maximum, then $x_i(O_t) = x_{ip}$.

PP3: Certainty associated to the objective feature.

    For $l = 1,...,l_n$

        For $b = 1,...,b_l$

            For $q = 1,...,\theta$

                $\forall O_t \in I_{lb}^q$

$$v\big(y(O_t) = y_q\big) = \dfrac{\left| I_{lb}^q \right|}{\left| \bigcup_{j=1}^{\theta} I_{lb}^j \right|} \tag{8}$$

PP4: If $x_i(O_t) = x_{ip}$ then $\zeta_i(O_t) = \zeta_i\big(x_i(O_t) = x_{ip}\big)$

PP5: If $y(O_t) = y_q$ then $v(O_t) = v\big(y(O_t) = y_q\big) \cdot \prod_{x_i \in K^C \cup K'} v(x_i(O_t))$

Since this certainty depends on the frequency with which the values appear in the base, it is necessary to calculate it every time a new case is added. Hence, the importance of using an efficient representation structure for its calculation.

Most Similar Cases Retrieval

The retrieval process involves two procedures: access and retrieval.
During the access phase, potential cases for the recovering process are selected, using the hierarchical structure of the case representation.

Algorithm 3. Access
Input: Problem to solve: O_0

     Level to consider: l
Output: Set of cases to recover: P
ACR1: $P = \{ \}$
ACR2: For $q = 1,..,\theta$

  i)   On each tree, select at level l the equivalence class corresponding to O_0. Be it

    I^q_{lb}

  ii) $P = P \bigcup I^q_{lb}$ (9)
Thus potential cases remain in set P.

Algorithm 4. Retrieval
Input: P, O_0, nc (number of cases to recover)
Output: Most Similar cases S
R1: $\forall O_t \in P$ calculate

$$\beta(O_0, O_t) = \frac{\sum\limits_{i=1}^{n} p_i\, \delta_i\big(x_i(O_t), x_i(O_0)\big) \cdot \big(1 - |\varsigma_i(O_t) - \varsigma_i(O_0)|\big)}{\sum\limits_{i=1}^{n} p_i} \qquad (10)$$

where:
n: Number of predictor features.

p_i: Weight or relevance of the feature i.

R2: Assign the most similar cases to S .

The new similarity function satisfies the following features:
I1: $0 \le \beta(O_0, O_t) \le 1$ (Boundary Condition)
I2: $\beta(O_t, O_t) = 1$ (Reflexivity)
I3: $\beta(O_0, O_t) = \beta(O_t, O_0)$ (Symmetry Condition)

Decision Determination

Once the most similar cases have been selected, it is possible for them to suggest different decisions. Therefore, it will be necessary to determine which decision to make. This selection is carried out considering the degree of similarity calculated in the previous procedure and the certainty of the decision of the recovered cases.

Algorithm 5. Adaptation
A1: $\forall O_t \in S$ do:

$$\mu(O_t) = \gamma \cdot \beta(O_0, O_t) + (1 - \gamma) \cdot v(O_t) \tag{11}$$

where γ is a parameter that is selected according to the experts' criteria. If γ tends to 1, it means that more importance is given to the similarity between the new problem and the recovered case than to the certainty of the solution of that case.

A2: If $\mu(O_t)$ is maximum, select case O_t and take its decision for solving the new problem.

4. Empirical Evaluation

The model described has been implemented through URS (Uncertainty Reasoning Systems) and evaluated on the datasets related to heart diseases [8].
Next, we show the description of the validation process. For more details see [7]
Table 1 summarizes the characteristics of the datasets.
Each experiment randomly partitioned the data into a 90% training set and a 10% testing set.
The results obtained from the application of the similarity function of the Nearest Neighbor Algorithm with the handling of uncertainty (10) and the adaptation formula proposed (11) are compared to the use of that very function in its classical form (3) using the adaptation method by reinstantiation. To identify these two processes, the first one is called NNB N (New Model of the Nearest Neighbor and the second one NNB T (Traditional Model of the Nearest Neighbor).

Table 1. Characteristics of the datasets

Case-base	No. Cases	Continuous Features	Missing Values
Cleveland	303	yes	yes
Hungarian	294	yes	yes
Switzerland	123	yes	yes
Long Beach	200	yes	yes

The results are averaged to analyze the system efficiency. Figures 1 shows the results.

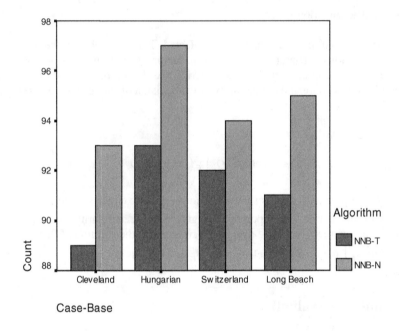

Fig. 1. Percentage of well-classified cases using the NNB T and NNB N algorithms

With little or no domain-specific background knowledge it could be observed that the knowledge organization and the retrieval and adaptation mechanisms with uncertainty handling produce meaningful results.

5. Conclusions

This research focuses the problem of decision-making under uncertainty in a Case-Based System pursuing a new structure for the organization of a case-base capable of combining the use of Decision Trees with the Rough Set Theory. Besides allowing a more efficient access to cases, the structure proposed makes the calculation of the existing uncertainty in their values easier. The algorithms for the calculation and handling of the uncertainty in the retrieval and adaptation modules were implemented in the URS Computational System, successfully applied in the making of decisions while diagnosing.

Acknowledgements. The authors are grateful to Dr. Zdzislaw Pawlak, whose comments on versions of this work and directions to related references have been most valuable.

References

1. Baldwin, J.F., Ribliro R.: Fuzzy reasoning by call for decision support systems. Int. Journal of uncertainty, fuzziness and knowledge-based systems, vol. 2, no 1, pages 11-24, 1994.
2. Chen, S-J., Hwang C-L.: Fuzzy Multiple Attribute Decision Making, Methods and Applications, Springer Verlag, 1992.
3. Churn-Jung L.: An Overview of Rough Set Semantics for Modal and Quantifier Logic. Journal of Uncertainty, Fuzziness and Knowledge-Based Systems Vol. 8, No. 1, pages 93-118, 2000.
4. Gutiérrez, I., Bello, R.: La Problemática de la Incertidumbre en los Sistemas Basados en Casos. Revista de Ingeniería de la Universidad de Antioquia, 1998.
5. Gutiérrez, I., Bello,R., Díaz de Villegas, A. Tellería, A.: Una Métrica de Similaridad Probabilista para el Módulo de Recuperación de un Sistema Basado en Casos. Proceeding del 7mo Congreso de Nuevas Tecnologías y Aplicaciones Informáticas. La Habana, 2000.
6. Gutiérrez I., Bello, R.: Determinación y Manejo de la Incertidumbre en un sistema Basado en Casos. Proceedings of the 7th Joint International Iberoamerican Conference. Conference on Artificial Intelligence, 15th Brazilian Conference on Artificial Intelligence Iberamia-SBIA 2000, 2000.
7. Gutiérrez, I., Bello, R.: URS, Uncertainty Reasoning System. Revista de Ingeniería de la Corporación Universitaria de Ibagué, Colombia, 2002.
8. Merz, C. J.,Murphy, P.M.: UCI Repository of Machine Learning Databases. Irvine, CA: University of California Irvine, Department of Informatics and Computer Science, 1996.
9. Myllymaki. P. ,Tirri, H.: Massively parallel case-based reasoning with probabilistic similarity metrics. In K-D. Althoff, K. Richter, and S. Wess, editors, Proceedings of the First European Workshop on Case-Based Reasoning, Kaiserslautern pages 48-53, 1993.
10. Parsons, S. :Current Approaches to handling Imperfect Information in Data and Knowledge Bases. IEEE Transactions on Knowledge and Data Engineering, Vol 8, No 3, 1996.
11. Pawlak, Z.: Vagueness and Uncertainty: a Rough Set Perspective. Computational Intelligence, Vol. 11, No 2., 1995.
12. Pawlak, Z: :Rough Sets: Present State and Perspectives. In: Proceedings of the Sixth International Conference "Information Processing and Management of Uncertainty in Knowledge-Based Systems (IPMU '96)" [1], pages 1137-1146, 1996.
13. Pearl, J.: Probabilistic Reasoning in Intelligent Systems. Palo Alto: Morgan Kaufmann, 1988.
14. Sankar, K., Skowron, P.: Rough Fuzzy Hybridization: A New Trend in decision-Making. Springer, Singapore, 1999.

Modeling Motion Qualitatively: Integrating Space and Time

Lledó Museros[1] and M. Teresa Escrig Monferrer[2]

[1]Alicer, Ceramic Design Technology Institute, Avda. Mar 42, E -12003
Castellón (Spain).
lledo@alicer.es
[2]Universidad Jaume I, Engineering and Computer Science Department,
E-12071Campus Riu Sec, Castellón (Spain)
escrigm@icc.uji.es

Abstract. Motion can be seen as a form of spatio-temporal change. This concept is used in this paper to present a qualitative representational model for integrating qualitatively time and topological information for reasoning about dynamic worlds in which spatial relations between regions may change with time. The calculus here presented exploits Freksa's notion of *conceptual neighbourhood* and defines a *topological neighbourhood* of the topological calculus about point-like, linear and areal 2D regions defined by Isli, Museros et alters. According to this, two topological relations can be called conceptual neighbours if one can be transformed into the other one by a process of gradual, continuous change which does not involve passage through any third relation. The calculus described consists of a constraint-based approach and it is presented as an algebra akin to Allen´s (1983) temporal interval algebra. One advantage of presenting the calculus in this way is that Allen's incremental constraint propagation algorithm can then be used to reason about knowledge expressed in the calculus. The algorithm is guided by composition tables and a converse table provided in this contribution. The algorithm will help, for instance, during the path-planning task of an autonomous robot by describing the sequence of topological situations that the agent should find during its way to the target objective.

1 Introduction

There are several approaches handling with spatio-temporal data [1,2,3,4,5]. If we want to construct a truly autonomous AI system then practical ways of reasoning with spatio temporal information must be found. Time and space are closely interconnected: much information that is referenced to space is also referenced to time and may vary with time. Motion is an example as it can be seen as a form of spatial change and it is used in such an interpretation in this paper.

There is of a large amount of work in qualitative theories as a basis for commonsense reasoning [6]. Our work in this paper is oriented to model motion in a qualitative framework. Our aim is to formalize the intuitive notion of spatio-temporal continuity for a qualitative theory of motion. Therefore, the paper presents a

M.T. Escrig Monferrer and F. Toledo Lobo (Eds.): CCIA 2002, LNAI 2504, pp. 64-74, 2002.
© Springer-Verlag Berlin Heidelberg 2002

qualitative representation model for integrating qualitative time and topological information for modeling motion and reasoning about dynamic worlds in which spatial relations between regions may change with time.

The representational model presented is a calculus which integrates a temporal algebra, in which variables represents time points and there are five primitive constraints: <<,==, >>, prev and next. As space the model presented integrates the topological calculus developed in [7] which reason about point-like, linear and areal 2D regions. The topological calculus chosen defines 9 topological relations which are: *touch, cross, overlap, disjoint, equal, completely-inside, touching-from-inside, completely-inside_i* and *touching-from-inside_i*.

The calculus described along the paper consists of a constraint-based approach and it is presented as an algebra akin to Allen's [8] temporal interval algebra, then Allen's incremental constraint propagation algorithm can be then used to reason about the knowledge expressed in the calculus. The algorithm is guided by composition tables and converse table that will be provided in this paper.

Usually composition tables have provided us with a mechanism for reasoning within static world. But in this paper we turn out our attention to the task of reasoning about dynamic worlds exploiting the Freksa's notion of conceptual neighborhood [9, 10]. The composition tables of the calculus described here can be regarded as an instance of conceptual neighborhood, and we will call it *topological neighborhood*. According to this, two relations drawn from a pair wise exclusive and jointly exhaustive set, such as the topological calculus defined in [7], can be called topological neighbors if one can be transformed into the other one by a process of gradual, continuous change which does not involve passage through any third region.

A prominent application of the calculus is the autonomous robot navigation, in which the robot has a topological map of the environment in which it has to move on. Then the spatio-temporal calculus presented here can help during the path-planning task to the autonomous robot, represented as a mobile spatial region moving along the static topological map it has. The calculus will help by describing the sequence of topological situations that the robot should find during its way from the start region to the target objective.

2 Overview of the Topological Calculus

To make this paper self-contained we now give a concise summary of the topological calculus selected. A fuller explanation can be found in [7]. We have chosen this topological calculus because it is presented as an algebra akin to Allen's [8] temporal interval algebra and it allows us to reason about point-like, linear and areal entities, which will allow us the use of different granularities of the same map. The calculus defines 9 topological relations, which are described below, that are mutually exclusive, that is, giving 2 entities, the relation between them must be one and only one of the 9 relations defined.

Before given the formal definition of each topological relation we define a number of basic topological concepts needed to understand the definition of the topological relations:

Definition 1. The boundary of an entity h, called δh is defined as:
- We consider the boundary of a point-like entity to be always empty.
- The boundary of a linear entity is the empty set in the case of a circular line or the 2 distinct endpoints otherwise.
- The boundary of an area is the circular line consisting of all the accumulation points of the area.

Definition 2. The interior of an entity h, called $h°$ is defined as $h°=h-\delta h$

Definiton 3. The function dim, which returns the dimension of an entity of either the types we consider, or of the intersection of 2 or more of such entities, is defined as follows:

If $S \neq \varnothing$ then
$\qquad$ $dim(S) = 0$ if S contains at least a point and no lines and no areas.
$\qquad$ $dim(S) = 1$ if S contains at least a line and no areas.
$\qquad$ $dim(S) = 2$ if S contains at least an area.
else $dim(S)$ is undefined.

A topological relation r between two entities h1 and h2, denoted by (h_1, r, h_2), is defined on the right hand side of the equivalence sign in the form of a point-set expression. The definitions of each topological relation are described below.

Definition 4. The *touch* relation:

$(h_1, \textbf{touch}, h_2) \Leftrightarrow h_1° \cap h_2° = \varnothing \wedge h_1 \cap h_2 \neq \varnothing$

Definition 5. The *cross* relation:

$(h_1, \textbf{cross}, h_2) \Leftrightarrow$

$\qquad$ $dim(h°_1 \cap h°_2) = max(dim(h°_1), dim(h°_2)) - 1 \wedge h_1 \cap h_2 \neq h_1 \wedge h_1 \cap h_2 \neq h_2$

Definition 6. The *overlap* relation:

$(h_1, \textbf{overlap}, h_2) \Leftrightarrow dim(h°_1) = dim(h°_2) = dim(h°_1 \cap h°_2) \wedge h_1 \cap h_2 \neq h_1 \wedge h_1 \cap h_2 \neq h_2$

Definition 7. The *disjoint* relation:

$(h_1, \textbf{disjoint}, h_2) \Leftrightarrow h_1 \cap h_2 = \varnothing$

We define the *equal, completely-inside* and *touching-from-inside* relations using the formal definition of the *in* relation:

$(h_1, \textbf{in}, h_2) \Leftrightarrow h_1 \cap h_2 = h_1 \wedge h°_1 \cap h°_2 \neq \varnothing$, then:

Definition 8. Given that (h_1, in, h_2) holds, next algorithm distinguishes between the *completely-inside*, the *touching-from-inside* and the *equal* relations:

$\qquad$ if (h_2, in, h_1) then $(h_1, \textbf{equal}, h_2)$
$\qquad$ else if $h_1 \cap \delta h_2 \neq \varnothing$ then $(h_1, \textbf{touching-from-inside}, h_2)$
$\qquad$ else $(h_1, \textbf{completely-inside}, h_2)$.

Definition 9. The *completely-inside$_i$* relation:

$(h_1,$ **completely-inside$_i$,** $h_2) \Leftrightarrow (h_2,$ completely-inside, $h_1)$

Definition 10. The *touching-from-inside$_i$* relation:

$(h_1,$ **touching-from-inside$_i$,** $h_2) \Leftrightarrow (h_2,$ touching-from-inside, $h_1)$.

3 The Calculus

As mentioned in the introduction, our aim is to propose a constraint-based approach to integrate the topological calculus developed in [7] and a temporal algebra. The topological relations of the calculus in [7] has been described in the previous section. But we still have to describe the temporal algebra that we have chosen for the integration. We will use a temporal algebra in which variables represent time points and there are five primitive constraints: <<, ==, >>, prev and nex, which are defined as:

Definition 11. Given two time points, t and t', t == t' iff has not occurred a change between t and t' (or between t' and t) on any relation.

Definition 12. Given two time points, t an t', t' **next** t iff t' > t and some relation or relations have changed to a neighbor relation between t and t'.

Definition 13. Given two time points, t and t', t' **prev** t iff t' < t and some relation or relations have changed to a neighbor relation between t and t'.

Definition 14. Given two time points, t and t', t' **>>** t iff t' > t and a relation has changed strictly more than once to a neighbor relation.

Definition 15. Given two time points, t and t', t' **>>** t iff t' < t and a relation has changed strictly more than once to a neighbor relation.

According to this, time is represented by disjunctive binary constraints of the form $X\{r_1, ..., r_n\}Y$, where each r_i is a relation that is applicable to X and Y. $X\{r_1, ..., r_n\}Y$ is a disjunction of the way $(Xr_1Y) \vee .... \vee (Xr_nY)$ and r_i is also called primitive constraints.

We have used this time algebra because we are only interested in the point of the time in which one region is transformed into its topological neighborhood. The topological neighborhood of a region is that region to which the original region can be transformed to by a process of gradual, continuous change which does not involve passage through any third region.

To reason about these temporal constraints we need to define the converse and composition operations and construct the converse and composition tables.

First of all we need to define what we understand as a general relation of the calculus because we are going to define the converse and composition operation in terms of general relations.

Definition 16. A **general relation** R of the calculus is any subset of the set of all atomic relations.

Definition 17. The **converse** of a general relation R, called $R^\cup$ is defined as:

$$\forall(X,Y) ((X,R,Y) \Leftrightarrow (Y,R^\cup,X)) \qquad (1)$$

Definition 18. The **composition** $R1 \otimes R2$ of two general relations R1 and R2 is the most specific relation R such that:

$$\forall (h_1, h_2, h_3) ((h_1, R1, h_2) \wedge (h_2, R2, h_3) \Rightarrow (h_1, R, h_3)) \qquad (2)$$

The last three definitions are suitable for temporal constraints chosen and the topological calculus defined in [7].

Below, we find table 1 and 2 which are the converse table and composition table respectively for the time algebra.

Table 1. The converse table for the time algebra.

r	$r\cup$
==	==
<<	>>
>>	>>
next	prev
prev	next

Table 2. The composition table for the time algebra.

r_1 \ r_2	<<	prev	==	Next	>>
<<	{<<}	{<<}	{<<}	{prev,<<}	{<<,prev,==,next,>>}
prev	{<<}	{<<,prev}	{prev}	{==,prev,next}	{next,>>}
==	{<<}	{prev}	{==}	{next}	{>>}
next	{<<,prev}	{prev,==,next}	{next}	{>>,next}	{>>}
>>	{<<,prev,==,next,>>}	{>>,next}	{>>}	{>>}	{>>}

The composition and converse tables for topological relations can be found in [7].

3.1 The Representation of the Spatio-Temporal Algebra

The first step to define the spatio-temporal algebra of this paper is to create the representational model of topology and qualitative time points. The representational model follows the formalism used by Allen for temporal interval algebra [8]. The Allen style formalism will provide to our approach the possibility of reasoning with topology in dynamic worlds by applying the Allen's constraint propagation algorithm.

As we have mentioned, the representational model uses the topological calculus developed in [7] and the time algebra defined in previous sections.

The binary relations between two objects, which can be points, lines or areas, h_1 and h_2 of the algebra in a point of time t are defined as tertiary constraints or propositions where the topological relation r between h_1 and h_2 in the point of time t is denoted by $(h_1,r,h_2)_t$. From this definition we define a **general relation R** of the algebra during time t as:

$$\forall(h_1,h_2) ((h_1,R,h_2)_t \Leftrightarrow U_{r\in R} (h_1,r,h_2)_t) \qquad (3)$$

3.2 The Operations

Definition 19. The **converse** of a general relation R in time t, denoted as $R^\cup$, in defined as follows:

$$\forall(h_1,h_2)\ ((h_1,R,h_2)_t \Leftrightarrow (Y,R^\cup,X)_t) \tag{4}$$

From this definition we observe that the converse of the algebra defined including topology and time is the same as the converse defined only for topological relations because the converse is calculated in the same point of time, therefore time does not affect to the converse operation. In table 3 we find the converse table constructed from this definition.

Table 3. The converse table for the spatio-temporal algebra

r	$r^\cup$
touch	touch
cross	cross
overlap	overlap
disjoint	disjoint
equal	equal
completely-inside	completely-inside$_i$
touching-from-inside	touching-from-inside$_t$
completely-inside$_i$	completely-inside
touching-from-inside$_t$	touching-from-inside

To define an algebra like Allen's the next step is to define the **composition** operation between the relations of the model. The composition for the model including topology and time has to be defined to include all the possibilities in four different ways as follows:

Definition 20. The resulting general relation R obtained from the **composition** ($\otimes$) operation can be calculated as:

a) $(A,R1,B)t_0 \otimes (B,R2,C)t_0 \Rightarrow (A,R,C)t_0$

b) $(A,R1,B)t_0 \otimes (t_0, \text{Reltime}, t_1) \Rightarrow (A,R,B)t_1$

c) $(A,R1,B)t_0 \otimes (B,R2,C)t_1 / (t_0, \text{Reltime}, t_1) \Rightarrow ((A,R1,B)t_0 \otimes (t_0, \text{Reltime}, t_1)) \otimes (B,R2,C)t_1 \Rightarrow (A,R',B)t_1 \otimes (B,R2,C)t_1 \Rightarrow (A,R,C)t_1$

d) $(A,R1,B)t_0 \otimes (A,R1,B)t_0 \Rightarrow (A,R1,B)t_0$

The first type of composition (*Definition20.a*) is the composition of the topological relations between three regions A, B and C, at the same point of time, where A, B, C belong to {point, line, area}. In this case it is the usual topological composition, since time does not have any effect. To calculate this composition we will use the 18 composition tables and the converse table defined in [7]. An example of these tables is depicted in table 4, which represents the PPP-table, which is the composition table between (A,r_1,B) and (B, r_2, C), r_1 and r_2 being atomic relations and A, B and C point entities. The rest of the tables can be found in [7].

Table 4. PPP–table .

r₂ r₁	equals	disjoint
equals	{equals}	{disjoint}
disjoint	{disjoint}	{equals, disjoint}

The second type of composition (*Definition20.b*) is the composition which implements Freksa's conceptual neighborhood notion. It looks for the possible topological relations which will appear between two regions as time changes. To reason about this we need to construct 6 composition tables that will be referred to as XY_t–table where the regions X and Y belong to {point (P), line (L), area (A)} and t represents the dimension of time of the algebra. We would need 9 composition tables (3^2) if we consider all possibilities with X and Y being a point-like, a linear or an areal entity. However, we construct only 6 tables from which the other 3 tables can be obtained using the converse operation. We construct the AA_t-table, LA_t-table, PA_t-table, LL_t-table, PL_t-table and the PP_t-table, which are depicted in tables 5 to 10 respectively. Note: due to limitation restrictions the topological relation are represented in the next way: *touch* is represented by T, *cross* by C, *overlap* by O, *disjoint* by D, *completely-inside* by CI, *touching-from-inside* by TFI, *equal* by E, *touching-from-inside*ᵢ by TFIᵢ and *completely-inside*ᵢ by CIᵢ. And due to limitation space we have depicted in a common column the case for "next" and "prev" and a common column for the case of "<<" and ">>" because their entries are the same. From the tables we can also infer that the = time relation represents the identity.

Table 5. AAt-table

Reltime RelTop	next or prev	<< or >>	==
T	{D,O,T}	{T,E,TFI,CI,TFIi,Cli,TFli}	{T}
O	{T,TFI,O}	{O,D,E,CI,TFIi,Cli}	{O}
D	{T,D}	{D,O,E,TFI,CI,TFIi,Cli,TFli}	{D}
E	{O,E,}	{E,T,D,TFI,CI, TFIi,Cli}	{E}
TFI	{O,CI,TFI}	{TFI,T,D,E,CI, TFli, Cli}	{TFI}
CI	{TFI,CI}	{CI,T,O,D,E,TFIi,Cli}	{CI}
TFIi	{O,Cli,TFi}	{TFli,T,D,E,CI,TFI}	{TFIi}
Cli	{TFli,Cli}	{Cli,T,O,D,E,TFI,CI}	{Cli}

Table 6. LAt-table

Reltime Reltop	next or prev	<< or >>	==
T	{C,D,T}	{T,TFI,CI}	{T}
C	{D,TFI,C}	{C,T,CI}	{C}
D	{T,D}	{D,C,TFI,CI}	{D}
TFI	{C,CI,TFI}	{TFI,T,D}	{TFI}
CI	{TFI,CI}	{CI,T,C,D}	{CI}

Table 7. PAt-table

Reltime Reltop	next or prev	<< or >>	==
T	{D,CI,T}	{T}	{T}
D	{T,D}	{D,CI}	{D}
CI	{T,CI}	{CI,D}	{CI}

Table 8. LLt-table

Reltime Reltop	next or prev	<< or >>	==
T	{D,O,C,T}	{T,E,TFI,CI, TFi,Cli}	{T}
D	{T,C,D}	{D,O,E,TFI,CI, TFli,Cli}	{D}
O	{T,C,O}	{O,D,E,TFI,CI, TFli, Cli}	{O}
C	{T,D,C}	{C,O,E,TFI,CI, TFli, Cli}	{C}
E	{T,O,E}	{E,D,C,TFI,CI, TFli,Cli}	{E}
TFI	{C,CI,T,TFI}	{TFI,D,O,E, TFli,Cli}	{TFI}
CI	{TFI,C,CI}	{CI,T,D,O,E, TFli,Cli}	{CI}
TFli	{T,C,Cli,TFi}	{TFli,D,O,E, TFI,CI}	{TFli}
Cli	{C,TFli,Cli}	{Cli,T,D,O,E, TFI,CI}	{Cli}

Table 9. PLt-table

Reltime Reltop	next or prev	<< or >>	==
T	{D,CI,T}	{T}	{T}
D	{T,CI,D}	{D}	{D}
CI	{T,D,CI}	{CI}	{CI}

Table 10. PPt-table

Reltime Reltop	next or prev	<< or >>	==
E	{D,E}	{E}	{E}
D	{E,D}	{D}	{D}

As a relation t prev t' corresponds to a change of some topological relation to a neighbour relation, the tables always keep the possibility that a relation has not changed between time t and t', this situation model the fact that the time changes from t to t' because other topological relationship has changed and the relationship between X and Y (RelTop) has not changed.

The 3 tables not constructed can be obtained by applying the converse operation. For example, the AL_t-table is not constructed but we can get any of its entries using the LA_t-table. This means that we have to find the most specific relation R such that, if X and Y are an areal and a linear entity respectively:

$$(X, Reltop, Y)_{t0} \otimes (t_0, Reltime, t_1) \Rightarrow (X, R, Y)_{t1} \qquad (4)$$

From the LA_t-table and using the converse operation we will get the relation R as follows:

$$(Y, Reltop^\cup, X)_{t0} \otimes (t_1, Reltime^\cup, t_0) \Rightarrow (Y, R', X) \qquad (5)$$

Then the relation R that we are looking for is $R=(R')^\cup$.

For the third case of composition (*Definition20.c*) we want to infer the composition R at time t_1 between 3 regions, X, Y and Z knowing the topological relation in time t_0 between X and Y, the topological relation at time t1 between Y and Z and the qualitative time relation between times t_0 and t_1. To get the composition relation R, first we have to obtain the topological relations that can appear between X and Y at time t_1 using the composition tables defined for the case of *Definition17.b* defined above. Then we have the general relation R' which appears between X and Y during

t_1; this together with the general relation R2 between Y and Z at t_1 allows us to apply the usual composition tables as explained for the case of *Definition17.a* and we can obtain the general composition relation R.

Finally the last composition case (*Definition20.d*) is the composition between the same two regions in the same point of time, sharing the relation R1, and the result is the relation R1 itself. We do not infer more information from this case.

Conclusions and Future Work

We have proposed a constraint-based approach for modelling motion. What we have obtained is a calculus consisting of atomic relations in time and of the algebraic operations of converse and composition. As such, the calculus is an algebra in the same style as the one provided by Allen [8] for temporal interval.

The objects manipulated by the calculus are point-like, linear and areal entities, contrary to most constraint-based frameworks in the qualitative spatial and temporal reasoning literature, which deal with only one type of entities. This will allow us to reason with different granularities.

Reasoning about knowledge expressed in the presented calculus can be done using a constraint propagation algorithm like the one in [8], guided by the composition and converse tables presented in this paper. Such an algorithm has the advantage of being incremental: knowledge may be added without having to revise the processing steps achieved so far.

The representational model presented here could help us to reason about the sequence of topological situations that an autonomous robot should find during its way from a starting region to a target objective. It can also help to detect situations in which the robot is loosing its direction of movement (way). This is our future work: to apply this representational model to the autonomous robot navigation problem. For instance, if we have a situation as the one depicted in figure 1a) in time t_0 and we want that the robot goes from $region_1$ to $region_2$, we know that the sequence of topological relations between the robot (interpreted as a mobile region) and the origin region, called $region_1$, and the target region, called $region_2$, is the next one:

$(Robot,CI_i,Region_1)_{t0}$ and $(Robot,D,Region_2)_{t0}$,
$(Robot,TFI_i,Region_1)_{t1}$ and $(Robot,T,Region_2)_{t1}$,
$(Robot,O,Region_1)_{t2}$ and $(Robot,O,Region_2)_{t2}$,
$(Robot,T,Region_1)_{t3}$ and $(Robot,TFI_i,Region_2)_{t3}$,
$(Robot,D,Region_1)_{t4}$ and $(Robot,CI_i,Region_2)_{t4}$
where t0 prev t1 prev t2 prev t3 prev t4.

Note that we have used the same notation for the topological relations as the one used for the composition tables.

If during its way until the target objective we find a situation which does not follow the sequence, for instance we find $(Robot,TFI_i,Region_1)_{t1}$ and $(Robot,D,Region_2)_{t1}$, the robot is losing its way. Therefore we want to use this knowledge to help us during the navigation of an autonomous robot integrating this knowledge to other qualitative spatial information such as orientation, distance and cardinal directions in the same way as it has been done in [11]. A preliminary result of that application has been obtained by using qualitative representation of such spatial aspects for the autonomous simulated navigation of a Nomad-200 robot, on a structured environment of an easy corridor (with offices in only one side) in a building [12].

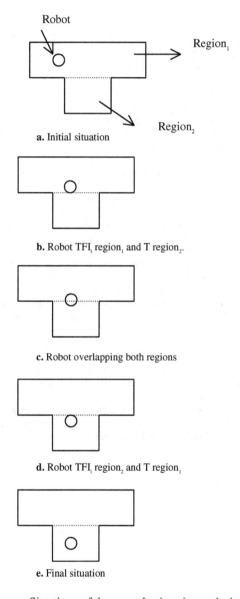

Robot

Region$_1$

a. Initial situation

Region$_2$

b. Robot TFI$_1$ region$_1$ and T region$_2$.

c. Robot overlapping both regions

d. Robot TFI$_1$ region$_2$ and T region$_1$

e. Final situation

Fig. 1. Graphical Sequence Situations of the example given in conclusions.

Acknowledgements. This work has been partially supported by CICYT under grant number TAP99-0590-002-02, and by Alicer, Ceramic Design Technology Institute.

References

[1]   A. Belussi, E.Bertino and B.Catania. "An extended algebra for constraint databases". *IEEE TKDE,* 10(5):686-705, 1998.

[2]   M.H. Böhlen, C.S. Jensen and M.O. Scholl, editors. *Spatio-Temporal Database Management*, volume 1678 of *LNCS*, Springer 1999.

[3]   S. Grumbach, P. Rigaux and L. Segoufin. "Spatio-Temporal Data Handling with Constraints". In *ACM GIS:*106-111. ACM Press, 1998.

[4]   A. Raffaetà, T. Frühwirth. "Spatio-Temporal Annotated Constraint Logic Programming". Third international Workshop on Practical Aspects of Declarative Languages (*PADL'01*), Las Vegas, USA, March 2001.

[5]   A. Mukerjee and F. T. Schnorrenberg. "Hybrid Systems: Reasoning across Scales in Space and Time". *AAAI Symposium on Principles of Hybrid Reasoning*, November 15-17, 1991.

[6]   A.G. Cohn and M. Hazarika. "Qualitative Spatial Representation and reasoning: An overview" *Fundamenta Informaticae*, 46(1-2):1-29, 2001.

[7]   A. Isli, Ll. Museros, T. Barkowsky and M. Reinhard. "A Topological Calculus for Cartographic Entities". In *Lecture notes in Artificial Intelligence 1849. Spatial Cognition II. Integrating Abstract Theories, Empirical Studies, Formal Methods and Practical Applications. Spatial Cognition.* Springer-Verlag, pp. 225 – 239, 2000

[8]   J. Allen, "Maintaining Knowledge about Temporal Intervals", *Communications of the ACM* , Vol. 26, No. 11. pag. 832-843, 1983.

[9]   C. Freksa. "Conceptual neighborhood and its role in temporal and spatial reasoning". *Technical Report Tech. RPt. FK1-146-91*, Institute of Information, University of Munich, 1991.

[10] C. Freksa. "Temporal Reasoning based on semi-interval". *Artificial Intelligence 54*, 199-227, 1992.

[11] M.T. Escrig and F. Toledo." Autonomous Robot Navigation using human spatial concepts". *International Journal of Intelligent Systems*, Vol.15, No.3, pp.165-196, 2000, March 2000. ISBN 0884-8173.

[12] L. Museros and M.T. Escrig. "Combining Qualitative Spatial Information : The Integration of Topology, Time, Orientation and Distances for Spatial Reasoning ", accepted to ECAI 2002 Workshop on Spatial and Temporal Reasoning.

Qualitative Comparison of Temporal Series. *QSI*

J.A. Ortega[1], F.J. Cuberos[2], R.M. Gasca[1], M. Toro[1], and J. Torres[1]

[1] Dpto. de Lenguajes y Sistemas Informáticos.
University of Seville.
Avda. Reina Mercedes s/n. Sevilla, Spain
{ortega, gasca,mtoro,jtorres}@lsi.us.es
[2] Dpto. de Planificación. Radio Televisión de Andalucía,
Ctra. San Juan-Tomares km. 1,3. S. J. Aznalfarache - Sevilla, Spain
fjcuberos@rtva.es

Abstract. In this paper, the study of systems that evolve in time by means of the comparison of time series is proposed. An improvement in the form to compare temporal series with the incorporation of qualitative knowledge by means of qualitative labels is carried out. Each label represents a rank of values that, from a qualitative perspective, may be considered similar. The selection of labels of a single character allows the application of algorithms of string comparison. Finally, an index of similarity of time series based on the similarity of the obtained strings is defined.

1 Introduction

The study of the temporal evolution of systems is an incipient research area. The development of new methodologies to analyze and to process the time series obtained from the evolution of these systems is necessary. A time series is a sequence of real values, each one representing the value of a magnitude at a point of time. These time series are usually stored in databases.

We are interested in databases obtained from the evolution of dynamic systems. A methodology to simulate semiqualitative dynamic systems and to store the data into a database is proposed in [13]. This database may also be obtained by means of the data acquired from sensors installed in the real system. Anyway, there is a variety of applications that produce and store time series.

One of the biggest problems of working with time-series databases is to calculate the similarity between two given time series. The interest of a similarity measure is multiple: finding the different behaviour patterns of the system stored in a database, looking for a particular pattern, reducing the amount of relevance series previously to the application of analysis algorithms, etc.

Many approaches have been proposed to solve the problem of an efficient comparison. In this paper, we propose to carry out this comparison from a qualitative perspective, taking into account the variations of the time series values. The idea of our proposal is to abstract the numerical values of the time series and to concentrate on the comparison in the shape of the time series.

M.T. Escrig Monferrer and F. Toledo Lobo (Eds.): CCIA 2002, LNAI 2504, pp. 75–87, 2002.

In this paper, time series with noise are not taken into account, and this is postponed for future works.

The remain of this paper is structured as follows: first, some related works that have been used to define our index will be analyzed. Next the *Shape Definition Language* will be introduced, which is appropriated to carry out the translation of the original values, and the problem of the *Longest Common Subsequence (LCS)* will also be explained. Next section will introduce our approach, the *Qualitative Similarity Index*. Finally, this index is applied to a semiqualitative logistics growth model with a delay.

2   Related Work

In the literature, different approximations have been developed to study time series. The shape definition language *(SDL)* is defined in [2]. This language *SDL* is suitable for retrieving objects based on shapes contained in the histories associated with these objects. An important feature of the language is its ability to perform blurry matching where the user cares only about the overall shape. This work is the key to translate the original data into a qualitative description of its evolution.

On the other hand, the study of the problem of the Longest Common Subsequence *(LCS)* is also related to this paper, because we use *(LCS)* algorithms as the baseline to define *QSI*. A complete review of the most known solutions to this problem is collected in [15].

There have been many works on comparison of time series [7]. Most of them propose the definition of indexes, which are applied to a subset of values obtained from the original data. These indexes provide an efficient comparison of time series. They are defined taking into account only some of the original values. This improvement of speed produces a decrease in the accuracy of the comparison. These indexes are obtained applying a transformation from the time series values to a lower dimensionality space.

Other approaches differ in the way to carry out this mapping or in the selected target space. One option is to select only a few coefficients of a transformation process to represent all the information of the original series. In this approach, the change from the time domain to the frequency domain is carried out. The Discrete Fourier Transform *(DFT)* is used in [1] to reduce the series to the first Fourier Coefficients. A solution based in the Discrete Wavelet Transform *(DWT)* in a similar way is proposed in [5].

Other approaches reduce the original data in the time series, selecting a subset of the original values. A piece-wise linear segmentation of the original curve is used in [9]. In [10], the Dynamic Time Warping algorithm is applied over the segmented data, and finally in work [11] a straight dimensionality reduction with Piece-wise Constant Approximation is made, selecting a fixed number of values of the original data. This is known as *PCA-indexing*.

The last option is to generate a 4-tuple-feature vector extracted from every sequence [12]. A new distance function is defined as the similarity index.

In paper [6], the study of series with different time scales from a qualitative perspective is proposed.

3   Shape Definition Language (SDL)

This language, proposed in [2], is very suitable to create queries about the evolution of values or magnitudes along the time.

For any set of values stored for a period of time, the fundamental idea in *SDL* is to divide the range of the possible variations between adjacent values in a collection of disjoint ranges, and to assign a label for each one of them.

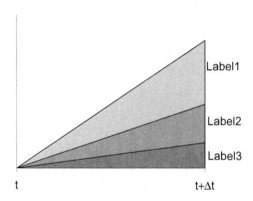

Fig. 1. Possible assignment of labels

Figure 1 represents a sample division into three regions of the positive axis. The behaviour of a time series may be described taking into account the transitions between consecutive values. A derivative series is obtained by means of the difference of amplitude among the consecutive values of the time series. The value of this difference matches in one of the disjoint ranges, and therefore this definition of the value produces a label of the alphabet.

This translation generates a sequence of transitions based on an alphabet. The symbols of this alphabet describe the magnitude of the increments of the time series values. Every symbol is defined by means of four descriptors. The firsts two are the lower and upper bounds of the allowed variation from the initial value to the final value of the transition. The last two specify the constraints on the initial and final value of the transition respectively.

The alphabet proposed in [2] has only 8 symbols. This translation gives priority to the shape over the original values of the time series. This affirmation will be later explained. Figure 2 shows an example of a translation using the set of symbols (*Down, down, stable, zero, up, Up*). Every string of symbols may describe an infinite number of curves. All of them verify the constraints imposed for the symbols to the represented transitions. Figure 3 shows three different curves with the same sequence of symbols, even though the curves have different initial points. The *SDL* language is used to translate a time series described

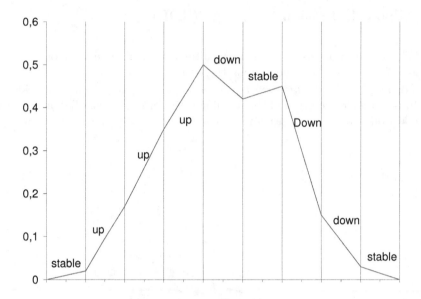

Fig. 2. Example of translation

by means of their numerical values into a string of symbols which represent the variations between adjacent values.

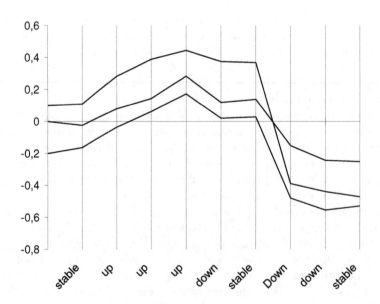

Fig. 3. Translation with identical sequence

4   Longest Common Subsequence (LCS)

Working with different kinds of sequences, from strings of characters to DNA chains, one of the most used similarity measure is the *Longest Common Subsequence* (LCS) of two or more given sequences. LCS is the longest collection of elements which appears in both sequences and in the same order.

The algorithms to compute LCS are well known and a deeper analysis of them is detailed in [15].

Our interest in LCS comes from a double point of view:

• The SDL language generates a string of symbols from the original numeric values of the time series.Therefore, it is possible to apply the LCS algorithm in order to find a "distance" between two time series, abstracting the shapes of the curves.

• LCS is a special case of the Dynamic Time Warping (DTW) algorithm, reducing the increment of distance of each comparison to the values 0 or 1. This reduction depends on the presence or absence of the same symbols. Thus, LCS inherits all the DTW features.

DTW is an algorithm intensively used in the speech recognition area because it is appropriated to detect similar shapes that are non-aligned in the time axis. This lack of alignment induces catastrophic errors in the comparison of shapes which use the Euclidean distance.

The idea of DTW is to find a set of ordered mappings between the values of two series, so the global distance warping cost is minimized.

5   Qualitative Similarity Index (QSI)

The idea of this index is the inclusion of qualitative knowledge in the comparison of time series. A measure based in the matching of qualitative labels that represent the evolution of the series values is proposed. Each label represents a range of values that may be assumed as similar from a qualitative perspective. Different series with a qualitatively similar evolution produce the same sequence of labels.

The proposed approximation performs better comparisons than previously proposed methods. This improvement is mainly due to two characteristics of the index: on the one hand, it maximizes the exactness because it is defined using all the information of the time series; and on the other hand, it focuses the comparison on the shape and not on the original values because it considers the evolution of groups as similar. It is interesting to note that the time series are supposed to be noise-free between two samples and with a linear and monotonic evolution.

Let $X = \langle x_0, ..., x_f \rangle$ be a time series. Our proposed approach is applied in three steps. First, a normalization of the values of X is performed, yielding $\tilde{X} = \langle \tilde{x}_0, ..., \tilde{x}_f \rangle$. Using this series, the difference series $X_D = \langle d_0, ..., d_{f-1} \rangle$ is obtained, which is translated into a string $S_X = \langle c_1, ..., c_{f-1} \rangle$. The similarity between two time series is calculated by means of the comparison of the two strings obtained from them, applying the previous transformation process, and then using the LCS algorithm. The result is used as a similarity measure with the original time series.

5.1   Normalization

Keeping in mind the qualitative comparison of the series, a normalization of the original numerical values in the interval [0,1] is performed. This normalization is carried out to allow the comparison of time series with different quantitative scales.

Let $X = \langle x_0, ..., x_f \rangle$ be a time series, and let $\tilde{X} = \langle \tilde{x}_0, ..., \tilde{x}_f \rangle$ be the normalized temporal series obtained from X, as follows:

$$\tilde{x}_i = \frac{x_i - min(x_0, ..., x_f)}{max(x_0, ..., x_f) - min(x_0, ..., x_f)} \tag{1}$$

where min and max are operations that return the maximum and minimum values of a numerical sequence respectively.

Let $X_D = \langle d_0, ..., d_{f-1} \rangle$ be the series of differences obtained from $\tilde{X}$ as follows:

$$d_i = \tilde{x}_i - \tilde{x}_{i-1} \tag{2}$$

This difference series will be used in the labelling step to produce the string of characters corresponding to X. It is interesting to note that every $d_i \in X_D$ is a value in the [-1,1] interval, as a consequence of the normalization process.

5.2   Labelling Process

The proposed normalization in the previous section is focused on the slope evolution and not on the original values. A label may be assigned to every different slope, so the range of all the possible slopes is divided into groups and a qualitative label is assigned to every group.

The range division is defined depending on the parameter δ which is supplied by experts according to their knowledge about the system. The value of this parameter has a direct influence in the quality of the results. Therefore, this is an open research area of this paper that will be detailed in future works.

Label	Range	Symbol
High increase	$[1/\delta, +\infty]$	H
Medium increase	$[1/\delta^2, 1/\delta]$	M
Low increase	$[0, 1/\delta^2]$	L
No variation	0	0
Low decrease	$[-1/\delta^2, 0]$	l
Medium decrease	$[-1/\delta, -1/\delta^2]$	m
High decrease	$[-\infty, -1/\delta]$	h

In this table, the first column represents the qualitative label for every range of
derivatives, which is shown in the second row. The last column contains the character assigned to each label. The proposed alphabet contains three characters for
increase and three for decrease ranges, and one additional character for constant
range. It is important to note that in our approach there is no application of the
constraints presented in SDL [2].

This alphabet is used to obtain the string of characters $S_X = \langle c_1, ..., c_{f-1} \rangle$
corresponding to the time series X, where every c_i represents the evolution
of the curve between two adjacent points of time in X. It is obtained from
$X_D = \langle d_0, ..., d_{f-1} \rangle$ assigning to every d_i its character in accordance with the
table above.

This translation of the time series into a sequence of symbols abstract from
the real values and focus our attention on the shape of the curve. Every sequence
of symbols describes a complete family of curves with a similar evolution.

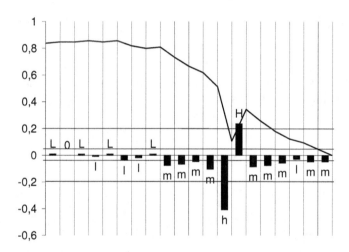

Fig. 4. Sample of translation

Figure 4 shows a normalized curve with their derivative values and the assigned label to each transition between adjacent values. This example has been
obtained with $\delta = 5$.

5.3   Definition of QSI Similarity

Let X, Y be two time series, $X = \langle x_0, ..., x_f \rangle$ and $Y = \langle y_0, ..., y_f \rangle$. Let S_X, S_Y
be the strings obtained when X, Y are normalized and labelled.

The QSI similarity between the strings S_X, S_Y is defined as follows

$$QSI(S_X, S_Y) = \frac{\nabla(LCS(S_X, S_Y))}{m} \tag{3}$$

where ∇S is the counter quantifier applied to string S. The counter quantifier yields the number of characters of S. On the other hand, m is defined as $m = max(\nabla S_X, \nabla S_Y)$. Therefore, the QSI similarity may be understood as the number of ordered symbols that may be found in the same order in both sequences simultaneously divided by the length of the longest sequence.

Properties of QSI. We are going to describe two properties of QSI.

Let S_X, S_Y, S_Z be three strings of characters obtained from the transformation of three temporal series X, Y, Z respectively. The definition of QSI similarity verifies that:

Property 1. $QSI(S_X, S_Y)$ is a number in the interval $[0, 1]$. If X is absolutely different of Y it is 0.

$$\text{If } LCS(S_X, S_Y)) = \emptyset$$
$$\Downarrow$$
$$\nabla LCS(S_X, S_Y)) = 0 \tag{4}$$
$$\Downarrow$$
$$QSI(S_X, S_Y) = 0.$$

The $QSI(S_X, S_Y)$ value increases according to the number of coincident characters. This number is 1 if $S_X = S_Y$.

$$\text{If } LCS(S_X, S_Y)) = S_X$$
$$\Downarrow$$
$$\nabla LCS(S_X, S_Y)) = S_X \tag{5}$$
$$\Downarrow$$
$$QSI(S_X, S_Y) = 1.$$

Property 2. The length of the strings to compare has also an important influence. In this sense, two strings with approximated lengths and with a number of coincident symbols are more similar than two strings with the same number of coincident symbols but with different lengths:

$$\nabla S_X \approx \nabla S_Y, \nabla S_X \approx \nabla S_Z,$$
$$\nabla LCS(S_X, S_Y) \approx \nabla LCS(S_X, S_Z)$$
$$\Downarrow \tag{6}$$
$$QSI(S_X, S_Y) > QSI(S_X, S_Z)$$

5.4   Comparison with Other Approaches

When a new approach is introduced, it is interesting to test its validity and the improvements with respect to the other approaches appeared in the literature. In this paper, our approach is going to be compared with the algorithm introduced in [10], called Segmented Dynamic Time Warping (*SDTW*). This algorithm carries out a clustering process with a set of time series. Every clustering process joins sets of data in subsets trying to minimize the similarity among the elements of every subset and the similarity between different subsets.

The *SDTW* algorithm was tested with the Australian Sign Language Dataset from the UCI KDD [4] choosing 5 samples for each word. The data in the database are the 3-D position of the hand of five signers, recorded by means of a data glove.

In order to carry out the comparison between both approaches, the same 10 words used in [10] from the 95 words included in the database have been chosen. Next, for every possible pairing of different words (45), the 10 sequences (5 of each word) have been clustered, using a hierarchical average clustering with two different distance measures. First, the distance defined in the classic *DTW* algorithm applied to the original numerical values of the series was used. The result was 22 correct clustering from 45. Then, the similarity *QSI* index, proposed in this paper, over the string obtained from the translation of the original values of the series was used. This time, the result was 44 correct clustering from 45. Therefore, our index obtains a 97.7% of accuracy. The *QSI* error is clearly lower than the obtained with *DWT*.

The total success obtained with *DWT* is exactly the same reported by [10], but the success obtained with *QSI* similarity is better.

6 Application of *QSI* to a Logistics Growth Model with a Delay

The following generic names: logistic, sigmoidal, and s-shaped processes are given to those systems in which an initial phase of exponential growth is followed by another phase of approaching to a saturation value asymptotically (figure 5). This growth is exhibited by those systems for which exponential expansion is truncated by the limitation of the resources required for this growth. In literature, these models have been profusely studied. They abound both in natural processes, and in social and socio-technical systems. These models appear in the

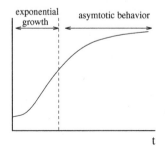

Fig. 5. Logistics growth curve

evolution of bacteria, in mineral extraction, in world population growth, economic development, learning curves, some diffusion phenomena within a given population such as epidemics or rumors, etc. In all these cases, their common behaviours are shown in figure 6. There is a bimodal behaviour pattern attractor: A stands for normal growth, and O for decay. It can be observed how it combines exponential with asymptotic growth. This phenomenon was first modelled by the Belgian Sociologist P.F. Verhulst in relation with human population growth. Nowadays, it has a wide variety of applications, some of which have just been mentioned.

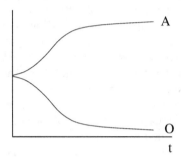

Fig. 6. Logistics growth model

Let S be the qualitative model. If a delay in the feedback paths of S is added, then its differential equations are

$$\Phi \equiv \begin{cases} \dot{x} = x(n\,r - m), \\ y = delay_\tau(x), \quad x > 0, \quad r = h_1(y), \\ h_1 \equiv \{(-\infty, -\infty), +, (d_0, 0), +, (0, 1), \\ \qquad +, (d_1, e_0), -, (1, 0), -(+\infty, -\infty)\} \end{cases}$$

being n the increasing factor, m the decreasing factor, and h_1 a qualitative continuous function defined by means of points and the derivative sign among two consecutive points. These functions are explained in detail in [14]. This function has a maximum point at (x_1, y_0). The initial conditions are

$$\Phi_0 \equiv \begin{cases} x_0 \in [LP_x, MP_x], \\ LP_x(m), \\ LP_x(n), \\ \tau \in [MP_\tau, VP_\tau] \end{cases}$$

where LP, MP, VP are the qualitative unary operators *slightly positive, moderately positive and very positive* for the x, τ variables.

The methodology described in [13] is applied to this model in order to obtain the database of time series. This methodology transforms this semiqualitative model into a family of quantitative models. Stochastic techniques are applied to choose a quantitative model of the family. The simulation of one selected quantitative model generates a time series that is stored into the database. We would like to classify the different behaviours of the system applying the QSI similarity to the obtained database. Figure 7 contains the table obtained when this index is applied between every two time series of the database. Figure 7 shows some of these time series. According to the obtained value QSI, three different

54X	55X	1X	18X	77X	17X	73X	Series
0,87	0,872	0,41	0,44	0,494	0,43	0,376	50X
	0,994	0,292	0,314	0,388	0,384	0,35	54X
		0,294	0,316	0,39	0,384	0,35	55X
			0,758	0,792	0,598	0,586	1X
				0,754	0,58	0,552	18X
					0,632	0,62	77X
						0,93	17X

Fig. 7. QSI similarity of the model

behaviours appear in figure 7. These results to obtain the behaviour patterns of the system are in accordance to others appeared in the bibliography [3] and [8], where the results are concluded by means of a mathematical reasoning.

Figure 8 shows the time series grouped by these behaviours. The 50x, 55x and 54x time series have a behaviour which is labelled as *decay and extinction*. In a similar way, the 18x, 1x and 77x time series whose behaviour is classified as *recovered equilibrium* and, finally, the 17x and, 73x time series whose behaviour is labelled as *retarded catastrophe* are shown.

7 Conclusions and Further Work

In this paper, the QSI index to measure the similarity of the time series depending on its qualitative features has been introduced. Furthermore, the proposed similarity index achieves better results than previous works with a similar computational cost.

In order to apply the QSI similarity index between two time series, first of all, a normalization process is necessary. Next, the sequence of differences is obtained from this normalized series. Finally, this sequence is translated into a string of characters using a qualitatively defined alphabet. The LCS algorithms are used to calculate the index QSI. The results obtained are in accordance with other previous works, although our approach produces an improved classification.

In the future, the idea is the automation and the optimization of the division into ranges of the possible slopes by studying the number of regions and their limits.

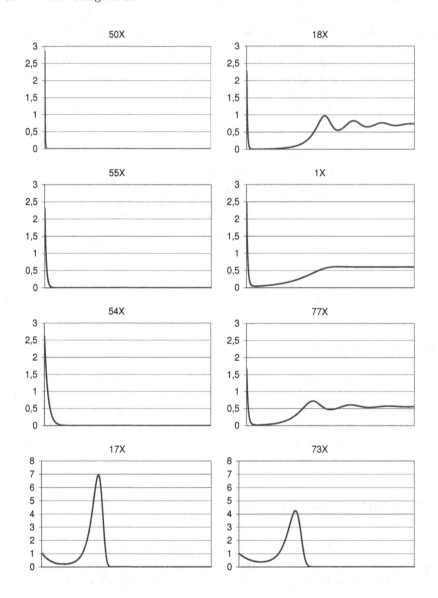

Fig. 8. Representations

Acknowledgments. This work was partially supported by the Spanish Interministerial Committee of Science and Technology by means of DPI2001-4404-E and DPI2000-0666-C02-02 programs.

References

1. *Agrawal R., Lin K.I., Sawhney H.S. and Shim K.* Fast similarity search in the presence of noise, scaling, and translation in time series databases. *The 21st VLDB Conference* Switzerland, (1995).

2. *Agrawal R., Psaila G., Wimmers E.L. and Zaït M.* Querying shapes of Histories. *The 21st VLDB Conference* Switzerland, pp. 502-514 (1995).

3. *Aracil J., Ponce E. and Pizarro L.* Behavior patterns of logistic models with a delay *Mathematics and computer in simulation* 44: 123–141, (1997).

4. *Bay S.* UCI Repository of KDD databases (http://kdd.ics.uci.edu/). Irvine, CA: University of California, Departamet of Information and Computer Science. (1999).

5. *Chan K. and Wai-chee F.A.* Efficient time series matching by wavelets *Proc.* 15th *International Conference on Data Engineering*, (1999).

6. *Cheung J.T. and Stephanopoulos G.* Representation of process trend - Part II. The problem of scale and qualitative scaling, *Computers and Chemical Engineering* 14(4/5), pp. 511-539, (1990).

7. *Faloutsos C., Ranganathan M., and Manolopoulos Y.* Fast subsequence matching in time-series databases. *The ACM SIGMOD Conference on Management of Data*, pp. 419-429 (1994).

8. *Karsky M. Dore J.-C. and Gueneau P.* Da la possibilité d'apparition de catastrophes différès. *Ecodecision No 6*, (1992).

9. *Keogh E.J. and Pazzani M.J.* An enhaced representation of time series wich allows fast and accurate classification, clustering and relevance feedback *Proc.* 4th *International Conference of Knowledge Discovery and Data Mining*, pp. 239-241, AAAI Press (1998).

10. *Keogh E.J. and Pazzani M.J.* Scaling up Dynamic Time Warping to massive datasets, *Proc. Principles and Practice of Knowledge Discovery in Databases*, (1999).

11. *Keogh E.J. and Pazzani M.J.* A simple dimensionality reduction technique for fast similarity search in large time series databases, (2000).

12. *Kim S-W, Park S. and Chu W.W.* An Index-Based Approach for Similarity Search Supporting Time Warping in Large Sequence Databases. *Proc. 17th IEEE Int'l Conf. on Data Engineering*, Heidelberg, Germany, (2001).

13. *Ortega J.A., Gasca R.M. and Toro M.* A semiqualitative methodology for reasoning about dynamic systems. 13th *International Workshop on Qualitative Reasoning*. Loch Awe (Scotland), 169–177, 1999.

14. *Ortega J.A.* Patrones de comportamiento temporal en modelos semicualitativos con restricciones. Ph.D. diss., Dept. of Computer Science, Seville Univ, (2000).

15. *Paterson M. and Dancík V.* Longest Common Subsequences. *Mathematical Foundations of Computer Science* vol. 841 de LNCS, pp.127-142, (1994).

Integrating 3D Orientation Models

Julio Pacheco, M. Teresa Escrig Monferrer, Francisco Toledo Lobo

Department of Computer Science and Engineering
Universitat Jaume I
Castellón, (Spain)
{pacheco | escrigm | toledo}@icc.uji.es

Abstract. The 2-D orientation model of Freksa and Zimmerman has been extended by us into a 3-D orientation model for fine information. When the information provided to the system is coarse or it is advisable to reduce the processing time of the reasoning process, it is necessary to define a coarse 3-D orientation model. Our orientation model has been coarse into three models, (a length coarse model, a height coarse model and a general coarse model) which have been explained in this paper. The management of different levels of granularity and the integration between the coarse and the fine 3-D orientation models has also been explained.
Keywords: Model-Based Reasoning, Spatial Reasoning, Qualitative Reasoning, Qualitative Orientation.

1. Introduction

In recent years, many qualitative spatial models have been developed to manage properly the imprecise knowledge about different aspects of space. Qualitative Spatial Reasoning is a field which has developed within the field of Artificial Intelligence. It is still an open field where many problems remain unsolved.

We want simpler and faster algorithms hence in most of the cases we sacrifice speed by memory or memory by speed. In qualitative algorithms we must decide if we want complexity or sureness. As much complex an algorithm is less uncertainty we have, but sometimes the facts are not as precise as we want, therefore we need less complexity (by other hand is traduced in a faster algorithm), although we will have more uncertainty.

The key will be in combine (when it would be necessary) both kinds of algorithms; fine algorithms with coarse algorithms (and its models).

The principal goal of the Qualitative Spatial Reasoning field is to represent our everyday common sense knowledge about the physical world, and the underlying abstractions used by engineers and scientists when they create quantitative models. Kak [11] points out that the behaviour of the intelligent machine of the future might carry out temporal reasoning, spatial reasoning and also reason over interrelated entities occupying space and changing in time with respect to their attributes and spatial interrelationships. Spatial information that we obtain through perception is coarse and imprecise, thus qualitative models which reason with distinguishing

M.T. Escrig Monferrer and F. Toledo Lobo (Eds.): CCIA 2002, LNAI 2504, pp. 88–100, 2002.
© Springer-Verlag Berlin Heidelberg 2002

characteristics rather than with exact measures seems to be more appropriate to deal with this kind of knowledge.

There exist mainly two qualitative models for orientation in 3D: Guesgen's approach [8] (which is a straightforward extension of Allen's temporal reasoning) and our approach [13, 14, 17, 18] (which is an extension of Freksa and Zimmerman model).

In general it is important in the Qualitative Spatial Orientation approaches to distinguish between models based on projections (as Guesgen's approach [8]) and models not based on projections (as Pacheco, Escrig and Toledo's approach [13, 14]).

In models based on projections, the relative orientation of objects is obtained by using (orthogonal or non-orthogonal) projections of objects into external axes, and then reasoning in one-dimension, by using Allen's temporal logic. There exist mainly three qualitative approaches for orientation which are based on projections: Guesgen's approach [8]; Chang et al. approach [1], and Mukerjee and Joe's approach [12]. Models based on projections might provide inconsistent representation of objects whose sides are not parallel to the axes. To overcome this problem, qualitative models not based on projections have been developed.

There exist mainly three qualitative models for orientation which are not based on projections into external reference systems (RS): Freksa and Zimmermann's model [3, 4, 5, 6]; Hernández's approach [9, 10]; and Frank's approach [7]. In these models not based on projections, space is divided into qualitative regions by means of RSs, which are centred on the reference objects (i.e. the RS are local and egocentric). Spatial objects are always simplified to points, which are the representational primitives.

From the two models on three dimensions, we consider our model to define some coarse models that make faster the algorithm (and it would be able when we have not more information) to calculate the positions in 3D.

In order to deal with this algorithm, firstly of all we are going to explain the base of the models and secondly we are going to reason to manage from the fine granularity to the coarse granularity.

We are going to explain briefly the Freksa and Zimmerman orientation representation (which is the base in the two dimensions of the model); in this model, we will see the differences between a fine and a coarse model and we are going to explain our model and how the 3-D space is represented (iconically and the names of every part in the space).

The structure of the paper will be:

(1) The representation of the previous models;

(2) The definition of the coarse models

(3) The management of different levels of granularity

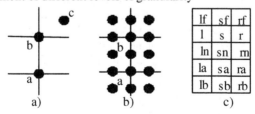

Fig. 1. a) The fine 2-D orientation RS; b) the 15 qualitative regions and c) their names in iconic representation.

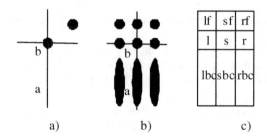

Fig. 2. *a) The coarse 2-D orientation RS; b) the 9 qualitative regions and c) their names in iconic representation.*

2. The 2-D Zimmerman and Freksa Orientation Representation

In [3,4,5,6] approach, the orientation RS is defined by a point and a director vector *ab*, which defines the left/right dichotomy. It can be interpreted as the direction of movement. The RS also includes the perpendicular line by the point *b*, which defines the first front/back dichotomy, and it can be seen as the straight line that joins our shoulders. This RS divides space into 9 qualitative regions (figure 2 a). A finer distinction could be made in the back regions by drawing the perpendicular line by the point *a*. In this case, the space is divided into 15 qualitative regions (figure 1). The point *a* defines the second front/back dichotomy of the RS. An iconic representation of the fine RS and the names of the regions are shown in figure 1 b) and c) for the fine RS and in figure 2 b) and c) for the coarse RS.

The information represented in both the coarse and the fine RSs is where is the point *c* with respect to the RS *ab*, that is, *c wrt ab*. This information can also be expressed of four different ways as a result of applying the following four operations: Homing, Homing Inverse, Shortcut and Shortcut Inverse.

3. The 3-D Pacheco, Escrig, and Toledo Orientation Model

In [13, 14, 17, 18] approaches, the three dimensional orientation model is defined adding, to the 2-D Freksa and Zimmerman representation, the height.

Therefore, our 3-D model divides the space in 75 qualitative orientation regions. The three dimensional space is divided in the breadth wise, by a plane which join the two main points of the RS *a* and *b*, in the lengthwise by two parallel planes passing, one of them by the point *a* and the other plane by the point *b*; and high wise by two parallel[1] planes more (perpendicular planes to the rest of the planes related before), also passing one of them by the point *a* and the other plane by the point *b*. (figure 3).

---

[1] Those planes are the reference planes. The reference plane chosen will be parallel planes to the floor (or to the base of the robot in a robotic application). In the case we do not have any specific plane to make reference, we must decide it first. When we said a

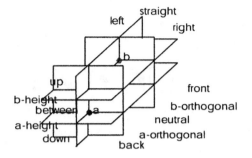

Fig. 3. *The 3-D orientation RS*

The names in the space depending where they are will be: *left*, *straight* and *right* (across), *front*, *b-orthogonal*, *neutral*, *a-orthogonal* and *back* (along) and *up*, *b-height*, *between*, *a-height* and *down* (high).

The names of every region are defined according to the position they are. They use acronyms as `ulf` if it position is in *up-left-front*; `usf` for *up-straight-front*; `urf` for *up-right-front*, and so on (figure 4).

As a matter of clarity, the 3-D representation has been translated into 2-D iconic representation, as it is shown in figure 5. In this 2-D iconic representation it is easier to perceive conceptual neighbourhood.

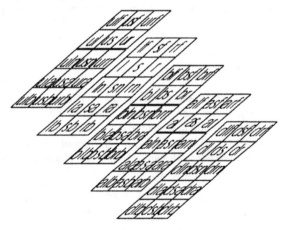

Fig. 4. *The names inside of the 3-D iconic representation*

reference plane (as the point *a* could be in any height) we refer to all the family of planes parallel to the reference plane.

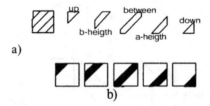

a)

b)

Fig. 5. *a) A single cell divided into five heights and the names of every part; b) the representation of the different heights.*

The information to be represented with this 3-D orientation RS (c *wrt ab*) can also be expressed of four different ways (as well as the original 2-D orientation RS) that is: Homing, Homing Inverse, Shortcut and Shortcut Inverse. These operations will be defined in the algebra.

4. The Coarse Models

Sometimes the information provided to the system is coarse or it is advisable to reduce the processing time of the reasoning process, in that case, it is necessary to define a coarse 3-D orientation model. Our 3-D orientation model has been coarsening into three models: a length coarse model, a height coarse model and a general coarse model.

4.1. The Length Coarse Model

From the original fine 3-D model approach, we can consider the coarse division with respect to the length. In that case we will have divided the space in the lengthwise by only one plane passing by the point *b*. (figure 6)

Therefore the names along will be: *front, b-orthogonal,* and *back-coarse-length*. And the 2-D iconic representation is shown in figure 7. (As a consequence of join the figure 2 c with the division of each cell appeared in figure 5)

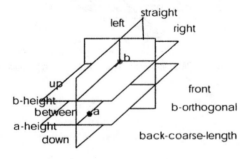

Fig. 6. *The length coarse RS.*

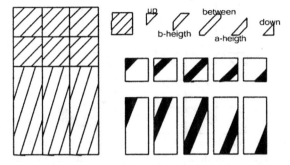

Fig. 7. *The length coarse iconic representation (It divides the main grid in 9 parts and every cell in five)*

4.2. The Height Coarse Model

Similarly, we can consider the coarse division with respect to the height. In that case we will have divided the heightwise space and by only one plane also by the point b. (figure 8).

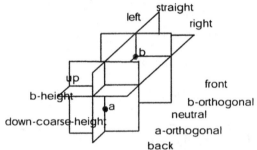

Fig. 8. *The height coarse RS.*

The names in the different heights are now: *up*, *b-height*, and *down-coarse-height*. In this case we will divide every cell in only three parts considering only the three different heights named. Therefore the 2-D iconic representation will remain as it is shown in figure 9.

4.3. The General Coarse Model

Considering the two model explained before, we join both in the general coarse RS. This model consists in reduce the divisions in the space to only 27 qualitative regions. It will be made contemplating only the planes which pass by the point b, in the original model.

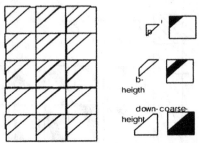

Fig. 9. *The height coarse iconic representation. (It divides every cell in three parts)*

The general coarse RS is defined by the plane which join the points *a* and *b*, defining the first left/right dichotomy, it includes the perpendicular plane by the point *b*, which separate the second front/back dichotomy and the reference parallel (to the floor) plane, also passing by the point *b*, which defines the last dichotomy up/down. (figure 10).

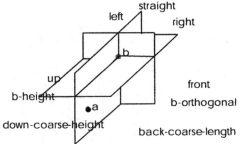

Fig. 10. *The general coarse RS..*

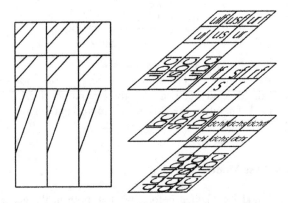

Fig. 11. *The 2-D iconic representation of the general coarse RS*

As a consequence of that the 2-D iconic representation is modified as it is shown in figure 11, where we can see how every cell is divided in three parts and the names of every region are defined using acronyms knowing that *down-coarse-height* will be dch and *back-coarse-length* bcl. In that case, for example, if the position is *down-coarse-height-straight-front* the acronym used will be dchsf, or urbcl if the position is *up-right-back-coarse-length*.

4.4. The Algebra of the General Coarse Model

The algebra consists on seven operations. The operations have been implemented as facts in a PROLOG database (as in [15, 16], but we have not extended in that aspect in this paper).

4.4.1 Identity

We will represent the identity operation as ID. The algebraic notation is: ID(*c wrt ab*) = *c wrt ab*. The 2-D iconic representation of this operation is presented in Figure 12 with all different positions in all models explained in this paper.

In figure 12 we can compare the 2-D iconic representations of the 3-D qualitative spatial orientations "*c wrt ab*". The figure 12 a) show the table of the fine model [13, 14, 15], the figure 12 b) the table of the length coarse model, the figure 12 c) the table of the height coarse model and the figure 12 d) the table of the general coarse 3-D qualitative spatial orientation.

In this paper we will show how to pass from one model to the other (from one table to the other).

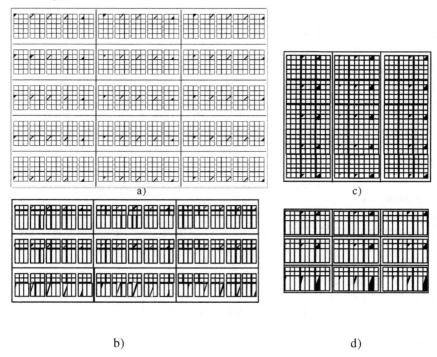

a)

c)

b)

d)

Fig. 12. *The 2-D iconic representations of the 3-D qualitative spatial orientation models* "c wrt ab". *a) the fine model, b) the length model, c) the height model and d) the general coarse model.*

4.4.2 Inversion

The inversion operation (INV) corresponds to the task of seeing the third point with respect to the RS *ba*. (See figure 13). The algebraic notation is: INV(*c wrt ab*) = *c wrt ba*.

4.4.3 Spin

The spin operation (SP) is the result of rotating 180 degrees the RS by the axis which passes by the two main points a and b of the RS [13, 14]. This operation implies that anything which was up and right will be down and left, respectively, after applying the operation.

4.4.4 Homing

In the homing (HM) operation we ask about the point *a* with respect to the RS formed by *bc*. (See the transformation in Figure 13). The algebraic notation is: HM(*c wrt ab*) = *a wrt bc*. Here disjunction also appears (as in Pacheco et al. database [15, 16]), for example: hm(us,[dchlf, dchsf, dchrf, dchl, dchs, dchr, dchlbcl, dchsbcl, dchrbcl]).

Although we have uncertainty here, we have less qualitative regions than in the fine RS, therefore the algorithm will work faster.

4.4.5 Homing Inverse

The homing inverse (HMI) operation is the result of applying the INV operation after the HM operation.
The algebraic notation is: HMI(*c wrt ab*) = INV(HM(*c wrt ab*)) = *a wrt cb*. The homing inverse operation is presented in figure 13. Also disjunctions appear here, for example: hmi(us,[ulf, usf, urf, ul, us, ur, ulbcl, usbcl, urbcl]).

4.4.6 Shortcut

In the shortcut (SC) operation we ask about the point *b* with respect to the *ac* RS. The algebraic notation is: *SC(c wrt ab)* = *b wrt ac*. The shortcut operation is presented in figure 13.

4.4.7 Shortcut Inverse

The shortcut inverse (SCI) operation is the result of applying the INV operation after the SC operation to the original orientation representation. The algebraic notation is: SCI(*c wrt ab*) = INV(SC(*c wrt ab*)) = *b wrt ca*. The shortcut inverse operation is presented in figure 13.

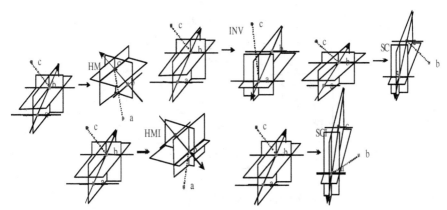

Fig. 13. *a) The 2-D iconic representation of the 3-D qualitative spatial orientation "c wrt ab". b) the 2-D iconic representation of the general coarse of the 3-D QSO "c wrt ab".*

5. The Management of Different Levels of Granularity

The key to pass from the any coarse models to the fine model or from the coarse models among them is provided by the algorithm in [2, 15, 16, 18], which contain the following steps: the definition and the relationship between the labels at different levels of granularity (for our model it is defined in figure 14); (2) the definition of the basic step of inference process (BSIP) for each granularity level and (3) the definition of the BSIP for each comb ination of the granularity level.

There is an injective relation between the finer model to the coarser model. Therefore, every qualitative orientation region in the finer model only correspond one region in the coarser, but one region in the coarser model could correspond to one or more qualitative regions in the finer model. (i.e. the region `ulf` always is named with this label, but `uln` in the fine model is labelled as `ulbc` in the length coarse model or `ulbcl` in the general coarse model, and the qualitative region named `dchrbcl` in the general coarse model, correspond in the fine model to the regions `brn`, `bra`, `brb`, `arn`, `ara`, `arb`, `drn`, `dra` and `drb`).

In figure 15 you can see as each region in a coarse model corresponds to one or more regions in the fine model.

The fine 3-D model (which is the finest) is finer representation than the length coarse model representation and the height coarse model representation, and those both are finer than the general coarse model (there is not a direct relation between the length coarse model and the height coarse model). Those relations are shown in figure 16.

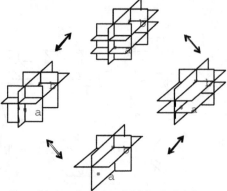

Fig. 14. *The step between the models (* up*: the fine model;* left*: the height coarse model;* right*: the length coarse model and* down *'the general coarse model*

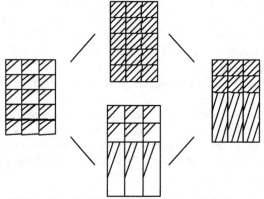

Fig. 15. *The relation between fine model and height model (on left) and length model (on right). In left relation every cell transforms his five divisions in only three (only the three cells of the first row are paint), in right relation only the back part is transformed.*

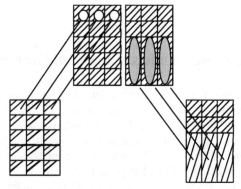

Fig. 16. *The relation between 2Dd iconic representations*

Conclusions and Future Work

We have achieved to integrate different spatial qualitative models in 3D.
In cases that we cannot to have got complete information we can use those coarse models to continue reasoning on the model.

Also we can pass between representations having more or less complexity or certain (depending on we want or we need)

We have left of this paper:

(1) How to represent the coarse models in an algorithm,
(2) the explanation of this algorithm,
(3) the application of the 3D orientation models to mobile robots with an arm manipulator on it.

Acknowledgements

This work has been partially supported by CICYT under grant number TAP99-0590-002-02.

References

[1]   Chang, S.K., Jungert, E., "A Spatial Knowledge structure for image information systems using symbolic projections", Proceedings of the National Computer Conference, Dallas, Texas, November 26, pag. 79-86, 1986.

[2]   Escrig, M.T., Toledo, F., "Reasoning with compared distances at different levels of granularity " in the 9th Conference of Spanish Association of Artificial Intelligence, 2001. ISBN: 84-932297-0-9

[3]   Freksa, c., "Conceptual Neighbourhood and its role in temporal and spatial reasoning", Proceedings of the IMACS Workshop on Decision Support Systems and Qualitative Reasoning, pag. 181-187, 1991.

[4]   Freksa, c., "Temporal reasoning based on semi-intervals", in Artificial Intelligence, vol. 54, pag. 199-227, 1992.

[5]   Freksa, c., "Using Orientation Information for Qualitative Reasoning", in a. U. Frank, I. Campari, and U. Formentini (editors). Theories and Methods of Spatio-Temporal Reasoning in Geographic Space. Proceedings of the International Conference on GIS-From Space to Territory, Pisa, volume 639 of Lecture Notes in Computer Science, Springer, Berlin, pag. 162-178, 1992.

[6]   Freksa, c., Zimmermann, K., "On the Utilization of Spatial Structures for Cognitively Plausible and Efficient Reasoning", in Proceedings of the IEEE International Conference on Systems, Man and Cybernetics, pag. 18-21, 1992.

[7]   Frank, a.U., "Qualitative Spatial Reasoning with cardinal directions", in Proceedings of the Seventh Austrian Conference on Artificial Intelligence, Wien, Springer, Berlin, pag. 157-167, 1991.

[8]   Guesgen, H.W., "Spatial reasoning based on Allen's temporal logic", Technical Report TR-89-049, International Computer Science Institute, Berkeley, 1989.

[9]   Hernández, D., "Diagrammatical Aspects of Qualitative Representations of Space", Report FKI-164-92, Technische Universität München, Germany, 1992.

[10] Hernández, D., ``Qualitative Representation of Spatial Knowledge". In volume 804 of Lecture Notes in Artificial Intelligence. Ed. Springer-Verlag, 1994.
[11] Kak, a., "Spatial Reasoning", AI Magazine, vol.9, no. 2, p. 23, 1988.
[12] Mukerjee, a. and Joe, G., "A Qualitative Model for Space". In the 8th American Association for Artificial Intelligence, pag. 721-727, 1990.
[13] Pacheco, J., Escrig, M.T., "An Approach to 3-D Qualitative Orientation of Point Objects" in the 4th Catalan congress of Artificial Intelligence, 2001.
[14] Pacheco, J., Escrig, M.T., Toledo, F. "A model for Representing and Reasoning with 3-D Qualitative Orientation " in the 9th Conference of Spanish Association of Artificial Intelligence, 2001. ISBN: 84-932297-2-5
[15] Pacheco, J., Escrig, M.T., Toledo, F. "Representing and Reasoning on Three-Dimensional Qualitative Orientation Point Objects" Proceedings in the 10th Potuguese Conference on Artificial Intelligence, EPIA 2001, Porto Portugal. In Pavel Brazdil, Alípio Jorge (ed.). Progress in Artifitial Intelligence. Lecture Notes in Artifitial Intelligence vol 2258, Springer, pag. 298-305, 2001. ISBN: 3-540-43030-X
[16] Pacheco, J., Escrig, M.T., Toledo, F. "Three-Dimensional Qualitative Orientation Point Objects: Model and Reasoning" Workshop on Logic programming for artificial Intelligence and Information System (LPAI) EPIA 2001, Porto Portugal. Proceedings edited by José Alferes and Salvador Abreu, pag. 59-74, 2001.
[17] Pacheco, J., Escrig, M.T., Toledo, F. "The First Steps towards Reasoning on 3-D Qualitative Orientation" in Inteligencia Artificial, Revista Iberoamericana de inteligencia Artificial. No 15 pag. 39-48 (2002) ISSN: 1137-3601
[18] Pacheco, J., Escrig, M.T., Toledo, F. "Qualitative Spatial Reasoning on Three-Dimensional Orientation Point Objects" Accepted paper in Sixteenth International workshop on Qualitative Reasoning. Qualitative Reasoning 2002, Sitges, Barcelona, España.

Improving Reliability in Classification of Microcalcifications in Digital Mammograms Using Case-Based Reasoning

Carles Vallespí[1], Elisabet Golobardes[1], and Joan Martí[2]

[1] Grup de Recerca en Sistemes Intelligents, departament d'Informàtica, Enginyeria i Arquitectura La Salle,
Pb. Bonanova 8,
08022 Barcelona, Spain
{cvalles, elisabet}@salleURL.edu
[2] Institut d'Informàtica i Aplicacions, Universitat de Girona,
Avda. Lluís Santaló s/n,
17071 - Girona, Spain
{joanm}@eia.udg.es

Abstract. Case-based classifiers try to solve given cases using the solutions of the most similar cases. In several medical domains, sometimes they do not perform well because of their reliability. In this paper we build a Case-Based Classifier in order to diagnose mammographic images. We explain different methods and behaviours that have been added to a Case-Based Classifier in order to improve its reliability and make it suitable for this complex domain where an error may be fatal.

1 Introduction

Automatic breast cancer detection has been proved a good practical tool for detecting and removing breast cancer prematurely, and it also increases the survival percentage in women [24]. There are several approaches to *Computer Aided Diagnosis* (CAD), but we focus on the breast cancer diagnosis using mammographic images. Radiologists agree on microcalcifications relevance when they are diagnosing a new case. Mammographic images are processed in order to find their microcalcifications and a set of features is extracted from them.

A Case-Based Reasoning algorithm is used for classifying these cases into benign or malignant cases. We have to be aware that Case-based Reasoning means using previous experience in form of cases to understand and solve new problems. A case-based reasoner remembers former cases similar to the current problem and attempts to modify their solutions to fit the current case [1]. The underlying idea is the assumption that similar cases have similar solutions. Though this assumption is not always true, it holds for many practical domains [20]. However, in this domain, reliable hypotheses are required because a single wrong prediction could be fatal (for example, take the case of a patient with a malignant tumour classified as a benign tumour). Therefore it's very important

M.T. Escrig Monferrer and F. Toledo Lobo (Eds.): CCIA 2002, LNAI 2504, pp. 101–112, 2002.

to take care with reliability (percentage of well predicted cases out of predicted cases), considering the accuracy as a second goal (percentage of well predicted cases out of all cases predicted).

Thus the purpose of this paper is twofold. First, to improve reliability in Case-based Reasoning classifiers, and second, to try to increase the final accuracy. In this paper, a total number of 216 mammograms were analysed in order to build a reliable classifier to predict the cancer risk.

This paper is organised as follows. First, the problem and related work are exposed. Then, a set of methods are presented in order to improve the reliability, and we explain how they are used in a Case Based Classifier System. Finally, we experiment with real cases and compare the results with other classifiers.

2   Related Work

2.1   Materials and Methods

A set of mammograms was used in order to analyse the incidence of features in the malignant character of the microcalcifications. The real diagnosis was known in advance from biopsies.

In order to evaluate the performance of the selected features for characterizing the microcalcifications and the power of the statistical model, the diagnosis provided by the model was compared to the real diagnosis given by the biopsies. Finally, this evaluation was compared to the diagnosis issued by 3 expert radiologists.

Conventional mammograms, in which the positions of clustered microcalcifications were determined by well experienced radiologists, were digitised using a CCD camera at a pixel size ranging from 12 to 37 micrometers and a twelve-bit gray scope, producing a 1524 × 1012 matrix image. An unshap-mask filter was applied to enhance the high-frequency component in the digitised images, simply to make it easier for the observers to recognise the microcalcifications at the stage of annotated image display (see figure 1).

The whole set of digitised mammograms compose an unpublished database formed by patients of the Regional Health Area of Girona, now available upon request, which in the future may contribute to increasing the digital mammogram databases.

The microcalcifications are segmented using a region-growing algorithm based on *Shen* segmentation techniques [23]. After segmenting the microcalcifications in every digitised mammogram, a set of features is extracted. The whole process is described in [16].

Taking into account that shapes and sizes of clustered microcalcifications have been associated with a high risk of carcinoma based on different subjective measures, such as whether or not the calcifications are irregular, linear, vermiform, branched, rounded or ring like, our efforts were directed at obtaining a feature set related to the shape.

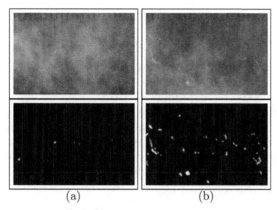

Fig. 1. Four examples of microcalcification segmentation, based on *Shen* algorithm: (a) well defined and big microcalcifications, (b) poor defined and small microcalcifications.

2.2 Improving Reliability

Classifiers often try to achieve the best accuracy by classifying all the test cases, without worrying about reliability. In some domains, reliability is not very important; however, in medical domains the penalty that we have to pay for each error can be very high. How should we achieve the best accuracy without sacrificing reliability? There are some methods to improve reliability by combining classifiers. They are bagging [5,4], boosting [9] and stacking [7]. However, these methods are not good enough because they sacrifice reliability in order to improve accuracy. This is not the main goal in medical domains. Therefore, they can be used for improving reliability without improving accuracy. We will see this in next section. There are some rule-based methods, as described in [11] that try to improve accuracy by combining Rule-Based and Case-Based Reasoning. We have not studied Rule-Based classifiers in this domain.

3   Improving Reliability

3.1   Case-Based Classifiers and Similarity Functions

Case-Based Reasoning integrates in one system two different characteristics: machine learning and problem solving capabilities. CBR uses a human-inspired philosophy: it tries to solve new cases by using previously solved ones [1]. The process of solving new cases also updates the system by providing the system with new information and new knowledge. This new knowledge can be used for solving other future cases. The basic method can be easily described in terms of its four phases. The first phase *retrieves* old solved cases similar to the new one. Then, in the second phase, the system tries to *reuse* the solutions of the previously retrieved cases to solve the new case. Next, the third phase *revises* the proposed solution. Finally, the fourth phase *retains* the useful information obtained when solving the new case.

The *reuse* phase has been simplified. It classifies the new case using the same class of the most similar retrieved one. We have previous works in medical domains (see [10]). One key point in the whole algorithms is the concept of *most similar* case used in the *retrieval* phase of CBR.

The notion of similarity between two cases is computed using different similarity measures. In this article, we use *the Nearest Neighbour Algorithm (NNA)*, which computes the similarity between two cases using a global similarity metric. The practical implementation of these distance functions use *Minkowski's metric*.

Minkowski's metric is defined as:

$$Similarity(Case\_x, Case\_y) = \sqrt[r]{\sum_{i=1}^{F} w_i \times |x_i - y_i|^r} \qquad (1)$$

Where *Case_x* and *Case_y* are two cases, whose similarity is computed; F is the number of features that describes the case; x_i, y_i represent the value of the *ith* feature of cases *Case_x* and *Case_y* respectively; and w_i is the weight of the *ith* feature.

Other distance metrics have been implemented as well, related to spheres and ellipsoids, like the Euler and the Mahalanobis [6] distance, respectively. Classifiers based on spheres or ellipsoids divide the training data into sets having the same class and then compute the mean for each class using these cases. The Euler and the Mahalonobis distances are used in order to compute the distance of an input case to each class. The main difference between both distances is the probability function used. Euler distance assumes the same probability for all the classes. Moreover, the Mahalanobis distance approximates the probability distribution function of the training data using a gaussian probability function which is different for each class. This function is set with two parameters (mean and standard deviation) easily computed using the training set.

$$\vec{C} * M^{-1} * \vec{C}' \qquad (2)$$

Where C is the case to classify and M is the covariance matrix for a given class.

If the training set is representative enough then Mahalanobis distance performs better than Euler distance. However, a lot of training cases are needed in order to estimate a good covariance matrix. And, sometimes, it is not possible to compute the matrix inverse because the matrix is not well conditioned. Both situations can be solved. For example, if training data is poor, Eigen vectors and Eigen values can be computed in order to reduce dimensionality. Thus, matrix covariance will be minor and it will be well estimated with fewer cases. Moreover, this technique reduces the noise of the training data (which is very important in real problems), but it is not possible to reduce the dimensionality a lot because important data may be lost.

In the mammogram domain we have not yet explained how to compare two cases. Notice that the cases are composed of a variable number of 21-dimension vectors (as exposed in 2.1). When we use a similarity function based on the Minkowski distance we have to compare only two vectors. However, we have two data matrix with a probably different number of rows. The first approach was to represent a case like a vector. This was a mean vector computed using the different vectors describing each microcalcification in the mammographic image. The results were published in [16].

However, using this method to compare two mammograms is suboptimal because an amount of data is lost. For this reason, we thought of using a similarity function that could compare both matrixes using all the data in them. In order to do this, we use PCA, applied to a data matrix describing one case. In this domain, when we use PCA, we can find the principal directions of energy, which can be very useful because we can see wether a mammogram has longer microcalcifications or not (because the direction of the first eigenvector is closer to the feature describing the size of the microcalcification), or wether the microcalcifications are very rough or not, and so on. This analysis allows us to compare two cases easily, by computing the angle formed between the principal vectors of two cases, and weighting the solution using the PCA auto-values.

3.2   Improving Performance in Classifiers

The combination of classifiers has long been proposed as a method to improve the accuracy achieved in isolation by a single classifier [17]. It allows us to obtain different points of view. Of course, in the end, *the best point of view* will be decided. But most of the times it is heuristic. Stacking [7] allows us to combine different decisions of each classifier to obtain a definitive prediction. There are several ways that stacking can be used for this task. For example, training a genetic algorithm using the outputs of each classifier to train them. However, it is not always good to train another classifier to make the final decision. Sometimes the best way is to use heuristic rules. For example, if the two classifiers that perform best classify the same, then we take their decision ignoring the other classifiers. This will be explained in the following sections.

Bagging and boosting [5,4,9] have been used to improve the accuracy of classification over a single classifier learned on the entire data. The Bagging technique uses repeated random samples of the dataset whereas in boosting the samples are weighted. These methods can be applied to Case-Based Reasoning Classifiers and we can use them for improving the performance of these classifiers.

3.3   Applying Bagging to CBR

As we have commented, bagging is used for improving the performance of a single classifier. Bagging builds different datasets from the original dataset by repeating randomly samples (there are more techniques for creating different datasets from the one original as described in [17]). Then a classifier is built from each dataset. Thus using one training dataset, the bagging method builds N classifiers, where N is the number of training datasets created. Finally, each input case is classified using the N classifiers, and the outputs are recombined in order to find the most suitable class. A policy may be chosen; for instance, the input class can be classified in the class with most votes. Furthermore, a threshold can be used for deciding if a case must be classified or unclassified. For example, if the difference of votes between the class most voted and the class with the second-highest number of votes is higher than a threshold then the case is classified in the class most voted. Otherwise, the case remains unclassified. It is very useful for improving reliability and classifying only those cases that are more likely to be well classified.

We tested this method replacing the case memory of the CBR classifiers with the datasets created by removing randomly samples instead of repeating them. So we randomly created smaller case memories, and we trained a CBR classifier for each case memory created. We used a previously tuned threshold for deciding which cases must be classified and which not. We will see the obtained results below.

3.4   Applying Stacking to CBR

Stacking methods are used to improve the performance achieved with a single classifier by combining the outputs of several classifiers. In the mammogram problem we use three classifiers, all CBR based, but each one is configured with different parameters. The first of these classifiers is a CBR classifier using a Minkowski similarity function and combined with bagging method (explained in 3.3). The second one is a classifier using a Mahalanobis similarity function, and the last one is a CBR classifier using a Principal Component Analysis (PCA) similarity function adapted to the mammogram problem (we will detail this in the next section, 3.5).

An input case must be classified for all three classifiers and then, all the outputs are combined using an heuristic method.

3.5   Heuristic Improvements

The mammogram problem is very complex because of the noise in the input data. As we described in 2.1 there are 21 features describing a microcalcification, and each case comprises N microcalcifications, where N takes a different value in each case. These features are extracted in a relatively complex process that adds noise. Moreover, this process depends on the microcalcifications detected or marked by the specialist in a mammographic image. But, we have not proved that the number of microcalcifications can be determinant for the final diagnosis. Thus, the number of microcalcifications can be one feature more when comparing cases. The classifier performs better adding the number of microcalcifications as an additional feature.

In previous publications we compared each test case with all the training cases; however, it does not make any sense to compare two mammograms composed of a very different number of microcalcifications, because CBR tries to recover similar cases solved in the past, and then try to adapt their solution to the new case. However if we select two cases composed of a very different number of microcalcifications then the cases are different enough and we do not need to compare them using Minkowski or Mahalanobis distances. When we did this optimisation, the classifier improved its accuracy, and its computational time.

3.6   Building the New Classifier

Many classifiers can be built by combining some of these methods (described in this section), in order to compare the methods exposed here and how well they perform in mammogram domain. One of them is a **Case Base** classifier **Using BAgging (CBUBA)**. This classifier is a Case Base Reasoning Classifier combined with bagging method. Another one is a **Mahalanobis Classifier (MC)** which uses mahalanobis measure as a distance metric. The **Case Based** classifier **Using Principal Component Analysis and bagging (CBUPCA)** is a mixture of a case based classifier and bagging, and uses PCA as a distance metric.

The results of these classifiers made possible to build the classifier used in the result tables of the next section. This classifier is called **Improved Reliability** classifier of **Microcalcifications** in digital m**Ammograms (IRMA)**. It is a Case Based Reasoning Classifier that uses the ideas seen in this section, furthermore it uses three different classifiers trained with a different similarity distance function for each one. The similarity distance functions used are the Mahalanobis, the Minkowski and the PCA similarity distance functions. Their outputs are combined using stacking method as described in 3.4. Moreover, the bagging method is used in the classifiers that use Minkowski similarity distance function. In addition, the heuristic improvements detailed in 3.5 have been added.

4   Experiments

First, we evaluate the performance of IRMA classifying mammograms and then we also evaluate the results obtained using a CBR approach [16,12,22]. All these results are compared with those obtained by human experts and the statistical model proposed in [15], as well as with six other well-known classifier schemes provided by machine learning.

4.1   Dataset

The dataset is formed by 216 instances (121 *benign* and 95 *malignant*) previously diagnosed by surgical biopsy. First, after an image processing step [15] -using the dataset described at section 2.1-, a mammographic image is reduced to a $m \times n$ matrix. This matrix contains as many rows, m, as the number of microcalcifications (μCa) present in the image, and as many columns (n=21) as the number of features that describe one μCa. Next, this $m \times 21$ matrix is transformed into a vector. This transformation computes the average value for each column (feature) across all the rows (μCas present in the image). Finally, the computed vector is labelled using the class (*benign* or *malign*) obtained from the diagnosis done by surgical biopsy.

4.2   Classifier Schemes

The results presented summarise different studies addressing this problem.

There are six classifier schemes chosen for the comparison which come from different learning theories. All these algorithms are obtained from the *Weka* package [25] developed at the University of Waikato in New Zealand, available from the http address: http://www.cs.waikato.ac.nz/ml/weka. The chosen algorithms are: *a,b*) instance-base learning IB1 and IBK with *k*=3 [2], *c*) statistical modelling, Naive Bayes (NB) [13], *d*) tree induction, C4.5 revision 8 [19], *e*) rule learning, PART [8], and *f*) support vector machines, SMO [18]. All these algorithms are run with the default configuration provided by *Weka* and they are compared with IRMA classifier described in section 3.5.

4.3   Experimental Set-up

We performed two kinds of experiments in order to compare the performance of the different algorithms. First, we maintained the proportion of original images - now, a set of features for each image- as training and test sets proposed by human experts. Thus, we compared the results obtained by IRMA and other classifiers with those achieved by human experts, and the statistical model [15] in terms of classification accuracy (*accuracy*). We also included in this comparison the true positive (*malignant* cases) rate of classified examples (*sensitivity*) and the true negative rate of classified examples (*specificity*). Although *accuracy* is computed using all the available examples, *sensitivity* and *specificity* just take into account the classified examples (the ones marked as *benign* or *malignant*).

The IRMA classifier has a parameter to be tuned which specifies if the classifier will be conservative or not. Therefore, The IRMA-6 specifies a very conservative classifier, and thus fewer cases will be classified. Moreover, the classified cases will probably classify well. The IRMA-1 is not a conservative classifier, and it will try to classify most of the cases without taking into account reliability.

The group of experiments computes the *accuracy* using stratified ten-fold cross-validation runs [25]. In other words, we divide the dataset into ten disjointed datasets that contain the same number of instances. These sets also maintain the class distribution presented in the original dataset (*stratified folds*). Next, we run the algorithms ten times, holding one different set each time for testing the classification accuracy, whereas the other nine sets are used as the training set of examples. Finally, the *accuracy* is computed averaging the accuracy of the ten runs. We also compute the *sensitivity* and *specificity* obtained across the ten-fold cross-validation runs.

4.4   Results

Table 1 summarises the results obtained across the different experiments conducted using the original training and test sets. This table includes the results obtained by IRMA, the CBR approach (CaB-CS [16] -Hamming, Euclidean and Cubic- and BASTIAN -Clark and PRS using Rough Sets weighting method-systems [21]) and the GA approach (GENIFER [14]-MDA and RA- , GALE and XCS systems [3]) as well as the ones obtained by the human experts (H-E) and the statistic model (SM), both introduced in [15]. The last five results use the methods described in this paper:

1. IRMA-1 (described in 3.6) uses a tuned non conservative threshold.
2. Case Based classifier Using BAgging (**CBUBA**) is described in section 3.3
3. Mahalanobis Classifier (**MC**) (described in section 3.1).
4. Case Based classifier Using Principal Component Analysis and bagging(**CBUPCA**).
5. IRMA-6 (described in section 3.6) uses a tuned conservative threshold.

The results show that accuracy in our classifier schemes is higher than the accuracy obtained by the human experts and the statistical model. However, human experts and the statistical model show a better specificity than the ones obtained by CBR and GA techniques. But, it is better to obtain a higher sensitivity in this domain (as explained in 1), and the IRMA-6 achieves **95.6%** of sensitivity (see table 1).

Table 1. Results obtained using the original training and test sets.

Variant	Unclas.	Sens.	Spec.	Accuracy
H-E	38.57	70.59	**92.59**	52.86
SM	52.86	81.82	90.48	40.00
Hamming	0.00	80.95	69.39	72.86
Euclidean	0.00	66.67	75.51	72.86
Cubic	0.00	66.67	77.55	74.29
Clark	0.00	66.66	81.63	77.14
PRS	0.00	66.66	83.67	78.57
MDA	0.00	23.80	93.87	72.86
RA	0.00	47.61	85.71	74.29
GALE	0.00	52.38	85.71	75.71
XCS	1.42	61.90	64.45	62.85
IRMA-1	0.47	92.18	66.47	**80.95**
CBUBA	1.91	85.48	68.77	76.52
MC	0.0	81.81	52.33	70.11
CBUPCA	2.38	87.77	54.91	72.42
IRMA-6	23.81	**95.92**	66.69	64.72

Machine learning algorithms tend to be more specific than sensitive. Usually, higher specificity rates are obtained. Results summarised in table 2 show this fact.

5 Conclusions and Further Work

The use of the bagging method applied to CBR classifier in this domain has improved the results obtained previously and, furthermore, it enables a threshold for improving reliability to be added (by being more conservative and do not

Table 2. Results obtained using stratified ten-fold cross-validation runs.

Variant	Uncl.	Sens.	Spec.	Accuracy	Std
Hamming	0.0	56.84	66.94	62.50	14.47
Euclidean	0.0	56.84	69.42	63.89	12.43
Cubic	0.0	60.00	68.60	64.81	9.62
Clark	0.0	57.10	62.88	60.40	12.73
PRS	0.0	63.15	68.60	66.20	11.12
MDA	0.0	52.63	70.25	62.50	11.20
RA	0.0	43.16	76.86	62.04	9.95
GALE	0.0	64.21	76.86	71.30	**5.93**
XCS	1.42	56.84	70.25	64.30	6.40
IB1	0.0	56.84	67.77	62.96	12.42
IB3	0.0	60.00	69.42	65.28	6.29
C4.5 (r8)	0.0	70.53	60.33	64.81	6.36
NB	0.0	60.00	68.60	64.81	7.66
PART	0.0	80.00	47.93	62.04	4.17
SVM-SMO	0.0	52.63	78.51	67.13	7.37
IRMA-1	0.47	92.18	66.47	**80.95**	8.37
CBUBA	1.91	85.48	**68.77**	76.52	11.15
MC	0.0	81.81	52.33	70.11	9.99
CBUPCA	2.38	87.77	54.91	72.42	7.81
IRMA-6	**23.81**	**95.92**	66.69	64.72	8.31

classifying all the cases of the entire test set). Likewise, the addition of new similarity functions to the previously used CBR classifier, has added new points of view and has improved a the sensitivity a little, but not the accuracy. The use of different classifiers (CBR based classifiers and Mahalanobis Classifiers) allows stacking methods to be used, by combining the outputs of these classifiers. However, in spite of the fact that the combination of different classifiers does not improve the final accuracy, it allows reliability to be improved by using heuristic rules (for instance, it does not classify if at least one of the outputs of a classifier is different from the other).

In conclusion, the use of the bagging method has improved accuracy and the use of a stacking method and different similarity functions (Mahalanobis and PCA) has improved reliability while maintaining accuracy.

However, none of these methods have been tested in other domains. In the future, they must be tested in other domains in order to analyse wether they improve the reliability and the accuracy, too. We must also design an algorithm to construct the stacking rules (now heuristic) automatically.

Acknowledgements. This work is supported by the *Ministerio de Sanidad y Consumo, Instituto de Salud Carlos III, Fondo de Investigación Sanitaria* of Spain, Grant No. 00/0033-02. We wish to thank *Enginyeria i Arquitectura La Salle* (Ramon Llull University) for their support to our Research Group in Intelligent Systems.

References

1. A. Aamodt and E. Plaza. Case-Based Reasoning: Foundations Issues, Methodological Variations, and System Approaches. In *AI Communications*, volume 7, pages 39–59, 1994.

2. D. Aha and D. Kibler. Instance-based learning algorithms. *Machine Learning, Vol. 6*, pages 37–66, 1991.
3. E. Bernadó, X. Llorà, and J. M. Garrell. XCS and GALE: a Comparative Study of Two Classifier Systems with Six Other Learning Algorithms on Classification Tasks. In *Proceeding of the International Workshop on Learning Classifier System*, 2001.
4. L. Breiman. Bagging predictors. *Machine Learning*, 24(2):123–140, 1996.
5. P. Buhlmann and B. Yu. Explaining bagging, 2000.
6. N. Campbell. Robust procedures in multivariate analysis i: Robust covariance estimation, 1980.
7. P. Chan. An extensible meta-learning approach for scalable and accurate inductive learning, 1996.
8. E. Frank and I.H. Witten. Generating Accurate Rule Sets Without Global Optimization. In J. Shavlik, editor, *Machine Learning: Proceedings of the Fifteenth International Conference*, pages 144–151. Morgan Kaufmann, 1998.
9. Y. Freund and R. E. Schapire. Experiments with a new boosting algorithm. In *International Conference on Machine Learning*, pages 148–156, 1996.
10. J.M. Garrell, E. Golobardes, E. Bernadó, and X. Llorà. Automatic diagnosis with Genetic Algorithms and Case-Based Reasoning. *Elsevier Science Ltd. ISSN 0954-1810*, 13:367–362, 1999.
11. A. R. Golding and P. S. Rosenbloom. Improving accuracy by combining rule-based and case-based reasoning. *Artificial Intelligence*, 87(1-2):215–254, 1996.
12. E. Golobardes, X. Llorà, M. Salamó, and J. Martí. Computer Aided Diagnosis with Case-Based Reasoning and Genetic Algorithms. *Knowledge Based Systems*, 2001.
13. G. H. John and P. Langley. Estimating Continuous Distributions in Bayesian Classifiers. In *Proceedings of the Eleventh Conference on Uncertainty in AI*, pages 338–345. Morgan Kaufman Publishers, 1995.
14. X. Llorà and Josep M. Garrell. GENIFER: A Nearest Neighbour based Classifier System using GA. In *Proceedings of the Genetic and Evolutionary Computation Conference (GECCO99)*, 1999.
15. J. Martí, X. Cufí, J. Regincós, and et al. Shape-based feature selection for microcalcification evaluation. *Proceedings of the SPIE Medical Imaging Conference on Image Processing*, 3338:1215–1224, 1998.
16. J. Martí, J. Español, E. Golobardes, J. Freixenet, R. García, and M. Salamó. Classification of microcalcifications in digital mammograms using case-based reasoning. In *International Workshop on digital Mammography*, 2000.
17. O. Hall N. Chawla, S. Eschrich. Creating Ensembles of Classifiers. Technical Report ISL-01-01, Department of Computer Science and Engineering, University of South Florida, 2001.
18. J. C. Platt. Fast Training of Support Vector Machines using Sequential Minimal Optimization. *Advances in Kernel Methods - Support Vector Learning*, MIT Press, 1998.
19. R. Quinlan. *C4.5: Programs for Machine Learning*. Morgan Kaufmann Publishers, 1993.
20. L. Gierl R. Schmidt. Case-based Reasoning for Medical Knowledge-based Systems, 2000.
21. M. Salamó and E. Golobardes. BASTIAN: Incorporating the Rough Sets theory into a Case-Based Classifier System. In *III Congrés Català d'Intel·ligència Artificial*, pages 284–293, October 2000.

112   C. Vallespí, E. Golobardes, and J. Martí

22. M. Salamó and E. Golobardes. Rough Sets reduction techniques for Case-Based Reasoning. In *Proceedings of the International Conference on Case-Based Reasoning*, 2001.
23. L. Shen, R.M. Rangayyan, and J.L. Dessautels. Detection and classification of mammographic calcifications. In *In State of the Art in Digital Mammographic Image Analysis*, pages 198–212, 1994.
24. D. Winfields, M. Silbiger, G.S. Brown, and et al. Technology transfer in digital mammography. *Report of the Joint National Cancer Institute. Workshop of May 19–20, Invest. Radiol.*, pages 507–515, 1994.
25. I. H. Witten and E. Frank. *DataMining: practical machine learning tools and techniques with Java implementations*. Morgan Kaufmann Publishers, 2000.

Fusion of Qualitative Preferences with Different Vocabularies

Aïda Valls[1] and Vicenç Torra[2]

[1] Computer Science and Mathematics Department, ETSE, URV
Avda.Països Catalans, 26, 43007 Tarragona, Spain
`avalls@etse.urv.es`
[2] Artificial Intelligence Research Institute, CSIC
Campus UAB, s/n, 08193 Bellaterra, Spain
`vtorra@iiia.csic.es`

Abstract. We present a method for the aggregation of qualitative preferences. This method is specially indicated when the set of criteria that is expressing the preferences is not homogeneous. That is, criteria have vocabularies with completely different terms, vocabularies with some common terms with different semantics or vocabularies with different granularity. The goal of the fusion process is to obtain a new ordered qualitative criterion expressing the overall preference over a set of alternatives. Our approach uses *clustering techniques* as an aggregation tool, and the *principal components analysis* to obtain a ranking of the alternatives.

1 Introduction

Fusion methods are applied to data sets with a collection of alternatives (f.i. objects, individuals) described with different criteria (f.i. properties, points of view) in order to obtain an overall value for each alternative, which summarises the information provided by the collection of criteria.

In this paper we will focus on alternatives that are described using qualitative preferences. This type of criteria uses a set of ordered values to indicate the preference of each alternative according to some aspect (f.i. the adequacy with respect to a particular goal, the degree of certainty of a desired fact). Many fusion methods for numerical values can be applied in this case, such as the weighted mean or the OWA operator (see [1] for a review of numerical operators). However, when data is uncertain, the values are usually not numerical, but qualitative. A qualitative preference criterion is the one that uses an ordered collection of terms (i.e. linguistic labels) to describe the alternatives, which is called 'vocabulary'.

In addition to the vocabulary, we have to consider how to explain the meaning of each term: its semantics. The most common solution is the use of fuzzy sets [2]. However, it is often argued that the definition of the membership functions can be difficult for the user. Other possibility is the use of a negation-based semantics, where the user explains the meaning of the terms in relation to their antonyms [3]. In this paper we are not going to give details about the semantics behind the vocabularies,

M.T. Escrig Monferrer and F. Toledo Lobo (Eds.): CCIA 2002, LNAI 2504, pp. 113–124, 2002.
© Springer-Verlag Berlin Heidelberg 2002

because we will concentrate on a specific part of the fusion process (the ranking), which is independent of the semantics representation.

To design a fusion method for a qualitative set of preferences we must take into consideration some questions that difficult the process:

- Is the number of terms equal in all the vocabularies?
- Are there different terms in the vocabularies?
- Are vocabularies equal but the meaning of the terms is different?

The first case is known as *Multigranularity* problem [4]. This situation arises when each criterion has a different uncertainty degree, then the terms are the same in all the criteria, but in each one the cardinality of the vocabulary is different. This is a situation in which the experts have different degrees of precision, that is, different degrees of knowledge about the problem.

The other situations can be denoted as *Heterogeneous Data* problems. In this case, not only the granularity is different, but also the terms have a different semantics. If each criterion is provided by a different expert, we can find vocabularies with different terms (each person uses his own words) or with the same terms but with different meaning (the same word can be interpreted in slightly different ways).

To sort out these problems, a common solution consists of including an initial phase where a mapping between each of the vocabularies and a fixed one is established, then all of the expert's vocabularies are translated into this common one [5]. However, this approach introduces error due to the approximations done in order to make the translation possible.

One of the key points of our method is that it can deal with different types of variables without introducing a pre-processing.

In the next sections we will explain the process of fusion. The goal is to obtain a ranking of the alternatives considering a unique preference criterion. This new criterion has a vocabulary with an ordered set of terms provided by the user, and a negation function to express the meaning of these terms. Values from this vocabulary will be selected in order to describe each alternative.

In section 2 the main steps of the fusion procedure are introduced. This paper focuses on the ranking process, which is explained in section 3. Some quality measures that can help the user to understand the result are defined in section 4. Section 5 is devoted to present some examples of applications in which fusion is useful. Finally, in section 6 we will review the results of tests on reduced data sets.

2 The Fusion Procedure

Our fusion method will be applied to a data matrix, X, with n alternatives (rows) and p preference criteria (columns), like the one in Fig.1 (left side). The result will be a ranking of the alternatives regarded to an overall preference criterion (right side of Fig.1). In addition to the ranking, we will attach a linguistic term to each alternative in order to make explicit the degree of preference.

	Weight	*Size*	*Waiting time*	*RESULT*
A	inadequate	feasible	short	not-recom.
B	good	feasible	very_long	good
C	good	good	very_long	good
D	feasible	feasible	acceptable	not-recom.
E	good	good	long	good
F	optimum	good	acceptable	recommendable
G	good	optimum	acceptable	very_good

Fig. 1. Example of fusion of 3 criteria

The fusion procedure can be divided up into two steps: (i) aggregation of the values in the data matrix, and (ii) ranking of the alternatives.

In the first step, the values of each alternative are analysed in order to find another evaluation for the alternative that allows us to compare it with the others and obtain the order among them. In the second step, the alternatives are compared and ranked on the basis of the value given in the aggregation phase.

In this paper we will focus on the ranking process, but first we will give some details about the aggregation step.

When working with qualitative criteria, each column of the data matrix is defining a partition on the set of alternatives. The alternatives that have the same value form a class, because they are indistinguishable for the user. For example, in Fig.1, alternatives B, C and E are preferred in the same degree (good) with regard to the *weight* characteristic. Therefore, we can say that, in this case, the aggregation goal is to obtain a new partition that summarises the information given by the values of the criteria. Each class in this partition corresponds to a new linguistic value in the domain of the new social (i.e. agreed) criterion. To obtain this partition we propose the use of a clustering method [6].

In any clustering process, the objects are grouped according to their similarity. To find these groups or clusters, each object is compared to the others using the values in the data matrix. In the example of Fig.1, we obtain 4 classes: $\alpha=\{A,D\}$, $\beta=\{B,C,E\}$, $\delta=\{F\}$ and $\gamma=\{G\}$.

After the clustering, each alternative belongs to a single class. Each class is given automatically a symbolic name, which is its aggregation value (f.i. α, β, δ, γ).

Then, the second step of the fusion process can start: the ranking. We will devote the main part of this paper to explain in detail the ranking process.

After the ranking, we proceed to change the artificially generated names of the clusters by other linguistic terms. These terms are selected from a preference vocabulary given by the user. For each class, we have defined an algorithm [7] that selects the most appropriate term from the vocabulary, using the negation-based semantics of the terms. In the example of Fig.1, the vocabulary available for the description of the classes was: {*ideal, very_good, good, recommendable, acceptable, not-recommendable, bad, terrible*}, and the terms selected where: *very_good* for class {G}, *good* for class {B,C,E}, *recommendable* for class {F} and *not-recommendable* for class {A,D}.

3 Ranking Using PCA

In the second stage of the fusion process, the classes obtained in the aggregation must be ordered according to the preference values of their components. We propose the use of a well-known multivariate statistical technique called *Principal Components Analysis* (PCA) [8].

To obtain a good ranking with PCA, criteria are required to be correlated with each other. This situation happens when the criteria are the opinions of different experts about the alternatives. Although the experts may have different opinions, it can be supposed to be an "ideal preference ranking" which they are trying to explain.

In the next subsections we will see the mathematical basis of the PCA, some measures to interpret and evaluate the result, and the steps that must be followed to rank the set of classes obtained in the aggregation stage.

3.1 The Principal Components Analysis Method

The *Principal Components Analysis* is a multivariate statistical method that obtains linear transformations of a set of correlated variables such that the new variables are not correlated. The new variables define a multi-dimensional space, whose axes are called principal components.

Considering that we have a data matrix, X, where the alternatives are defined in a certain basis, the PCA will make a change in the basis, so that, the new space is defined by orthogonal axes. However, PCA is not applied directly to the matrix X [9]. We use a $p \times p$ symmetric, non-singular matrix, M.

Principal Components are generated one by one. To find the first principal component we look for a linear combination of the variables that has maximum sample variance. Then, the second vector will be obtained with the same goal subject to the fact of being orthogonal to the first vector, and so on. The solution to this maximisation problem is based on the fact that the matrix M can be reduced to a diagonal matrix L by premultiplying and postmultiplying it by a particular orthonormal matrix U. This diagonalisation is possible because M is a $p \times p$ symmetric, non-singular matrix.

$$U'MU = L \tag{1}$$

With this diagonalisation we obtain p values, $l_1, l_2, ..., l_p$, which are called the characteristic roots or eigenvalues of M. The columns of U, $u_1, u_2, ..., u_p$, are called the characteristic vectors or eigenvectors of M. Geometrically, the values of the these vectors are the direction cosines of the new axes related to the old.

Having the set of data, X, described by p variables, $x_1, x_2, ..., x_p$, we can obtain the eigenvectors corresponding to this data and produce new p uncorrelated variables, $z_1, z_2, ..., z_p$. The transformed variables are called the *principal components* of X.

The new values of the alternatives are called z-scores, and are obtained with this transformation:

$$z = U'x^* \tag{2}$$

where x^* is $p \times 1$ vector that has the values of an alternative after some scaling.

The matrix M, from which the principal components are calculated, is obtained with equation (3). The matrix Y can have different forms, which deals to different results.

$$M = \frac{Y'Y}{n} \qquad (3)$$

Product matrix:

The first approach consists of taking $Y = X$, that is, performing the analysis from the raw data. However, there are not many inferential procedures that can be applied in this case.

Covariance matrix:

The second approach consists of centring the data, so that, $Y = X - \overline{X}$. In this case, we transform the variables such that they have mean equal to 0. With this transformation we perform a translation of the data. It is important to notice that, in this case, the matrix M obtained is the covariance matrix of X. In this case, the principal components are obtained with (4).

$$z = U'\left[x - \overline{x}\right] \qquad (4)$$

where x is a $p \times 1$ vector that has the values of an alternative on the original variables, and $\overline{x}$ is also a $p \times 1$ vector that has the mean of each variable.

Statistical analysis with the PCA method is usually done from the covariance matrix, because the inferential procedures are better developed for this kind of matrix than for any other type [9]. However, there are some situations in which the covariance matrix should not be used: (i) when the original variables are expressed in different units or (ii) when the variances are different (even though the variables are in the same units). The use of a covariance matrix in these two situations will give undue weight to certain variables (i.e. those that have a large range of values or a large variance).

To avoid this weighting of certain variables, a third approach is possible.

Correlation matrix

It corresponds to the centring and standardisation of the data in X using (5). Then, the variables in Y have mean equal to 0 and unit deviation. In this case, the matrix M is the correlation matrix of X.

$$Y = \frac{X - \overline{X}}{\sqrt{variance(X)}} \qquad (5)$$

The use of correlation matrices is also very common in PCA and it is usually the default option in some computer packages (f.i. Minitab). Inferential procedures for this type of matrices are well defined.

The z-scores are obtained using (6).

$$z = U'D^{-1}[x - \bar{x}]$$
(6)

where x is $p \times 1$ vector, corresponding to a single variable of X, and D is the diagonal matrix of standard deviations of the variables.

To perform the ranking of alternatives during a fusion process, we recommend the use of the **correlation matrix**, since we can be dealing with variables with different units or different variances.

The Principal Component Analysis allows us to reduce the multidimensionality of the data, and to represent the information of the initial data set in a k-space smaller than the original (with p variables), that is, $k \ll p$. In the k-space the data is easily interpretable. However, the determination of which should be the value k is not straightforward. The larger k is, the better the fit of the PCA model; the smaller k is, the simpler the model will be.

There are different stopping criteria (see [9]). They are based in the fact that the characteristic roots, $l_1, l_2, ..., l_p$, are decreasingly ordered, that is, $l_1 > l_2 > ... > l_p$. That means that the first characteristic vector is the one that accounts for a higher proportion of variability. That is, it conserves the highest information of the original data as possible in one dimension.

For the case of the correlation matrix, the most frequently used stopping criterion is the selection of the components whose eigenvalues are greater than one. The rationale for this criterion is that any components should account for more "variance" than any single variable (remember that variances are equal to 1 because data have been centred and standardised).

PCA is usually performed for descriptive purposes. In this framework, we use it to represent our data in a single axis. Therefore, after applying the stopping criterion, it is useful to know the proportion of the total information that can be represented with only the first component. There is a direct relationship between the sum of the original variances and the sum of the characteristic roots obtained with the PCA.

$$Tr(L) = l_1 + l_2 + l_3 + ... l_p$$
(7)

In the case of doing the PCA with the correlation matrix, $Tr(L) = p$ because the variables have been previously standardised.

The value $Tr(L)$ can be used to calculate the proportion of the total "variance" attributable to the i-th component, which is $l_i/Tr(L)$.

If variables are highly correlated, the percentage of information represented using the first principal component is high (around 70-80 %). This is enough to obtain a good ranking with this method. If more than one component are needed (considering the stopping criterion and the variance measurement), PCA will not give good results. In addition, the quality measures we define in section 4, will not be calculable for the case of needing more that one axis. In this case, we must discard this ranking technique and use another approach [7].

The analysis of principal components obtained from the data matrix, X, gives us a new p-space where the alternatives can be represented. However, it is also possible to make a dual analysis from X^T. That is, transposing the data matrix we consider the alternatives as columns (or variables) and the variables as rows (or alternatives). Then, using the PCA, we can obtain an n-space where we can represent the variables in terms of a set of uncorrelated axis (that represent uncorrelated alternatives). An important property is that this n-space is related to the p-space obtained with matrix X. With this relation, we can use the p-space to represent the variables without having to perform the second analysis.

To obtain the coordinates of the alternatives in the new space, we calculate the z-scores (2). To represent the variables we must calculate the V-vectors, which indicate the direction of the variables in the space of the principal components.

$$v_i = u_i \sqrt{l_i} \qquad (8)$$

The correlations among the variables and the principal components are interesting to interpret the results, as it will be seen in the next subsection.

3.2 Application of the PCA to Rank Order

Now, we are going to see in detail the process that must be followed to obtain the rank order of the partition of alternatives that we have got in the clustering phase.

Before applying the PCA, we build the prototype of each class. The prototype is the pattern of the class. For each criterion, the prototype takes the value that appears more times in the alternatives that belong to the class. These prototypes are the objects to be ranked.

With the prototypes we can build another matrix B. Following the example in Figure 1, we can see here the matrix B with the prototypes of the 4 classes obtained in the aggregation stage (Table 1).

Table 1. Example of Prototypes matrix

	Weight	Size	Waiting time
Class α: A+D	inadequate	feasible	short
Class β: B+C+E	food	good	very_long
Class δ: F	optimum	good	acceptable
Class γ: G	good	optimum	acceptable

Then, we have two data matrices which can be used to obtain the first principal component: the original data matrix, X, and the prototypes matrix, B. In principle, the PCA could be performed in each of the two matrices. However, the second one has a very short number of objects (between 4 and 9, which are the usual cardinalities of linguistic vocabularies). This is not good for PCA, which is a technique to be used when the number of variables is much more small than the number of alternatives (i.e. classes or objects). Moreover, the values in the matrix of prototypes have not been provided by the experts, they are the result of some computations over the original values, which can introduce error in the interpretation of the result. So, although the objects that we want to rank are the ones in matrix B, we should not perform the PCA directly with these data matrix. The PCA will be done in the original data matrix and then the prototypes of the classes will be introduced in the new space in order to be ranked.

We can distinguish 5 sequential steps in the process of applying the Principal Components Analysis to our data. At the end, we will have a ranking of the classes and some values that will be used to measure the goodness of the result and to infer the relationships among the variables (i.e. preference criteria).

STEP 1 – Apply the PCA using the correlations matrix. Obtain the eigenvalues, l_i, eigenvectors, u_i and V-vectors, v_i.

STEP 2 – Check if the first component is enough to perform the ranking, using the stopping criterion: we need all components u_i such that $l_i>1$.

If we need more than one principal component to represent our data, we execute step 4 and end.

STEP 3 – Use the first V-vector to know the meaning of the first component. If $v_1(x_j)$ is near zero, it means that the variable x_j has no influence in the interpretation of the component, while the higher $v_1(x_j)$ is, the more the component is saying the same than the variable x_j. Moreover, we can apply (9) to calculate the relationship (i.e. correlation) between a variable, x_j, and the first axis.

$$CORR_1\left(x_j\right)= v_1^{\ 2}\left(x_j\right) \tag{9}$$

The sign of the elements of v_1 indicates the direction of each variable in relation to the component. This is particularly interesting because we must determine which is the direction of the first component in order to know which are the best alternatives. In our case, all the variables are expressing preferences, where the higher the value, the more preferred an alternative is. Thus, the sign of coefficients of v_1 should be the same if all the criteria agree. Therefore, we will stop the fusion process if the size of variables that are positively correlated with the first component is similar to the size of variables that are negatively correlated with this component, because in this case the direction of the first component cannot be established.

STEP 4 – Calculate the contribution of each variable to the formation of the first principal component (5). If a variable has not contributed to the formation of the first axis, it means that this variable does not give any useful information for the determination of axis to be used in the ranking. If a variable does not contribute to any axis, it means that it can be eliminated from the analysis and the result would not be significantly different.

$$CTR_1(x_j) = \frac{v_1^2(x_j)}{l_1} = u_1^2(x_j) \tag{10}$$

STEP 5 – Find the z-scores of the prototypes in the first principal component, z_1, using equation (6), where x are the columns of the prototypes matrix.

The z-scores tell us the position of each class into a line, which defines a total order among them. The direction of the director vector of this line determines which are the best and worse positions. This direction has been found in step 3. Thus, the ranking of the classes we were looking for is already set.

4 Quality Measures

In this section we define some quality measures that can be useful for the user in order to decide the reliability of the result. In many applications where fusion techniques are required, it is interesting to know to what extent the result of the process is acceptable. In addition, if the person that is executing the fusion process is a non-specialised end user, the ignorance about the way the result is obtained often causes a mistrust feeling, and the consequent abandon of the system to continue doing the processes by hand.

For this reason, we have studied in detail the techniques applied at each stage of this new method. Some quality measures have been defined using information available at the different stages. We are now going to define a goodness measure to evaluate the ranking stage, which is the focus of this paper.

This quality measure takes into account the quality of the representation of the classes by the first principal component, and also, the agreement of the criteria in relation to the first component.

$$GOODNESS_{PCA} = \frac{\dfrac{\sum_{j=1}^{p} s \cdot CORR_1^2(x_j)}{p} + \dfrac{\sum_{j} QLT_1(j)}{\text{number of classes}}}{2} \qquad (11)$$

where s depends on the direction of the first component. If the x_j is positively correlated to the first component, $s = 1$. Otherwise, $s = -1$.

The best value of $GOODNESS_{PCA}$ is 1. The worst value is 0, which would correspond to a situation where the classes were not well represented and the criteria did not agree with the first component.

In the numerator, the first addend is measuring the correlation of the variables, using equation (9). The second addend is related to the quality of representation of the classes, which is measured using (12). If a class obtains a value near to 0, it means that it is bad represented by the first component, if the value is 1, the class is perfectly explained by the axis.

$$QLT_1(j) = \frac{z_i^2(j)}{d^2(j,G)} \qquad (12)$$

being d the Euclidean distance between the alternative j and the centre of gravity (0 in our case, because we work with the correlations matrix).

5 Applications

This fusion method can be applied to any problem that works with qualitative preferences. Some fields that use fusion techniques to sort out these kinds of problems are: decision making with multiple criteria (MCDM) and data mining.

MCDM is a particular subset of decision-making problems, in which the decision maker is faced with a set of alternatives described by different criteria, and his goal is to find either the best alternative or a ranking of the alternatives with respect to the decision problem. The main difficulty in MCDM problems lies in the fact that usually there is no objective or optimal solution for all the criteria. Thus, some trade-off must be done among the different points of view to determine an acceptable solution. If these criteria are qualitative preferences over the set of decision alternatives, we can use the methodology explained in this paper to find a ranking of the alternatives. Then, the decision maker can use this ranking to make the selection of the best alternative.

The second application field that we are interested in, data mining, is completely different. In this case, information aggregation can be applied to improve different data mining techniques. For example, we can use aggregation operators to build models from a dataset or to combine previously build data models. As well as, at the pre-processing stage, we can improve the quality of the data (f.i. avoid missing values, correct erroneous values) using information coming from different sources. Besides of increasing the quality of data, information aggregation can be also used to relate previously unrelated data. This is the case of re-identification procedures used to link records in separate files that relate to the same object (individual, company or household). Statistical Disclosure Control is an example of the use of interest of the study of re-identification tools.

We have applied this fusion method in these two application examples with good results (more details in [7,10]).

6 Results and Conclusions

As we are not able to see in detail the previous applications, we will explain a smaller case study. We performed 5 tests of this fusion methodology with data obtained from 5 experts describing 25 different countries. Each expert was required to use a qualitative preference vocabulary to describe the following aspects the countries: *Dimension, Temperature, Degree of Development, Individual Freedom* and *Degree of Conflicts*. Each person has used his/her mother tongue, so the terms are difference but some of them have the same meaning.

We have analysed each aspect separately. For each one, we have build the data matrix, X. See for instance Table 2.

Table 2. Data matrix for the Dimension of countries

	E1	*E2*	*E3*	*E4*	*E5*
Portugal	Small	Petit	Peque	Petit	Mig
Italy	Medium	Mitjà	Peque	Petit	Mig
Ireland	Small	Petit	MPeque	Petit	Petit
Canada	Big	Gran	Mgrande	Gran	Gran
Brazil	Big	MGran	Mgrande	Gran	Gran
...	...	...	...	...	...
Greece	Medium	Petit	Normal	Petit	Mig

After making the clustering and applying the Principal Components Analysis to each data set, we have obtained the following results (Table 3).

- **%A:** Proportion of information explained with the first axis, which is the degree of agreement between the qualitative preference criteria (between the 5 experts in this case).
- **G:** value of $GOODNESS_{PCA}$, which measures the quality of the ranking.

Table 3. Results with Countries Data

	%A	G
Dimension	66	0.673
Temperature	79	0.813
Degree of Development	73	0.646
Individual Freedom	84	0.719
Degree of Conflicts	86	0.774
Average	**77.6**	**0.725**

Analysing the data, we have seen that in the first test (*dimension*) effectively there is a higher disagreement between the five experts. In this case, the stopping criterion selects only one component, but the second one has an eigenvalue of 0.74, which is not far from the cutting value, 1. Calculating the degree of correlation between each criterion and the first principal component, we can see that there are two experts (E3 and E5) with correlations 0.46 and 0.57, respectively. This indicates that these experts have a slightly different opinion with respect to the result obtained. We obtain a higher degree of agreement in the other concepts. The *degree of conflicts* of the countries is the criterion in which the experts have a most similar opinion.

However, the degree of agreement is not enough to evaluate the goodness of the ranking. Using the measure defined in section 4, we can see that the best result corresponds to the *temperature*. In this test, all the classes are well represented by the first axis. Otherwise, regarding the *degree of conflicts* criterion, we can find that one of the classes is not well represented (see equation (12)). We have checked that this because the experts do not agree with the degree of conflict of the countries that belong to this class.

With these experiments we have tested our fusion method. We can see that we can extract useful information about the process. This in an important feature that is not considered in other fusion techniques.

Acknowledgements. This work is supported by the EU project CASC (IST-2000-25069) and the CICYT project STREAMOBILE (TIC2001-0633-C03-01/02). We also acknowledge the valuable help of Dr. Karina Gibert.

References

1. Marichal, J.-L.: Aggregation operators for multicriteria decision aid, PhD. Thesis, University of Liège, Belgium (1998)
2. Wang, P.P. (ed.): Computing with words, John Wiley & Sons (2001)
3. Torra, V.: Negation functions based semantics for ordered linguistic labels, Int. Journal of Intelligent Systems, vol.11 (1996) 975-988
4. Herrera, F., Herrera-Viedma. E., Martínez, L.: A fusion approach for managing multigranularity linguistic term sets in decision making, Fuzzy Sets and Systems, 114 (2000) 43-58
5. Herrera, F., Herrera-Viedma, E.,: Linguistic decision analysis: Steps for solving decision problems under linguistic information, Fuzzy Sets and Systems, 115 (2000) 67-82
6. Valls, A., Torra, V.: Using classification as an aggregation tool in MCDM, Fuzzy Sets and Systems, vol.115-1, Special issue on Soft Decision Analysis (2000) 159-168
7. Valls, A., Moreno, A., Sánchez, D.: A multi-criteria decision aid agent applied to the selection of the best receiver in a transplant, 4th. International Conference on Enterprise Information Systems, Ciudad Real, Spain (2002) 431-438
8. Pearson, K.: On the lines and planes of closest fit to systems of points in space, Phil. Mag. Ser. B, 2 (1901) 559-572
9. Jackson, J.E., A user's guide to principal components, John Wiley & Sons (1991)
10. Valls, A., Torra, V., Domingo-Ferrer, J.: Aggregation methods to evaluate multiple protected versions of the same confidential data set, 1st.Int.Workshop on Soft Methods in Probability and Statistics, Poland, September (2002) in press

FUTURA: Hybrid System for Electric Load Forecasting by Using Case-Based Reasoning and Expert System

Raúl Vilcahuamán[1,2], Joaquim Meléndez[1], and Josep Lluis de la Rosa[1]

[1] Institut d'Informàtica i Aplicacions, Universitat de Girona,
Campus Montilivi, Edifici P.4. Girona, Spain.
[2] Facultad de Ingeniería de Sistemas.
Universidad Nacional del Centro del Perú,
Calle Real 160, Huancayo, Perú.

r.vilcahuaman@ieee.org, {quimmel,peplluis}@eia.udg.es

Abstract. The results of combining a numeric extrapolation of data with the methodology of case-based reasoning and expert systems in order to improve the electric load forecasting are presented in this contribution. Registers of power consumption are stored as cases that are retrieved and adapted by an expert system to improve a numeric forecasting given by numeric algorithms. FUTURA software has been developed as a result of this work. It combines the proposed techniques in a modular way while it provides a graphic user interface and access capabilities to existing data bases.

1 Introduction

When an electric power system, whether for transmission or for distribution, is being planned, the power engineer must know how much power is expected to be served and where and when it has to be supplied. Consequently, the load forecasting includes knowing the location (Where) of each element, the magnitude (How much), and its timing characteristics (When). Nowadays systems used for load forecasting take into consideration just registered numeric information and the forecast is limited to extrapolation algorithms with *rough* results in a medium term. The limits that these methods present have motivated the development of FUTURA software which incorporates Artificial Intelligence techniques (AI) in order to benefit from another forecasting knowledge.

FUTURA consists of four main modules that use different techniques to solve forecasting partial aspects appealing to the available knowledge to do so.

- The first module operates with a *Curve Fitting* algorithm implemented according to recommendations of the Electric Power Research Institute (EPRI) [10].

M.T. Escrig Monferrer and F. Toledo Lobo (Eds.): CCIA 2002, LNAI 2504, pp. 125-138, 2002.
© Springer-Verlag Berlin Heidelberg 2002

- The second module uses the *case-based reasoning* (CBR) methodology to adjust the result obtained by the previous module in the different purchase/sale points of the electric companies for any future day/month/year (date) with a 15-minute resolution.

- The third module is an *expert system* whose knowledge base considers indicators such as PBI (gross domestic product GDP) growing, population, urban growing, inflation, electric rates, investments among the main partners. It is used to adapt the former results to the new socioeconomic context.

- The fourth module is an utility to make reports with respect to the analyzed values from either the future or historically-registered ones such as load factor, demand factor, coincidence factor, peak demand, minimum demand, single-line diagram, etc.

FUTURA allows to administer a great amount of data and generate reports to be used in power flows, planning and optimum expansion programs, and calculation of marginal costs in electric power systems. FUTURA is being used in Peru for the study of the *Valor Agregado de Distribución 2001 (VAD-2001)*- yard stick competition- in order to obtain the electric rates in Peru for the next 4 years.

2   Electric Load Forecasting

The raise of demand is expected in different places where the load already exists. Raises will also be experimented in areas where there is no demand for electric energy, and in less proportion there will also be a decrease of the peak load along the time particularly due to actions that the distributor may take and the procedures in demand side management (DSM). An adequate load forecasting requires the use of all the information available for the user. Fig.1 depicts the main agents that influence the electric load.

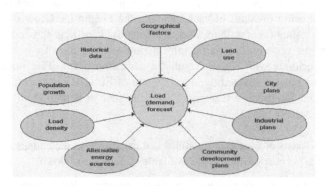

Fig. 1. Factors which affect the forecasting of electric demand

The load forecasting for the electric energy covers short, medium, and long terms for the operation and planning.

For example, in the very short term, which fluctuates from an hour to 24 hours, these models are used for planning the electricity costs and the operation guides of the units. In the short term these models are used for the operation of generating units. In a medium term, which may go from a month to a year, these models are used to make contracts with the important customers as long as the suppliers. And for more-than-a-year-long forecasts they are used for the acquisition of generators.

The present liberation of the electric market makes the load forecasting be especially important since it is the base to negotiate the consumption to be contracted in each point and hence the price to be paid for it.

The importance of this fact relies on not contracting more than what will be consumed and at the same time not contracting an inferior volume. In the first case it is implied that we will pay for electricity which we will not use (but that has been contracted, and therefore it will be produced). Meanwhile in the second case, a high electricity demand implies an important penalty due to the excess of consumption. That is why the importance of a well adjusted and adequate forecast. The forecasting objectives which are being pursued in this work are under this line.

3 Models for the Electric Load Forecasting

Various demand forecasting methods have been proposed. They can be divided into three big categories: parametric, non-parametric, and artificial intelligence based methods.

3.1 Parametric Models

The parametric models formulate mathematics or statistic load model by examining the quantitative relationships between the load and the factors which affect the load. Some of the models used are explicit time functions, polynomial functions, ARMAX [14], Fourier series, and/or multiple lineal regression.

3.2 Non-parametric Methods

The non-parametric models allow a load forecast to be calculated directly from the historic data. For example, by using non-parametric regression [6], it is possible to make load forecasts given by local load averages observed in the past with the size of the next "neighbour" and the specific weights of the loads defined by a multivariable kernel product.

3.3 Artificial Intelligence Based Methods

Various artificial intelligence (AI) technologies such as expert systems, artificial neural networks, fuzzy logic, and genetic algorithms have been applied, at least as prototypes in the electric industry [9], [8], [20]. Among these proposals the ones which stand out are the expert systems [18], [19]. Thus, the load forecasts are obtained based upon logic relationships (typically rules) among the diverse indicators such as GDP, population growth, rates, weather, etc. In the case of the holidays' forecast, the knowledge to be used might be more simplified.

The application of fuzzy systems also allows to treat imprecision in theses contexts, and it is often done paying attention to probabilistic criteria as in [2]. Other widely used techniques are the artificial neural networks [11], [22], [4], [5] and the combination of them with fuzzy systems [2]. In most of neural networks based works, they use not only the registered power measurements (historic load patterns) but other types of data (weather data, social activities, types of loads, etc.) In that area, the perceptron multi-layer has been widely used to forecast demands because of its capacity to approximate non-lineal functions.

The proposal of using deterministic annealing (DA) clustering is also used to classify the input data in clusters [22]. DA is very similar to simulated annealing (SA) since they both start from the analogy of statistics mechanisms. The main difference between both is that SA uses a probabilistic search while DA uses a deterministic technique. The principal disadvantage of the systems based on neural networks is that once the system is trained and by any chance the system changes its topology (reconfiguration of the electric network) the system simply does not respond adequately.

The idea of using methodology belonging to Case-Based Reasoning (CBR), as it is presented in the following sections, is new in this field although it has been proposed for the forecast in other fields (for example [13]).

4   Combination of Knowledge-Based Methods and Numeric Methods for Electric Load Forecasting

The use of individual methodologies, either based on numeric computing (like Curve Fitting) or AI techniques, has given partial results [2], [3], [5] for the electric load forecasting. Thus, the development of a system which combines the advantages of each method involved is proposed. The developed package uses firstly the Curve Fitting (CF) technique to obtain a forecasting polynomial curve based on a criterion of minimum quadratic error. By using such technique a *gross* or softened forecast is obtained. Next this curve is adapted for each predicted day by applying the methodology of case-based reasoning (CBR).

Since the consumption under normal conditions responds to a monotonous growing function, last year data is recovered to adjust to the result obtained through Curve Fitting considering an adaptation of such data according to the values that certain indicators (GDP growth, population, urban growth, inflation, electric rates, etc.) take in the forecasting point.

For the case adaptation an expert system (ES) is proposed to be used. In the following paragraphs these forecast stages are detailed.

4.1 Polynomial Model Curve Fitting (CF)

It is based on the extrapolation of historic loads. A strong computing support is required in order to handle a wide data range. The EPRI [10] recommends the polynomial, L_n, to be a third order one and the historic data base to be used must contain data from up to 6 years -Equation (1)-.

In general the Curve Fitting method is applied with the purpose of extrapolating peak loads because of two main reasons: First, the peak load is the most important value for planning since the peak load is the one which has a higher impact in the system requirements. Second, the electric companies can easily obtain the annual peak load from records.

$$L_n(t) \approx a_n t^3 + b_n t^2 + c_n t + d_n .$$ (1)

In the equation, $L_n(t)$ represents the load for the substation n in the instant t. $C_n = \lfloor a_n, b_n, c_n, d_n \rfloor$ are the coefficients of the polynomial which better approximates the load in such substation n. These coefficients are obtained by minimising the total quadratic error among the polynomial and the available measurements (vector L_n) according to expression (2):

$$C_n = \left[P^T P \right]^{-1} . P^T L_n .$$ (2)

Being P the sampling matrix (rectangular) defined as:

$$P = \begin{bmatrix} 1^3 & 1^2 & 1^1 & 1^0 \\ 2^3 & 2^2 & 2^1 & 2^0 \\ \vdots & \vdots & \vdots & \vdots \\ N^3 & N^2 & N^1 & N^0 \end{bmatrix}_{N \times (3+1)}$$ (3)

With the purpose of reducing the computing cost, FUTURA performs a data preprocessing which takes into account only the highest and lowest values of the measurements in the peak hour (typically it is taken at 19:00 h according to the EPRI recommendations) and they are separated by days of the week [19].

Three forecasting curves are obtained with them for each day of the week (dL, dM, dX, dJ, dV, dS, dD). They are the highest, lowest and medium (the average of two previous ones) value curves.

Let's call $L_{CF}(t)$ the forecast obtained in the instant t from the polynomial C_n.

As it was stated, the interest in the peak hour is based on that the use of the forecast will be the contracting, and if sometime this is inferior to the consumption, the supplying company will punish the customer.

4.2   Case-Based Reasoning Hybrid System

The previous method is obtained from the criteria of a least mean square error. Then the forecast obtained will be valid as demand tendency or gross estimation. With the purpose of refining this forecast case-based reasoning has been used as a methodology which proposes to retrieve real data that responds to a similar description of the current problem to be solved. Fig. 2 represent the 4-R CBR cycle and the main tasks associated (Retrieve, Reuse, Revise, Retain) [1].

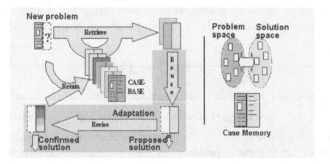

Fig. 2. Cases and CBR cycle: retrieve, reuse, retain and revise. From [17].

In our case the problem definition is determined by the forecasting point, the forecasting instant and the contextual conditions (political, economic, etc.) relative to the forecasting point and instant. The forecasting point (*substation n*) will be the one which will determine the use of one historical data base or another ($L_n(t)=L(t)$). It is not considered substations in the neighbourhood because we have worked only with substations where previous records existed. Load records have been indexed according forecasting time. The forecasting time has defined to differentiate years (*a*), months (*m*) -mEn, mFb, mMr, mAb, mMy, mJn, mJl, mAg, mSp, mOc, mNv, mDc- and the days (*d*) of the week (dL, dM, dX, dJ, dV ,dS, dD, dE). Where dE corresponds to special days as national holidays and special days relative to exceptional situations such as elections, catastrophes, sports events (soccer finals, Olympic Games, etc.) and similar events. For every day hourly periods (h) of 15 minutes are differentiated according to the cadence of the available records.

Thus, we consider the load records *r(t)* as instances which associate time instants *(t)* with load values $L(t)$ in such instants.

$$r(t) = \langle t, L(t) \rangle \quad con \quad t = (a, m, d, h) . \tag{4}$$

Once the forecasting curves are obtained through the Curve Fitting method (L_{CF}), these are adapted according to the following relationship:

$$L_P(t) = L_{CF}(t) \cdot L_{CBR}(t) \; . \tag{5}$$

Where $L_{CBR}(t)$ represents the retrieved and adapted value for each instant to be forecasted.

4.3   Case Retrieval

Up until now the algorithm used for the retrieval is designed to assist medium-term forecasting needs. It can be different if the short term would be considered. This considers the weather and season characteristics in Peru, where the variations in a month are not significant and thus neither are the electricity consumption characteristics. On the contrary the variations which depend on the day of the week and the time are in fact important. From these considerations the daily consumption curves for each month to be forecasted are recovered (15 minutes x 24 hours = 96 points per curve). They are averaged according to the day of the week. That is, the criterion of the *k-Nearest Neighbours* is considered for the retrieve of a whole month (k = nsem., number of weeks of the recovered month), considering as likeness criterion the nearest year (typically the previous one) and the coincidence of the attributes *month (m)* and *day (d)*.

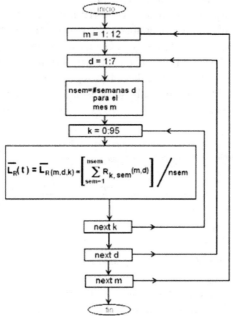

Fig. 3. Case retrieve for a month

In order to soften the possible errors, the recovered values for each day of the week are averaged. The figure 3 shows this average of the cases for each day of the week, where m represents the months, d represents the days, and k is an interval of 15 minutes (measurements every 15 minutes). $L_R(t)$ is the average case recovered and normalised respect to the highest value for each day of the week (dL, ..., dD).

The normalisation assures a coherent modification of the forecast given by CF when applying equation (5). The special days (dE) are put aside and do not intervene in the average. They are managed in separated and individual way.

4.4   Expert System for the Adaptation of Cases

Once the average case, $L_R(t)$, is retrieved for each day of the week (dL, ..., dD) in the month to be forecasted (at resolution intervals of 15 minutes), we proceed to its adaptation according to the socioeconomic context. An adaptation factor, $K(t)$, is obtained from considering of the forecasting point and the available contextual information and used to influence the retrieved cases. Equation (6) represents this action.

$$L_{CBR}(t) = L_R \cdot K(t) .$$ (6)

The adaptation factor $K(t)$ is obtained through an expert system (ES) which evaluates socioeconomic indices in the measurement point regarding to what is considered as a normal situation. This perform a fine tune of the forecasting curve ($L_P(t)$). It is obtained for the month under study from the previous values retrieved and adapted.

The knowledge base of the expert system (ES) developed for this purpose comes from the knowledge of network operators as long as reports of the electric companies and documents of the regulating entity – Gerencia Adjunta de Regulación Tarifaría (GART- OSINERG) del Perú [12], [15], [18], [19]. From this point the expert system was organised as it is represented in the following Ishikawa diagram. The knowledge base considers rules for special loads such as mines, refineries, The Child effect (fenómeno del niño), etc.

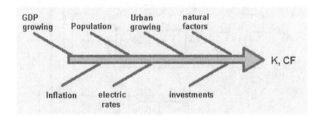

Fig. 4. Ishikawa diagram for the expert system

The $K(t)$ factor under usual situations can introduce variations of up to 20% over the recovered cases. In exceptional cases these variations can reach to 60%. That is the case when considering the effects of the Child Effect -Fenómeno del Niño.

5 Results

Below are shown some FUTURA functionalities. A consultation of historic data is presented for three different days in Fig. 5.

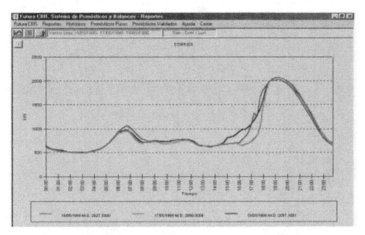

Fig. 5. Historic data for a Saturday, Sunday, and Monday.

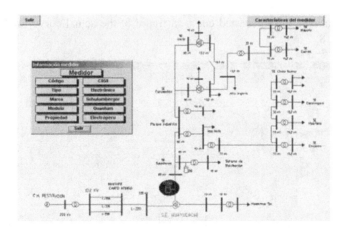

Fig. 6. Single line diagram (purchase point and meter data)

The next graphic (Fig. 7) belongs to a load forecast in which the power engineer wants to know the load diagram for Wednesday 17 of the next year. In order to do this task we will use the available data for two years (1998-1999). It is necessary to mention that the forecast given by FUTURA will be done for the highest demand, average demand, and lowest demand. Under strict rigor the forecast which seems to be interesting is the average value, but for distribution companies the most important fore-

casting values are the highest and the lowest ones since their energy purchase contracts include a range where there is no overcharge for consumption out of place.

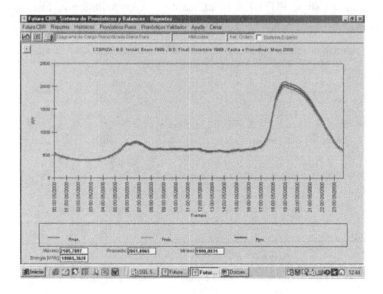

Fig. 7. Load diagram forecasted for May 17 of the next year

In order to validate the forecasted curve in figure 8, the actual curve for May 17 is
shown in Fig. 8.

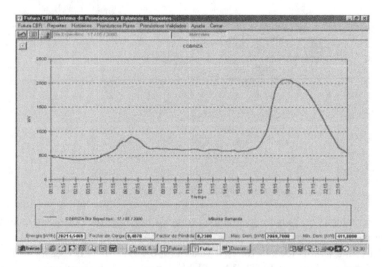

Fig. 8. Real load diagram

To evaluate the medium term load forecast performance of the proposed methodology it is used to forecast two months ahead for one week in October. The load forecast error by days is shown below:

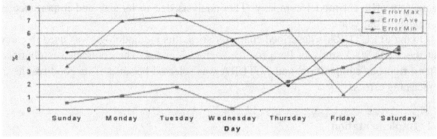

Fig. 9. Error for a week two months ahead

Fig. 10 shows a comparative study of FUTURA in contrast with other models. Met 1: uses CF 2 with real data. Met 2: Uses CF2 with validated data. Met 3: Use CF3 with real data.

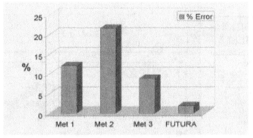

Fig. 10. Comparative study for one week

With FUTURA model we obtained a 1.86% of average error. In [14] reports feeder forecasting errors for SAS package from 2.29% to 4.27% and for evolutionary programming from 1.87% to 2.27%.

In the proposed model we use the term "validated forecasting", it means that abnormal weather and systems conditions, such as thunderstorms or distribution outages are treated as abnormal events with bad real-time readings and are not considered.

It is important to mention that this value tends to decrease once more reliable data is supplied to the expert system and the case to be analysed by the CBR is most similar. The results reported are obtained performing tests with data bases from different points with records from 3 to 10 years of length.

5.1   Result Exploitation

The distribution electric systems are considered nowadays as a monopolistic activity which should be regulated through a legislation able to encourage efficiency and participation of private companies. Under this activity concessions are granted to install networks dedicated to give distribution service in a determined geographic area existing the obligation to do so [7]. In Latin America the methodology called Valor Agregado de Distribución –VAD or *yardstick competition* is mainly used to determine the income got from the distribution activity. In it the distribution company competes against an efficient model company. This analysis due to its size and importance is done every four years.

Owing to FUTURA's described characteristics, this methodology was used to carry out the VAD 2001 study in Peru for the sectors 3 and 4. The contract was obtained after a rigorous competition, and FUTURA was selected because of its good results in forecasting errors.

5.2 Implementation

FUTURA has entirely been programmed in Power Builder (Case base, methods belonging to the 4R of CBR, knowledge base, inference engine and GUI, and so on. The data base was built in SQL.

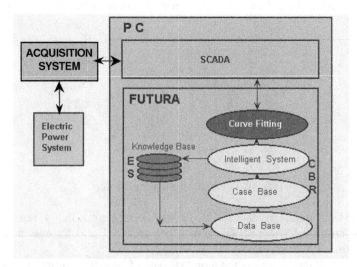

Fig. 11. Implementation shema.

Referring to the implementation of the CBR methodology, under this environment, it has been done from the knowledge analysis to be used according to the *containers* proposed by Richter [21] adapted to supervisory schema proposed in [16] and [17]. The analysis of the sector's own vocabulary and the existing records in the standard data base have led to the definition and case indexation that have been exposed.

The mechanism to retrieve data is done by the temporary neighbour criterion. However, some other alternatives are being studied based on weighted similarity. Finally, the adaptation of these done by the ES, based on the socioeconomic indices in the measurement point is applied by the user using a precompiled expert system built from an intensive collection of socieconomic information and evaluating its influence in the power consumption.

6   Conclusions

The proposed methodology improves substantially the electric load forecasting against methods which work individually. This happens because it benefits from the advantages of each method.

The advantages contributed by the CBR methodology resides in the flexibility of the knowledge representation (this can be redistributed among the four containers – according to the application needs). We can also mention fewer maintenance efforts, reuse of real measurements, continuous learning, time improvement and adaptation to changes in the environment.

The expert system module uses the expert engineers' knowledge in demand growth. The knowledge base can be done as sophisticated as the power systems analyst wants.

FUTURA is in conditions to administer great demand information amounts. It permits to do consultations and to make reports by magnetic or printed means.

7   Future Work

The system described above reuses a substation's records for its future demand forecasting. It is also proposed to widen the use of these records to predict "behaviors" in similar substations which, because of different reasons, do not have enough data records. But there should be defined an adequate method for these new cases to evaluate the similarity between substations (typology and number of customers, load characterization, consumption profiles, habits, season characteristics, etc.)

Acknowledgements. Authors want to thank the grant support received from Agencia Española de Cooperación Internacional AECI/ALE 2002 and the resources used within the project "Supervisión Experta de la Calidad de Servicio", SECSE. DPI2001-2198 funded by MCYT from the Spanish Government and European Union (FEDER funds).

References

1. Aamodt, A., Plaza, E.(1994) Case-Base Reasoning: foundational issues, methodological variations and system approaches. AI Communications. IOS Press, Vol. 7: 1 pp 39-59.
2. Bartkiewicz, W. (2000) Neuro-Fuzzy Approaches to Short-Term Electrical Load Forecasting. Proceedings of the IEEE-INNS-ENNS International Joint Conference on Neural Networks (IJCNN'00).
3. Bartkiewicz, W. Gontar Z. and Zielinski, J. (2000) Uncertainty of the Short-Term Electrical Load Forecasting in Utilities. Proc. of the IEEE-INNS-ENNS -IJCNN'00.
4. Carpentiero, O., Silva A., Feichas C. (2000) A Hierarchical Neural Model in Short-Term Load Forecasting. Proceedings of the IEEE-INNS-ENNS - IJCNN'00.

5. Charytoniuk, W. y Mo-Shing Chen (2000). Very short-term load forecasting using artificial neural networks. IEEE Trans. on Power Systems, Vol. 15 No. 1, 263 – 268.
6. Charytoniuk, W.; Chen, M.S.; Van Olinda, P. (1997) Nonparametric Regression Based Short-Term Load Forecasting. U. of Texas at Arlington. PE-891-PWRS-0-08-1997
7. Comisión de Tarifas de Energía (2001) Estudio de Costos del Valor Agregado de Distribución. Gerencia Adjunta de Regulación tarifaría(ex CTE) – OSINERG. Lima.
8. Dabbaaghchi I, Cristie R., et al. (1997). Al Aplication Areas in Power Systems, IEEE Expert, January February
9. De la Rosa, J.(1999) Sistemes experts a temps real, Publicación de Universitat de Girona, España.
10. Electric Power Research Institute (1979) Research into Load Forecasting and Distribution Planning, EPRI Report EL-1198, EPRI, Palo Alto, CA.
11. Garcia, A et al.(1994) A Neural System for Short-Term Load Forecasting Based on Day-Type Classification, Proc. ISAP94, pp. 353-360.
12. GART-OSINERG. Anuario Estadístico 1996-1997-1998-1999-2000. Gerencia Adjunta de Regulación Tarifaría.- Organismo supervisor de la inversión en energía GART OSINERG. Lima – Perú.
13. Hansen, B. (2000) Analog forecasting of ceiling and visibility using fuzzy sets. Maritimes Weather Centre, Darmouth, Nova Scotia.
14. Hong-Tzer, Y, et al(1996) Identification of ARMAX Model for short term load forecasting: an evolutionary programming approach. IEEE Trans. on Power Systems, Vol. 11, No. 1, 403-408.
15. Lee, H. (1996) Spatial Electric Load Forecasting, Marcel Dekker, Inc.
16. Melendez J. Macaya D., Colomer J., (2001), Case Based Reasoning methodology for process suprvision" CG proceedings of the ECC'01, European Control Conference
17. Melendez J, Colomer J, de la Rosa JL, (2001), "Expert Supervision Based on Cases", Proceedings of the 8th IEEE International Conference on Emerging Technologies and Factory Automation, ETFA'0 1, pp: 431-440.
18. Vilcahuamán, R. et al. (1999) Sistema experto para el pronostico de la demanda. CONIMERA XXV, Lima, Perú.
19. Vilcahuamán, R. Medina, I. y Trelles, A. (2000) PRONOS: Sistema experto para el pronostico de la demanda. Facultad de Ingeniería de Sistemas. Universidad Nacional del Centro del Perú.
20. Third international conference on case-based reasoning (1999) Engineering Applications of Case-Based Reasoning. Special Issue of The International Journal. Engineering Applications of Artificial Intelligence. Volume 12(6) 1999.
21. Richter, M. The Knowledge Contained in Similar Measures. University of Kaiserlautern.
22. Mori, H., y Yuihara, A. (2001) Deterministic Annealing clustering for ANN-based short-term load forecasting. IEEE Trans. on Power Systems, Vol. 16, No. 3, 545-552.

Minimal and Redundant SAT Encodings for the All-Interval-Series Problem

T. Alsinet, R. Béjar, A. Cabiscol, C. Fernàndez, and F. Manyà

Dept. of Computer Science
Universitat de Lleida, Jaume II, 69, E-25001 Lleida, Spain
{tracy,ramon,alba,cesar,felip}@eup.udl.es

Abstract. The SAT encodings defined so far for the all-interval-series (`ais`) problem are very hard for local search but rather easy for systematic algorithms. We define different SAT encodings for the `ais` problem and provide experimental evidence that this problem can be efficiently solved with local search methods if one chooses a suitable SAT encoding.

1 Introduction

In the last years, the AI community has investigated the generic problem solving approach which consists in modeling hard combinatorial problems as instances of the propositional satisfiability problem (SAT) and then solving the resulting encodings with algorithms for SAT. The success in solving SAT-encoded problems depends on both the SAT solver and the SAT encoding used. While there has been a tremendous advance in the design and implementation of SAT solvers, our understanding of SAT encodings is very limited and is yet a challenge for the AI community working on propositional reasoning.

In this paper we define different SAT encodings for the all-interval-series (`ais`) problem and provide experimental evidence that this problem can be efficiently solved with local search if one chooses a suitable SAT encoding. The `ais` problem is presented as a difficult benchmark for local search methods in the libraries CSPlib and SATLIB. [1] Hoos [1], and more recently Schuurmans & Southey [5], showed that the `ais` problem of size 12 causes great difficulties even for the best local search methods for SAT. In a note of the CSPlib, Simonis and Beldiceanu showed that CHIP, using global constraints, can find a single solution without search, but finding all solutions or more irregular solutions is difficult even with the efficient cycle constraint. Our best encoding allows WalkSAT [6] to find solutions (not always the same) of the `ais` problem of size 18 in less than one minute.

This paper is structured as follows. In the next section, we define the `ais` problem. Then, we define a variety of SAT encodings for the `ais` problem. Finally, we present our experimental investigation and some concluding remarks.

---

[1] http://www-users.cs.york.ac.uk/~tw/csplib, http://www.satlib.org

M.T. Escrig Monferrer and F. Toledo Lobo (Eds.): CCIA 2002, LNAI 2504, pp. 139–144, 2002.
© Springer-Verlag Berlin Heidelberg 2002

2   The All-Interval-Series Problem

The ais problem is inspired by a well-known problem occurring in serial musical composition, which can be easily formulated as an instance of a more general arithmetic problem in $\mathbb{Z}_n$, the set of integer residues modulo n: given a positive integer n, find a vector $s = (s_1, \ldots, s_n)$, such that

1. s is a permutation of $\mathbb{Z}_n = \{0, 1, \ldots, n-1\}$; and
2. the interval vector $v = (|s_2 - s_1|, |s_3 - s_2|, \ldots, |s_n - s_{n-1}|)$ is a permutation of $\mathbb{Z}_n - \{0\} = \{1, 2, \ldots, n-1\}$.

A vector v satisfying these conditions is called an ais of size n; and the problem of finding such a series is called the ais problem of size n, and denoted by ais$n$.

3   *SAT* Encodings for the All-Interval-Series Problem

Our minimal *SAT* encoding for the ais$n$ problem is defined as follows:

1. The set of propositional variables is

$$\left\{ s_i^j \mid 1 \le i \le n, j \in \mathbb{Z}_n \right\} \cup \left\{ v_i^j \mid 1 \le i \le n-1, j \in \mathbb{Z}_n - \{0\} \right\}$$

and its cardinality is $n^2 + (n-1)^2$. The intended meaning of variable s_i^j is that element s_i of vector s takes the value j, and the intended meaning of variable v_i^j is that element v_i of vector v takes the value j.
2. *The vector s is a permutation of $\mathbb{Z}_n$.* For each i $(1 \le i \le n)$, we define the clause

$$s_i^0 \vee \cdots \vee s_i^{n-1}; \tag{1}$$

and for each i_1, i_2 $(1 \le i_1 < i_2 \le n)$ and for each $j \in \mathbb{Z}_n$, we define the clause

$$\neg s_{i_1}^j \vee \neg s_{i_2}^j \tag{2}$$

in order to ensure that the set of variables s_i^j encodes a valid permutation of the set $\mathbb{Z}_n$.
3. *The interval vector $v = (v_1, \ldots, v_{n-1})$ is a permutation of $\mathbb{Z}_n - \{0\}$ and is the interval vector associated with the encoded permutation in the variables s_i^j.*
   a) For each i $(1 \le i \le n-1)$, we define the clause

   $$v_i^1 \vee \cdots \vee v_i^{n-1}; \tag{3}$$

   and for each i_1, i_2 $(1 \le i_1 < i_2 \le n-1)$ and for each $j \in \mathbb{Z}_n - \{0\}$, we define the clause

   $$\neg v_{i_1}^j \vee \neg v_{i_2}^j \tag{4}$$

   in order to ensure that the set of variables v_i^j encodes a valid permutation of the set $\mathbb{Z}_n - \{0\}$.

b) For each $x, y \in \mathbb{Z}_n$ $(x \neq y)$ and for each i $(1 \leq i \leq n - 1)$, we define the clause

$$\neg s_i^x \vee \neg s_{i+1}^y \vee v_i^z, \tag{5}$$

where $z = |x - y|$, in order to ensure that the permutation encoded in the variables v_i^j corresponds to the interval vector associated with the permutation encoded in the variables s_i^j.

We define below three different sets of clauses, containing redundant information, which were added to our minimal encoding in order to conduct our experimental investigation.

1. *A set of clauses that ensures that at most one element of $\mathbb{Z}_n$ is assigned to each element s_i of vector s.* For each two different $j_1, j_2 \in \mathbb{Z}_n$ $(j_1 < j_2)$ and for each i $(1 \leq i \leq n)$, we define the clause

$$\neg s_i^{j_1} \vee \neg s_i^{j_2} \tag{6}$$

2. *A set of clauses that ensures that at most one element of $\mathbb{Z}_n - \{0\}$ is assigned to each element v_i of vector v.* For each two different $j_1, j_2 \in \mathbb{Z}_n - \{0\}$ $(j_1 < j_2)$ and for each i $(1 \leq i \leq n - 1)$, we define the clause

$$\neg v_i^{j_1} \vee \neg v_i^{j_2} \tag{7}$$

3. *A set of clauses that ensures that certain values cannot be assigned to elements s_i and s_{i+1} of vector s if element v_i of vector v has assigned a given value k such that $k > \dfrac{|\mathbb{Z}_n|}{2}$.* [2] For each variable of the form v_i^k, where $k > \dfrac{|\mathbb{Z}_n|}{2}$, and for each value m, where $|\mathbb{Z}_n| - k \leq m \leq k - 1$, we define the clauses

$$(\neg v_i^k \vee \neg s_{i-1}^m) \wedge (\neg v_i^k \vee \neg s_i^m) \tag{8}$$

The set of clauses (6) (resp. (7)) together with the set of clauses (1) (resp. (3)) ensures that exactly one value of $\mathbb{Z}_n$ (resp. $\mathbb{Z}_n - \{0\}$) occurs in each element of vector s (resp. v). Nevertheless, it is straightforward to see that (6) and (7) add redundant information when one encodes the concept of permutation.

The set of clauses (8) also contains redundant information because, in our minimal encoding, we encode the values that *can* take elements s_i and s_{i+1} of vector s if element v_i of vector v takes a given value k. The additional clauses add the values that *cannot* be assigned to s_i and s_{i+1} if $v_i = k$. For instance, if $\mathbb{Z}_n = \{0, 1, \dots, 9\}$ and $v_3 = 8$, then s_3 and s_4 cannot be $2, 3, 4, 5, 6$ and 7 because $|s_4 - s_3| \neq 8$ if s_3 or s_4 are $2, 3, 4, 5, 6$ or 7.

In the following we refer to the encodings for $\texttt{ais}n$ by $\texttt{ais-x}_6\texttt{x}_7\texttt{x}_8\texttt{-}n$, where $\texttt{x}_i$ is $\texttt{r}$ if the set of redundant clauses (i) is added to our minimal SAT encoding; otherwise, x_i is $\texttt{m}$ (minimal). Thus, $\texttt{ais-mmm-8}$ denotes the minimal encoding for $\texttt{ais8}$, and $\texttt{ais-rrw-8}$ denotes the encoding that adds to $\texttt{ais-mmm-8}$ the clauses of (6) and (7).

[2] We assume that the cardinality of $\mathbb{Z}_n(|\mathbb{Z}_n|)$ is even. In our experiments we always consider $\texttt{ais}$ problems of even size.

4   Experimental Results

We conducted an experimental investigation for knowing the computational behavior of the different encodings when solved with *WalkSAT* [6,4]. We considered 6 encodings: ais-mmm-n, ais-rmm-n, ais-mmr-n, ais-rmr-n, ais-rrm-n
and ais-rrr-n; and n ranged from 8 to 18. We do not report on experimental
results for encodings ais-mrm-n and ais-mrr-n because their performance with
WalkSAT is very poor.

The ais instances of the SATLIB use encoding ais-rrm-n, but the sets of
clauses (2) and (4) appear twice. Actually, for each clause of (2) of the form
$\neg s_{i_1}^j \vee \neg s_{i_2}^j$, there is also the redundant clause $\neg s_{i_2}^j \vee \neg s_{i_1}^j$. The same happens
for the clauses of (4). As we observed that encoding ais-rrm-n outperforms the
SATLIB encoding, we did not considered SATLIB instances.

Table 1 and Table 2 contain the experimental results obtained when the instances were solved with *WalkSAT* using heuristics *Best* [6] and *R-Novelty* [4].[3]
Both tables show the mean time needed to solve each instance, the noise parameter setting (ω) employed, and the mean number of flips needed to solve
each instance. Each instance was executed 1000 times (100 times for size 16 and
18) using approximately optimal noise parameters and an extremely high cutoff
value for obtaining a solution in every try. Such results were obtained on a 250
MHz Sun UltraSparc with 512 MB of memory.

Our experimental results provide experimental evidence that adding the set
of redundant clauses (8) to encodings ais-mmm-n and ais-rmm-n is a decisive
factor for obtaining good performance, while no redundancy (ais-mmm-n), full
redundancy (ais-rrr-n), and particularly redundancy of set (7) give rise to very
poor performance.

As a conclusion we can say that the ais problem is not a difficult problem
for local search methods for SAT if one chooses a suitable SAT encoding. We
solved the ais problem of size 18 in less than one minute obtaining one solution in
every try. The challenge continues being to understand why some encodings have
a good computational performance for local search methods while others cause
great difficulties. We were not able to solve that challenge, but our encodings,
as well as the encodings defined in [2] for the quasigroup completion problem,
provide a well-suited test-bed for improving our understanding of SAT encodings.

Although in this paper we focus on local search, it is worth mentioning that
we also observed dramatic differences in the time needed to solve an instance
when our SAT encodings were solved with the systematic algorithm *Satz* [3]. For
instance, while encoding ais-mmm-14 cannot be solved after 12 hours, encoding
ais-mrm-14 is solved in less than 2 seconds. Finally, it is interesting to notice that
a good performing encoding for local search is not necessarily a good performing
encoding for systematic search.

---

[3] In Table 2, experimental results for encoding ais-rrm-n are not reported because
its performance with *R-Novelty* is very poor.

Table 1. Experimental results for *WalkSAT* with *Best*

instances	time	ω	flips	instances	time	ω	flips
ais-mmm-8	0.07 sec	16	16489	ais-mmm-14	15.07 sec	5	2038926
ais-rmm-8	0.08 sec	18	16600	ais-rmm-14	17.30 sec	5	1988276
ais-mmr-8	0.04 sec	18	8807	ais-mmr-14	3.23 sec	5	419190
ais-rmr-8	0.04 sec	19	8275	ais-rmr-14	3.89 sec	5	409446
ais-rrm-8	0.13 sec	38	23933	ais-rrm-14	72.43 sec	9	7109993
ais-rrr-8	0.06 sec	26	11073	ais-rrr-14	14.43 sec	10	1317726
ais-mmm-10	0.36 sec	9	70052	ais-mmm-16	96.64 sec	4	12217374
ais-rmm-10	0.43 sec	12	68315	ais-rmm-16	138.76 sec	4	13475144
ais-mmr-10	0.16 sec	12	29626	ais-mmr-16	15.48 sec	4	1696485
ais-rmr-10	0.19 sec	15	28143	ais-rmr-16	19.54 sec	3	1711560
ais-rrm-10	0.92 sec	19	126852	ais-rrm-16	731.18 sec	4	62256356
ais-rrr-10	0.36 sec	20	47168	ais-rrr-16	106.62 sec	6	7858553
ais-mmm-12	2.73 sec	7	432741	ais-mmm-18	554.53 sec	2	60961874
ais-rmm-12	3.13 sec	6	419505	ais-rmm-18	747.81 sec	2	60852334
ais-mmr-12	0.91 sec	9	128405	ais-mmr-18	50.70 sec	2	5052630
ais-rmr-12	1.02 sec	7	125758	ais-rmr-18	72.02 sec	2	5442343
ais-rrm-12	10.49 sec	9	1216994	ais-rrm-18	5481.60 sec	3	305046936
ais-rrr-12	2.18 sec	14	241433	ais-rrr-18	501.73 sec	4	34244876

Table 2. Experimental results for *WalkSAT* with *R-Novelty*

instances	time	ω	flips	instances	time	ω	flips
ais-mmm-8	0.02 sec	23	4608	ais-mmm-14	5.44 sec	10	697538
ais-rmm-8	0.02 sec	25	4671	ais-rmm-14	6.31 sec	9	662785
ais-mmr-8	0.01 sec	27	2402	ais-mmr-14	1.55 sec	12	184273
ais-rmr-8	0.01 sec	26	2635	ais-rmr-14	2.01 sec	12	196450
ais-rrr-8	0.05 sec	37	7870	ais-rrr-14	35.36 sec	13	3027817
ais-mmm-10	0.12 sec	17	22283	ais-mmm-16	42.54 sec	7	4755468
ais-rmm-10	0.16 sec	19	24039	ais-rmm-16	49.56 sec	8	4579118
ais-mmr-10	0.05 sec	20	9267	ais-mmr-16	8.21 sec	10	867117
ais-rmr-10	0.06 sec	22	9402	ais-rmr-16	9.88 sec	10	838852
ais-rrr-10	0.47 sec	32	53447	ais-rrr-16	337.40 sec	10	24254964
ais-mmm-12	1.00 sec	13	146779	ais-mmm-18	254.01 sec	7	24838322
ais-rmm-12	1.12 sec	10	141380	ais-rmm-18	277.58 sec	7	21883436
ais-mmr-12	0.37 sec	15	48137	ais-mmr-18	29.218 sec	8	2683459
ais-rmr-12	0.37 sec	15	43581	ais-rmr-18	40.99 sec	7	2967321
ais-rrr-12	5.04 sec	24	480813	ais-rrr-18	2077.63 sec	9	118819048

References

1. H. H. Hoos. *Stochastic Local Search – Methods, Models, Applications*. PhD thesis, Department of Computer Science, Darmstadt University of Technology, 1998.
2. H. Kautz, Y. Ruan, D. Achlioptas, C. Gomes, B. Selman, and M. Stickel. Balance and filtering in structured satisfiable problems. In *Proceedings of the International Joint Conference on Artificial Intelligence, IJCAI'01, Seattle/WA, USA*, 351–358. Morgan Kaufmann, 2001
3. C. M. Li, and Anbulagan. Heuristics based on unit propagation for satisfiability problems. In *Proceedings of the International Joint Conference on Artificial Intelligence, IJCAI'97, Nagoya, Japan*, 366–371. Morgan Kaufmann, 1997.
4. D. McAllester, B. Selman, and H. Kautz. Evidence for invariants in local search. In *Proceedings of the 14th National Conference on Artificial Intelligence, AAAI'97, Providence/RI, USA*, pages 321–326. AAAI Press, 1997.
5. D. Schuurmans and F. Southey. Local search characteristics of incomplete SAT procedures. In *Proceedings of the 17th National Conference on Artificial Intelligence, AAAI-2000, Austin/TX, USA*, pages 297–302. AAAI Press, 2000.
6. B. Selman, H. A. Kautz, and B. Cohen. Noise strategies for improving local search. In *Proceedings of the 12th National Conference on Artificial Intelligence, AAAI'94, Seattle/WA, USA*, pages 337–343. AAAI Press, 1994.

PN to CSP Methodology: Improved Bounds

Daniel Riera[1], Miquel A. Piera[1], and Antoni Guasch[2]

[1] Enginyeria de Sistemes i Automàtica,
Universitat Autònoma de Barcelona, Bellaterra, Spain
{Daniel.Riera,MiguelAngel.Piera}@uab.es
[2] Instituto de Robótica e Informática Industrial,
UPC/CSIC, Barcelona, Spain
Guasch@esaii.upc.es

Abstract. Traditional production planning techniques are constrained by large numbers of decision variables, uncertainty in demand and time production, and non-deterministic system behaviour (intrinsic characteristics in manufacturing). This paper presents an improvement to a methodology in the area of Knowledge Based Systems (KBS) which generates automatically Constraint Satisfaction Problems (CSP), using Petri-nets (PN) to model the problem and Constraint Programming (CP) in the solution.

The methodology combines the modelling power of PN to represent both manufacturing architecture and production logistics, together with the optimisation performance given by CP. While PN can represent a whole production system, CP is effective in solving large problems, especially in the area of planning. The improvement raises from the design of a more complete algorithm to calculate the transitions firings bounds, and hence to remove useless problem variables.

1 Introduction

In the last few years, many methods and tools have been developed to improve production performance in the manufacturing industry. These approaches try to tackle changes in production objectives such as *high production diversity* (instead of *high production volume*), *make to order* (instead of *make to stock*), and *zero stock* (instead of *just in time*) policies.

Scheduling problems arise when multiple types of job types are processed by multiple kinds of shared resources according to technological precedence constraints. Production scheduling problems have been proved to be NP-hard [1]. Artificial Intelligence (AI) approaches to tackle these problems can be classified as:

- Heuristic dispatching rules: Widely used in practice, and based mainly on experience. Their disadvantage lies in the difficulty of finding more comprehensive models. Furthermore, optimal results cannot be guaranteed.
- Computational intelligence based approaches (ie. genetic algorithms, neural networks, etc.): widely used to improve bounded production subsystems.

M.T. Escrig Monferrer and F. Toledo Lobo (Eds.): CCIA 2002, LNAI 2504, pp. 145–158, 2002.
© Springer-Verlag Berlin Heidelberg 2002

However formulation difficulties appear when they are used to tackle the whole production system — performance depending on several logistic aspects (difficult to describe).
- KBS: Powerful approach. However, the production system performance is highly coupled (sensitive) in relation to the acquired knowledge.

Petri-nets have shown to be successful tools for modelling Flexible Manufacturing Systems (FMS) due to several advantages such as the conciseness of embodying both the static structure and the dynamics, the availability of the mathematical analysis techniques, and its graphical nature [5,8,3]. Furthermore, PN are very suitable to model and visualize patterns of behaviour comprising concurrency, synchronization and resources sharing, which are the main characteristics of a FMS.

CP has been mainly chosen because of its good optimisation performance. Since CP is usually embedded in declarative programming, the user need not write an algorithm to solve the problem but need only model the problem to be solved. Therefore, once the model is generated, CP can optimise it without requiring an expert to rule it.

This paper improves the methodology presented in [6] where the main aspects of a PN analysis methodology to deal automatically with all the constraints of a production system are presented. This methodology automatises the constraints modelling phase of a production system — described previously in PN formalism — in order to generate an optimal scheduling for a particular system state and production goal, making the optimisation phase hidden from the user (See Fig. 1). The addition of a new stage in the transitions firing bounding algorithm makes the search faster due to the removal of unfeasible solutions.

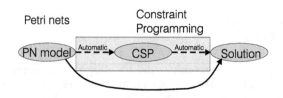

Fig. 1. Presented methodology

Although CP offers a powerful technology to deal with the best planning policy for a production system, it requires a deep knowledge in both the production system and the CP technology, and time to develop the CP model. Thus, the present work tries to combine the main advantages of both methodologies in order to offer good scheduling policies, minimizing the time spent in the modelling and optimization tasks.

Apart from the improved algorithm, the foundations for the analysis on a PN model and the generation of the CP model are presented. The analysis is made by detecting structures in the PN, which are translated directly into the CSP constraints.

In sections 2 and 3 PN and CP backgrounds are presented. Section 4 introduces the methodology, including the proposed algorithm. Section 5 illustrates the methodology by means of an example. Finally, Sections 6 and 7 discuss the benefits, and present the conclusions and future work.

2   Petri-Nets Background

A *Petri-net* (PN) is a particular kind of directed graph, together with an initial state called the *initial marking*. An ordinary PN is a 5-tupla $N = (P, T, I, O, M_0)$:

- $P = \{p_1, \ldots, p_n\}$ is the set of places, represented graphically by circles.
- $T = \{t_1, \ldots, t_m\}$ is the set of transitions, represented graphically by bold lines or rectangles.
- $I : (P \times T) \to \mathbb{N}$ is a function that defines the weight of directed arcs from places to transitions.
- $O : (T \times P) \to \mathbb{N}$ is a function that defines the weight of directed arcs from transitions to places.
- M_0 is the initial marking.

A *marking* is an array that assigns to each place a non-negative integer. If a marking assigns to place p a value k $(k \in \mathbb{Z}^+)$, p is marked with k tokens, represented graphically by black dots.

A transition t_i is said to be enabled by a marking M, if $\forall p \in P : M(p) \geq I(p, t_i)$. The firing transition generates a new marking M' which can be computed by withdrawing $I(p_k, t_i)$ tokens from each p_k input place of t_i, and by adding $O(p_j, t_i)$ tokens to each p_j output place of t_i.

In manufacturing terms, *transitions* are used to model operations (firing a transition can represent a task or process initiation or an ending of a task), *places* are used to model buffers and resources status, connecting *arcs* specify logical relationships and resource constraints among operations, and *tokens* represent material and resources conditions.

Although several PN classes have been defined in the literature, the current methodology only works with deterministic timed PN [7].

3   Constraint Programming Background

Constraints arise in most areas of human endeavour. A constraint is simply a logical relation among several unknowns (or variables), each taking a value in a given domain. The constraint thus restricts the possible values that variables can take. CP is the study of computational systems based on constraints. The main idea is to solve problems by stating constraints (requirements) about the problem area and, consequently, finding a solution satisfying all the constraints.

The earliest ideas leading to CP may be found in the AI with the *scene labelling* problem [10] and the *interactive graphics* [9].

Gallaire [2] and Jaffar and Lassez [4] noted that logic programming was just a particular kind of CP. The basic idea behind Logic Programming (LP), and declarative programming in general, is that the user states *what* has to be solved instead of *how* to solve it, which is very close to the idea of constraints.

Recent advances promise that CP and Operations Research (OR), can exploit each other, in particular, the CP can serve as a roof platform for integrating various constraint solving algorithms including those developed and checked to be successful in OR.

Then, CP combines ideas from a number of fields including Artificial Intelligence, Combinatorial Algorithms, Computational Logic, Discrete Mathematics, Neural Networks, Operations Research, Programming Languages and Symbolic Computation.

The problems solved using CP are called Constraint Satisfaction Problems. A CSP is defined as:

- a set of variables,

$$X = \{x_1, \ldots, x_s\},$$

- for each variable x_i, a finite set D_i of possible values (its *domain*), and
- a set of *constraints* restricting the values that the variables can simultaneously take.

4   Petri-Net to CP Models

4.1   CSP Components Identification

In order to analyse the PN model and generate the CSP problem, the first step is to identify the elements composing the CSP. These elements are:

- Variables
  There is a variable for each firing of a PN transition. Hence, every transition is associated to a list of times. The length of this list is given by the number of times the transition is fired (or a higher bound if unknown). These are called *transition variables*.
  The second set of variables are those representing the number of firings of the transitions. These variables are called *firing variables*.
  Apart of these, there are also *Boolean variables* which indicate the paths followed by tokens in bifurcations.
- Domains
  The domains on the *transition variables* are defined using the knowledge about the problem. Usually the fact of reducing the domains on the variables makes the search faster. *Firing variables* depend on the bounds found by the *Transitions Firings Bounding* algorithms (See Alg.1 and 2).
- Constraints
  They are generated in the PN structures detection phase (See Section 4.3) and restrict the paths which can be followed by every token and the times when transitions can be fired.

4.2   Calculation of the Bounds of the Transitions Firings

Different kinds of preprocessing can be made in a CSP. Domains preprocessing is used typically to help the search to avoid impossible, worthless or redundant solutions. An example can be seen in Section 4.3: symmetries removal.

Apart from the domains preprocessing, in this methodology, the number of variables used for the time firings is not constant. It is not possible to know the number of firings of a transition previously — this is another variable in the problem — but a higher bound can be found (Λ). The tighter the bound, the fewer the number of generated branches of the tree search.

In the presentation of the methodology, an algorithm based in the initial marking of the PN was presented. This paper presents a two-phases algorithm — by the addition of a new part based on the final marking — which improves the bounds calculations.

Hence, the 2-phases algorithm dependent on the PN and the initial (M_0) and final (M_f) markings of the problem is proposed:

Algorithm 1 *Transitions Firings Bounding I*

Step 1: Initialisation *of Λ_0' by applying rules $T{\to}' P$ and $P{\to}' T$ (See below) for each place — using the initial marking (M_0) — and transition respectively. First $T{\to}' P$ is applied to every place in the PN and later $P{\to}' T$ calculates the initial λ'–values for every transition.*

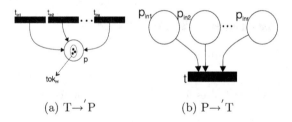

(a) $T{\to}' P$ (b) $P{\to}' T$

Fig. 2. General cases for place and transition feeding from M_0

$T{\to}' \mathbf{P}$ *is used to calculate the maximum number of tokens each place $p \in P$ can contain during all the system run. This is calculated applying to the general case shown in Fig.2(a) the formula presented in Eq.1.*

$$tok'(p) = tok_{\text{ini}}(p) + \sum_{i=1}^{m} \lambda_i' \cdot O_{t_i,p}, \qquad (1)$$

where $tok_{\text{ini}}(p)$ is the number of tokens of place p in the initial marking (M_0).

P→'T *initialises the number of times each transition $t \in T$ might be fired during the total execution of the system. The number or expression (if there are unknown values) is given by the application of the formula in Eq.2 to the general case shown in Fig.2(b).*

$$\lambda'(t) = \min_{i=1,\ldots,n} \left\lfloor \frac{tok'(p_i)}{I_{p_i,t}} \right\rfloor \mid I_{p_i,t} \neq 0. \tag{2}$$

Step 2: Propagation *of the λ'–values in Λ'_i from its values in Λ'_{i-1}. In this step both numbers and expressions are propagated.*

Step 3: Resolution *of the expressions in Λ'_i. If an expression representing λ'_j contains itself (λ'_j), it is not considered, and is substituted by infinity (∞). After this simplification, min functions are applied, if possible.*

Step 4: *if $\exists \lambda'_j \in \Lambda'_i \mid \lambda'_j \notin \mathbb{Z}^+$ then go to Step 2 else End.*

Algorithm 2 *Transitions Firings Bounding II*

Step 1: Initialisation *of Λ_0 (in a similar way than in Alg.1) by applying rules P→T and T→P (See below). In this phase, the results found by the previous algorithm (e.g. Λ') are used.*

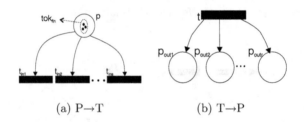

(a) P→T   (b) T→P

Fig. 3. General cases for place and transition feeding from M_f

P→T *is equivalent to T→'P but applying to the general case shown in Fig.3(a) the formula presented in Eq.3.*

$$tok(p) = tok_{\text{fin}}(p) + \sum_{i=1}^{m} \lambda_i \cdot I_{p,t_i}, \tag{3}$$

where $tok_{\text{fin}}(p)$ is the number of tokens of place p in the final marking (M_f).

T→P *is equivalent to P→'T but applying the formula in Eq.4 to the general case shown in Fig.3(b).*

$$\lambda(t) = \min \left(\lambda'(t), \min_{i=1,\ldots,n} \left\lfloor \frac{tok(p_i)}{O_{t,p_i}} \right\rfloor \right) \mid O_{t,p_i} \neq 0. \tag{4}$$

Step 2: Propagation *of the λ–values in Λ_i from its values in Λ_{i-1}. In this step both numbers and expressions are propagated.*

Step 3: Resolution *of the expressions in Λ_i. If a expression representing λ_j contains itself (λ_j), it is not considered, and is substituted by infinity (∞). After this simplification, min functions are applied, if possible.*

Step 4: *if $\exists \lambda_j \in \Lambda_i \mid \lambda_j \notin \mathbb{Z}^+$ then go to* **Step 2** *else* **End**.

4.3   Petri-Net Structures Detection

In this step, the PN structures are extracted in order to generate the constraints and reduce the search space. Each structure corresponds to a set of constraints which are automatically generated:

Structure T (*Transition*). T constraints (See Eq.5) are generated for every single transition in the PN. This is not a structure but a way of removing symmetries from the problem. Since there is a variable for each firing of a transition, by using T constraints, the values of these variables (and hence the firings) are given a unique order.

$$t_{i_j} \geq t_{i_{j-1}} \forall j = 2, \ldots, l, \ \ \mathtt{length}(T_i) = l. \tag{5}$$

Structure S (*Sequence*). This structure includes two consecutive transitions (with a direct path between them). Each firing time of the exit transition is related with one of the source transition (See Eq.6).

$$t_{i_j} \geq t_{k_j} + \mathtt{time}_k \forall j = 1, \ldots, l, \ \ \mathtt{length}(t_i) = \mathtt{length}(t_k) = l, \tag{6}$$

where $\mathtt{time}_k$ is the processing time associated to transition k.

These constraints are not generated if both transitions (forming S) belong to a more complex structure (i.e. B, M or MB).

Structure IS (*Initial Stock*). This represents an initial stock (i.e. an isolated place feeding two or more transitions). IS structure does not add temporal constraints but constraints related with the number of firings of the exit transitions (See Eq.7).

$$\sum \lambda'_i \leq tok_{\mathrm{ini}}(p_{\mathrm{in}}) \forall i \mid \mathtt{feeds}(p_{\mathrm{in}}, t_i), \tag{7}$$

where p_{in} is the place representing the initial stock.

Structure B (*Branch*). This structure is formed by a single transition, which feeds a set of transitions through a single place (See Fig.4). A list of *Boolean variables* are used to select the path followed by each token in the structure. These variables enable or disable constraints depending on their correspondence to the selected path (See Eq.8).

$$t_{\text{out}_i} \geq (t_{\text{in}_j} + \text{time}_{\text{in}}) \cdot B_{\text{out}_j} - B_{\text{diff}} \cdot M$$
$$\forall j = 1, \ldots, n, \ \ \text{length}(T_{\text{in}}) = n,$$
$$\forall i = 1, \ldots, m, \ \ \text{length}(T_{\text{out}}) = m, \tag{8}$$
$$B_{\text{diff}} = \text{diff}(i, \sum_{k=1}^{j} B_{\text{out}_k}),$$

where function diff returns zero (0) if the parameters are equal and one (1) if they are different, and M is an integer that dominates the expression (a 'big-M' term).

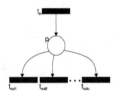

Fig. 4. Structure B

Structure M (*Meet*). This is complementary to structure B. A set of transitions feed a single transition through a unique place (See Fig.5). *Boolean variables* are also necessary in this case (See Eq.9).

$$t_{\text{out}_i} \geq (t_{\text{in}_j} + \text{time}_{\text{in}}) \cdot B_{\text{in}_i} - B_{\text{diff}} \cdot M$$
$$\forall j = 1, \ldots, n, \ \ \text{length}(T_{\text{in}}) = n,$$
$$\forall i = 1, \ldots, m, \ \ \text{length}(T_{\text{out}}) = m, \tag{9}$$
$$B_{\text{diff}} = \text{diff}(j, \sum_{k=1}^{i} B_{\text{in}_k}).$$

Structure MB (*Meet-Branch*). This is the most complex structure, where a list of input transitions feeds an output list of transitions (See Fig.6). This structure also requires the use of *Boolean variables* (See Eq.10).

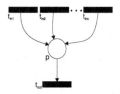

Fig. 5. Structure M

$$T_{\text{out}_i} \geq (T_{\text{in}_j} + \texttt{time}_{\text{in}}) \cdot B_{\text{in},\text{out}_j} - B_{\text{diff}} \cdot M$$
$$\forall j = 1, \ldots, n, \quad \texttt{length}(T_{\text{in}}) = n,$$
$$\forall i = 1, \ldots, m, \quad \texttt{length}(T_{\text{out}}) = m, \qquad (10)$$
$$B_{\text{diff}} = \texttt{diff}(i, \sum_{in} \sum_{k=1}^{j} B_{\text{in}_k}).$$

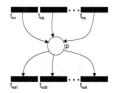

Fig. 6. Structure MB

4.4   CSP Labelling Definition

Since the aim of this methodology is to find the optimum, not only a solution has to be found but optimality must be proved. Although a possibility is to generate the complete solutions tree, this would mean a high computational cost.

On the other hand optimality can be proved by labelling the variable to optimise first, and selecting its values from better to worse solutions. This means that, in the moment a solution is found, all the possible better solutions have been already rejected. Optimality is proved and further search is not necessary.

Transition and *Boolean variables* are labelled only once for each instance of the variable to optimise (any of their feasible values gives an optimal solution). Paths are selected by labelling *Boolean variables* first. *Transition variables* are labelled later.

5   Example

Process and Assemble Factory. The system is composed by two machines which perform the next operations: M1 makes two different operations depending on the type of piece it is working with. This is a shared resource. Hence it is necessary to plan the order the pieces are put into it. On the other hand, M2 is used to assemble two processed pieces (A and B). The system can be seen in Fig. 7.

The aim is, given 10 pieces of type A and 5 pieces of type B, to perform 5 pieces (processed and assembled).

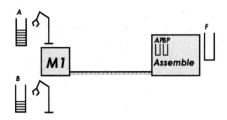

Fig. 7. The studied system

5.1   Petri-Net of the System

The PN of the studied system (See Fig.8) has the next components:

Places:
        p1: Stock of pieces A.
        p2: Stock of pieces B.
        p3: Piece A being processed in M1.
        p4: Piece B being processed in M1.
        p5: M1 free.
        p6: Stock of pieces A processed.
        p7: Stock of pieces B processed.
        p8: M2 free.
        p9: M2 assembling a final piece.
        p10: Stock of assembled pieces.
Transitions:
        t1: Move piece A to M1 (1 hour).
        t2: Move piece B to M1 (1 hour).
        t3: Retire piece A from M1 (2 hours).
        t4: Retire piece B from M1 (4 hours).
        t5: Move processed pieces A and B to M2 (1 hour).
        t6: Retire final piece from M2 (3 hours).
Initial and final markings:
        $M_0 = [10, 5, 0, 0, 1, 0, 0, 1, 0, 0]$
        $M_f = [-, -, -, -, -, -, -, -, -, 5]$

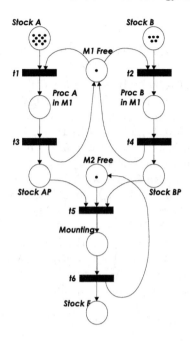

Fig. 8. The Petri-net of the system

5.2   Transitions Firings Bounding

In order to calculate the higher bounds of the transitions firings, Algorithms presented in Section 4.2 are applied to M_0 and M_f respectively:

$$\Lambda_0' = [\min(10, 1 + \lambda_3' + \lambda_4'), \min(5, 1 + \lambda_3' + \lambda_4'),$$
$$\lambda_1', \lambda_2', \min(\lambda_3', \lambda_4', 1 + \lambda_6'), \lambda_5']$$
$$\Lambda_1' = [\min(10, 1 + \lambda_1' + \lambda_2'), \min(5, 1 + \lambda_1' + \lambda_2'),$$
$$\min(10, 1 + \lambda_3' + \lambda_4'), \min(5, 1 + \lambda_3' + \lambda_4'),$$
$$\min(\lambda_1', \lambda_2', 1 + \lambda_5'),$$
$$\min(\lambda_3', \lambda_4', 1 + \lambda_6')] =$$
$$= [\min(10, \infty), \min(5, \infty), \min(10, \infty),$$
$$\min(5, \infty), \min(\lambda_1', \lambda_2', \infty),$$
$$\min(\lambda_3', \lambda_4', \infty)] =$$
$$= [10, 5, 10, 5, \min(\lambda_1', \lambda_2'), \min(\lambda_3', \lambda_4')]$$
$$\Lambda_2' = [10, 5, 10, 5, \min(10, 5), \min(10, 5)] =$$
$$= [10, 5, 10, 5, 5, 5] = \Lambda'$$

$$\Lambda_0 = [\min(\lambda_1', \lambda_3), \min(\lambda_2', \lambda_4),$$
$$\min(\lambda_3', \min(\lambda_1 + \lambda_2, \lambda_5)),$$
$$\min(\lambda_4', \min(\lambda_1 + \lambda_2, \lambda_5)),$$
$$\min(\lambda_5', \lambda_6), \min(\lambda_6', \min(\lambda_6, 5))] =$$
$$= [\min(10, \lambda_3), \min(5, \lambda_4), \min(10, \lambda_1 + \lambda_2, \lambda_5),$$
$$\min(5, \lambda_1 + \lambda_2, \lambda_5), \min(5, \lambda_6), \min(5, \lambda_6)] =$$
$$= [\min(10, \lambda_3), \min(5, \lambda_4), \min(10, \lambda_1 + \lambda_2, \lambda_5),$$
$$\min(5, \lambda_1 + \lambda_2, \lambda_5), \min(5, \lambda_6), 5]$$
$$\Lambda_1 = [\min(10, \min(10, \lambda_1 + \lambda_2, \lambda_5)),$$
$$\min(5, \min(5, \lambda_1 + \lambda_2, \lambda_5)),$$
$$\min(10, \min(10, \lambda_3) + \min(5, \lambda_4), \min(5, \lambda_6)),$$
$$\min(5, \min(10, \lambda_3) + \min(5, \lambda_4), \min(5, \lambda_6)),$$
$$\min(5, 5), 5]$$
$$= [\min(10, \infty + \lambda_2, \lambda_5), \min(5, \lambda_1 + \infty, \lambda_5),$$
$$\min(\min(10, \infty) + \min(5, \lambda_4), 5, \lambda_6),$$
$$\min(5, \min(10, \lambda_3) + \min(5, \infty), \lambda_6), 5, 5] =$$
$$= [\min(10, \lambda_5), \min(5, \lambda_5), \min(5, \lambda_6),$$
$$\min(5, \lambda_6), 5, 5]$$
$$\Lambda_2 = [\min(10, 5), \min(5, 5), \min(5, 5),$$
$$\min(5, 5), 5, 5] =$$
$$= [5, 5, 5, 5, 5, 5] = \Lambda$$

5.3   Structures Found

The structures found and automatically translated into constraints are as follows:

T: t1, t2, t3, t4, t5 and t6
S: p3, p4, p6, p7, p8 and p9
IS: p1, p2
B: $\emptyset$
M: $\emptyset$
MB: p5

5.4   Results

The firing times found after the optimisation phase are the next:

```
Firings(t1)=[20, 23, 26, 29, 37]
Firings(t2)=[0, 5, 10, 15, 32]
Firings(t3)=[21, 24, 27, 30, 38]
Firings(t4)=[1, 6, 11, 16, 33]
Firings(t5)=[23, 27, 31, 35, 40]
Firings(t6)=[24, 28, 32, 36, 41]
```

Then, the optimal time for the performance of 5 pieces (processed and assembled) is 44 hours ($t_{6_5} + \text{time}_6$).

6   Benefits of the Purposed Methodology

The proposed approach improves several aspects of actual scheduling tools, some of which are:

- The specification of the logistics of complex production systems using the PN formalism together with the presented analysis tool is a useful procedure to improve the overall system performance.
- The use of the CP technology to avoid local optimisation in front of global optimisation gives better solutions.
- The possible validation of the scheduling policy by means of a PN simulator. Note that the CP model does not consider the stochastic aspects of manufacturing systems.

7   Conclusions and Future Work

This methodology has proved to work for academic examples, making the improved algorithm the tree generation faster. Although only structural constraints extracted from the PN are used, new constraints are being studied. These may raise from relations like symmetries, t-invariants, etc. and also constraints which can be added by experts on the studied system. The addition of these constraints makes the search faster. Likewise, more complex PN models are going to be considered [11].

Another work line is the hierarchial structuring of the search in order to perform the optimisation in different steps: splitting the system in more general structures first and, specializing later.

Acknowledgements. The authors wish to acknowledge the financial support received from the CICYT Spanish program DPI2001-2051-C02.

References

1. French, S.: Sequencing and Scheduling: An Introduction to the Mathematics of the Job-Shop. Willey, New York (1982)
2. Gallaire, H.: Logic Programming: Further developments. IEEE Symposium on Logic Programming. Boston (1985)
3. Guasch, A., Piera, M.A., Casanovas, J., Figueras, J.: Modelado y simulación. Edicions UPC, Barcelona (2002)
4. Jaffar, J., Lassez, J.L.: Constraint Logic Programming. The ACM Symposium on Principles of Programming Languages. ACM (1987)
5. Jensen, K.: Coloured Petri-Nets: Basics Concepts, Analysis Methods and Practical Use. Springer-Verlag, Vol. 1. Berlin (1997)
6. Riera, D. and Piera, M.A. and Guasch, A.: CSP Generation from Petri-nets Models. IFAC b'02. 15th World Congress. Barcelona (2002)
7. Silva, M.: Las Redes de Petri: en la Automática y la Informática. AC, Madrid (1985)

8. Silva, M., Valette, R.: Petri Nets and Flexible Manufacturing. Lecture Notes in Computer Science, Vol. 424. Advances in Petri-Nets, (1989) 374–417

9. Sutherland, I.: Sketchpad: a man-machine graphical communication system. Proc. IFIP Spring Joint Computer Conference (1963)

10. Waltz, D.L.: Understanding line drawings of scenes with shadows, in: Psycology, of Computer Vision. McGraw-Hill, New York (1975)

11. Wang, L., Wu, S.: Modeling with Colored Timed Object-Oriented Petri Nets for Automated Manufacturing Systems. Computers and Industrial Engineering, Vol. 34, **2**, (1998) 463–480

Disjunction of Non-binary and Numeric Constraint Satisfaction Problems

Miguel A. Salido and Federico Barber

Departamento de Sistemas Informáticos y Computación,
Universidad Politécnica de Valencia
Camino de Vera s/n, 46071
Valencia, Spain
{msalido, fbarber}@dsic.upv.es

Abstract. Nowadays, many researchers are working on Constraint Satisfaction Problems (CSPs). Many CSPs can be modelled as non-binary CSPs and, theoretically, they can be transformed into an equivalent binary CSP, using some of the current techniques. However, this transformation may be an inadequate or inefficient way to manage certain types of non-binary constraints. In this paper, we propose an algorithm called *DHSA* that solves numeric non-binary CSPs with disjunctions in a natural way, as non-binary disjunctive CSP solver. This proposal extends the class of *Horn constraint*, originally studied by Koubarakis, since DHSA manages disjunctions of linear inequalities and disequations with any number of inequalities per disjunction. This proposal works on a polyhedron whose vertices are also polyhedra that represent the non-disjunctive problems. This non-binary disjunctive CSP solver translates, in a preprocess step, the disjunctive problem into a non-disjunctive one by means of a statistical preprocess step. Furthermore, a Constraint Ordering Algorithm (COA) classifies the resultant constraints from the most restricted to the least restricted one. This preprocess step can be applied to other disjunctive CSP solvers in order to find a solution earlier.

Keywords: CSPs, non-binary constraints, Disjunctive constraints.

1 Introduction

Over the last few years, many researchers have been working on Constraint Satisfaction Problems (CSPs), as many real problems can be efficiently modelled as constraint satisfaction problems (CSPs) and solved using constraint programming techniques. Some examples are scheduling, planning, machine vision, temporal reasoning, medical expert systems and natural language understanding. Most of these problems can be naturally modelled using non-binary (or *n*-ary) constraints, that involve any number of variables. In the constraint satisfaction literature, the need to address issues regarding non-binary constraints has only recently started to be widely recognized. Research has traditionally focused on binary constraints (i.e., constraints between pairs of variables) [17]. The basic

M.T. Escrig Monferrer and F. Toledo Lobo (Eds.): CCIA 2002, LNAI 2504, pp. 159–172, 2002.

reasons are the simplicity of dealing with binary constraints compared to non-binary ones and the fact that any non-binary constraint satisfaction problem can be transformed into an equivalent binary one [9]. However, this transformation has several drawbacks:

- Transforming a non-binary into a binary CSP produces a significant increase in the problems' size, so the transformation may not be practical [3] [6]. The translation process generates new variables, which may have very large domains, causing extra memory requirements for algorithms. In some cases, solving the binary formulation can be very inefficient [1].
- A forced binarization generates unnatural formulations, which cause extra difficulties for constraint solver interfaces with human users [4].

When trying to solve a problem with non-binary constraints, we are faced with a crucial modelling decision. Do we convert the problem into a binary one or do we leave it in its non-binary representation? If we convert the problem into a binary one, then we can use some of the widely studied algorithms and heuristics for binary constraints to solve the problem. If we leave the problem in its non-binary representation, we have to use algorithms and heuristics for non-binary constraints. Such algorithms and heuristics have not been studied extensively. Our objective is to study the disjunctive non-binary CSP in its natural representation.

Disjunctions of linear constraints over real values are important in many applications [5]. The problem of deciding consistency for an arbitrary set of disjunctions of linear constraints is NP-complete [16].

In [7], Lassez and McAloon studied the class of *generalized linear constraints*, this includes linear inequalities (e.g., $x_1 + 2x_3 - x_4 \leq 4$) and disjunctions of linear disequations (e.g., $3x_1 - 4x_2 - 2x_3 \neq 4 \lor x_1 + 3x_2 - x_4 \neq 6$). They proved that the problem consistency for this class can be solved in polynomial time.

Koubarakis in [5] extends the class of *generalizad linear constraints* to include disjunctions with an unlimited number of disequations and *at most one* inequality per disjunction. (e.g., $3x_1 - 4x_2 - 2x_3 \leq 4 \lor x_1 + 3x_2 - x_4 \neq 6 \lor x_1 + x_3 + x_4 \neq 9$). This class is called *Horn constraints*. He proved that deciding consistency for this class can be done in polynomial time.

In this paper, we propose an algorithm for solving problems with numeric non-binary disjunctive constraints. This algorithm called "Disjunctive Hyper-polyhedron Search Algorithm" (DHSA) manages non-binary disjunctive CSPs in a natural way as a non-binary CSP solver. This proposal extends the class of *Horn constraint* originally studied by Koubarakis [5] since DHSA manages disjunctions of linear and non-linear disequation and linear inequalities with any number of inequalities per disjunction. The objective of our non-binary CSP is more ambitious since besides of deciding consistency, DHSA obtains the minimal domains of the variables and the solutions that the user requires. This algorithm carries out the search through a polyhedron that maintains the problem inequalities in its faces and updates itself when new constraint is studied. This proposal overcomes some of the weaknesses of other proposals like *disjunctive Forward-checking* and *disjunctive Real Full Look-ahead* keeping its complexity unchanged when the domain size and the number of disequations increase.

2 Preliminaries

Briefly, a numeric constraint satisfaction problem $P = (X, D, C)$ is defined by:

- a set of variables $X = \{x_1, x_2, ..., x_n\}$;
- a set of domains $D = \{D_1, ..., D_n\}$ where each variable $x_i \in X$ has a set D_i of possible values (its domain);
- a set of constraints $C = \{c_1, c_2, ..., c_p\}$ restricting the values that the variables can simultaneously take.

A solution to a CSP is an assignment of a value from its domain to every variable such that all constraints are satisfied. The objective in a CSP may be determining:

- whether a solution exists, that is, if the CSP is consistent;
- all solutions or only one solution, with no preference as to which one;
- the minimal variable domain;
- an optimal, or a good solution by means of an objective function defined in terms of certain variables.

2.1 Notation and Definitions

Definition 1[8]

Let $P=(X,D,C)$ be a numeric CSP, P is globally consistent if and only if $\forall x_i \in X$, $\forall a \in D_i$, $x_i = a$ belongs to a solution to P.

We will summarize the notation that will be used in this paper.

Generic: The number of variables in a CSP will be denoted by n. The constraints will be denoted by c with an index, for example, c_1, c_i, c_k, Also, all constraints are global constraints, that is, all constraints have the maximum arity n.

Variables: To represent variables, we will use x with an index, for example, x_1, x_i, x_n.

Domains: The domain of the variable x_i will be denoted by $D_i = [l_i, u_i]$, so that the domain length of the variable x_i is $d_i = u_i - l_i$. We assume continuous domains for variables.

Constraints: Let $X = x_1, ..., x_n$ be a set of real-valued variables. Let α be a polynomial of degree 1 (i.e. $\alpha = \sum_{i=1}^{n} p_i x_i$) over X, and let b, p_i be real numbers. A *linear relation* over X is an expression of the form $\alpha r b$ where $r \in \{<, \leq, =, \neq, \geq, >\}$. Specifically, a *linear disequation* over X is an expression of the form $\alpha \neq b$ and a *linear equality* over X is an expression of the form $\alpha = b$. In accordance with previous definitions, the constraints that we are going to manage are linear relations of the form:

$$Inequalities : \sum_{i=1}^{n} p_i x_i \leq b \tag{1}$$

$$Disequations: \sum_{i=1}^{n} p_i x_i \neq b \tag{2}$$

$$Non-linear \ \ Disequations: F(x) \neq b \tag{3}$$

where x_i are variables ranging over continuous intervals and $F(x)$ is a non-linear function. Using the above constraints, equalities can be written as conjunctions of two inequalities. Similarly, strict inequalities can be written as the conjunction of an inequality and a disequation. Thus, we can manage all possible relations in $\{<, \leq, =, \neq, \geq, >\}$.

2.2   Constraints

Traditionally constraints are considered *additive*, that is, the order of imposition of constraints does not matter, all that matter is that the conjunction of constraints be satisfied [2]. Our framework will manage internally the constraints in an appropriate order with the objective of reducing the temporal and spatial complexity.

The *arity* of a constraint is the number of variables that the constraint involves. A *unary* constraint is a constraint involving one variable. A *binary* constraint is a constraint involving a pair of variables. A non-binary constraint is a constraint involving an arbitrary number of variables. When referring to a non-binary CSP, we mean a CSP where some or all of the constraints have an arity of more than 2. DHSA is a CSP solver that manages non-binary constraints.

Example. The following are examples of atomic non-binary constraints that DHSA can manage:

$$2x_1 - 5x_2 + 3x_3 - 9x_4 \leq 4, \ 3x_1^4 + 6\sqrt[3]{x_5} - 2x_4^3 \neq 9, \ x_1 - 2x_2 - 4x_3 + x_4 < 4$$

The first and second constraints are managed directly by DHSA. The last constraint is transformed into two constraints:

$$x_1 - 2x_2 - 4x_3 + x_4 < 4 \Rightarrow x_1 - 2x_2 - 4x_3 + x_4 \leq 4 \wedge x_1 - 2x_2 - 4x_3 + x_4 \neq 4$$

In this paper, we assume a non-binary CSP where variables are bounded in continuous domains (for example: $x_i \in [l_i, u_i]$) and a collection of non-binary constraints of the form (1)(2) and (3).

3   Specification of DHSA

DHSA is considered to be a CSP solver that manages non-binary disjunctive constraints. In Figure 1, a general scheme of DHSA is presented. Initially, DHSA studies the significant parameters such as number of variables and number of disjunctive inequalities. Depending on these parameters DHSA runs a preprocess step in which two algorithms are carried out: a heuristic process to translate the disjunctive problem into a non-disjunctive one, and the *Constraint Ordering Algorithm* (COA) to classify the most restricted constraints first, reducing the temporal complexity considerably. Then, using the resultant ordered and non-disjunctive problem, DHSA carries out the consistency study with the resultant problem as a classic CSP solver.

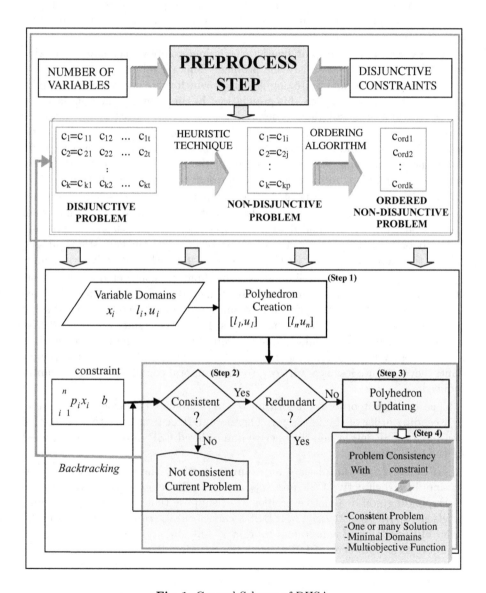

Fig. 1. General Scheme of DHSA

3.1   Preprocess Step

Solving disjunctive constraint problems requires considering an exponential number of non-disjunctive problems. For example, if the problem has k disjunctive constraints composed by l atomic constraints, the number of non-disjunctive problems is l^k.

DHSA uses a preprocessing heuristic technique to obtain the non-disjunctive problem that is likely to satisfy the problem. This technique can be compared with the sampling from a finite population, in which there is a population, and a sample is chosen to represent this population. In this context, the population is the convex hull of all solutions generated by means of the Cartesian Product of variable domain bounds. This convex hull may be represented by a polyhedron with n dimensions and 2^n vertices. However, the sample that the heuristic technique chooses is composed by n^2 vertices of the complete polyhedron[1]. These vertices are well distributed in order to represent the entire population.

With the selected sample of vertices (n^2), the heuristic technique studies how many vertices $v_{ij} : v_{ij} \leq n^2$ satisfy each atomic constraint c_{ij} . Thus, each atomic constraint c_{ij} is labelled with p_{ij}: $c_{ij}(p_{ij})$, where $p_{ij} = v_{ij}/n^2$ represents the probability that c_{ij} satisfies the whole problem. Thus, the heuristic technique selects, the atomic constraint with the highest p_{ij} for each disjunctive constraint.

As we remarked in the preliminaries, constraints are considered *additive*, that is, the order in which the constraints are studied does not make any difference [2]. However, DHSA carries out an internal ordering of the constraints. If some constraints are more restricted than others, these constraints are studied first in order to reduce the resultant polyhedron. Thus, the remaining constraints are more likely to be redundant. However, if the remaining ones are not redundant, they generate less new vertices, so the temporal complexity is significantly reduced.

The constraint ordering algorithm (COA) classifies the atomic constraints in ascending order of the labels p_{ij}. Therefore, DHSA translates the disjunctive non-binary CSP into a non-disjunctive and ordered CSP in order to be studied by the CSP solver.

In Figure 2, we can observe an example in which the atomic selected constraints in a disjunctive CSP are: (c_{12}, c_{21}, c_{32}). Therefore, DHSA will run the corresponding non-disjunctive problem. Let suppose that the atomic constraint labels are $(c_{12}(3), c_{21}(2), c_{32}(1))$. If DHSA carries out the consistency study in the order of imposition of constraints (option 1) (c_{12}, c_{21}, c_{32}), DHSA will generate 6 new vertices. However, if DHSA runs the ordering algorithm, which classifies the constraints in ascending order (option 2) (c_{32}, c_{21}, c_{12}), DHSA will generate only one new vertex with the corresponding time reduction.

If the selected and ordered non-disjunctive problem is not consistent, the algorithm backtracks and the the heuristic technique selects the following set of atomic constraints that is more likely to satisfy the problem.

---

[1] The heuristic selects n^2 items if $n > 3$, and 2^n vertices, otherwise

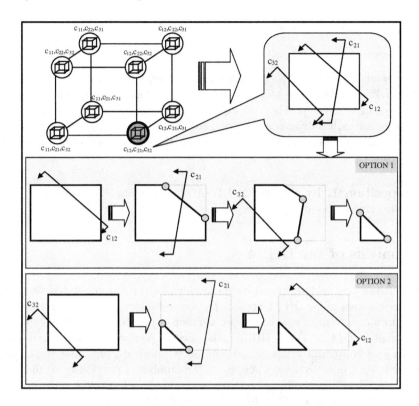

Fig. 2. Example of the Constraint Ordering Algorithm

3.2   CSP Solver

The CSP solver used by DHSA is a complete CSP solver [11] [13]. It generates an initial polyhedron (step 1) with 2^n vertices created by means of the Cartesian product of the variable domain bounds $(D_1 \times D_2 \times ... \times D_n)$. DHSA classifies the selected constraints (by the preprocess step) in two different sets: the inequality set and the disequation set. For each ($\leq$) constraint, the CSP solver carries out the consistency check (step 2). If the ($\leq$) constraint is not consistent, the CSP solver returns *not consistent current problem* and it backtracks to the preprocess step in order to select a new non-disjunctive problem. If the constraint is consistent, the CSP solver determines whether the ($\leq$) constraint is not redundant, and updates the polyhedron (step 3), i.e. the CSP solver eliminates the inconsistent vertices and creates new ones. Finally, when all inequalities have been studied, DHSA studies the consistency with the disequations. Therefore, the solutions to CSP are all vertices, and all convex combinations between any two vertices that satisfy all disequations.

DHSA can obtain some important results such as: the problem consistency; one or many problem solutions; the minimal domain of the variables; the vertex of the polyhedron that minimises or maximises some objective or multi-objective function.

Theorem 1. The CSP solver is sound and complete.

Proof: The CSP solver is sound and complete because it always maintains the solution set in a convex polyhedron whose faces are the problem ($\leq$) constraints. If the resultant polyhedron is not empty, each solution found by the CSP solver is correct, and all solutions can be found into the convex hull of the resultant polyhedron.

Proposition 1. By theorem 1, DHSA obtains global consistency in each non-disjunctive problem.

4   Analysis of the DHSA

DHSA spatial cost is determined by the number of vertices generated. Initially, in the preprocess step, DHSA studies the consistency of the n^2 vertices with the atomics constraints, where n is the number of problem variables. Thus, the spatial cost is $O(n^2)$. Then, DHSA generates 2^n vertices. In the worst case, for each ($\leq$) constraint (step 2), DHSA might eliminate only one vertex and generate $n + c_\leq$ new vertices, where $c_\leq$ is the number of previously studied ($\leq$) constraints. Thus, the number of vertices is $2^n + k(n + c_\leq)$, where k is the number of disjunctive constraints. Therefore, the spatial cost is $O(2^n)$.

The temporal cost can be divided into five steps: Preprocess, initialization, consistency check with ($\leq$) constraints, actualization and consistency check with ($\neq$) constraints. The preprocess cost is $O(ktn^2)$ where t is the maximum number of atomic constraints in a disjunctive constraint. The initialization cost (step 1) is $O(2^n)$, because the algorithm generates 2^n vertices. For each ($\leq$) constraint (step 2), the consistency check cost depends linearly on the number of polyhedron vertices, but not on the variable domains. Thus, the temporal cost is $O(2^n)$. Finally, the actualization cost (step 3) and the consistency check with ($\neq$) constraints depend, on the number of vertices, that is $O(2^n)$. In the worst case, if all non-disjunctive problems must be checked, these three steps must be carried out l^k. Thus, the temporal cost in the worst case is: $O(ktn^2) + O(2^n) + l^k(k \cdot (O(2^n) + O(2^n)) + O(2^n)) \implies O(l^k 2^n)$. Note, that in practice this complexity is much smaller because the heuristic technique obtains statistically the more appropriate non-disjunctive problem at the preprocess step, so it is not necessary to try all possibilities.

5   Evaluation of the Polyhedron Search Algorithm

In this section, we compare the performance of DHSA with some of the more current CSP solvers. We have selected Forward-checking [4] (FC) and Real Full

Look-ahead [10] (RFLA)[2] because they are the most appropriate techniques that can manage this CSP typology. We have used a PIII-800 with 256 Mb. of memory and Windows NT operating system.

Generally, the benchmark sets are used to test algorithms for particular problems, but in recent years, there has been a growing interest in the study of the relation between the parameters that define an instance of CSP in general (i.e., the number of variables, domain size, density of constraints, etc..).

In this empirical evaluation, each set of random constraint satisfaction problems was defined by the 5-tuple $< n, c_\leq, c_\neq, d, t >$, where n was the number of variables, $c_\leq$ the number of disjunctive ($\leq$) constraints, $c_\neq$ the number of ($\neq$) constraints, d the length of variable domains and 't' the number of atomic constraints for each disjunctive ($\leq$) constraint. The problems were randomly generated by modifying these parameters. We considered all constraints as global constraints, that is, all constraints had maximum arity. Thus, each of the graphs shown sets four of the parameters and varies the other one in order to evaluate the algorithm performance when this parameter increases. We tested 100 test cases for each type of problem and each value of the variable parameter, and we present the mean CPU time for each of the techniques. Four graphs are shown which correspond to the four significant parameters (Figures 3, 4, 5, 6). The domain length parameter is not significant for DHSA, so we do not include this graph. Each graph summarizes the Mean CPU time for each technique. Here, for unsolved problems in 200 seconds, we assigned a 200-second run-time. Therefore, these graphs contain a horizontal asymptote in $time = 200$.

In Figure 3, the number of variables was increased from 3 to 11, the number of ($\leq$) and ($\neq$) constraints, the variable domain length and the number of atomic constraints were set $< n, 6, 20, 2000, 6 >$ respectively. The graph shows a global view of the behaviour of the algorithms. The mean CPU time in FC and RFLA increased faster than DHSA. When the unsolved problems were set to time=200 and the others maintained their real-time cost, we observed that FC was worse than RFLA. However, DHSA always had a better behaviour and was able to solve all the problems satisfactorily.

In Figure 4 , the number of variables, the number of ($\neq$) constraints, the variable domain length and the number of atomic constraints were set $< 11, c, 40, 2000, 6 >$, and the number of random ($\leq$) constraints ranged from 2 to 10. The graph shows that the mean CPU times in FC and RFLA increased exponentially and were near the horizontal asymptote for problems with 10 ($\leq$) constraint. The number of unsolved problems increased in FC and RFLA much more than in DHSA.

In Figure 5, the number of variables, the number of ($\leq$) constraints, the variable domain length and the number of atomic constraints were set $< 11, 6, c, 2000, 6 >$, and the number of random ($\neq$) constraints ranged from 10 to 1000.

---

[2] Forward-checking and Real Full Look-ahead were obtained from CON'FLEX, which is a C++ solver that can handle constraint problems with continuous variables with disjunctive constraints. It can be found in:
http://www-bia.inra.fr/T/conflex/Logiciels/adressesConflex.html.

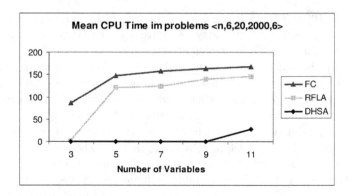

Fig. 3. Mean CPU Time when the number of variables increased

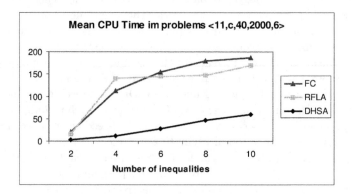

Fig. 4. Mean CPU Time when the number of inequalities increased

The graph shows that the behavior of FC and RFLA got worse when the number of ($\neq$) constraints increased. DHSA did not increase its temporal complexity due to the fact that it carried out the consistency check of the ($\neq$) constraints in low complexity. The number of unsolved problems was very high for both FC and RFLA, while DHSA had a good behavior. Note that DHSA was proved with an amount of 10^5 disequations and it solved them in few seconds (< 3 sc.)

In Figure 6, the number of variables, the number of ($\leq$) and ($\neq$) constraints and the variable domain length were set $< 10, 6, 10, 200, t >$, and the atomic constraints were increased from 4 to 14. To study the behaviour of the algorithms when the number of atomic constraints increased, we chose $t - 1$ non-consistent atomic constraints and only one consistent atomic constraint. That is, if the number of atomic constraints was 8, the random constraint generator generated 7 non-consistent atomic constraints and 1 consistent constraint.

Thus, we could observe the behaviour of the algorithm when the number of atomic constraints increased. FC and RFLA had worse behaviour than DHSA. DHSA makes a preprocess step in which it selects the most appropriate non-

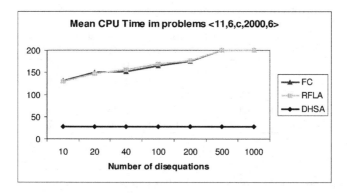

Fig. 5. Mean CPU Time when the number of disequations increased

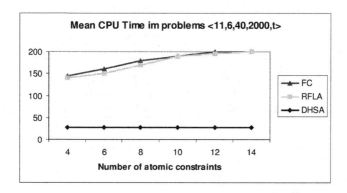

Fig. 6. Mean CPU Time when the number of atomic constraints increased

disjunctive problem. Also, this preprocess step is made in polynomial time, so the temporal cost is very low.

We present a comparison between DHSA without the Constraints Ordering Algorithm (N-COA) and DHSA with the Constraints Ordering Algorithm (Y-COA) in Table 1. This comparison was carried out in two different contexts: in non-consistent problems and in consistent problems. It can be observed that the number of vertices generated was higher in DHSA N-COA than DHSA Y-COA in both cases due to the fact that the Constraints Ordering Algorithm first selects the more appropriate non-disjunctive problems.

Following, we present a comparison between RFLA and FC with the proposed preprocess step (Y-RFLA and Y-FC) and without it (N-RFLA and N-FC) in Table 2. The random generated constraints had the following properties: the number of variables, the number of ($\neq$) constraints, the variable domain length and the number of atomic constraints were set $< 5, c, 5, 10, 2 >$ and the number of ($\leq$) constraints were increased from 5 to 30. We can observed that the preprocess

Table 1. Number of vertices generated in problems $< 9, c, 40, 100, 10 >$

Const	Non-Consist Prob.		Consist Prob.	
	N-COA	Y-COA	N-COA	Y-COA
2	560	0	1050	588
5	1500	420	2920	870
10	2800	872	4215	1625
15	3200	1054	6538	2135
20	3520	1314	7346	2627

step reduced the temporal cost in both algorithms. This temporal cost would be reduce if the number of atomic constraints was higher than 2.

Table 2. Mean CPU time in solved problems $< 5, c, 5, 10, 2 >$

Algor.	Number of disjunctive constraints				
	5	10	15	20	30
N-FC	0.3	9.33	22.7	45.4	75.6
Y-FC	0.15	4.5	18.7	32.1	59.7
N-RFLA	0.25	11.3	25.5	41.2	62.5
Y-RFLA	0.2	8.7	14.5	20.1	43.2

6   Conclusion

In this paper, we have proposed an algorithm called DHSA that solves non-binary disjunctive CSP solver. This proposal extends the class of *Horn constraint* originally studied by Koubarakis [5] since DHSA manages disjunctions of linear and non-linear disequation and linear inequalities with any number of inequalities per disjunction. The objective of our non-binary CSP solver may be: to obtain the problem consistency; to get the minimal domains of the variables and to obtain the solutions that the user requires.

This proposal carries out a consistency study using an algorithm composed of two preprocess algorithms. The first algorithm translates the disjunctive problem into a non-disjunctive one and the other algorithm orders the atomic constraints in an appropriate form. Then, a complete algorithm is carried out over the resulting problem in order to study the consistency of the non-disjunctive problem. DHSA overcomes some weaknesses of other algorithms because its behavior is independent from the domain size and the number of atomic constraints, while other approaches depend exponentially on the number of variables, the number of constraints and the domain size.

Currently, we are working on a framework that is dynamically configured depending on the parameters. This framework is composed by DHSA as a complete CSP solver helped by heuristics such as OFHH (a linear heuristic) [14] and POLYSA (a cubic heuristic) [12]. Furthermore, we are applying these techniques to discrete CSPs [15].

Acknowledgments. This paper has been partially supported by grant UPV-20010980 from the Technical University of Valencia and grant DPI2001-2094-C03-03 from the Spanish government.

References

1. F. Bacchus and P. van Beek, 'On the conversion between non-binary and binary constraint satisfaction problems', *In proceeding of AAAI-98*, 311–318, (1998).
2. R. Barták, 'Constraint programming: In pursuit of the holy grail', *in Proceedings of WDS99 (invited lecture), Prague, June*, (1999).
3. C. Bessière, 'Non-binary constraints', *In Proc. Principles and Practice of Constraint Programming (CP-99)*, 24–27, (1999).
4. C. Bessière, P. Meseguer, E.C. Freuder, and J. Larrosa, 'On forward checking for non-binary constraint satisfaction', *In Proc. Principles and Practice of Constraint Programming (CP-99)*, 88–102, (1999).
5. M. Koubarakis, 'Tractable disjunction of linear constraints', *In Proc. 2nd International Conference on Principles and Practice of Constraint Programming (CP-96)*, 297–307, (1999).
6. J. Larrosa, *Algorithms and Heuristics for total and partial Constraint Satisfaction*, Phd Dissertation, UPC, Barcelona, 1998.
7. J.L. Lassez and K. McAloon, 'A canonical form for generalizad linear constraints', *In Advanced Seminar on Foundations of Innovative Software Development*, 19–27, (1989).
8. O. Lhomme, 'Consistency techniques for numeric CSPs', *In International Joint Conference on Artificial Intelligence (IJCAI-93)*, 232–238, (1993).
9. F. Rossi, C. Petrie, and V. Dhar, 'On the equivalence of constraint satisfaction problems', *In proceeding of European Conference of Artificial Intelligence*, 550–556, (1990).
10. D. Sabin and E.C. Freuder, 'Understanding and improving the MAC algorithm', *In proceeding of Principles and Practice of Constraint Programming*, 167–181, (1997).
11. M.A. Salido and F. Barber, 'An incremental and non-binary CSP solver: The Hyperpolyhedron Search Algorithm', *In Proc. of 7th International Conference on Principles and Practice of Constraint Programming (CP-01), LNCS 2239*, 799–780, (2001).
12. M.A. Salido and F. Barber, 'POLYSA: A polinomial algorithm for non-binary constraint satisfaction problems with <= and <>', *In Proceeding of EPIA-2001 Worshop on Constraint Satisfaction and Operation Research (CSOR01)*, 99–113, (2001).
13. M.A. Salido, A. Giret, and F. Barber, 'Constraint satisfaction by means of dynamic polyhedra', *In Operational Research Proceedings 2001, Springer Verlag*, **1**, 405–412, (2001).
14. M.A. Salido, A. Giret, and F. Barber, 'A non-binary constraint satisfaction solver: The One-Face Hyperpolyhedron Heuristic', *Research and Development in Intelligent Systems XVIII, Springer Verlag*, **1**, 313–324, (2001).

15. M.A. Salido, A. Giret, and F. Barber, 'Integration of Discrete and Non-binary CSPs with Linear Programming Techniques', *To appear in Proc. of CP-2002 Workshop on Cooperative Solvers in Constraint Programming*, (2002).
16. E. Sontag, 'Real addition and the polynomial time hierarchy', *Information Processing Letter*, **20**, 115–120, (1985).
17. E. Tsang, *Foundation of Constraint Satisfaction*, Academic Press, London and San Diego, 1993.

An Empirical Approach to Discourse Markers by Clustering

Laura Alonso[1], Irene Castellón[2], Karina Gibert[3], and Lluís Padró[4]

[1] CLiC (Centre de Llenguatge i Computació)
Department of General Linguistics
Universitat de Barcelona
lalonso@lingua.fil.ub.es
[2] Department of General Linguistics
Universitat de Barcelona
castel@lingua.fil.ub.es
[3] Department of Statistics and Operational Research
Universitat Politècnica de Catalunya
karina@eio.upc.es
[4] TALP Research Center
Software Department
Universitat Politècnica de Catalunya
padro@lsi.upc.es

Abstract. The problem of capturing discourse structure for complex NLP tasks has often been addressed by exploiting surface clues that can yield a partial structure of discourse. Discourse Markers (DMs) are among the most popular of these clues because they are both highly informative of discourse structure and have a very low processing cost. However, they present two main problems: first, there is a general lack of consensus about their appropriate characterisation for NLP applications, and secondly, their potential as an unexpensive source of discourse knowledge is weakened by the fact that information associated to them is usually hand-encoded. In this paper we will show how a combination of clustering techniques provides empirical evidence for a characterisation of DMs. This data-driven methodology provides generalisations helpful for reducing the cost of encoding the information associated to DMs, while increasing consistency of their characterisation.

1 Introduction

Some complex Natural Language Processing Applications, such as Machine Translation, Information Extraction, Dialogue Management or Text Summarisation, try to obtain a certain representation of the structure of a text as a whole, what is usually called *discourse*.

Discourse processing tools have traditionally relied on expensive sources of hand-coded knowledge, which implies a high computational cost when applied to real-world tasks. Seeking improvements in efficiency and coverage, some approaches exploit superficial textual clues to obtain a partial representation of discourse.

M.T. Escrig Monferrer and F. Toledo Lobo (Eds.): CCIA 2002, LNAI 2504, pp. 173–183, 2002.

Cue phrases such as *because, although* or *in that case*, usually called Discourse Markers (DMs) are among the most used of these clues. They are highly informative of discourse structure and they can be treated satisfactorily enough with shallow NLP techniques to guide discourse processing tasks such as segmentation, relevance and coherence assessment and even the derivation of a certain structure of discourse [15]. Punctuation, syntactic structures and other shallow textual clues can also have a similar discourse characterising function.

As a drawback to their low processing cost, resources based on DMs are usually built by labour-intensive description and encoding of the information associated to them. In addition, the lack of consensus on the characterisation of DMs has precluded re-usability of these costly resources.

The use of clustering techniques for a description of DMs could be helpful for solving both these problems. First, clustering algorithms can elicit a data-driven organisation of linguistic objects. Secondly, an empirical approach provides non-biased evidence to ground a characterisation of conflictive units such as DMs.

The main goal of clustering techniques is to identify partitions in an unstructured set of objects described by certain characteristics. Those partitions or classes contain similar objects according to some criteria, usually a distance or similarity function. They are expected to be different from each other, although sometimes they are not, since the method always produces classes, even if they are meaningless. All the objects in a class can be considered together as a whole, and consequently treated in the same way, if the classes can be semantically interpreted by the human analyst.

Therefore, clustering techniques may contribute in characterising DMs by eliciting classes that are empirically grounded and the possible sources of bias that human judgement may introduce. The obtained data organisation is represented in a structure that is easily interpretable by humans. Moreover, it is possible to work with an extensive set of features, comprehending many of the features proposed in heterogeneous approaches, and a high number of examples.

Most of the previous work on obtaining data-driven DM characterisation relies on hand-coded examples [17,14,7,12]. Common to the techniques of clustering and classification based on examples is their capacity of abstracting from a high number of examples and dealing with extensive sets of describing features. The main difference is that classification relies on pre-classified examples, which implies a high cost and unavoidable bias.

The underlying hypothesis of our work is that *DMs with a similar behaviour in naturally occurrent text will correspondingly have a similar behaviour as to the discourse processing instructions they elicit.* As follows, an automated classification of discourse markers according to features describing their occurrences in texts will mirror a taxonomy of the same items as discourse processing devices.

In this paper we present a data-driven classification of DMs in Spanish by clustering techniques. In section 2, we present the data, DMs and corpus, and the clustering tools used. In section 3, we present the results obtained together with a discussion, to finish with conclusions and future work.

2   Experiment

2.1   Discourse Markers

We are working with a set of 577 Spanish DMs, including cue phrases and syntactical structures. These DMs were gathered from previous work about DMs for NLP [15,13], and specific approaches to DMs in Spanish: grammatical [16], computational (the dictionary of the MACO morphological analyzer for Spanish [3]) and from a corpus study. They are stored in a lexicon of Spanish DMs, with syntactic, discourse segmental and rhetorical information (see Table 1).

Table 1. Sample of the cue phrase lexicon

DM	boundary	syntactic type	rhetorical type	direction	content
además	not appl.	adverbial	satellizer	inclusion	reinforcement
a pesar de	strong	preposition	satellizer	right	concession
así que	weak	subordinating	chainer	right	consequence
dado que	weak	subordinating	satellizer	right	enablement

Table 2. Defining features of DMs for clustering

in-lexicon features	values
DM form	*aunque, además, así que*, etc.
Rhetorical content	*cause, circumstance*, etc.
Syntactical type	adverb, coordinating, preposition, etc.
Rhetorical type	*connector, satellizer* (rhetorically subordinating), etc.
contextual features	**values**
Occurrence in initial sentence	yes/no
Occurrence in final sentence	yes/no
Occurrence in initial segment	yes/no
Occurrence in final segment	yes/no
Position of DM in segment	initial, middle, final
Previous word	noun, verb, adverb, adjective, etc.
Following word	grammatical category of the following word
Level of embedding	1 (no embedding), 2, 3, 4, 5, 6
Kind of segment of occurrence	given by the discourse segmenter[§]
Kind of parent segment	given by the discourse segmenter[§]
Kind of previous segment	given by the discourse segmenter[§]
Kind of following segment	given by the discourse segmenter[§]
Negation in the segment of occurrence	yes/no
Negation in the previous segment	yes/no
Negation in the following segment	yes/no

§ Kinds of segment given by the discourse segmenter: adjectival, adverbial, apposition, unmarked coordinated, marked weak, marked strong, non-personal, cite, marked, parenthetic, prepositional

Each DM instance to be clustered was described by a set of 19 features, upon which the clustering tool evaluated similarity (see Table 2). The choice of features was motivated by previous research on classification of DMs [17,14,7], which suggests that discourse structural features (level of embedding, segment markedness, surrounding words, ortography) are useful for describing DM behaviour. We additionally included features productive in the DM lexicon, like syntactical or rhetorical categories, taking care that they did not completely determine the classification.

Another factor that influenced the final choice of the working features was their availability, that is to say, whether they could be easily obtained, from NL Engineering resources such as the DM lexicon mentioned above or by shallow text processing.

2.2   Corpus

We extracted random paragraph-sized occurrences of DMs from a 16 million word corpus (5.5 million words balanced Spanish text (LEXESP) and 10.5 million newspaper text), resulting in a 1,270,993 words corpus with a total of 68,275 instances of DMs. To obtain some of the contextual features listed above, the corpus was previously morphosyntactically analysed [4] and unambiguous intrasentential discursive segments and DMs were identified by an automated discourse segmenter [1].

Unsupervised Corpus. All of the used text processing tools priorise precision over recall, which guarantees a high degree of reliability. In the case of DM recognition, however, the segmenter was modified so that all words which were formally identical to a DM were identified, regardless of their ambiguity as to discursive or sentential function, that is to say, insensitive to the fact that a word which was formally identical to a DM might not be performing a DM function in a particular instance.

In order to overcome the capacity limits of the clustering tool KLASS+ (see section 2.3), resampling techniques have been used to make bootstrap-oriented clustering. Accordingly, we worked with 5 random samples from this fully automatically annotated corpus, consisting of 200 objects each.

Hand-Tagged Corpus. The enhanced recall in DM recognition implied a decrease in precision of approximately 38%. This meant that 38% of the DM instances in the unsupervised samples were performing a non-discursive function in the original text.

To assess the impact of this error rate, we manually tagged a small part of the original corpus, obtaining 277 DM instances with unambiguous discursive function. Two 200-item random samples of this controlled set were clustered. Moreover, classifications of the two hand-tagged samples were taken as comparison ground to better evaluate the adequacy of the describing features.

2.3   Clustering Tools

Among all existing clustering techniques [8], the family of ascendant hierarchical methods (of quadratic cost) is the most popular, since it organizes objects in a binary tree and the number of final clusters may be decided after the clustering. However, other families, like partitioning methods (of linear cost) have become very used, partially because of their capacity to handle huge sets of objects.

The software used to perform the cluster analysis of DMs is KLASS+ [9], an autonomous clustering tool oriented to ill-structured domains. It applies an ascendant hierarchical method [6] that builds classes iteratively clustering the most similar pair of objects at each step[1].

Similarity is calculated according to some distance measure or transformation. KLASS+ permits to work with different distances and similarity coefficients, including mixed distances which enable simultaneously working with categorical and numerical variables. In this application, χ^2 metric was used. It is not order depending, so the final tree is always the same regardless of the objects ordering. In addition, KLASS+ implements *clustering based on rules* method [10] for finding the structure of a dataset.

KLASS+ offers some interpretation-oriented tools for helping in the analysis of the clustering results: using a heuristic criterion, it can recommend the best number of classes, it provides the prototypical description and the distribution of the variables for every class, either in numerical or graphical way, and it can identify *characteristic variables* [11,10], which can be used to identify the particularities and *meaning* of the final classes.

As an additional aid to overcome the capacity limits of KLASS+, we resorted to Autoclass-C [5], a clustering tool that applies a partitioning method and that could handle the whole set of 68,275 instances of DMs. The outcome of this tool is a non-hierarchical set of clusters and a list of features ordered by their influence values summed over all classes. We used Autoclass-C to further assess the relevance of features in the classes given by KLASS+.

3   Results

First of all, the 2 hand-tagged samples were clustered and a hierarchical tree was found for each of them. Using KLASS+ recommendations, classifications consisting of 3 and 6 classes were obtained. The descriptive tools proposed by KLASS+ showed that negation and segment-contextual features perturbed classification, so they were left out of the objects descriptions and the analysis was repeated without them. After that, we performed classifications of the 5 unsupervised samples. Recommended partitions are still on 3 and 6 classes.

3.1   Variable Relevance

Some of the features in the initial set, like *occurrence in initial/final segment* or *sentence* were not found to be characterising at any level of granularity, since they

---

[1] Chained reciprocal neighbours is the underlying cluster algorithm.

present very similar distribution in all the classes (Figure 1, left). In contrast, characterising features, like *position of the DM in the segment*, present different values across classes, thus constituting a distinguishing variable of the class, which can be used to identify it either totally or partially (Figure 1, right).

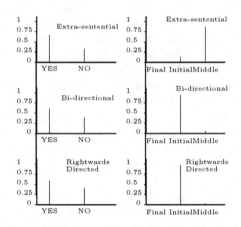

Fig. 1. Distribution across classes for features *occurrence in initial sentence* (left) and *DM position in the segment* (right).

The characterising function of features at different levels of partition motivated a hierarchy of DM classes that can be seen in Figure 2. We compared this hierarchy with the list of feature influence given by Autoclass-C and found a high degree of correlation. As can be seen in Table 3, the main discrepancy between them is that the *type of segment* and *position of DM in the segment* features are considered as more discriminating by Autoclass-C than by KLASS+, whereas *following word* has the opposite interpretation.

The hierarchy is organised as follows:

1. At the topmost level, *position of the DM in the segment* distinguishes DMs occurring mainly in segment initial position from those in other segment positions.
2. DMs integrated in the sentence are further distinguished by *level of embedding*, *type of segment of occurrence* and *type of parent segment*
3. *Syntactical type* subdivides the rightwards directed class, often in correlation with and *rhetorical type*.
4. *rhetorical content* further differentiates classes.
5. At very particular levels, *form of DM* is a highly discriminating feature.

3.2 Consistent Classes

The classifications performed by KLASS+ showed no important differences from one sample to another. Partitions in 3 classes gave the groups:

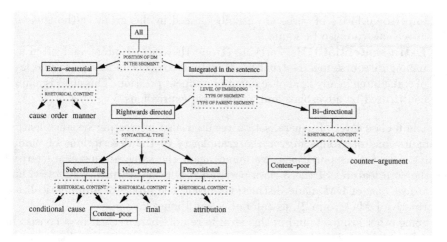

Fig. 2. Hierarchy of features according to their characterising function at subsequent levels of granularity

Table 3. Comparison of feature relevance as given by KLASS+ and Autoclass

	KLASS+		Autoclass-C	
relevance	feature		feature	influence
−	position of DM in the segment			
			following word	0.119
-	level of embedding		level of embedding	0.244
-	type of parent segment		type of parent segment	0.248
-	type of segment			
			position of DM in the segment	0.251
+	following word			
+	previous word		previous word	0.313
+	rhetorical type		rhetorical type	0.384
+	syntactical type		syntactical type	0.461
			type of segment	0.469
++	rhetorical content		rhetorical content	0.645
++	form of DM		form of DM	1.000

1. Highly **Bi-directional** DMs, usually in the middle position of a plain text segment. In hand-tagged corpus, relative pronouns are usually clustered with grammaticalized but informative DMs (group 2, below), whereas in unsupervised samples they are classed together with coordinating conjunctions and some instances of very frequent counterargumentative DMs. It seems that this discrepancy succeeds in signalling the non-discursive function of relative pronouns and coordinating conjunctions in the unsupervised sample.
2. **Rightwards directed** DMs, informative of rhetorical structure and content, prototypically found in first or second level of embedding, in initial position of a non-plain text segment. Prepositions, subordinating conjunctions and

impersonal forms of verbs are usually classed in this group, although some adverbials can also be found.

3. **Extra-sentential** DMs, carrying strong rhetorical content and often signalling discourse macro-structure, they tend to occur in first or second level of embedding in any kind of segment or segment position. This class is mainly constituted by adverbials and anaphorical expressions.

The 6-class level of generalisation resulted also interesting because feature configurations of groups mirror the granularity of the descriptions of human analysts. In 6-class partitions, we found again the same groups characterised by the core features of the 3-class partitions, but the features *syntactical* and *rhetorical type* of DM made distinctions inside the group of grammaticalized-informative DMs (group 2), as can be seen in Figure 2.

Some other groups found in this level were not characterised by a consistent core of features, and the hierarchy of features was not clear, either. This is a usual phenomenon when clustering ill structured domains [9], like natural language, since clustering is based on syntactic-like criteria (metrics, similarities) which are not able to capture semantic structures present on data.

Clustering based on rules is a proposal [10] to overcome syntactic limitations by combining the clustering with a partial knowledge base on the domain. The results of the experiment so far enable us to deal with such semantic specifications, the use of rules for finding an improved classification of DMs is currently in progress.

3.3 Supervised *vs.* Unsupervised

The main difference between the classifications of unsupervised and hand-tagged samples is that highly ambiguous DMs, such as coordinating conjunctions and relatives, are classed together with extra-sentential DMs in unsupervised classifications, while they are more adequately placed within the grammaticalized DMs in hand-tagged ones. In the latter classifications, a clearcut distinction is made between subordinating and coordinating DMs, both rhetorically and syntactically (Figure 3, right). But in unsupervised classifications, the distinction is made between DMs with vacuous rhetorical content and those having meaningful content (Figure 3, left). The reason for this is that, in hand-tagged samples, these DMs have been correctly characterised in respect to their position in the segment, which is initial when they perform a discursive function. In automated parsing, many might-be-DMs in segment middle position are identified. Consequently, they are classed together with DMs occurring in this position, which are typically extra-sentential.

Taking this into account, hand-tagged classifications can be considered as a reference point or golden standard to assess the discursive function of DMs in unsupervised classifications. As we have shown in [2], divergences between an unsupervised classification and the golden standard allow parametrising prototypicality of DMs. This notion of prototypicality helps in detecting DMs that are possibly misanalysed as to their discursive function.

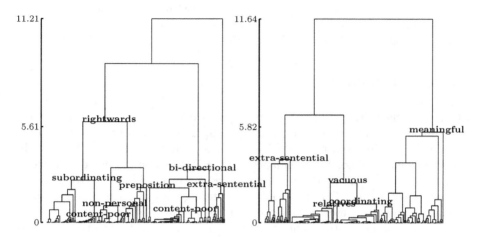

Fig. 3. Right: Dendrogram from a hand-tagged sample, left: Dendrogram from unsupervised corpus

4   Future Work

Once the behaviour of the proposed features has been established, an improved representation of DMs can be pursued. The results of the experiment direct possible enhancements of the set of defining features, by including others that are similar to the ones found more characterising. Moreover, given the success of this preliminary approach to clustering DMs, it seems worthy to perform a deeper analysis of the corpus to obtain DM features that are more informative of discourse processing, such as thematisation, co-reference or an improved representation of polarity.

To overcome capacity limits in clustering, we will:

- Combine the trees of several independent random samples from the same corpus and use the result to estimate the structure of the whole corpus
- Combine complementary clustering tools, for example, by identifying similarity groups within the whole set of DMs with a system capable of dealing with huge amounts of data, like Autoclass-C, and further working them out with a hierarchical tool such as KLASS+

The results of clustering will be used to improve the information in the Spanish DMs lexicon. The hierarchical configuration of the features will enable the use of inheritance in a classification of DMs for reducing the cost of encoding information, and it will also guarantee consistency of the data. Another use of clustering is the assessment as to the discursive function of automatically extracted DMs. A typical classification of prototypical DMs (Figure 3, right) can be taken as a reference point. To detect DMs not performing a discursive function, a classification of might-be-DMs can be evaluated in comparison to this reference point. Divergences arising between these two classifications should identify conflictive spots where non-discursive elements are most probably located.

5 Conclusions

Our work shows the utility of clustering as a portable and scalable technique for discourse processing technologies. This approach reduces the cost and inconsistency found in extensive use of hand-encoded information, which has already been applied to eliminate redundancies in the DM lexicon presented in Table 1.

The classifications found by KLASS+ have clearly delimited DM groups across a variety of samples. Groups found by clustering correspond to analysts' intuitions, and objects present consistent meanings within classes. Classes are defined by a stable core of features with varying degree of specificity directly related to the granularity of the groups, which can also be expressed in terms of a hierarchy of features. The method of hierarchical clustering has been specially adequate to explore this kind of feature organisation.

Moreover, these groups allow us to determine the degree of prototypicality of DMs. Might-be-DMs with a doubtful discursive function are classed differently in unsupervised and hand-tagged classifications. This has two main implications: First, it constitutes an empirical approach to delimit the concept of DM. Second, hand-tagged classifications can be taken as a comparison ground, so that differences with this reference point serve to signal elements with unprobable discursive function in unsupervised classifications.

Acknowledgements. This research has been conducted thanks to a grant associated to the X-TRACT project, PB98-1226 of the Spanish Research Department. It has also been partially funded by projects HERMES (TIC2000-0335-C03-02) and PETRA (TIC2000-1735-C02-02).

References

1. L. Alonso and I. Castellón. Towards a delimitation of discursive segment for natural language processing applications. In *First International Workshop on Semantics, Pragmatics and Rhetoric*, Donostia - San Sebastián, November 2001.
2. L. Alonso, I. Castellón, L. Padró, and K. Gibert. Discourse marker characterisation via clustering: extrapolation from supervised to unsupervised corpora. In *SEPLN*, Valladolid, September 2002.
3. M. Arévalo, L. Alonso, M. Taulé, and M.A. Martí. Documentación sobre el analizador morfológico para el castellano (amcas). Technical Report X-Tract 01/01 Working Paper, CLiC, Universitat de Barcelona, 2001.
4. J. Carmona, S. Cervell, L. Màrquez, M. A. Martí, L. Padró, R. Placer, H. Rodríguez, M. Taulé, and J. Turmo. An environment for morphosyntactic processing of unrestricted spanish text. In *First International Conference on Language Resources and Evaluation (LREC'98)*, Granada, Spain, 1998.

5. P. Cheeseman and J. Stutz. Bayesian classification (AutoClass): Theory and results. In U. M. Fayyad, G. Piatetsky-Shapiro, P. Smyth, and R. Uthurusamy, editors, *Advances in Knowledge Discovery and Data Mining*. AAAI Press/MIT Press, 1996.
6. C. De Rham. La classif. hierarch. selon la méthode des voisins réciproques. *Cahiers d'Analyse des Données*, V(2):135–144, 1997.
7. B. Di Eugenio, J.D. Moore, and M. Paolucci. Learning features that predict cue usage. In *ACL-EACL97, Proceedings of the 35th Annual Meeting of the Association for Computational Linguistics*, pages 80–87, Madrid, Spain, 1997.
8. B. Everitt. *Cluster Analysis*. Heinemann, London, 1981.
9. K. Gibert. The use of symbolic information in automation of statistical treatment of ill-structured domains. *Artificial Intelligence Communications*, 1997.
10. K. Gibert, T. Aluja, and U. Cortés. Knowledge discovery with clustering based on rules. interpreting results. In *Principles of Data Mining and Knowledge Discovery*. Springer-Verlag, 1998.
11. K. Gibert, U. Cortés, and I. Rodríguez-Roda. Identifying characteristic situations in wastewater treatment plants. In *Workshop in Binding Environmental Sciences and Artificial Intelligence*, 2000.
12. J.H. Kim, M. Glass, and M.W. Evens. Learning use of discourse markers in tutorial dialogue for an intelligent tutoring system. In *COGSCI 2000, Proceedings of the 22nd Annual Meeting of the Cognitive Science Society*, Philadelphia, PA, 2000.
13. A. Knott. *A Data-Driven Methodology for Motivating a Set of Coherence Relations*. PhD thesis, University of Edinburgh, Edinburgh, 1996.
14. D.J. Litman. Cue phrase classification using machine learning. *Journal of Artificial Intelligence Research*, 5:53–94, 1996.
15. D. Marcu. *The Rhetorical Parsing, Summarization and Generation of Natural Language Texts*. PhD thesis, Department of Computer Science, University of Toronto, Toronto, Canada, 1997.
16. M.A. Martín Zorraquino and J. Portolés. Los marcadores del discurso. In Ignacio Bosque and Violeta Demonte, editors, *Gramática Descriptiva de la Lengua Española*, volume III, pages 4051–4213. Espasa Calpe, Madrid, 1999.
17. E.V. Siegel and K.R. McKeown. Emergent linguistic rules from inducing decision trees: Disambiguating discourse clue words. In *AAAI94, Proceedings of the 12th Conference of the American Association for Artificial Intelligence*, pages 820–826, 1994.

The Role of Interval Initialization in a GBML System with Rule Representation and Adaptive Discrete Intervals

Jaume Bacardit and Josep Maria Garrell

Enginyeria i Arquitectura La Salle,
Universitat Ramon Llull,
Psg. Bonanova 8, 08022-Barcelona,
Catalonia, Spain, Europe. {jbacardit,josepmg}@salleURL.edu

Abstract. This paper examines some initialization methods for a genetic based machine learning (GBML) rule representation [2] which works with adaptive discretization intervals. The methods studied apply different degrees of uniformness to the initial intervals of the population. The tests done show that except the test problems with more attributes, the differences between the tested methods accuracies are not significant. This proves that we only have to be aware of it in a limited kind of problems.

Keywords: Evolutionary Computation, Machine Learning, Adaptive Discretization.

1 Introduction

The application of the Genetic Algorithms (GA) to classification problems is a field with a lot of work done, and traditionally it has been addressed from two different points of view: the Pittsburgh approach, and the Michigan approach, early exemplified by LS-1 [17] and CS-1 [9], respectively.

The classical solution proposed by those systems is a set of rules which use a prefixed finite number of intervals to handle real-valued attributes. If the discretization intervals are not good, the accuracy of the solution probably will not be good enough.

A simple approach to apply discrete rules is the use of a high number of prefixed uniform discretization intervals. However, it has the problem that the search space grows easily, which slows the evolution process without a clean accuracy improvement of the solution.

Lately, several alternatives to the discrete rules were developed in the genetic-based classifier systems field [19,5,13]. Those alternatives present better performance on problems with real-valued attributes but also have more computational cost.

A middle point between these two point of view is the use of a smart discretization algorithm [7,12,11] , which usually is more accurate and faster than

M.T. Escrig Monferrer and F. Toledo Lobo (Eds.): CCIA 2002, LNAI 2504, pp. 184–195, 2002.

the uniform discretization, but they are not robust enough in some domains as was shown in our previous work [2].

As a more robust alternative, in this paper we present a work on a rule representation with adaptive discrete intervals which split and merge through the evolution process in the training stage. This approach avoids the higher computational cost of the approaches which work directly with real values and finds a good discretization only expanding the search space with small intervals where necessary.

This representation was first presented at [2] and in this paper we focus on a specific issues: the method used to create the initial intervals. The initialization method has to generate enough diversity in the initial pool to make sure that the evolution will converge to a good solution, and we want to test which degree of diversity is the correct.

The paper is structured as follows: After the related work in section 2 we describe the framework of the work presented in this paper in section 3 and the initialization methods in section 4. Next, the description of the test suite in section 5, its results in section 6 and finally, there are the conclusions and further work in section 7.

2 Related Work

There exist several alternatives to discrete rules for handling problems with real-valued attributes inside the evolutionary computation field. Some of these alternatives work on rules composed by interval predicates with real numbers [19], fuzzy rules [5], instances and decision trees [13]. The field of discretization methods is also rich, There are methods that work with the entropy of the information [7], the χ^2 statistic [12] or a multi-dimensional non-uniform discretization [11].

About the intervals initialization, there is not much work published or it is not very clear, because usually it is taken for granted some kind of random initialization, but it is not explained well. Moreover, most of the systems following the Michigan approach rely on a covering operator to fill the population, avoiding the initialization stage.

Anyway, some examples can be found in the literature. Aguilar et al. [1] evolve axis-parallel hyper-rectangles where the the interval for each hyper-rectangle dimension is centered on a random value from the training set attributes and have a random width.

Other loosely related work can be found in the genetic fuzzy systems also. Cordón et al. [5] evolve fuzzy set membership functions initializing them from previously known ones, but each individual with little variations.

3 Framework

In this section we describe the main features of our classifier system, called GAssist (*Genetic Algorithms based claSSIfier sySTem*) [8], a Pittsburgh style classifier system inspired by GABIL [6]. Also, we will describe the working of the adaptive intervals rule representation. The structure of the rules, the crossover and the fitness computation have been borrowed from GABIL. The uncommon parts of the system are explained in the following subsections.

3.1   Matching Strategy

The matching process evaluates the rules using a "if .... then .... else if ... then..." structure usually called *Decision List* [16]

3.2   Mutation Operators

The variable-length individuals that we have in this system makes more difficult the sizing of the the classic gene-based mutation probability. To simplify this sizing, we will define p_{mut} as the probability that an individual has of being mutated. After an individual is selected for mutation with this probability, we choose a random gene inside its chromosome which is mutated.

3.3   Control of the Individuals Length

Like all the systems following the Pittsburgh approach, and, in general, most of the representations with variable-length individuals [18], the control of the size of the individuals is a very important issue. This control is achieved with two operators:

Rule deletion. We delete the rules of the individuals which do not match any training example after the evaluation process. This rule elimination is done after the fitness computation. It has the following constraints:

- The elimination process is activated after some number of iterations, to prevent a great loss of diversity in the early stage of the evolution process.
- The number of rules of an individual never is reduced below a certain minimum value. This minimum can be decided using information of the problem domain or with the following options:
  - The minimum number of rules that let the crossover operator generate longer individuals again.
  - The number of classes in the problem.
- We follow the second policy in the tests done in this work.

Selection based on individual size. The selection operator, as usual, is guided by the fitness (the accuracy), but it also gives certain degree of importance to the size of the individuals. We use tournament selection because its local behavior lets apply this policy. The criterion of the tournament will be given by an operator called "size-based comparison" [3], defined as follows:

- The operator will not be active until a minimum number of iterations have been reached, using only the fitness to do the selection.
- Given two individuals a and b, each one with fitness f_a and f_b and size (in rules) r_a and r_b.
- We will define a "distance" parameter called d_{comp} which will act in the following way:
  - If $|f_a - f_b| < d_{comp}$ then:
    * If $r_a < r_b$ then a is better than b
    * If $r_a > r_b$ then b is better than a
    * If $r_a = r_b$ then we will use the general case
  - Else, we use the general case: we select the individual with higher fitness.

3.4   Discrete Adaptive Intervals Rule Representation

Our aim is to find good discretization intervals without a great expansion of the search space. To achieve this objective, we present a rule representation with discrete adaptive intervals where the discretization intervals are not fixed, and evolve through the iterations, merging and splitting between them.

In order to make this representation achieve a reasonable computational cost and to control well the search space, it has to follow the next constraints:

- We define a number of "low level" uniform and static intervals for each attribute which we call *micro-intervals*.
- The adaptive intervals are built joining *micro-intervals*.
- Attributes with different number of *micro-intervals* can coexist in the population, but attributes can not change its number of *micro-intervals* during the evolution.
- For computational cost reasons, we will have a upper limit in the number of intervals allowed for an attribute, which in most cases will be less that the number of *micro-intervals* assigned to each attribute.
- When we split an interval, we select a random point in its *micro-intervals* to apply the operator.
- When we merge two intervals, the value of the resulting interval is taken from the one which has more *micro-intervals*. If both have the same number of *micro-intervals*, the value is chosen randomly.
- The initial number of micro-intervals is chosen form a predefined set.
- The number and size of the initial intervals is selected randomly

The adaptive intervals and the split and merge operations are represented in figure 1.

In order to make the interval splitting and merging part of the evolutionary process, we have to include it in the GA's genetic operators. We have chosen to add to the GA cycle two special stages applied to the offspring population after the mutation stage. The new cycle is represented in figure 2. For each stage (split and merge) we have a probability (p_{split} or p_{merge}) of applying a split or merge operation to an individual. If an individual is selected for split or merge, a random point inside its chromosome is chosen to apply the operation.

This representation requires some changes to the other parts of the GA:

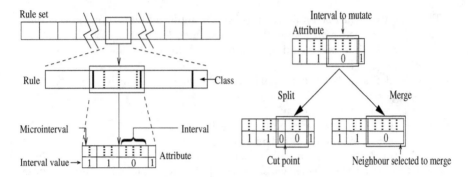

Fig. 1. Diagrams of the adaptive intervals representation and the split and merge operations.

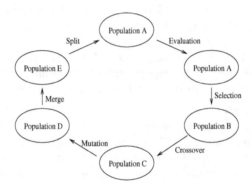

Fig. 2. Cycle of the GA with the added *split* and *merge* operators.

- The crossover operator can only select points of crossover in the attribute boundaries.
- The "size-based comparison" operator uses the length (number of genes) of the individual instead of the number of rules, because now the size of a rule can change when the number of intervals that contains change. This change also makes the GA prefer the individuals with fewer intervals in addition to fewer rules, further simplifying and generalizing them [3].

The correct sizing of p_{split} and p_{merge} will be critical for achieving a good evolution process. A value too small will prevent a good exploration, and a value too big can bring over-learning to the rule set. The sizing of these two probabilities depends on the number of attributes of the problem domain, because the probabilities are defined as affecting individuals. So, domains with very different number of attributes will have also a very different sizing of p_{split} and p_{merge}.

4 Initialization of the Adaptive Intervals

In the previous section we stated that the number and size of the initial intervals is chosen randomly. In this section we present some alternative initialization policies, with different degrees of randomness that will range from an uniform initialization to the previous used one. These policies explained in this section are applied after a number of *micro-intervals* has been selected for an attribute, and decide two aspects: (a) having uniform or non-uniform interval size and (b) the number of initial intervals for each attribute term.

Initial number of intervals for each attribute. In this point we can choose two policies:

- Uniform number of intervals: All the attributes of the population have a predefined number of intervals.
- Non-Uniform number of intervals: Initialize each attribute of the population with a random number of intervals between two and the maximum number of intervals allowed for an attribute.

Size (in micro-intervals) of the intervals. We can have three different policies:

- Uniform intervals size: All intervals have the same number of micro-intervals.
- Non-Uniform intervals size: Fully random-length interval.
- Semi-Uniform intervals size: A policy with a behavior which resides in the middle of the two previous ones. We will choose a size ranging from one to the double of the size of the uniform interval size, that is:

$$[1 : 2 \cdot \frac{\text{Total number of micro-intervals}}{\text{Total number of intervals}}]$$

These three initialization methods are represented in the example in figure 3.

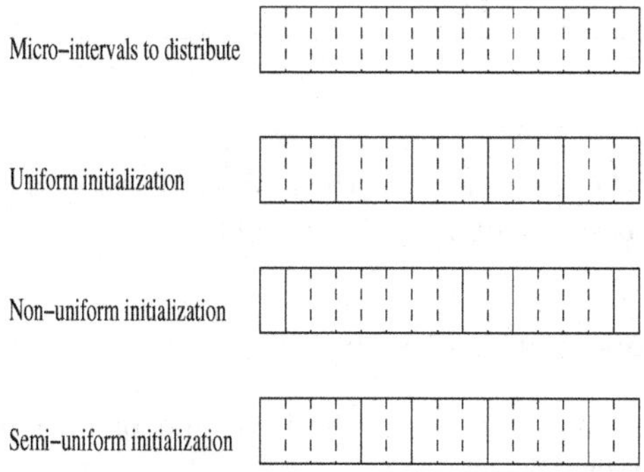

Fig. 3. Initialization policies dealing with the intervals size.

If we combine the two kind of policies, we can have 6 initialization methods with more or less uniformity.

5   Test Suite

In this section we describe the tests that have been done to evaluate the accuracy and simplicity of the methods presented in this paper and also the sizing of their control parameters.

5.1   Test Problems

The test problems selected for this paper include different classes of problems, in order to give us a broad overview of the performance of the methods being tested.

First of all, we will have a synthetic problem (*Tao* [13]) which has non-orthogonal frontiers between classes. Also, we use several problems of the University of California at Irvine (UCI) repository [4]. The problems selected are: Pima-indians-diabetes (*Pima*), *Iris*, *Glass* and breast-cancer-winsconsin (*Breast*). Finally we will use three problems of our own private repository. The first two deal with diagnosis of breast cancer, biopsies (*Bps* [15]) and mammograms (*Mamm* [14]) and the last one with the prediction of student qualifications (*Lrn* [8]). The characteristics of the problems are listed in table 1.

Table 1. Characteristics of the test problems.

Name	examples	real attr.	discrete attr.	Classes
Tao	1888	2	-	2
Pima	768	8	-	2
Iris	150	4	-	3
Glass	214	9	-	6
Breast	699	-	9	2
Bps	1027	24	-	2
Mamm	216	21	-	2
Lrn	648	4	2	5

The partition of the examples into the train and test sets has been done using *stratified ten-fold cross-validation* method [10].

5.2   Configurations of the GA to Test

We have tested the combinations of the two kind of initialization policies explained in the previous section, giving the 6 test configurations shown in table 2.

The parameters of the GA for the tests are shown in table 3 which are distributed in two tables. The first one contains the common parameters for all the tests while the second table contains the parameter which take a different value for each problem. Most of these parameters have been determined empirically with some short tests.

Table 2. Configurations of the GA to test

Configuration	Number of Intervals	Size of Intervals
conf1	Uniform	Uniform
conf2	Uniform	Semi-Uniform
conf3	Uniform	Non-Uniform
conf4	Non-Uniform	Uniform
conf5	Non-Uniform	Semi-Uniform
conf6	Non-Uniform	Non-Uniform

The reader can see that the sizing of both p_{split} and p_{merge} is the same for all the test problems except the tao problem, where giving a similar value to p_{merge} than p_{split} produced a solution with too small number of rules and intervals, and less accurate than the results shown in the next section. This is an issue that needs further study.

In these tests, as we have explained in the framework section, we will have attributes with different number of intervals coexisting in the population, instead of the tests done in a previous paper [2] where all the attributes of the population have the same number of *micro-intervals* and can achieve better results in some of the problem domain. The reason is simple, the *multi-adaptive* tests will be more sensitive to the initialization method as there is more diversity in the population. This can give more clear results about which initialization method is best.

Table 3. Common and problem-specific parameters of the GA.

Parameter	Value
Crossover probability	0.6
Iter. of rule deletion activation	30
Iter. of size comparison activation	30
Sets of *micro-intervals* used	5,6,7,8,10,15,20,25
Tournament size	3

Code	Parameter
#iter	Number of GA iterations
p_{mut}	Probability of mutating an individual
popsize	Size of the population
d_{comp}	Distance param. in the "size-based comparison"
p_{split}	Probability of splitting an interval
p_{merge}	Probability of merging an interval

Probl.	Parameter					
	#iter	p_{mut}	popsize	d_{comp}	p_{split}	p_{merge}
Tao	1500	0.8	200	0.0005	0.3	0.6
Pima	1500	0.6	200	0.01	0.25	0.25
Iris	500	0.8	500	0.02	0.25	0.25
Glass	1500	0.6	300	0.015	0.6	0.6
Breast	1250	0.6	200	0.01	0.7	0.7
Bps	1000	0.6	200	0.015	0.6	0.6
Mamm	1000	0.6	300	0.01	0.8	0.8
Lrn	2000	0.7	200	0.01	0.3	0.3

6   Results

In this section we will show the results of the tests done. The objective of the tests was to compare the method presented in their accuracy, but also to detect if the evolution process works well and generates an accurate but also minimal solution. For these reasons, the results that follow show, for each tested method and test problem: the average and standard deviation values of the percentage of correct classification adjusted by the test fold size and the size of the individuals in number of rules and also intervals per attribute.

Finally, for each configuration, test and fold, 15 runs with different initial seeds are done. After the tests have been explained, the results of them are showed in the table 4. These results are summarized with the ranking of the table 5 build based on the accuracy on each of the test problems.

The first thing we can see in the results is that in only two problems (*Bps* and *Mamm*, the two problems with more attributes) the differences between the test configurations are quite significant in accuracy but specially in the number of rules and intervals per attribute, showing that these problems are quite sensitive to the initialization method. Another significant aspect of the results for these two problems is that the best method for both (conf6) gives also the most reduced solution.

Also, we can observe a curious situation in the domains *Pima, Iris, Glass* and *Breast*, where the number of intervals per rule is less than two. This means that there are several attributes with only one interval which indicates that they are irrelevant in the rules where they appear.

Finally, if we try to extract a global meaning of the results looking at the ranking table, we see that the methods with a non-uniform number of intervals (configurations 4, 5 and 6) have a better ranking than the other three methods (1, 2 and 3). If we group the results with the other kind of policy, the size of the intervals, The method with uniform-size intervals is the best.

7   Conclusions and Further Work

In this paper we have presented several initialization methods for our adaptive discretization intervals rule representation. The objective of the tests done was to detect the degree of sensitivity of the final result to the initialization method.

The results show that, except the two problems with more attributes, there is no significant difference between the accuracy results obtained by the tested methods, and limits the type of problems where we have to be aware to choose a good initialization method. If we have to choose a method, the ranking table shows that the configuration with non-uniform number of intervals but uniform-length intervals is the more regular.

As a further work, we consider that it is important to study the effect of the sizing of the control parameters of the representation, p_{split} and p_{merge}, but also d_{comp}, the parameter of the size-based comparison operator. These parameters,

Table 4. Mean and standard deviation of the accuracy (percentage of correctly classifier examples) and number of rules for each method tested. Bold entries show the method with best results for each test problem and type of result.

Problem	Config	Accuracy	# of Rules	Interv. per Attr.
Tao	conf1	**94.5±0.9**	15.7±3.2	3.9±0.5
	conf2	94.2±0.9	15.4±3.2	3.8±0.5
	conf3	93.8±1.2	**14.5±3.3**	**3.5±0.5**
	conf4	94.4±1.1	15.5±3.0	3.8±0.5
	conf5	94.0±0.7	15.6±3.6	3.8±0.5
	conf6	94.0±1.1	14.6±3.4	3.6±0.6
Pima	conf1	74.4±2.7	5.2±1.9	1.5±0.3
	conf2	73.9±3.2	4.5±1.4	**1.3±0.2**
	conf3	74.3±3.3	**4.0±1.5**	**1.3±0.2**
	conf4	74.4±3.0	6.3±3.0	1.8±0.5
	conf5	74.3±3.1	5.4±2.5	1.5±0.4
	conf6	**74.6±3.1**	4.4±1.4	**1.3±0.2**
Iris	conf1	**96.3±1.9**	**3.4±0.6**	1.3±0.2
	conf2	96.0±2.6	3.6±1.4	1.3±0.2
	conf3	96.0±2.2	3.6±0.8	1.3±0.2
	conf4	95.9±2.4	3.7±1.1	1.3±0.2
	conf5	95.9±2.2	3.7±1.0	1.3±0.2
	conf6	95.6±2.2	3.6±0.8	**1.3±0.1**
Glass	conf1	65.5±4.4	7.9±2.2	1.7±0.2
	conf2	**65.8±3.2**	7.5±2.0	1.6±0.2
	conf3	64.9±3.5	7.3±1.9	1.6±0.2
	conf4	65.7±3.0	7.3±2.2	1.6±0.2
	conf5	64.9±3.0	7.2±1.9	1.6±0.2
	conf6	65.3±3.4	**7.1±2.0**	1.6±0.2
Breast	conf1	95.2±2.2	2.5±0.8	1.3±0.2
	conf2	95.1±2.4	2.5±0.8	**1.3±0.1**
	conf3	95.2±2.5	2.6±0.8	1.3±0.2
	conf4	95.2±2.3	2.7±0.8	**1.3±0.1**
	conf5	**95.5±2.4**	**2.4±0.6**	**1.3±0.1**
	conf6	95.2±2.1	2.5±0.6	**1.3±0.1**
Bps	conf1	75.2±3.0	20.3±10.0	4.5±0.6
	conf2	75.1±2.8	20.1±9.9	4.5±0.6
	conf3	77.8±3.1	13.1±6.7	4.2±0.4
	conf4	79.4±3.0	8.9±5.4	2.7±0.4
	conf5	79.5±2.9	6.2±3.8	2.3±0.4
	conf6	**80.1±2.9**	**5.2±3.2**	**2.1±0.4**
Mamm	conf1	64.0±4.7	11.6±3.2	3.5±0.3
	conf2	63.5±4.4	9.8±3.1	3.2±0.3
	conf3	64.9±4.9	7.7±3.0	2.7±0.4
	conf4	64.2±4.5	11.0±3.5	3.1±0.4
	conf5	63.8±4.8	10.1±3.6	3.0±0.5
	conf6	**66.2±4.9**	**6.8±2.8**	**2.6±0.5**
Lrn	conf1	65.8±4.3	8.8±3.1	3.0±0.2
	conf2	66.3±4.7	8.5±2.9	3.0±0.2
	conf3	66.7±3.8	8.2±3.1	2.9±0.2
	conf4	**66.8±4.4**	7.4±2.4	2.9±0.1
	conf5	66.5±3.9	6.9±2.0	**2.8±0.1**
	conf6	66.4±4.1	**6.8±2.0**	**2.8±0.1**

if correctly sized, allow a correct exploration of the search space, but also can bring a premature convergence if their value is not good.

Also as further work, it can be interesting to analyze the results of the tests presented in this paper from the computational cost point of view. If the differences of the accuracy are not significant, maybe the differences in computational

Table 5. Performance ranking of the tested methods. Lower number means better ranking.

Problem	Conf1	Conf2	Conf3	Conf4	Conf5	Conf6
Tao	1	3	6	2	4	5
Pima	2	6	5	3	4	1
Iris	1	3	2	5	4	6
Glass	3	1	6	2	5	4
Breast	3	5	6	4	1	2
Bps	6	5	4	3	2	1
Mamm	4	6	2	3	5	1
Lrn	6	5	2	1	3	4
Average	3.25	4.25	4.125	2.875	3.5	3
Final rank	3	6	5	1	4	2

time resulting from a good initialization method and also from the adjust of the control parameters can be bigger.

Acknowledgments. The authors acknowledge the support provided under grant numbers 2001FI 00514, CICYT/Tel08-0408-02 and FIS00/0033-02. The results of this work were partially obtained using equipment cofunded by the *Direcció General de Recerca de la Generalitat de Catalunya (D.O.G.C. 30/12/1997)*. Finally we would like to thank Enginyeria i Arquitectura La Salle for their support to our Intelligent Systems Research Group.

References

1. Jesús Aguilar, José Riquelme, and Miguel Toro. Three geometric approaches for representing decision rules in a supervised learning system. In *Late Breaking Papers of the Genetic and Evolutionary Computation Conference (GECCO'99)*, pages 8–15, 19919999.
2. Jaume Bacardit and Josep M. Garrell. Evolution of adaptive discretization intervals for a rule-based genetic learning system. In *Proceedings of the Genetic and Evolutionary Computation Conference (GECCO-2002) (to appear)*, 2002.
3. Jaume Bacardit and Josep M. Garrell. Métodos de generalización para sistemas clasificadores de Pittsburgh. In *Proceedings of the "Primer Congreso Iberoamericano de Algoritmos Evolutivos y Bioinspirados (AEB'02)"*, pages 486–493, 2002.
4. C. Blake, E. Keogh, and C. Merz. Uci repository of machine learning databases, 1998. Blake, C., Keogh, E., & Merz, C.J. (1998). UCI repository of machine learning databases (www.ics.uci.edu/mlearn/MLRepository.html).
5. O. Cordón, M. del Jesus, and F. Herrera. Genetic learning of fuzzy rule-based classification systems co-operating with fuzzy reasoning methods, 1998. Cordn, O., del Jesus, M.J and Herrera, F. (1998), Genetic learning of fuzzy rule-based classification systems co-operating with fuzzy reasoning methods, International Journal of Intelligent Systems, Vol. 13 (10/11), pp.1025-1053.
6. Kenneth A. DeJong and William M. Spears. Learning concept classification rules using genetic algorithms. *Proceedings of the International Joint Conference on Artificial Intelligence*, pages 651–656, 1991.
7. Usama M. Fayyad and Keki B. Irani. Multi-interval discretization of continuous-valued attributes for classification learning. In *IJCAI*, pages 1022–1029, 1993.

8. Elisabet Golobardes, Xavier Llorà, Josep Maria Garrell, David Vernet, and Jaume Bacardit. Genetic classifier system as a heuristic weighting method for a case-based classifier system. *Butlletí de l'Associació Catalana d'Intel.ligència Artificial*, 22:132–141, 2000.

9. John H. Holland. Escaping Brittleness: The possibilities of General-Purpose Learning Algorithms Applied to Parallel Rule-Based Systems. In Mitchell, Michalski, and Carbonell, editors, *Machine learning, an artificial intelligence approach. Volume II*, pages 593–623. Morgan Kaufmann, 1986.

10. Ron Kohavi. A study of cross-validation and bootstrap for accuracy estimation and model selection. In *IJCAI*, pages 1137–1145, 1995.

11. Alexander V. Kozlov and Daphne Koller. Nonuniform dynamic discretization in hybrid networks. In *Proceedings of the 13th Annual Conference on Uncertainty in AI (UAI)*, pages 314–325, 1997.

12. H. Liu and R. Setiono. Chi2: Feature selection and discretization of numeric attributes. In *Proceedings of 7th IEEE International Conference on Tools with Artificial Intelligence*, pages 388–391. IEEE Computer Society, 1995.

13. Xavier Llorà and Josep M. Garrell. Knowledge-independent data mining with fine-grained parallel evolutionary algorithms. In *Proceedings of the Genetic and Evolutionary Computation Conference (GECCO-2001)*, pages 461–468. Morgan Kaufmann, 2001.

14. J. Martí, X. Cufí, J. Regincós, and et al. Shape-based feature selection for microcalcification evaluation. In *Imaging Conference on Image Processing, 3338:1215-1224*, 1998.

15. E. Martínez Marroquín, C. Vos, and et al. Morphological analysis of mammary biopsy images. In *Proceedings of the IEEE International Conference on Image Processing (ICIP'96)*, pages 943–947, 1996.

16. Ronald L. Rivest. Learning decision lists. *Machine Learning*, 2(3):229–246, 1987.

17. Stephen F. Smith. Flexible learning of problem solving heuristics through adaptive search. In *Proceedings of the 8th International Joint Conference on Artificial Intelligence (IJCAI-83)*, pages 421–425, Los Altos, CA, 1983. Morgan Kaufmann.

18. Terence Soule and James A. Foster. Effects of code growth and parsimony pressure on populations in genetic programming. *Evolutionary Computation*, 6(4):293–309, Winter 1998.

19. Stewart W. Wilson. Get real! XCS with continuous-valued inputs. In L. Booker, Stephanie Forrest, M. Mitchell, and Rick L. Riolo, editors, *Festschrift in Honor of John H. Holland*, pages 111–121. Center for the Study of Complex Systems, 1999.

Feature Subset Selection in an ICA Space

Marco Bressan and Jordi Vitrià*

Centre de Visió per Computador, Dept. Informàtica,
Universitat Autònoma de Barcelona, 08193 Bellaterra, Barcelona, Spain.
Tel. +34 93 581 30 73 Fax. +34 93 581 16 70
{marco, jordi}@cvc.uab.es

Abstract. Given a number of samples possibly belonging to different classes, we say these samples live in an ICA space if all their class-conditional distributions are separable and thus can be expressed as a product of unidimensional distributions. Since this hypothesis is unfrequent on real-world problems we also provide a framework through class-conditional Independent Component Analysis (CC-ICA) where it can be held on stronger grounds. For this representation, we focus on the problem of feature subset selection for classification, observing that divergence arises as a simple and natural criterion for class separability. Since divergence is monotonic on the dimensionality, optimality can be ensured without the need for an exhaustive search for features. We adapt the Bayes decision scheme to our independence assumptions and framework. A first experiment on Trunk's artificial dataset, where class-conditional independence is already known, illustrates the robustness and accuracy of our technique. A second experiment, on the UCI letter database, evaluates the importance of the representation when assuming independence. A third experiment on the Corel database illustrates the performance of our criterion on high dimensional data.

Keywords: Feature Selection, Divergence, Independent Component Analysis, Naive Bayes.

1 Introduction

Feature selection methods are necessary in presence of high dimensional data computed from hyperspectral sensors, multi-sensor fusion or multiple data model integration. These methods require a criterion that evaluates the goodness of any feature subset. In order to produce an optimal subset of features, generally an exhaustive sequential feature selection procedure is required, so the size of the problem grows combinatorially on the dimension. Additionally, standard feature selection criteria, such as the Bhattacharya distance among classes, require costly and completely new calculations for each possible subset, despite their heavy assumptions on the class-conditional distributions. A whole different perspective arises if the features can be considered statistically independent. In this case, discriminant functions such as divergence, Bhattacharya distance, (generalized) Fisher ratio or Jeffries-Matusita distance are greatly simplified. In this paper, we

---

* This work is supported by CICYT and EU grants TAP98-0631 and 2FD97-0220 and the Secretaría de Estado de Educación, Universidades, Investigación y Desarrollo from the Ministerio de Educación y Cultura de España.

M.T. Escrig Monferrer and F. Toledo Lobo (Eds.): CCIA 2002, LNAI 2504, pp. 196–206, 2002.

focus on divergence due to its simplicity and general assumptions on class-conditional distributions. Independence can also provide simplicity to the classifiers where the Naive Bayes Rule is a well-known example.

Of course, class-conditional independence is not a light assumption so we also provide an alternative representation using class-conditional Independent Component Analysers for ensuring the assumption of statistical independence among features. In this case, it would be more proper to talk about feature extraction instead of feature selection. We adapt divergence and the Naive-Bayes classifier to this representation.

In Section 2 we introduce the concept of independence and conditional independence, making some observations that justify our choice for a class-conditional representation. Section 3 introduces Independent Component Analysis (ICA) and explains the way it can be employed, through local representations, to force independence on the random vector representing a certain class. In Section 4 we deal with the consequences upon divergence of assuming independence of the feature vectors representing each class. A property of order is exposed, showing that, with these assumptions and criterion, a feature subset of any cardinality can be found without involving any search procedure. By interpreting divergence in terms of expected log-likelihood ratios we can formulate a divergence-based criterion good for evaluating local features and obtaining class-dependent optimal feature subsets. We then focus on the problem of classifying the selected independent features. In Section 5 we adapt the Bayes Decision Scheme to our local representation, resulting in a modified Naive Bayes classifier. Experiments on one artificial and two benchmark databases were performed showing the performance of our method. These experiments evaluate robustness to class-distributions and dimensionality, and the importance of the independence assumption on the Naive Bayes classifier.

2   Conditional Independence

Let X and Y be random variables and $p(x,y), p(x), p(y)$ and $p(x|y)$ be, respectively, the joint density of (X,Y), the marginal densities of X and Y, and the conditional density of X given $Y = y$. We say that X and Y are independent if any of the following two equivalent definitions hold [1]:

$$p(x,y) = p(x)p(y) \tag{1}$$
$$p(x|y) = p(x) \tag{2}$$

It proves useful to understand independence from the following statement derived from (2): Two variables are independent when the value one variable takes gives us no knowledge on the value of the other variable. For the multivariate case $(X_1, ..., X_N)$, independence can be defined by extending (1) as $p(x) = p(x_1)...p(x_N)$.

In the context of statistical classification, given K classes in $\Omega = \{C_1, ...C_K\}$ and a set of features represented by N-dimensional random vector $\mathbf{x} = (x_1, ..., x_N)$, the Maximum A Posteriori (MAP) and the Maximum Likelihood (ML) solutions both make use of the class-conditional densities $p(\mathbf{x}|C_k)$. A frequent mistake is to think that the independence of the features implies class-conditional independence, being Simpson's paradox [2] probably the most well known counterexample. For this particular case, in which class-conditional independence is not true, we now introduce a local representation where this assumption can be held on stronger grounds.

2.1   Independent Component Analysis

The ICA of an N dimensional random vector is the linear transform which minimizes the statistical dependence between its components. This representation in terms of independence proves useful in an important number of applications such as data analysis and compression, blind source separation, blind deconvolution, denoising, etc. [3,4,5,6]. Assuming the random vector we wish to represent through ICA has no noise, the ICA Model can be expressed as $\mathbf{W}(\mathbf{x} - \overline{\mathbf{x}}) = \mathbf{s}$, where $\mathbf{x}$ corresponds to the random vector representing our data, $\overline{\mathbf{x}}$ its mean, $\mathbf{s}$ is the random vector of *independent components* with dimension $M \leq N$, and $\mathbf{W}$ is called the *filter* or *projection matrix*. This model is frequently presented in terms of $\mathbf{A}$, the pseudoinverse of $\mathbf{W}$, called the *mixture matrix*. Names are derived from the original blind source separation application of ICA. If the components of vector $\mathbf{s}$ are independent, at most one is Gaussian and its densities are not reduced to a point-like mass, it can be seen that $\mathbf{W}$ is completely determined [7]. Estimation of the filter matrix $\mathbf{W}$ and thus the independent components can be performed through the optimization of several objective functions such as likelihood, network entropy or mutual information. Though several algorithms have been tested, the method employed in this article is the one known as FastICA. This method attempts to minimize the mutual information by finding maximum negentropy directions, proving to be fast and efficient [6].

As mentioned, global feature independence is not sufficient for conditional independence. In [8] we introduced a class-conditional ICA (CC-ICA) model that, through class-conditional representations, ensures conditional independence. This scheme was successfully applied in the framework of classification for object recognition. The CC-ICA model is estimated from the training set for each class. If $\mathbf{W}_k$ and $\mathbf{s}_k$ are the projection matrix and the independent components for class C_k with dimensions $M_k \times N$ and M_k respectively, then from the ICA model,

$$\mathbf{s}^k = \mathbf{W}^k(\mathbf{x} - \overline{\mathbf{x}^k}) \tag{3}$$

where $\mathbf{x} \in C_k$ and $\overline{\mathbf{x}^k}$ is the class mean, estimated from the training set. Assuming the class-conditional representation actually provides independent components, we have that the class-conditional probability noted as $p^k(\mathbf{s}) \overset{def}{=} p(\mathbf{s}^k)$ can now be expressed in terms of unidimensional densities,

$$p(\mathbf{x}|C_k) = \nu_k p^k(\mathbf{s}) = \nu_k \prod_{m=1}^{M_k} p^k(s_m) \tag{4}$$

with $\nu_k = (\int p^k(\mathbf{s})ds)^{-1}$, a normalizing constant. From now on we will say Ω is an *ICA Space* if all its class-conditional distributions correspond to independent variables and thus can be expressed as a product of unidimensional distributions.

3   Divergence

Class separability is a standard criterion in feature selection for classification. Measures for class separability are generally obtained from the distance among the previously estimated class-conditional distributions. A commonly used distance measure for (class-conditional) densities, for its connection with information theory, is the Kullback-Leibler distance,

$$KL(C_i, C_j) = \int_\Omega p(\mathbf{x}|C_i) \log \frac{p(\mathbf{x}|C_i)}{p(\mathbf{x}|C_j)} d\mathbf{x} \tag{5}$$

where $1 \leq i, j \leq K$. The asymmetry of Kullback-Leibler motivates the symmetric measure of divergence, long ago used for feature selection [9], defined as

$$\hat{D}_{ij} = \hat{D}(C_i, C_j) = KL(C_i, C_j) + KL(C_j, C_i) \tag{6}$$

Besides being symmetric, divergence is zero between a distribution and itself, always positive, monotonic on the number of features and provides an upper bound for the classification error [10]. The two main drawbacks of divergence are that it requires density estimation and has a nonlinear relationship with classification accuracy. The first drawback is specially problematic in high dimensional spaces, precisely where we would require feature selection techniques. The second one is related with the fact divergence increases without bound as class separability increases. Swain and Davis [11] heuristically solved this inconvenient by introducing the following transformed divergence,

$$D_{ij} = 2[1 - \exp(-\frac{\hat{D}_{ij}}{8})] \tag{7}$$

Transformed divergence has a saturating behaviour asymptotyc to 2, and is lower bounded by the (also asymptotyc to 2) Jeffries-Matusita distance. It has also been shown that transformed divergence is computationally more economical, comparably as effective as the JM distance and considerably better than simple divergence [12].

3.1   Independent Component Divergence

If our features lie on an ICA space as defined in section 2.1, introducing (1) in (6) it can be seen that divergence is additive on the features,

$$\hat{D}_{ij} = \sum_{n=1}^{N} \hat{D}_{ij}^n \tag{8}$$

So, for this particular case, unidimensional density estimation can be performed and the calculation of divergence for a feature subset $S \subseteq \{1, ..., N\}$ (noted by $\hat{D}_{ij}^S$) is straightforward. This additive rule is not true for the transformed divergence, but working with a transformed unidimensional divergence is still desirable so we define $D_{ij}^n = 2[1 - \exp(-\hat{D}_{ij}^n/8)]$. Transformed divergence for any feature subset can be obtained by using that

$$D_{ij}^S = 2[1 - \prod_{n \in S}(1 - D_{ij}^n/2)]. \tag{9}$$

A very important property besides montonicity shared by transformed divergence and divergence, is that

$$(n_1 \notin S, n_2 \notin S) \wedge (D_{ij}^{n_1} \le D_{ij}^{n_2}) \Rightarrow (D_{ij}^{S \cup n_1} \le D_{ij}^{S \cup n_1}) \tag{10}$$

This property of order suggests that, at least for the two class case, the best feature subset is the one that contains the features with maximum marginal (transformed) divergence, and thus provides a very simple rule for feature selection without involving any search procedure.

Although, transformed divergence only provides a measure for the distance between two classes there are several ways of extending it to the multiclass case, providing an effective feature selection criterion. The most common is taking the average over all class pairs

$$D_A^n = \frac{1}{K(K-1)} \sum_{i=1}^{K-1} \sum_{j=1}^{K} D_{ij}^n \tag{11}$$

D_A^n represents the average divergence present in feature n. This approach (noted by D_A) is simple and preserves the exposed property of order for feature subsets, but it is not reliable as the variance of the pairwise divergences increases. A more robust approach is to sort features by their maximum minimum (two-class) divergence D_M. This works fine for small subsets but decays as the size of the subset increases: sorting features by maximum minimum divergence is a very conservative election.

Additional criterions that prove adequate for particular problems can be thought of heuristically. For instance, ranking the features maximizing the divergence in all classes, minimizing the influence of already well separated classes over the choice of features.

3.2   Divergence in Class-Conditional Representations

If our features do not lie in an ICA space, through (3) we have K local linear representations, each one making $\mathbf{x}|C_k$ independent. With this local approach, the selection of a single feature for the whole ICA space involves the selection of possibly distinct single features belonging to different representations. We now provide an alternative definition of divergence, adapted to local representations.

The log-likelihood ratio (L) is defined as,

$$L_{ij}(\mathbf{x}) = \log p(\mathbf{x}|C_i) - \log p(\mathbf{x}|C_j) \tag{12}$$

$L_{ij}(\mathbf{x})$ measures the overlap of the class-conditional densities in $\mathbf{x}$. It can be seen from (6) that $D_{ij} = E_{C_i}(L_{ij}) + E_{C_j}(L_{ji})$ where E_{C_i} is the class-conditional expectation operator. Approximating $E_{C_i}(g(x)) \approx (1/\#C_i) \sum_{x \in C_i} g(x) \overset{def}{=} \overline{g(x)}_{C_i}$, and reordering the terms, we have

$$D_{ij} \approx \left(\overline{\log p(x|C_i)}_{C_i} - \overline{\log p(x|C_i)}_{C_j} \right)$$
$$+ \left(\overline{\log p(x|C_j)}_{C_j} - \overline{\log p(x|C_j)}_{C_i} \right) \tag{13}$$
$$\overset{def}{=} D'_{ij} + D'_{ji}$$

D'_{ij} measures the difference in the expected likelihood of classes i and j, assuming all samples are taken from class i. It is no longer symmetric but still additive for conditionally independent variables. Introducing (4) D'_{ij} can be expressed as,

$$D'_{ij} = \nu_i \sum_{m=1}^{M_i} \left(\overline{\log p^i(s_m)}_{C_i} - \overline{\log p^i(s_m)}_{C_j} \right)$$
$$\overset{def}{=} \nu_i \sum_{m=1}^{M_i} D'^m_{ij} \tag{14}$$

Divergence is maximized by maximizing both D'_{ij} and D'_{ji}. The assymetry and locality of the latter will cause different feature subsets on each class representation, meaning that while certain features might be appropriate for separating class C_i from class C_j in the ith representation, possibly distinct features will separate class C_j from class C_i in the jth representation.

As with divergence, we have that D'_{ij} only provides a measure of distance between two classes in a certain representation. Extension to the multiclass case can be performed in a very simmilar manner. For instance, having fixed the representation, the average has to be taken over only one index,

$$D'^m_{A_i} = \frac{1}{K-1} \sum_{j=1, j\neq i}^{K} D'^m_{ij} \tag{15}$$

The same with the minimum criterion. As for the algorithm for D_{MAX}, it can be easily adapted to D' by fixing one of the class indexes.

4   Bayes for Independent Features

Even though our feature selection criterion is not classifier driven, the independence assumption can be also used in classification. In this section we expose the result of using the independence assumption in a Bayes Decision scheme. The ML (or MAP) solution assuming class-conditional independence of the features (that is, assuming the features live in an ICA space) is known as the Naive Bayes Classifier [13]. In this context a test sample described by features $\mathbf{x}_{Test}$ is assigned to class C_{Naive} if

$$C_{Naive} = \arg \max_{k=1...K} \prod_{n=1}^{N} p(x_n|C_k) \tag{16}$$

If independence is not known in advance and a CC-ICA representation is used then, by replacing (4) in (16) and using log-likelihoods [8],

$$C_{Naive} = \arg\max_{k=1...K} \sum_{m=1}^{M_k} \log P^k(s_m) + log(\nu_k) \tag{17}$$

If a subset of features has been selected for class C_k using (14), then the sum in (17) is only performed on the corresponding features. The class-conditional marginal densities $P^k(s_m)$ can be estimated using classical density estimation techniques such as Gaussian Mixture Models, Laplace Mixture Models or nonparametric Kernel methods. It can be seen that maximization of mutual information results in strongly nongaussian distributions. This a priori knowledge can be used to restrict possible densities to particular density families such as the generalized Gaussian.

5   Experiments

A first experiment is performed on the artificial two-class example Trunk used to illustrate the curse of dimensionality [14]. The two classes have multivariate normal 20-dimensional distributions with covariance given by the identity matrix and means $\mu 1 = [1/\sqrt{1}, 1/\sqrt{2}, ..., 1/\sqrt{20}]$, $\mu 2 = -\mu 1$. In a recent survey on feature selection [15], Jain and Zongker propose this example to investigate the quality of certain feature subsets considering that the optimal d-feature subset is known in advance: the first d features. They propose a measure of average quality for the feature selection criterion varying the number of training patterns per class and averaging the results of five artificially generated data sets on every possible d-feature subset. The maximum possible value for this average quality is one, meaning that the 20 possible feature subsets were the optimal subset for the five data sets.

Notice that this data set is actually an ICA space: the class-conditional densities are uncorrelated gaussians, thus independent. So there is no need to transform the data. We use (7) to calculate the unidimensional divergence values. In Fig. (1) we reproduce the results in [15] using the Mahalanobis distance between means as a criterion and the optimal branch and bound feature subset selection algorithm. We also plot the results of our method, estimating the marginal densities with a 2-Gaussian Mixture Model (no prior knowledge of the data assumed) and with a Gaussian with unknown mean and deviation (Gaussian data assumed). For the latter, divergence has a closed form [16]. From Fig. (1) we observe divergence is a fairly robust criterion with performance above Jain's criterion, even though both make use of only first and second order statistics. Gaussian Mixture Models do not perform well when the number of samples is similar to the dimensionality but soon recovers, meaning that we can do without the prior knowledge on the data distribution without seriously affecting the results.

A second experiment is performed on the Letter Image Recognition Data [17]. Each instance of the 20000 images within this database represents a capital typewritten letter in one of twenty fonts. Each letter is represented using 16 integer valued features corresponding to statistical moments and edge counts. Training is done on the first 16000 instances and test on the final 4000. There are approximately 615 samples per class in the

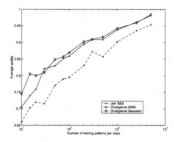

Fig. 1. Quality of selected feature subsets as a function of the size of the training data.

training set. In this case feature independence cannot be assumed so we use a CC-ICA Representation of the data. Fig. (2) illustrates the results of the Naive Bayes Classifier for different representations and feature subsets. The divergence feature selection criterion was used for ICA (a global ICA representation), CC-ICA and ORIG (the original representation), while for PCA, features were selected as ordered by the representation. The results of Maximum Likelihood classification on PCA were also included as a reference.

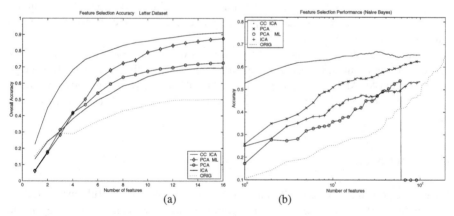

Fig. 2. Naive Bayes performance on different representations and feature selection criteria on the (a) UCI Letter dataset and (b) Corel Database histogram-based classification. The importance of the independence assumption on Naive Bayes performance is observed. Maximum Likelihood on a PCA representation is added as a reference.

We can observe in Fig. 2(a) the importance of the independence assumption when using, both Naive Bayes and the divergence criterium. The CC-ICA representation, by seeking this independence, achieves much better results than all the other implementations. On this database we also tried Naive Bayes on 10000 random 8-feature combinations for each class, resulting that no combination achieved our classification results (83.17%).

A third experiment was performed in order to illustrate the performance of independent feature selection on high dimensional data. In this case 8-bin local color histograms (dimension=512) were extracted from different representative regions of 948 images belonging to the Corel Database [18]. The regions belong to ten different classes corresponding to clouds, grass, ice, leaves, rocky mountains, sand, sky, snow mountains, trees and water. A total of 40000 samples (histograms) were extracted, of which 30000 were used for training and the remaining for test. The number of class samples was equal among both traning and test sets. In all cases, the true class dimensionality was considerably below 512: classes have very restricted color variation. So the CC-ICA was performed after PCA dimensionality reduction (preserving 98.5% of the variance) and whitening. This technique is a frequent preprocessing stage for ICA [6]. The final dimensions for the class-conditional representations varied between 42 (ice) and 85 (leaves). Fig. 2(b) accounts for the results of Naive-Bayes classification using under various representations. As with the letter database, the CC-ICA scheme (17) outperforms the global representations notoriously for a low number of features. The performance of this method drops after 40 features, precisely the dimension of the least dimensional class. The answer to why PCA outperforms ICA for Naive-Bayes has to be found on the fact that independence does not imply conditional independence and the consequence this has over our feature selection criterion and the Naive-Bayes classifier. ORIG represents a K-NN classification on the original data using a mean Bhattacharyya distance for feature selection, and PCA-ML stands for Maximum Likelihood classification and is illustrated as a reference. This last drops to zero once the covariance matrix for a certain class becomes rank-defficient.

Accuracy results in (2(b)) are really not impressive: below 70% in the best case. This is due to the high confusion the class signatures (color). This is the reason why the average match percentile (AMP) is used to evaluate the results of this type of experiment, where a rank in the classification proves sufficient. The AMP for our best case (31 features) is 92.64%.

6   Conclusions

It has been shown that statistically independent features provide useful representations for the data in terms of interesting projections, as well as conditionally independent features greatly simplify pattern classification in terms of unidimensional density estimation. In this paper we show how (conditional) independence can also be useful for the problem of feature selection. Since independence is not usually encountered on real-world data we first provide a context where class-conditional independence can be assumed on stronger grounds (CC-ICA). In this context, it is known that the separability measure of divergence is reduced to a sum of unidimensional divergences. So we adapt this measure to the introduced context and specify the way it can be used as a feature selection criterion. We show that, under our assumptions, a feature subset of any cardinality can be found without involving any search procedure. We then focus on the problem of classification making use of the selected independent features. Even though, no assumption is made on the classification method, the assumption of independence is also useful for this stage. From a stochastic perspective, the maximum likelihood solution is actually the Naive Bayes solution. The three different experiments performed illustrate the robustness and performance of the introduced techniques on artificial, real-world benchmarked and high dimensional data, as well as comparing the results with alternative approaches.

The CC-ICA representation is still a linear approximation of a highly nonlinear problem, so actual independence is seldom achieved and the assumptions made for our method weakened. Even though, current research on nonlinear or overcomplete independent component analysis could eventually provide a framework where the exposed theory can be even more effectively put into practice. Another major inconvenient of our approach is the fact that ICA learning requires a large number of samples, particularly on high dimensional data so we need a large number of samples per class. When this condition is not met we cannot find trustable class conditional representations nor make any assumption on the divergence. Future research aims to evaluate the performance of alternative separability measures such as the JM distance or generalized Fisher ratio, also simplified in the context of independent features.

References

1. Dawid, A.P.: Conditional independence in statistical theory (with discussion). Journal of the Royal Statistical Society, Ser. B **41** (1979) 1–31
2. Simpson, E.: The interpretation of interaction in contingency tables. Journal of the Royal Statistical Society, Ser. B **13** (1951) 238–241
3. Bell, A., Sejnowski, T.: The 'independent components' of natural scenes are edge filters. Neural Computation **11** (1999) 1739–1768
4. Lee, T., Lewicki, M., Seynowski, T.: A mixture models for unsupervised classification of non-gaussian sources and automatic context switching in blind signal separation. IEEE Transactions on PAMI **22** (2000) 1–12
5. Vigario, R., Jousmäki, V., Hämäläinen, M., Hari, R., Oja, E.: Independent component analysis for identification of artifacts in magnetoencephalographic recordings. Advances in Neural Information Processing Systems **10** (1998) 229–235
6. Hyvärinen, A., Karhunen, J., Oja, E.: Independent Component Analysis. John Wiley and Sons (2001)
7. Comon, P.: Independent component analysis - a new concept? Signal Processing **36** (1994) 287–314
8. M.Bressan, D.Guillamet, J.Vitria: Using an ica representation of high dimensional data for object recognition and classification. In: IEEE CSC in Computer Vision and Pattern Recognition (CVPR 2001). Volume 1. (2001) 1004–1009
9. Marill, T., Green, D.: On the effectiveness of receptors in recognition systems. IEEE Trans. on Information Theory **9** (1963) 1–17
10. Kailath, T.: The divergence and bhattacharyya distance measures in signal selection. IEEE Trans. on Communication Technology COM-15 **1** (1967) 52–60
11. Swain, P., Davis, S.: Remote sensing: the quantitative approach. McGraw-Hill (1978)
12. Swain, P., King, R.: Two effective feature selection criteria for multispectral remote sensing. In: Proceedings of the 1st International Joint Conference on Pattern Recognition, IEEE 73 CHO821-9. (1973) 536–540
13. Duda, R., Hart, P., Stork, D.: Pattern Classication. John Wiley and Sons, Inc., New York, 2nd edition (2001)

14. Trunk, G.: A problem of dimensionality: A simple example. IEEE Trans. on Pattern Analysis and Machine Intelligence **1** (1979) 306–307
15. Jain, A.K., Zongker, D.E.: Feature selection: Evaluation, application, and small sample performance. IEEE Trans. on Pattern Analysis and Machine Intelligence **19** (1997) 153–158
16. Fukunaga, K.: Introduction to Statistical Pattern Recognition, Second Edition. Academic Press, Boston, MA (1990)
17. Blake, C., Merz, C.: Uci repository of machine learning databases (1998)
18. Corporation, C.: Corel stock photo library. Ontario, Canada (1990)

Validating Distance-Based Record Linkage with Probabilistic Record Linkage

Josep Domingo-Ferrer[1] and Vicenç Torra[2]

[1] Universitat Rovira i Virgili, Dept. of Computer Science and Mathematics,
Av. Països Catalans 26, 43007 Tarragona, Catalonia, Spain,
jdomingo@etse.urv.es
[2] Institut d'Investigació en Intel·ligència Artificial,
Campus de Bellaterra, 08193 Bellaterra, Catalonia, Spain
vtorra@iiia.csic.es

Abstract. This work compares two alternative methods for record linkage: distance based and probabilistic record linkage. It compares the performance of both approaches when data is categorical. To that end, a distance over ordinal and nominal scales is defined. The paper shows that, for categorical data, distance-based and probabilistic-based record linkage lead to similar results in relation to the number of re-identified records. As a consequence, the distance proposed for ordinal and nominal scales is implicitly validated.

1 Introduction

Re-identification procedures are tools developed to detect the presence of the same individual in different data files. Record linkage is a particular strategy for re-identification which links records in separate files that correspond to the same individual. While these procedures can be developed under various assumptions (see [4] and [9] for a detailed description of the alternative approaches: e.g. files share or not share variables; two or more files to be re-identified; types of the variables) we restrict here the work to the case of linking only two data files that share a set of variables.

Note that re-identification in the case of common variables is far from trivial because it is usually the case that a matching procedure among pairs of records is not enough to establish links between them. This is so due to the presence of errors in the files (the usual case).

In the case of re-identification assuming common variables, the two most successful re-identification methods are probabilistic record linkage and distance-based record linkage. [6] describes both approaches and includes a comparison for numerical data files. An alternative promising method based on clustering techniques is describe in [5]. The rationale of the latter proposal is similar to the one of [4].

In this work we focus on probabilistic and distance-based record linkage. The characteristics of these methods are as follows:

M.T. Escrig Monferrer and F. Toledo Lobo (Eds.): CCIA 2002, LNAI 2504, pp. 207–215, 2002.

Probabilistic record linkage: Probabilistic record linkage applied to files A and B is based on the computation of an index for each pair of records (r_A, r_B) where r_A and r_B are records of file A and B, respectively. Then, some index thresholds are used to label the pair as a linked pair (LP), a clerical pair (CP) or a non-linked pair (NP). A clerical pair is one that cannot be automatically classified as linked or non-linked; human inspection is needed to classify it.

To use probabilistic record linkage in an effective way, we need to set the thresholds (*e.g.* the values *linkThreshold* and *nonLinkThreshold*) and the conditional probabilities used in the computation of the indices. In plain words, thresholds are computed from: (i) the probability of linking a pair that is an unmatched pair (a *false positive* or *false linkage*) and (ii) the probability of not linking a pair that is a match pair (a *false negative* or *false unlinkage*). Conditional probabilities used for the indices are usually estimated using the EM algorithm [10].

For a detailed description of this method see [7], [8] and [2].

Distance-based record linkage: In general, for each record in file A, the distance to every record in file B is computed. Then the *nearest* record in file B is considered. A record in file B is labeled as *linked* when the nearest record in file A turns out to be its corresponding original record (the one that generated the distorted record). In all other cases, records are not linked. Details on this method are given in [11].

These two approaches are radically different. The following aspects can be underlined:

- Distance-based record linkage methods are simple to implement and to operate. The main difficulty consists of establishing appropriate distances for the variables under consideration. In particular, distances for categorical variables (in ordinal and nominal scales) are required. On the other hand, distance-based record linkage allows the inclusion of subjective information (about individuals or variables) in the re-identification process.
- Probabilistic record linkage methods are less simple. However, they do not assume rescaling or weighting of variables and require the user to provide only two probabilities as input: the probabilities of false positive and false negative.

For numerical data, it has been proven (see [6]) that both approaches lead to similar re-identification results. For categorical data, no comparison is available in the literature, probably because distances over categorical data are less straightforward than distances over numerical data.

In this work we consider two distances for categorical data (one for ordinal sccales and the other for nominal scales). We compare then probabilistic and distance-based record linkage. The comparison is based on extensive experimentation. Results show that the behavior of both approaches is similar as in the numerical case, and thus it validates the proposed distances.

The structure of the rest of this paper is as follows. In Section 2, we describe the methodology to compare both record linkage approaches. In particular, this section proposes distances for categorical data. Section 3 describe the results obtained and Section 4 contains some conclusions and mentions future work.

Table 1. Variables used in the analysis.

Variable	Meaning	u	l	s	m	o	N. Categ.
BUILT	year structure was built	X	X			X	25
DEGREE	long-term average degree days				X	X	8
GRADE1	highest school grade	X	X			X	21
METRO	metropolitan areas				X		9
SCH	schools adequate				X		6
SHP	shopping facilities adequate				X		6
TRAN1	means of transportation to work	X			X		12
WHYMOVE	primary reason for moving	X	X				18
WHYTOH	main reason for choice of house	X			X		13
WHYTON	id. for choosing this neighborhood	X			X		13

2   Methodological Considerations

To compare the probabilistic and distance-based re-identification methods, and due to the lack of benchmarks for this purpose, we have performed a set of experiments based on the ones used by National Statistical Offices to evaluate masking procedures and to determine the re-identification risk for a particular data file prior to its publication.

Thus, we have applied re-identification procedures between an original data file and some masked data files obtained through application of several masking methods on the original file. This is consistent with the methodology proposed in [6] for the case of continuous variables.

Several re-identification experiments were performed in order to mitigate the dependency of results on a single dataset. Thus, different sets of variables, different masking methods and different method parameterizations were considered. In this section, we detail the experiments obtained so far. We first describe the original data file used (a publicly available data file). Then, we describe how masking methods were applied to obtain different masked data files. We then propose some distances for categorical. Results of the experiments are reported in the next section.

2.1   Test Data Collection

Data from the *American Housing Survey 1993* were used (these data can be obtained from the U.S. Census Bureau using the Data Extraction System at http://www.census.gov/DES/www/welcome.html). A set of 10 categorical variables (see Table 1). Five groups of variables were defined over the set of selected variables, and the same analysis was performed for each of them. First, three groups were defined by grouping variables with a similar number of categories. Let 's', 'm' and 'l' denote the groups of variables with small, medium and large number of categories, respectively. A fourth group denoted by 'u' was defined that corresponds to the union of the groups 'm' and 'l'; thus, 'u' corresponds to the group of variables with medium or large number of categories. Finally, a fifth group 'o' was defined as the subset of ordered variables (variables that range in an ordinal scale). This latter group was defined after analyzing the meaning of each category in the range of variables. Table 1 gives for each variable, in which groups is present and also the number of categories.

To allow a substantial amount of experiments in reasonable time, we took only the first 1000 records from the corresponding data file.

2.2   Generation of File Pairs for Re-identification

The generation of pairs of files to perform re-identification was achieved by masking the original data file. Each pair was formed by the original data set and one masked version of it. To generate masked versions of the original data, several masking methods were applied to the original 1000-record file containing the 10 variables in Table 1. Four masking methods were considered and for each one nine different parameterizations were applied. Masking methods were selected among those commonly used by National Statistical Offices to protect data files. Different parameterizations were taken so that different levels of data protection were experimented with. The consideration of both aspects led to $4 * 9 = 36$ different masked data files.

The following masking methods were considered (see [13] for a detailed description of masking methods): Top and Bottom coding, Global recording and PRAM (Post-Randomization Method). 9 different parameterizations (with parameter $p = 1, \cdots, 9$ – the larger the p, the larger the distortion) where considered for each method. The application of these four masking methods above with nine different parameterizations per method led to 36 different masked data files.

2.3   Re-identification Experiments

For each record linkage method (probabilistic record linkage and distance-based record linkage) and for each pair of *(original-file, masked-file)*, five re-identification experiments were performed. More specifically, each of the five experiments corresponded to one of the five groups of variables 'u', 'l', 's', 'm' and 'o' defined in Table 1. Since there were 36 different file pairs, 36*5=180 re-identification experiments were performed for each record linkage method.

The implementation of probabilistic record linkage used in the experimentation was the U.S. Census Bureau software provided by W. Winkler [15], [3] with some additions. The EM algorithm was used for the estimation of the probabilities. The implementation of distance-based record linkage was especially written

Table 2. Re-identification results for the 's' group of variables using probabilistic (left) and distance-based (right) record linkage

parameter	Bottom	Global	PRAM	Top	Bottom	Global	PRAM	Top
1	1000	1000	966	1000	502	986	978	853
2	699	1000	921	891	263	861	938	617
3	577	917	897	749	176	651	916	447
4	447	730	881	493	101	326	905	200
5	279	835	843	429	66	103	882	95
6	161	695	803	458	43	83	828	78
7	79	355	789	688	36	9	792	42
8	51	51	759	45	3	3	780	42
9	51	51	734	188	3	3	753	42

in C for the experimental work reported in this paper. An essential point was to define a distance for categorical variables, which was done as follows:

Definition 1. *1. For a nominal variable V, the only permitted operation is comparison for equality. This leads to the following distance definition:*

$$d_V(c, c') = \begin{cases} 0 \text{ if } c = c' \\ 1 \text{ if } c \neq c' \end{cases}$$

where c and c' correspond to categories for variable V.

2. For an ordinal variable V, let $\leq_V$ be the total order operator over the range of V. Then, the distance between categories c and c' is defined as the number of categories between the minimum and the maximum of c and c' divided by the cardinality of the range (denoted by $D(V)$):

$$d_V(c, c') = \frac{|c'' : min(c, c') \leq_V c'' \leq_V max(c, c')|}{|D(V)|}$$

The distance for pairs of records was computed assuming equal weight for all variables.

3   Results

Results of both re-identification procedures turn out to be similar. In Tables 2-6, the number of correctly re-identified records is displayed for the groups of variables (PRL is the probabilistic based record linkage and DBRL corresponds to distance-based one. It can be seen that for some of the experiments (some particular combination of masking method and parameterization), PRL lead to better results than DBRL and that for some of the experiments is DBRL which performs best.

The average number of re-identified records per experiment was computed as a measure of similarity between both record linkage methods. The following expression was used:

Table 3. PRL (left) and DBRL (right) results for the 'm' group

parameter	Bottom	Global	PRAM	Top	Bottom	Global	PRAM	Top
1	195	118	118	114	722	995	1000	966
2	448	104	117	88	372	984	997	878
3	428	93	114	74	340	967	997	836
4	410	83	115	54	332	917	994	805
5	386	93	109	52	323	802	990	797
6	372	148	101	38	313	493	985	758
7	367	448	96	77	302	243	981	503
8	367	576	102	356	272	202	980	275
9	593	559	98	325	156	167	981	255

$$\frac{\sum \text{number of correct re} - \text{identifications}}{\text{number of experiments}}$$

For distance-based record linkage, an average number of 593.06 re-identified records (over 1000) was obtained. For probabilistic record linkage, the average was 579.32 re-identified records. Thus, the performance of both methods is similar.

Note 1. It is important to point out that, even though both methods yields similar average numbers of re-identified records, the re-identified records are not the same. Furthermore, it can be seen e.g. in Tables 3 and 4 that, for a particular masking method, parameterization and set of variables, not even the number of re-identified records is similar for both approaches. Therefore, both record linkage methods should be regarded as complementary rather than as antagonistic.

Note 2. Distance-based record linkage seems to perform better for PRAM masked data while probabilistic record linkage seems to perform better for the other masking methods. As PRAM is the only non-deterministic masking method, seems that for the re-identification of data with stochastic errors, distance based record linkage is more appropriate.

Additional analyses have been carried to assess the performance of both record linkage methods ([9] describe correlation statistics between the number of correctly re-identified records and some information loss measures). These results also show that both approaches to re-identification lead to similar results.

In the experiments reported in this paper, no information is fed to record linkage procedures about the masking method applied to protect the original file. In fact, this is not the usual case in disclosure risk assessment. It can be proven that, if a distance is used which takes into account the masking method applied, the distance-based record linkage largely improves its results. A simple way for a distance to take masking into account is as follows: assign a distance *infinity* when category c cannot be recoded as c' using the current masking method. In this case, the average number of correctly re-identified records increases to 663.49, which should be compared to 593.06 for the original distance-based record linkage and to 579.32 for probabilistic record linkage.

Table 4. PRL (left) and DBRL (right) results for the 'u' group

parameter	Bottom	Global	PRAM	Top	Bottom	Global	PRAM	Top
1	530	415	414	389	572	994	986	906
2	799	402	411	318	352	899	956	746
3	828	380	438	280	225	767	943	589
4	824	379	421	246	171	556	939	357
5	691	385	413	233	126	355	914	259
6	690	464	402	190	92	226	896	179
7	666	882	378	266	68	68	880	105
8	570	856	391	509	22	23	877	58
9	598	782	387	425	11	9	849	50

Table 5. PRL (left) and DBRL (right) results for the 'o' group

parameter	Bottom	Global	PRAM	Top	Bottom	Global	PRAM	Top
1	1000	999	988	1000	876	965	987	925
2	932	993	952	914	746	912	970	793
3	749	962	936	783	570	815	925	652
4	553	833	909	574	442	711	917	473
5	428	685	906	404	309	563	877	338
6	357	518	865	350	265	423	861	261
7	318	295	853	386	213	240	862	244
8	329	300	829	440	186	215	848	207
9	305	338	801	398	169	197	833	177

4   Conclusions and Future Work

Two record linkage methods for re-identification of categorical microdata have been studied in this paper: probabilistic and distance-based. Since distance-based record linkage only existed in the literature for numerical data, a distance for categorical data has been defined to extend this kind of linkage to categorical data. We have shown that the number of re-identifications is similar for both record linkage procedures, but that the re-identified individuals/records are not the same. This is consistent with existing comparisons of both record linkage methods for numerical data. Beyond implicit validation of the proposed distance for categorical data, results in this paper show that both methods are complementary rather than antagonistic and best results are obtained if they are combined.

Table 6. PRL (left) and DBRL (right) results for the 'l' group

parameter	Bottom	Global	PRAM	Top	Bottom	Global	PRAM	Top
1	1000	999	997	997	952	996	992	970
2	993	997	993	968	937	992	985	909
3	992	993	980	950	921	969	973	874
4	983	986	975	917	907	946	973	825
5	954	979	976	862	740	912	964	772
6	936	934	967	798	723	863	975	716
7	889	894	959	730	686	824	958	661
8	826	844	961	676	608	753	960	554
9	780	785	948	571	568	687	953	476

It has also been pointed out that distance-based record linkage can substantially improve (and thus outperform probabilistic record linkage) if information about the masking method is embedded into the distance function.

Future refinements of distance-based record linkage is to give a different weight to each variable when computing the distance. This would be problem-dependent and would require a learning mechanism to adjust weights beforehand.

Acknowledgments. Partial support of the European Community under the contract "CASC" IST-2000-25069 and of the CICYT under the project "STREAMOBILE" (TIC2001-0633-C03-01/02) is acknowledged.

References

1. L. Sweeney, "Information explosion", in *Confidentiality, Disclosure, and Data Access: Theory and Practical Applications for Statistical Agencies*, eds. P. Doyle, J. I. Lane, J. M. Theeuwes and L. M. Zayatz, Elsevier, 43–74, 2001.
   H. B. Newcombe, J. M. Kennedy, S. J. Axford and A. P. James, "Automatic linkage of vital records", *Science*, vol. 130, 954–959, 1959.
2. W. E. Winkler, "Matching and record linkage", in *Business Survey Methods*,ed. B. G. Cox, Wiley, 355–384, 1995.
   J. F. Robinson-Cox,"A record-linkage approach to imputation of missing data: analyzing tag retention in a tag-recapture experiment", *Journal of Agricultural, Biological and Environmental Statistics*, vol. 3, 48–61, 1998.

3. W. E. Winkler, "Advanced methods for record linkage", *Proc. of the American Statistical Assoc. Section on Survey Research Methods*, 467–472, 1995.
4. V. Torra, "Towards the re-identification of individuals in data files with non-common variables", in *Proceedings of ECAI'2000*, 326–330.
   V. Torra, "Re-identifying individuals using OWA operators", *Proceedings of the 6th Intl. Conference on Soft Computing*, Iizuka, Fukuoka, Japan, 2000.
5. J. Bacher, S. Bender and R. Brand, "Empirical re-identification – Evaluation of a simple clustering technique", *Intl. Journal of Uncertainty, Fuzziness and Knowledge-Based Systems*, forthcomming.
6. J. Domingo-Ferrer and V. Torra, "A quantitative comparison of disclosure control methods for microdata", in *Confidentiality, Disclosure, and Data Access: Theory and Practical Applications for Statistical Agencies*, eds. P. Doyle, J. I. Lane, J. M. Theeuwes, L. M. Zayatz, Elsevier, 111–133, 2001.
7. I. P. Fellegi and A. B. Sunter, "A theory of record linkage", *Journal of the American Statistical Association*, vol. 64, 1183–1210, 1969.
8. M. A. Jaro, "Advances in record-linkage methodology as applied to matching the 1985 Census of Tampa, Florida", *Journal of the American Statistical Association*, vol. 84, 414–420, 1989.
9. J. Domingo-Ferrer, V. Torra, Distance-based and probabilistic record linkage for re-identification of records with categorical variables, *Butlletí de l'ACIA*, 27, 2002.
10. A. P. Dempster, N. N. Laird and D. B. Rubin, "Maximum likelihood from incomplete data via the EM algorithm", *Journal of the Royal Statistical Society*, vol. 39, 1–38, 1977.
11. D. Pagliuca and G. Seri, *Some Results of Individual Ranking Method on the System of Enterprise Accounts Annual Survey*, Esprit SDC Project, Deliverable MI-3/D2, 1999.
12. F. Felsö, J. Theeuwes and G. G. Wagner, "Disclosure limitation methods in use: results of a survey", in *Confidentiality, Disclosure, and Data Access: Theory and Practical Applications for Statistical Agencies*, eds. P. Doyle, J. I. Lane, J. M. Theeuwes and L. M. Zayatz, Elsevier, 17–42, 2001.
13. L. Willenborg and T. de Waal, *Elements of Statistical Disclosure Control*, Springer-Verlag, 2001.
14. P. Kooiman, L. Willenborg and J. Gouweleeuw, *PRAM: A Method for Disclosure Limitation of Microdata*, Research Report, Voorburg NL: Statistics Netherlands, 1998.
15. U. S. Bureau of the Census, *Record Linkage Software: User Documentation*. Available from U. S. Bureau of the Census, 2000.

Evaluating Feature Selection Algorithms

Luis Carlos Molina, Lluís Belanche, and Àngela Nebot

Universitat Politècnica de Catalunya
Departament de Llenguatges i Sistemes Informàtics
Jordi Girona 1-3, Campus Nord C6-201,
08034, Barcelona, Spain.
{lcmolina,belanche,angela}@lsi.upc.es

Abstract. In view of the substantial number of existing feature selection algorithms, the need arises to count on criteria that enables to adequately decide which algorithm to use in certain situations. In this work a step is made is this direction by assessing the performance of several fundamental algorithms in a controlled scenario. A scoring measure ranks the algorithms by taking into account the amount of relevance, irrelevance and redundance on sample data sets of varying sizes. This measure computes the degree of coincidence between the output given by the algorithm and the known optimal solution.

1 Introduction

A feature selection algorithm (FSA) is a computational solution that is motivated by a certain definition of *relevance*. The generic purpose pursued is the improvement of the inductive learner, either in terms of learning speed, generalization capacity or simplicity of the representation. However, the relevance of a feature –as seen from the inductive learning perspective– may have several definitions depending on the objective that is looked for [1]. An irrelevant feature should not be useful for induction, but not all relevant features are necessarily useful for induction [2]. The notion of relevance has not yet been rigorously justified on a common agreement [3].

The FSAs can be classified according to the kind of output they yield: (1) those algorithms giving a (weighed) linear order of features and (2) those algorithms giving a subset of the original features. Both types can be seen in an unified way by noting that in (2) the weighting is binary.

A FSA should be seen as a computational approximation corresponding to a precise definition of relevance. The *continuous* feature selection problem then refers to the assignment of weights w_i to each feature $x_i \in X$ in such a way that the order corresponding to its theoretical relevance is preserved. The *binary* feature selection problem refers to the assignment of binary weights. This can be carried out directly (like many FSAs in machine learning [4,5]), or *filtering* the output of the continuous problem solution.

In this research, several fundamental algorithms found in the literature are studied to assess their performance in a controlled scenario. To this end, a measure to evaluate FSAs is proposed that takes into account the particularities

M.T. Escrig Monferrer and F. Toledo Lobo (Eds.): CCIA 2002, LNAI 2504, pp. 216–227, 2002.
© Springer-Verlag Berlin Heidelberg 2002

of relevance, irrelevance and redundance on the sample data set. This measure computes the degree of matching between the output given by a FSA and the known optimal solution. Sample size effects are also studied. The results illustrate the strong dependence on the particular conditions of the FSA used and on the amount of irrelevance and redundance in the data set description, relative to the total number of features.

The paper is organized as follows: in section 2 the feature selection problem is reviewed and the main characteristics of a FSA are presented in an unified framework. In section 3 the aspects of the experimental evaluation are set forth as well as an *scoring* criterion to evaluate the performance of different algorithms. In section 4 the specific algorithms used in this study are described together with the experimental methodology. Finally, in section 5 the obtained results are shown and discussed. The paper ends with the conclusions about the knowledge gained.

2   Feature Selection

Let X be the original set of features, with cardinality $|X| = n$. Let $J(X')$ be an evaluation measure to be optimized (say to maximize) defined as $J : X' \subseteq X \to \mathbb{R}$. The selection of a feature subset can be seen under three considerations:

- Set $|X'| = m < n$. Find $X' \subset X$, such that $J(X')$ is maximum.
- Set a value J_o, this is, the minimum J that is going to be tolerated. Find the $X' \subseteq X$ with smaller $|X'|$, such that $J(X') \geq J_o$.
- Find a compromise among minimizing $|X'|$ and maximizing $J(X')$ (general case).

Notice that, with these definitions, an optimal subset of features is not necessarily unique.

2.1   Characterization of a FSA

There exist in the literature several considerations to characterize feature selection algorithms [1,6,7]. In view of them it is possible to describe this characterization as a search problem in the hypothesis space as follows:

Search Organization: General strategy with which the space of hypothesis is explored. This strategy is in relation to the portion of hypothesis explored with respect to their total number. Three categories can be distinguished: *exponential* $O(2^n)$, *sequential* $O(n^k)$ and *random*.

Generation of Successors: Mechanism by which possible variants (successor candidates) of the current hypothesis are proposed. In this case up to five categories can be distinguished: *forward, backward, compound, weighting* and *random*.

Evaluation Measure: Function by which successor candidates are evaluated, allowing to *compare* different hypothesis to guide the search process. These may be classified into: *distance*, *dependence*, *information*, *consistency*, *accuracy* and *divergence* measures.

All FSA can be represented in a space of characteristics according to the criteria of: search organization (Org), generation of successor states (GS) and evaluation measures (J). This space <Org, GS, J> encompasses the whole spectrum of possibilities for a FSA [8]. New proposals for evaluation measures (not expressible as a combination of the already existent) would extend the vertical axis. Notice that the search organization and the generation of successor states are coordinates whose elements are, in principle, exclusive of each other, in the sense that a certain FSA will use only one combination organization/generation. We then speak of a *hybrid* FSA when it requires more than a point in the same coordinate to be characterized. This is unusual in the literature, although recent works seem to point in this direction [9].

3   Empirical Evaluation

The first question arising in relation to a feature selection experimental design is: what are the aspects that we would like to evaluate of a FSA solution in a given data set? In this study we decided to evaluate FSA performance with respect to four particularities: relevance, irrelevance, redundance and sample size. To this end, several fundamental FSAs are studied to assess their performance on synthetic data sets with known relevant features. Then sample data sets of different sizes are corrupted with irrelevant and/or redundant features. The experiments are designed to test the *endurance* of different FSAs (e.g., behaviour against the ratio number-of-irrelevant vs. number-of-relevant features).

3.1   Particularities to Be Evaluated

Relevance: Different families of problems are generated by varying the number of relevant features N_R. These are features that, by construction, have an influence on the output and whose role can not be assumed by the rest (i.e., there is no redundance).

Irrelevance: Irrelevant features are defined as those features not having any influence on the output, and whose values are generated at random for each example. For a problem with N_R relevant features, different numbers of irrelevant features N_I are added to the corresponding data sets (thus providing with several subproblems for each choice of N_R).

Redundance: In these experiments, a redundance exists whenever a feature can take the role of another (perhaps the simplest way to model redundance). This is obtained by choosing a relevant feature randomly and replicating it in the data set. For a problem with N_R relevant features, different numbers of redundant features $N_{R'}$ are added in a way analogous to the generation of irrelevant features.

Sample Size: It refers to the number of instances $|S|$ of a data sample S. In these experiments, it is defined as $|S| = \alpha k N_T c$, where α is a constant, k is a multiplying factor, N_T is the total number of features $(N_R + N_I + N_{R'})$ and c is the number of classes of the problem. Note this means that the sample size will depend linearly on the total number of features.

3.2 Evaluation of Performance

The *score* criterion expresses the degree to which a solution obtained by a FSA matches the correct solution. This criterion behaves as a similarity $s(x, y)$: $X \times X \rightarrow [0, 1]$ in the classical sense [10], satisfying:

1. $s(x, y) = 1 \Longleftrightarrow x = y$
2. $s(x, y) = s(y, x)$

where $s(x, y) > s(x, z)$ indicates that y is more similar to x than z is.

Let us denote by X the total set of features, partitioned in $X = X_R \cup X_I \cup X_{R'}$, being $X_R, X_I, X_{R'}$ the subsets of relevant, irrelevant and redundant features of X, respectively and call $X^* \subseteq X$ the ideal solution. Let us denote by $\mathcal{A}$ the feature subset selected by a FSA. The idea is to check how much $\mathcal{A}$ and X^* have in common. Let us define $\mathcal{A}_R = X_R \cap \mathcal{A}$, $\mathcal{A}_I = X_I \cap \mathcal{A}$ and $\mathcal{A}_{R'} = X_{R'} \cap \mathcal{A}$. In general, we have $\mathcal{A}_T = X_T \cap \mathcal{A}$ (hereafter T stands for a subindex in $\{R, I, R'\}$). Since necessarily $\mathcal{A} \subseteq X$, we have $\mathcal{A} = \mathcal{A}_R \cup \mathcal{A}_I \cup \mathcal{A}_{R'}$. The *score* $S_X(\mathcal{A})$: $P(X) \rightarrow [0, 1]$ will fulfill the following conditions:

- $S_X(\mathcal{A}) = 0 \Longleftrightarrow \mathcal{A} = X_I$
- $S_X(\mathcal{A}) = 1 \Longleftrightarrow \mathcal{A} = X^*$
- $S_X(\mathcal{A}) > S_X(\mathcal{A}')$ indicates that $\mathcal{A}$ is more similar to X^* than $\mathcal{A}'$.

The score is defined in terms of the similarity in that for all $\mathcal{A} \subseteq X, S_X(\mathcal{A}) = s(\mathcal{A}, X^*)$. This scoring measure will also be parameterized, so that it can ponder each type of divergence (in relevance, irrelevance and redundance) to the optimal solution. The set of parameters is expressed as $\alpha = \{\alpha_R, \alpha_I, \alpha_{R'}\}$ with $\alpha_T \geq 0$ and $\sum \alpha_T = 1$.

Intuitive Description
The criterion $S_X(\mathcal{A})$ penalizes three situations:

1. There are relevant features lacking in $\mathcal{A}$ (the solution is incomplete).
2. There are more than enough relevant features in $\mathcal{A}$ (the solution is redundant).
3. There are some irrelevant features in $\mathcal{A}$ (the solution is incorrect).

An order of importance and a weight will be assigned (via the α_T parameters), to each of these situations.

Formal Description
The precedent point (3.) is simple to model: if suffices to check whether $|\mathcal{A}_I| > 0$, being $\mathcal{A}$ the solution of the FSA. Relevance and redundance are strongly related

given that, in this context, a feature is relevant or not depending on what other relevant features are present in $\mathcal{A}$.

Notice then that the optimal solution X^* is not unique, though all of them should be equally valid for the *score*. To this end, the features are broken down in *equivalence classes*, where elements of the same class are redundant to each other (i.e., any optimal solution must comprise only one feature of each equivalence class).

Being $\mathcal{A}$ a feature set, we define a binary relation between two features $x_i, x_j \in \mathcal{A}$ as: $x_i \sim x_j \iff x_i$ and x_j represent the same information. Clearly $\sim$ is an equivalence relation. Let $\mathcal{A}^\sim$ be the quotient set of $\mathcal{A}$ under $\sim$, that is $\mathcal{A}^\sim = \{[x] \mid x \in \mathcal{A}\}$; any optimal solution $\mathcal{A}^*$ will satisfy:

1. $|\mathcal{A}^*| = |X_R|$
2. $\forall [x_i] \in \mathcal{A}^\sim : \exists x_j \in [x_i] : x_j \in \mathcal{A}^*$

We denote by $\mathcal{A}^*$ *any* of these solutions.

Construction of the *Score*

In the present case, the set to be split in equivalence classes is formed by all the relevant features (redundant or not) chosen by a FSA. We define then:

$$\mathcal{A}_R^\sim = (\mathcal{A}_R \cup \mathcal{A}_{R'})^\sim$$

(equivalence classes in which the relevant features chosen by a FSA are split)

$$X_R^\sim = (X_R \cup X_{R'})^\sim$$

(equivalence classes in which the original set of features is split)

Let $\mathcal{A}_R^\sim \uplus X_R^\sim = \{[x_i] \in X_R^\sim \mid \exists [x_j] \in \mathcal{A}_R^\sim : [x_j] \subseteq [x_i]\}$ and define, for Q quotient set:

$$F(Q) = \sum_{[x] \in Q} (|x| - 1)$$

The idea is to express the *quotient* between the number of redundant features chosen by the FSA and the number it could have chosen, given the relevant features present in its solution. In the precedent notation, this is written (provided the denominator is not null):

$$\frac{F(\mathcal{A}_R^\sim)}{F(\mathcal{A}_R^\sim \uplus X_R^\sim)}$$

Let us finally build the *score*, formed by three terms: relevance, irrelevance and redundance. Defining:

$$I = 1 - \frac{|\mathcal{A}_I|}{|X_I|}, \qquad R = \frac{|\mathcal{A}_R^\sim|}{|X_R|}, \quad \text{with } \mathcal{A}_R^\sim = (\mathcal{A}_R \cup \mathcal{A}_{R'})^\sim$$

$$R' = \begin{cases} 0 & \text{if } F(\mathcal{A}_{\tilde{R}} \uplus X_{\tilde{R}}) = 0 \\ \frac{1}{|X_{R'}|}\left(1 - \frac{F(\mathcal{A}_{\tilde{R}})}{F(\mathcal{A}_{\tilde{R}} \uplus X_{\tilde{R}})}\right) & \text{otherwise.} \end{cases}$$

for any $\mathcal{A} \subseteq X$ the score is defined as $S_X(\mathcal{A}) = \alpha_R R + \alpha_{R'} R' + \alpha_I I$.

Restrictions on the α_T

We can establish now the desired restrictions on the behavior of the score. From the more to the less severe: there are relevant features lacking, there are irrelevant features, and there is redundancy in the solution. This is reflected in the following conditions on the α_T:

1. Choosing an irrelevant feature is better than missing a relevant one:
   $\frac{\alpha_R}{|X_R|} > \frac{\alpha_I}{|X_I|}$
2. Choosing a redundant feature is better than choosing an irrelevant one:
   $\frac{\alpha_I}{|X_I|} > \frac{\alpha_{R'}}{|X_{R'}|}$

We also define $\alpha_T = 0$ if $|X_T| = 0$. Notice that the denominators are important for, as an example, expressing the fact that it is not the same choosing an irrelevant feature when there were only two that when there were three (in the latter case, there is an irrelevant feature that could have been chosen when it was not).

Practical Considerations

In order to translate the previous inequalities into workable conditions, a parameter $\epsilon \in (0, 1]$ can be introduced to express the exact relation between the α_T. Let $\underline{\alpha}_T = \frac{\alpha_T}{|A_T|}$. The following two equations have to be satisfied:

$$\beta_R \underline{\alpha}_R = \underline{\alpha}_I, \qquad \beta_I \underline{\alpha}_I = \underline{\alpha}_{R'}$$

for suitable chosen values of β_R and β_I. In this work we take $\beta_R = \epsilon/2$ and $\beta_I = 2\epsilon/3$. This means that, at equal $|A_R|, |A_I|, |A_{R'}|$, α_R is at least twice more important than α_I (because of the $\epsilon/2$) and α_I is at least one and a half times more important than $\alpha_{R'}$. Specifically, the minimum values are attained for $\epsilon = 1$ (i.e., α_R counts twice α_I). For $\epsilon < 1$ the differences widen proportionally to the point that, for $\epsilon \approx 0$, only $\alpha_R R$ will count on the overall score.

4   Experimental Evaluation

In this section we detail the experimental methodology and quantify the various parameters of the experiments. The basic idea consists on generating sample data sets with known particularities (synthetic functions f) and hand them over to the different FSAs to obtained a hypothesis H. The divergence between the defined function and the obtained hypothesis will be evaluated by the *score* criterion. This experimental design is illustrated in Fig. 1.

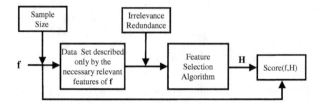

Fig. 1. FlowChart of the Experimental Design.

4.1   Description of the Used FSAs

The ten FSAs used in the experiments were : E-SFG, QBB, LVF, LVI, C-SBG, RELIEF, W-SBG, W-SFG (see [7]), SFBG and SFFG [11] (Table 1). The algorithms E-SFG, W-SFG are versions of SFG using entropy and the accuracy of a C4.5 inducer, respectively. The algorithms C-SBG, W-SBG are versions of SBG using consistency and the accuracy of a C4.5 inducer, respectively. During the course of the experiments the algorithms FOCUS, B&B, ABB and LVW (see [7]) were put aside due to their unaffordable consumption of resources.

Table 1. FSAs used in the experiments.

Algorithm	Search Organization	Generation of Succesors	Evaluation Measure
LVF	Random	Random	Consistency
LVI	Random	Random	Consistency
QBB	Random/Expon.	Random/Backward	Consistency
RELIEF	Random	Weighting	Distance
C-SBG	Sequential	Backward	Consistency
E-SFG	Sequential	Forward	Entropy
SFBG	Exponential	Compound	Consistency
SFFG	Exponential	Compound	Consistency
W-SBG	Sequential	Backward	Accuracy(C4.5)
W-SFG	Sequential	Forward	Accuracy(C4.5)

4.2   Modifications to the FSA

For purposes of comparison, some modifications were performed to the FSAs, without affecting the nucleus of each algorithm. On the other hand, a filtering criterion was established to binarize the outputs of the algorithms that give a linear order of features.

Resource: We consider that all the FSAs should have approximately the same opportunities to compete, in what regards the computational resources. This means the exponential algorithms can be finished before its natural stopping condition. In our case, this only happens to the QBB algorithm, which may be forced to give the best solution obtained until that moment. For the case of LVI, it should be pointed out that only 50% (on average) of the data set is sampled, so that double resources are assigned.

Filtering Criterion: Since RELIEF and E-SFG give as output an ordered list of features x_i according to their weight w_i, a filtering criterion is necessary to transform this solution to a subset of features. The procedure used here is simple: since the interest is in determining a good cut point, first those w_i further than two variances from the mean are discarded (that is to say, with very high or very low weights). Then define $s_i = w_i + w_{i-1}$ and $\sigma_j = \sum_{i=2}^{j} s_i$. The objective is to search for the feature x_j such that:

$$1 - \frac{\sigma_j}{\sigma_n} \frac{n-j}{n} \quad \text{is maximum.}$$

The cut point is then set between x_j and x_{j+1}.

4.3   Implementations of Data Families

A total of twelve families of data sets were generated studying three different problems and four instances of each, by varying the number of relevant features N_R. Let $x_1, \ldots, x_n$ be the relevant features of a problem f. The selected problems are:

Parity: This is the classic binary problem of parity n, where the output is $f(x_1, \cdots, x_n) = 1$ if the number of $x_i = 1$ is odd and $f(x_1, \cdots, x_n) = 0$ otherwise.

Disjunction: A disjunctive task, with $f(x_1, \cdots, x_n) = 1$ if $(x_1 \wedge \cdots \wedge x_{n'}) \vee (x_{n'+1} \wedge \cdots \wedge x_n)$, with $n' = n \operatorname{div} 2$ if n is even and $n' = (n \operatorname{div} 2) + 1$ if n is odd.

GMonks: This problem is a generalization of the classic *monks* problems [12]. In its original version, three independent problems were applied on sets of $n = 6$ features that take values of a discrete, finite and unordered set (nominal features). Here we have grouped the three problems in a single one computed on *each* segment of 6 features. Let n be multiple of 6, $k = n \operatorname{div} 6$ and $b = 6(k' - 1) + 1$, for $1 \leq k' \leq k$. Let us denote by '1' the first value of a feature, by '2' the second, etc. The problems are the following:

1. $P_1 : (x_b = x_{b+1}) \vee x_{b+4} = 1$
2. $P_2 :$ two or more $x_i = 1$ in $x_b \cdots x_{b+5}$
3. $P_3 : (x_{b+4} = 3 \wedge x_{b+3} = 1) \vee (x_{b+4} \neq 3 \wedge x_{b+1} \neq 2)$

For each segment, the boolean condition $P_2 \wedge \neg(P_1 \wedge P_3)$ is checked. If this condition is satisfied for s or more segments with $s = n_s \operatorname{div} 2$ (being n_s the number of segments) the function *GMonks* is 1; otherwise, it is 0.

4.4   Experimental Setup

The experiments were divided in three groups. The first group refers to the relationship between irrelevance vs. relevance. The second refers to the relationship between redundance vs. relevance. The last group refers to sample size. Each group uses three families of problems (*Parity*, *Disjunction* and *GMonks*) with four different instances for each problem, varying the number of relevant features N_R.

Relevance: The different numbers N_R vary for each problem, as follows: {4, 8, 16, 32} (for *Parity*), {5, 10, 15, 20} (for *Disjunction*) and {6, 12, 18, 24} (for *GMonks*).

Irrelevance: In these experiments, we have N_I running from 0 to 2 times the value of N_R, in intervals of 0.2 (that is, eleven different experiments of irrelevance for each N_R).

Redundance: Similarly to the generation of irrelevant features, we have $N_{R'}$ running from 0 to 2 times the value of N_R, in intervals of 0.2.

Sample Size: Given the formula $|S| = \alpha k N_T c$ (see §3.1), different problems were generated considering $k \in \{0.25, 0.5, 0.75, 1.0, 1.25, 1.75, 2.0\}$, $N_T = N_R + N_I + N_{R'}$, $c = 2$ and $\alpha = 20$. The values of N_I and $N_{R'}$ were fixed as $N_I = N_{R'} = N_R \, div \, 2$.

5   Results

A sample of the results is presented in Fig. 2. In all the plots, each point represents the average of 10 independent runs with different random data samples. The Figs. 2 (a), (b) and (c) are examples of irrelevance vs. relevance for four instances of the problems, (d) is an example of redundance vs. relevance and (e) and (f) are examples of sample size experiments. In all cases, the horizontal axis represents the ratios between these particularities as explained above. The vertical axis represents the average results given by the score criterion.

In Fig. 2 (a) the results of the algorithm C-SBG can be appreciated for the four instances of the *Parity* problem. In this case, the algorithm shows excellent performance for N_{R_4} (note the performance curve is on top of the graphic). However, it rapidly degrades for increasing numbers of irrelevant features.

In Fig. 2 (b) it can be observed that the algorithm W-SBG is in general more robust than the previous C-SBG, although it still shows a definite downward trend in performance both for increasing problem sizes and for increasing ratios N_I/N_R. Fig. 2 (c) illustrates one of the salient characteristics of RELIEF, namely its robustness against irrelevance.

In what concerns redundance, Fig. 2 (d) shows the way it affects an algorithm, in this case C-SBG. It can be seen how increasing problem sizes do affect performance, though to a lesser extent than irrelevance (compare to Fig. 2(a)).

In Fig. 2(e), the *curse of dimensionality* can be appreciated [13]. In this figure, LVI presents an increasingly poor performance (see the figure from top

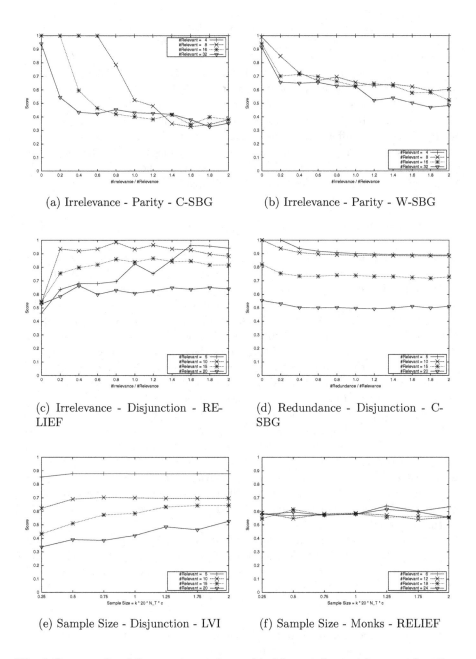

(a) Irrelevance - Parity - C-SBG

(b) Irrelevance - Parity - W-SBG

(c) Irrelevance - Disjunction - RE-LIEF

(d) Redundance - Disjunction - C-SBG

(e) Sample Size - Disjunction - LVI

(f) Sample Size - Monks - RELIEF

Fig. 2. Some results of the experiments in graphical format. See text for an explanation.

to bottom) with the number of features, provided the number of examples is being increased in a linear way. However, in general, as long as more examples are added, performance is better (see the figure from left to right). However, in

Fig. 2(f), the algorithm RELIEF shows a very stable performance (though only a fair one) in the same conditions for a more difficult problem.

The overall results (not shown) indicate that, in the case of *irrelevance vs. relevance*, the algorithms SFFG, RELIEF and W-SFG have a good performance for the majority of the experiments of this group. In the case of *redundance vs. relevance*, the results present the algorithms LVF, C-SBG, QBB, SFBG and SFFG as the overall best. Regarding the sample size experiments, the aim was to find out which algorithms suffer more drastic changes in performance when the sample size increases or decreases. In this respect, it can be observed that the algorithms W-SFG, SFFG, RELIEF and QBB look more stable than the rest, in the sense that their performance is less affected by these changes.

6   Conclusions

In this work, a way to evaluate feature selection algorithms (FSA) has been proposed in order to understand their general behavior on the particularities of relevance, irrelevance, redundancy and sample size on synthetic data sets. To achieve this goal, a set of controlled experiments using artificially generated data sets is designed and carried out. The set of optimal solutions is then compared with the output given by the FSAs (the obtained hypotheses). To this end, a scoring measure has been defined to express the degree of approximation of the FSA solution to the real solution. The final outcome of the experiments can be seen as an illustrative step towards gaining useful knowledge that enables to decide which algorithm to use in certain situations.

In this vein, it is pointed out how the general behavior of different FSAs can differ greatly depending on these different particularities. This is due to the fact that they are based on different underlying definitions of relevance, use different biases and implement quite different ways of exploring the search space. This means that the best solution for each algorithm can be quite diverse, showing the danger in relying in a single algorithm, and pointing in the direction of new hybrid algorithms or combinations thereof for a more reliable assessment of feature relevance.

As future works, this study can be extended in many ways to carry up richer evaluations, such as considering features strongly *correlated* with the class or with one another, more complex definitions of redundance (such as linear combinations), noise in the data sets, other kinds of data (e.g., continuous data), missing values, and the use of combined evaluation measures.

Acknowledgements. This work is supported by the Spanish project CICyT TAP99-0747 and the Mexican Institute of Petroleum.

References

1. A. L. Blum and P. Langley. Selection of Relevant Features and Examples in Machine Learning. In R. Greiner and D. Subramanian (eds.), *Artificial Intelligence on Relevance*, Vol. 97, Artificial Intelligence (1997) 245–271.
2. R. A. Caruana and D. Freitag. How Useful is Relevance? Tech. Report, Fall'94 AAAI Symposium on Relevance (1994).
3. D. Bell and H. Wang. A Formalism for Relevance and its Application in Feature Subset Selection. *Machine Learning* Vol. 41(2) (2000) 175–195.
4. H. Almuallim and T. G. Dietterich. Learning with Many Irrelevant Features. In *Proc. of the 9th National Conference on Artificial Intelligence*, Vol. 2, AAAI Press (1991) 547–552.
5. R. A. Caruana and D. Freitag. Greedy Attribute Selection. In *Proc. of the 11th International Conference on Machine Learning*, Morgan Kaufmann, New Brunswick, NJ (1994) 28–36.
6. J. Doak. An Evaluation of Feature Selection Methods and their Application to Computer Security. Tech. Report CSE–92–18, Davis, CA: University of California (1992).
7. H. Liu and H. Motoda. *Feature Selection for Knowledge Discovery and Data Mining*. Kluwer Academic Publishers, London, GB (1998).
8. L. C. Molina, L. Belanche, and À. Nebot. Caracterización de Algoritmos de Selección de Variables. In *Proc. of the 4th. Congrés Català d'Intel.ligencia Artificial*, Barcelona (2001) 16–23.
9. J. Bins and B. Draper. Feature Selection from Huge Feature Sets. In *International Conference on Computer Vision*, Vol. 2, Vancouver (2001) 159–165.
10. S. Chandon and L. Pinson. *Analyse Typologique*. Masson Editions (1981).
11. P. Pudil, J. Novovicová, and J. Kittler. Floating Search Methods in Feature Selection. *Pattern Recognition Letters* Vol. 15(11), (1994) 1119–1125.
12. S. B. Thrun et al. The MONK's Problems: A Performance Comparison of Different Learning Algorithms. Tech. Report CS-91-197, Carnegie Mellon University (1991).
13. A. K. Jain and D. Zongker. Feature Selection: Evaluation, Application, and Small Sample Performance. *Transactions on Pattern Analysis and Machine Intelligence*, Vol. 19(2), IEEE (1997) 153–158.

KDSM Methodology for Knowledge Discovery from Ill-Structured Domains Presenting Very Short and Repeated Serial Measures with Blocking Factor

Jorge Rodas[1], Karina Gibert[2], and J. Emilio Rojo[3]

[1] Software Department, Technical University of Catalonia, Barcelona, Spain
jr@lsi.upc.es
[2] Department of Statistics and Operational Research, Barcelona, Spain
karina@eio.upc.es
[3] Hospital of Bellvitge, Barcelona, Spain
jrojo@csub.scs.es

Abstract. This paper is an introduction of Knowledge Discovery in Serial Measurement (KDSM) methodology for analyzing repeated and very short serial measures with a blocking factor in *ill-structured domains* (ISD).

KDSM arises from the results obtained in a real application of psychiatry (presented in the previous issue of CCIA [11]). In this application domain, common statistical analysis (time series analysis, multivariate data analysis...) and artificial intelligence techniques (knowledge based methods, inductive learning), employed independently, are often inadequate due to the intrinsic characteristics of ISD.

KDSM is based on both the combination of statistical methods and artificial intelligence techniques, including the use of *clustering based on rules* (introduced by Gibert in 1994).

Keywords: Classification, Clustering, Knowledge Discovery, Serial Measures, Ill-Structured Domains.

1 Introduction

The second half of the XXth century has witnessed a growing interest in computation, which has allowed data manipulation, information in general and in particular like experts' knowledge in very restricted domains (e.g. illness diagnosis or economic data classification) to be represented in a code way for computer use [2].

However, the integration of information into computers is a difficult, expensive process. Hence, better methods to sort out valuable information from non-valuable information are being searched for.

This great development in computation has been transmitted to sciences like Artificial Intelligence (where valuable information means knowledge) and

M.T. Escrig Monferrer and F. Toledo Lobo (Eds.): CCIA 2002, LNAI 2504, pp. 228–238, 2002.

Statistics. The former's goal is to *develop programs that learn and enhance both their own knowledge and the user's*, and the latter aims to *synthetically and understandably present the compilation and analysis of all kinds of information* [13].

Nowadays, society automatically generates an enormous quantity of data, of useful and superfluous information (e.g. the Internet, investigations which—to achieve a goal—make use of certain data, overlooking other more relevant data, etc.) Such explosion of information is increasingly hindering access to the desired information [14].

This situation has aroused the present interest in processes that allow information and its research to be correctly manipulated. In an effort to build a communication and cooperation bridge between Artificial Intelligence and Statistics researchers, Douglas H. Fisher and Bill Gale—among others—established a line of research which combined both sciences and founded the *Society for Artificial Intelligence and Statistics*, an organization that boosts this line of research, thus giving rise to interdisciplinary work. KDSM is framed within the Artificial Intelligence and Statistics line, which focuses on some rapidly developing areas, such as Knowledge Discovery in Databases (KDD) and Data Mining.

Moreover, it is often a difficult task to obtain valuable data from information coming from domains with an inadequate structure, as is the case of psychiatry [12]. Such domains are named *ill-structured domains* (ISD) by [6]. Some of their relevant characteristics are: *heterogeneous data matrices, additional information on domain structure* and *partial non-homogenous knowledge*.

The paper is structured as follows: Sect. 2 is concerned with the formulation of the problem, which gave rise to our KDSM methodology. The KDSM methodology is introduced in Sect. 3. Some interesting results obtained with KDSM are given in Sect. 4. Finally, Sect. 5 is devoted to the conclusions and future work.

2   Problem Formulation

In this section, the problem that gave rise to the KDSM methodology is stated.

In Fig. 1, the representation of a series of *individuals* $(i_1..i_n)$ can be see, in which m occurrences of a given *event* E take place at different time points $(E_{i,1} \ldots E_{i,m})$. Linked to each event occurrence, there exists an *attribute of interest* Y which affects the individual's behavior. The study of its evolution over a given period of time $[t_1, t_r]$ following each occurrence of E is the objective of this research.

Thus, a certain fixed number of measurements (r) of Y is taken at fixed time intervals, beginning from the occurrence of each E, for each individual and each occurrence of E.

This scenario generates information that can be structured as follows:

1. For each i a set of quantitative and/or qualitative characteristics $X_1 \ldots X_K$ is available. This gives rise to matrix X, which corresponds to $[x_{ik}]$, where $i = \{1 \ldots n\}$ and $k = \{1 \ldots K\}$.

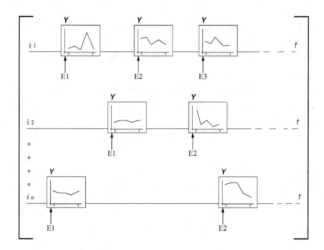

Fig. 1. Measure of Y after each occurrence of E for each i

2. For each occurrence of E, a sequence of serial measures of Y at all fixed time points is obtained. Let E_{ij} $i = \{1 \ldots n\}$ and $j = \{1 \ldots m\}$ be the j-th occurrence of event E in individual i. Hence, for a given individual i there exists a number m of occurrences of E. Considering that time resets at 0 for each occurrence of E, it is possible to set $t_1 \ldots t_r$ as the time points when interest attribute Y will be measured after the occurrence of E. The measures of Y generate a second matrix Y, corresponding to $[Y_{ij}^t]$; $i = 1 \ldots n$ and $j = 0 \ldots m$.

3. For each E a set of quantitative and/or qualitative characteristics $Z_1 \ldots Z_L$ is available. This gives rise to matrix Z, which corresponds to $[z_{ijl}]$, where $i = \{1 \ldots n\}$, $j = \{1 \ldots m\}$ and $l = \{1 \ldots L\}$.

The measures of the attribute of interest are given by Y_{ij}^r, where $i = \{1 \ldots n\}$ is the individual, $j = \{1 \ldots m\}$ indicates the j-th occurrence of E on the individual i and $r = \{1 \ldots R\}$ indexes the time instant from the occurrence of E_{ij} when interest attribute Y was measured. It must be pointed out that *the measurement times are the same* with respect to the occurrence of all the events for all the individuals.

Once an i, j has been determined, the measures of interest attribute Y in the time period of $t_1 \ldots t_r$ may be represented by *very short curves (where r is small)* apparently independent of each other.

In fact, each individual is independent of the others. Consequently, the *number of events* and the *time instant* at which they occur may differ from individual to individual without any underlying pattern.

Nevertheless, all the events on the same individual are affected by his/her own characteristics, which causes all serial measures relative to a particular individual $\{Y_{ij}^1 \ldots Y_{ij}^r\}$, $j = \{1 \ldots m\}$ to receive the individual's influence.

As a result, on matrix Y, individual i may be regarded as a *blocking factor*[18] defining *packs* of curves which are not independent of each other (see Table 1).

Table 1. *Serial measures blocks.*

	t_1	t_2	$\ldots$	t_R	
E_{11}	Y_{11}^1	Y_{11}^2	$\ldots$	Y_{11}^r	
$\vdots$	$\vdots$	$\vdots$	$\vdots$	$\vdots$	block 1
E_{1m}	Y_{1m}^1	Y_{1m}^2	$\ldots$	Y_{1m}^r	
$\vdots$	$\vdots$	$\vdots$	$\vdots$	$\vdots$	
E_{n1}	Y_{n1}^1	Y_{n1}^2	$\ldots$	Y_{n1}^r	
$\vdots$	$\vdots$	$\vdots$	$\vdots$	$\vdots$	block n
E_{nm}	Y_{nm}^1	Y_{nm}^2	$\ldots$	Y_{nm}^r	

A block is therefore constituted by all serial measures $\{Y_{ij}^1 \ldots Y_{ij}^r\}$, $j = \{1 \ldots m\}$ following any occurrence of E on the same individual i. These series are composed of a *small number* of measurements over a specific time period where few observations are present. However, the number of measurements is the same after each event, and so is the distribution over time with respect to the event occurrence. In particular, *a set of very short serial measures over time with a blocking factor* will be analyzed.

The objective of KDSM is to find the pattern followed by the serial measures $\{Y_{ij}^1 \ldots Y_{ij}^r\}$ and the characteristics of the individual $(X_1 \ldots X_K)$ and the event $(Z_1 \ldots Z_L)$ related to the temporal evolution of the attribute of interest Y. Nonetheless, considering the descriptions of matrices X, Y, and Z in previous paragraphs, it is obvious that they may not be related because of their incompatibility. Thus, a way to manipulate these matrices must be found to be able to analyze them.

If there were a common pattern for occurrences of E on all individuals, a single series per individual could be considered and analyzed by means of the *intervention policy* [4] of statistical time series. However, this is not the case. For this reason, it is inadequate to resort to a classical temporal analysis. This situation would imply too rigid a hypothesis for many of the real situations to be covered.

For like problems, a method of analysis based on Matthews's ideas [8,3] is often employed. The method consists in reducing the number of series of each individual to a single series that summarizes the whole set either through the *mean* of each instant (*thick line* in Fig. 2), the *mean area* per series or *mean tendency* per series. This would allow the measures of interest attribute Y to be reduced to a single row per individual, and matrices X, Y, and Z would enable a classical analysis. Nevertheless, relevant information would often be lost, since variability depends on both each event and each *individual effect* (see Fig. 2).

The conclusions drawn from the study of such transformation may therefore be far from reality.

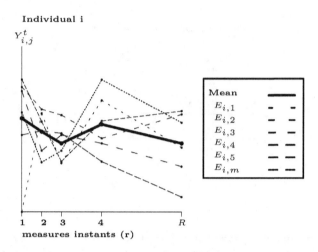

Fig. 2. Example curves of serial measures related to an individual i

Fig. 2 shows a hypothetical situation for an individual i, where the curves represent the recorded serial measures after each event E at the different measure instants r. Despite describing a general tendency of individual i, the mean (thick line) summarizes information excessively, and therefore details that might be significant are lost.

In conclusion, our formal problem is as follows:

Given a set of individuals $I = \{i_1 \ldots i_n\}$, a set of attributes (quantitative and /or qualitative) $X_1 \ldots X_K$ which define I, a matrix $X = [x_{ik}]_{nK}$, $i = \{1 \ldots n\}$, $k = \{1 \ldots K\}$, x_{ik} being the value of X_K for i; given the attribute of interest configuring the serial measures $\{Y_{i,j}^t\}$, $t = \{0 \ldots r\}$, for $i = \{1 \ldots n\}$, $j = \{1 \ldots m\}$, the matrix containing all the serial measures over time $[Y_{ij}^t]_{Nr}$, $N = \sum_1^i m$, $t = \{0..r\}$; a set of events $E = \{E_{i,1} \ldots E_{i,m}\}$, a set of attributes (quantitative and/or qualitative) $Z_1 \ldots Z_K$ which characterize E, matrix $Z = [z_{ijl}]_{nmL}$, $i = \{1 \ldots n\}$, $j = \{1 \ldots m\}$, $l = \{1 \ldots L\}$, z_{ijl} being the value of Z_L for E; and considering:

- *the individuals $I = \{i_1 \ldots i_n\}$ act as a blocking factor on matrix Y,*
- *the measure points $t = \{0..r\}$ represent a fixed number over time for all the serial measures,*
- *the number of observations per serial measure r is small, and*
- *for each i there exists a variable number of serial measures m*

a model for the behavior of serial measures will be established. The model will specify:

- *the pattern(s) for the behavior of the serial measures $\{Y_{i,j}^t\}$ and*
- *their relationship with matrices X and Z.*

3   KDSM Methodology

Based on our experience in real application, the steps of the KDSM methodology are presented in this section. Its justification is provided in the technical report [9].

KDSM performs three main tasks:

1. identification of the individuals'different initial profiles by studying the baseline serial measures, $Y_{i_0}^t$, and their relationship with matrix X,
2. from the knowledge induced in the previous task, the serial measures $\{Y_{ij}^t\}$, $t = \{0 \ldots r\}$ are studied and the possible patterns for these measures are obtained, and
3. the results of the previous task are crossed with matrix Z to find relationships between them and to obtain new knowledge.

The steps of the *methodology for knowledge discovery in serial measures* (KDSM) are the following:

1. *Extraction of a baseline matrix Y_0 from a database containing very short and repeated serial measures over time (taking $Y_0 = [Y_{i0}^t]$, $i = \{1 \ldots n\}$, $t = \{0 \ldots r\}$).*

   This matrix will contain the data which represent the individuals' initial conditions.

2. *Hierarchical clustering of I using the baseline matrix Y_0.*

   This step allows the *a priori* structure of the individuals to be found before occurrence of the first event E.

3. *Interpretation of the resulting classes of Y_0 from the individuals'characteristics (matrix X).*

4. *Rules induction from comparison between classes, on the basis of attributes X_k.*

   The relevant characteristics which determine the *a priori* structure are searched for.

   In this step, multiple boxplots are used as a first alternative for comparison. The resulting rules, type *crisp*[1] are the basis for the initial and partial knowledge (KB_0) of the domain. Other methods are currently being analyzed, like the CIADEC method [16,17], based on fuzzy rules and others developed from the Kruskal-Wallis method [15].

---

[1] Predicates' logic rules.

5. *Construction of the matrix* $D = [Y_t^{ij} - Y_t^{ij-1}]$ *to measure the effect of a given event on the attribute of interest.*

   The data contained in matrix D measure the effect *per se* of a given event, irrespective of the individual's characteristics; that is, matrix D eliminates the blocking factor that i exerts upon E. These data take into account only the improvement or deterioration of interest attribute Y resulting from the occurrence of E by comparing what happens before and after such occurrence.

6. *Classification Based on Rules of matrix D with knowledge base KB_0.*

   The main idea of the classification based on rules is to compile additional knowledge of the domain as a set of rules and to use it for segmenting the set of objects into meaningful subsets that will be respected during clustering (further details in [6]). The results will represent the structure suggested by KB_0. In this case, the goal is to find groups of individuals with similar effects of event E, regarding groups of like individuals at the beginning of the process (KB_0).

7. *Interpretation of resulting classes.*

   The general pattern of curves of each class is characterized, and internal variability in each class and between them is studied and graphically represented by: a) the curves of each class plus the mean curve, and b) the mean curves of all the classes.

8. *Class analysis.*

   The characteristics of matrix Z are projected over the classes generated from matrix D, and those which are relevant and determine a particular behavior of the individuals are searched for.

4   Results

In this section, the last important results, phase 3, obtained after application of the KDSM methodology in psychiatry are provided. It must be born in mind that this paper reports on the formalization of KDSM and the significant achievements of its application in this field, and that all the details of the analysis of the domain, of the matrices' data and results of classifications appeared in the paper [10] of CCIA01.

As a brief reminder, the case study of psychiatry was developed from two *Clinical Databases*[2] relative to the Electro-Convulsive Therapy or electroshock-based therapy (ECT) performed on a group of patients. The former contains characteristics of the patients and the latter contains serial measures of the attribute of interest and information on characteristics of the events (electroshocks) constituting ECT.

KDSM was applied on these data by performing a three-phase analysis:

---

[2] On a first step of data handling the matrices X, Y and Z were obtained from those clinical databases.

1. *Baseline classification.* This phase's objective is to find useful information to discover possible profiles of patients which are being treated with ECT, and to observe if there is an *a priori* structure in the group of patients which can establish differences in the effects of electroshock (ES). Knowledge in the shape of rules (KB_0) describing the group of patients is derived.

2. *Classification Based on Rules of matrix D.* This type of classification was applied to matrix D, using the rules obtained in the previous phase as a knowledge base. Matrix D (of differences) was employed to eliminate the individual effect (in this case, patient effect) on the events (ES) occurred during ECT, and to study its effect separately. This study revealed the nature of the patients' evolution after each ES during ECT. In this particular case, the use of KDSM improved the quality of the results and the interpretability of the classes thanks to the combination of the knowledge base and clustering processes, irrespective of the fact that the KB_0 used was simple enough for conventional AI techniques to be applied.

3. *Projection of Z on P.* To finish the analysis, all the attributes in Z were projected on the classes obtained in the previous phase. That is, all the attributes that characterize the ES were taken and their respective multiple boxplots were performed with respect to the four classes obtained (Table 2, *patients* **p** where the classes are: *young patients who show a positive trend* **yp** *young patients who show a deterioration trend* **yd**, *mature patients who show a positive trend* **mp**, and *mature patients who show a deterioration trend* **md**). By analyzing the boxplots that KDSM identified as relevant attributes by the Kruskal-Wallis method, the expert (psychiatrist) found out that some attributes mark important differences between classes. Such differences allowed the identification of a set of factors which are related to the fact that an isolate ES has a strong influence on the patient's behavior. For instance, it is surprising that the values of attribute **PI** (a patient's identifier) are not projected in association with one single class. In Table 2, we can observe how the quantity of ES relative to each patient is distributed in the four classes obtained. This emphasizes the fact that they group to the different classes without the need for a patient to be associated with only one class. Hence, among the 13 ES applied to p05, a young patient, 9 are in **yd** (class of young patients showing a deterioration trend) whereas the other 4 are in **yp** (class of young patients showing a positive trend).

   In addition, by projecting all the Z on the classes, additional relevant results of great interest for the expert were obtained. They are currently being analyzed by a specialized team of psychiatrists. The most significant results concern blood pressure, impedance, pulses, diastolic pressure, systolic pressure, oxygen drops, convulsion energy and convulsion time.

The result obtained in the last phase is particularly revealing because it shows that what makes the patient get better or deteriorate after an ES does not depend only on him/her. An ES can have a different effect on the same patient throughout ECT. This fact reveals the need to further study ECT, since this

Table 2. *Patient and his/her ES quantity per class.*

PI	yp	yd	md	mp
p01	3	3		
p02			5	1
p03	1	4		
p05	4	9		
p06	2	7		
p07			4	2
p08	4	4		
p10	2	6		
p11			6	1
p12			6	6
p13	3	3		

therapy's efficacy could be enhanced if the tendencies shown by these attributes were confirmed.

5   Conclusions and Future Work

5.1   Conclusions

This work is concerned with the study of very short repeated serial measures of an attribute of interest presented at specific time points. These series constitute blocks relative to each individual.

Based on a real life application in psychiatry, KDSM has been designed. This methodology allows new knowledge on serial measures periodically repeated in a group of individuals to be gained.

Application of KDSM to the measurements of the electro-convulsive therapy (ECT) has yielded excellent results from the point of view of psychiatry. They revealed that the serial measures of the attribute of interest of each patient are neither inherent to the patient nor to the global observation of the therapy. Instead, the same patient may have a different reaction after each electroshock (ES), which clearly indicates that his/her evolution throughout ECT is not monotonous.

Until now, psychiatrists had regarded ECT (the set of events, ES, applied to a patient during the treatment) as a single unit, analyzing the effect of the *whole* therapy before and after the therapy globally [1].

KDSM has shown that too much information has been summarized, and that a significant phenomenon was concealed, namely the same patient reacts in a different way in each session. If the whole treatment had been summarized in one single observation, this would never have been discovered.

In view of these results, experts believe that this fact is due to external or internal causes of each patient, but which may or may not be present in each session. They have not yet been identified, though psychiatrists have begun to work with several hypotheses.

This new knowledge in psychiatry has changed the research orientation in this field. KDSM is therefore a methodology for discovering knowledge which combines AI and Statistics and which has helped to identify new useful relevant knowledge in the application area, in agreement with KDD's classical requirements [5].

5.2 Future Work

The work so far conducted has led us to identify some future tasks. For example, it is necessary to introduce a specific notation for baselines, matrices, etc. for improvement of the problem formulation and establishment of the "final" version of KDSM to solve our problem. A precise, formal description of each step will also be provided.

Furthermore, we are working on the formal design of the pattern of knowledge on the objective domain and the development of a result interpretation mechanism (some progress has been made thanks to boxplots [7]).

As far as new tests are concerned, a second stage of application of KDSM in the field of psychiatry, where some preliminary results have already been obtained, has started.

Finally, we are going to work on data from the State Employment Department and the Economic and Social Information Centre of the Government of the State of Chihuahua in Mexico.

References

1. Abrams, R.: Electroconvulsive Therapy. Ed. Oxford University Press. Third Edition. NY.US (1997)
2. Adrians, P. and Zantinge, D.: Data Mining, Addison-Wesley. Third Edition (1998)
3. Bin, Xia B.: Similarity Search in Time Series Data Sets. Simon Fraser University Press. (1997)
4. Box, G. and Jenkins, G. and Reinsel, G.: Time Series Analysis, Forecasting and Control. Prentice Hall. Third Edition (1994)
5. Fayyad, U. and Piatetsky-Shapiro, G. and Smyth, P.: From Data Mining to Knowledge Discovery in Databases (a survey). AI Magazine, Vol. 17:3. (1996) 37–54
6. Gibert, K. and Cortés, U.: Weighing quantitative and qualitative variables in clustering methods. Mathware and Soft Computing, Vol. 4:3. (1997) 251–266
7. Gibert, K. and Roda, I. and Cortés, U. and Sànchez-Marrè, M.: Identifying characteristic situations in wastewater treatment plants. Workshop in Binding Environmental Sciences and Artificial Intelligence, Vol. 1. (2000) 1–9
8. Matthews, J.N.S.: A refinement to the analysis of serial data using summary measures. Statistics in Medicine, Vol. 12. (1993) 27–37
9. Rodas, J. and Gibert, K. and Rojo, J. and Cortés, U.: A methodology of knowledge discovery in serial measurement applied to psychiatric domain. Technical University of Catalonia Press, LSI-01-53-R. (2001)
10. Rodas, J. and Gibert, K. and Rojo, J.: Influential factors determination on an ill-structured domain response. Technical University of Catalonia Press, LSI-01-6-R. (2001)

11. Rodas, J. and Gibert, K. and Rojo, J.: The use of Clustering Base on Rules for Electroshock Effects Identification. Butlleti de l'ACIA, Number 25. (2001) 145–153
12. Rodas, J. and Gibert, K. and Rojo, J.: Electroshock Effects Identification Using Classification Techniques. Springer's Lecture Notes of Computer Science Series, Vol. Crespo, Maojo and Martin (Eds.). (2001) 238–244
13. Rodas, J. and Gibert, K. and Vázquez, R.: Artificial Intelligence and Statistics : Common Things. Actas del SICI 00. (2000) 45–50
14. Rodas, J. and Gramajo, J.: Classification and Clustering Study in Incomplete Data Domain. Technical University of Catalonia Press, LSI-01-11-R. (2000)
15. Siegal, S. and Castellan, N.J.: Nonparametric statistics for the Behavioral Sciences, Minimum mean Rank differences. McGraw Hill. Second Edition. (1988) 206–215
16. Vázquez, F. and Gibert, K.: Generación Automática de Reglas Difusas en Dominios Poco Estructurados con Variables Numéricas. CAEPIA, Vol. 1. (2001) 143–152
17. Vázquez, F.: Automatic Characterization and Interpretation of Conceptual Descriptions in Ill-Structured Domains using Numerical Attribute. Technical University of Catalonia Press, LSI-02-51-R. (2002)
18. Walpole, R. and Myers, R. and Myers S.: Probability and Statistics for Engineers and Scientists. Prentice Hall. Sixth Edition. (1998)

On Filtering the Training Prototypes in Nearest Neighbour Classification[*]

J.S. Sánchez[1], R. Barandela[2], and F.J. Ferri[3]

[1] Dept. Llenguatges i Sistemes Informàtics, U. Jaume I, 12071 Castelló, Spain
[2] Instituto Tecnológico de Toluca, Av. Tecnológico s/n, 52140 Metepec, México
[3] Dept. d'Informàtica, U. València, 46100 Burjassot (València), Spain

Abstract. Filtering (or editing) is mainly effective in improving the classification accuracy of the Nearest Neighbour (NN) rule, and also in reducing its storage and computational requirements. This work reviews some well-known editing algorithms for NN classification and presents alternative approaches based on combining the NN and the Nearest Centroid Neighbourhood of a sample. Finally, an empirical analysis over real data sets is provided.

1 Introduction

Given a set of n labelled prototypes or training set (TS), the k-NN classifier [7, 8] consists of assigning an input sample to the class most frequently represented among the k closest prototypes in the TS according to a certain dissimilarity measure. A particular case of this rule is when $k = 1$, in which each input sample is assigned to the class indicated by its closest neighbour.

The asymptotic classification error of the k-NN rule (that is, when n grows to infinity) tends to the optimal Bayes error rate as $k \to \infty$ and $k/n \to 0$. If $k = 1$, the error is bounded by approximately twice the Bayes error [10]. This behaviour in asymptotic classification performance combines with a conceptual and implementational simplicity, which makes it a powerful classification technique capable of dealing with arbitrarily complex problems, provided a large enough TS is available.

Nevertheless, the NN classifiers also exhibit some practical disadvantages. An obvious drawback comes from the fact that, in the case of having large sets of prototypes, it necessarily implies a considerable computational burden to search for the k neighbours. On the other hand, the performance of these rules, as with any non-parametric method, is extremely sensitive to incorrectness in the TS.

Extensive efforts have been devoted to overcome these drawbacks. Condensing [2,18,14,9,26,33,5,22] and fast NN search algorithms [13,15,31] try to alleviate the high computational cost of these classifiers. Optimal distance measures [29,

---

[*] This work has partially been supported by grants TIC2000-1703-C03-03 from the Spanish CICYT, SAB2001-0004 from the Spanish MECD, and 32016-A from the Mexican CONACyT.

M.T. Escrig Monferrer and F. Toledo Lobo (Eds.): CCIA 2002, LNAI 2504, pp. 239–248, 2002.

25], sample re-combination [16], and editing [32,30,10,27,3,4,1] contribute to improving the classification performance of the NN rules.

Joint use of edited and condensed NN rules has been proposed to pick out an appropriate subset of prototypes with computational efficiency and accuracy as ultimate goals. While condensing aims at selecting a sufficiently small subset of prototypes that leads approximately the same performance than the NN rule using the whole TS, the purpose of editing is to eliminate possible outliers from the original TS which strongly degrade the performance of the NN rules and also to clean possible overlap among regions of different classes.

In the frame of edited NN rules, this paper focuses on introducing a group of algorithms based on the Nearest Centroid Neighbours (NCN) [6], which define a kind of surrounding neighbourhood around a sample. Experiments with real data are provided to compare the performance of the alternative schemes proposed here to that of some classical edited NN rules.

The organization of the rest of this paper is as follows. Section 2 provides a review of several well-known editing techniques. Section 3 presents alterntive algorithms to filter the TS. Section 4 describes the real-world data sets and the experiments carried out. Section 5 discusses the empirical results obtained on those databases. Finally, some concluding remarks are given in Sect. 6.

2   Some Filtering Algorithms for NN Classifiers

As already mentioned, filtering or editing is primarily aimed at improving the performance of the NN rule by preprocessing the TS. As a by-product, it also obtains a decrease in the TS size and accordingly, a reduction in the computational burden of the corresponding classifier.

The first work on editing corresponds to that of Wilson [32], and then many other proposals have followed [30,21,27,3,33]. Differences among most approaches refer to the classifier employed for editing along with the error estimate and the stopping criterion considered [12]. The error estimate is only used in this context to decide which prototypes need to be removed from the TS. On the other hand, the stopping criterion provides the possibility of applying editing in an iterative way.

2.1   Wilson's Editing

This technique consists of applying the k-NN rule to estimate the class label of all prototypes in the TS and discard those samples whose label does not agree with the class associated with the largest number of the k neighbours [32]. This is a non-iterative editing based on the leaving-one-out estimate.

1. Let $S = X$. (X is the original TS, and S will be the edited set)
2. For each $x_i \in X$ do:
   - Discard x_i from S if it is misclassified using the k-NN rule with prototypes in $X - \{x_i\}$.

2.2   All-k-NN Editing

This scheme can be seen as a different realization of the original Wilson's editing that utilizes all the l-NN classification rules, with l ranging from 1 through k, for a predetermined value of k [30].

1. Let $S = X$.
2. For each $x_i \in X$ do:
   - Set $l = 1$
   - While $l < k + 1$ do:
     - Discard x_i from S if it is misclassified using the l-NN rule with prototypes in $X - \{x_i\}$, go to Step 2.
     - Set $l = l + 1$

2.3   Holdout Editing

In the case of the algorithms based on the leaving-one-out error estimate (that is, Wilson's scheme and its relatives), the statistical independence between test and training prototypes cannot be assumed because their functions are interchanged. In order to achieve this statistical independence, the classification of prototypes can be performed in a holdout manner.

Holdout editing [10] consists of randomly partitioning the initial TS into $b > 2$ blocks of prototypes, $B_1, ..., B_b$, and then eliminating prototypes from each block using only two independent blocks at the same time.

1. Let $S = X$ and randomly divide X into b blocks, $B_1, ..., B_b$.
2. For each $B_i, i = 1, ..., b$ do:
   - For each $x_j \in B_i$ do:
     - Discard x_j from S if it is misclassified using the k-NN rule with prototypes in $B_{(i+1) \bmod b}$.

2.4   Multiedit

Devijver and Kittler introduced the well-known Multiedit algorithm [10], which consists of a repetitive version of the Holdout editing scheme. This technique is also based on the holdout error estimate, but using the 1-NN classification rule and iterating the editing process.

1. Let $S = \emptyset$ and randomly divide X into b blocks, $B_1, ..., B_b$.
2. For each $B_i, i = 1, ..., b$ do:
   - For each $x_j \in B_i$ do:
     - Add x_j to S if it is misclassified by the NN rule with prototypes in $B_{(i+1) \bmod b}$.
3. If $S = X$ during the last I iterations, then exit with the final set S.
4. Let $X = S$ and go to Step 1.

The Multiedit algorithm has been proven to be asymptotically optimal [10]. Nevertheless, in practice it shows a poor behaviour when applied to finite sets of prototypes [21,27].

2.5   Generalized Editing

The Generalized editing technique [20] was proposed out of concern for too many prototypes being removed from the TS by classical Wilson's method. In Generalized editing, two parameters are defined: k and k', in such a way that $(k + 1)/2 \leq k' \leq k$. Algorithmically, this scheme can be written as follows:

1. Let $S = X$.
2. For each $x_i \in X$ do:
   - Find the k-NN of x_i in $X - \{x_i\}$.
   - If some class has at least k' representatives from the k neighbours, change the label of x_i according to that class. Otherwise, discard x_i from S.

2.6   Depuration

This filtering approach [3] consists of removing some suspicious prototypes from the TS, while changing the class labels of some other instances. It is based on the Generalized editing scheme introduced in the previous section.

The Depuration methodology involves several applications of the Generalized editing followed by the employment, also repeatedly, of Wilson's algorithm. Iteration in the application of each one of these procedures stops if one of the following criteria is fulfilled:

1. Stability in the structure of the TS has been reached (no more removals and no more relabellings).
2. Estimate of the misclassification rate (leaving-one-out, see [17]) has begun to increase.
3. One class has resulted emptied (all its representatives in the TS have been removed or transferred to another class) or has resulted in a very small size/dimensionality rate (less than five training prototypes for each considered feature).

It is to be noted that when the size/dimensionality rate is not adequate, some feature selection algorithm [23] must be previously used to allow further depuration of the TS.

2.7   Editing with Proximity Graph

Sánchez et al. proposed [27] to employ some cases of proximity graphs [19], such as the Gabriel Graph (GG) and the Relative Neighbourhood Graph (RNG), for editing the NN rule. Any of these graphs can be efficiently computed by heuristic approaches [19]. In brief, these editings try to set a geometrical relation between a sample and its neighbours in order to improve the performance of the NN rule by using a suitably reduced set of prototypes.

This editing technique is based on the leaving-one-out estimate as Wilson's method, but it utilizes the graph neighbours of each sample instead of the Euclidean distance neighbourhood. Two samples x and y are said to be *graph neighbours* in a proximity graph $G = (V, E)$ if there exists an edge $(x, y) \in E$ between them. Thus, taking into account the definitions of GG and RNG [19], the graph neighbourhood of a point requires that no other point lies inside the union of the zones of influence (i.e., hypersphere or lune, respectively) corresponding to all its graph neighbours. From this relation, it seems possible to surround a prototype by means of all its graph neighbours.

The simplest editing based on proximity graphs can be summarized as follows: after computing the graph neighbourhood of every sample in the TS, all the graph neighbours of a prototype "vote" for its class. In other words, all prototypes around a sample take part in the process of estimating whether it is mislabelled or not, regardless of their actual distance to the sample.

1. Compute the GG (or RNG) associated with the given TS.
2. Discard those prototypes that are misclassified according to their graph neighbours.

3   Alternative Filtering Techniques

A new algorithm was proposed in [11] as a way of improving the behaviour of classical editing in the finite sample size case. This technique corresponds to a slight modification of the original work of Wilson and basically consists of using the leaving-one-out error estimate with the k-NCN classifier [28].

From a practical point of view, the k-NCN rule is thought to obtain more suitable information about prototypes in the TS and specially, for those close to decision boundaries. This can be achieved by taking into account not only the proximity of prototypes to a given input sample, but also their *symmetrical distribution* around it. In general, when applied to editing, this results in a practical improvement of the corresponding procedure [11].

1. Let $S = X$.
2. For each x_i in X do:
   - Discard x_i from S if it is misclassified by the k-NCN rule with patterns in $X - \{x_i\}$.

3.1   Combining NN and k-NCN Classifiers to Filter the TS

The scheme proposed in this section combines information about proximity with that related to the spatial distribution of prototypes in the TS. This kind of fusion tries to guarantee that prototypes used for editing are correctly labelled according to the NN rule. Although, in general, it is not possible to remove only prototypes lying in wrong class regions, this method can be seen as a way of reducing the number of "correct" prototypes discarded during the editing process.

After searching for the k NCNs of a prototype, only those whose NN belongs to their same class will be considered. This can be understood as an ensemble of two editings: first, editing the k NCNs by using the NN rule and second, editing a prototype by the $j \leq k$ NCNs not discarded in the previous stage.

1. Let $S = X$.
2. For each x_i in X do:
   - Identify the k NCNs of x_i in $X - \{x_i\}$.
   - Select the $j \leq k$ NCNs correctly labelled according to the NN rule.
   - Discard x_i from S if it is misclassified by the j-NCN rule with patterns in $X - \{x_i\}$.

Alternatively, one might use the k-NN decision rule (instead of the particular 1-NN for editing the set of the NCNs (Step 2.b). On the other hand, although this scheme is based on the leaving-one-out estimate, other error estimates as holdout and B-fold cross-validation are also directly applicable.

4   Databases and Experiments

Experiments over eight standard data sets (see Table 1) taken from the UCI Database Repository [24] have been carried out to study the behaviour of the different editing algorithms introduced in the previous sections. In particular, Wilson's editing ($W(k)$), All-k-NN editing ($A(k)$), Holdout editing ($H(b, k)$), Multiedit ($M(b, I)$), Depuration ($D(k, k')$), GG-based editing (GG), RNG-based editing (RNG), k-NCN editing ($NCN(k)$) and the combined approach ($C(k)$), have been considered. The results for each original TS (i.e., no editing, NoE) has also been included for comparison purposes.

Table 1. The data sets used in the experiments.

Data set	No. classes	No. features	TS size	Test set size
Glass	6	9	174	40
Liver	2	6	276	69
Pima	2	6	615	153
Vehicle	4	18	678	168
Vowel	11	10	429	99
Cancer	2	9	546	137
Heart	2	13	216	54
Wine	3	13	144	34

Five different random partitions of the original database into training and test sets have been used to obtain the performance results. The experiments consist of applying the NN rule to each of the test sets, where the training portion has been preprocessed by different editing algorithms. In our experiments, all schemes have employed the Euclidean distance function.

The results correspond to the average over the five random partitions. Only one typical set of parameters ($k = 3$, $k' = 2$, $b = 5$, $I = 5$) has been tried for each editing. To obtain more reliable results, for those editing schemes involving internal randomization (i.e., Holdout and Multiedit), the results were computed by taking the average over five trials for each partition.

5 Results

Table 2 provides the average classification accuracy obtained by the NN rule with the resulting edited sets. Highlight indicates the best filtering method for each database. Table 3 reports the resulting TS size after editing. In this case, italic refers to the best technique in terms of accuracy.

Table 2. Classification rates of the NN rule over different edited sets

	Glass	Liver	Pima	Vehicle	Vowel	Cancer	Heart	Wine	Average
NoE	70.0	65.2	63.9	64.3	97.6	95.6	58.2	72.3	73.4
W(3)	63.0	69.3	72.0	59.6	86.7	96.0	64.4	**71.8**	72.9
A(3)	64.2	68.1	71.7	59.6	86.7	96.3	65.2	67.7	72.4
H(5,3)	62.0	64.1	71.5	59.6	70.1	96.3	64.1	70.0	69.7
M(5,5)	41.9	55.4	68.9	42.7	13.6	96.4	59.9	68.9	56.0
D(3,2)	67.0	**70.3**	**75.9**	61.3	83.2	**96.7**	**69.3**	70.6	74.3
GG	67.0	69.3	74.1	59.6	61.4	95.9	67.8	70.0	70.6
RNG	67.5	68.1	72.0	**63.2**	**92.9**	96.3	65.9	68.8	74.4
NCN(3)	**68.0**	69.9	72.9	60.9	89.7	96.0	67.4	68.2	74.1
C(3)	67.0	68.1	72.2	61.4	89.7	96.3	67.8	70.0	74.1

Results in Table 2 show that in general, the best alternatives for these data sets correspond to Depuration, k-NCN editing, and RNG-based algorithm. Classification accuracy achieved by the combined method is very similar to that of the best option for each database. What is clear is the fact that the behaviour of the Multiedit is much worse than any other filter almost without exception under all the cases, but specially in the Vowel database (79.3% less accuracy than the best choice). The rationale is that, in some experiments, the Multiedit algorithm systematically discarded all prototypes from some classes.

It is also interesting to note that the NN rule without editing (NoE) leads to the best results in four cases; this suggests that the sets available for these experiments are not large enough for properly applying the current editing techniques, specially taking into account the size to dimensionality ratio of such data sets.

Examining the edited set size in Table 3, the results show that, as is to be expected, the Multiedit generally obtains the highest reduction rate. These results also indicate that, in almost all the experiments, Depuration and RNG-based editings retain more prototypes than Wilson's and the schemes based on NCN. In fact, concerning the Depuration method, this result is to be expected:

Table 3. Number of prototypes in the resulting edited sets

	Glass	Liver	Pima	Vehicle	Vowel	Cancer	Heart	Wine	Average
NoE	174	276	615	678	429	546	216	144	384.8
W(3)	114.8	176.0	427.8	423.2	407.0	529.6	138.2	*100.2*	289.6
A(3)	111.0	145.4	363.2	377.2	406.4	519.8	115.0	92.8	266.4
H(5,3)	94.6	167.0	427.0	348.8	192.6	524.6	134.2	97.2	248.3
M(5,5)	**44.8**	**39.4**	**261.2**	**155.6**	**24.2**	501.2	**56.4**	65.6	143.6
D(3,2)	142.4	*232.0*	*403.6*	601.4	426.0	***338.2***	*183.8*	109.8	304.7
GG	105.6	190.4	472.8	342.8	119.4	530.8	147.8	110.8	252.6
RNG	132.2	195.2	474.6	*469.0*	*397.4*	532.0	152.4	118.0	308.9
NCN(3)	*115.8*	174.4	429.0	433.2	412.8	529.6	143.0	103.4	292.7
C(3)	114.6	176.8	424.0	431.8	412.2	527.4	135.2	103.8	290.7

from this, some prototypes that would be removed by other approaches are now relabelled and retained in the TS. The parameter values employed in the experiments here reported ($k = 3, k' = 2$) produce no elimination of prototypes during the first steps of the algorithm (that is, when Generalized editing is being applied) over those databases with only two classes.

Confidence levels for the statistical significance (two-tailed Student's t-tests) of the difference in accuracy of C(3) with regard to that achieved by the rest of algorithms are reported in Table 4. Values in brackets indicate that classification accuracy of the corresponding method is higher than that of C(3). Cells in blank mean that differences are not statistically significant. As can be seen, this alternative editing procedure is significantly better than the methods based on the holdout estimate in most cases. With respect to Wilson's editing and its relative (A(3)), differences in accuracy are statistically significant in four out of the eight databases. Finally, when comparing with proximity-graph-based algorithms, C(3) is better than GG in two cases and better than RNG only in one database.

Table 4. Statistical significance of differences with C(3)

	Glass	Liver	Pima	Vehicle	Vowel	Cancer	Heart	Wine
W(3)	0.01			0.001	0.005			0.001
A(3)	0.05			0.001	0.005			0.005
H(5,3)	0.01	0.001	0.1	0.001				0.005
M(5,5)	0.001	0.001	0.05	0.001	0.001			0.01
D(3,2)		(0.05)	(0.001)		0.005			(0.05)
GG				0.005	0.001			
RNG				(0.001)	(0.005)			0.01
NCN(3)		(0.025)	(0.025)	0.01				

6   Concluding Remarks

Some experiments have been carried out over eight real data sets using both standard and alternative editing algorithms. These schemes are primarily based on using the NCNs of a sample and also on some kind of information fusion derived from distinct realizations of neighbourhood. More specifically, these approaches combine the 1-NN and the k NCNs of a pattern in order to eliminate erroneously labelled prototypes from the TS.

The results here reported clearly indicate that some filtering approaches yield high classification accuracy but retain a very large number of prototypes; this occurs with Depuration and RNG-based editings, which obtained the best results in terms of accuracy but discarded only about 20% of training patterns. On the contrary, those filtering methods based on the holdout estimate achieve the highest reduction rates but also show an important degradation in accuracy (specially, with the Multiedit).

With regard to the set of alternative filtering algorithms introduced in Sect. 3, it appears to constitute a good trade-off with both high accuracy and a moderate number of prototypes retained. As a first conclusion, it seems that this kind of editings can be established as the best choice for the experiments carried through in the present paper.

References

1. Aha, D.W., Kibler, D., Albert, M.K.: Instance-based learning algorithms, *Machine Learning* **6** (1991) 37-66.
2. Alpaydin, E.: Voting over multiple condensed nearest neighbors. *Artificial Intelligence Review* **11** (1997) 115-132.
3. Barandela, R., Gasca, E.: Decontamination of training samples for supervised pattern recognition methods, In *Advances in Pattern Recognition*, Lecture Notes in Computer Science 1876, Springer Verlag (2000) 621-630.
4. Brighton, H., Mellish, C.: Advances in instance selection for instance-based learning algorithms, *Data Mining and Knowledge Discovery* **6** (2002) 153-172.
5. Chang, C.L.: Finding prototypes for nearest neighbor classifiers, *IEEE Trans. on Computers* **23** (1974) 1179-1184.
6. Chaudhuri, B.B.: A new definition of neighborhood of a point in multi-dimensional space, *Pattern Recognition Letters* **17** (1996) 11-17.
7. Cover, T.M., Hart, P.E.: Nearest neighbor pattern classification. IEEE Trans. on Information Theory **13** (1967) 21-27.
8. Dasarathy, B.V.: *Nearest Neighbor Norms: NN Pattern Classification techniques*, IEEE Computer Society Press, Los Alamos, CA, 1991.
9. Dasarathy, B.V.: Minimal consistent subset (MCS) identification for optimal nearest neighbor decision systems design, *IEEE Trans. on Systems, Man, and Cybernetics* **24** (1994) 511-517.
10. Devijver, P.A., Kittler, J.: *Pattern Recognition: A Statistical Approach*, Prentice Hall, Englewood Cliffs, NJ, 1982.
11. Ferri, F.J., Sánchez, J.S., Pla, F.: Editing prototypes in the finite sample size case using alternative neighbourhoods, In: *Advances in Pattern Recognition*, Lecture Notes in Computer Science 1451, Springer Verlag (1998) 620-629.

12. Ferri, F.J., Albert, J.V., Vidal, E.: Considerations about sample-size sensitivity of a family of edited nearest-neighbor rules, *IEEE Trans. on Systems, Man, and Cybernetics-Part B: Cybernetics* **29** (1999) 667-672.
13. Fukunaga, K., Narendra, P.M.: A branch and bound algorithm for computing k-nearest neighbors, *IEEE Trans. on Computers* **24** (1975) 750-753.
14. Gates, G.W.: The reduced nearest neighbor rule. *IEEE Trans. on Information Theory* **18** (1972) 431-433.
15. Grother, P.J., Candela, G.T., Blue, J.L.: Fast implementation of nearest neighbor classifiers, *Pattern Recognition* **30** (1997) 459-465.
16. Hamamoto, Y., Uchimura, S., Tomita, S.: A bootstrap technique for nearest neighbor classifier design, *IEEE Trans. on Pattern Analysis and Machine Intelligence* **19** (1997) 73-79.
17. Hand, D.J.: *Construction and Assessment of Classification Rules*, John Wiley & Sons, Chichester, UK, 1997.
18. Hart, P.E.: The condensed nearest neighbor rule, *IEEE Trans. on Information Theory* **14** (1968) 515-516.
19. Jaromczyk, J.W., Toussaint, G.T.: Relative neighbourhood graphs and their relatives, *Proc. of IEEE* **80** (1992) 1502-1517.
20. Koplowitz, J., Brown, T.A.: On the relation of performance to editing in nearest neighbor rules, *Pattern Recognition* **13** (1981) 251-255.
21. Kuncheva, L.I.: Editing for the k-nearest neighbors rule by a genetic algorithm, *Pattern Recognition Letters* **16** (1995) 809-814.
22. Lipowezky, U.: Selection of the optimal prototype subset for 1-NN classification, *Pattern Recognition Letters* **19** (1998) 907-918.
23. Liu, H., Motoda, H.: *Feature Selection for Knowledge Discovery and Data Mining*, Kluwer Academic Publishers, Boston, 1998.
24. Merz, C.J., Murphy, P.M.: *UCI Repository of Machine Learning Databases*, Dept. of Information and Computer Science, University of California, Irvine, CA, 1998.
25. Ricci, F., Avesani, P.: Data compression and local metrics for nearest neighbor classification, *IEEE Trans. on Pattern Analysis and Machine Intelligence* **21** (1999) 380-384.
26. Ritter, G.L., Woodritz, H.B., Lowry, S.R., Isenhour, T.L.: An algorithm for selective nearest neighbor rule. *IEEE Trans. on Information Theory* **21** (1975) 665-669.
27. Sánchez, J.S., Pla, F., Ferri, F.J.: Prototype selection for the nearest neighbour rule through proximity graphs, *Pattern Recognition Letters* **18** (1997) 507-513.
28. Sánchez, J.S., Pla, F., Ferri, F.J.: On the use of neighbourhood-based non-parametric classifiers, *Pattern Recognition Letters* **18** (1997) 1179-1186.
29. Short, R.D., Fukunaga, K.: The optimal distance measure for nearest neighbor classification, *IEEE Trans. on Information Theory* **27** (1981) 622-627.
30. Tomek, I.: An experiment with the edited nearest neighbor rule, *IEEE Trans. on Systems, Man and Cybernetics* **6** (1976) 448-452.
31. Vidal, E.: An algorithm for finding nearest neighbours in (approximately) constant average time", *Pattern Recognition Letters* **4** (1986) 145-147.
32. Wilson, D.L.: Asymptotic properties of nearest neighbor rules using edited data sets, *IEEE Trans. on Systems, Man and Cybernetics* **2** (1972) 408-421.
33. Wilson, D.R., Martinez, T.R.: Reduction techniques for instance-based learning algorithms. *Machine Learning* **38** (2000) 257-286.

Classification of Abnormal Situations in a Waste Water Treatment Plant

Adama Traoré[1], Monique Polit[1], Cecilio Angulo[2], and Andreu Català[2]

[1] Université de Perpignan, Laboratoire de Physique Appliquée et d'Automatique,
F-66860 Perpignan Cedex, France
[2] Universitat Politècnica de Catalunya, Knowledge Engineering Research Group,
E-08800 Vilanova i la Geltrú, Spain

Abstract. The waste water treatment plants are very unstable and the waters to be treated are ill defined. The command of those processes needs to be done with advanced methods of control and supervision. They have to take into account the bad knowledge of the processes. The most important situations that imply problems for the plant are listed. Parameters for comparison between crisis and normal situation are measured. Fuzzy logic and support vector machines methods are used and compared to distinguish the different situations in order to take a decision. The method is tested in simulation and on a real plant.

1 Introduction

The waste water treatment plants are most of the time unstable and ill defined by the water to be treated. The European restrictions require enhancing the monitoring and control systems in order to meet them. The treatment of waste water from the city has to be optimized before rejection in the river.

A system of supervision must have two functions: monitoring and control. During the monitoring of the plant, the system has to be able to decide if the system is in a normal state or not. If the system detects an abnormal situation, it has to characterize it, for undertaking a correcting action. In order to classify the abnormal situations that imply a quick acting, we identify 15 scenarios among the problems that can occur in the plant. At that time, there is almost no on-line sensor, able to identify the state of the process. So the use of online measurements coupled with rules given the state of the system is necessary.

The classification is realized on a hand, with fuzzy rules on simulated data and on data measured on a real plant. On the other hand, the K-SVCR algorithm [1], a modified procedure based on support vectors, is also studied for comparison.

2 The Waste Water Treatment Plant and the Simulator

The studied processes are two plants for the pollution removal on waste water from cities. The first one alternates anaerobic and aerobic areas [2]. A database

M.T. Escrig Monferrer and F. Toledo Lobo (Eds.): CCIA 2002, LNAI 2504, pp. 249–256, 2002.

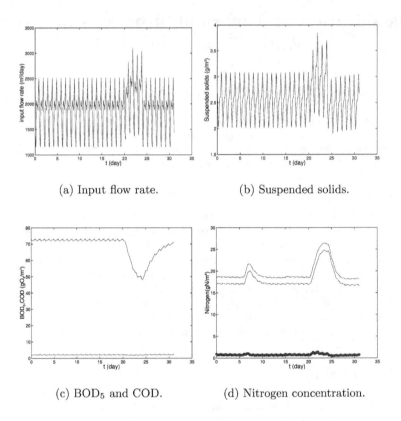

(a) Input flow rate.   (b) Suspended solids.

(c) BOD$_5$ and COD.   (d) Nitrogen concentration.

Fig. 1. Variations of parameters for the rain.

was build using three months of working. The variables measured every day at the input and at the output of the processes are input flow rate, BOD$_5$, COD, suspended solids, total nitrogen, ammonia, nitrate and pH. Those variables are chosen, because they greatly influence the water quality.

With those experimental values, a database is created, using the software GPS-X (Hydromantis), developed to simulate waste water treatment plant.

After that, four perturbation situations are defined, characterized by variations applied to the input flow rate. They are rain, storm, excess of pollution and excess of nitrogen. Variations are applied relatively to the normal situation on the parameters that represent the abnormal situation.

The data evolution is the following: the first 20 days, dynamics is left free to reach the normal situation. The twentieth day the perturbation is applied, and modifies the process dynamic during about 5 days. The process returns to a normal working after about 5 days.

On Fig. 1, input flow rate, suspended solids, BOD$_5$ (lower curve), COD (upper curve) and nitrogen concentration (N, lower curve, NO$_3$+NO$_2$, middle curve, NH$_4$, upper curve) are depicted for the rain scenario.

Table 1. Example of rules for the inference table.

IF Q_{in} very big AND	COD_{in} minus AND	N small THEN	norma $mf5$
Q_{in} very big	COD_{in} minus	N big	norma $mf6$
Q_{in} very big	COD_{in} zero	N small	norma $mf5$
Q_{in} very big	COD_{in} zero	N big	norma $mf6$
Q_{in} very big	COD_{in} plus	N small	norma $mf5$
Q_{in} very big	COD_{in} plus	N big	norma $mf6$
Q_{in} big	COD_{in} minus	N small	norma $mf4$
Q_{in} big	COD_{in} minus	N big	norma $mf6$

3   Related Work

Several approaches to this problem have been early elaborated from different perspectives of the machine learning research community. So, in [3] a real-time knowledge-based supervision of a waste water treatment plant is implemented. The operation scheme includes organic matter removal, like in our approach, nitrification/denitrification, and enhanced biological phosphorous removal.

Another possibilities include a case-based system approach [4], or a distributed control based on agent architecture [5]. This late case is of a particular interest, because the knowledge is organized in several distributed agents, representing the available knowledge for every sub process of the waste water treatment plant, improving previous developments with monolithic Knowledge Based Systems.

4   Fuzzy Classification of the Situations

As several authors already exposed it, fuzzy logic is well adapted to model biological process [6,7]. The chosen variables for the classification of abnormal situation are the input flow rate Q_{in}, COD_{in} and total nitrogen, N.

The fuzzification, the inference table and the defuzzification are made in a classical manner [8], [9]. The fuzzy toolbox of Matlab$^{©}$ is used. Variations of Q_{in} and COD_{in} are divided into three subsets (trapezium) and those of N into 2 subsets (see Fig. 2(a), 2(b), 2(c)). The inference table has 18 rules; some of them are depicted in Table 1.

The output (*norma*) is divided into 6 subsets (see Fig. 2d), each of them corresponding to a precise situation as,

1. excess of pollution
2. excess of ammonium
3. normal situation
4. rain
5. storm

and the last one corresponding to an undetermined case (0.5).

For the defuzzification the mean of maximum (mom) method is used.

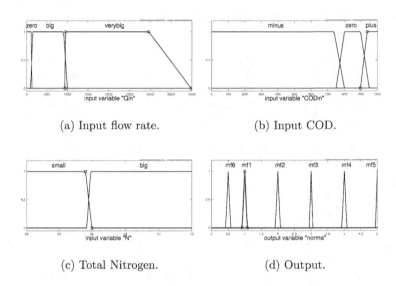

(a) Input flow rate.   (b) Input COD.

(c) Total Nitrogen.   (d) Output.

Fig. 2. Fuzzy subsets for the input variables and the output variable.

5   K-SVCR Classification of the Situations

In the last years, the Support Vector Machine (SVM) paradigm has obtained a great amount of success between the research community. Its generalisation ability is a well-known feature of SVMs, and it is interesting for wastewater problems because, usually, information about the process is very poor.

Recently, a new algorithm has been developed mixing advantages from SVM for classification and SVM for regression problems, the K-SVCR method. This procedure improves the usual multi-category, 1-versus-1 and 1-versus-rest, extensions of the binary SVM classification because is more robust against wrong partial predictions [1].

Learning is made by defining a K-SVCR for each scenario pairs. Each machine assigns +1 if the entry belongs to the first associated scenario, −1 in the case of an entry belonging to the second scenario and 0 for any other entry.

6   Application to the Detection of Problems

6.1   Fuzzy Classification

The fuzzy classifier is used to detect abnormal situation on the simulator. Unknown successions of situations (normal and abnormal) are put at the classifier input. The classification is always well done. Two examples are given on Fig. 3(a), 3(b). In the first one, a situation of ammonia excess and after a situation of rain is detected. In the second one, the classifier detects a situation of ammonium and a situation of rain.

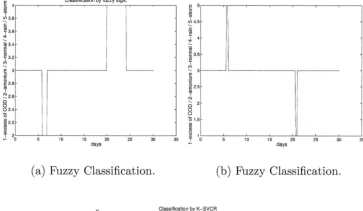

(a) Fuzzy Classification.   (b) Fuzzy Classification.

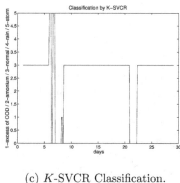

(c) K-SVCR Classification.

Fig. 3. Fuzzy detection and K-SVCR detection of abnormal situations.

6.2 K-SVCR Classification

To consider the data evolution, the entries after the perturbation have been eliminated for the training phase. It has been only considered data from the eleventh to the fifteenth day. So, transition phase is not used for training. This data window is similar for all the considered scenarios.

To capture the process dynamics, SVM input data has been created by using two entries in a day during two days (there exists data every hour). In short, machines are evaluated on a $\mathbb{R}^{36}$ input space with a very short training data set (110 entries).

As evaluation kernels, gaussian functions have been used and the weights in the machines have been limited to $C = 2500$. This election is heuristic, and another values could be employed.

Results from example in Fig. 3(c) are similar to Fig. 3(b). Some inputs are classified with '0-label' for the K-SVCR ensemble machines to indicate no-classification. This region is a transition phase between two classification zones and the kernel machine was not trained here.

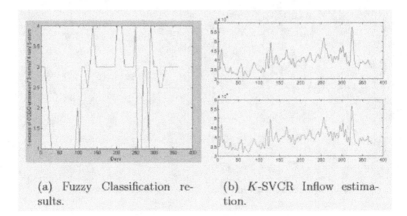

(a) Fuzzy Classification re-   (b) K-SVCR Inflow estima-
sults.   tion.

7   Application to a Real Plant

7.1   Experimental Conditions

The real plant in which we applied the fuzzy classification and the Support
Vector paradigm is the waste water treatment plant for the city of Perpignan.
The necessity of detecting problems very early is evident, especially because the
water is rejected after treatment in a river, very close from the sea.

In this plant several quantities are recorded at the input and at the output
of the installation, like for example: date, quantity of rain, flow rate, pH, solid
suspended matter, total nitrogen, COD. The plant receives only few industrial
waste waters.

Unfortunately, these quantities are measured only once by day and for some
of them once every 4 days. Recorded data for one year of running were studied.
We keep only the data containing all the parameters that we need: quantities
of rain, input flow rate, COD and total nitrogen at the input. The input fuzzy
subsets were slightly modified in order to adapt them to the real plant data and
the last inference rule was modified.

7.2   Results with Fuzzy Logic

The classification results are depicted on Fig. 4(a). On this figure, only 3 points
correspond to a situation between two possibilities (output = 2.5). In fact these
points correspond at recording after a period of storm during which the data
were not recorded (except flow rate).

In three other cases, the detection of an excess of COD corresponds in fact
to a low input flow rate.

The other situations were all well classified.

7.3   Discussion of the Classification Results

The classification results are very satisfactory. Especially we can observe that
the classification was obtained with the same fuzzy subsets for the whole year.

In fact the mean input flow rate is higher during summer and autumn due to storms and to an increasing use of water. A better classification would be certainly obtained, changing the subsets for this period of the year.

In order to build an automatic control of the station for anticipating the problems, it is necessary to detect them upstream before the input of the plant. So it would be possible to react before the arrival of the problem. To do that it seems possible to implement the fuzzy classification in the different pumping stations that work before the input of the plant.

7.4   Results with Support Vector Machines

To observe the ability of support vector machines to generalize, a second experiment has been elaborated. The only parameters containing daily data are quantity of rain and input flow rate. So, we would like to determine the forthcoming flow rate from the data in the past two days and the actual data (6 entries).

Training data has been created selecting, in a random manner, five days for each month during a year. In this moment we are using only 1/6 of total information to train our machine for regression. The input flow rate evolution is depicted on Fig. 4(b) (up) and the results are depicted down on the same subfigure.

On the graphic, days are represented in the X-axis and normalized input flow rate (original and predicted) is represented in the Y-axis. It can be observed as predicted input flow rate is very close to the actual input flow evolution. Even in some cases where input flow is very large, error rate is very low.

8   Conclusions

The fuzzy classification is well adapted to the detection of abnormal situation in waste water treatment plant. Results obtained with the Support Vector technique on simulated and real data are very promising, too.

The difficulties to solve known are of two types. The first of them is to have online and real time sensors at different points of the plant (especially at the input) for quantities like COD or total nitrogen.

The second problem to be solved is to detect abnormalities that have not been classified until now.

After that, a supervision system could be installed on the plant in order to control it very early, which means before the input of the station.

Acknowledgements. This study has been carried out with financial support from the "Communauté de Travail des Pyrénées", specific RTD programme 2001-2002, MIPEDAR (Monitoring Intelligent prédictif des stations d'Epurations des eAux Résiduelles).

The authors gratefully acknowledge their partners in that project for their help. They thank also the CGE office in Perpignan for placing the data at their disposal.

256 A. Traoré et al.

References

1. Angulo, C., Català, A.: K-SVCR, A multi-class support vector machine. Lecture Notes in Computer Sciences. **1810** (2000) 31–38
2. Millis, N.F., Ip, S.Y.: Effect of uncoupling phosphorylation on the economics of the activated sludge process. Chemical Eng. Communications **45** (1986) 1–6
3. Baeza, J.A., Ferreira, E.C., Lafuente J.: Knowledge-based supervision and control of wastewater treatment plant: a real-time implementation. Water Science and Technology **41** (2000) 129–137
4. Roda, I.R., Sànchez-Marrè, M., Comàs, J., Cortès U., Poch, M.: Development of a case-based system for supervision of an activated sludge process. Environmental Technology **22** (2001) 477–486
5. Baeza, J., Gabriel, D., Béjar, J., Lafuente, J.: A distributed control system based on agent architecture for wastewater treatment. Computer-Aided Civil and Infrastructure Eng. **17** (2002) 93–103
6. Estaben, M., Polit, M., Steyer, J.P.: Fuzzy Control for an anaerobic digester. Control Engineering Practice **9** (1997) 1303–1310
7. Heinzle, E., Dunn, I.J., Ryhiner, G.B.: Modeling and control for anaerobic wastewater treatment. Advances in Biochemical Engineering Biotechnology **48** (1993) 79–114

Ant Colonies for the RCPS Problem

Joaquín Bautista and Jordi Pereira

Universitat Politécnica de Catalunya.
ETSEIB. Avda. Diagonal 647, Planta 7. 08028 Barcelona (Spain)
{Joaquin.bautista, jorge.pereira}@upc.es

Abstract. Several approaches based on Ant Colony Optimization (ACO) are developed to solve the Resource Constrained Project Scheduling Problem (RCPSP). Starting from two different proposals of the metaheuristic, four different algorithms adapted to the problem characteristics are designed and implemented. Finally the effectiveness of the algorithms are tested comparing its results with those previously found in the literature for a data set used as a the benchmark instance set for the problem.

1 Introduction

The Resource Constrained Project Scheduling Problem (RCPSP) is a classical problem from the Industrial Engineering area, which has extensively received the attention of the literature, see [13], [16] and [21]. The problem consists on finding a feasible schedule minimizing the makespan, the total duration, for a project built by a set of activities with known and deterministic durations subject to precedence constraints between activities and accumulative constraints related to resource availability and resource consumption by the activities.

Several exact solution approaches have been developed, being the most effective those based on branch and bound procedures, see [17] and [18], able to solve problems with up to thirty activities optimally; but due to the NP-Hardness character of the problem, several heuristics [13] and metaheuristics [2], [3] and [9] have been developed for solving real size instances of the problem. Between the heuristics approaches, the greedy heuristics based on progressive construction of the solution using a priority rule and serial or parallel, [1] and [11], scheduling scheme are the most famous. The priority rules combine or refer some characteristics of the instance, like activities duration, the total slack of the activities, their number of successors, the resource consumption of the activities, etc., to order the activities in each iteration of the greedy procedure, and select the most promising activity between a set of candidate activities compatible with the current partial schedule.

The application of these type of algorithms offer good mean solutions, usually improving when the number of characteristics taken into account by the priority rule increases. Unfortunately, no single priority rule can be considered to dominate all other rules for any instance of the problem, and they only provide a single solution unless some randomness is added to the procedure.

M.T. Escrig Monferrer and F. Toledo Lobo (Eds.): CCIA 2002, LNAI 2504, pp. 257-268, 2002.

Between the metaheuristics developed for the problem, simulated annealing (SA) [3], tabu search (TS) [2] and genetic algorithms (GA) [9] are the most well known. These heuristics provide alternative ways to explore the solution neighborhood in a space limited by the neighborhood definition, but due to their generality, they cannot take profit of the knowledge present in the greedy heuristics, unless some special operators are designed to take them into account.

This work shows several implementations of the ACO, Ant Colony Optimization [6], metaheuristic which combine some elements from the greedy heuristics, and their knowledge of the problem, with a neighborhood structure defined by previously high quality solutions. A local search procedure, known as justification is added to obtain a fast procedure with good performance results.

2 Greedy Procedures for the RCPSP

2.1 Problem Definition

Formally, a RCPSP problem can be described as follows. Let $X_0=\{0,...,n+1\}$ denote the set of n activities of a project, M be the set of m resource types while $R_0=\{R_{01},...,R_{0m}\}$ is the set of resource capacities where resource consumption is constrained to R_i. Each activity $i \in X_0$ has an associated completition time d(i) and a resource requirement r(i,1),...r(i,m) where r(i,j) is the requirement for a resource of type j per time unit by the activity i.

Let P_i be the set of immediate predecessors of activity i. 0 is the only start activity, that has no predecessor and n+1 is the only end activity, which has no successor. We assume that the start activity and the end activity have processing time zero, and thus usually known as dummy tasks. A schedule for the project is represented by the vector $(s_0,s_1,...,s_{n+1})$ where S(i) is the starting time of activity $i \in X_0$. If S(i) is the start time of activity i, then F(i)=S(i)+d(i) is its finishing time. The makespan of a project is the difference between finish time and start time. Observe that the start time of a schedule equals S(0) and the finish time equals F(n+1). A schedule is feasible if it satisfies the following constraints: I) activity $i \in X_0$ must not be started before all its predecessors are finished, that is S(i)≥S(i)+d(i) for every S(i)∈P(i), and II) the resource constraints have to be satisfied, that is at every time unit t the sum of the resource requirements of all scheduled activities does not exceed the resource capacities, that is for every resource and every time unit the solution holds:

$$\sum_{S(i) \in X_0 ; S(i) \le t < S(i)+d(i)} r(i,j) \le R_0(j)$$

The RCPSP problem consists in finding a feasible schedule with minimal makespan for a given project.

2.2 Scheduling Schemes and Solution Representations

The literature of the problem shows several scheduling schemes and solution representation formats.

The two most common scheduling schemes found in the literature are the serial scheduling scheme and the parallel scheduling scheme. Both return the total duration of the project, known as the project makespan, C_{max}, a compatible schedule defined by the starting and ending instant of each activity and, if needed a list of tasks ordered by the decision step when they were scheduled. Both schemes follow an iterative pattern, but the difference lies on how the algorithm goes from one iteration to the next one.

The serial scheduling scheme is based on activity advances, so in each iteration an activity is selected for scheduling, while the parallel scheme uses a clock advance scheme, in each iteration as many activities as possible are scheduled until no other activity can be scheduled. Even though the parallel scheduling scheme is easier to implement, it's more intuitive and has good results with classic scheduling rules, Kolish [12] showed that the parallel scheduling scheme builds solutions in the set of non-delay schedules, a subset of the active schedules where optimal solutions lie. As the non-delay schedule is a subset of the set containing the optimal solutions it's possible that the optimal solution is not included in the non-delay set, so a parallel scheduling scheme might not generate an optimal solution even if all possible schedules are generated. This demonstration has leaded to an increase in the use of the serial scheduling scheme, which will also be used in the present work.

The scheduling scheme also relies on the format used to represent a solution. Three different methods have been applied to codify it. The first, known as rule representation, is based on associating a priority value to each activity (a set of priority rules found in the literature is shown in the Appendix I) that any scheduling scheme can transform in a solution to the problem. In the second representation, known as activity list representation, the solution is represented as an ordered vector of activities compatible with precedence constraints. A third approach, known as rule list, is based on associating a priority rule to each scheduling decision step, and select the activity whose priority index for this rule is higher.

2.3 Serial Scheduling Scheme

The scheduling scheme used in this work is shown afterwards.

Parameters:
n   Number of activities
m   Number of resources
i   Activity index, $0 \leq i \leq n+1$
j   Resource index, $1 \leq j \leq m$
k   Programming decision index, $0 \leq k \leq n+1$
t   Time index $1 \leq j \leq Bound[C_{max}]$
d(i)   Duration of activity i.
W   Set of scheduled activities
X   Set of non-scheduled activities. Initially X_0.
Pi   Set of immediate predecessors of activity i

Y_k Set of activities with precedence activities already scheduled ($Y_k \subseteq X$) in the k-th scheduling step.

S(i)   Starting time of activity i

F(i)   Finishing time of activity i

$R_0(j)$ Availability of resource j

R(t,j) Availability of resource j at the time t, initially equal to $R_0(j)$ for any t.

r(i,j) Resource consumption of resource j by the activity i.

Algorithm scheme:

1. Initialization: W={$\varnothing$}, R(t,j)=R_0(j) for each t.
2. For k=1 to n do
3. Calculate Y_k (composed by the activities whose predecessors are part of the set W)
4. Select activity$\in Y_k$
5. Assign S(activity) and F(activity)
6. Update R(t,j) for each t between I(activity) and F(activity) for each j.
7. W=W $\cup$ { activity }
8. X=X$\cap$ { activity }
9. End For
10. Cmax=max{F(i)}

In this algorithm, steps 4 and 5 are not fully formalized. Step 5, assigning S(activity) and F(activity) consists on finding the minimal feasible starting time, where precedence relationships are fulfilled (S(activity)$\geq$F(predecessor) for any predecessor of activity) and enough available resources for the duration of the activity exist (R(t,j)$\geq$r(i,j) for any resource and any S(activity)$\leq$t<F(activity)). The finishing time will be the starting time plus the duration of the activity.

The selection step, 4, relies on the particular algorithm and schedule representation. The algorithms can define different policies to select the activities ranging from a random selection between candidates to more sotisfied proposals. Some of the heuristics shown here will make use of a probabilistic rule based on information obtained by previous solutions and a priority rule. In other circumstances, e.g. use of a activity list representation used in the local search procedure shown afterwards, step 3 is not needed, because the definition of the activity list representation assures that the k-th activity on the list will be precedence compatible with the previously selected activities.

2.4 Serial Scheduling Scheme

The following heuristics, see section three and four, make use of a double justification procedure as a local search embedded in the global scheme.

This procedure exploits the reversibility property of the instances of the problem to try to minimize the makespan. The reverse instance of an instance is the instance obtained by reversing the precedence relationships while keeping the resource consumption of each activity. Obviously each solution for the reverse instance can be transformed in a solution for the direct instance by substrating the finishing time of the activity to the makespan of the problem to get the starting time of the activity for the direct problem.

The justification procedure consists on generating a schedule for the reverse instance of a problem from a solution to the direct problem. The schedule for the reverse instance starts with an activity list representation of tasks ordered by decreasing finishing times from the original solution, using the lexicographic order to break any possible ties. This procedure obtains an alternative solution whose makespan is equal to or inferior the original solution makespan.

The double justification procedure is based on applying the justification step twice: first the original solution is justified to the "right", creating an activity list as shown before and evaluating it, and afterwards the solution is justified to the "left", justifying the solution obtained by right-justifying and obtaining a new solution for the direct instance, whose makespan will be smaller than or equal the original makespan.

3 The ACO Metaheuristic

3.1 Introduction to the ACO Metaheuristic

The ACO, Ant Colony Optimization, metaheuristic is an evolutive heuristic procedure used to solve combinatorial optimization problems, inspired on the behave of real ants. More precisely, the metaheuristic uses an analogy with the indirect communication used by ants to solve real life problems, like food foraging, using a multi-agent collaboration scheme. Its main characteristics are: (1) Use of positive feed-back (speeding up the discovering of good quality solutions), (2) distributed computing (the structure of the algorithm allows a simple and natural parallelization scheme) and (3) the use of greedy constructive heuristics.

In the ACO metaheuristic [7], a colony of "artificial ants" search in a collective fashion high quality solutions for a considered optimization problem. Each ant builds a solution by several iterations. In each decision point a activity is selected from a set of possible candidates using a probabilistic transition rule, based on heuristic information of the instance and historical information (a trail of "pheromones") from previously built solutions.

The historical information that ants use during the construction steps consists on a matrix on indices that keep track of characteristics of previously found good quality solutions.

It's not hard to see the relationships between the outlined heuristic and the serial scheduling scheme from section 2.2. Each ant will create a solution using the serial scheduling scheme and a unique probabilistic priority rule based in one heuristic rule from the literature, see appendix I, and the trail available from previous solutions.

Once the ants have built a solution, the ant leaves trail in some of the attributes of the solution, proportionally to the quality of the solution the ant has built, favoring the exploration of solutions "near" the best solutions found previously.

From the initial proposal for the metaheuristic, several implementation for different problems have appeared, between them the travelling salesman problem [6], the jobshop problem [4], or the resource constrained project scheduling problem shown here [15] and several variations from the original scheme, between them the

MINMAX-ACO, from Stützle and Hoos [Stültze 97], the ACS from Dorigo and Gambardella [5], the HAS from Gambardella, Taillard and Dorigo [8] and the FANT from Taillard [20].

3.2 Characteristics of the Proposed Implementation

The basic scheme of the proposed implementation is based on the subcolony concept. Each subcolony is an independent set, built up by functional units called ants. Each ant is independent from the rest and is able to create its own list of activities using the probabilistic rule shown afterwards and evaluate the list using the serial scheduling scheme. The probabilistic rule will be built from the trail information and one of the priority rules shown in appendix I. This modification, the use of different priority rules for the same procedure, allow the use of different source of knowledge, the priority rules, on the same procedure, taking profit of all of them. Additionally, only the best ant of each subcolony will lay trail, a concept known as elitism [5]. Two different policies of depositing trail have been tested. In the first one, the trail is left between correlative pairs of activities in the activity list representation of the solution, while in the second the trail is left between the activity and the position it occupies in the activity list.

In each scheduling decision (step 4 from the algorithm shown in 2.2) the probabilities to choose the activity i from a set D of candidate activities is determined using the following pondered probability rule (1), where α and β are two algorithm parameters representing the importance given to the trail information τ and the heuristic information, η, on activity selections

$$p_{ij} = \frac{[\tau_{ij}]^{\alpha}[\eta_j]^{\beta}}{\sum_{h \in D}[\tau_{ih}]^{\alpha}[\eta_h]^{\beta}} \tag{1}$$

Three different policies to leave the trail information τ_{ij} are used. The first one is identical to the original proposal from Dorigo, and reads the trail between correlative activities in the activity list, leaving trail as commented before. The second consists on obtaining the trail between the activity to schedule and the decision step, which could occupy in the activity list if it was scheduled in this position. Finally, the third is based on the trail left between the activity and the summation of trails between the first scheduling decision and the decision in which in may be scheduled. The later two approaches will leave trail between the activity and the position of the list when trail updating occurs.

Due to the difference of range adopted by each proposed priority rule, its associated values are normalized before using (1) between 1 and the cardinality of the cardinality of the set D of candidates, using a linearization.

Once finished the generation of solutions of each subcolony, the trail-updating step follows. This step is divided in two phases. In a first phase a small quantity of trail is "evaporated" to add diversity to the search using (2) where ρ is a parameter of the algorithm known as evaporation.

$$\tau_{ij} = (1 - \rho) \cdot \tau_{ij} \tag{2}$$

In the second phase the trail is deposited depending on the trail management policy using formula 3, where UB is a known upper bound for the problem, the best solution found until now, and makespan is the total duration of the solution leaving trail.

$$\tau_{ij} = \tau_{ij} + \frac{UB}{makespan} \cdot \rho \tag{3}$$

The double justification procedure shown before is applied to each solution generated by the ants and the resulting activity list is used as a base to leave trail.

3.3 Global Scheme of the Heuristics

Once shown the particular details of the proposed implementations, we show the algorithm for the problem and the subcolony procedure.
   Algorithm: ACO Algorithm
1. Initialize trail to a small constant.
2. Create a subcolony.
3. The subcolonies form a solution using the trail information and their priority rule.
4. Update trail with the best found solution of the subcolony.
5. If final condition reached, end. Else, go to step 2
   Procedure: Ants subcolony
1. Build an ant with its own priority rule.
2. Build a solution using the priority rule, the trail information and the serial scheduling scheme.
3. Apply double justification to the solution provided by step 2.
4. While there are ants to generate go to 1.
5. Return the best solution obtained by the subcolony.

The ant algorithm shown before calls the subcolony procedure in step 3, which uses the serial scheduling scheme and double justification to obtain a solution. Each subcolony will thus generate 39 solutions (thirteen ants, one for each priority rule, and three evaluations for each ant, one for the construction and two for double justification), where only the best solution will update the trail.

4 Hybrid Ant System

Following Gambardella, Dorigo and Taïllard proposal for the Quadratic Assignment Problem [8] another version of the ACO heuristic which radically differs from the previous ones has also been implemented.

   In the HAS (Hybrid Ant System) scheme, the ants do not build solutions from scratch but use the trail information to generate small perturbations on the original solution that allow the reoptimization of the solution in course.

   The algorithm is shown afterwards:

Algorithm: HAS
1. Generate an initial solution
2. Apply a perturbation to the solution
3. Apply a local search procedure to the perturbed solution
4. Update the trail information
5. If ending condition is satisfied: end. Else go to 2.

In this algorithm the trail information will notify how to make the perturbation movements. The initial solution is built using the heuristic EFT, shown in the Appendix I, while the rest of the algorithm is symmetric to the proposed in section 3; the local search procedure used is double justification, and the trail management policy is based on leaving trail between the activity and its position in the activity list.

The perturbation procedure makes nc changes on the initial solution, where nc is a parameter of the algorithm corresponding to the number of exchanges which will be done on the initial solution on each call to the perturbation routine. This parameter was fixed to 5 during the computational experience shown afterwards, and should vary depending on the size of the problem.

Each one of the exchanges, chooses an activity at random, determines all activities which could exchange their positions in the list by the position occupied by the random activity creating a new list of activities fulfilling precedence constraints and choosing one using one of the next two policies.

With probability p (fixed in the algorithm to 5%) a intensification policy is used, choosing to exchange the activity whose trail summation between the first position and the new position is maximal.

With probability $1-p$ a diversification policy is used choosing an activity with probability (4) between the candidate list.

$$p_i = \frac{\sum_{j=1}^{np} \tau_{ij}}{\sum_{h \in D} \sum_{j=1}^{np} \tau_{ij}} \qquad (4)$$

where np correspond to the position occupied by the random selected activity.

5 Computational Experience

The heuristics were implemented in C language and have been tested with the dataset j120 from the PSPLIB [14] collection. The dataset is built by 600 instances to the problem with 120 activities each and four types of resources. This dataset is the hardest available from the PSPLIB and is used as a benchmark set for the algorithms to measure their quality in the literature. As a measure of the computing time, the number of solutions constructed by the heuristics (100, 1000 and 5000 solutions) is used. This method is also the used in the literature for comparing results between different computers and implementations. Running times for each evaluation were around 0.03 seconds per iteration for the HAS algorithm and 0.022 seconds for the ACO algorithms. The following parameters were used: α, trail importance, equal to 0.25; β, heuristic importance, equal to 0.75; and ρ, trail evaporation, equal to 0.1. As the number of evaluations done by each ACO subcolony is thirty-nine, the number of subcolonies used is 3, 25 and 128 subcolonies. For the heuristic proposed in section 4, the number of iterations will be 33, 333 and 1666. The algorithms will be marked in the results as ACO-T (ACO with trail left between activities), ACO-P (ACO with trail left between activity and position) and ACO-MP (ACO with trail left between activity and positions and read in an accumulative fashion) for the heuristics of section 3 and HAS for the heuristic in section 4.

The following table shows, for each heuristic and each number of generated solutions, the mean deviations between the obtained results, the best solution found compared to the best solution known and the bound obtained by relaxing the resource consumption constraints, obtained by any minimum path algorithm, and known as the CPM method in project scheduling.

Table 1. Results obtained by each heuristic for a given number of generated solutions.

	Dev. Best solution (%)	Dev. CPM (%)	Optimum found
ACO-T-100	7.69	40.11	147
ACO-T-1.000	7.65	40.01	147
ACO-T-5.000	6.82	38.8	159
ACO-P-100	7.34	39.5	148
ACO-P-1.000	6.72	38.7	159
ACO-P-5.000	6.72	38.6	159
ACO-AP-100	7.38	39.65	149
ACO-AP-1.000	6.36	38.14	167
ACO-AP-5.000	6.36	38.1	167
HAS-100	7.65	40.06	150
HAS-1.000	6.07	37.72	166
HAS-5.000	5.16	36.42	177

The results show that the proposed heuristics converge to high quality solutions fast, keeping a small deviation to the best known solution of the problem. This converge can even be considered as premature for some algorithms. For example, the heuristics ACO-AP and ACO-P obtain similar results for 1000 and 5000 generated solutions, making use of the trail information to obtain improvements between 100 and 1000 iterations to reach a stable solution forbidding diversification.

The ACO-T heuristic were strong improvements are located between the 1000 and 5000 solutions. The HAS procedure, even if it substantially improve between the 100 and 1000 solutions, it continues improving the quality obtained.

The following table shows a comparative between several procedures present in the literature. The number of solutions reported for these heuristics is equal to 1000 and 5000 solutions and are compared with the solutions obtained by 1000 and 5000 generated solutions offered by the procedure. The results obtained by Baar's et al. tabu search [2] are not shows as no results for problems over 90 activities were reported.

Table 2. Comparative results with those found in the literature.

Procedure	Author	Dev. CPM(%)-1000	Dev.CPM(%)-5000
HAS	Present	37.72	36.42
AS-RCPSP	[15]	---	36.65
GA-serial activity list	[9]	39.37	36.74
SA-serial activity list	[3]	42.81	37.68
ACO-MP	Present	38.14	38.1
ACO-P	Present	38.7	38.6
Sampling-LFT-paralelo	[11]	39.60	38.75
ACO-T	Present	40.1	38.8

The HAS procedure seems to be more effective than the genetic algorithm due to Hartmann, considered as the best algorithm available for the problem. The difference between both algorithms for 1000 and 5000 solutions diminishes, alerting on possible improvements by using a some long-term diversification scheme. The rest of algorithms presented are competitive for 1000 generated solutions limit, but they cannot compete on the long term with the ACO heuristic proposed by Merkle et al. [15] for 5000 ants. In should be said that our ACO heuristics only generate 1666 ants, and not 5000 as Merkle's one, and don't use an exhaustive 2-opt exchange mechanism used by Merkle et al. which increase the computation times.

6 Conclusions

The Ant Colony Algorithms seem to be a competitive approach for solving resource constrained scheduling problems. The heuristics shown obtain the best solutions limited to 1000 schedules generated, and the best algorithm, the HAS algorithm, from those shown here, improves the performance shown by the best available procedure from the literature.

Appendix: Heuristic Rules

Nomenclature:

$P(i)$ Processing time of activity I

$R(i,j)$ Resource j consumption by activity I

$R_0(j)$ Available resource j

$i \Rightarrow h$ Successors of activity I

$ns(i)$ Number of immediate successors of activity I

$nts(i)$ Number of successors of activity I

$CPM(i)$ Length of the critical path between the starting and activity i of the project, obtained by a shortest path algorithms

Number	Name	Rule
1	SIO *Shortest Imminent Operation.*	$v(i) = -P(i)$
2	GRD *Greatest Resource Demand*	$v\,(i) = P(i)\sum_{j=1}^{M} R(i,j)$
3	GRPW *Greatest Rank Positional Weight.*	$v(i) = P(i)\sum_{i\Rightarrow h} P(h)$
4	WRUP	$v(i) = w_p ns(i) + w_r \sum_{j=1}^{M} \dfrac{R(i,j)}{R_0(j)}$ $w = 1 - w_r;\quad w_r = (0.0, 0.1, ..., 0.9, 1$
5	WRUP2	$v(i) = w_p \sum_{i\to h} P(h) + w_r \sum_{j=1}^{M} \dfrac{R(i,j)}{R_0(j)}$
6	MTS *Most Total Successors*	$v(i) = nst(i)$
7	WRUP3	$v\,(i) = w_p P(i) + w_r \sum_{j=1}^{M} \dfrac{R(i,j)}{R_0(j)}$
8	WRUP5	$v(i) = w_p nst\,(i) + w_r \sum_{j=1}^{M} \dfrac{R(i,j)}{R_0(j)}$
9	MIT *Most Immediate Successors*	$v(i) = ns(i)$
10	Batcharjee-Sahu	$v(i) = SIO(i) + d(i)$
11	GPW *Greatest Positional Weight.*	$v(i) = \sum_{i\Rightarrow h} P(h)$
12	Weighted duration and resource consumption	$v(i) = SIO(i) + \sum_{j=1}^{M} d(i) * r(i,j)$
13	EFT. Earliest Finishing time	$v(i) = -(CPM\,(i) + d(i))$

Acknowledgements. This work has been partially funded by CYCIT grant DPI2001-2169. We would also like to thank two anonymous reviewers for their suggestions to improve this work.

References

1. Álvarez-Valdés, R., Tamarit, J.M. (1989) Heuristic algorithms for a resource constrained project scheduling: A review and an empirical analysis, Advances in Project Scheduling, R. Slowinski, J. Weglarz (Ed.). Elsevier, Amsterdam. 1989, pp. 113-134.
2. Baar T., Brucker P., Knust S. (1998) Tabu-search algorithms and lower bounds for the resource-constrained project scheduling problem in: S.Voss, S.Martello, I.Osman, C.Roucairol (eds.): *Meta-heuristics: Advances and Trends in Local Search Paradigms for Optimization, Kluwer,* 1-18.
3. Bouleimen, K., Lecocq , H. (1998) A new efficient simulated annealing algorithm for the resource-constrained project scheduling problem. *Technical Report, Service de Robotique et Automatisation,* Université de Liège.

4. Colorni A., Dorigo M, Maniezzo V y Trubian M. (1994) Ant System for job-shop scheduling. *JORBEL- Belgian Journal of Operations Research, Statistics and Computer Science*, 34(1) 39-53
5. Dorigo M. y Gambardella M. (1997) Ant Colony System: A cooperative learning approach to the traveling salesman problem. *IEEE Transactions on Evolutionary Computation*, 1(1) 53-66.
6. Dorigo M., Maniezzo V. y Colorni A. (1991) The Ant System: An autocatalytic optimizing process. *Thechnical Report 91-016 Revised, Dipartimento di Electronica*, Politecnico di Milano, Italy.
7. Dorigo M., Maniezzo V. y Colorni A. (1996) The Ant System: Optimization by a colony of cooperating agents. *IEEE Transactions on Systems, Man., and Cybernetics – Part B*, 26(1) 29-41.
8. Gambardella L.M., Taillard E.D. y Dorigo M. (1999) Ant colonies for the quadratic assignment problem. Journal of the Operational Research Society, 50(2) 167-176
9. Hartmann, S. (1997) A competitive genetic algorithm for resource-constrained project scheduling. *Technical Report 451, Manuskripte aus den Instituten für Betriebswirtschaftslehre der Universität Kiel.*
10. Hartmann, S., Kolisck, R. (1998) Experimental Evaluation of State of Art Heuristics for the Resource Constrained Project Scheduling Problem. *Wp. IBUK*, No. 476.
11. Kolisch, R. (1996) Efficient priority rules for the resource-constrained project scheduling problem. *Journal of Operations Management*, 14, 179-192.
12. Kolisch, R. (1996) Serial and parallel resource-constrained project scheduling methods revisited: Theory and computation. European *Journal of Operational Research*, 90, 320-333.
13. Kolisch, R., Hartmann S. (1998) Heuristic Algorithms for solving the resource-constrained project scheduling problem: Classification and computational analysis. *Handbook on Recent Advances in Project Scheduling*. Kluwer, Amsterdam.
14. Kolisch R., Sprencher A. (1996) PSPLIB – A project scheduling problem library. *European Journal of Operational Research*, 96. 205-216
15. Merkle, D., Middedorf M., Schmeck H. (2000) Ant Colony Optimization for Resource Constrained Project Scheduling. GECCO-2000
16. Özdamar, L., Ulusoy, G. (1995) Survey on the resource-constrained project scheduling problem. *IIE Transactions*, 27-5, 574-586.
17. Patterson, J.H.. (1984) A comparison of exact approaches for solving the multiple constrained resource, project scheduling problem. *Management Sc.*, 30-7, 854-867.
18. Simpson, W.P., Patterson, J.H. (1996) A multiple-tree search procedure for the resource-constrained project scheduling problem. *EJOR*, 89, 525-542.
19. Stützle T., Hoos H.H. (1997) The MAX-MIN Ant Syste and local search for the traveling salesman problem. *In T.Bäck, Z.Michalewicz and X.Yao, eds., Proceedings of the 1997 IEEE International Conference on Evolutionary Computation (ICEC'97)*, pp. 309-314. IEEE Press, Piscataway NJ
20. Taillard É. D., FANT: Fast ant system, *Technical report IDSIA-46-98*, IDSIA, Lugano, 1998.
21. Weglarz, J. Ed. (1998) *Handbook on Recent Advances in Project Scheduling*. Kluwer, Amsterdam.

A Multi-agent Architecture Integrating Learning and Fuzzy Techniques for Landmark-Based Robot Navigation

Dídac Busquets[1], Ramon López de Màntaras[1], C. Sierra[1], and T.G. Dietterich[2]

[1] Artificial Intelligence Research Institute (IIIA)
Spanish Council for Scientific Research (CSIC)
Campus UAB, 08193 Bellaterra, Barcelona, Spain
{didac,mantaras,sierra}@iiia.csic.es
[2] Oregon State University
Corvallis, OR, 97331 USA
tgd@cs.orst.edu

Abstract. This paper extends a navigation system implemented as a multi-agent system (MAS). The arbitration mechanism controlling the interactions between the agents was based on manually-tuned bidding functions. A difficulty with hand-tuning is that it is hard to handle situations involving complex tradeoffs. In this paper we explore the suitability of reinforcement learning for automatically tuning agents within a MAS to optimize a complex tradeoff, namely the camera use.

1 Introduction

In landmark-based navigation, the robot must be able to start in an unknown location and navigate to a desired target using visually-acquired landmarks. The specific scenario that we are studying assumes that there is a target landmark that the robot is able to recognize visually. The target is visible from the robot's initial location, but it may subsequently be occluded by intervening objects. The challenge for the robot is to acquire enough information about the environment (locations of other landmarks and obstacles) so that it can move along a path from the starting location to the target position. The robot should do this quickly but safely.

In this paper, we build upon the multi-agent architecture for outdoor landmark based navigation described in [14]. Each of the agents in the navigation system has a bidding function that is controlled by a set of internal parameters. These parameters need to be tuned to achieve the best performance of the Navigation system and of the overall system. Adjusting these parameters manually can be very difficult, particularly because of the tradeoffs confronting the top-level agents. An alternative to manual tuning is to employ machine learning techniques, specifically reinforcement learning (RL) methods. In this paper, we describe some experiments to test the feasibility of applying RL within this multi-agent system.

M.T. Escrig Monferrer and F. Toledo Lobo (Eds.): CCIA 2002, LNAI 2504, pp. 269–281, 2002.

RL is most needed and most appropriate in cases where there is a complex, quantitative tradeoff between behaviors. In such cases, manual tuning is difficult, and the quantitative criterion of maximizing expected reward, which is the goal of RL, permits us to represent the tradeoff nicely. In the navigation system, such a tradeoff appears with the use of the camera, since several agents compete for using it. Moreover, its use is expensive, so we want to minimize it.

Section 2 is devoted to relevant related work. The multi-agent architecture of the navigation system is described in Section 3. Section 4 describes the learning task. The details of the RL algorithm we have used are explained in Section 5. The experiments are presented in Section 6. Finally, the paper concludes with Section 7.

2   Related Work

Since Brooks proposed the subsumption architecture [4], many other coordination mechanisms for robotic systems have been proposed (Maes [10], [1]). Regarding multi-agent architectures, Liscano et al [7], Isik [8], and Stentz [15], among others, use hierarchical centralized architectures with arbitration to decide which activity takes control of the robot. Our approach, however, is completely decentralized, which means that the broadcast of information is not hierarchical. This approach is easier to program and is more flexible and extensible than centralized approaches. We propose a model for cooperation and competition between activities based on a simple bidding mechanism. A similar model was proposed by Rosenblatt [13] in CMU's DAMN project, in which voting was used to coordinate a set of modules to control the robot.

The map building approach we use is based on the work by Prescott [12], who proposed a network model that stores the spatial relationships among landmarks for robot navigation. By matching a perceived landmark with the network, the robot can find its way to a target, provided it is represented in the network. While Prescott's approach is quantitative, ours uses a fuzzy extension of his model to work with fuzzy qualitative information about distances and directions. Levitt and Lawton [9] also proposed a qualitative approach to the navigation problem, but assume unrealistically accurate distance and direction information between the robot and the landmarks. Another qualitative method for robot navigation was proposed by Escrig and Toledo [6], using constraint logic. However, they assume the robot has some a priori knowledge of the spatial relationship of the landmarks, while we build these relationships while exploring the environment.

3   The Multiagent Architecture

The architecture is composed of three systems (see Figure 1). Each system competes for two available resources: motion and vision. The three systems have the following responsibilities. The Pilot is responsible for all motions of the robot. It selects these motions to carry out commands from the Navigation system and

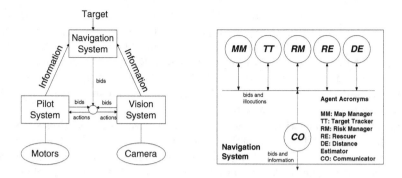

Fig. 1. Left: Robot architecture. Right: Navigation System.

(independently) to avoid obstacles. The Vision system is responsible for identifying and tracking landmarks (including the goal) and for detecting obstacles to support obstacle avoidance. The process of identifying landmarks requires comparing images taken before and after suitable robot motions, so the Vision system must ask the Pilot system to carry out certain motions to support perception. Finally, the Navigation system is responsible for choosing higher-level robot motions to move the robot to a specified goal. This requires requesting the Vision system to identify and track landmarks, to build a map of the environment, and requesting the Pilot to move the robot in various directions (to aid the Vision system or to move the robot toward the goal position or toward some intermediate target position).

From this brief description, two observations can be made. First, these three systems must cooperate to achieve the overall task of reaching the goal landmark position. For instance, the Pilot needs the Vision system to identify obstacles, and it needs the Navigation system to select a path to the goal. Second, the systems are also competing–there are some tradeoffs between them. For example, the Pilot and the Navigation system both compete for the Vision system. The Pilot needs vision for obstacle avoidance, while the Navigation system needs vision for landmark detection and tracking.

To manage this cooperation and competition, we use a bidding mechanism. Each system generates bids for the services offered by the Pilot and Vision systems. The service actually executed by each system depends on the winning bid at each point in time. We have manually written the bidding functions to obtain good performance from the combined system.

The Navigation system itself is also implemented as a MAS (see Figure 1). This system is composed of six agents with the following responsibilities: keep the target located with maximum precision and reach it (*Target Tracker*), keep the risk of losing the target low (*Risk Manager*), recover from blocked situations (*Rescuer*), keep the error in the distance to landmarks low (*Distance Estimator*), and keep the information on the map consistent and up-to-date (*Map Manager*). There is an additional agent, *Communicator*, which manages the communication between the Navigation system with the robot's other systems. As with the overall system, the Navigation system employs a bidding mechanism to coordinate these agents. Each agent bids for the action it wants the robot to perform. These bids are sent to the *Communicator* agent, which determines the winning action. The selected action is then sent as the Navigation system's bid for the services of the Vision and Pilot systems. Each action can involve a combination of requests to the Vision and the Pilot systems.

For map representation and wayfinding, we have extended Prescott's beta-coefficients system [12]. Prescott's model stores the relationships among the landmarks in the environment to build a map. The location of a landmark is encoded based on the relative locations (headings and distances) of three other landmarks. This relationship is unique and invariant to viewpoint. Once this relationship has been stored, the location of each landmark can be computed from the locations of the three landmarks encoding it, no matter where the robot is located as long as the robot can compute the heading and distance to each of the three landmarks.

As the robot explores the environment, it stores the relationships among the landmarks it sees. This creates a network of relationships among the landmarks in the environment. If this network is sufficiently-richly connected, then it provides a computational map of the environment. Given the headings and distances to a subset of currently-visible landmarks, the network allows to compute the locations of all of the remaining landmarks, even if they are currently not visible from the robot.

If there are landmarks associated with all known obstacles in the environment, then this network can also be employed to plan a path from the current location of the robot to the goal. Because of obstacles, this path may not be a straight line from the current location to the goal. Instead, it typically consists of a sequence of intermediate targets, called diverting targets, such that if the robot travels from one diverting target to the next, it will eventually reach the goal.

Prescott's model assumes that the robot is able to measure the exact location of the landmarks. But this is not the case in our robot: the vision system gives only imprecise information about the location of the landmarks, and we cannot rely on the odometry of the robot, as it is also imprecise. To deal with this unavoidable imprecision, our extended model represents all the network coordinates as fuzzy numbers and carries out all map computations using fuzzy arithmetic [3].

4   The Learning Task

Within the Navigation system, a tradeoff exists between the *Target Tracker* agent, the *Risk Manager*, and the *Distance Estimator*. For instance, the *Target Tracker* wants to know the exact heading and distance to the target at all times, while the *Risk Manager* wants to ensure that the robot is surrounded by a rich network of landmarks so that the robot does not get lost. These agents' goals

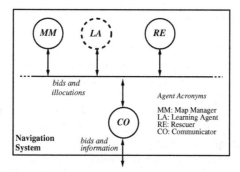

Fig. 2. Modified navigation system, with the new agent

compete for the control of the camera. In addition to this conflict between these agents, the Navigation system also must not monopolize the camera, because the Pilot needs to use the camera for obstacle avoidance as well.

We propose to replace the *Target Tracker*, the *Risk Manager*, and the *Distance Estimator* with a new *Learning Agent* whose bidding function will be tuned by RL. We formulate the reward function for this agent so that it is rewarded for reaching the current target while minimizing the use of the camera. The two remaining agents have very different roles. The *Map Manager* maintains the beta-coefficient map, but does not bid on actions. The only remaining active agent is the *Rescuer*, which is responsible for the higher-level choice of diverting targets whenever the robot becomes blocked. This activity is better-implemented by path planning algorithms than by RL, so we have not included the *Rescuer*'s responsibilities within the *Learning Agent*. The new architecture for the Navigation system is shown in Figure 2.

The task confronting the *Learning Agent* is to choose actions (for both motion and vision) to reach the current target while minimizing the use of the camera. The current target is determined by the *Rescuer*, and the *Map Manager* provides the map information needed by the *Learning Agent*. If the robot becomes blocked, the *Rescuer* will choose a diverting target, and then the *Learning Agent* will take control and choose actions to reach that new target. Once the diverting target is reached, the *Rescuer* may be able to set the current target to be the original goal, and then the *Learning Agent* will attempt to move to that target.

5   The RL Algorithm

There are two general styles of RL algorithms: Model-based and Model-free. Model-based algorithms learn a transition model $P(s'|s, a)$ for the environment, where s is the state of the environment at time t, a is an action to be executed, and s' is the resulting state of the environment at time $t + 1$. Model-based algorithms also learn a reward model $R(s, a, s')$ which gives the expected one-step reward of performing action a in state s and making a transition to state s'.

For robot learning model-free methods are impractical, because they require many more interactions with the environment to obtain good results.

Hence, for our experiments, we have chosen the model-based algorithm known as Prioritized Sweeping [11].

We represent both the transition model $P(s'|s, a)$ and the reward model $R(s, a, s')$ by three-dimensional matrices with one cell for each combination of s, s', and a. This technique will only work if the state and action spaces are small. Hence, the most challenging aspect of applying RL is the proper design of the state representation.

5.1   State Representation

We want the *Learning Agent* to learn a general policy that works for any environment, independent of the locations of the landmarks and targets. Hence, our state representation must not directly employ the locations of the landmarks. Moreover, the robot cannot directly observe the complete state of the environment, which would include the location of the robot, all obstacles, and all landmarks! Instead, the task of the robot is to learn under conditions of incomplete knowledge about the locations of obstacles, landmarks, and targets.

State spaces that encode incomplete knowledge are known as "belief state spaces" [5]. The purpose of a belief state representation is to capture the current *state of knowledge* of the agent, rather than the current state of the external world. We do not use the term belief state in the restricted sense of a probability distribution over states; the main reason to use a belief state representation is that it allows us to treat the states as observable. In our case, the learning agent is trying to move from a starting belief state in which it knows nothing to a goal belief state in which it is confident that it is located at the target state. Along the way, it seeks to avoid getting lost (a belief state in which it does not know its location relative to the target).

To explain our state representation, we begin by defining a set of belief state variables. Then we explain how these are discretized to provide a small set of features each taking on a small set of values so that $P(s'|s, a)$ and $R(s, a, s')$ can be represented with small tables.

At any given point in time, the headings to all objects (landmarks and the target position) are divided into six sectors of 60 degrees each. The field of view of the robot is 60 degrees, so at any point in time, the robot can observe one sector. For each sector, we represent information about the number of landmarks believed to be in that sector and the precision of our beliefs about their headings and distances.

Given these sectors, the following state variables can be defined:

- Distance to target, and its imprecision, $D(t), I_d(t)$
- Heading to target, and its imprecision, $H(t), I_h(t)$
- The landmarks in each sector, $L(s) = \{l_1, ..., l_{n_s}\}$

- Number of landmarks in each sector, $N(s) = \min(4, |L(s)|)$
- Average imprecision of landmarks in each sector,

$$\overline{I}(s) = \tfrac{1}{N(s)} \sum_{l \in Best(4, L(s))} I(l)$$

We now explain each of these. The distance $D(l)$ to a landmark (or $D(t)$ to the target) is a fuzzy number in the range $[0, \infty]$. The heading to a landmark $H(l)$ (or $H(t)$ to the target) is a fuzzy number with range $[0, 2\pi]$. For each of these, the imprecision ($I_d(l)$ for distance, $I_h(l)$ for heading) is defined by taking the interval corresponding to the 70% α-cut of the fuzzy number (see Figure 3).

The imprecision of a landmark is computed by combining the imprecision in the heading and in the distance as follows. First, $I_h(l)$ is normalized by dividing by its maximum value of 2π. Second, $I_d(l)$ is normalized by applying the hyperbolic tangent function, which maps it into the $[0, 1]$ interval. Finally, the two imprecisions are combined according to: $I(l) = \lambda \cdot \tanh(\beta \cdot I_d(l)) + (1 - \lambda) \cdot \frac{I_h(l)}{2\pi}$ where λ weighs the relative importance of the two imprecisions, and β controls how quickly the transformed I_d approaches 1. In our experiments, we set $\beta = 1$ and $\lambda = 0.2$.

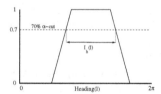

Fig. 3. Computation of imprecision from a fuzzy number

We summarize the agent's knowledge of the landmarks in each sector by averaging the imprecision of the four most-precisely-known landmarks. The function $Best : N \times 2^L \to 2^L$ selects a subset, $B = Best(n, L)$, of a group of landmarks, $L = \{l_1, ..., l_m\}$, such that $|B| \leq n \wedge \forall_{l \in B} \forall_{l' \in L-B} I(l) \leq I(l')$. Having 4 landmarks in one sector is already very good, since only 3 landmarks are needed to use the beta-coefficient system network. Furthermore, we do not want these measures to be affected by bad landmarks when we have some that are good enough. That is why we use $Best(4, L(s))$ when computing $\overline{I}(s)$.

5.2 Features

After computing these state variables, we discretize them to define a small number of features each of which takes on a small number of values. We employ the following features:

- Target Distance, $D(t)$, discretized to 5 intervals.
- Target Location Imprecision: measure of imprecision on the location of the target, $I(t)$, discretized to 7 intervals.

- Landmark Count: average number of landmarks over the six sectors, $\overline{C} = \frac{1}{6} \sum_{s=0}^{5} N(s)$, discretized to 4 intervals.
- Landmark Imprecision: average imprecision of landmarks' locations in each sector, $\overline{I} = \frac{1}{6} \sum_{s=0}^{5} \overline{I}(s)$, discretized to 7 intervals.

This gives a total of 980 belief states.

5.3   Actions

Just as RL requires careful design of the state space to ensure that it is compact, it also requires careful design of the action set to ensure that it is small but also sufficient for the robot to achieve its goals. This is even more important when we are planning based on dynamic programming, then we must keep the state and action spaces small.

Physically, the robot is able to simultaneously perform two types of actions: *moving* and *looking* actions. Moving actions make the robot move in a given direction. Looking actions employ the camera to identify or track landmarks in the environment in specified sectors. The vision system can either search for new landmarks or re-acquire already-detected landmarks, but it is not able to do both things at the same time, because different image processing routines are required for each. In either case, however, the vision system returns the heading and distance to the landmarks it detects.

An additional constraint on the design of actions is that the vision system is most effective when the robot is moving in certain directions relative to the landmarks being observed.

Given these constraints, we have designed the following set of actions for the *Learning Agent*:

- Move Blind (MB): move toward the target (i.e., in the direction in which the target is *believed* to lie). Do not use the vision system.
- Move and Look for Landmarks (MLL): move toward the target. Point the camera in the sector that contains the fewest number of known landmarks, and look for new landmarks in this sector.
- Move Orthogonally to Target (MOT): move orthogonally to the direction of the target. Point the camera at the target and attempt to improve the precision of the heading and distance to the target.
- Move and Verify Landmarks (MVL): move toward the target. Point the camera to the sector with the maximum imprecision, $\overline{I}$, and attempt to re-acquire known landmarks and measure their heading and distance more accurately.
- Move and Verify Target (MVT): move toward the target. Point the camera at the target and attempt to re-acquire it and measure its heading and distance more accurately.

These actions should affect the state variables as follows. All actions except MOT will make the distance to the target decrease. MB will make all impre-cisions grow. MLL should increase the number of detected landmarks. MOT should reduce the imprecision about the target's location, while MVL should reduce the overall imprecision. MVT will also reduce the imprecision of the target's location, but not as much as MOT. All actions require that the heading to the target is known (at least approximately). The heading is choosen as the center of the fuzzy interval for $H(t)$. If the heading is completely unknown, the center of this interval will be π. This causes the robot "pace" back and forth, turning 180 degrees (π radians) each time an action is executed.

We have assigned an immediate reward to each action to reflect the load on the vision and the motion systems. The rewards are negative, because they are costs. MB is the cheapest action, since it does not use the camera. It has a reward of -1. MVL and MVT produce a reward of -5, since they make moderate demands on the vision system. MOT gives a reward of -6, because it requires more motion in addition to the same image processing as MVL and MVT. Finally, MLL is the most expensive, with a reward of -10, because it must do extensive image processing to search for new landmarks and verify that they are robust to changes in viewpoint.

The system receives a reward of 0 when it reaches the target. The RL objective is to maximize the total reward. In our case, it is equivalent to minimize the total cost of the actions taken to reach the target.

6   Experimentation

We employ the Webots[1] simulator to perform our experiments. This simulator has a very high realism, adding noise to the robot movement and sensing. Figure 4 shows a picture of the simulated environment. This simulated environment contains a set of landmarks, one of which is designated as the target. There is also a wall that surrounds the region in which the robot is navigating. The landmarks are the only objects in the environment. There are no obstacles, as obstacle avoidance is handled by the Pilot system. However, the robot can be blocked by the landmarks or by the wall. In each trial, the robot starts at a random location in this environment, and it has to reach the target. The trial terminates under three conditions: (a) if the robot reaches the target (and is confident that it has reached the target), (b) if the robot takes 500 steps without reaching the target, or (c) if the robot is blocked.

In order to see if the performance of the system improves after learning, we compare it with a hand-coded policy. The hand-coded policy uses the same discretized features as the learning algorithm. If the robot is far from the target and there are few landmarks, it executes an MLL; if there are enough landmarks but they are highly imprecise, an MVL is executed; if the landmarks are good enough, an MOT is executed if the target's location has a high imprecision, and an MB is executed otherwise. If the robot is not far from the target but its location is highly imprecise, then an MVL or an MVT is executed, depending on whether the overall imprecision of landmarks is high or not; if the target's location has low imprecision, then if the robot is really near the target it executes

---

[1] Webots simulator, www.cyberbotics.com

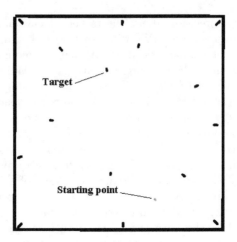

Fig. 4. Simulated environment

an MVT, and an MB is executed if the distance is medium. This hand-coded policy is not the same as the policy produced by the hand-coded bidding functions previously reported [14]. We have chosen this policy because it allows us to debug and test the *Learning Agent* separately from the rest of the multi-agent system.

The *Learning Agent* was trained for 2000 simulated trials. At regular intervals, the learned value function was tested by placing the robot in 99 randomly-chosen starting locations, running one trial from each location, and measuring the total reward, the total number of actions, and whether the robot succeeded in reaching the target position. The same set of 99 starting locations was employed in each testing period. The hand-coded policy was also evaluated on these 99 starting locations. Figure 5 shows that even after only 99 trials, the *Learning Agent* is already out-performing the hand-coded policy. After 2000 trials, the *Learning Agent* succeeds in reaching the target in 84 of the trials, compared to only 24 for the hand-coded policy.

Table 1. Comparison of the *Learning Agent* (LA) and the hand-coded policy (HC) after 2000 training trials. RPT: Reward per trial. APT: Actions per trial

	RPT	APT	MB	MOT	MVT	MVL	MLL
HC	−858	153.33	4.94	18.59	0.52	121.96	7.32
LA	−336	49.95	11.41	6.52	5.61	4.97	21.43

We can also compute the average reward per trial, the number of actions per trial, and the number of actions of each type. Table 1 displays this information after 2000 training trials. Each value is averaged over five test runs. The only difference between test runs is the random number seed for the Webots

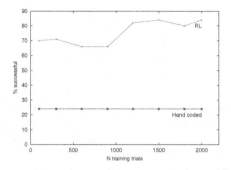

Fig. 5. Number of successful test trials as a function of training steps.

simulator. We see that while the hand-coded policy receives an average of −858 units of reward, the learned policy only receives −336 units, which is a huge improvement. In addition, the *Learning Agent* on the average only requires 50 steps to terminate a trial (reach the goal, become blocked, or execute 500 steps) compared to 153 steps for the hand-coded policy. The *Learning Agent* never terminates because of the 500-step limit.

Looking at Table 1, we see that the *Learning Agent* has learned to perform fewer MOT and MVL actions and more MB, MVT, and MLL actions. Note particularly that the learning agent is executing an average of 11.4 MB actions per trial, compared to only 4.9 for the hand-coded policy. One of the goals of applying RL was to find a policy that freed the camera for use by the low-level obstacle avoidance routines, and this is exactly what has happened. On the other hand, we were surprised to see that the *Learning Agent* chooses to execute the most expensive action, MLL, so often (21.4 times per trial, compared to only 7.3 times per trial for the hand-coded policy). Evidently, it has found that a mix of MLL and MB gives better reward than the combination of MVL and MOT that is produced by the hand-coded policy. The *Learning Agent* spends much more time looking for new landmarks and much less time verifying the direction and distance to known landmarks.

7   Conclusions and Future Work

The long-term goal of our research is to apply RL to automatically learn bidding functions in a multi-agent system. In this paper, we have taken a step toward this goal by showing that RL can learn to select actions to resolve a complex tradeoff that arises in our multi-agent robot control system. The results of our experiments show that the *Learning Agent* achieves a higher rate of success than the hand-coded policy in the Navigation multi-agent system. Furthermore, the *Learning Agent* accomplishes this while performing many fewer actions and while performing a different mix of actions. This underlines the value of employing RL rather than attempting to resolve complex tradeoffs by hand-coding.

The next step will be to integrate the *Learning Agent* into the overall multi-agent system and compare the performance of the *Learning Agent* with the performance of the hand-coded bidding functions described in [14]. This will require that we find a way to scale the learned value function so that it provides appropriate bids within the MAS. We may also find that the *Learning Agent* should place a higher or lower cost on using the camera than we employed in the experiments described here. We can easily change the reward function to reflect increased or decreased costs and then retrain the *Learning Agent*.

Additional future work will also test the robustness of these results to changes in the set of features and the set of actions. The current sets of features and actions reflects lessons from three previous design iterations. A challenge was to design features and actions that were well-matched in the sense that the actions should frequently lead to a change in the feature values so that RL can detect progress in moving toward (or away from) the goal. If the actions operate at a finer grain than the features can represent, most actions appear to leave the state unchanged, and learning becomes impossible. This has been termed the "state-action deviation problem" [2]. It can be fixed by using more levels of discrete values for each feature, but this slows learning by requiring that the robot perform more interactions with the environment. Asada et al. [2] suggest another solution in which self-loops (cases where the state is unchanged) are ignored in the transition model. We plan to evaluate the suitability of this approach in future experiments.

In designing the current set of actions, we sought to minimize the number of actions to keep the branching factor of the exploratory search small. However, a consequence of this is that most of the actions have "built-in" decisions. For example, MLL always looks for new landmarks in the sector with the fewest landmarks, and this might not always be best. However, we did not want to introduce six different "look-for-landmarks" actions, one for each sector, because this would increase the branching factor and make the initial exploration very slow. Nonetheless, we would like to study whether it might be possible to introduce such finer-grained actions after the *Learning Agent* has found a good initial policy. This might allow the learner to improve its performance further. In conclusion, RL is a promising method for tuning the behavior of agents in a multi-agent system.

Acknowledgements. This research has been supported by the Fulbright Joint Research Project and Plan Nacional Project DPI 2000-1352-C02-02. Dídac Busquets holds the CIRIT doctoral scholarship 2000FI-00191.

References

1. R.C. Arkin. Motor schema-based mobile robot navigation. *Int. J. Robotics research*, 8(4):92–112, 1989.
2. M. Asada, S. Noda, S. Tawaratsumida, and Koh Hosoda. Purposive behavior acquisition for a real robot by vision-based reinforcement learning. *Machine Learning*, 23:279–303, 1996.

3. G. Bojadziev and M. Bojadziev. *Fuzzy sets, fuzzy logic, applications*, volume 5 of *Advances in Fuzzy Systems*. World Scientific, 1995.
4. R. Brooks. A robust layered control system for a mobile robot. *IEEE J. of Robotics and Automation*, RA-2(1):14–23, 1986.
5. A. R. Cassandra, L. P. Kaelbling, and M. L. Littman. Acting optimally in partially observable stochastic domains. In *Proc. of the Twelfth National Conference on Artificial Intelligence*, pages 1023–1028, Cambridge, MA, 1994. AAAI Press/MIT Press.
6. M. Teresa Escrig and F. Toledo. Autonomous robot navigation using human spatial concepts. *Int. J. of Intelligent Systems*, 15:165–196, 2000.
7. R. Liscano et al. Using a blackboard to integrate multiple activities and achieve strategic reasoning for mobile-robot navigation. *IEEE Expert*, 10(2):24–36, 1995.
8. C. Isik and A.M. Meystel. Pilot level of a hierarchical controller for an unmanned mobile robot. *IEEE J. Robotics and Automation*, 4(3):242–255, 1988.
9. T.S. Levitt and D.T. Lawton. Qualitative navigation for mobile robots. *Artificial Intelligence Journal*, 44:305–360, 1990.
10. P. Maes. The dynamics of action selection. In *Proc. of IJCAI'89*, pages 991–997, 1989.
11. A. W. Moore and C. G. Atkeson. Prioritized sweeping: Reinforcement learning with less data and less time. *Machine Learning*, 13:103, 1993.
12. T.J. Prescott. Spatial representation for navigation in animats. *Adaptive Behavior*, 4(2):85–125, 1996.
13. J. Rosenblatt. Damn: A distributed architecture for mobile navigation. In *Proc. of the 1995 AAAI SpringSymposium on Lessons Learned from Implemented Software Architectures for Physical Agents*. AAAI Press, March 1995.
14. C. Sierra, R. López de Màntaras, and D. Busquets. Multiagent bidding mechanisms for robot qualitative navigation. In *Intelligent Agents VII. Lectures Notes in Artificial Intelligencee (Proc. of ATAL-2000)*, pages 198–212. Springer, Verlag, 2001.
15. A. Stentz. The codger system for mobile robot navigation. In C.E. Thorpe, editor, *Vision and Navigation, the Carnegie Mellon Navlab*, pages 187–201, Boston, 1990. Kluwer Academic Pub.

SIMBA: An Approach for Real-Time Multi-agent Systems

V. Julian, C. Carrascosa, M. Rebollo, J. Soler, and V. Botti

Departament de Sistemes Informàtics i Computació,
Universitat Politècnica de València, Spain
{vinglada,carrasco,mrebollo,jsoler,vbotti}@dsic.upv.es

Abstract. The use of the agent/multi-agent system paradigm has increased sharply as an important field of research within the Artificial Intelligence area. In recent times, the application of this paradigm seems appropriate for solving complex problems which require intelligence and bounded response times. This paper presents SIMBA : an architecture based on ARTIS agents as its main component for the development of real-time multi-agent systems. The ARTIS agent architecture guarantees an agent response that satisfies all its critical temporal restrictions in a real-time environment. The main feature of SIMBA systems is their applicability for complex, distributed, real-time domains. The architecture allows the communication among agents taking into account their hard temporal restrictions.
In order to show the use of systems of this kind, the paper describes the design of a multi-agent system for the distributed intelligent control of a residential building.

Keywords: agents, multi-agent systems, real-time AI.

1 Introduction

Over the last few years, the application of the agent / multi-agent paradigm in real-time environments arises from the required capacities of new real-time systems. This paradigm attempts to incorporate flexibility and distribution in new real-time designs. A *Real-Time System (RTS)* is a system in which the correctness of the system depends not only on the logical result of computation, but also on the time at which the results are produced [15]. It is well-known that a RTS is formed by a set of tasks characterised by a deadline, a period, a worst-case execution time and an assigned priority. A *deadline* defines the greatest time interval in which the system can provide a response. If the response is obtained after this time, it will probably not be useful. Researchers differentiate between two types of RTS. The first, called *Hard Real-Time System*, is a RTS where the execution of a task after its deadline is completely useless. Systems of this kind are critical systems and if timing responses are not satisfied, this will result in severe consequences. The second, called *Soft Real-Time System*, is characterised by the fact that the execution of a task after its deadline only decreases the

M.T. Escrig Monferrer and F. Toledo Lobo (Eds.): CCIA 2002, LNAI 2504, pp. 282–293, 2002.

quality of the task result [16]. Different techniques are needed for hard and soft RTS.

On the other hand, a multi-agent system which involves several agents that collaborate towards the achievement of a joint objective is viewed as a team of agents. Most proposed teamwork structures [10] [3] rely on agents in a multi-agent system to negotiate and/or contract with each other in order to initiate team plans. However, in dynamic, real-time domains with limited communication, complex negotiation protocols may take up too much time. Therefore, these protocols are not suitable for time-bounded problems.

Our work has been focused in time critical environments in which the full system can be controlled by autonomous agents that need communication to improve the system goal. This focus motivates the introduction of Social Real-Time Domains. In such domains, agents need to act autonomously while still working towards a common system goal. Time-critical environments require real-time response and, therefore, they eliminate the possibility of excessive communication among agents.

According to these concepts, it is possible to define a *Real-Time Agent* as an agent with temporal restrictions. These restrictions may be hard, soft or both. A real-time agent should guarantee its temporal restrictions and, concurrently, it should try to accomplish its goals. Finally, if a real-time agent is included as a component of a multi-agent system, this system can be considered as a *Real-Time Multi-Agent System*. It is important to highlight that the agent may have its interactions bounded. This modification will affect all the communication processes in the multi-agent system.

An architecture for a real-time multi-agent system is presented in this paper. The proposal is called SIMBA (Multi-Agent System Based on ARTIS) and it constitutes a significant extension of the ARTIS agent architecture approach for real-time environments [2]. SIMBA can be seen as a set of ARTIS agents and their interactions. This proposal increases the applicability of the ARTIS agent architecture for problems where a multi-agent approach is more suitable than a centralised one.

The rest of the paper is structured as follows: section 2 focuses on the features of social real-time domains. Section 3 presents an overview of the SIMBA architecture for real-time environments and its main component, the ARTIS agent. Section 4 goes into the communicative aspects of this type of agents. In section 5, an intelligent building management system is described as an example. Finally, some conclusions are mentioned in section 6.

2   Social Real-Time Domains

We define a social real-time domain as a domain with the following characteristics:

- There is a team of autonomous agents $\mathcal{A}$ that collaborate to achieve a common long-term goal $\mathcal{G}$.

- Periodically, each agent can read or send messages m with no adverse effects upon the achievement of $\mathcal{G}$.
- The domain is dynamic and time-bounded. This means that team performance is adversely affected if an agent fails to act for a period. Each agent is able to manage hard real-time restrictions and to solve a system subproblem.
- The domain has unreliable communication, either in terms of transmission reliability or bandwidth limits. If an agent $a_i \in \mathcal{A}$ sends a message m to agent $a_j \in \mathcal{A}$, then m arrives with some probability; or an agent a_i can only receive x messages every y time units. That is, sending a message does not guarantee its reception.
- A message m has a maximum length K, and an agent can send and receive at least one message m with a period p_i.

In the extreme case, the communication channel lose all the messages, then an interval of no communication will appear, requiring the agents to act completely isolated. If agent a_i cannot carry on with its action until receiving a message from a_j, then the team's performance could suffer. Because of the unreliable communication, the message might not get through on the first try. And because of the dynamic, real-time nature of the domain, the team's likelihood or efficiency of achieving $\mathcal{G}$ is reduced. However, if a message is received, it will be treated in a finite amount of time.

Intelligent building sensing and control is a social real-time domain since a set of agent controls different subsystems and they need to communicate with each other in order to maintain the global objective [13] [1]. There are several other examples of social real-time domains, such as port container terminal management, factory maintenance, distributed industrial process control and robot team control.

3   SIMBA Architecture

SIMBA is an architecture for multi-agent systems to work properly in social real-time domains. The SIMBA architecture constitutes the natural evolution of the ARTIS agent architecture, since it allows for the development of different related agents for hard real-time environments.

Basically, a SIMBA system is formed by a set of ARTIS agents (AA) with probably hard temporal restrictions. This set of agents controls the subsystem of the real-time environment with hard critical constrains. Additionally, the system may integrate different types of agents, which cover other non-critical activities on the system. For this reason, SIMBA must be prepared to incorporate heterogeneous agents using standard agent-interaction processes.

As mentioned above, the main component of the SIMBA architecture is the ARTIS agent, so, the architecture of this special type of agent is presented in the following point. Later, the formal approach and design aspects of the SIMBA architecture are described.

3.1   The ARTIS Agent Architecture

The ARTIS architecture is an extension of the blackboard model [12] which has been adapted to work in hard real-time environments. This architecture includes the use of well-known techniques of Real Time Artificial Intelligence Systems [9]. This approach guarantees reacting on the environment in a dynamic and flexible way. It incorporates all the necessary aspects that the agency features provide to a software system, but adapted to hard real-time environments.

The ARTIS agent architecture guarantees an agent response that satisfies all the critical temporal restrictions of the system, its capacities for problem-solving, for adaptability and for proactivity help to provide the best answer for the current environment status. Its critical timing requirements are 100% guaranteed by means of an off-line schedulability analysis as detailed in [8].

Basically, the agent must perceive an environment through a set of sensors. After this, the system must compute and transmit a response to other agents or the environment using a set of effectors. The response can be obtained after a reflex process or a deliberative process. Furthermore, the agent must work with hard temporal restrictions in dynamic environments.

Though the basic AA is designed to work properly under hard real-time restrictions, some of the optional features (such as communication with other agents) may prevent this real-time behaviour due to the unpredictable actions they involve. Therefore, it is the agent designer's decision to choose which features (and, therefore, which behaviours) the agent is going to have.

The AA architecture could be labeled as a vertical-layered, hybrid architecture with added extensions to work in a hard real-time environment [11]. It is formed by the following elements (see Figure 1):

- A set of sensors and effectors to be able to interact with the environment. Perception and action processes are time-bounded. The communication acts are included into these processes. So, the ARTIS agent has a Communication Module (CoMo) which is in charge of controlling the sending and arrival of messages.
- A *set of in-agents* (internal agents) that models the AA behaviours in order to achieve the AA goals. An *in-agent* is an internal entity that has the necessary knowledge to solve a particular problem (this knowledge can incorporate IA techniques that provide intelligence for solving the problem). Basically, this entity periodically performs a specific task (which may or may not be complex). The main reason for splitting the whole problem-solving method into smaller entities is to provide an abstraction which organises the problem-solving knowledge in a modular and gradual way. Depending on the temporal restrictions and the intelligence used in its problem-solving method, in-agents can be classified as *critical* or *acritical*. A *critical* in-agent is characterised by a period and a deadline. The available time for the in-agent to obtain a valid response is bounded. It must guarantee a basic response to the current environment situation. It is formed by two layers (see Figure 1): the reflex layer and the real-time deliberative layer. The first one assures a

minimal quality response and the second one tries to improve this response. The reflex layer of all the in-agents make up the AA mandatory phase. On the other hand, the real-time deliberative layers form the optional phase. An *acritical* in-agent only has the real-time deliberative layer. Almost all the in-agents for real-time environments are critical in-agents.

- A *set of beliefs* comprising a world model (with all the domain knowledge which is relevant to the agent) and the internal state. This set is stored in a frame-based blackboard. Temporal extensions have been incorporated allowing the reasoning entities to manage time naturally.

- The *Control Module* that is responsible for the real-time execution of the in-agents that belong to the AA. The temporal requirements of the two in-agent layers (reflex and deliberative) are different. Thus, the control module must employ different execution criteria for each one. The control module of an AA is divided into two submodules: the reflex server and the deliberative server.

  • Reflex server (RS) This module is in charge of controlling the execution of reactive components, that is, the components with critical temporal restrictions. Due to these restrictions, it is integrated within a Real-Time Operating System (RTOS).

  • Deliberative server (DS) This module is in charge of controlling the execution of deliberative components. Therefore, this server is the intelligent element of the control module, but with temporal restrictions.

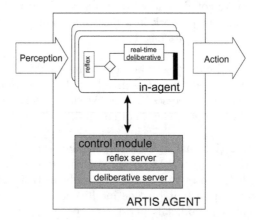

Fig. 1. ARTIS Agent Architecture

3.2 Formal Approach

Once the ARTIS agent architecture is presented, a formal view of the SIMBA approach is described. This formal view allows us to explain the architecture in a more concrete way.

Definition 1 *A* SIMBA *architecture is an structure:*

$$\text{SIMBA} = \langle A, O, L, I \rangle$$

where:

- $A = \{AA_i\}$, *a countable set of* ARTIS *agents, which are formalised below.*
- $O = $ *a domain ontology, which specifies the common vocabulary in order to represent the system environment.*
- $L = $ *a communication language to be employed by the agents for the interaction processes.*
- $I = \{(AA_i, AA_j)/AA_i, AAj \in A\}$, *a set of interactions represented by AA pairs. These interactions show the relations in the system organisation.*

As can be seen, the main component of a SIMBA system is the ARTIS agent, which can be formally defined as follows:

Definition 2 *An* ARTIS *agent is an structure:*

$$AA_i = \langle Behav_i, G_i, B_i, \beta_i \rangle$$

where:

- $Behav_i$ *is a set of different behaviours of the AA_i for different situations.*
- $G_i = \{g_1^{[t_1,t_2]}, g_2^{[t_2,t_3]}, \ldots, g_n^{[t_n,t_m]}\}$, *a set of AA goals, representing the motivations and restrictions of the agent. The goals are designed as desired states and they can be temporal bounded. These temporal restrictions show the interval in which the goal must be obtained. The goals can be expressed as RTCTL* formulae [5].*
- B_i *is the AA_i belief set in the current instant. All the data in this set are time stamped using a temporal logic as explained in [4].*
- $\beta_i : G_i \times B_i \rightarrow Behav_i$, *a selection function that determines the current behaviour of the AA_i according to its goals and its beliefs. This function corresponds to the AA Control Module.*

Each behaviour is defined as follows

Definition 3 *A behaviour beh $\in$ Behav_i is a set of in-agents*

$$beh = \{a_{ij}\}$$

A behaviour contains the problem-solving knowledge. As stated above, an in-agent gives a solution for a particular problem of the ARTIS agent.

Definition 4 *An in-agent is an structure*

$$a_{ij} = \langle \rho_{ij}, f\rho_{sel}, \sigma_{ij}, f\sigma_{sel}, B_{ij}, D_{ij}, T_{ij} \rangle$$

where:

- ρ_{ij} is a set of reflex actions that can be executed by the in-agent.
- $f\rho_{sel} : B_{ij} \times (D_{ij}, T_{ij}) \to \rho_{ij}$, a selection function that determines the appropriate reflex action to execute by the in-agent according to its current state and temporal restrictions.
- σ_{ij} is a set of cognitive actions that can be executed by the in-agent.
- $f\sigma_{sel} : B_{ij} \times (D_{ij}, T_{ij}) \to \sigma_{ij}$, a selection function that determines the appropriate cognitive action to execute by the in-agent according to its current state and temporal restrictions.
- $B_{ij} \subset B_i$, is a set of beliefs representing the internal state and environment of the in-agent. These beliefs are part of the belief set (B_i) of the AA_i that the in-agent belongs to.
- D_{ij} is a deadline, which indicates the greatest time interval in which the in-agent should have executed an action.
- T_{ij} is the period, which determines the activation frequency of the in-agent. This period is needed due to the external environment's own dynamic of RTS. At each period, the in-agent execution begins reading the new incoming values of the data (perceptions) through the appropriate sensors. These new values update the B_{ij} of the in-agent.

This organisation among AA, behaviours and in-agents provides a hierarchy of abstractions which structures the problem-solving knowledge in a modular and gradual way. One of the main reasons for doing this is to employ the advantages of modular programming, that is, complexity split and code reusability.

3.3   Architecture Design

The SIMBA architecture design is FIPA-compliant in order to allow for future inter-communication with outer agents from other platforms. A FIPA agent platform is defined as software that implements the set of FIPA specifications. To be considered FIPA-compliant, an agent platform implementation must at least implement the Agent Management [7] and Agent Communication Language specifications [6]:

- The Agent Management Specification forces the implementation of a Directory Facilitator (DF) that provides yellow-pages service to the agents involved and an Agent Management System (AMS) which maintains the addresses for agents registered in the platform (white-pages service).
- The Agent Communication Language Specification contains the message description set to be employed in agent interactions.

A graphical view of the SIMBA architecture is shown in Figure 2 in accordance with these considerations. As can be seen, it is formed by several ARTIS agents and a mediator agent which integrates the DF and the AMS services. This mediator agent is the SIMBA interface with agents that do not follow the ARTIS agent architecture. Moreover, the communication language in SIMBA will obviously be FIPA-ACL.

With respect to each ARTIS agent design, a single AA is implemented through a graphical toolkit named InSiDE (Integrated Simulation and Development Environment) [14] which facilitates the design and debugging of an AA. InSiDE is a visual toolkit which was developed to allow for agent-oriented implementation and management of ARTIS agents. It incorporates an off-line schedulability analysis, which assures that all the temporal restrictions are guaranteed a priori. By means of this toolkit, a user can build a prototype of an ARTIS Agent, which is directly executable over the RT-Linux operating system [8].

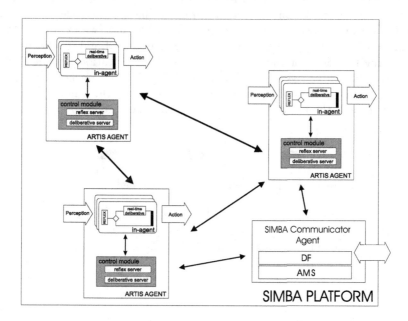

Fig. 2. SIMBA Platform

4   ARTIS Agent Communicative Aspects

The communication process has to be time-bounded in some way in order to be considered within a real-time restricted system such as the AA. On the other hand, the whole execution time of this process cannot be bounded, due to the multiple factors that may affect it, making it very difficult to assure the sending and reception of answers. Moreover, the foreseen interaction processes may be complex, and they may need to send several messages in the same process.

The main use of the AA communication is to ask for a service. According to its possible uses, it doesn't seem appropriate to consider the unfulfillment of a communication process as catastrophic. So, even though the communication process has soft real-time restrictions, it is not possible to assign critical temporal restrictions to manage it.

As has been previously mentioned, the part of the Control Module in charge of controlling the execution of the non-critical tasks of the AA is the Deliberative Server (DS). The DS controls the execution of the Communication Module. This module is in charge of controlling all the low-level peculiarities of a communication process such as message construction (according to the communication language), physical media sending and receiving, parsing, syntactic checking, etc.

Figure 3 shows a possible execution stage of an AA by a timing diagram. In this example, the AA is comprised by two in-agents (*a* and *b*). Black boxes represent the processor time intervals assigned to the in-agent reflex layer execution. Between these executions, there exists available time (white boxes). At the beginning of each one of these slacks, the DS is executed and it schedules this time taking into account the execution of the Communication Module and the real-time deliberative layers of the in-agents. The DS only launches the Communication Module if there is enough slack time to assure the sending of at least one message and the reception of at least another message.

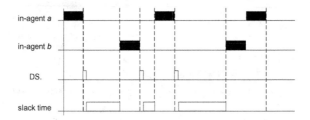

Fig. 3. Timing diagram example

This way of controlling the communication makes it possible to communicate without interfering in the fulfillment of critical AA restrictions.

5   Example: Intelligent Buildings

In this paper, we present a prototype of a system, developed according to our approach, which emphasises the multi-agent architecture presented in previous sections. The system we present controls an intelligent building. An intelligent building is one that utilises computer technology to autonomously govern the building environment so as to optimise user comfort, energy-consumption, safety and monitoring-functions [13]. In this example, we consider a residential building that has distributed different sensor and actuator devices which can be controlled and monitored. Due to the limits of the paper only some aspects of the example are sketched.

Three main functionalities can be extracted from the given definition of an intelligent building:

- Safety & Security: the system must take into account system failures such as gas or water leaks and detection of intruders.
- Comfort: all the aspects related to the building habitability and resident preferences.
- Energy-consumption: related to an effective management of energy resources such as electricity, gas, diesel or water.

This system belongs to the social real-time domains explained in section 2. There exist critical temporal constraints such as alarm activation or closing/opening valves. Moreover, there exists a clear distribution in the system activities. The coordination among the entities in the system will improve the global functionality but is not critical for the fulfillment of the critical constraints.

In this case, the SIMBA system is formed by three agents (see Figure 4): the safety/security agent, the comfort agent and the energy agent. Each one is in charge of controlling its corresponding subsystem.

$$A = \{AA_{safety}, AA_{comfort}, AA_{energy}\}$$

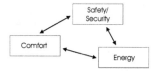

Fig. 4. Intelligent building control system

Each one of these agents is an ARTIS agent. SIMBA allows for the interaction with external, non-ARTIS agents through the services supplied by the mediator agent. For instance, it is possible for an agent to ask the system about one of the residents. The system can verify whether this person is at home or not. Some interactions in the system are:

- The safety/security agent informs about a system failure to the rest of the agents.
- The safety/security agent informs the comfort agent that the building is empty in order to minimise its functionalities.
- The energy agent and the comfort agent negotiate different energy resources consumption.

Due to the limits of this paper, we will focus on the safety/security agent. Depending on the presence or absence of residents in the building, the agent shows two different behaviours. If there is nobody in the building, then this agent is the only entity responsible for safety and security. The difference between them lies in the control that the agent must exert on the building. When it is unoccupied, the safety/security agent assumes all the responsibilities.

Additionally, another case can be detected: when a failure has happened—leak or intrusion—and the agent must change its monitoring behaviour to another, more critical and reactive, to handle it. Figure 5 shows the different behaviours of the safety/security agent as an state diagram.

$$Behav_{safety} = \{beh_{occ}, beh_{empty}, beh_{emerg}\}$$

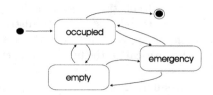

Fig. 5. State diagram. Safety agent behaviours

Each behaviour must deal with two responsibilities—leaks and intruders—. So, it seems adequate to assign an in-agent to each one. In such a case, the in-agents for each behavior only vary their temporal parameters—deadline and period—. Their knowledge and their reactions must be the same ones.

$$beh_{empty} = \{a_{leak}, a_{secur}\}$$

Temporal characteristics of in-agents will take into account the differences in the sensors and actuators sampling. One usual security measure in classic control systems is to achieve that the period of the system is $\frac{T}{2}$, where T is the period of the highest-frequency device. The deadline estimation depends on the dynamic of the environment. It must be such a deadline that allows to solve the problem in a satisfactory way for the user. For instance, to raise the fire alarm 2 seconds later from to detect smoke. It always must be lower than the period.

$$a_{leak} = \{\rho_{leak}, 5, 2\} \quad a_{secur} = \{\rho_{secur}, 30, 10\}$$

It must be always guarantee that the system can achieve its goals. That's why temporal intervals which characterise the goals must be less restrictive than the deadline and period of the in-agent responsible of the goal.

$$\Box G(smoke = TRUE \rightarrow \Box F^{\leq 10} alarm = ON)$$

In this RTCTL* expression, we are asking the system for a deadline of 10 seconds from the detection of smoke to the alarm raising.

6   Conclusions

This paper shows the SIMBA architecture, which is a real-time multi-agent system architecture. This architecture shows how a multi-agent oriented paradigm can be applied to solve problems in social real-time domains. To do so, it is needed software architecture with the appropriate components along with development artifacts adapted to build this kind of systems.

The work described in this paper is the result of an investigation effort with respect to the application of interaction processes in an ARTIS agent. Several questions remain open with respect to new protocols for ARTIS agents in order to do complex cooperation or coordination processes. We are currently working on the implementation of a complete version of the example described in this paper. This prototype will allow us to analyse the influence of the communication processes within the real-time behaviour and to prove new interaction protocols.

References

1. M. Boman, P. Davidsson, and H. Younes. Artificial decision making under uncertainty in intelligent buildings. In *Proceedings of UAI'99*, 1999.
2. V. Botti, C. Carrascosa, V. Julian, and J. Soler. Modelling agents in hard real-time environments. In *MAAMAW'99 Proceedings*, volume 1647 of *LNAI*, pages 63–76. Springer-Verlag, 1999.
3. P. Cohen, H. Levesque, and I. Smith. On team formation. In *Contemporary Action Theory. Synthese*. J. Hintikka and R. Tuomela, editors, 1998.
4. A. Crespo, V. Botti, F. Barber, D. Gallardo, and E. Onaindia. A temporal blackboard for real-time process control. *Engineering Applications of Artificial Intelligence*, pages 225–256.
5. E. Emerson, A. Mok, A. Sistla, and J. Srinivasan. Quantitative temporal reasoning. *Real-Time Systems*, (4):331–352, 1992.
6. FIPA. Agent acl message structure specification. Technical Report XC00061E, 2001.
7. FIPA. Agent management specification. Technical Report XC00023H, 2001.
8. A. Garcia-Fornes, A. Terrasa, V. Botti, and A. Crespo. Analyzing the schedulability of hard real-time artificial intelligence systems. *Engineering Applications of Artificial Intelligence*, pages 369–377, 1997.
9. A. Garvey and V. Lesser. A survey of research in deliberative real-time artificial intelligence. *The Journal of Real-Time Systems*, (6):317–347, 1994.
10. B. J. Grosz. Collaborative systems. *AI Magazine*, 17(2):67–85, 1996.
11. J. P. Muller. A conceptual model for agent interaction. In *Proceedings of the second International Working Conference on Cooperating Knowledge Base Systems*, pages 213–234, DAKE Centre, University of Keel, 1994. Deen, S. M. (Ed.).
12. P. Nii. Blackboard systems: The blackboard model of problem solving and the evolution of blackboard architectures. *The AI Magazine*, pages 38–53, Summer 1986.
13. S. Sharples, V. Callaghan, and G. Clarke. A multi-agent architecture for intelligent building sensig and control. *Sensor Review*, 19(2):135–140, 1999.
14. J. Soler, V. Julian, C. Carrascosa, and V. Botti. Applying the artis agent architecture to mobile robot control. In *Proceedings of IBERAMIA'2000. Atibaia, Sao Paulo, Brasil*, volume I, pages 359– 368. Springer Verlag, 2000.
15. J. Stankovic. Misconceptions about real-time computing. *IEEE Computer*, 12(10):10–19, 1988.
16. J. Stankovic. Distributed real-time computing: The next generation. *Journal of the Society of Instrument and Control Engineers of Japan*, 1992.

Cooperative Case Bartering for Case-Based Reasoning Agents

Santiago Ontañón and Enric Plaza

IIIA, Artificial Intelligence Research Institute
CSIC, Spanish Council for Scientific Research
Campus UAB, 08193 Bellaterra, Catalonia (Spain).
{santi,enric}@iiia.csic.es, http://www.iiia.csic.es

Abstract. Multiagent systems offer a new paradigm to organize AI Applications. We focus on the application of Case-Based Reasoning to Multiagent systems. CBR offers the individual agents the capability of autonomously learn from experience. In this paper we present a framework for collaboration among agents that use CBR. We present explicit strategies for case bartering in order improve individual case bases and reduce bias in the case bases. We also present empirical results illustrating the robustness of the case bartering process for several configurations of the multiagent system. Finally, a bias and variance analysis of the effects of bartering is included.

Keywords: Cooperative CBR, Multiagent CBR, Collaboration Policies, Bartering, Multiagent Learning.

1 Introduction

Multiagent systems offer a new paradigm to organize AI applications. Our goal is to develop techniques to integrate CBR into applications that are developed as multiagent systems. CBR offers the multiagent system paradigm the capability of autonomously learn from experience. In this paper we present a framework for collaboration among agents that use CBR and some experiments illustrating how they can improve its performance using case bartering strategies.

The individual case bases of the CBR agents are the main issue here, if they are not properly maintained, the overall system behavior will be suboptimal. In a real system, there will be agents that can very easily obtain certain kind of cases, and that will very costly obtain other types of cases, and for sure that other agents in the system will be in the inverse situation. It will be beneficial for both agents if they reach an agreement to trade cases. This is a very well known strategy in the human history called *bartering*. Using case bartering, agents that have a lot of cases of some kind will give them to another agents in return to more interesting cases for them.

Our research focuses on the scenario of separate case bases that we want to use in a decentralized fashion by means of a multiagent system, that is to say a collection of CBR agents that manage individual case bases and can communicate (and collaborate) with other CBR agents. In this paper we focus on case bartering. We present two protocols for case bartering that improve the overall performance of the system and of the individual

M.T. Escrig Monferrer and F. Toledo Lobo (Eds.): CCIA 2002, LNAI 2504, pp. 294–308, 2002.

CBR agents without compromising the agent's autonomy. This protocols will try to minimize the individual case base bias (how far is a case base of being a good sample of the overall distribution).

The structure of the paper is as follows. First, we present the collaboration scheme that the agents use, then the individual case base bias measurement is introduced. After that, the case bartering mechanism, including the bartering protocols is presented. Finally, the experiments are explained and the paper closes with related work and conclusion sections.

2 Collaboration Scheme

A multiagent CBR ($\mathcal{MAC}$) system $\mathcal{M} = \{(A_i, C_i)\}_{i=1...n}$ is composed on n agents, where each agent A_i has a case base C_i. In the experiments reported here we assume that initially case bases are disjunct ($\forall A_i, A_j \in \mathcal{M} : C_i \cap C_j = \emptyset$), i.e. initially there is no case shared by two agent's case bases. In this framework we restrict ourselves to analytical tasks, i.e. tasks (like classification) where the solution is achieved by selecting from an enumerated set of solutions $K = \{S_1 \ldots S_K\}$. A case base $C_i = \{(P_j, S_k)\}_{j=1...N}$ is a collection of pairs problem/solution.

When an agent A_i asks another agent A_j help to solve a problem the interaction protocol is as follows. First, A_i sends a problem description P to A_j. Second, after A_j has tried to solve P using its case base C_j, it sends back a message that is either :sorry (if it cannot solve P) or a solution endorsement record (SER). A SER has the form $\langle\{(S_k, E_k^j)\}, P, A_j\rangle$, where the collection of *endorsing pairs* (S_k, E_k^j) mean that the CBR method of the agent A_j has found E_k^j cases in case base C_j endorsing solution S_k—i.e. there are a number E_k^j of cases that are relevant (similar) for endorsing S_k as a solution for P. Each agent A_j is free to send one or more endorsing pairs in a SER record.

2.1 Voting Scheme

The voting scheme defines the mechanism by which an agent reaches an aggregate solution from a collection of SERs coming from other agents. The principle behind the voting scheme is that the agents vote for solution classes depending on the number of cases they found endorsing those classes. However, we want to prevent an agent having an unbounded number of votes. Thus, we will define a normalization function so that each agent has one vote that can be for a unique solution class or fractionally assigned to a number of classes depending on the number of endorsing cases.

Formally, let $\mathcal{A}^t$ the set of agents that have submitted their SERs to the agent A_i for problem P. We will consider that $A_i \in \mathcal{A}^t$ and the result of A_i trying to solve P is also reified as a SER. The vote of an agent $A_j \in \mathcal{A}^t$ for class S_k is

$$Vote(S_k, A_j) = \frac{E_k^j}{c + \sum_{r=1...K} E_r^j}$$

where c is a constant that on our experiments is set to 1. It is easy to see that an agent can cast a fractional vote that is always less than 1. Aftern aggregating the votes from different agents the winning solution class is the class with more votes in total.

This voting scheme can be seen as a variation of *Approval Voting* [2]. In *Approval Voting* each agent vote for all the candidates they consider as posible solutions without giving any weight to its votes. In our scheme, *Approval Voting* can be implemented making $Vote(S_k, A_j) = 1$ if $E_k^j \neq 0$ and 0 otherwise.

There are two differences between the standard *Approval Voting* and our voting scheme. The first one is that in our voting scheme agents can give a weight to each one of its votes. The second difference is that the sum of the votes of an agent is bounded to 1. Thus we can call it *Bounded-Weighted Approval Voting* (BWAV). In the experiments section we will show some experiments illustrating the effect of changing the voting scheme.

We will show now the $Committee$ collaboration policy that uses this voting scheme (see [8] for a detailed explanation and comparison of several collaboration policies).

2.2   Committee Policy

In this collaboration policy the agent members of a $\mathcal{MAC}$ system $\mathcal{M}$ are viewed as a committee. An agent A_i that has to solve a problem P, sends it to all the other agents in $\mathcal{M}$. Each agent A_j that has received P sends a solution endorsement record $\langle\{(S_k, E_k^j)\}, P, A_j\rangle$ to A_i. The initiating agent A_i uses the voting scheme above upon all SERs, i.e. its own SER and the SERs of all the other agents in the multiagent system. The problem's solution is the class with maximum number of votes.

Notice that the agents participating in the Committee Policy have no reason or incentive to lie when providing a SER. First of all, it is rational for an agent to participate in the Committee Policy because it improves the accuracy of the agent itself in classification. Secondly, once an agent has joined the Committee Policy there is no incentive to cheat the others (there is no benefit in the others being worse). On the contrary, if agents start to cheat causing the Committee Policy accuracy to diminish, the agents would decide simply to leave the Committee Policy. Thus, it is rational to participate in the Committee Policy and cheating provides no immediate or long term benefit.

3   Case Base Bias

In a previous work [8] we showed how agents can obtain better results using the *Committee* collaboration policy that working alone. However, in those experiments we assumed that every agent had a representative sample of cases in its case base. When an agent has a case base that is not representative of the overall distribution, we say that the agent has a biased case base.

In this section we are going to define a measure of the degree of biasing of an individual case base (*ICB* bias or *Individual Case Base bias*), then we will show how the performance of the *Committee* degrades as the *ICB* bias of the agents grow. Later sections introduce bartering policies to improve the *Committee* performance.

Table 1. Classification accuracy for the marine sponge classification problem for systems with several mean Individual Case Base bias.

$\mathcal{MAC}$ ICB	3 Ag.	5 Ag.	8 Ag.	10 Ag.
0.0	88.36%	88.12%	87.50%	86.75%
0.1	86.07%	87.50%	85.35%	85.00%
0.2	81.46%	83.53%	83.00%	82.00%

Let be $d_i = \{d_i^1, \ldots, d_i^K\}$ the individual distribution of cases for an agent A_i, where d_i^j is the number of cases with solution S_j in the case base of A_i. Now, we can estimate the overall distribution of cases $D = \{D^1, \ldots, D^K\}$ where D^i is the estimated probability of the class S_i, $D^j = \frac{\sum_{i=1}^{n} d_i^j}{\sum_{i=1}^{n} \sum_{l=1}^{K} d_i^l}$

To measure how far is the case base C_i of a given agent A_i of being a representative sample of the overall distribution we will define the *Individual Case Base* (ICB) bias, as the square distance between the distribution of cases D and the (normalized) individual distribution obtained from d_i:

$$ICB(C_i) = \sum_{l=1}^{K} \left(D^l - \frac{d_i^l}{\sum_{j=1}^{K} d_i^j} \right)^2$$

In order to see how the ICB bias affects the performance of the system, Table 1 shows the accuracy of several multiagent systems with increasing ICB bias (the $\mathcal{MAC}$ ICB bias is calculated as the mean of all the ICB bias of the agents in the system). There we can see that when the agents have case bases that are not representative (those with a high ICB) the agents using the *Committee* policy obtains lower accuracies. In the following sections, we will show how case bartering improves accuracy by lowering the individual biases.

4   Case Bartering

In the physical world, bartering involves the interchange of two goods. But as our agents will barter with cases (that are just information) they will only send a copy of the cases to the other agents without losing them. It's a matter of the internal case deletion policy of each agent if a case must be forgotten or not. Deletion policies have been studied [13] but we will not be considering them in these experiments.

In this section, we are going to present the Case Bartering protocol that the agents use in order to improve the overall performance.

4.1   Case Bartering Mechanism

To reach a bartering agreement for bartering between two agents, there must be an offering agent A_i that sends an offer to another agent A_j. Then A_j has to evaluate whether the offer of interchanging cases with A_i is interesting, and accept or reject the offer. If the offer is confirmed, we say that A_i and A_j have reached a bartering agreement, and they will interchange the cases in the offer.

Formally an offer is a tuple $o = \langle A_i, A_j, S_{k_1}, S_{k_2} \rangle$ where A_i is the offering agent, A_j is the receiver of the offer, and S_{k_1} and S_{k_2} are two solution classes, meaning that the agent A_i will send one of its cases with solution S_{k_2} and A_j will send one of its cases with solution S_{k_1}.

4.2   Making and Accepting Offers

The Case Bartering Protocol is not restrictive in how many offers can an agent send at a time. So, many strategies can be used here, but in our experiments, the agents use a very simple one to choose which are the most interesting offers, as follows for a given agent A_i:

- For each solution class $S_{k_1} \in \{S_1 \ldots S_K\}$
- A_i looks if increasing by one its number of cases with solution S_{k_1} will decrease its *ICB* bias.
- If so, A_i chooses which agent A_j of the others is the best one to ask for cases of solution S_{k_1} (Currently the chosen A_j is the one with more cases of the solution class S_{k_1}).
- Now A_i determines which is its best class S_{k_2} (the class for which it has more cases), and makes the offer $o = \langle A_i, A_j, S_{k_1}, S_{k_2} \rangle$, i.e. A_i offers to A_j a case of solution S_{k_2} if A_j gives one of solution S_{k_1} to A_i.

When an agent receives a set of offers, it has also to choose which of these offers to accept and which not. In our experiments the agents use the simple rule of accepting every offer that reduces its own *ICB* bias. Thus, we will define the set of interesting offers *Interesting*(O, A_i) of a set of offers O for an agent A_i as those offers that will reduce the *ICB* bias of A_i. Moreover, an agent cannot send twice the same case to the same agent. So, the agents will only accept those interesting offers that can satisfy (i.e. can provide a new case for interchanging).

4.3   Case Bartering Protocol

We are going to present two different protocols for Case Bartering, both synchronous (i.e. there are preestablished stages ("rounds") where the agents can send their offers, then the protocol moves to the next stage, etc). The first one is called the *Simultaneous Case Bartering Protocol*, and the second one the *Token-Passing Case Bartering Protocol*.

When an agent member of the $\mathcal{MAC}$ wants to enter in the bartering process, it sends an initiating message to all the other agents in the $\mathcal{MAC}$. Then all the other agents answer whether or not they enter the bargaining process. This initiating message contains a parameter t_R, corresponding to the time that each round of the protocol will last.

Simultaneous Case Bartering Protocol (SCBP). In this protocol, in every round all the agents send their offers simultaneously. When all the offers have been sent, all the agents send a message for the offers they accept.

1. Each agent A_i broadcasts its individual distribution d_i.
2. Each agent computes the overall distribution estimation D.
3. The agents send their bartering offers.
4. Each agent chooses a subset of accepted offers from the set of received offers from the other agents and sends messages accepting them.
5. When the maximum time t_R is over, all the unaccepted offers are considered as rejected.
6. Each agent that has some bartering agreements sends the cases to interchange to the corresponding agents.
7. Each agent broadcasts its new individual distribution d_i.
8. If there have been no interchanged cases, the protocol ends, otherwise go to 3.

Token-Passing Case Bartering Protocol (TPCBP). The main difference between this protocol and the previous one is the introduction of a Token-Passing mechanism, so that only the agent who has the Token can make offers to the others.

1. Each agent broadcasts its local statistics d_i.
2. Each agent computes the overall distribution estimation D.
3. Each agent computes the *ICB* bias of all the agents taking part in the bartering (including itself), and sorts them. This defines the order in which the Token will be passed through.
4. The agent with highest *ICB* bias is the first to have the Token.
5. The agent who has the Token sends its bartering offers.
6. Each agent chooses a subset of accepted offers from the set of received offers from the owner of the token and sends messages accepting them.
7. When the maximum time t_R is over, all the unaccepted offers are considered as rejected.
8. Each agent that has some bartering agreements sends the cases to interchange to the corresponding agents.
9. Each agent broadcasts its new individual distribution d_i.
10. If the Token belongs to the last agent, go to 11, otherwise the Token is given to the next agent and we go to 5.
11. If there have been no interchanged cases, the protocol ends, otherwise go to 3.

In both protocols, if an offer is not accepted neither rejected within the period time t_R, the offer is considered as rejected, and the protocol moves to the next round.

To ensure the convergence of both protocols, we have only to have in mind the only restriction that we have imposed: an agent cannot send twice the same case to the same agent. With this restriction it's easy to see that both protocols cannot run indefinitely, because each agent has a limited number of cases to trade with. So, we can say that in a bounded number of rounds both protocols will end.

Comparing the protocols, we can see that the *Simultaneous* protocol has the problem that an agent has to decide if accept offers or not without knowing if its own offers are going to be accepted. The *Token-Passing* protocol tries to solve this problem by letting only one agent to send offers at a time. TPCBP is not really sensible to the order in which the token is passed on, because many rounds are needed, and each round with a recomputed order.

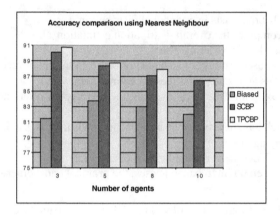

Fig. 1. Accuracy comparison of systems where the agents use nearest neighbor with and without using case bartering

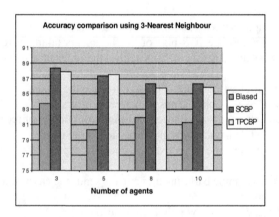

Fig. 2. Accuracy comparison of systems where the agents use 3-nearest neighbor with and without using case bartering

5   Experimental Results

In this section we want to show how the classification accuracy of the agents improve using the case bartering protocols with respect to systems where the agents do not use them. We also show results concerning case base sizes after the bartering and the number of rounds needed to converge to a stable case distribution.

We use the marine sponge identification (classification) problem as our test bed. Sponge classification is interesting because the difficulties arise from the morphological plasticity of the species, and from the incomplete knowledge of many of their biological and cytological features. Moreover, benthology specialists are distributed around the world and they have experience in different benthos that spawn species with different characteristics due to the local habitat conditions.

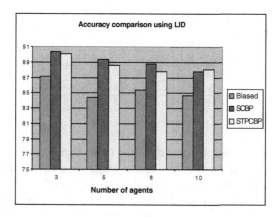

Fig. 3. Accuracy comparison of systems where the agents use LID with and without using case bartering

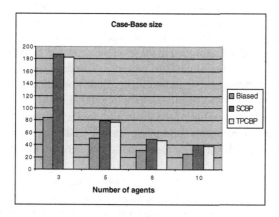

Fig. 4. Comparison of the case base size before and after the bartering process

In order to show the improvements obtained in the system when the agents use case bartering, we have designed an experimental suite with a case base of 280 marine sponges pertaining to three different orders of the *Demospongiae* class (*Astrophorida*, *Hadromerida* and *Axinellida*). In an experimental run, cases are randomly distributed among the agents (e.g. if the training set is composed of 252 cases and we have a 4 agents system, each agent will receive about 63 cases). In the testing phase, problems arrive randomly to one of the agents. The goal of the agent receiving a problem is to identify the correct biological order given the description of a new sponge. Once an agent has received a problem, he will use the *Committee* collaboration policy to obtain the prediction.

For experimentation purposes, we force biased case bases in every agent. Specifically, we increase the probability of each agent to have cases of some classes and decrease the probability to have cases of some other classes. For example, in the 3 agent scenario,

Table 2. $\mathcal{MAC}$ *ICB* biases of the multiagent systems used in the experiments before and after the case bartering process.

$\mathcal{MAC}$ *ICB*	*3 Ag.*	*5 Ag.*	*8 Ag.*	*10 Ag.*
Before	0.2	0.2	0.23	0.15
After SCBP	$4.0E^{-5}$	0.0003	0.0004	0.0004
After TPCBP	$3.0E^{-5}$	0.0002	0.0002	0.0003

the 70% of the cases for the class *Astrophorida* in the training set are in the individual case base of Agent 1, and the other two agents only have a 15% of them. Analogously, the 70% of the cases for the classes *Hadromerida* and *Axinellida* are in the case bases of the Agents 2 and 3 respectively. This process increases the individual case-base bias of the agents in the $\mathcal{MAC}$; the first row of Table 2 shows the average over Individual Case-Base (ICB) biases for the agents in the experiments.

Table 2 also shows the average *ICB* biases for the agents in the experiments after the bartering process. We can see that both protocols are able to reduce the ICB bias to very small values. This shows that the bartering protocols effectively interchange cases until all agents drastically reduce their *ICB* bias; only then the process ends and the overall accuracy has indeed improved to the level we expected. Finally, notice that when agents have a greater volume of cases to barter (e.g. in the 3 agents scenario) the *ICB* bias obtained after bartering is one order of magnitude lower than when the agents have fewer cases (from 0.00003 in 3 agents scenario to 0.0003 in the 10 agents scenario).

In order to test the generality of the protocols, we have tested them using systems with 3, 5, 8 and up to 10 agents, and using several CBR methods: nearest neighbor, 3-nearest neighbor and LID [1]. The results presented here are the average of 5 10-fold cross validation runs.

The figures 1, 2 and 3 show the results of applying the two case bartering protocols. Three bars are shown for each scenario, the *biased* results represent the average accuracy obtained by the $\mathcal{MAC}$ without using case-bartering with biased individual case bases; and the *SCBP* and *TPCBP* results represent the average accuracy obtained by the $\mathcal{MAC}$ after using the *Simultaneous Case Bartering Protocol* and *Token-Passing Case Bartering Protocol* respectively. We can see in those figures that in all the scenarios, the $\mathcal{MAC}$ systems using case bartering obtain a significative gain in accuracy than those systems that do not use case bartering. This shows the independence of the bartering protocols from the CBR method used by the individual agents. Those figures also show that case bartering is robust even when the size of the case bases decreases and the number of cases an agent can barter is very small, as we can see for the 10 agents scenario where each agent has only about 25 cases (i.e. less than 9 cases per class).

Comparing the accuracy obtained by the two protocols *SCBP* and *TPCBP* we see that both have nearly the same accuracy in all the scenarios. We can see that there is never a difference greater than 1% between the results of the Simultaneous protocol and the results of the Token-Passing protocol. Therefore no bartering protocol is significantly better than another but both are significantly better than using no bartering protocol.

A naive way to solve the ICB bias problem colud be to centralize all data in one location and adopt a completely cooperative multiagent approach where each agent

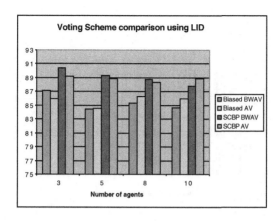

Fig. 5. Comparison between *Bounded-Weighted Approval Voting* and standard *Approval Voting* for agents using LID.

sends its cases to all the other agents. In this approach, each agent will have aquired all the cases known in the system. To see that bartering is better than this approach, we have performed experiments where all the agents have all the cases and the accuracy obtained for LID was 88.37% versus the 90.36% achieved by a 3 agent system using the SCBP in the copy mode.

Figure 4 shows the case base sizes reached after case bartering. The *biased* bar shows the case base size before case bartering, and the other two show the case base size after applying case bartering. We see that the agents stop interchanging cases before each agent acquires all known cases in the system. Moreover, except in the 3 agents scenario, the case base sizes do not increase very much. The 3 agents scenario is special because the initial case bases of the agents are quite big, and to repair their *ICB* biases the number of cases needed to be bartered is much greater than in the 5, 8 or 10 agent scenarios. We also see that the case base sizes obtained using the Token-Passing protocol are slightly smaller than the ones obtained using the Simultaneous protocol.

For comparison purposes Figures 5 and 6 show some results where the agents use standard *Approval Voting* instead of the *Bounded-Weighted Approval Voting*. These figures show a comparison between the two voting schemes for two different scenarios: in the first one the agents do not use case-bartering, and in the second one they use the *SCBP*. The results show the accuracy for LID and 3-Nearest Neighbour (since in 1-Nearest Neighbour agents vote for only one class, there is no difference between *AV* and *BWAV*). Figures 5 and 6 show that there is no significant difference between the two voting schemes. When the agents use LID, *BWAV* works better for systems where there are fewer agents (and thus more cases per case-base). But when the agents use 3-Nearest Neighbour this difference is not so clear. When the case-bases are biased, standard *AV* is worse than *BWAV* with 3-Nearest Neighbour (specially in the 3 and 8 agents scenario). However, after the bartering process (when *ICB* bias is low), both voting schemes obtain nearly the same result. Sumarizing, both voting schemes behave similarly, but *BWAV* is more robust with higher biased conditions.

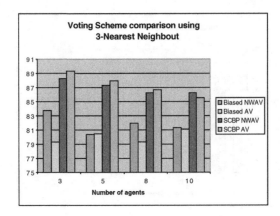

Fig. 6. Comparison between *Bounded-Weighted Approval Voting* and standard *Approval Voting* for agents using 3-nearest neighbour.

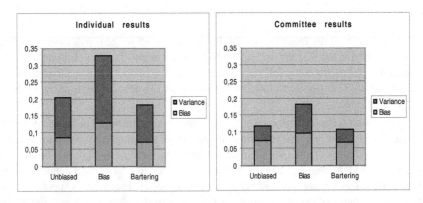

Fig. 7. Bias plus variance decomposition of the classification error for a system with 5 agents both solving problems individually and using the Committee collaboration policy.

5.1   Bias Plus Variance Analysis

Bias plus Variance decomposition of the error [7] is a useful tool to provide an insight of learning methods. Bias plus variance analysis breaks the expected error as the sum of three non-negative quantities:

- Intrinsic target noise: this is the expected error of the Bayes optimal classifier (lower bound on the expected error of any classifier).
- Squared bias: measures how closely the learning algorithm's prediction matches the target (averaged over all possible training sets of a given size).
- Variance: this is the variance of the algorithm's prediction for the different training sets of a given size.

Figure 7 shows the bias plus variance decomposition of the error (obtained using the model presented in [7]) for a system composed of 5 agents using NN. the left hand of

Figure 7 shows the bias plus variance decomposition of the error when the agents solve the problems individually, and the right hand shows the decomposition when agents use the committee collaboration policy to solve problems. Three different scenarios are presented for each one: *unbiased*, representing a situation where the agents have unbiased case bases; *biased*, representing a situation where the agents have biased case bases; *bartering*, where the agents have biased case bases and they use case bartering.

Comparing the Committee collaboration policy with the individual solution of problems, we see that the error reduction obtained with the Committee is only due to a reduction in the variance component. This result is expected since a general result of machine learning tells that we can reduce the classification error of any classifier by averaging the prediction of several classifiers when they make uncorrelated errors due to a reduction in the variance term [5].

Comparing the *unbiased* and the *biased* scenarios, we can see that the effect of the ICB bias in the classification error is reflected in both bias and variance components. The variance is the one that suffers a greater increase, but bias is also increased.

If the agents apply case bartering they can greatly reduce both components of error— as we can see comparing the *biased* and the *bartering* scenarios. Comparing the *bartering* scenario with the *unbiased* scenario, we can also see that case bartering can make agents in the *biased* scenario to achieve greater accuracies that agents in the *unbiased* scenario. Looking with more detail, we see that in the *bartering* scenario the bias term is slightly smaller than the bias term in the *unbiased* scenario. This is due to the increased size of individual case bases, because as noted in [10], when the individual training sets are smaller the bias tends to increase. The variance term is also slightly smaller in the *bartering* scenario than in the *unbiased* scenario.

Sumarizing, the Committee collaboration policy is able to reduce the variance component of the error. Case Bartering can make a system with biased case bases to achieve grater accuracies than a system with unbiased case bases because of two reasons: as the ICB bias is reduced, the accuracy of a system with unbiased case bases is recovered, and as the size of individual case bases is slighly increased, the bias term of error is reduced and the accuracy can be greater than in the *unbiased* scenario.

6   Related Work

Several areas are related to our work: multiple model learning (where the final solution for a problem is obtained through the aggregation of solutions of individual predictors), case base competence assessment, and negotiation protocols. Here we will briefly describe some relevant work in these areas that is close to us.

A general result on multiple model learning [6] demonstrated that if uncorrelated classifiers with error rate lower than 0.5 are combined then the resulting error rate must be lower than the one made by the individual classifiers. The BEM (*Basic Ensemble Method*) is presented in [9] as a basic way to combine continuous estimators, and since then many other methods have been proposed: *Bagging* [3] or *Boosting* [4] are some examples. However, all these methods do not deal with the issue of "partitioned examples" among different classifiers as we do—they rely on aggregating results from multiple classifiers that have access to *all* data. Their goal is to use multiplicity of classifiers to increase accuracy of existing classification methods. Our intention is to combine the decisions of autonomous classifiers (each one corresponding to one agent), and to see how can they cooperate to achieve a better behavior than when they work alone. A more similar approach is the one proposed in [15], where a MAS is proposed for pattern recognition. Each autonomous agent being a specialist recognizing only a subset of all the patterns, and where the predictions were then combined dynamically.

Learning from biased datasets is a well known problem, and many solutions have been proposed. Vucetic and Obradovic [14] propose a method based on a bootstrap algorithm to estimate class probabilities in order to improve the classification accuracy. However, their method does not fit our needs, because they need the entire testset available for the agents before start solving any problem in order to make the class probabilities estimation.

Related work is that of case base competence assessment. We use a very simple measure comparing individual with global distribution of cases; we do not try to assess the aeras of competence of (individual) case bases - as proposed by Smyth and McKenna [12]. This work focuses on finding groups of cases that are competent.

In [11] Schwartz and Kraus discuss negotiation protocols for data allocation. They propose two protocols, the sequential protocol, and the simultaneous protocol. These two protocols can be compared respectively to our *Token- Passing Case Bartering Protocol* and *Simultaneous Case Bartering Protocol*, because in their simultaneous protocol, the agents have to make offers for allocating some data item without knowing the other's offers, and in the sequential protocol, the agents make offers in order, and each one knows which were the offers of the previous ones.

7   Conclusions

We have presented a framework for cooperative Case-Based Reasoning in multiagent systems, where agents use a market mechanism (bartering) to improve the performance both of individuals and of the whole multiagent system. The agent autonomy is maintained, because if an agent does not want to take part in the bartering, he just has to do nothing, and when the other agents notice that there is one agent not following the protocol they will ignore it during the remaining iterations of the bartering process.

We have shown a problem arising when data is distributed over a collection of agents, namely that each agent may have a skewed view of the world (the individual bias). Comparing empirical results in classification tasks we saw that both the individual and the overall performance decreases when bias increases. The process of bartering shows that the problems derived from distributed data over a collection of agents can be solved using a market-oriented approach. Each agent engages in a barter only when it makes sense for its individual purposes but the outcome is an improvement of the individual and overall performance.

As we have previously said in the experiments section, the naive way to solve the ICB bias problem could be to centralize all data in one location or adopt a completely cooperative multiagent approach where each agent sends its cases to all other agents. We have shown, that we can obtain better results with the bartering approach that with this completely cooperative one. Moreover, another problem with this completely cooperative approach is that redundancy increases and there may be scaling up problems; the bartering approach tries to interchange cases only to the amount that is necessary and not more.

In the experiments reported in this paper, the agents use strategies for choosing which offers to generate and send to other agents and for choosing which offers to accept from other agents. Currently, both strategies try to minimize the *ICB* bias measure. The *ICB* bias estimates the difference between the individual and global case distribution over the classes. However, we plan to study other kinds of biases that may characterize the individual agents' case base. In order to compute these new bias measures, the agents may need to make public more information. Thus, a modification in the bartering protocols would be needed to manage the information required.

We have focused on bartering for agents using lazy learning but future work should address the usefulness of bartering for eager (inductive) learning techniques.

Acknowledgements. The authors thank Josep-Lluís Arcos and Eva Armengol of the IIIA-CSIC for their support and for the development of the Noos agent platform and the LID CBR method respectively. Support for this work came from CIRIT FI/FAP 2001 grant and projects and IST-1999-19005 "IBROW".

References

[1] E. Armengol and E. Plaza. Lazy induction of descriptions for relational case-based learning. In *12th European Conference on Machine Learning*, 2001.

[2] Steven J. Brams and Peter C. Fishburn. *Approval Voting*. Birkhauser, Boston, 1983.

[3] Leo Breiman. Bagging predictors. *Machine Learning*, 24(2):123–140, 1996.

[4] Yoav Freund and Robert E. Schapire. Experiments with a new boosting algorithm. In *Proc. 13th ICML*, pages 148–146. Morgan Kaufmann, 1996.

[5] Jerome H. Friedman. On bias, variance, 0/1 - loss, and the curse-of-dimensionality. *Data Mining and Knowledge Discovery*, 1(1):55–77, 1997.

[6] L. K. Hansen and P. Salamon. Neural networks ensembles. *IEEE Transactions on Pattern Analysis and Machine Intelligence*, 1(12):993–1001, 1990.

[7] Ron Kohavi and David H. Wolpert. Bias plus variance decomposition for zero-one loss functions. In Lorenza Saitta, editor, *Machine Learning: Proceedings of the Thirteenth International Conference*, pages 275–283. Morgan Kaufmann, 1996.

[8] S. Ontañón and E. Plaza. Learning when to collaborate among learning agents. In *12th European Conference on Machine Learning*, 2001.

[9] M. P. Perrone and L. N. Cooper. When networks disagree: Ensemble methods for hydrid neural networks. In *Artificial Neural Networks for Speech and Vision*. Chapman-Hall, 1993.

[10] richard A. Olshen and L. Gordon. Almost sure consistent nonparametric regression from recursive partitioning schemes. *Multivariate Analysis*, 15:147–163, 1984.

[11] R. Schwartz and S. Kraus. Bidding mechanisms for data allocation in multi-agent environments. In *Agent Theories, Architectures, and Languages*, pages 61–75, 1997.

[12] B. Smyth and E. McKenna. Modelling the competence of case-bases. In *EWCBR*, pages 208–220, 1998.

[13] Barry Smyth and Mark T. Keane. Remembering to forget: A competence-preserving case deletion policy for case-based reasoning systems. In *IJCAI*, pages 377–383, 1995.

[14] S. Vucetic and Z. Obradovic. Classification on data with biased class distribution. In *12th European Conference on Machine Learning*, 2001.

[15] L. Vuurpijl and L. Schomaker. A framework for using multiple classifiers in a multiple-agent architecture. In *Third International Workshop on Handwriting Analysis and Recognition*, 1998.

Integrating the Organ and Tissue Allocation Processes through an Agent-Mediated Electronic Institution

Javier Vázquez-Salceda[1], Ulises Cortés[1], and Julian Padget[2]

[1] Departament de Llenguatges i Sistemes Informàtics.
Universitat Politècnica de Catalunya.
c/ Jordi Girona 1-3. E08034 Barcelona, Spain.
{jvazquez,ia }@lsi.upc.es
Phone: 34 934017016 Fax: 34 934017014
[2] Department of Computer Science. University of Bath. Bath, BA2 7AY. United Kingdom.
jap@cs.bath.ac.uk
Phone 34 932919335 Fax 34 932919410

Abstract. In this paper we present a first approach to the formalization of Carrel, a virtual organization for the procurement of organs and tissues for transplantation purposes, in order to model the allocation processes of organs and tissues in a integrated way. We show how it can be formalized with the ISLANDER formalism. Also we present a first mechanism to federate the institution in several geographically-distributed platforms.

Keywords: Electronic Institutions, Multi-agent systems, Transplants.

1 Introduction

Organ transplantation from human donors is the only option available when there is a major damage or malfunction in an organ. At the time of writing, more than one million people in the world have successfully received an organ, and thereafter, in most cases, lead normal lives.

Over the years, transplant techniques have evolved, knowledge of donor-recipient compatibility has improved and so have immunosuppressant drug regimes, leading to an increase in the number of organs that can be transplanted, but also in the range of transplants, moving beyond organs (heart, liver, lungs, kidney, pancreas) to tissues (bones, skin, corneas, tendons). However, the allocation process for tissues is quite different from that for organs, because of the time such pieces can be preserved outside the human body. Tissues are clusters of quite homogeneous cells, so the optimal temperature for preservation of all the cells composing the tissue is almost the same. Thus, tissues can be preserved for several days (from six days in the case of corneas to years in the case of bones) in tissue banks. For tissues, the allocation process is triggered when there is a recipient with a need for a certain tissue, at which time some number of tissue banks are searched for a suitable one.

Organs, on the other hand, are very complex structures with several kinds of cell types with different optimal preservation temperatures. That fact leads to quite short preservation times (hours), no need for an organ bank, and an allocation process that is triggered when a donor appears, taking the form of a search for a suitable recipient in some number of hospitals.

M.T. Escrig Monferrer and F. Toledo Lobo (Eds.): CCIA 2002, LNAI 2504, pp. 309–321, 2002.
© Springer-Verlag Berlin Heidelberg 2002

1.1   The Case for Software Systems for Organ and Tissue Management

The increasing rate of success of tissue transplants is leading to an increase in the number of requests. This volume is starting to overwhelm the human coordinators and furthermore is leading to tissue loss, because available tissues are not being assigned due to lack of time to process all requests.

In the case of organs, successful transplants have also led to an increase in demand for organs for transplantation purposes. However, there is not an increasing volume of donations to match the demand. Much research has been done to create policies for donor identification (to increase the number of available donors), organ allocation (to find a suitable recipient for each organ) and in extraction, preservation and implant procedures (to increase the chances of success).

The relative scarcity of (organ) donors has led to the creation of international coalitions of transplant organizations. This new, more geographically distributed, environment makes an even stronger case for the application of distributed software systems to solve:

– *the data exchange problem:* exchange of information is a major issue, as each of the actors collects different information and stores it in different formats. The obvious, and easily stated, solution is the definition of standard data interchange.
– *the communication problem:* countries typically use different languages and terminologies to tag the same items or facts. Either a standard notation or a translation mechanism needs to be created to avoid misunderstandings.
– *the coordination issues:* in order to manage requests at an international level, there is the need to coordinate geographically distributed surgery teams, and to coordinate piece delivery at an international level.
– *the variety of regulations:* an additional issue is the necessity to accommodate a complex set of, in some cases conflicting, national and international regulations, legislation and protocols governing the exchange of organs. These regulations also change over time, making it essential that the software is adaptable.

The first two points can largely be resolved using standard software solutions. For instance, the EU projects RETRANSPLANT, TECN have devoted most of their effort to the creation of a) standard formats for the storage and exchange of information about pieces, donors and recipients among organizations, b) telematic networks, or c) distributed databases. Another project, ESCULAPE, uses conventional software to help in matching tissue histocompatibility.

The third point (coordination) is harder to solve with conventional software. A sound alternative is the use of *software agents*, where an *Agent* is a computer program capable of taking its own decisions with no external control (*autonomy*), based on its perceptions of the environment and the objectives it aims to reach [18]. It not only reacts to the environment (*reactivity*) but also *proactively* takes initiatives. The *social ability* of agents allow them to group together (in *agencies*) sharing common objectives and dividing the tasks to reach those objectives. All these attributes suggest that multi-agent systems are well-suited to solve coordination issues.

It is the last point (the variety of regulations changing over time) which underpins our case for the use of so-called *electronic institutions*, whose purpose is to provide overarching frameworks for agent interaction, where agents may reason about the norms [6, 2,3,5], in the same way as physical institutions and social norms do in the real world. Electronic institutions and the norms that govern them are the key to a system that is able to adapt automatically to changes in regulations.

In summary, our proposal address all four issues, by the use of multi-agent technology, not only for coordination and regulation but also serving as a language interface among teams using different terminology, and actively distributing the information to be shared.

2 An Institution for the Distribution of Organs and Tissues

The Carrel institution is an agent platform which hosts a group of agents (an *agency*) responsible for the allocation of organs and tissues. In the case of tissues, the allocation process comprises:

1. The tissue banks keeping the institution updated about tissue availability
2. The agency receiving requests from the hospitals for tissues. For each request (brought by an agent representing the hospital) the institution tries to allocate the *best* tissue available from all the tissue banks that are known.

In the case of organs, the process comprises:

1. Each hospital informing the institution about patients that have been added to or removed from the waiting list of that hospital, or patients either to be added to or removed from the national-wide Maximum Urgency Level[1] Waiting List.
2. When a donor appears, the hospital informs the institution of all the organs suitable for donation in the form of *offers* sent to the organ allocation organization, which then assigns the organs.

Figure 1 depicts all the entities that interact with the Carrel system. There are a) the hospitals that create the tissue requests b) the Tissue Banks, and c) the national organ transplantation organizations, that own the agent platform and act as observers—the figure shows the organizations in Spain: the Organización Nacional de Transplantes[2] (ONT) [14] and the Organitzaciò CATalana de Transplantaments[3] (OCATT). In the proposed system all hospitals, even those owning a Tissue Bank, should make their requests for tissues or their organ offers through Carrel in order to ensure a fair distribution of pieces and to ease the tracking of all pieces from extraction to implantation, as the ONT and OCATT currently require for organs.

2.1 Role of the Carrel Institution

The role of the Carrel Institution can be summarized by the following tasks:

- to make sure that all the agents which enter into the institution behave properly (that is, that they follow the behavioral norms).
- to be up to date about all the available pieces in the Tissue Banks, and all the recipients that are registered in the waiting lists.
- to check that all hospitals and tissue banks fulfill all the requirements needed to interact with Carrel.
- to take care of the fulfillment of the commitments undertaken inside the Carrel system.
- to coordinate the piece delivery from one facility to another.
- to register all incidents relating to a particular piece.

---

[1] In Spain the Maximum Urgency Level is called Urgency-0
[2] National Transplant Organization
[3] Catalan Transplant Organization

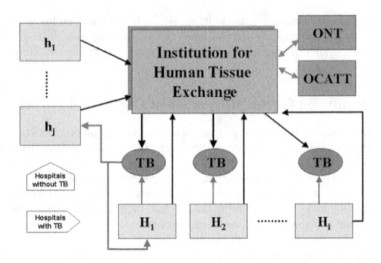

Fig. 1. Carrel: An Agent Mediated Institution for Tissues Assignment

2.2   The UCTx Agency

The participation of hospitals in Carrel is based on the notion of membership. That is, hospitals belong to the Institution and respect the negotiation (assignation) rules, and the agents that represent them inside Carrel are unable to break these conventions. A Hospital interacts with Carrel through the Transplant Coordination Unit Agency (*UCTx*). A version of the UCTx agent architecture that handles tissue requests can be found in [4].

   Adapting the UCTx agency in order to assist not only in the tissue allocation process but also in the organ allocation process is not difficult. In the case of tissues, it is surgeons who are responsible for creating the tissue requests through their **Surgeon Agent** [4]. In contrast, for organs it is the *Hospital Transplant Coordinator* who is responsible for issuing organ offers to the institution or answering a call for recipients. So the architecture presented in [4] does not need to be modified but instead just the functionality of the **Coordinator Agent** is extended.

3   Formalizing the Carrel Institution

To give a formal description of the interaction among agents in the Carrel system we will follow the ISLANDER formalism [7]. It views an agent-based electronic institution as a type of *dialogical system* where all the interactions inside the institution are a composition of multiple dialogic activities (message exchanges). These interactions (called *illocutions* [13]) are structured through agent group meetings called *scenes* that follow well-defined protocols.

3.1   The Performative Structure

The connected graph of scenes constitutes the *performative structure*. It is a network of scenes that defines the possible paths for each agent role. In accordance with its role, an agent may or may not be permitted to follow a particular path through the performative structure, and ultimately, may be required to leave the institution.

In the case of the Carrel institution, the set of scenes to model the organ and tissue allocation processes is:

– *Reception Room*: is the scene where all external agents should identify themselves in order to be assigned the roles they are authorized to play. If these agents carry either a request for one or more tissues or an offer of one or more organs, then this information is checked to make sure that it is well-formed.

– *Consultation Room*: is the scene where the institution is updated about any event or incident related to a piece. Agents coming from tissue banks should update the institution about tissue availability, while agents coming from hospitals should update the institution about the waiting lists and also inform it about the reception of all pieces (organs or tissues) they have received, the transplant operation and the condition of recipients.

– *Exchange Room*: is the scene where assignation of pieces takes place. There are specific exchange rooms for tissue requests (*Tissue Exchange Room*) and for organ offers (*Organ Exchange Room*).

– *Confirmation Room*: is the scene where the provisional assignments made in one of the exchange rooms are confirmed, whereafter a delivery plan is constructed, or cancelled, because a new request of higher priority has arrived.

A key element of the ISLANDER formalism is the definition of agent *roles*. Each agent can be associated to one or more roles, and these roles determine the scenes an agent can enter and the protocols it should follow (the *scene protocols* are defined as multi-role conversational patterns). There are two kinds of roles: the *external roles* (roles for incoming agents) and the *institutional roles* (roles for agents that carry out the management of the institution). The external roles are the following:

Hospital Finder Agent (hf): agents sent by hospitals with tissue requests or organ offers that are seen from the point of view of the institution as requests for finding an acceptable tissue or recipient, respectively.

Hospital Contact Agent (hc): agents from a certain hospital that are contacted by the institution when an organ has appeared for a recipient on the waiting list of that hospital. The agent then enters the institution to accept the organ and to receive the delivery plan.

Hospital Information Agent (hi): agents sent by hospitals to keep the Carrel system updated about any event related to a piece or the state of the waiting lists. They can also perform queries on the Carrel database through the **DB Agent** (see §3.2).

Tissue bank notifier (tb): agents sent by tissue banks in order to update Carrel about tissue availability.

The institutional roles consist of one agent to manage each scene and one agent to coordinate all the scene relationships:

Institution Manager (im): agent coordinating all the scene managers.

Reception Room Manager (rrm): manager of the *Reception Room* scene.

Tissue Exchange Room Manager (trm): manager of a *Tissue Exchange Room* scene.

Organ Exchange Room Manager (orm): manager of a *Organ Exchange Room* scene.

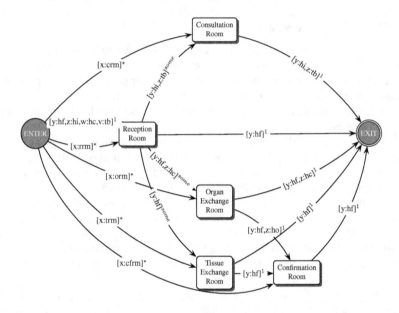

Fig. 2. The Carrel Institution performative structure

Confirmation Room Manager (cfrm): manager of the *Confirmation Room* scene.
Consultation Room Manager (crm): manager of the *Consultation Room* scene.

With all the scenes and roles identified in the previous section, the performative structure can be drawn, as depicted in figure 2. Nodes are the scenes listed above plus *enter* and *exit* nodes which define the begin and end points of the diagram. Arcs are labelled with tags *variable:role*, where variable is an $agent_i$ and role is one among the identified Carrel's roles. The diagram in figure 2 shows, for instance, that scene's managers go directly from the *enter* point to the scene they should manage (the * means that they are the ones creating the scene), while all the external agents must proceed through the *Reception Room* scene in order to be registered and then be directed to the proper scene according to their roles.

Authentication of external agents. As explained above, in the *Reception Room* external agents enter and are registered inside the platform. In this room an authentication mechanism based in electronic certificates ensures that external agents come only from authorized organizations (which previously received the electronic certificate to be used). Once the sender has been identified and authorized, the external agents are then directed to the proper room according to their roles.

The protocol of this scene can be seen in figure 3: an $agent_i$ requests for admission (1) and may be accepted (messages 3a, 3b, 3c, 3d) or refused (message 2, exit state w_1). According to the role of the incoming $agent_i$:

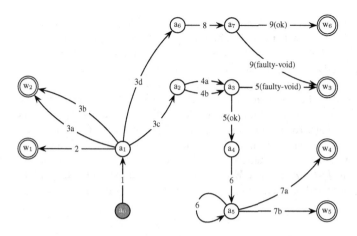

Fig. 3. The conversation graph for the Reception room

- it is headed to the *Consultation Room* (exit state w_2),
- if it brings a request from a hospital, the request is checked (messages 4 and 5). Then agent$_i$ waits until the appropriate *Exchange Room* is available for the assignation (messages 6 and 7a for tissues, 6 and 7b for organs).
- if it was called by the institution to receive an organ offer, the information it brings about the recipient is checked and, if all is correct, it is then directed to the *Organ Exchange Room* that sent the call.

The content of the messages that appear in this conversation graph and the following ones are specified in [17].

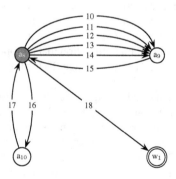

Fig. 4. Conversation graph for the Consultation room

Registering the recipients and the available pieces. In order to manage the assignation of organs and tissues, the Carrel institution needs up to date information on a) all the available tissues for transplantation, b) the state of hospitals waiting list for each kind of organ, and c) the whereabouts about all pieces that have been assigned by Carrel.

The *Consultation Room* allows agents coming from hospitals or tissue banks to keep Carrel updated about all the facts mentioned above. The protocol of this scene is shown in figure 4. The incoming agents can perform notifications (messages 10 to 14) and are informed if the notification is successful (message 15). The agents coming from hospitals—which represent the Hospital Transplant Coordinator [4]—can also perform queries (message 16) about historical facts (e.g. statistics on, say, successful cornea transplantations over a certain period). The queries are answered (message 17) with the level of detail that is permitted for a certain role, as all access to the database is controlled through a *Role-Based Access Model* [10]. When the incoming agents have performed all the queries and notifications, they exit the Carrel system (message 18).

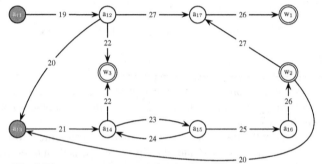

Fig. 5. The conversation graph for the Organ Exchange room

Allocating organs. For organ assignment, a new scene, the *Organ Exchange Room* has been added. The protocol of this scene, depicted in figure 5, can be divided in two parts:
- the arrival of an Agent$_i$ (hospital *Finder Agent*) with an offer of an available organ (states a_{11} and a_{12}), waiting for a notification that a proper recipient has been found (message 22, exit state w_3) or not (message 27 leading to an exit request through state w_1).
- the loop of the scene manager looking for recipients. Based on the information of the waiting lists stored in Carrel's database, the scene manager sends a call to a hospital (message 20) where there is a suitable recipient. Then an Agent$_j$ (hospital *Contact Agent*) enters the scene to answer the call, saying whether it accepts the organ or not (message 20). Sometimes Agent$_j$, representing the hospital Transplant Coordinator, expresses the intention to use the organ in a different recipient (message 23), a change that, depending on the reasons given, can either be accepted or rejected (messages 24 and 25). If the scene manager and Agent$_j$ agree, then Agent$_i$ is notified of the recipient, otherwise Agent$_j$ exits the scene and the loop starts again with a call to another hospital for another recipient.

The search and assignment processes by the scene manager are driven by knowledge of donor-recipient compatibility that is coded in the form of rules such as the following ones for kidneys:

```
1- (age_donor <= 1)
     -> (age_recipient < 2)

2- (age_donor > 1) AND (age_donor < 4)
     -> (age_recipient < 4)

3- (age_donor >= 4) AND (age_donor < 12)
     -> (age_recipient > 4) AND (age_recipient < 60)

4- (age_donor >= 12) AND (age_donor < 60)
     -> (age_recipient >= 12) AND (age_recipient < 60)

5- (age_donor >= 60) AND (age_donor < 74) AND (creatinine_clearance > 55 ml/min)
     -> (age_recipient >= 60) AND (transplant_type SINGLE-KIDNEY)

6- (age_donor >= 60) AND (age_donor < 74) AND (glomerulosclerosis <= 15%)
     -> (age_recipient >= 60) AND (transplant_type SINGLE-KIDNEY)

7- (age_donor >= 60) AND (glomerulosclerosis > 15%) AND (glomerulosclerosis <= 30%)
     -> (age_recipient >= 60) AND (transplant_type DUAL-KIDNEY)

8- (weight_donor = X)
     -> (weight_recipient > X*0.8) AND (weight_recipient < X*1.2)

9- (disease_donor Hepatitis_B)
     -> (disease_recipient Hepatitis_B)

10-(disease_donor Hepatitis_C)
     -> (disease_recipient Hepatitis_C)

11-(disease_donor VIH)
     -> (DISCARD-DONOR)

12-(glomerulosclerosis > 30%)
     -> (DISCARD-KIDNEY)

13- (HLA_compatibility_factors < 3)
     -> (DONOR-RECIPIENT-INCOMPATIBILITY)
```

Rules 1 to 8 are related to size compatibility, either considering age ranges (rules 1 to 7) or weight differences, here the criterion permits a 20% variation above or below. Rules 5 to 7 consider quality of the kidney and assess not only the limit that is acceptable but also the transplant technique to be used (to transplant one or both kidneys). Rules 9 to 10 are examples of diseases in the donor that do not lead to discarding the organ for transplantation, if a proper recipient is found (in the example, a recipient that has had also the same kind of hepatitis B or C in the past). Finally, rules 11 to 13 are examples of rejection rules, as determined by current medical knowledge.

It is important that such policies not be hard-coded in the system, as such rules evolve with practice (for instance, some years ago donors with any kind of Hepatitis were discarded). Expressing the knowledge in the form of rules is a technique that allows the system to be adaptable to future changes in medical practice.

Allocating tissues. The *Tissue Exchange Room* is the place where negotiation over tissues is performed. The protocol of this scene is shown in figure 6: Agent$_i$ (hospital *FinderAgent*) asks the scene manager for tissue offers (tissues matching the requirements included in their petition). Then the scene manager gives a list of available tissues (message 29) that is evaluated by the external agent$_i$ (message 30). With this information the scene manager can make a provisional assignment and solve collisions (two agents

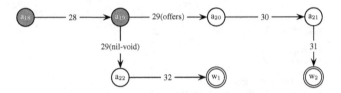

Fig. 6. The conversation graph for the Tissue Exchange room

interested in the same tissue). When this provisional assignment is delivered (message 31) then agent$_i$ exits the scene to go to the *Confirmation Room* represented by state w_2. There is an alternative path for the case when there are no available pieces matching the requirements described in the petition (message 9 with null list). In this case agent$_i$ requests an exit permission from the institution (message 32, exit state w_1), including the reason for leaving. The reason provided is recorded in the institution logs to form an audit trail for the relevant authorities to inspect. For further information about this negotiation process see [16].

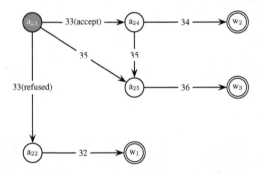

Fig. 7. Conversation graph for the Confirmation room

Confirming the assignation. In the *Confirmation Room* scene, the provisional assignments made in a *Tissue Exchange Room* or an *Organ Exchange Room* are either confirmed or withdrawn. Figure 7 shows the protocol of this scene: the agent$_i$ can analyze the assigned piece data and then accept or refuse it (message 33). If the agent$_i$ accepts the piece and no higher-priority requests appear during a certain time window then the provisional assignment is confirmed and a delivery plan is given to the agent$_i$ (message 34), and then it exits the Carrel system (exit state w_2). When there is a request with higher priority that needs the piece provisionally assigned to agent$_i$ a conflict arises. To resolve the conflict the scene manager notifies the agent$_i$ that the assignment has been withdrawn (message 35) and that he is then entitled to a fresh request for another piece, if available, (message 36) to be negotiated again in the *Exchange Room* whence it came.

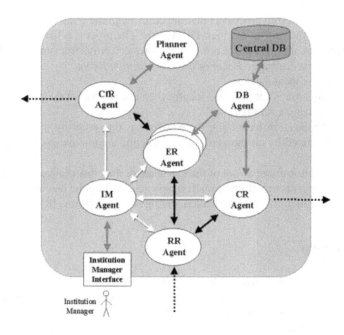

Fig. 8. The multi-agent architecture of a Carrel platform

3.2   The Multi-agent Architecture

The agent architecture that performs the *institutional roles* is shown in figure 8. There is
one agent managing each of the scenes: the **RR Agent** managing the *Reception Room*,
the **CR Agent** managing the *Consultation Room*, an **ER Agent** for each *Exchange
Room* (either the ones for organs or the ones for tissues), and a **CfR Agent** managing
the *Confirmation Room*. Also there is an agent (the **IM Agent**) playing the *institution
manager* role.

In order to assist those agents, two agents are added for specific tasks: the **Planner
Agent**, to build the delivery plans that are needed in the *Confirmation Room*, and the **DB
Agent**, which is devoted to the role-based access control of the internal Database.

4   A Network of Carrel Institutions

In the previous sections the Carrel system has been described as an institution that
works alone, managing all the requests and offers coming from the hospitals. However a
distributed system is needed in order to manage the allocation problem at an international
level (one of the aims of our scheme).

To do so, we propose to create a federation of geographically-distributed Carrel
platforms. Hospitals and Tissue banks register themselves to the "nearest" platform and
interact as described in previous sections.

As a result, the search process is distributed through the platforms, exchanging information among themselves via their **DB Agents**. The process is the following:

- The **DB Agent** of a certain platform$_i$ receives a query, either from an *Organ Exchange Room*, a *Tissue Exchange Room* or the *Consultation Room*
- It accesses the local database.
- If the information is not available locally, then it sends part of the query to other **DB Agents** in other Carrel Platforms.
- All the diferences in terminology are solved at this point by the use of domain ontologies shared by all the platforms that define a common exchange format for the information.

All Carrel platforms are aware of the existence of the other platforms. The communication among agents on different platforms is acheived by the mechanism defined in the FIPA specification for communication among Agent platforms [8].

5   Conclusion

We have presented here an Agent-Mediated Electronic Institution for the distribution of organs and tissues for transplantation purposes. Our aim with this work is not only to apply multi-agent technologies to model the organ and tissue allocation problem but we also have devoted part of our efforts in formalization, following the recommendations in [9] about the need of formal design methods when applying agents to the medical domain in order to ensure the *safety* and *soundness* of the resulting system. In our case we have chosen a formalism called ISLANDER [7], based on the dialogical framework idea, to get an accurate description of the interactions among the agents. By means of such formalism we have been able to design a system that combines the strengths of agents with the adventages of formal specifications.

As far as we know, there are very few references in the literature about the use of agents in the transplant domain. [15] and [12] describe single agents to solve specific tasks needed for this domain (respectively, a receiver selection algorithm based on multicriteria decision techniques and a planner for transport routes between hospitals for organ delivery). [11] proposes a multi-agent system architecture to coordinate all the hospital members involved in a transplant. [1] also proposes a static hierarchical agent architecture for the organ allocation problem, but no formalism is used in the development of the architecture, and no mechanism is presented to make the architecture adaptive to changes in policies or regulations. For an extended discussion see [16].

Future work aims to extend the methodology to introduce explicit representations of norms to allow agents to reason about the norms. The agents will be able to make better choices in special circumstances. We will follow Dignum's work in [6], incorporating the abstract norms and values of real organizations' statutes and formally connecting them with their implementation in the electronic institution's procedures and protocols. In doing so we will get a full description of an institution, from the abstract (higher) level to the implementation (lower) one.

Acknowledgements. U. Cortés, and J. Vázquez-Salceda want to acknowledge the IST-2000-28385 Agentcities.NET and the IST-1999-10176 A-TEAM projects. The views in this paper are not necessarily those of Agentcities.NET and A-TEAM consortia.

References

1. A. Aldea, B. López, A. Moreno, D. Riaño, and A. Valls. A multi-agent system for organ transplant co-ordination. In Barahona Quaglini and Andreassen (Eds.), editors, *Proceedings of the 8th. European Conference on Artificial Intelligence in Medicine, Portugal, 2001.*, Lecture Notes in Artificial Intelligence 2101: Artificial Intelligence in Medicine, pages 413–416., 2001.

2. C. Castelfranchi, F. Dignum, C. Jonker, and J. Treur. Deliberate normative agents: Principles and architecture, 1999.

3. R. Conte and C. Castelfranchi. Are incentives good enough to achieve(info)social order? In V. Shankararaman, editor, *Workshop on Norms and Institutions in Multi-Agent Systems.* ACM-AAAI, ACM Press, 2000.

4. U. Cortés, J. Vázquez-Salceda, A. López-Navidad, and F. Caballero. UCTx: A multi-agent system to assist a transplant coordinator unit. *Applied Intelligence. Accepted*, 2002.

5. C. Dellarocas and M. Klein. Contractual Agent Societies: Negotiated shared context and social control in open multi-agent systems. In V. Shankararaman, editor, *Workshop on Norms and Institutions in Multi-Agent Systems*, pages 1–11, 2000.

6. F. Dignum. Abstract norms and electronic institutions. In *Proceedings of the International Workshop on Regulated Agent-Based Social Systems: Theories and Applications (RASTA '02), Bologna*, 2002.

7. Marc Esteva, Julian Padget, and Carles Sierra. Formalizing a language for institutions and norms. In Milinde Tambe and Jean-Jules Meyer, editors, *Intelligent Agents VIII*, Lecture Notes in Artificial Intelligence. Springer Verlag, 2001. To appear.

8. The Foundation for Intelligent Phisical Agents, http://www.fipa.org/repository/fipa2000.html. *FIPA Specifications*, 2000.

9. J. Fox and S. Das. *Safe and Sound.* MIT Press, 1st edition, 1999.

10. A. Lin. Integrating policy-driven role-based access control with common data secutiry architecture. Technical Report HPL-1999-59, HP Laboratories Bristol, 1999.

11. A. Moreno, A. Valls, and J. Bocio. Management of hospital teams for organ transplants using multi-agent systems. In Barahona Quaglini and Andreassen (Eds.), editors, *Proceedings of the 8th. European Conference on Artificial Intelligence in Medicine, Portugal, 2001*, Lecture Notes in Artificial Intelligence 2101: Artificial Intelligence in Medicine, pages 374–383, 2001.

12. A. Moreno, A. Valls, and A. Ribes. Finding efficient organ transport routes using multi-agent systems. In *IEEE 3rd International Workshop on Enterprise Networking and Computing in Health Care Industry (Healtcom), L'Aquilla, Italy*, 2001.

13. P. Noriega. *Agent-Mediated Auctions: The Fishmarket Metaphor.* Number 8 in IIIA Monograph Series. Institut d'Investigació en Intel.ligència Artificial (IIIA), 1997. PhD Thesis.

14. Organización Nacional de Transplantes. http://www.msc.es/ont.

15. A. Valls, A. Moreno, and D. Sánchez. A multi-criteria decision aid agent applied to the selection of the best receiver in a transplant. In *4th. International Conference on Enterprise Information Systems, Ciudad Real, Spain*, 2002.

16. J. Vázquez-Salceda, U. Cortés, and J. Padget. Formalizing an electronic institution for the distribution of human tissues. In *Artificial Intelligence in Medicine.* Accepted, 2002.

17. J. Vázquez-Salceda, U. Cortés, J. Padget, A. López-Navidad, and F. Caballero. Extending the carrel system to mediate in the organ and tissue allocation processes: A first approach. Technical Report LSI-02-32-R, Departament de Llenguatges i Sistemes Informàtics, 2002.

18. M. Wooldrige and N.R. Jennings. Intelligent agents: Theory and practice. *The Knowledge Engineering Review*, 10(2):115–152, 1995.

Modelling the Acquisition Geometry of a C-Arm Angiography System for 3D Reconstruction

Cristina Cañero[1,2], Eduardo Nofrerías[3], Josefina Mauri[3], and Petia Radeva[1,2]

[1] Computer Vision Center, Edifici O Campus UAB, 08190 Cerdanyola, Spain.
[2] Computer Science Department, Universitat Autònoma de Barcelona, Spain
[3] Hospital Universitari Germans Tries i Pujol, Badalona, Spain
cristina@cvc.uab.es

Abstract. This paper is concerned with the calibration of the intrinsic and extrinsic parameters of a X-ray angiographic system for 3D reconstruction of coronary vessel centerlines. We discuss whether the isocentric model is an accurate model for the movement of the C-arm, and analyse the assumptions made by this model. We propose a methodology which takes into account these facts and we propose for each model a calibration method. The calibration only needs a phantom that is commonly available by the physicians, since it is used to calibrate geometrical distortion. Then, we test the models with the calibration grid, as well as with a phantom imaged three months later. Experimental results show that by using the proposed models, it is not necessary neither a calibration nor a refinement at each acquisition.

1 Introduction

Digital X-ray angiography provides high quality images of coronary vessels. Assessing the percentage of stenosis and measuring the lesion length are applications with a great clinical interest. These measurements are obtained in clinical practice by comparing the size of the lesion to the width of the catheter appearance in the image disregarding the imprecision due to the perspective projection. In order to obtain reliable vessel measurements, a 3D reconstruction of vessels is a must. Other applications that need 3D reconstruction of vessels from angiography are the determination of optimal views [1] and the fusion of angiography with other medical image modalities like the intravascular ultrasound images to obtain a real volumetric 3D reconstruction of the vessel [2,3]. However, in order to obtain an accurate 3D reconstruction of a point, the acquisition geometry must be known with a high precision. In the angiographic frame, the model proposed by Dumay et al. in [1] is commonly used to predict the acquisition geometry. Nevertheless, authors in [4] state that the classical isocentric model could not satisfy the accuracy required, and thus proposes to use a variable isoaxis instead of a variable isocenter. Chen et al. in [5] proposes also the refining of the geometry for each acquisition for the same reason. Other authors, as Hoffman et al. in [6] propose to calibrate the imaging geometry using a phantom consisting on a cube with 12 lead markers attatched on it at a known position. Although these

M.T. Escrig Monferrer and F. Toledo Lobo (Eds.): CCIA 2002, LNAI 2504, pp. 322–335, 2002.
© Springer-Verlag Berlin Heidelberg 2002

approaches provide a satisfying accuracy to the 3D reconstruction, they require a calibration at each acquisition, which becomes a time-consuming and tedious task in clinical practice.

We propose an improved model of the movement of the C-arm and an associated calibration technique, which only needs a phantom that is commonly available by the physicians. Experimental results show that the calibration must be performed only once. This fact highly simplifies the clinical application of diagnostic techniques involving 3D reconstruction from angiographies.

2   Materials and Methods

2.1   Extrinsic and Intrinsic Parameters Calibration

Given the general problem of pinhole camera calibration, Zhang in [7] proposes a technique to calibrate both the intrinsic and extrinsic parameters by using a planar pattern. This method can also be applied on the angiographic frame provided that the distance from the Image Intensifier (II) to the X-ray source remains constant for all views.

Zhang's Method. This technique only requires the camera (or angiography acquisition system) to observe a planar pattern shown at a few (at least two) different orientations. Either the camera or the planar pattern can be freely moved. The motion need not to be known. Thus, we can use the calibration grid used to estimate the geometrical distortion in [8] as calibration pattern.

Let $\tilde{\mathbf{m}} = [u, v, 1]^T$ be an augmented 2D point. A 3D point is denoted by $\widetilde{\mathbf{M}} = [X, Y, Z, 1]^T$. A camera is then modeled by the usual pinhole:

$$s\tilde{\mathbf{m}} = \mathbf{A} \left[\mathbf{R}\ \mathbf{t} \right] \widetilde{\mathbf{M}} \tag{1}$$

with

$$\mathbf{A} = \begin{bmatrix} \alpha & \gamma & u_0 \\ 0 & \beta & v_0 \\ 0 & 0 & 1 \end{bmatrix}$$

where s is an arbitrary scale factor, $(\mathbf{R}, \mathbf{t})$ the rotation and translation which relates world coordinates with camera coordinates, and $\mathbf{A}$ is the camera intrinsic matrix, with (u_0, v_0) the coordinates of the principal point, α and β the scale factors and γ the skew factor.

In this method, the point is to assume that the model plane is on $Z = 0$ of the world coordinate system, so we can denote $\widetilde{\mathbf{M}} = [X, Y, 1]^T$. Therefore, a model point on world coordinates can be expressed in image coordinates by applying the homography $\mathbf{H}$:

$$s\tilde{\mathbf{m}} = \mathbf{H}\widetilde{\mathbf{M}} \quad \text{with} \quad \mathbf{H} = \mathbf{A} \left[\mathbf{r_1}\ \mathbf{r_2}\ \mathbf{t} \right]$$

where $\mathbf{r_1}, \mathbf{r_2}$ are the first and second columns of $\mathbf{R}$. $\mathbf{H}$ is defined up to a scale factor and can be estimated for each view (see [7]).

Using the knowledge that $\mathbf{r_1}$ and $\mathbf{r_2}$ are orthonormal, we can define the following constraints for each view:

$$\begin{bmatrix} \mathbf{v}_{12}^T \\ (\mathbf{v}_{11} - \mathbf{v}_{22})^T \end{bmatrix} \mathbf{b} = \mathbf{0} \tag{2}$$

where

$$\mathbf{v}_{ij} = [\, h_{i1}h_{j1}, h_{i1}h_{j2} + h_{i2}h_{j1}, h_{i2}h_{j2},$$
$$h_{i1}h_{j3} + h_{i3}h_{j1}, h_{i2}h_{j3} + h_{i3}h_{j2}, h_{i3}h_{j3}]^T,$$

$$\mathbf{b} = [B_{11}, B_{12}, B_{22}, B_{13}, B_{23}, B_{33}]^T$$

and

$$\mathbf{B} = \lambda \mathbf{A}^{-T}\mathbf{A}^{-1} \equiv \lambda \begin{bmatrix} B_{11} & B_{12} & B_{13} \\ B_{21} & B_{22} & B_{23} \\ B_{31} & B_{32} & B_{33} \end{bmatrix}$$

For n images of the model plane, we can stack equations of (2) as:

$$\mathbf{V}\mathbf{b} = \mathbf{0} \tag{3}$$

Imposing the skewless constraint $\gamma = 0$, i.e., $[0, 1, 0, 0, 0, 0]\mathbf{b} = 0$[1] we can add an additional equation to (3). This allows us to obtain the remaining parameters by only using 2 views. The solution to 3 is the eigenvector of $\mathbf{v}^T\mathbf{v}$ associated with the smallest eigenvalue. Once $\mathbf{B}$ is estimated, all camera intrinsic parameters can be computed as follows:

$$u_0 = -\frac{B_{13}}{B_{11}} \qquad v_0 = -\frac{B_{23}}{B_{22}}$$

$$\lambda = \frac{-B_{13}^2 B_{22} - B_{23}^2 B_{11} + B_{33} B_{22} B_{11}}{B_{22} B_{11}}$$

$$\alpha = \sqrt{\frac{\lambda}{B_{11}}} \qquad \beta = \sqrt{\frac{\lambda}{B_{22}}}$$

And the extrinsic parameters for each view are:

$$\mathbf{r_1} = \frac{\mathbf{A}^{-1}\mathbf{H_1}}{\|\mathbf{A}^{-1}\mathbf{H_1}\|}, \qquad \mathbf{r_2} = \frac{\mathbf{A}^{-1}\mathbf{H_2}}{\|\mathbf{A}^{-1}\mathbf{H_2}\|},$$
$$\mathbf{r_3} = \mathbf{r_1} \times \mathbf{r_2}, \qquad \mathbf{t} = \frac{\mathbf{A}^{-1}\mathbf{H_3}}{\|\mathbf{A}^{-1}\mathbf{H_1}\|}$$

For further details, see [7].

---

[1] In practice, we impose $[0, 1000, 0, 0, 0, 0]\mathbf{b} = 0$, since it makes somewhat stronger this constraint.

Using Zhang's Method in the Angiographic Frame. The calibration pattern required by Zhang's method can be easily constructed by printing a checkerbox or a grid onto a paper and then fixing it to a rigid planar surface, for instance to a hard-covered book. Although this approach is not applicable when working with X-rays, we can use the same grid we used when calibrating Image Intensifiers's distortion in [8] as calibration pattern. Thus, we propose to place the grid on the examination table, and acquire it by changing the anatomical angles for each view. Zhang's method [7] can then be applied to obtain the intrinsic parameters, represented by matrix $\mathbf{A}$, and the extrinsic parameters, corresponding for each view i to matrices $\hat{\mathbf{R}}_i$ and $\hat{\mathbf{t}}_i$.

Nevertheless, this calibration is only valid for the acquired views, and we are interested in being able to compute the extrinsic parameters $\hat{\mathbf{R}}$, $\hat{\mathbf{t}}$ for any given configuration of the C-arm, determined by the anatomical angles α and β. To do that, we need to define a model of the movement of the C-arm, as the one proposed by Dumay et al. in [1], and then estimate the parameters of this model from the obtained $\hat{\mathbf{R}}_i$ and $\hat{\mathbf{t}}_i$ using Zhang's method.

2.2 Modelling the Movement of the C-Arm

Modelling the movement of the C-arm means defining how to compute the extrinsic parameters $\mathbf{R}$, $\mathbf{t}$ for any given configuration of the C-arm, determined by the anatomical angles α and β.

Dumay et al. defined in [1] the characteristic movements of a ceiling-mounted C-arm. First we will analize this model and then introduce some modifications to improve its accuracy.

Dumay's Model (M0). In the model proposed by Dumay et al. in [1], the fixed axis of rotation is directed horizontally and in longitudinal direction to the table. This axis is always projected 'vertically' in the images, i.e. its projection coincides with the y-axis on the image matrix. The projection of this fixed axis is therefore chosen as vector $\mathbf{l}$ on the image plane. The axis perpendicular to $\mathbf{l}$ on the image plane is denoted as $\mathbf{k}$ and defined as:

$$\mathbf{k} = [0, -\cos\alpha, \sin\alpha]^T$$

The position of the plane, $\mathbf{C} = \|C\|\mathbf{c}$, where $\mathbf{c}$ can be computed as:

$$\mathbf{c} = [\sin\beta, \sin\alpha\cos\beta, \cos\alpha\cos\beta]^T$$

The local reference system is chosen as a left-hand oriented orthogonal system, and thus the remaining axis $\mathbf{l}$ is solved from:

$$\mathbf{l} = \mathbf{c} \times \mathbf{k}$$

From this model, we can define the extrinsic parameters $\mathbf{R}'$, $\mathbf{t}'$ as:

$$\mathbf{R} = \bar{\mathbf{R}} \qquad \mathbf{t} = \bar{\mathbf{t}} \tag{4}$$

where

$$\bar{\mathbf{R}} = \left[\, \mathbf{k}\, \mathbf{l}\, \mathbf{c}\,\right]^T$$

and

$$\bar{\mathbf{t}} = [0, 0, \|C\|]^T$$

where $\|C\|$ is defined as the distance fom the isocenter of rotation to the entrance screen of the image intensifier.

However, the model proposed by Dumay et al. makes the following assumptions:

- Vector $\mathbf{l}$ coincides with the y axis on the image, and $\mathbf{k}$ coincides with the x axis on the image.
- The imaging equipment is properly aligned and thus the central beams intersect at the isocenter of rotation.
- The rotation and angulation axes do intersect, i.e. there is an isocenter.
- The rotation and angulation axes are perfectly orthogonal.
- The central beam is orthogonal to the angulation axis.

We will analyse each assumption and, if necessary, we will define a model for each case.

Model with Image Rotation (M1). Vector $\mathbf{l}$ and $\mathbf{k}$ may not coincide with the y axis and x axis on the image, respectively, since the Image Intensifier (II) introduces a distortion with a rotational effect. Our undistortion method presented in [8] fixed image rotation and other distortions, even the orientation-dependent ones, by estimating the distortion model from the anatomical angles. Nevertheless, and since the ground truth orientation of the image is unknown, the resulting undistorted image will be in general rotated from the ideal undistorted one. Moreover, rotation and angulation axis of the isocentric model could be not aligned with the ideal image.

Therefore, image rotation can stem both from II's distortion and from image misalignment. For simplicity, we will combine both rotations on a unique rotation matrix $\mathbf{R_d} = R_z(\theta)$, which will be applied before projecting. Since this rotation is not in general performed on the origin of coordinates, we should add a displacement vector $\mathbf{t_d} = [d_x, d_y, 0]^T$ after rotating[2]. Thus, the extrinsic parameters defined by this model are:

$$\mathbf{R} = \mathbf{R_d}\bar{\mathbf{R}} \qquad \mathbf{t} = \mathbf{R_d}\bar{\mathbf{t}} + \mathbf{t_d}$$

since $\bar{\mathbf{t}}$ is a displacement among z axis, matrix $\mathbf{R_d}$ has no effect on it, and thus:

$$\mathbf{R} = \mathbf{R_d}\bar{\mathbf{R}} \qquad \mathbf{t} = \bar{\mathbf{t}} + \mathbf{t_d} \tag{5}$$

---

[2] Although the rotation related to angulation and rotation angles misalignement is performed before projecting and the one related to II distortion is performed after, it is very easy to show that we can do this simplification.

Non Intersecting Central Beams. If the imaging equipment is not properly aligned, the central beam does not intersect the isocenter of rotation, i.e., the isocenter is also displaced (ϵ_x, ϵ_y) from the central beam in the plane perpendicular to it. We assume that this displacement is constant for all views. Although this situation is possible, it can be modelled with the previous model, since parameters d_x, d_y can compensate this effect. Therefore, we will not define a model for this situation.

Non Intersecting Rotation Axis (M2). If the two rotation axis do not intersect, the isocentric model is not valid. Instead, we should define a model with a displacement between the two rotation axis and perpendicular to both. Since rotation, defined by α angle, is performed around the y axis and angulation around the x axis, this displacement will be along the z axis after α rotation. Let ϵ be this displacement, then we can define the following model for the external parameters:

$$\mathbf{R} = \mathbf{R_d} R_x(\beta) R_y(\alpha)$$
$$\mathbf{t} = \bar{\mathbf{t}} + \mathbf{t_d} + \mathbf{R_d}(\mathbf{I} - R_x(\beta))[0; 0; \epsilon]^T \qquad (6)$$

where $R_y(\alpha)$ corresponds to the rotation and $R_x(\beta)$ to the angulation[3].

Non Orthogonal Rotation Axes (M3). Although the rotation axes are expected to be orthogonal, perfect orthogonality is hard to achieve, and thus the angulation axis will be slighty rotated from its ideal position. Moreover, the anatomical angles could be measured as $\alpha' = \alpha + \triangle\alpha$ and $\beta' = \beta + \triangle\beta$. This fact would have an equivalent effect on the extrinsic parameters as the non orthogonality of the rotation axes. Therefore, we introduce the rotation matrix $\mathbf{R_p}$ in our model, and the extrinsic parameters will be:

$$\mathbf{R} = \mathbf{R_d} R_x(\beta) \mathbf{R_p} R_y(\alpha)$$
$$\mathbf{t} = \bar{\mathbf{t}} + \mathbf{t_d} + \mathbf{R_d}(\mathbf{I} - R_x(\beta)\mathbf{R_p})[0; 0; \epsilon]^T \qquad (7)$$

Central Beam Non Orthogonal to Angulation Axis (M4). In theory, the central beam should be perpendicular to the angulation axis. Nevertheless, this may not be true, and hence we introduce matrix $\mathbf{R_b}$ in the model. This matrix will describe the rotation between the central beam and the ideal one, which is perpendicular to the angulation axis. Thus, the model will be **M3**, but

---

[3] Note that if we compute $R_x(\beta) R_y(\alpha)$ we will not obtain $\bar{\mathbf{R}}$, but $\bar{\mathbf{R}} \mathbf{R_a}$, where

$$\mathbf{R_a} = \begin{bmatrix} 0 & -1 & 0 \\ 1 & 0 & 0 \\ 0 & 0 & 1 \end{bmatrix}$$

This is not important to obtain a 3D reconstruction, nor have effect when callibrating.

replacing $\mathbf{R_d}$ by $\mathbf{R_b}$. Thus, we obtain the following expression for the extrinsic parameters:

$$\mathbf{R} = \mathbf{R_b}R_x(\beta)\mathbf{R_p}R_y(\alpha)$$
$$\mathbf{t} = \bar{\mathbf{t}} + \mathbf{t_d} + \mathbf{R_b}(\mathbf{I} - R_x(\beta)\mathbf{R_p})[0; 0; \epsilon]^T \qquad (8)$$

2.3   Calibrating the C-Arm's Movement Model

Zhang's approach assumes that the world coordinate system is placed on the calibration pattern. This coordinate system does not in general coincide with the rotation and angulation axes. Thus, there is a rigid transform, represented by $\mathbf{R_w}$, $\mathbf{t_w}$ between the two coordinate systems. If the model is exact and well calibrated, the extrinsic parameters $\mathbf{R}_i$, $\mathbf{t_i}$ predicted by the model and the matrices $\hat{\mathbf{R}}_i$, $\hat{\mathbf{t}}_i$, estimated using Zhang's approach, should fulfill the following:

$$\hat{\mathbf{R}}_i = \mathbf{R}_i\mathbf{R_w} \qquad \hat{\mathbf{t}}_i = \mathbf{R}_i\mathbf{t_w} + \mathbf{t}_i \qquad (9)$$

Our aim is thus to estimate the parameters of each model and the rigid transform $\mathbf{R_w}$, $\mathbf{t_w}$, which fits the best the estimated matrices $\hat{\mathbf{R}}_i$, $\hat{\mathbf{t}}_i$ using Zhang's approach to the ideal matrices $\mathbf{R}_i$, $\mathbf{t_i}$ of each model.

M0 Calibration. The parameters to be estimated are $\mathbf{R_w}$, $\mathbf{t_w}$ and $\|C\|$. Using equation (4) and (9), we can state the following:

$$\hat{\mathbf{R}}_i = \bar{\mathbf{R}}_i\mathbf{R_w} \qquad \hat{\mathbf{t}}_i = \bar{\mathbf{R}}_i\mathbf{t_w} + \bar{\mathbf{t}}_i$$

For each view i, we can compute an estimation of $\mathbf{R_w}$ as:

$$\mathbf{R_w}^i = \bar{\mathbf{R}}_i^T\hat{\mathbf{R}}_i$$

The estimated $\mathbf{R_w}$ can then be assumed to be the mean of $\mathbf{R_w}^i$. To estimate the mean of a set of rotations, we use the approach proposed in [9].

On the other hand, for each view we can define the following set of linear constraints:

$$\begin{bmatrix} \bar{\mathbf{R}}_i & [0,0,1]^T \end{bmatrix} \begin{bmatrix} \mathbf{t_w} \\ \|C\| \end{bmatrix} = \hat{\mathbf{t}}_i$$

These constraints can be stacked to construct an overdetermined linear system of equations, which can be resolved by applying any linear least squares approach. Since there are 4 independent unknown variables - namely, $\mathbf{t_w}$ and $\|C\|$ -, we need at least 2 views.

M1 Calibration. Using equations (5) and (9), we obtain:

$$\hat{\mathbf{R}}_i = \mathbf{R_d}\bar{\mathbf{R}}_i\mathbf{R_w} \qquad \hat{\mathbf{t}}_i = \mathbf{R_d}\bar{\mathbf{R}}_i\mathbf{t_w} + \bar{\mathbf{t}}_i + \mathbf{t_d} \qquad (10)$$

Note that $\mathbf{R_w}$, $\mathbf{t_w}$, $\mathbf{R_d}$, $\mathbf{t_d}$ and $\bar{\mathbf{t}}_i$ should be constant for all views.

First, we need to estimate $\mathbf{R_d}$. Given two views i, j with $i \neq j$, we can compute the following:

$$\hat{\mathbf{R}}_i \hat{\mathbf{R}}_j^T = \mathbf{R_d} \mathbf{R}_i \mathbf{R_w} \mathbf{R_w}^T \mathbf{R}_j^T \mathbf{R_d}^T$$

and using that $\mathbf{R_w}$ is a rotation matrix and thus $\mathbf{R_w} \mathbf{R_w}^T = \mathbf{I}$, we can state that:

$$\hat{\mathbf{R}}_i \hat{\mathbf{R}}_j^T = \mathbf{R_d} \mathbf{R}_i \mathbf{R}_j^T \mathbf{R_d}^T$$

Since $\mathbf{R_d}$ is uniquely determined by the angle θ, this non-linear system is very easy to solve by applying any standard non-linear least squares approach. In this work, we have applied the Gauss-Newton method to estimate θ. To construct the error function, we have used the metric proposed in [9] to compute the distance between two rotations.

Once we have an estimate of $\mathbf{R_d}$, we can proceed to estimate the other parameters. First, for each view i, we can compute an estimate of $\mathbf{R_w}$ as:

$$\mathbf{R_w}^i = \bar{\mathbf{R}}_i^T \mathbf{R_d}^T \hat{\mathbf{R}}_i$$

The estimated $\mathbf{R_w}$ can then be assumed to be the mean of $\mathbf{R_w}^i$, which can be computed as proposed in [9].

Second, for each view we can define the following set of linear constraints:

$$\begin{bmatrix} \mathbf{R_d} \mathbf{R_i} & \mathbf{I} \end{bmatrix} \begin{bmatrix} \mathbf{t_w} \\ \mathbf{t_i} + \mathbf{t_d} \end{bmatrix} = \hat{\mathbf{t}}_\mathbf{i}$$

where

$$\mathbf{t_i} + \mathbf{t_d} = [d_x, d_y, \|C\|]^T$$

These constraints can be stacked to construct an overdetermined linear system of equations, which can be resolved by applying any linear least squares approach. Since there are 6 independent unknown variables - namely, $\mathbf{t_w}$, d_x, d_y and $\|C\|$ -, we need at least 2 views.

The obtained parameters θ, $\mathbf{R_w}$, $\mathbf{t_w}$, d_x, d_y and $\|C\|$ can then be refined by using a non-linear least squares minimization method using as error function the sum of the squared distances between the detected intersection points on the images and the predicted ones using the model.

M2 Calibration. Using equations (6) and (9), we obtain the following relation:

$$\hat{\mathbf{R}}_i = \mathbf{R_d} R_x(\beta_i) R_y(\alpha_i) \mathbf{R_w}$$
$$\hat{\mathbf{t}}_i = \mathbf{R_d} R_x(\beta_i) R_y(\alpha_i) \mathbf{t_w} + \bar{\mathbf{t}}_i + \mathbf{t_d} +$$
$$\mathbf{R_d}(\mathbf{I} - R_x(\beta_i))[0, 0, \epsilon]^T$$

To estimate the parameters of the model, we first estimate θ by using the non-linear approach used to calibrate the previous model, replacing $\hat{\mathbf{R}}_i$ by

$R_x(\beta_i)R_y(\alpha_i)$. Once we have an estimate of θ, and thus of $\mathbf{R_d}$, we can define the following set of linear constraints for each view i:

$$\left[\mathbf{R_d}R_x(\beta_i)R_y(\alpha_i) \; \mathbf{b} \; \mathbf{I} \right] \begin{bmatrix} \mathbf{t_w} \\ \epsilon \\ d_x \\ d_y \\ \|C\| \end{bmatrix} = \hat{\mathbf{t_i}}$$

where

$$\mathbf{b} = \mathbf{R_d}(\mathbf{I} - R_x(\beta_i))[0,0,1]^T$$

These constraints can be stacked to construct an overdetermined linear system of equations, which can be resolved by applying any linear least squares approach. Since there are 7 independent unknown variables - namely, $\mathbf{t_w}$, ϵ, d_x, d_y and $\|C\|$ -, we need at least 3 views.

Finally, the obtained parameters θ, $\mathbf{R_w}$, $\mathbf{t_w}$, ϵ, d_x, d_y and $\|C\|$ can be refined by using a non-linear least squares minimization method to fit the predicted positions of the intersection points of the grid to the detected ones on the images, as we have done with model **M1**.

M3 Calibration. Using equations (7) and (9), we can state the following:

$$\hat{\mathbf{R}}_i = \mathbf{R_d}R_x(\beta)\mathbf{R_p}R_y(\alpha)\mathbf{R_w}$$
$$\hat{\mathbf{t}}_i = \mathbf{R_d}R_x(\beta)\mathbf{R_p}R_y(\alpha)\mathbf{t_w} + \bar{\mathbf{t}}_i + \mathbf{t_d} + \mathbf{R_d}(\mathbf{I} - R_x(\beta)\mathbf{R_p})[0,0,\epsilon]^T$$

Since we have not found a closed form solution to estimate the parameters of this model, we propose to fit model **M2** and then use the obtained parameters θ, $\mathbf{R_w}$, $\mathbf{t_w}$, ϵ, d_x, d_y and $\|C\|$ and the added $\mathbf{R_p} = \mathbf{I}$ as starting guess for a non-linear minimization procedure. As before, the error functional to be minimized will be the squared distance between the predicted positions of the intersections on the grid and the detected ones on the images.

M4 Calibration. Using equations (8) and (9), we can obtain the following expression for matrices $\hat{\mathbf{R}}_i$, $\hat{\mathbf{t}}_i$:

$$\hat{\mathbf{R}}_i = \mathbf{R_b}R_x(\beta)\mathbf{R_p}R_y(\alpha)\mathbf{R_w}$$
$$\hat{\mathbf{t}}_i = \mathbf{R_b}R_x(\beta)\mathbf{R_p}R_y(\alpha)\mathbf{t_w} + \bar{\mathbf{t}}_i + \mathbf{t_d} + \mathbf{R_b}(\mathbf{I} - R_x(\beta)\mathbf{R_p})[0,0,\epsilon]^T$$

To estimate the parameters of this model, we can start with the parameter estimate for model **M3** as initial guess (with $\mathbf{R_b} = \mathbf{R_d}$), and run a non-linear minimization procedure. Again, the error function will be the squared distance betweeen the positions of the intersections on the grid predicted by the model and the detected ones on the images.

3   Experimental Results

The experimental results presented in this work were performed using a SIEMENS Cathcor 3.3 C-arm angiography acquisition system in the University Hospital "Germans Trias i Pujol" (Badalona, Spain). This system is laterally mounted instead of ceiling-mounted, and thus we must replace α by $-\alpha$ and β by $-\beta$ in the formulae proposed. Figure 1 illustrates how anatomical angles are defined in our system.

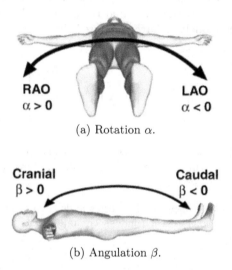

(a) Rotation α.

(b) Angulation β.

Fig. 1. Anatomic angles for a laterally mounted SIEMENS Cathcor 3.3 C-arm, which define the orientation of the detector.

3.1   Zhang's Calibration on a C-Arm Angiographer from SIEMENS

We have acquired the grid for different positions of the C-arm, namely for $\alpha \in \{-30, -15, -5, 0, 5, 15, 30\}$ and $\beta \in \{-20, -15, -10, 0, 10, 15, 20\}$. First, we have detected the intersections for each view i, thus obtaining $\hat{\mathbf{u}}_i, \hat{\mathbf{v}}_i$, the distorted positions on the image of the intersection points on the grid, and $\mathbf{x}_i, \mathbf{y}_i$, the real positions in world coordinates (in cm). After, we have applied the undistortion method proposed in [8] to obtain the undistorted coordinates $\mathbf{u}_i, \mathbf{v}_i$. Third, we have applied Zhang's method to $\mathbf{u}_i, \mathbf{v}_i$ and $\mathbf{x}_i, \mathbf{y}_i$, obtaining matrices $\mathbf{A}$, $\hat{\mathbf{R}}_i$ and $\hat{\mathbf{t}}_i$. Finally, we have computed the following expression for each view i and detected position j:

$$E_{ij} = \begin{bmatrix} u_{ij} \\ v_{ij} \end{bmatrix} - \mathbf{A}[\mathbf{R_i} - \mathbf{t_i}] \begin{bmatrix} x_{ij} \\ y_{ij} \\ 0 \\ 1 \end{bmatrix}$$

The standard desviation of E_{ij} was of 0.13 pixels, and the maximum value of $\|E_{ij}\|$ was of 0.8 pixels.

3.2   Accuracy of the Proposed Models

The aim of this experiment is to determine which model fits the best to the real movement of the C-arm. In order to do that, we have first divided the acquired views of the previous experiment in two sets: the calibration and the test set. Then, we have estimated the parameters of each model for each view of the calibration set, using the estimated $\hat{\mathbf{R}}_i$ and $\hat{\mathbf{t}}_i$ of the previous experiment. Finally, and for each model, we have computed the following expression for each view i and position j:

$$E_{ij} = \begin{bmatrix} u_{ij} \\ v_{ij} \end{bmatrix} - \mathbf{A}[\mathbf{R_i}^k \mathbf{t_i}^k] \begin{bmatrix} x_{ij} \\ y_{ij} \\ 0 \\ 1 \end{bmatrix}$$

where matrices $\mathbf{R_i}^k$ and $\mathbf{t_i}^k$ are the predicted extrinsic parameters for view i and model $\mathbf{Mk}$, using the estimated parameters. Table 1 shows the results obtained.

Table 1. Displacement E (in pixels) between the detected intersection points on the grid and predicted positions for each model, computed both for calibration and test sets.

	Calibration		Test	
	std(E)	max $\|E\|$	std(E)	max $\|E\|$
M0	6.81	33.38	5.63	23.00
M1	1.80	10.15	1.85	9.77
M2	1.98	13.14	1.96	11.07
M3	1.08	8.49	1.00	4.77
M4	0.91	5.39	0.86	5.44

From these results, we can state that the model which better fits is **M4**. Note the large maximal errors introduced by model **M0**. Since the distance between wires on the grid is of 1cm and the projected gap on the image measures a mean of 40 pixels, an error of 30 pixels is very important.

3.3   3D Reconstruction of a Phantom

Three months after the calibration date, we have acquired a phantom consisting on a wavy wire, simulating a vessel. The wire was imaged for different views, namely, for $\alpha \in [30^o, 0^o, -30^o]$ and $\beta \in [15^o, 0^o, -15^o]$.

We have then estimated for each model the corresponding extrinsic parameters for all views by using the calibration performed in the previous experiment.

Table 2. Here D is the distance from each projected point of the curve to the nearest position on the image corresponding to wire. $|D|$ is the mean of distance D for all views, and $max|D_i|$ is the maximum value of the mean distance computed for each view. All values are in pixels.

	Ignoring distortion		Including distortion	
Model	$|D|$	max $|D_i|$	$|D|$	max $|D_i|$
M0	4.0	7.9	3.4	7.5
M1	0.6	1.5	0.6	1.4
M2	0.5	1.5	0.5	1.4
M3	0.4	0.9	0.2	0.5
M4	0.3	0.6	0.1	0.3

For the intrinsic parameters, it must be noted that the distance from the X-ray source to the Image Intensifier's screen was different from the calibration acquisitions, i.e. whereas when calibrating it was of 95cm, in this experiment was of 100cm. Therefore, to determine the intrinsic parameters, i.e. matrix $\mathbf{A}$, we have recomputed components A_{11} and A_{22} as $A_{11} = 100/95\hat{A}_{11}$ and $A_{22} = 100/95\hat{A}_{22}$, where $\hat{\mathbf{A}}$ is the matrix estimated using Zhang's method.

From each model, we have reconstructed the phantom using a biplane snake (for a description of biplane snakes, see [10]) and views $[\alpha_1 = 30^o, \beta_1 = 0^o]$ and $[\alpha_2 = -30^o, \beta_2 = 0^o]$. We have done two reconstructions: ignoring the distortion introduced by the Image Intensifier, and using the distortion/undistortion model proposed in [8].

Finally, we have projected the reconstructed curve on the other views, to see whether the projection of the curve fits the image. Figure 3.3 shows the obtained curve projected for a view with $\alpha = 0$ and $\beta = 15$, for each model. Note that the curve fits pretty accurately for models **M3** and **M4**. Numerical results are presented in table 2.

4 Discussion

We have proposed a method to calibrate the extrinsic and intrinsic parameters of a C-arm by using a phantom which is commonly available by the physicians, since it is the one used to calibrate geometrical distortion.

Then, we have discussed whether the isocentric model is an accurate model for the movement of the C-arm. In particular, we question whether the rotation axis and the angulation axis do intersect, if there is not a perfect orthogonality between the two axes, and also if the central beam is orthogonal to the angulation axis. We have therefore proposed models which take into account these facts, and estimated its parameters by using a calibration grid. Then, we have tested the models with a phantom imaged three months later. Experimental results lead us to believe that our models perform better than the traditional isocentric model. In particular, they conduct us to select model **M4** as the model to be used for 3D reconstruction purposes. Moreover, the accuracy obtained in the experiments

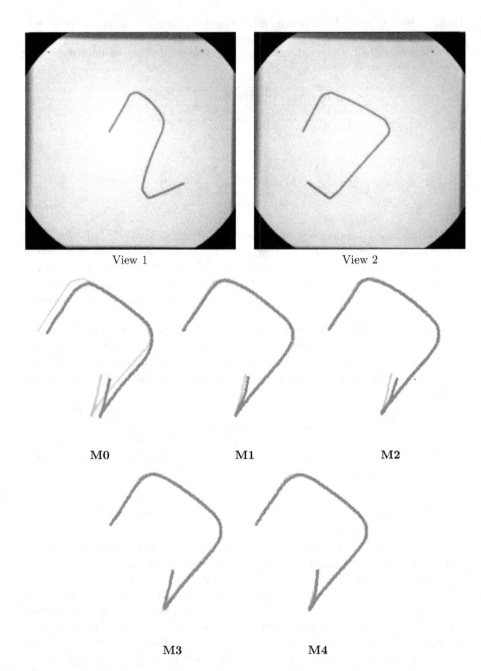

Fig. 2. Projection of the reconstructed 3D curve (dark) using each model at $\alpha = 0, \beta = 15$. The curve was obtained from views $\alpha = 30, \beta = 0$ (view 1) and $\alpha = -30, \beta = 0$ (view 2). Geometrical distortion introduced by the Image Intensifier was taken into account.

encourauges us to state that by using model **M4**, it shall not be necessary a calibration nor a refinement at each acquisition, as proposed in [4,5,6], but only a periodic calibration. This fact is very important, since it highly simplifies the clinical application of diagnostic techniques involving 3D reconstruction from angiographies.

Acknowledgments. This work was supported in part by the catalonian *Departament d'Universitats, Recerca i Societat de la Informació* under the grant 1999FI 00753 APTIND CVC and by the spanish *Ministerio de Ciencia y Tecnología* under the projects TIC2000-1635-C04-04 and TIC2000-0399-C02-01.

References

1. Dumay, A., Reiber, J., Gerbrands, J.: Determination of optimal angiographic viewing angles: Basic principles and evaluation study. IEEE Transactions on Medical Imaging **13** (1994)
2. Pujol, O., Cañero, C., Radeva, P., Toledo, R., Saludes, J., Gil, D., Villanueva, J., Mauri, J., García, B., Gómez, J., Cequier, A., Esplugas, E.: Three-dimensional reconstruction of coronary tree using intravascular ultrasound images. In: Computers in Cardiology. (1999) 265–268
3. Wahle, A., Prause, G., DeJong, S., Sonka, M.: Geometrically correct 3-D reconstruction of intravascular ultrasound images by fusion with biplane angiography - methods and validation. IEEE Transactions on Medical Imaging **18** (1999)
4. Wahle, A., Wellnhofer, E., Mugaragu, I., Sauer, H., Oswald, H., Fleck, E.: Assessment of diffuse coronary artery disease by quantitative analysis of coronary morphology based upon 3-D reconstruction from biplane angiograms. IEEE Transactions on Medical Imaging **14** (1995) 230–241
5. Chen, S., Metz, C.: Improved determination of biplane imaging geometry from two projection images and its application to three-dimensional reconstruction of coronary arterial trees. Medical Physics **25** (1997) 633–654
6. Hoffmann, K., Williams, B., Esthappan, J., Chen, S.Y., Carroll, J., Harauchi, J., Doerr, V., Kay, G., Eberhardt, A., Overland, M.: Determination of 3D positions of pacemaker leads from biplane angiographic sequences. Medical Physics **24** (1997) 1854–1862
7. Zhang, Z.: A flexible new technique for camera calibration. IEEE Transactions on Pattern Analysis and Machine Intelligence **22** (2000) 1330–1334
8. Cañero, C., Vilariño, F., Mauri, J., Radeva, P.: Predictive (un)distortion model and 3D reconstruction by biplane snakes. IEEE Transactions on Medical Imaging, to appear (2002)
9. Pennec, X.: Computing the mean of geometric features. Application to the mean rotation. Technical report, INRIA (1998) Available at http://www-sop.inria.fr/rapports/sophia/RR-3371.html.
10. Cañero, C., Radeva, P., Toledo, R., Villanueva, J., Mauri, J.: 3D curve reconstruction by biplane snakes. In: Proceedings of International Conference on Pattern Recognition. Volume 4. (2000) 563–566

Non-negative Matrix Factorization for Face Recognition*

David Guillamet and Jordi Vitrià

Computer Vision Center-Dept. Informàtica
Universitat Autònoma de Barcelona
08193 Bellaterra, Barcelona, Spain
{davidg, jordi}@cvc.uab.es

Abstract. The computer vision problem of face classification under several ambient and unfavorable conditions is considered in this study. Changes in expression, different lighting conditions and occlusions are the relevant factors that are studied in this present contribution. Non-negative Matrix Factorization (NMF) technique is introduced in the context of face classification and a direct comparison with Principal Component Analysis (PCA) is also analyzed. Two leading techniques in face recognition are also considered in this study noticing that NMF is able to improve these techniques when a high dimensional feature space is used. Finally, different distance metrics (L1, L2 and correlation) are evaluated in the feature space defined by NMF in order to determine the best one for this specific problem. Experiments demonstrate that the correlation is the most suitable metric for this problem.

1   Introduction

Face recognition is one of the most challenging problems to be solved in the computer vision community. Until now, several methods and sophisticated approaches have been developed in order to obtain the best recognition results using some specific face databases. Due to this huge number of methods and face databases, there is no uniform way to establish the best method because nearly all of them have been designed to work with some specific face situations. Even though, some of these methodologies have lead to the development of a great number of commercial face recognition systems. Most of the face recognition algorithms can be classified into two classes, image template based or geometry feature based. Template based methods compute a measure of correlation between new faces and a set of template models to estimate the face identity. Several well-known statistical techniques have been used to define a template model, such as Support Vector Machines (SVM) [12], Linear Discriminant Analysis (LDA) [1], Principal Component Analysis (PCA) [11] and Independent

---

* This work is supported by Comissionat per a Universitats i Recerca del Departament de la Presidencia de la Generalitat de Catalunya and Ministerio de Ciencia y Tecnologia grant TIC2000-0399-C02-01.

M.T. Escrig Monferrer and F. Toledo Lobo (Eds.): CCIA 2002, LNAI 2504, pp. 336–344, 2002.

Component Analysis (ICA) [2]. Usually, these approaches are focused on extracting global face features, and occlusions are difficult to handle. Geometry feature-based methods analyze explicit local facial features, and their geometric relationships. Some examples of these methods are the active shape model [4], the elastic bunch graph matching algorithm for face recognition [13] and the Local Feature Analysis (LFA) [10].

In this paper we address the problem of recognizing frontal faces captured in different illumination conditions and containing natural occlusions such as individuals wearing sunglasses and/or scarfs. In order to obtain comparable results with the most important techniques, we have used a face database that has been extensively used by the computer vision community, the AR face database [7]. Furthermore, in this paper we introduce the Non-negative Matrix Factorization (NMF) [5,6] technique in a face classification framework noticing its ability to deal with natural occlusions. As NMF is based on a subspace definition, we have also introduced the Principal Component Analysis (PCA) for a direct comparison. We also present some preliminary results concerning to the determination of which distance metric should be used in the feature space created by the positive restrictions of NMF. In order to evaluate the introduction of NMF in such a framework, we have taken as a reference the results of a previous work [3] that used the same face database for analyzing two leading commercial face recognition techniques.

2   PCA and NMF Techniques

Due to the high dimensionality of data, similarity and distance metrics are computationally expensive and some compaction of the original data is needed. Principal Component Analysis (PCA) is an optimal linear dimensionality reduction scheme with respect to the mean squared error (MSE) of the reconstruction. For a set of N training vectors $X = \{x^1, \ldots x^N\}$ the mean $(\mu = \frac{1}{N} \sum_{i=1}^{N} x^i)$ and covariance matrix $(\Sigma = \frac{1}{N} \sum_{i=1}^{N} (x^i - \mu)(x^i - \mu)^T)$ can be calculated. Defining a projection matrix E composed of the K eigenvectors of Σ with highest eigenvalues, the K-dimensional representation of an original, n-dimensional vector x, is given by the projection $y = E^T(x - \mu)$.

Non-negative Matrix Factorization (NMF) is a method to obtain a representation of data using non-negativity constraints. These constraints lead to a part-based representation because they allow only additive, not subtractive, combinations of the original data [5]. Given an initial database expressed by a $n \times m$ matrix V, where each column is an n-dimensional non-negative vector of the original database (m vectors), it is possible to find two new matrices (W and H) in order to approximate the original matrix $V_{i\mu} \approx (WH)_{i\mu} = \sum_{a=1}^{r} W_{ia}H_{a\mu}$. The dimensions of the factorized matrices W and H are $n \times r$ and $r \times m$, respectively. Each column of matrix W contains a basis vector while each column of H contains the weights needed to approximate the corresponding column in V using the bases from W. Defining an objective function given by $F = \sum_{i=1}^{n}\sum_{\mu=1}^{m}[V_{i\mu}\log(WH)_{i\mu} - (WH)_{i\mu}]$ that is related to the likelihood of generating the images in V from the bases W and encodings H. An iterative approach to reach a local maximum of this objective function is given by the following rules [5]: $W_{ia} \leftarrow W_{ia}\sum_{\mu}\frac{V_{i\mu}}{(WH)_{i\mu}}H_{a\mu}$, $W_{ia} \leftarrow \frac{W_{ia}}{\sum_{j}W_{ja}}$, $H_{a\mu} \leftarrow H_{a\mu}\sum_{i}W_{ia}\frac{V_{i\mu}}{(WH)_{i\mu}}$. Initialization is performed using positive random initial conditions for matrices W and H. The convergence of the process is also ensured. See [5,6] for more information.

3   Experimental Results

Our experiments are based on the direct comparison of principal component analysis (PCA) and non-negative matrix factorization (NMF) techniques using a well-known face database, the AR [7]. Furthermore, the obtained results are compared to two leading techniques (see [3]) used in the computer vision community: the FaceIt and Bayesian techniques. FaceIt technique is based on the Local Feature Analysis (LFA) [10] and the Bayesian technique [9] models large non-linear variations in facial appearance using a PCA approach as a probability density estimation tool. Also, our experiments consider different distance metrics in order to find the most suitable one for the NMF technique.

The AR database [7] contains images of 116 individuals (63 males and 53 females). Original images are 768×576 pixels in size with 24-bit color resolution. This database is very interesting because subjects were recorded twice at a 2-week interval. During each session 13 conditions with varying facial expressions, illumination and occlusion were captured. Original images were reduced to 40×48 pixels because our representation becomes more manageable and faces were aligned by manually localizing both eye positions. In order to avoid external influences of background, we have only considered the part of a face inside an elliptical region. Fig. 1 shows an example of an individual taken under different conditions and the elliptical region considered.

Faces are projected in a low dimensional space that in this particular study is limited to 50, 100 and 150 dimensions in order to have a general idea of how results can change when the dimensionality of the feature space is modified. As known, Non-negative Matrix Factorization is a part based technique and Principal Component Analysis a global one and this behaviour is reflected in the bases obtained by both techniques. Fig. 2 shows some of the bases where we can initially see that NMF provides a more sparse representation instead of the global one provided by PCA.

In our experiments, training images consist of two neutral poses of each individual that were captured in two different days (instance labelled as AR 01 in Fig. 1). In order to see how each technique can deal with expressions, images labelled as AR 02, AR 03 and AR 04 are used as a testing set because they contain smile, anger and scream expressions. Table 1 shows the results of both algorithms with respect to the FaceIt and Bayesian techniques. The first impression is that L2 is not the most suitable metric when working with NMF

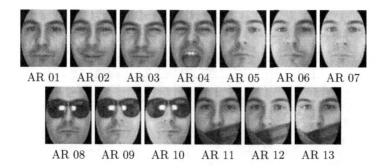

AR 01   AR 02   AR 03   AR 04   AR 05   AR 06   AR 07

AR 08   AR 09   AR 10   AR 11   AR 12   AR 13

Fig. 1. Conditions of an individual of the AR face database: (1) neutral, (2) smile, (3) anger, (4) scream, (5) left light on, (6) right light on, (7) both lights on, (8) sunglasses, (9) sunglasses/left light, (10) sunglasses/right light, (11) scarf, (12) scarf/left light, (13) scarf/right light

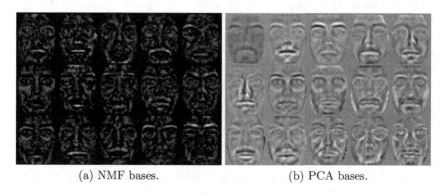

(a) NMF bases.   (b) PCA bases.

Fig. 2. Bases obtained by both techniques, PCA and NMF

and both L1 and correlation metrics could be a good choice. Expression AR 02 is better classified by FaceIt and AR 03 is better classified when using NMF in a high dimensional space. But expression AR 04 demonstrates that is a very difficult expression and both PCA and NMF are not able to deal with.

Illumination conditions are also a factor to take into account in a face recognition framework. This conditions are reflected in images AR 05, AR 06 and AR 07. Table 1 shows that PCA can not deal with illumination conditions as good as the NMF and when dimensionality increases, NMF can improve the FaceIt and Bayesian approaches.

Occlusions have been considered a topic of research in the computer vision community. AR 08 contains sunglasses that occlude both eyes and AR 09 and AR 10 consider the same situation but including left and right illuminations. AR 11 images consider a scarf and that means that mouth is occluded. AR 12 and AR 13 also consider a scarf but with the addition of illumination conditions. Table 1 shows all results obtained when considering these two kinds of occlusions.

Table 1. Expression, illumination and occlusion (with sunglasses and scarf) results

		Facial Expression			Illumination Changes			Sunglasses Occlusions			Scarf Occlusions	
		AR 02	AR 03	AR 04	AR 05	AR 06	AR 07	AR 08	AR 09	AR 10	AR 11	AR 12	AR 13
FaceIt		0.96	0.93	0.78	0.95	0.93	0.86	0.10	0.08	0.06	0.81	0.73	0.71
Bayesian		0.72	0.67	0.41	0.77	0.74	0.72	0.34	0.35	0.28	0.46	0.43	0.40
PCA-50+L2 Norm		0.67	0.82	0.18	0.77	0.76	0.57	0.16	0.12	0.18	0.44	0.38	0.37
NMF-50 +	L2 Norm	0.61	0.78	0.14	0.91	0.84	0.67	0.16	0.10	0.12	0.47	0.35	0.28
	L1 Norm	0.72	0.80	0.19	0.93	0.87	0.69	0.19	0.10	0.20	0.59	0.35	0.32
	Correlation	0.73	0.77	0.18	0.94	0.89	0.76	0.23	0.12	0.17	0.61	0.45	0.35
PCA-100+L2 Norm		0.80	0.88	0.24	0.86	0.86	0.69	0.23	0.15	0.22	0.59	0.50	0.47
NMF-100 +	L2 Norm	0.62	0.85	0.09	0.94	0.85	0.67	0.14	0.11	0.12	0.47	0.36	0.25
	L1 Norm	0.85	0.91	0.29	0.97	0.94	0.87	0.24	0.15	0.21	0.66	0.55	0.46
	Correlation	0.89	0.90	0.28	0.99	0.94	0.88	0.32	0.19	0.24	0.76	0.62	0.59
PCA-150+L2 Norm		0.83	0.90	0.29	0.85	0.87	0.71	0.26	0.16	0.24	0.62	0.57	0.48
NMF-150 +	L2 Norm	0.66	0.87	0.09	0.93	0.84	0.64	0.17	0.12	0.09	0.53	0.31	0.24
	L1 Norm	0.88	0.92	0.30	0.98	0.97	0.92	0.31	0.21	0.23	0.73	0.57	0.48
	Correlation	0.93	0.95	0.36	0.99	0.96	0.91	0.38	0.21	0.23	0.75	0.62	0.56

Under the presence of sunglasses, recognition rates decrease considerably as can be seen in table 1. This means that eyes are a very important feature to take into consideration when classifying faces. It is interesting to note that when sunglasses are considered without considering lighting influences (AR 08), NMF obtains the best recognition results. But, when lighting conditions are present, the Bayesian technique gives the best results. Thus, NMF is a good choice when partial occlusions are present but when lighting conditions affect to the scene, it turns out that NMF can not deal with a more general change in the scene. Table 1 shows a similar behaviour when considering a scarf because the NMF, when no lighting conditions are present (AR 11) in the scene, can have a high recognition rate, even comparable to the best one obtained with FaceIt, but when lighting conditions are present (AR 12 and AR 13) all recognition rates decrease considerably.

In general, the first impression of these first experiments is that NMF performs better than PCA in the same dimensional space. This behaviour was expected because PCA is based on a global transformation of the original space and NMF on a local one. Thus, it turns out that when we are considering local effects as occlusions, changes in expression or even changes in the illumination, PCA is not able to represent them as well as NMF. In terms of performances with respect to the FaceIt and Bayesian techniques, NMF has comparable recognition rates and, in some situations, is even better than these two methods. The reason of this high performance is mainly justified by its natural definition of representing data using a combination of bases that are part-based. Finally, it is clear that L2-norm is the worst metric to use with NMF and the correlation metric is the best one.

3.1   Gender Classification

It is clear that if we try to distinguish between males and females, local features corresponding to each gender are different. Thus, this means that Non-negative Matrix Factorization (NMF) can be a suitable technique for capturing these local differences. This motivates to create a gender classifier based on the NMF and when a testing face is correctly classified according to its gender, we can use this information to recognize the face using a more specific face classifier. In our study, we have learned two gender classifiers: one with PCA and the other with NMF with the same parameters as in the previous experiments. Fig. 3 shows the gender classification results when using 50,100 and 150 dimensional spaces.

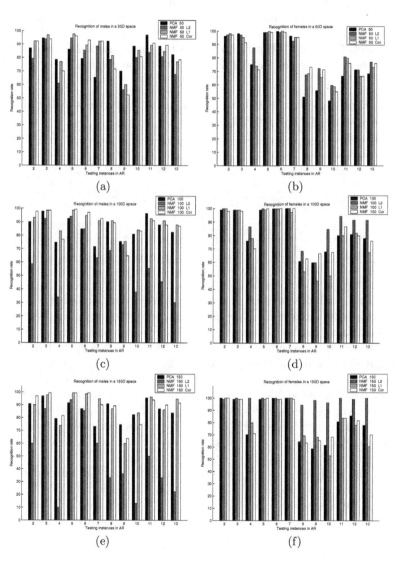

Fig. 3. Gender classification results when trying to classify males (a) and females (b) using a 50 dimensional feature space. (c) and (d) are the results when using a 100 dimensional space and (e) and (f) in a 150 dimensional space

Fig. 3 depicts a general behaviour for both PCA and NMF techniques: females are better recognized in this set of situations: AR 02, AR 03, AR 05, AR 06, AR 07 and males in the other ones. These recognition differences must be studied more deeply but this means that both genders have some local features that are better identified depending on the face situation. But images with occlusions, as AR 08, AR 09 and AR 10 are very difficult to identify even when trying to determine whether it is a male or female.

Considering that NMF is based on capturing local behaviours we can think that a more specific classifier based only on males or females should improve the initial recognition rates presented before. We have learned both PCA and NMF models for gender identification with the same internal parameters as in the previous experiments. Table 2 shows the obtained results.

Table 2. Expression, illumination and occlusion (with sunglasses and scarf) results when considering a previous gender classifier

		Facial Expression			Illumination Changes			Sunglasses Occlusions			Scarf Occlusions		
		AR 02	AR 03	AR 04	AR 05	AR 06	AR 07	AR 08	AR 09	AR 10	AR 11	AR 12	AR 13
PCA-50+L2 Norm		0.74	0.87	0.22	0.82	0.82	0.62	0.21	0.13	0.20	0.52	0.44	0.40
NMF-50 +	L2 Norm	0.68	0.83	0.17	0.91	0.86	0.68	0.20	0.10	0.14	0.51	0.34	0.31
	L1 Norm	0.81	0.87	0.25	0.94	0.89	0.76	0.24	0.14	0.22	0.60	0.41	0.37
	Correlation	0.85	0.84	0.25	0.96	0.92	0.84	0.29	0.17	0.24	0.67	0.51	0.45
PCA-100+L2 Norm		0.83	0.91	0.28	0.86	0.86	0.70	0.25	0.16	0.23	0.64	0.55	0.49
NMF-100 +	L2 Norm	0.65	0.87	0.14	0.92	0.89	0.73	0.16	0.15	0.13	0.50	0.32	0.24
	L1 Norm	0.90	0.92	0.31	0.97	0.96	0.89	0.26	0.17	0.21	0.71	0.56	0.51
	Correlation	0.91	0.94	0.34	0.98	0.97	0.92	0.35	0.21	0.25	0.79	0.62	0.57
PCA-150+L2 Norm		0.84	0.91	0.28	0.86	0.87	0.71	0.27	0.17	0.25	0.63	0.57	0.51
NMF-150 +	L2 Norm	0.70	0.88	0.13	0.94	0.89	0.69	0.18	0.13	0.10	0.53	0.36	0.27
	L1 Norm	0.90	0.93	0.33	0.98	0.98	0.92	0.32	0.20	0.24	0.73	0.58	0.52
	Correlation	0.93	0.94	0.35	0.98	0.97	0.93	0.36	0.24	0.26	0.79	0.65	0.61

In general, with the addition of a gender classifier both techniques (PCA and NMF) are slightly improved. This improvement is not very significant in face images containing hard occlusions such as those faces containing sunglasses or a scarf. However, these results motivate to build up a face classifier divided into a global gender detector and two specific face classifiers, one for males and another for females. This configuration must work out much better than only considering a face classifier because NMF is based on the representation of local features. Fig. 4 summarizes previous results showing all the recognition rates obtained according to the method used (PCA or NMF) in conjunction with their internal parameters. We have to note that the overall recognition rate for the FaceIt technique is 65.83% and 52.42% for the Bayesian one.

From the analysis of Fig. 4, we can appreciate that the introduction of a gender classifier improves the whole recognition rates even using PCA or NMF. Obviously, this behaviour is justified because it is more easy to classify a face into a male or female than recognizing the face directly. But it is clear that this improvement is more remarkable in low dimensional spaces.

If we directly compare the overall results obtained using PCA and NMF with respect to the FaceIt and Bayesian techniques, we can state that performances are comparable depending on the low dimensional space. The best configuration of our scheme is the one that uses the NMF in a 150 dimensional space using the

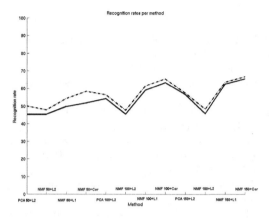

Fig. 4. Recognition rates according to the method used without a gender classifier (solid line) and with a gender classifier (dashed line)

correlation metric where we obtain a recognition rate of 66.74% that is greater than the recognition rate of 65.83% obtained by the FaceIt technique. Of course, this behaviour is not observed in all the face situations but it is clear that for some certain situations one technique will be more convenient than another one.

4   Conclusions

This paper analyzes the Non-negative Matrix Factorization (NMF) technique in the problem of recognizing faces captured under non favorable conditions such as changes in expressions, changes in the lighting conditions and occlusions. Results are also compared with the well-known Principal Component Analysis (PCA) technique because both algorithms are based on finding a subspace where our data can be expressed. Our experiments demonstrate that NMF allows high recognition rates in comparison with PCA, which treats its input data in a global a way. It is clear that these results are justified by the fact that our face database contains local variations of faces, not global ones. In this present study, we have alse analysed L1, L2 and correlation metrics noticing that the last is the most suitable one. A gender classifier stage has also been introduced in order to obtain the best results. Finally, we have compared our results to the two leading face recognition techniques (FaceIt and Bayesian), noticing that our scheme is more adapted to the problem of recognizing faces under several unfavorable conditions. This is justified because these two techniques have been designed to work with faces that contain specific changes in expressions, but not the whole range of conditions that we have exposed in this current work.

References

1. Belhumeur, P.N., Hespanha J.P., Kriegman D.J.: Eigenfaces vs. fisherfaces: Recognition using class specific linear projection. IEEE Transactions on Pattern Analysis and Machine Intelligence, 19(7):711-720, 1997
2. Comon P.: Independent component analysis - a new concept ? Signal Processing, 36:287-314, 1994
3. Gross R., Shi J., Cohn J.F.: Quo vadis Face Recognition? In: Proc. third Workshop on Empirical Evaluation Methods in Computer Vision, December, 2001
4. Lanitis A., Taylor C.J., Cootes T.: Automatic interpretation and coding of face images using flexible models. IEEE Transactions on Pattern Analysis and Machine Intelligence, 19(7):743-756, 1997
5. Lee D., Seung H.: Learning the parts of objects by non-negative matrix factorization. Nature, 401:788-791, 1999
6. Lee D., Seung H.: Algorithms for non-negative matrix factorization. In: Advances in Neural Information Processing Systems, 2000
7. Martinez A., Benavente R.: The AR face database. Technical report 24, Computer Vision Center (CVC). Barcelona, Spain, June 1998
8. Moghaddam B.: Principal Manifolds and Probabilistic Subspaces for Visual Recognition. IEEE Trans. on Pattern Analysis and Machine Intell., 24(6), June 2002
9. Moghaddam B., Pentland A.P.: Probabilisitc visual learning for object representation. IEEE Trans. on Pattern Analysis and Machine Intell., 19(7):696-710,1997
10. Penev P., Atick J.: Local feature analysis: A general statistical theory for object representation. Neural Systems, 7:477-500, 1996
11. Turk M., Pentland A.P.: Eigenfaces for recognition. Journal of Cognitive Neuroscience, 3(1):71-86, 1991
12. Vapnik V. N.: The nature of statistical learning theory. Springer Verlag, Heidelberg, DE, 1995
13. Wiskott L., Fellous J.M., Kruger N., Malsburg C. von der: Face recognition by elastic bunch graph matching. IEEE Transactions on Pattern Analysis and Machine Intelligence, 10(7):775-779, July 1997

Efficient Path Planning Using Harmonic Functions Computed on a Non-regular Grid*

Pedro Iñiguez[1] and Jan Rosell[2]

[1] Dept. Eng. Electrònica Elèctrica i Automàtica (URV),
Av. Països Catalans 26, 43007-Tarragona, SPAIN, pinyigue@etse.urv.es
[2] Institut d'Organització i Control de Sistemes Industrials (UPC),
Diagonal 647, 08028-Barcelona, SPAIN, rosell@ioc.upc.es

Abstract. Robot path planning is devoted to the planning of a trajectory for the robot to perform a collision-free motion between to configurations. Potential fields methods have been used to guide the robot through the obstacles in the robotic cell. The use of harmonic functions allows the definition of a potential field without local minima and with the ability to be incrementally updated. In order to efficiently use this approach to motion planning in higher dimensional C-spaces, the paper presents a hierarchical and dynamic method to compute harmonic functions on a non-regular grid.

1 Introduction

Motion planning is usually done in Configuration Space [1] (C-space), were the robot is mapped to a point. Potential fields (introduced by Kathib [2]) is one of the main approaches to path planning, despite its drawbacks as the creation of minima other than the goal and the difficulty to cope with high dimensional C-spaces.

To cope with the local minima problem, the use of harmonic functions was proposed by Connolly [3,4], giving rise to a practical path planning approach described in Section 2. In a similar line, the approach of Yang et al. [5] present a neural network topologically organized as a grid, where the dynamic environment is represented by the neural activity landscape with only a global minimum located at the goal. Potential field approaches usually work in a regular grid decomposition of C-space, which aids the computation of the potential field.

This paper follows the harmonic function approach, since harmonic functions allow a reactive behavior and can be incrementally updated, besides having a unique minimum. These features makes the harmonic function approach suitable for uncertain environments. In order to be able to use this approach in high dimensional C-spaces, this paper proposes a hierarchical and dynamic method to compute harmonic functions on a non-regular grid decomposition of Configuration Space.

---

* This work was partially supported by the CICYT projects TAP99-0839 and DPI2001-2202.

M.T. Escrig Monferrer and F. Toledo Lobo (Eds.): CCIA 2002, LNAI 2504, pp. 345–354, 2002.

Similar hierarchical decompositions have been previously proposed but within the scope of different motion planners based on search methods in the discretized C-space. Bohlin [6] presents a resolution complete planner based on an implicit grid: first a search is done on a coarse subset of the grid, which is successively refined until a solution is found. In a similar approach, Henrich et al. [7] propose a hierarchical search (based on a best first algorithm) based on a merging of neighboring hypercubes resulting in larger stepsizes in free areas, while maintaining small steps in the vicinity of obstacles.

The paper is structured as follows. Section 2 reviews the harmonic function approach. Section 3 proposes a non-regular grid decomposition of C-space and Section 4 describes the algorithm to compute the harmonic function in the obtained grid. Finally, Section 5 evaluates the efficiency of the proposed method and Section 6 concludes the work.

2   Harmonic Functions

An harmonic function ϕ on a domain $\Omega \subset \Re^n$ is a function that satisfies Laplace's equation [3]:

$$\nabla^2 \phi = \sum_{i=1}^{n} \frac{\partial^2 \phi}{\partial x_i^2} = 0 \qquad (1)$$

Numerical solutions to Laplace's equation can be found using finite difference methods. For $n = 2$ let $u(i, j)$ be a regular sampling of ϕ on a grid with spacing h. Then, the discrete form of Laplace's equation is:

$$h^2 \nabla^2 \phi(i, j) = u(i+1, j) + u(i-1, j) + u(i, j+1) + u(i, j-1) - 4u(i, j) = 0 \quad (2)$$

and the solution is found by relaxation methods, like the Jacobi iteration method that simultaneously replaces, at iteration k, any non-boundary node of the grid with the average of its $2n$-Manhattan neighbors computed at iteration $k-1$. Being $u^k(i, j)$ the harmonic function value of the cell (i, j) computed at iteration k, the Jacobi iteration method for $n = 2$ is expressed as:

$$u^k(i, j) = \frac{1}{4} u^{k-1}(i+1, j) + u^{k-1}(i-1, j) + u^{k-1}(i, j+1) + u^{k-1}(i, j-1) \quad (3)$$

Two different solutions arise depending on the boundary condition used. Being $\partial\Omega$ the boundary of Ω and c a constant value, the Dirichlet boundary condition is:

$$\phi|_{\partial\Omega} = c \qquad (4)$$

This boundary condition specifies a gradient along the outward normal of the C-obstacles surface, and results in trajectories with maximum clearance.

Being $\mathbf{n}$ the vector normal to the boundary, the Newmann boundary condition is:

$$\frac{\partial \phi}{\partial \mathbf{n}}|_{\partial\Omega} = 0 \qquad (5)$$

This boundary condition specifies a gradient tangential to the C-obstacles surface, and results in trajectories that follow the C-obstacles's border. Being ϕ_D

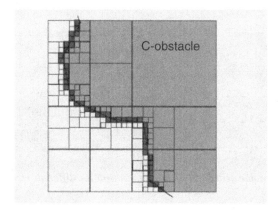

Fig. 1. *Hierarchical discretization of C-space.*

and ϕ_N the harmonic functions found using, respectively, the Dirichlet and New-mann boundary conditions, a new harmonic function that combines both effects can be defined as:

$$\phi = \alpha\phi_N + (1 - \alpha)\phi_D \quad \alpha \in [0,1] \tag{6}$$

Harmonic functions give rise to a practical path planning approach with the following main features [8]:

- A potential field with a unique minimum
- An efficient update of the potential field
- Completeness up to the discretization error in the environment.
- A robust and reactive behavior.

3 Hierarchical Decomposition of Configuration Space

Let $\mathcal{C}_k$ be a grid at a given level k in the hierarchy and c_k be a cell with sides of size s_k. A coarse regular grid, $\mathcal{C}_0$, is first considered with $s_0 = \Delta 2^m$ and $m \in \aleph^+$. Then, the cells over the C-obstacle border are refined by hierarchically halving the spacing, until c_m cells are reached, with $s_m = \Delta$ (Figure 1). The c_m cells that contain the border are considered as part of the C-obstacles. The obtained refined non-regular grid is $\mathcal{C}_m$. The potential field is computed over $\mathcal{C}_m$, as detailed in Section 4 (the initialization phase assumes the Dirichlet boundary condition and fixes the C-obstacles cells at a high potential and the goal cell at a low one). Using a non-regular grid decomposition of C-space, the relaxation methods to compute the harmonic functions converge quicker and less memory resources are required, which allows the use of this path planning approach to higher dimensional C-spaces.

In order to efficiently manage the computations in the non-regular grid, the following labelling convention is proposed. The cells of $\mathcal{C}_0$ are identified by its coordinates, as shown in Figure 2a for a 2D C-space. A subcell obtained by

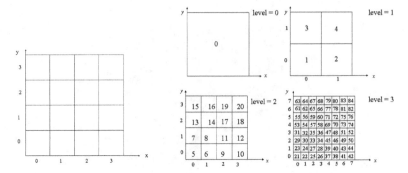

Fig. 2. *a) Initial regular grid C_0 b) Cell enumeration for different levels in the hierarchy in a 2D C-space.*

refinement is identified by the coordinates of its parent cell in C_0 and a label that univocally locates it, as shown in Figures 2b for different levels in the hierarchy for a 2D C-space. Figure 3 shows an example of hierarchical decomposition with the cell enumeration following the proposed convention.

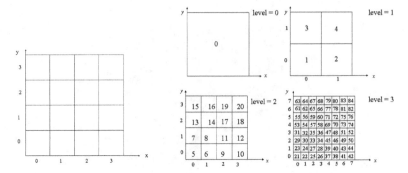

Fig. 3. *Example of hierarchical decomposition and cell enumeration in a 2D C-space.*

The labelling has the following relationship between consecutive levels in the hierarchy:

$$L_{(k+1)} = 2^n L_k + R \tag{7}$$

where L_k is the label of a cell in C_k, n is the dimension of the C-space and R is the relative position of the subcell with respect to its parent cell, as level 1 is enumerated with respect to level 0 (Figure 2b). This expression, frequently needed in the recurrent computation of the harmonic function, is a simple expression that results from the enumeration convention adopted.

The computation of the relative coordinates of a given subcell from its label, and the obtention of the label from the relative coordinates are basic operations

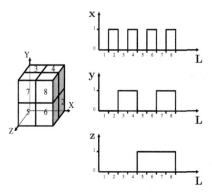

Fig. 4. *Cell labelling and relation to relative coordinates in a 3D C-space.*

needed during the computation of the harmonic function on the non-regular grid. Particularly, there is the need to compute the labels of the Manhattan neighbor cells of a given subcell. This is done changing from labels to relative coordinates, where the neighboring relations are trivial. For a two-dimensional C-space, the relation between the label L_r of a cell of the hierarchical partition level r and its relative coordinates (x,y) is the following:

$$L_r = F_r + x + 2!2^0\mathrm{int}\left(\frac{x}{2}\right) + 2!2^2\mathrm{int}\left(\frac{x}{4}\right) + \cdots + 2y + 2!2^1\mathrm{int}\left(\frac{y}{2}\right) + 2!2^3\mathrm{int}\left(\frac{y}{4}\right) + \cdots \quad (8)$$

where $F_r = \frac{2^{2r}-1}{2^2-1}$ is the label of the first cell (the one located at the left-bottom corner) of the hierarchical partition level r, and $\mathrm{int}(x)$ is a function that returns the integer part of x. Generalizing to n dimensions, the following expression results:

$$L_r = F_r + \sum_{j=1}^{n}\left\{2^{(j-1)}v_j + n!\sum_{i=0}^{r-1}2^{(j-1+ni)}\mathrm{int}\left(\frac{v_j}{2^{(i+1)}}\right)\right\} \quad (9)$$

where $(v_1, \cdots, v_n)$ are the relative coordinates and $F_r = \frac{2^{nr}-1}{2^n-1}$ is the label of the first cell.

The inverse procedure, i.e. how to compute the n relative coordinates of a subcell from its label L, is done by first computing the relative position in each partition and then computing consecutive binary conversions (as suggested in figure 4). The procedure is detailed in the following algorithm, that computes the coordinates $(v_1, \cdots, v_n)$ from the label L and uses the functions $\mathrm{int}(x)$ that computes the integer part of x and $\mathrm{fmod}(x, y)$ that computes the remainder of $\frac{x}{y}$.

```
Compute Coordinates(L)

    i = 1; level = 0; Ncell[i-1]=L;
    DO{
        Ncell[i]=int(Ncell[i-1]/2ⁿ);
        remainder[i]=fmod(Ncell[i-1],2ⁿ);
        IF (remainder[i]==0)
            Ncell[i]=Ncelda[i]-1;
            remainder[i]=2ⁿ;
        END IF
        ++level; ++i;
    }WHILE (Ncell[i-1]>0);

    x=0; y=0;
    FOR (i=level;i>0;i = i − 1)
        remainder[i] = remainder[i] - 1;
        FOR (j=0;j<n;j = j + 1)
            v[j] =2*v[j] + fmod(remainder[i],2);
            remainder[i] = int(remainder[i]/2);
        END FOR
    END FOR
END
```

This loop consecutively stores in remainder[i] the relative position of a cell Ncell[i] with respect to its parent cell (eq. (7)), until a cell of the initial grid C_0 is reached.

This loop finds the relative coordinates of the cell L with respect to its parent cell in C_0, by weighing the consecutive relative positions stored in remainder[i] according to their partition level.

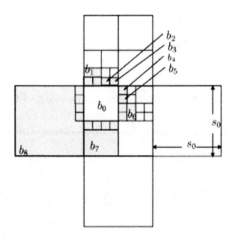

Fig. 5. *Neighbor cells of different size used to compute the harmonic function at b_0.*

4   Harmonic Function Computation

The computation on a grid C_m of the harmonic function value of a cell c_r with sides of size s_r must take into account that its neighbor cells may have different sizes, as shown in Figure 5. For $n = 2$ the potential u_i of a point located at (d_{ix}, d_{iy}) from the center of a given cell b_0 with potential u_0 is expressed, using Taylor's theorem, as:

$$u_i = u_0 + d_{ix}\frac{\partial u_0}{\partial x} + d_{iy}\frac{\partial u_0}{\partial y} + d_{ix}^2\frac{1}{2}\frac{\partial^2 u_0}{\partial x^2} + d_{iy}^2\frac{1}{2}\frac{\partial^2 u_0}{\partial y^2} + d_{ix}d_{iy}\frac{\partial^2 u_0}{\partial x \partial y} \qquad (10)$$

Let V be the number of neighbors of b_0, and b_i be one of them. If p_m is the maximum partition level and p_i the partition level of the cell b_i, then b_i contains $B_i = 2^{(p_m - p_i)}$ cells of maximum partition level that neighbor on b_0. Applying equation (10) to each of these cells, summing and taking into account the symmetry, the following expression is obtained:

$$\sum_{i=1}^{V} 2^{(p_m - p_i)}u_i = 2^{(p_m - p_0 + 2)}u_0 + D\left(\frac{\partial^2 u_0}{\partial x^2} + \frac{\partial^2 u_0}{\partial y^2}\right) \qquad (11)$$

where D is a constant value that depends on the distances from the center of b_0 to the center of its neighboring cells. This value is not important, since the harmonic functions satisfy Laplace's equation, that is: the sum of the second derivatives is zero. Therefore, the expression of u_0 obtained from (11) is:

$$u_0 = \frac{\sum_{i=1}^{V} 2^{(p_m - p_i)}u_i}{2^{(p_m - p_0 + 2)}} \qquad (12)$$

Generalizing to n dimensions, and taking into account that the denominator of (12) can be expressed as $2n2^{(p_m - p_0)}$, the following expression of u_0 is obtained:

$$u_0 = \frac{2^{(p_0 - 1)}}{n}\sum_{i=1}^{V}\frac{u_i}{2^{p_i}} \qquad (13)$$

Table 1. Comparative study of harmonic function computation between regular and hierarchical non-regular grid decomposition of C-space.

	Scenario 1	Scenario 2	Scenario 3
C_0	20 x 20	10 x 10	10 x 10
Partition level	2	3	4
N_u	80 x 80	80 x 80	160 x 160
N_h	859	646	1246
N_h/N_u	0.13	0.10	0.05
T_h (s)	4.67	5	12.02
T_u (s)	6.87	6.87	37.13
T_h/T_u	0.68	0.73	0.32

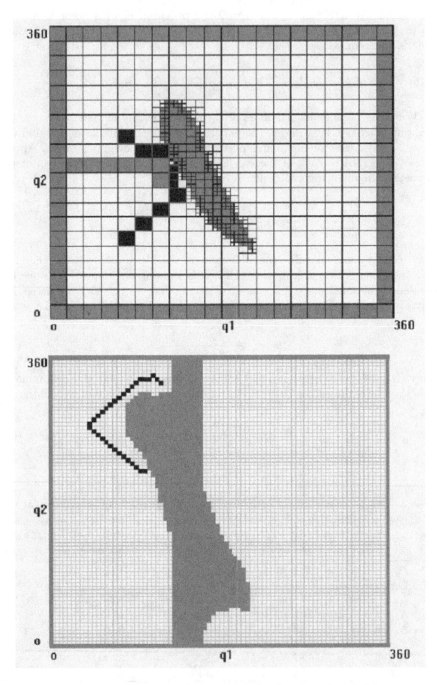

Fig. 6. *Collision-free trajectories: a) on a hierarchical non-regular grid decomposition of a 2D C-space b) on a regular grid decomposition of a 2D C-space.*

5 Comparative Study

A study has been performed to compare the cost of computing the harmonic function on a hierarchical non-regular grid decomposition of C-space vs. the cost of computing it on a regular grid. The software is implemented in C++ for Windows and runs on a PC with a Pentium@133 processor.

Table 1 shows the results of the comparison performed in three different scenarios, with different hierarchical partition levels and different maximum resolution. The computation times for the hierarchical decomposition and for the uniform decomposition are T_h and T_u, respectively, and the number of cells used are N_h and N_u. It can be seen that in all cases a considerable reduction in the computing time and in the number of cells is obtained.

Figure 6a shows a path computed following the negated gradient of the harmonic function computed on a hierarchical decomposition of C-space, where it can be seen that the precision is preserved on the obstacle boundary while the cells in free space are bigger. Figure 6b shows another scenario, where now a uniform decomposition is used.

6 Conclusions

The potential field method using harmonic functions is a practical approach to path planning. Moreover, its feature of robust and reactive behavior and the ability to be incrementally updated makes it suitable for motion planning in uncertain environments. To efficiently use the harmonic function approach to motion planning in higher dimensional C-spaces, this paper has presented a method to compute the harmonic function on a non-regular grid. The method, illustrated with examples in 2D C-space, is hierarchical, simple and computationally efficient, both in time and memory, as verified by the comparative analysis performed. Extensions to more degrees of freedom are straightforward and currently under development.

References

1. T. Lozano-Pérez. Spatial planning: A configuration space approach. *IEEE Trans. Comput.*, 32(2):108–120, 1983.
2. O. Khatib. Real-time obstacle avoidance for manipulators and mobile robots. In *Proc. of the IEEE Int. Conf. on Robotics and Automation*, pages 500–505, 1985.
3. C. I. Connolly, J. B. Burns, and R. Weiss. Path planning using Laplace's equation. In *Proc. of the IEEE Int. Conf. on Robotics & Automation*, pages 2102–2106, 1990.
4. C. I. Connolly and R. A. Grupen. The use of harmonic functions in robotics. *Journal of Robotic Systems*, 10(7):931–946, 1993.
5. S. X. Yang, X. Yuan, M. Meng, G. Yuan, and H. Li. Real-time planning and control of robots using shunting neural networks. In *Proc. of the IEEE/RSJ Int. Conf. on Intelligent Robots and Systems*, pages 1590–1595, 2001.
6. R. Bohlin. Path planning in practice: Lazy evaluation on a multi-resolution grid. In *Proc. IEEE/RSJ Int. Conf. on Intelligent Robots and Systems*, pages 49–54, 2001.

7. D. Henrich, C. Wurll, and H. Wörn. On-line path planning by heuristic hierarchical search. In *Proc. of the 24th Annual Conf. of the IEEE Industrial Electronics Society*, volume 4, pages 2239–2244, 1998.
8. K. Souccar, J. Coelho, C. Connolly, and R. Grupen. *Practical Motion Planning in Robotics*, chapter Harmonic Functions for Path Planning and Control, pages 277–301. John Wiley & Sons Ltd, 1998.

Image Texture Prediction Using Colour Photometric Stereo

Xavier Lladó[1], Joan Martí[1], and Maria Petrou[2]

[1] Institute of Informatics and Applications, University of Girona,
17071, Girona, Spain
{llado,joanm}@eia.udg.es
[2] Centre for Vision, Speech, and Signal Processing, University of Surrey,
GU2 5XH, Guildford, Surrey, England
m.petrou@ee.surrey.ac.uk

Abstract. The purpose of this work is to analyse what happens to the surface information when the image resolution is modified. We deduce how the surface texture appears if seen from different distances. Using Colour Photometric Stereo a method for predicting how surface texture looks like when changing the distance of the camera is presented. We use this technique on the recognition of textures seen from different distances. Real sets of images have been used in order to evaluate the performance of the recognition system.

1 Introduction

The main motivation for this paper is the problem of description of multicoloured surfaces invariant to the geometry. Recognition of 3-dimensional surface textures from 2-dimensional images is difficult. The 2-dimensional texture in the image, the *image* texture, is produced by variation in both surface reflectance and surface relief. The latter two constitute the *surface* texture. While the reflectance properties are intrinsic to the surface, the surface relief produces a pattern of shadings that depends strongly on the direction of the illumination [1]. Thus, the *image* texture created by a 3D *surface* texture changes drastically with the imaging geometry.

This paper uses *Colour Photometric Stereo* (CPS), as described in [2] and [3], to compute the detailed shape and colour of a rough surface when seen by a camera at the zenith of the surface. Photometric stereo is based on the fact that image intensities depend on the surface orientation and its reflectance. Hence, if several images are taken from the same viewing position but with different lighting directions, variation of pixel intensities in these images will be due to changes in the relative positions of the illuminant and the surface [4]. This constraint permits us to calculate the normal vectors, which represent the surface orientation of any point on the surface, and the reflectance factor or albedo, which describes the reflection properties of the surface.

We assume that in a database of textures, we have all the information concerning the surface texture constructed from the photometric stereo set. We

M.T. Escrig Monferrer and F. Toledo Lobo (Eds.): CCIA 2002, LNAI 2504, pp. 355–363, 2002.
© Springer-Verlag Berlin Heidelberg 2002

then assume that we are given the image of one of these textures captured by a camera at a different (longer) distance and with unknown direction of illumination. From the original information in the database, we predict how each surface would look like when seen from the new distance, for various directions of illumination. Thus we create a "virtual" database of image textures against which we compare the unknown image texture in order to classify it. Recognition of the texture allows us also to guess the approximate orientation of the illumination under which the image was captured. The image texture classifier we use is based on the co-ocurrence matrices [5].

The rest of this work is organised as follows. In section 2 and 3 the image prediction method is explained. In section 4, the method is validated using real sets of images in the context of texture recognition. Finally, the work ends with conclusions and future work.

2   Image Prediction Process

Our purpose is to predict how surface texture looks like if seen from a different distance. In order to do this, it is necessary to understand what happens with the colour and surface shape information if the distance of the camera is changed.

We shall start by considering two grids referring to the pixels of two images of the same surface, captured from two different distances. One of them must correspond to the higher resolution image and it must be finer than the other. Let us indicate by indices ij a pixel of the coarse grid. This pixel is made up from several pixels of the fine resolution grid, some of which contribute to it only partially. Let us for the moment ignore by how much each pixel of the fine resolution contributes to pixel ij of the coarse resolution, and let us simply say that "superpixel" ij corresponds to a tile of size $K \times L$ of fine resolution pixels. We shall refer to the pixels of the coarse resolution as "superpixels" and the term "pixel" will be used only for the fine resolution pixels. Each superpixel may be thought of as representing a surface patch characterised by a particular gradient vector $(p_{ij}, q_{ij}, 1)^T$ and a particular reflectance function $\rho_{ij}(\lambda)$. The superpixel will have intensity I_{ij}^u in the coarse resolution image, $u = 1, 2, 3$ or 4, each corresponding to a different direction of the illumination.

Each superpixel corresponds to a tile of pixels. We wish to keep track of the superpixel to which a pixel contributes. So, we shall give to every pixel three sets of indices: one tells us to which tile it belongs, one tells us where about in the tile it is, and one tells us its location in the fine resolution grid. Let us indicate by indices mn the position of pixels in the fine resolution grid. So, a pixel that contributes to superpixel ij will have indices $ij; kl\ mn$, where $k = 1, 2, ..., K$ and $l = 1, 2, ..., L$. Any other quantity associated with pixel $ij; kl$ mn will be indicated by the same notation as for superpixel ij. That is, pixel $ij; kl\ mn$ corresponds to a surface patch with gradient vector $(p_{ij;kl}^{mn}, q_{ij;kl}^{mn}, 1)^T$ and a reflectance function $\rho_{ij;kl}^{mn}(\lambda)$. Our problem is to predict I_{ij}^u, for a given direction of illumination u, given $\rho_{ij;kl}^{mn}(\lambda)$, $p_{ij;kl}^{mn}$ and $q_{ij;kl}^{mn}$ for all values of i, j, k and l. The values of $\rho_{ij;kl}^{mn}(\lambda)$, $p_{ij;kl}^{mn}$ and $q_{ij;kl}^{mn}$ have been computed from four images by Colour Photometric Stereo. We shall not go into details of this now as they have been published elsewhere [2,3]. Although the CPS scheme we use can deal with non-Lambertian surfaces, we assume here that the surface we are dealing with is Lambertian.

If the sensitivity of the sensor is $S(\lambda)$, the spectral distribution of the incident light is $\mathcal{L}(\lambda)$, and the reflectance funcion of the surface patch projected on superpixel ij is $\mathcal{R}(\lambda, N_{ij}, u)$, where N_{ij} is the normal to the surface vector and u the direction of illumination vector, then the intensity value registered by the sensor at superpixel ij is:

$$I_{ij}^u = \int S(\lambda)\mathcal{L}(\lambda)\mathcal{R}(\lambda, N_{ij}, u)d\lambda \tag{1}$$

$\mathcal{R}(\lambda, N_{ij}, u)$ could be separated in a geometric component $\mathcal{G}(N_{ij}, u)$ and a surface material component, $\rho_{ij}(\lambda)$. Assuming we are dealing with a Lambertian surface,

$$\mathcal{G}(N_{ij}, u) = \frac{N_{ij} \cdot u}{|N_{ij}||u|} \tag{2}$$

where N_{ij} is $(p_{ij}, q_{ij}, 1)^T$, so:

$$I_{ij}^u = \int S(\lambda)\mathcal{L}(\lambda)\mathcal{G}(N_{ij}, u)\rho_{ij}(\lambda)d\lambda \tag{3}$$

Superpixel ij is made up from several pixels each of which may have its own reflectance function, and its own orientation. So, $\mathcal{G}(N_{ij}, u)\rho_{ij}(\lambda)$ is really the sum of several such factors, one for each pixel that contributes to the superpixel. Then

$$I_{ij}^u = \int S(\lambda)\mathcal{L}(\lambda) \sum_{k,l=1}^{K,L} \mathcal{G}(N_{ij;kl}^{mn}, u)\rho_{ij;kl}^{mn}(\lambda)d\lambda \tag{4}$$

By exchanging the order of integration and summation, we obtain:

$$I_{ij}^u = \sum_{k,l=1}^{K,L} \int S(\lambda)\mathcal{L}(\lambda)\mathcal{G}(N_{ij;kl}^{mn}, u)\rho_{ij;kl}^{mn}(\lambda)d\lambda \tag{5}$$

Note that this formula is quite general: it allows us to predict the value of superpixel ij from the information we have on its constituent pixels, even when seen by a different sensor, under illumination with different spectral distribution and different orientation than those under which the original images, from which the surface information was extracted, were captured.

We shall restrict ourselves here to the case where the sensor and light source are the same. If we assume that the unknown illumination direction is the same as one of the illumination directions in the original data used by the photometric stereo, then this equation collapses to a trivial one:

$$I_{ij}^u = \sum_{k,l=1}^{K,L} I_{ij;kl}^{u;mn} \tag{6}$$

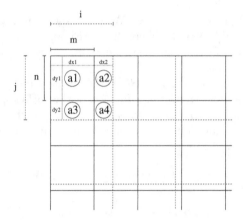

Fig. 1. General case of image resolution change.

This approach allows us to go straight to predicting how an image of the surface would look like when imaged under different conditions, from those under which the images in the database were imaged.

Now, we wish to analyse the general case, in which superpixel ij is made up of several pixels, some of which contribute only partially (see figure 1). In this situation, it is necessary to know by how much each pixel of the fine resolution (area a_{kl}) contributes to superpixel ij of the coarse resolution. In this sense we calculate the point spread function of the imaging device. Then it is not necessary to compute these areas a_{kl} which after all are only a crude approximation of the point spread function, but the weights arising from the point spread function itself can be used instead.

3   Point Spread Function

Practically every imaging system introduces some kind of degradation into the data it captures. A common phenomenon when deling with very fine textures is the spatial blurring that the imaging system introduces into the data. This phenomenon can be quantified in terms of how spread a point source appears to be when its image is captured. This is expressed by the *point spread function* (PSF) of the system.

As we explained at the end of section 2, in the more general case of our prediction method, it is not necessary to compute the areas a_{kl} which after all are only a crude approximation of the point spread function. Thus, the objective now is to obtain the PSF of the imaging system and use it in the prediction method.

In order to derive the PSF [6], an image with many edges of various known orientations is needed. However, it may not be necessary to use more than one orientation if the PSF of the sensor is circularly symmetric. To establish whether

Fig. 2. Test chart for the derivation of the point spread function.

the PSF of our sensor is circularly symmetric or not, a simple chart like the one in figure 2 is used. This chart can be used to measure the PSF at 0°, 45°, 90° and 135° degrees. The test chart is captured using the camera-grabber system used throughout our experiments, using the viewing and illumination conditions used for all the experiments reported.

To check the symmetry of the sensor, we compute the derivative of the image at 0°, 45°, 90° and 135° degrees using the Robinson operators [7].

The profiles of the resultant images along several lines orthogonal to the original edges are computed and averaged to produce the four profiles for 0°, 45°, 90° and 135° plotted in figure 3. These are the profiles of the point spread function. Note that first column shows the derivative images obtained. Two of the four profiles of the point spread function plotted there are narrower than the other two. This is because they correspond to orientations 45° and 135° and the distance of the pixels along these orientations is $\sqrt{2}$ longer than the distance of pixels along 0° and 90°.

In figures 4.a and 4.b we plot separately the two pairs of profiles and see that the system has the same behaviour along the 0°, 90° and 45°, 135° orientations. Taking into account the $\sqrt{2}$ correction for the 45° and 135°, we conclude that the point spread function of this imaging system is to a high degree circularly symmetric. Figure 4.c shows the plot of the four profiles while in figure 4.d we zoom into the central part of the plot of figure 4.c. Then, in our practical application these four profiles ara averaged to produce a single cross-section of a circularly symmetric point spread function.

When the profile of the PSF is known next step is to use this information in order to infer the weights of the filter which will be used in the prediction method instead of the areas a_{kl}. To do that, the obtained profile has been fitted to a gaussian distribution. The obtained gaussian distribution has $\mu = -0.038889$ and $\sigma = 1.157407$. Afterwards, the weights of the PSF filter which we shall refer as g are obtained as follows:

$$g_0 = 1$$
$$g_x = e^{-\frac{x^2}{2\sigma^2}}$$
$$g_N = e^{-\frac{N^2}{2\sigma^2}}$$

(7)

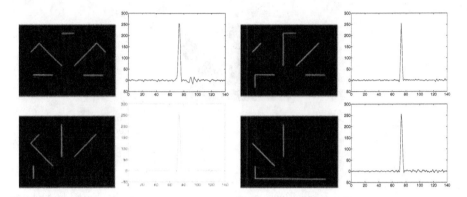

Fig. 3. Derivative images and PSF profiles at 0°, 45°, 90° and 135° degrees.

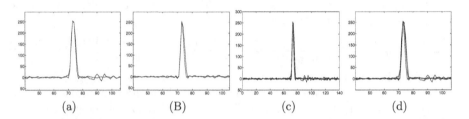

Fig. 4. The point spread function of the imaging system. (a) PSF profile for orientations 0° and 90°. (b) PSF profile for orientations 45° and 135°. (c) Four profiles of the PSF. (d) Zooming into (a).

In order to obtain the dimension of the filter we have imposed $g_N = 0.01$, consequently N can be obtained as

$$-\frac{N^2}{2\sigma^2} = \ln 0.01 \Rightarrow N = \lceil \sqrt{-2\sigma^2 \ln 0.01} \rceil \tag{8}$$

Furthermore, when the weights of the filter are obtained, a normalisation of them has done. We shall refer to the normalised filter as $\tilde{g}$ and it can be calculated as

$$\tilde{g}_{ij} = \frac{g_{ij}}{\sum_{i,j=1}^{N} g_{ij}} \tag{9}$$

As a result of this process our PSF filter $\tilde{g}$ is symmetric and of size 9×9.

Note that incorporating the use of PSF filter instead of areas a_{kl} the predicting method has replaced the exploration of a tile of size $K \times L$ pixels of the fine resolution by the exploration of a tile of size $N \times N$, where N is the dimension of the PSF filter. Hence, each pixel has a contibution in the superpixel ij equal to the weight of the PSF filter position which it corresponds.

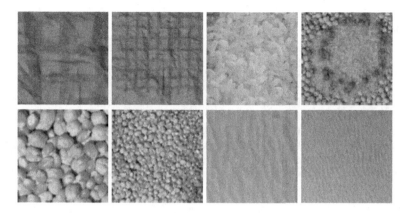

Fig. 5. First and third column: one image of the photometric stereo set. Second and fourth column: images captured from a longer distance.

4   Experimental Results

The proposed method was tested with several photometric sets consisting of four images each, obtained by placing the camera at a distance along the zenith of the surface. Other images of the same surfaces were captured from a longer distance for 4 different illumination directions. These are the images we shall want to classify, using as reference images those of the photometric stereo sets.

The photometric database consists of seven surfaces. First and third column of figure 5 show one of the photometric set images for four of the surfaces. From the information in the original database, we predict how each surface looks like when seen from the longer distance, for 4 different directions of illumination. Hence we create a "virtual" database of 28 image textures against which we compare the unknown image texture in order to classify it.

We start our classification system by obtaining a representative feature vector for each texture image in the "virtual" database, using the co-ocurrence matrices. The co-ocurrence matrices were implemented in an isotropic way for fixed distance d, computing two of the most typical features, contrast and homogeneity, for 60 different values of d. Among all the computed features, those which could discriminate between the different classes best were chosen. These turned out to be contrast at distance 29, and homogeneity at distance 2. After that we build a classifier for this set of features, which calculates the feature vector for the unknown image texture, and assigns it to one of the classes of the "virtual" database. Second and fourth column of figure 5 show examples of the unknown images we want to classify.

As these images are large, we produce from each one of them 9 subimages to be used for testing. Thus, we had in all $7 \times 9 \times 4 = 252$ test images of size 94×94 each (7 different surfaces, 4 different directions of illumination, 9 subimages).

Table 1. Confusion matrix and illuminant classification rates for the four illuminant directions (O_1,O_2,O_3,O_4).

	T1	T2	T3	T4	T5	T6	T7
T1	0.89	0.11	0.0	0.0	0.0	0.0	0.0
T2	0.25	0.47	0.08	0.0	0.0	0.17	0.03
T3	0.0	0.0	1.0	0.0	0.0	0.0	0.0
T4	0.0	0.0	0.0	0.97	0.03	0.0	0.0
T5	0.0	0.0	0.0	0.0	0.86	0.14	0.0
T6	0.0	0.0	0.0	0.0	0.14	0.86	0.0
T7	0.0	0.0	0.0	0.0	0.0	0.0	1.0

	O_1	O_2	O_3	O_4
T1	0.67	0.25	1.0	0.50
T2	0.50	0.57	0.0	0.0
T3	0.55	0.89	0.11	0.78
T4	0.89	0.33	0.75	0.44
T5	0.44	1.0	1.0	0.89
T6	0.55	0.44	0.83	0.29
T7	1.0	0.44	0.67	0.67

The texture classification rate obtained classifying the unknown images into one of the 7 surfaces (without considering illumination direction) was 84.74%. While the illuminant classification rate obtained (considering 7 surfaces and 4 different direction of illumination) was 64.87%.

In order to illustrate these classification results we used the so called *confusion matrices* $A = \alpha_{ij}$, where α_{ij} is the frequency with which a test example from class i is classified as belonging to class j. Ideally a confusion matrix should be the unit matrix. Table 1 shows the confusion matrix when we classify the test images to one of the texture classes of the database. Table 1 also shows the classification rate for the four illuminant directions.

In two alternative experiments we tried to classify the same patterns without going through the prediction stage, but just using features constructed from the original high resolution images (original database). In this case we only classified correctly into the 7 surfaces 22.28% of patterns. In a third experiment, we used again features constructed from the original images but we scaled up the distance d used for the construction of the co-ocurrence matrix according to the change in image resolution. In this case the texture recognition rate of the classifier was 33.69%. Hence, we demonstrate it is necessary to go through the prediction stage in order to extract the features which allows the best recognition results.

5   Conclusions

We presented a general framework for recognising textures when seen from different distances. The 4-source CPS has been used in order to obtain the reflectance and the surface shape information of the surface from a close by distance. The proposed method allows one to predict how the texture will look like when seen by a different sensor and under different imaging geometry with an illuminant of different spectral properties. It is based on the assumption of Lambertian surfaces, but it can easily be generalised to other types of surface. The method has been validated using real sets of images in the context of texture recognition when the test data have been captured from different distances than those in the database.

Our further studies will be focused on the inclusion of more features in order to characterise the textures. The idea is to introduce colour as well as additional textural features with the goal to improve the recognition rates of the classifier.

Acknowledgments. This work was supported by UdG grant BR00/03, and EPSRC grant GR/M73361.

References

1. Chantler, M.: Why illuminant direction is fundamental to texture analysis. IEE Proceedings in Vision, Image and Signal Processing **142** (1995) 199–206
2. Barsky, S., Petrou, M.: Colour photometric stereo: Simultaneous reconstruction of local gradient and colour of rough textured surfaces. In Proceedings 8th International Conference on Computer Vision (2001) II: 600–605
3. Petrou, M., Barsky, S.: Shadows and highlights detection in 4-source colour photometric stereo. In Proceedings International Conference on Image Processing (2001) 967–970
4. Woodham, R.: Gradient and curvature from the photometric-stereo method, including local confidence estimation. Journal of the Optical Society of America, A **11** (1994) 3050–3068
5. Haralick, R., Shanmugan, K., Dunstein, I.: Textural features for image classification. IEEE Transactions on Systems, Man, and Cybertinetics **3** (1973) 610–621
6. Petrou, M., Bosdogianni, P.: Image Processing. The Fundamentals. John Wiley & Sons, LTD (1999)
7. Robinson, G.: Edge detection by compass gradient mask. Computer Graphics and Image Processing **6** (1977) 492–501

Region-Boundary Cooperative Image Segmentation Based on Active Regions

Xavier Muñoz, Jordi Freixenet, Xavier Cufí, and Joan Martí

Institute of Informatics and Applications. University of Girona
17071 Girona, Spain
{xmunoz,jordif,xcuf,joanm}@eia.udg.es

Abstract. An unsupervised approach to image segmentation which fuses different sources of information is presented. The proposed approach takes advantage of the combined use of 3 different strategies: an appropriated placement, the control of decision criterion, and the results refinement. The new algorithm uses the boundary information to initialize a set of active regions which compete for the pixels in order to segment the whole image. The method is implemented on a multiresolution representation which ensures noise robustness as well as computation efficiency. The accuracy of the segmentation results has been proven through an objective comparative evaluation of the method.

1 Introduction

Image segmentation is one of the most important processes of image analysis, understanding and interpretation [1]. Many segmentation methods are based on two basic properties of the pixels in relation to their local neighbourhood: discontinuity and similarity. Methods based on some discontinuity property of the pixels are called boundary-based methods, whereas methods based on some similarity property are called region-based methods. Unfortunately, both techniques, boundary-based and region-based, often fail to produce accurate segmentation results.

Taking into account the complementary nature of the boundary-based and region-based information, it is possible to alleviate the problems related to each when considered separately. Although it is assumed that integration of both methods yields to get complementary information and, therefore, has long been a highly desirable goal [2], it becomes a non-trivial task due to the conflicts and incommensurate objectives it involves.

In this paper we propose a new segmentation method which combines different strategies to perform the integration: taking as a basis a previously developed segmentation algorithm [3], we have used the main contours of the image to adequately place the seeds in order to initialize the region models; then as these regions grow, they compete for the pixels of the image by using a decision criterion which ensures the homogeneity inside the region and the presence of edges at its boundary; finally, the method has been implemented on a multiresolution

M.T. Escrig Monferrer and F. Toledo Lobo (Eds.): CCIA 2002, LNAI 2504, pp. 364–374, 2002.

representation which allows us to refine the region boundaries from a coarse to a finer resolution.

The remainder of this paper is structured as follows: main strategies to perform the integration of region and boundary information are reviewed in Section 2. Section 3 describes the proposed segmentation technique, detailing the placement of the starting seeds and the growing of the active regions. The multiresolution representation is presented in Section 4, while experimental results proving the validity of our proposal appear in Section 5. Finally, conclusions are given in Section 6.

2   Related Work on Region-Boundary Integration

In the task of segmentation of some complex pictures, such as outdoor and natural images, it is often difficult to obtain satisfactory results using only one approach to image segmentation. The tendency towards the integration of several techniques seems to be the best solution in order to produce better results. Hence, with the aim of improving the segmentation process, a large number of new algorithms which integrate region and boundary information have been proposed over the past few years.

The existing main strategies to integrate region and boundary information [4] rely on the processes of:

- **Guidance of seed placement:** boundary information is used in order to decide the most suitable position to place the seed of the region growing process.
- **Control of decision criterion:** the inclusion of edge information in the definition of the decision criterion which controls the growth of the region.
- **Boundary refinement:** boundary information is used to refine the inaccurate boundaries obtained by a region based segmentation

2.1   Guidance of Seed Placement

The placement of the initial seed points can be stated as a central issue on the obtained results of a region-based segmentation. Despite their importance, the traditional region growing algorithm chooses them randomly or using a set a priori direction of image scan. In order to make a more reasonable decision, edge information can be used to decide what is the most correct position in which to place the seed. It is generally accepted that the growth of a region has to start from inside it (see [5,6]). The interior of the region is a representative zone and allows the obtention of a correct sample of the region's characteristics. On the other hand, it is necessary to avoid the boundaries between regions when choosing the seeds because they are unstable zones and not adequate to obtain information over the region. Therefore, this approach uses the edge information to place the seeds in the interior of the regions. The seeds are launched in placements free of contours and, in some proposals, as far as possible from them.

On the other hand, edge information can also be used to establish a specific order for the processes of growing. As is well known, one of the disadvantages of the region growing and merging processes is their inherently sequential nature. Hence, the final segmentation results depend on the order in which regions are grown or merged. The edge based segmentation allows for deciding this order, in some cases simulating the order by which humans separate segments from each other in an image (from large to small) [7], or in other proposals giving the same opportunities of growing to all the regions [3].

2.2   Control of Decision Criterion

Region growing algorithms are based on the growth of a region whenever its interior is homogeneous according to certain features as intensity, color or texture. The most traditional implementation starts by choosing a starting point called seed pixel. Then, the region grows by adding similar neighbouring pixels according to a certain homogeneity criterion, increasing step by step the size of the region. So, the homogeneity criterion has the function of deciding whether a pixel belongs to the growing region or not. The decision of merging is generally taken based only on the contrast between the evaluated pixel and the region. However, it is not easy to decide when this difference is small (or large) enough to take a decision. The edge map provides an additional criterion on that, such as the condition of contour pixel when deciding to aggregate it. The encounter of a contour signifies that the process of growing has reached the boundary of the region, so the pixel must not be aggregated and the growth of the region has finished.

The work of Xiaohan et al. [8] proposed a homogeneity criterion consisting of the weighted sum of the contrast between the region and the pixel, and the value of the modulus of the gradient of the pixel. A low value of this function indicates the convenience of aggregating the pixel to the region. A similar proposal was suggested by Falah et al. [9], where at each iteration, only pixels having low gradient values (below a certain threshold) are aggregated to the growing region. On the other hand, Gambotto [10] proposed using edge information to stop the growing process. His proposal assumes that the gradient takes a high value over a large part of the region boundary. Thus, the iterative growing process is continued until the maximum of the average gradient computed over the region boundary is detected.

Fuzzy logic becomes an interesting possibility to carry out the integration of edge information into the decision criterion. The fuzzy rule-based homogeneity criterion offers several advantages in contrast to ordinary feature aggregation methods. Among them is its short development time, due to the existing set of tools and methodologies, and the facility to modify or extend the system to meet the specific requirements of a certain application. Furthermore, it does not require a full knowledge of the process and it is intuitive to understand due to its human-like semantics. Additionally, it is possible to include such linguistic concepts as shape, size and colour, which are difficult to handle using most other mathematical methods. A key work in using fuzzy logic was developed by Steudel and Glesner [11], who proposed to carry out the segmentation on the basis of a region growing algorithm that uses a fuzzy rule-based system composed of a set of four fuzzy rules refereed to the contrast, gradient, size and shape of regions. A similar work can be found in [12], where the integration of a fuzzy rule-based region growing and a fuzzy rule-based edge detection is applied on colonoscopic images for the identification of closed-boundaries of intestinal lumen, in order to facilitate diagnosis of colon abnormalities.

2.3 Boundary Refinement

Region-based segmentation yields a good detection of true regions, although as is well known that the resultant sensitivity to noise causes the boundary of the extracted region to be highly irregular. This approach, which we have called boundary refinement, considers region-based segmentation as a first approxima-tion to segmentation. Typically, a region-growing procedure is used to obtain an initial estimate of a target region, which is then combined with salient edge information to achieve a more accurate representation of the target boundary. As in the over-segmentation proposals, edge information permits here, the re-finement of an initial result. Examples of this strategy are the works of Haddon and Boyce [13], Chu and Aggarwal [14] or the most recent of Sato et al. [15]. Nevertheless, two basic techniques can be considered as common ways to refine the boundary of the regions:

1. **Multiresolution**: this technique is based on the analysis at different scales. A coarse initial segmentation is refined by increasing the resolution.
2. **Boundary Refinement by Snakes**: another possibility is the integration of region information with dynamic contours, concretely snakes. The refine-ment of the region boundary is performed by the energy minimization of the snake.

Multiresolution. The multiresolution approach is an interesting strategy to carry out the refinement. The analysis operates on the image at different scales, using a pyramid or quadtree structure. The algorithm consists of an upward and a downward path; the former has the effect of smoothing or increasing the resolution in class space, at the expense of a reduction in spatial resolution, while the latter attempts to regain the lost spatial resolution, preserving the newly won class resolution. The assumption underlying this procedure is invariance across scales: those nodes in an estimate considered as interior to a region are given as the same class as their "fathers" at lower resolution.

The implemented algorithm is based on the work of Spann and Wilson [16], where the strategy uses a quadtree method using classification at the top level of the tree, followed by boundary refinement. A non-parametric clustering al-gorithm is used to perform classification at the top level, yielding an initial boundary, followed by downward boundary estimation to refine the result. A recent work following the same strategy can be found in [17].

Boundary Refinement by Snakes. The snake method is known to solve such problems by locating the object boundary from an initial plan. However, snakes do not try to solve the entire problem of finding salient image contours. The high grey-level gradient of the image may be due to object boundaries as well as noise and object textures, and therefore the optimization functions may have many local optima. Consequently, in general, active contours are sensitive to initial conditions and are only really effective when the initial position of the contour in the image is sufficiently close to the real boundary. For this reason, active contours rely on other mechanisms to place them somewhere near the desired contour. In first approximations to dynamic contours, an expert is responsible for putting the snake close to an intended contour; its energy minimization carries it the rest of the way. However, region segmentation could be the solution of the initialization problem of snakes. Proposals concerning integrated methods consist of using the region segmentation result as the initial contour of the snake. Here, the segmentation process is typically divided into two steps: First, a region growing with a seed point in the target region is performed, and its corresponding output is used for the initial contour of the dynamic contour model; Second, the initial contour is modified on the basis of energy minimization.

In the work of Chan et al. [18], the greedy algorithm is used to find the minimum energy contour. This algorithm searches for the position of the minimum energy by adjusting each point on the contour during iteration to a lower energy position amongst its eight local neighbours. The result, although not always optimal, is comparable to that obtained by variational calculus methods and dynamic programming. The advantage is that their method is faster. Similar proposals are the works of Vérard et al. [19] and Jang et al. [20]. Curiously, all these algorithms are tested on Magnetic Resonance Imaging (MRI) images, but this is not a mere coincidence. Accurate segmentation is critical for diagnosis in medical images. However, it is very difficult to extract the contour which exactly matches the target region in MRI images. Integrated methods seem to be a valid solution to achieve an accurate and consistent detection.

3   Active Region Segmentation

Our proposal combines these three strategies to perform the image segmentation. First, we use the main contours of the image to adequately place the seeds in order to initialize the region models. Then as these regions grow, they compete for the pixels of the image by using a decision criterion which ensures the homogeneity inside the region and the presence of edges at its boundary. Finally, the method has been implemented on a multiresolution representation which allows us to refine the region boundaries from a coarse to a finer resolution.

Recently, the concept of active regions as a way to combine the region and boundary information has been introduced. This model is a considerable extension on the active contour model since it incorporates region-based information with the aim of finding a partition where the interior and the exterior of the region preserve the desired image properties. The underlying idea is that the region moves through the image (shrinking or expanding) in order to contain a single, whole region. The competition algorithm proposed by Zhu and Yuille [21] and the geodesic active regions presented in Paragios and Deriche's work [22] are good examples of active region models.

The main contribution of our proposal is twofold:

- Unsupervised region initialization: the seeds which allow us to initialize the statistical measurements which model the region are automatically placed from the boundary information. Hence, it is not necessary user intervention or a previous learning phase.
- Integrated energy function: the energy function incorporates the homogeneity inside the region (region information) and the discontinuity at the contour (boundary information).

3.1 Initialization

To obtain a sample of each region large enough to model its homogeneity behaviour, initial seeds have to be placed completely inside the regions. Boundary information allows us to extract these positions in the "core" of the regions by looking for places far away from the contours. The seed placement is carried out according to the algorithm proposed in [3]. The method is based on the detection and extraction of the most relevant contours in the image characterized by an outstanding length within the global frame of the image and by any appreciable difference between the separated regions in chromatic and textural features. Further, seeds are placed in zones free of contours or, in other words, the "core" of the regions.

Each region is modeled by a Gaussian distribution, so the mean and the standard deviation, which are initialized from the seeds, describe the homogeneity region behaviour. Hence, the probability of a pixel (x, y) of belonging to a region characterized by (μ, σ) is

$$P_R((x, y)|(\mu, \sigma)) = \frac{1}{\sqrt{2\pi}\sigma} \exp\{-\frac{(I_{(x,y)} - \mu)^2}{2\sigma^2}\} \tag{1}$$

where $I_{(x,y)}$ is the intensity of the pixel (x, y). The background is treated as a single region having uniform probability distribution P_0.

3.2 Active Region Growing

The goal of image segmentation is to partition the image into subregions with homogeneous intensity (color or texture) properties in its interior and a high discontinuity with neighbouring regions in its boundary. With the aim of integrating both conditions in an optimal segmentation, the global energy is defined with two basic terms. Boundary term measures the probability that boundary pixels are really edge pixels. The probability of a given pixel (x, y) being at the real boundary is measured by $P_B((x, y))$, which can be considered as directly proportional to the value of the magnitude gradient of the pixel. Meanwhile, region term measures the homogeneity in the interior of the regions by the probability that these pixels belong to each corresponding region. As has been previously defined, $P_R((x,y)|(\mu,\sigma))$ measures the probability that a pixel (x,y) belongs to a region modeled by (μ,σ).

Some complementary definitions are required: let $\rho(R) = \{R_i : i\epsilon[0, N]\}$ be a partition of the image into $\{N + 1\}$ non-overlapping regions, where R_0 is the region corresponding to the background region. Let $\partial\rho(R) = \{\partial R_i : i\epsilon[1, N]\}$ be the region boundaries of the partition $\rho(R)$. The energy function is defined as

$$
\begin{aligned}
E(\rho(R)) = \\
(1 - \alpha)\textstyle\sum_{i=1}^{N} - \log P_B((x,y) : (x,y)\epsilon\partial R_i)) \\
+\alpha\textstyle\sum_{i=0}^{N} - \log P_R((x,y) : (x,y)\epsilon R_i|(\mu_i,\sigma_i))
\end{aligned}
\tag{2}
$$

where α is a model parameter weighing the two terms: boundary probability and region homogeneity. This function is then optimized by a region competition algorithm [21], which takes into account the neighbouring pixels to the current region boundaries $\partial\rho(R)$ to determine the next movement. Concretely, a region aggregates a neighbouring pixel when this new classification diminishes the energy of the segmentation.

Intuitively, all regions begin to move and grow, competing for the pixels of the image until an energy minimum is reached. When the minimization process finishes, if there is a background region R_0 not occupied by any seed regions, a new seed is placed in the background, and the energy minimization starts again.

4   MultiResolution Implementation

In order to further reduce the computational cost, a multiscale representation [16] is proposed which can be combined with the active region segmentation. Specifically, a pyramid of images at different scales is built upon the full resolution image. At lowest resolution level, the seeds are placed from the boundary information and start to compete for the image, obtaining a first segmentation result. This multiresolution structure is then used according to a coarse-to-fine strategy which assumes the invariance of region properties over a range of scales. Specifically, a boundary region is defined at coarsest level and then, at successive levels, the pixels not classified as boundary are used to initialize and model the regions. Further, segmentation by active region is performed to refine the candidate boundary by a factor of two using the multiresolution structure. As a result, the boundaries of the full image size are produced at the finest resolution.

Furthermore, the use of a multiresolution representation allows us to avoid the over-segmentation problems produced by the presence of noise in images. An initial coarse region segmentation is performed on a lower resolution achieving the effect of smoothing. Hence, the use of a multiresolution technique ensures noise robustness as well as computation efficiency.

Fig. 1. The segmentation results obtained over three images of the trial set.

5   Experimental Results

The performance of our proposal has been analyzed over a set of 22 test images including synthetic and real ones. The set of 12 synthetic images has been generated following the method proposed by Zhang [23], where the form of the objects of the images changes from a circle to an elongated ellipse. To make synthetic images more realistic, a 5×5 average low-pass filter is applied to produce a smooth transition between objects and background. Then, a zero-mean Gaussian white noise is added to simulate noise effect. On the other hand, 10 selected real images are well-known standard test images extracted from the USC-SIPI image database (University of Southern California-Signal and Image Processing Institute). All test images are size 256×256 pixels. Figure 1 shows an example of segmentation with three images belonging to the trial set.

In order to evaluate the results, we use the quality parameters (region-based and boundary-based) proposed by Huang and Dom [24]. The boundary-based approach evaluates segmentation in terms of both localization and shape accuracy of extracted regions. Two distance distribution signatures are used to measure the boundary quality, one from ground truth to the estimated, denoted by D_G^B, and the other from the estimated to ground truth, denoted by D_B^G. Instead, the region-based approach assesses the segmentation quality in terms of both size and location of the segmented regions. A region-based performance

Table 1. Summarized segmentation results of main strategies and our proposal over a set of 12 synthetic and 10 real test images.

Strategy	Region-based			Boundary-based				Time
	e_R^m	e_R^f	p	μD_G^B	σD_G^B	μD_B^G	σD_B^G	
Summary of Synthetic Images Evaluation								
GSP	0,059	0,025	0,957	1,003	0,708	0,993	0,843	0,340
CDC	0,202	0,011	0,893	0,954	0,658	0,965	0,877	0,290
BR	0,034	0,066	0,949	0,404	0,506	0,765	0,771	0,120
ARS	0,089	0,015	0,947	0,480	0,312	0,563	0,688	6,251
MARS	0,030	0,015	0,977	0,475	0,580	0,560	0,341	0,980
Summary of Real Images Evaluation								
GSP	0,066	0,033	0,949	2,121	3,018	2,160	3,389	0,430
CDC	0,174	0,044	0,890	1,828	1,297	1,544	3,125	0,380
BR	0,074	0,088	0,918	0,698	0,968	0,412	0,982	0,176
ARS	0,106	0,033	0,929	0,711	0,528	0,344	0,886	8,132
MARS	0,038	0,032	0,964	0,730	0,711	0,320	0,641	1,256

measure based on normalized Hamming distance is defined, p. Moreover, two types of errors are defined: missing rate e_R^m and false alarm rate e_R^f.

Furthermore, we have made a comparison of our proposal against other strategies to integrate region and boundary information. Thereby, we implemented the algorithms corresponding to the three previously described strategies. Concretely, our implementation of the **guidance of the seed placement** strategy (GSP) is based on a previous work [3], while the **control of decision criterion** strategy (CDC) is based on the proposal of Xiaohan et al. [8], and the **boundary refinement** strategy (BR) on the work of Wilson and Spann [16]. Table 1 shows the summarized results obtained for the three strategies; our proposal of active region segmentation (ARS), and our proposal implemented on a multiresolution representation (MARS).

Quantitative results successfully demonstrate the validity of our proposal. Although the active region segmentation (ARS) obtains useful results, the technique has some problems due to the presence of noise which causes an over-segmentation of the image and a relatively high computational cost. The implementation of this proposal on a multiresolution representation (MARS) solves these problems and achieves an optimal result.

6   Conclusions

A new strategy for image segmentation which integrates region and boundary information has been described. The algorithm uses boundary information in order to initialize, in an unsupervised way, a set of active regions, which later compete for the pixels minimizing an energy function which takes into account both region and boundary information. The method has been implemented on a multiresolution representation and has been tested on a set of synthetic and real images. The experimental results demonstrate the effectiveness of the proposed algorithm in estimating regions and their boundaries with high accuracy.

The algorithm can be directly adapted to perform color or texture segmentation assuming multi-variable Gaussian distributions to model each region. In this sense, future extensions of this work are oriented to the integration of grey level, color and texture cues.

Acknowledgments. This study has been partially developed thanks to the support of the *Departament d'Universitats, Recerca i Societat de la Informació de la Generalitat de Catalunya.*

References

1. Haralick, R., Shapiro, R.: Computer and Robot Vision. Volume 1 & 2. Addison-Wesley Inc, Reading, Massachussets (1992 & 1993)
2. Pavlidis, T., Liow, Y.: Integrating region growing and edge detection. IEEE Transactions on Pattern Analysis and Machine Intelligence **12** (1990) 225–233
3. Cufí, X., Muñoz, X., Freixenet, J., Martí, J.: A concurrent region growing algorithm guided by circumscribed contours. In: International Conference on Pattern Recognition. Volume I., Barcelona, Spain (2000) 432–435
4. Cufí, X., Muñoz, X., Freixenet, J., Martí, J.: A review on image segmentation techniques integrating region and boundary information. Advances in Imaging and Electronics Physics **120** (2002) 1–32
5. Benois, J., Barba, D.: Image segmentation by region-contour cooperation for image coding. In: International Conference on Pattern Recognition. Volume C., The Hague, Netherlands (1992) 331–334
6. Sinclair, D.: Voronoi seeded colour image segmentation. Technical Report 3, AT&T Laboratories Cambridge (1999)
7. Moghaddamzadeh, A., Bourbakis, N.: A fuzzy region growing approach for segmentation of color images. Pattern Recognition **30** (1997) 867–881
8. Xiaohan, Y., Yla-Jaaski, J., Huttunen, O., Vehkomaki, T., Sipild, O., Katila, T.: Image segmentation combining region growing and edge detection. In: International Conference on Pattern Recognition. Volume C., The Hague, Netherlands (1992) 481–484
9. Falah, R., Bolon, P., Cocquerez, J.: A region-region and region-edge cooperative approach of image segmentation. In: International Conference on Image Processing. Volume 3., Austin, Texas (1994) 470–474
10. Gambotto, J.: A new approach to combining region growing and edge detection. Pattern Recognition Letters **14** (1993) 869–875
11. Steudel, A., Glesner, M.: Fuzzy segmented image coding using orthonormal bases and derivative chain coding. Pattern Recognition **32** (1999) 1827–1841
12. Krishnan, S., Tan, C., Chan, K.: Closed-boundary extraction of large intestinal lumen. In: International Conference of the IEEE Engineering in Medicine and Biology Society, Baltimore, Washington (1994)
13. Haddon, J., Boyce, J.: Image segmentation by unifying region and boundary information. IEEE Transactions on Pattern Analysis and Machine Intelligence **12** (1990) 929–948

14. Chu, C., Aggarwal, J.: The integration of image segmentation maps using region and edge information. IEEE Transactions on Pattern Analysis and Machine Intelligence **15** (1993) 1241–1252

15. Sato, M., Lakare, S., Wan, M., Kaufman, A., Nakajima, M.: A gradient magnitude based region growing algorithm for accurate segmentation. In: International Conference on Image Processing. Volume III., Vancouver, Canada (2000) 448–451

16. Wilson, R., Spann, M.: Finite prolate spheroidial sequences and their applications ii: Image feature description and segmentation. IEEE Transactions on Pattern Analysis and Machine Intelligence **10** (1988) 193–203

17. Hsu, T., Kuo, J., Wilson, R.: A multiresolution texture gradient method for unsupervised segmentation. Pattern Recognition **32** (2000) 1819–1833

18. Chan, F., Lam, F., Poon, P., Zhu, H., Chan, K.: Object boundary location by region and contour deformation. IEE Proceedings-Vision Image and Signal Processing **143** (1996) 353–360

19. Vérard, L., Fadili, J., Ruan, S., Bloyet, D.: 3d mri segmentation of brain structures. In: International Conference of the IEEE Engineering in Medicine and Biology Society, Amsterdam, Netherlands (1996) 1081–1082

20. Jang, D., Lee, D., Kim, S.: Contour detection of hippocampus using dynamic contour model and region growing. In: International Conference of the IEEE Engineering in Medicine and Biology Society, Chicago, Ilinois (1997) 763–766

21. Zhu, S., Yuille, A.: Region competition: Unifying snakes, region growing, and bayes/mdl for multi-band image segmentation. IEEE Transactions on Pattern Analysis and Machine Intelligence **18** (1996) 884–900

22. Paragios, N., Deriche, R.: Geodesic active regions for supervised texture segmentation. In: International Conference on Computer Vision. Volume II., Corfou, Greece (1999) 926–932

23. Zhang, Y.: Evaluation and comparison of different segmentation algorithms. Pattern Recognition Letters **18** (1997) 963–974

24. Huang, Q., Dom, B.: Quantitative methods of evaluating image segmentation. In: International Conference on Image Processing. Volume III., Washington DC (1995) 53–56

Spherical Panoramas for Pan-Tilt Camera Motion Compensation in Space-Variant Images

Filiberto Pla and V. Javier Traver

Dep. de Llenguatges i Sistemes Informàtics
Universitat Jaume I,
E12080 Castelló, Spain
{pla,vtraver}@uji.es
http://vision.uji.es

Abstract. In active vision scenarios, the motion of the observer induces an apparent motion in the image plane. One approach for camera motion compensation is the use of panoramic images, representing the scene at the different positions of the camera. In this work, an approach to build spherical panoramic views from a pan-tilt camera is described, which is based on background updating techniques. Interestingly, panoramic representations allow motion detection and analysis to be performed independently from camera movements. This makes easier the detection of moving objects in active tracking tasks. Additionally, the advantages of combining spherical panoramas with log-polar images is discussed. An example of target segmentation by background difference is shown, which shows the effectiveness of panoramic representations in active vision systems.

1 Introduction

One of the problems to be solved in active vision systems, where the camera is moving, is to overcome the effect of *apparent motion* due to egomotion [6, 3]. This is the case of systems based on a pan-tilt camera performing known rotational movements. Active monocular target tracking with a pant-tilt head is a valid framework for some visual surveillance applications, like people or vehicle monitoring, where the system focuses its attention on certain target.

One way to achieve a representation in which camera motion is compensated consists of building a panoramic view [9]. A panoramic view acts as a reference image, which has compensated the effect of camera motion from all images taken by the camera into a single image representation. This approach has been used in video coding techniques [7] to extract moving objects from an image sequence.

The approach presented here has been inspired in works such as [1], where image mosaics built from a pan-tilt camera motion have been used to perform motion segmentation. Unlike this and similar works, a more adequate model of panoramic representation is proposed, to deal both, with a pan-tilt system and with the possibility of using a non-uniform image sampling sensor, like a log-polar imaging system [8].

M.T. Escrig Monferrer and F. Toledo Lobo (Eds.): CCIA 2002, LNAI 2504, pp. 375–387, 2002.

An accurate way to perform registration to build the panorama, based on a motion estimation technique previously developed in [5], is also proposed. Previous works on building panoramic images have focused on constructing image mosaics for visualization applications, where accuracy is not as important as it is in moving target segmentation and motion analysis tasks. Figure-ground segmentation is here done using an approach reported by [2], which is more independent from tuning parameters.

Next section describes the proposed panoramic model, pointing out its properties and the relation with non-uniform sampled images. Section 2 shows an example of how these panoramic representations can be used for motion detection and analysis. Section 3 presents the results of some experiments carried out using the described techniques. Finally, some conclusions from the present work and the way we can use it in future work are drawn in Sect. 5.

2   Building Panoramic Views

2.1   Notation

There are several types of panoramic representation to deal with image information in a scene. The kind most often used is an image plane projection onto a reference image frame [7,4]. Panoramic views (or image mosaics) generated from camera pan-tilt movements are also possible [1,2].

Other types of panoramic representations are cylindrical and spherical panoramas [9]. *Cylindrical* panoramas are quite adequate for building panoramas from pan camera movements, because given the camera focal length, we only have to bring out the pan angle rotated for the camera to match the image contents with the panoramic representation. *Spherical* panoramas could be a more natural way of building panoramic views generated from pan-tilt movements. In a spherical panorama, world coordinates of a point $p = (x, y, z)$ are mapped into 2D spherical coordinates (θ, ϕ), which represent the direction of point p in the world coordinates. These spherical coordinates are calculated from the 3D world coordinates as

$$\begin{cases} \theta = \arctan\left(\sqrt{x^2 + y^2}/z\right), & \theta \in [0, \pi] \\ \phi = \arctan\left(y/x\right) & , \quad \phi \in [-\pi, \pi] \end{cases}.$$

If a pin-hole camera model is assumed (Fig. 1), it is possible to compute $f(\theta, \phi)$, corresponding to a world point $p = (x, y, z)$ as

$$\begin{cases} \theta = \arctan\left(\sqrt{x'^2 + y'^2}/f\right) \\ \phi = \arctan(y'/x') \end{cases}, \tag{1}$$

where (x', y') are the image coordinates, and f the focal length of the camera.

In the case of a log-polar image $I(u, v)$, and under an ideal mathematical model, we have that $u = \log\left(\sqrt{x'^2 + y'^2}\right)$ and $v = \arctan(y'/x')$. Therefore, the spherical coordinates can be computed as

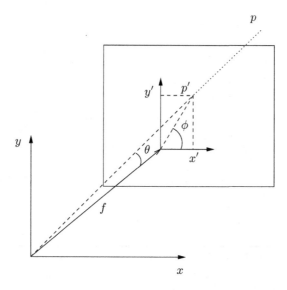

Fig. 1. Pin-hole camera model and spherical coordinates of a world point

$$\begin{cases} \theta = \arctan(e^u/f) \\ \phi = v \end{cases} . \tag{2}$$

When the camera rotates a pan angle of α radians about y axis, and a tilt angle of β radians about x axis (Fig. 2), the (θ_r, ϕ_r) spherical coordinates of p with respect to the new camera position are related to the coordinates (θ, ϕ) of the initial camera position as

$$\begin{pmatrix} \sin\theta_r \cos\phi_r \\ \sin\theta_r \sin\phi_r \\ \cos\theta_r \end{pmatrix} = \boldsymbol{A}(\alpha, \beta) \cdot \boldsymbol{B}(\theta, \phi) , \tag{3}$$

with

$$\boldsymbol{A}(\alpha, \beta) = \begin{pmatrix} \cos\alpha & \sin\alpha \sin\beta & \sin\alpha \cos\beta \\ 0 & \cos\alpha & -\sin\beta \\ -\sin\alpha & \cos\alpha \sin\beta & \cos\alpha \cos\beta \end{pmatrix} ,$$

and

$$\boldsymbol{B}(\theta, \phi) = \begin{pmatrix} \sin\theta \cos\phi \\ \sin\theta \sin\phi \\ \cos\theta \end{pmatrix} .$$

Thus, by knowing the pan and tilt angles (α, β) of the camera movement, a back-mapping can be performed from the spherical coordinates (θ, ϕ) of the image points, in a given camera position, with respect to the spherical coordinates of the initial coordinate system, which represents the panoramic representation.

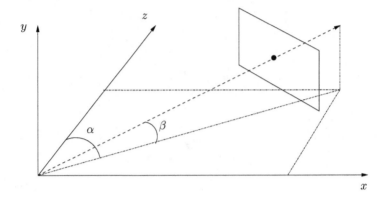

Fig. 2. Pan-tilt movement of a camera with respect to the reference coordinate system

---

Algorithm 1 Building a panoramic background image from a set of camera motions

---

1: Initialize the panoramic image $P(\theta, \phi)$ with ∞
2: Rotate camera a certain pan-tilt angles (α_i, β_i)
3: **for all** (θ, ϕ) in the panoramic image **do**
4:     Compute the corresponding (θ_r, ϕ_r) in the rotated camera axis by using the Equation (3).
5:     Compute the current image plane coordinates using the inverse relations either of (1) or of (2), depending on using either cartesian or log-polar images, that is:

$$\begin{cases} x' = f \tan\theta \cos\phi \\ y' = f \tan\theta \sin\phi \end{cases} \qquad \begin{cases} u = \log(f\tan\theta) \\ v = \phi \end{cases}$$

6:     **if** $P(\theta, \phi) = \infty$ **then**
7:         $P(\theta, \phi) \leftarrow I(x', y')$
8:     **else**
9:         $P(\theta, \phi) \leftarrow (1 - \lambda)P(\theta, \phi) + \lambda I(x', y'), \lambda \in [0, 1]$
10:     **end if**
11: **end for**

2.2   Algorithm

An accurate computation of the pan and tilt angles is important to perform a good mapping of the images taken at different camera positions and, in turn, to achieve a good accuracy in the panoramic representation. To that end, some kind of pan-tilt camera calibration is needed [10].

To build a panoramic background image from a set of different camera rotations (α_i, β_i) with respect to the initial camera position, Algorithm 1 is proposed.

The parameter λ is used in a simple auto-regressive filter to integrate the background information from the different views. In all cases, for log-polar images, $I(u, v)$ has to be used instead of $I(x', y')$.

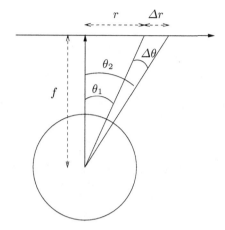

Fig. 3. Relation between the panoramic image and the image plane resolution

The heaviest computational effort in this procedure lies in computing the (θ_r, ϕ_r) coordinates in a rotated coordinate system after some pan-tilt camera movement (i.e., the operations described in Equation (3)). At this moment, this operation has to be performed for every pixel in the image. Alternative ways to perform this coordinates transform are possible (e.g., using quaternions), and should be investigated to increase the efficiency.

Calibration of the intrinsic camera parameters (f) can be done by means of some standard calibration algorithm [11]. The possible values of (x', y') or (u, v) for all predefined values of the panoramic image (θ, ϕ) can be precomputed and kept in LUTs.

The pan and tilt angles (α_i, β_i) rotated by the camera can be obtained more accurately after a movement by these steps:

1. Read the encoder pan-tilt positions of the camera motors.
2. Use these pan and tilt angles as initialization values to the translational motion estimation between the reference and the current image, by using a motion estimation algorithm [5].
3. Find out the initial translational input as $(x_0, y_0) = (x_r\alpha_i, y_r\beta_i)$, with x_r and y_r being constants worked out by the calibration process.
4. Approximate the pan and tilt angles by $(\alpha_i, \beta_i) = (x_0/x_r, y_0/y_r)$.

2.3   Image Resolution Issues

The resolution or size of the panoramic image can be chosen according to the desired resolution in the image plane. To take this decision, it has to be taken into account that, given a spherical panoramic representation, the projection of the panoramic information (stored in uniform resolution in θ, ϕ) into an image plane in a certain orientation, does not provide a uniform resolution in the x' and y' axes in the image plane. In fact, we can approximate (see Fig. 3) the

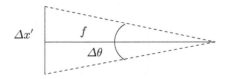

Fig. 4. Relation between spherical image resolution and image plane resolution

relation between the width of a pixel in the panoramic image $\Delta\theta$, and the width Δr of the area (pixel width) covered by a bin in the panoramic image into the image plane as

$$\Delta r = f \cdot \frac{\Delta\theta}{1 + \theta_1^2}$$

since

$$\tan(\theta_1) = r/f,$$
$$\tan(\theta_2) = (r + \Delta_r)/f$$
$$\Delta r = f(\tan(\theta_2) - \tan(\theta_1)),$$
$$\theta_2 = \theta_1 + \Delta\theta$$
$$\tan(\theta_1 + \Delta\theta) = \tan(\theta_1) + \Delta\theta/(1 + \theta_1^2)$$

Therefore, a *uniform* sampling in the spherical representation approximately becomes a *quadratic* sampling in the image plane, which means that resolution decreases in a quadratic way when we move away from the image center. This means that resources are wasted if cartesian images are used as a source to build spherical panoramic images. And this is so because the resolution of the image plane far away from the image center (the optical axis) is not used when this peripheral information is projected onto the surface of the sphere representing the panoramic image.

On the contrary, building spherical panoramas from log-polar images makes some sense, as it is illustrated in the following observations:

1. The fact of mapping the image plane information into the panoramic representation takes advantage of the decreasing resolution occurring in log-polar images far from the image center. It is true, however, that resolution in log-polar images decays exponentially, rather than quadratically.
2. Similarly, the back-projected information from the panoramic view to a log-polar image will not suffer from the decrease of the projected image resolution.
3. High-resolution spherical panoramic views could be built from different log-polar images, integrating the high fovea resolution at different views in a single representation.
4. There is a straightforward relation between the pixel coordinates in log-polar images and the corresponding spherical coordinates in the panoramic image (see Equation 2).

To have a spherical panorama with enough resolution to take advantage of the image resolution of the images the panoramic view is built from, if we would like to build a panoramic that covers half the 3D space, that is $\theta \in [0, \pi/2]$ and $\phi \in [-\pi, \pi]$, the following relation has to be taken into account (Fig. 4):

$$\Delta\theta = 2\arctan(\Delta x'/2f)$$
$$\pi/(2\Delta\theta) = M$$

with M being the number of bins along θ in P.

3   Motion Detection in Spherical Panoramas

Given that a panoramic view is a representation built in a incremental way from a sequence of images taken with different positions of the camera, the idea of building the panoramic image that represents the background, could be mixed with the process of detecting changes in the source image with respect to the panoramic representation when we are performing the mapping.

In other words, while updating the panoramic representation, which represents the background, some procedure could be done while doing the updating to extract information about what is moving with respect to the panoramic background. Thus, if the panoramic background is supposed to be static and free of the apparent movement created by the camera motion, any change in the present image when mapping it into the panoramic representation will be due either to a different motion present in the images or to a change in the scene illumination with respect to the camera.

A straightforward way to see the above mentioned effect is to use a difference-based approach to detect motion changes. In this case, the difference operation will be performed between the panoramic image representation $P(\theta, \phi)$ and the present image $I(x', y')$ taken at a given camera pan-tilt position (α, β) with respect to the reference coordinate system of the panoramic representation.

The algorithm used to perform this image difference or background subtraction, is based on the approach used by [2]. Therefore, the procedure described in Algorithm 2 is used to perform the panoramic background image updating and the detection of possible moving pixels in the current image.

$V(\theta, \phi)$ is a variance image where the evolution of the variance of the gray levels of a pixel in the panoramic view is kept and updated, integrating the actual variance (or standard deviation) of the pixel in the current image with respect to its mapping in the panoramic representation.

The binary image $T(x', y')$ resulting from the process will represent the possible moving pixels due to moving objects with respect to the static background, the latter being represented by the panoramic image. The procedure described above has the advantage of having no *a priori* thresholds to set up, thus getting rid of tuning parameters.

Other types of motion analysis could be done using the information of the current image taken by the camera. For instance, one can use log-polar images rather than cartesian images, and compare the contents of these images with the

Algorithm 2 Panoramic image updating and motion detection

1: Given an image $I(x', y')$ taken from a certain pan-tilt (α, β) camera movement
2: **for all** (θ, ϕ) in the panoramic image **do**
3:    Compute the corresponding (θ_r, ϕ_r) in the rotated camera axis by using the Equation (3.
4:    Compute the current image plane coordinates using the following expressions, depending on using either cartesian or log-polar images:

$$\begin{cases} x' = f \tan\theta \cos\phi \\ y' = f \tan\theta \sin\phi \end{cases} \qquad \begin{cases} u = \log(f \tan\theta) \\ v = \phi \end{cases}$$

5:    **if** $P(\theta, \phi) = \infty$ **then**
6:       $P(\theta, \phi) \leftarrow I(x', y')$
7:       $V(\theta, \phi) \leftarrow \sigma_0$ {some initial value}
8:    **else if** $|I(x', y') - P(\theta, \phi)| < V(\theta, \phi)$ **then**
9:       $P(\theta, \phi) \leftarrow (1 - \lambda)P(\theta, \phi) + \lambda I(x', y'), \ \lambda \in [0, 1]$
10:      $V(\theta, \phi) \leftarrow (1 - \lambda)V(\theta, \phi) + \lambda|I(x', y') - P(\theta, \phi)|$
11:      $T(x', y') \leftarrow 0$
12:   **else**
13:      $T(x', y') \leftarrow 1$
14:   **end if**
15: **end for**

Fig. 5. From left to right, frames 1, 5 and 17 in the sequence

current state of the panoramic representation to segment the target and estimate its motion parameters, with the advantage of having compensated the apparent motion of pan-tilt camera movement.

4   Experimental Results

A spherical panorama has been built from a real sequence of images taken from a pan movement, using a Sony EVI-G21 camera. In this case, a sequence of 17 images was taken. The pan angle was computed by the procedure described in Sect. 2, using also the algorithm reported in [5] to estimate more accurately the rotation performed, in order to calculate the mapping and updating of the panoramic view.

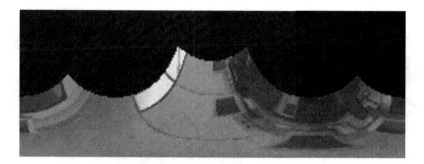

Fig. 6. Spherical panoramic view built from sequence in Fig. 5

Fig. 7. Panoramic view projected in the image plane of the first image in the sequence

Figure 5 shows some frames in the sequence, and Fig. 6 shows the spherical panoramic representation built. Rows in Fig. 6, image denote the θ angle, while columns denote the ϕ angle. Figure 7 represents the same panoramic image as that in Fig. 6, but represented in the image plane corresponding to the initial image in the sequence, in order to appreciate the quality of the mapping. A second experiment has been performed consisting of pasting on the sequence of images of Fig. 5, a target region that undergoes a movement of scaling, rotation and translation with respect to the image plane. Figure 8 shows three images of that sequence with an X-shaped target.

Therefore, if two subsequent images in the sequence were compared, two different movements will be detected, the one corresponding to the target and the one corresponding to the apparent motion of the pan movement of the camera. On the other hand, Fig. 9 shows the result of applying the algorithm described in Sect. 2 for simultaneous background updating and motion detection. In these

Fig. 8. From left to right, frames 1, 5 and 15 in the sequence with the pasted X-shaped target

Fig. 9. Moving and grey level changing pixels between the images in the sequence and the panoramic background image. From left to right, the moving pixels corresponding to frames, 5 and 15 in the sequence

images, we can see how, apart from the obvious detection of pixels at borders of objects because of the effect of occluding pixels from view to view, the main area of the moving target has been detected, while the background has been considered with no moving changes, due to the effect of camera motion compensation in the panoramic representation.

Figure 10 shows the same images in the sequence in Fig. 5, but with cartesian images reconstructed from log-polar images sized 64×128. The corresponding panoramic image projected in a cartesian image plane referred to the first image in the sequence is shown in Fig. 11. Note that, because of the rightward pan movement; the resolution in the middle of the image has increased when moving this direction, due to the effect of mixing the information of the fovea through the sequence.

Figure 12 shows the result of the algorithm for image change detection at some frames in the sequence. Note that, the results are quite similar to those in Fig. 9 but with a "smoothing" effect due to the lower resolution far from the image center. Therefore, these results provide an idea of the potential of this technique for motion analysis where camera motion is compensated in a pan-tilt camera. Moreover, the use of spherical panoramic images are a suitable approach to take advantage of space-variant images, like log-polar images, because of the

Fig. 10. From left to right, log-polar image 1, 5 and 17 in the sequence

Fig. 11. Panoramic view projected in the image plane of the first image in the sequence built from log-polar images

effects of the projection of the image plane information in the panoramic image, as commented in the previous section.

5   Conclusions

Camera motion compensation in a pan-tilt camera system can be achieved by building panoramic representations of a scene with a static background. The approach presented here describes a way of building spherical panoramas from a sequence of frames taken from a pan-tilt camera.

Spherical panoramas offer some properties that could be exploited by using log-polar images because: (i) this panoramic representations produces an effect of non-uniform image resolution when projecting its contents into an image plane in a given camera direction; and (ii) there exists a straightforward relation between spherical and log-polar coordinates.

Fig. 12. Moving and grey level changing pixels between the log-polar images in the sequence and the panoramic background image. From left to right, the moving pixels corresponding to frames 1, 5 and 15 in the sequence

The results of the experiments carried out show that panoramic representations can be used for the detection and analysis of targets that move with respect to a static background. An example of image difference technique has been shown, to illustrate how this process could be implemented, by fusing the panoramic image representation information with the contents of the current image taken from a given pan-tilt direction.

Future work could be done directly using the proposed approach to detect moving regions in a pan-tilt system for target monitoring, and combine it with log-polar image representation, in the way described in this work.

References

1. K.S. Bhat, M. Saptharishi, and P.K. Khosla. Motion detection and segmentation using image mosaics. In *IEEE International Conference on Multimedia and Expo*, volume 3, pages 1577–1580, 2000.
2. A.R.J. Fran ois. *Semantic, interactive manipulation of visual data*. PhD thesis, University of Southern California, 2000.
3. J.E. Ha and I.S. Kweon. Robust direct motion estimation considering discontinuity. *Pattern Recognition Letter*, 21(11):999–1011, 2000.
4. K. Mase and H. Nishira. Computing the field-of-view of a stitched panorama to create fov sensitive virtual environments. In *International Conference on Pattern Recognition, ICPR '96*, volume I, 1996.
5. R. Montoliu and F. Pla. Multiple parametric motion model estimation and segmentation. In *IEEE Intl. Conf. on Image Processing (ICIP)*, volume II, pages 933–936, Thessaloniki, Greece, October 2001.
6. J.M. Odobez and Bouthemy P. Detection of multiple moving objects using multi-scale mrf with camera motion compensation. In *International Conference on Image Processing, ICIP'94*, volume II, pages 257–261, 1994.
7. F. Odone, A. Fusiello, and E. Trucco. Robust motion segmentation for content-based video coding. In *6th RIAO (Recherche d'Informations Assist e par Ordinateur) International Conference*, Paris, France, 2000.
8. Fernando Pardo-Carpio. *Sensor Retínico Espacio Variante Basado en Tecnología CMOS*. PhD thesis, Dept. Informàtica i Electrònica, Universitat de València, September 1997.

9. R. Szeliski and H. Shum. Creating full view panoramic image mosaics and environment maps. In *Proceedings of SIGGRAPH*, pages 251–258, 1997.

10. V. J. Traver and F. Pla. Motion estimation-based self-calibration of a log-polar pan-tilt camera. In *Visualization, Imaging and Image Processing Conf.*, September 2002. (Accepted for VIIP'02).

11. R.Y. Tsai. A versatile camera calibration technique for high accuracy 3D machine vision metrology using off-the-self TV camera and lenses. *IEEE Journal of Robotics and Automation*, RA-3(4):323–344, 1987.

Unsupervised Parameterisation of Gaussian Mixture Models

Daniel Ponsa and Xavier Roca

Centre de Visió per Computador, Universitat Autònoma de Barcelona, 08193
Bellaterra (Barcelona), Spain,
daniel@cvc.uab.es

Abstract. In this paper we explain a new practical methodology to
fully parameterise Gaussian Mixture Models (GMM) to describe data set
distributions. Our approach analyses hierarchically a data set distribution to be modeled, determining unsupervisedly an appropriate number
of components of the GMM, and their corresponding parameterisation.
Results are provided that show the improvement of our method with
regard to an implementation of the traditional approach usually applied
to solve this problem. The method is also tested in the unsupervised
generation of shape models for visual tracking applications.

1 Introduction

Many Computer Vision problems require determining an appropriate representation for the distribution of a multivariate data set. For example, in pattern
recognition problems, models are usually generated from training data, generalising its variability in a less complex representation. This problem can be posed
as finding a description of the training set distribution, to delimit the space of
parameters of valid instances of the pattern to be modelised[1]. In other areas as
Image Segmentation, regions in the image need to be automatically isolated according to some measure of similarity. This can be posed as identifying similarity
clusters in the distribution of image features[2,3]. In these and other Computer
Vision problems, a solution can be obtained by describing the analysed data set
with a Mixture Model.

Mixture Models increases the representability of classical parametric distribution by stablishing a linear combination of several of them. In that way, they
can describe more precisely a data set distribution, while requiring an amount
of parameters reduced in comparison with the modeled data. The probability
density function of such models can be expressed as

$$p(x) = \sum_{i=1}^{M} p(x|i)P(i) \ , \tag{1}$$

where M indicates the amount of mixture components (the order of the model),
$p(x|i)$ the probability density function of the i-th component of the mixture, and

M.T. Escrig Monferrer and F. Toledo Lobo (Eds.): CCIA 2002, LNAI 2504, pp. 388–398, 2002.

$P(i)$ its weight or mixing coefficient. The values $P(i)$ are positive, and sum up to unity.

Given a Mixture Model with M components, their parameters $P(i)$ and the ones ruling $p(x|i)$ are usually determined by maximising their likelihood for a given data set. This is a non-trivial task in general terms, but various procedures exist when mixture components are gaussian density functions [4]. This methods follow an iterative scheme that fit a given initial parameterisation of the mixture model to data. However, depending on its initial condition, they can converge to a local maximum solution, which represent poorly the real data distribution. Moreover, they don't take into account the estimation of a very important parameter in mixture models: the amount of mixtures components. In this paper we propose a methodology to solve both problems, when gaussian mixture components are considered.

The rest of the paper is organized as follows: In Section 2, we review previous work on the problem of learning gaussian mixtures with an unknown number of components. Then, in Section 3 we describe our proposal to solve this problem, evaluating in Section 4 its performance in comparison with traditional approaches. Results obtained in the application of our method in the unsupervised generation of shape models are also shown. The paper ends with a brief discussion.

2 Previous Work

The majority of popular and computationally feasible techniques using mixture models consider Gaussian components, given by:

$$p(x|i) = \frac{1}{(2\pi)^{n/2}|\Sigma_i|^{1/2}} \exp^{-\frac{1}{2}(x-\mu_i)^T \Sigma_i^{-1}(x-\mu_i)} , \tag{2}$$

where n is the data dimensionality, and (μ_i, Σ_i) its mean and covariance. For a fixed number M of components, the mixture model is characterised by the parameters $\Phi = ((P(1), \mu_1, \Sigma_1) \cdots (P(M), \mu_M, \Sigma_M))$. Given an initial guess of parameters M and Φ_0, the EM algorithm [5] (detailed in Figure 1) is the standard method used to determine the maximum likelihood estimation of the parameters. As noted before, depending on Φ the algorithm can converge to a local maxima solution, as the likelihood of a Gaussian Mixture Model (GMM) is not unimodal, and obviously the value of M is crucial to correctly model the real distribution.

The traditional approach to infer the most probable number of components in GMM is based in an exhaustive search; Given a range of M values, which is supposed to contain the optimal number of components, the EM algorithm is used to converge several GMM of different order. Then, the converged GMM are evaluated with a defined criterion, and the solution with the number of components that maximizes (or minimizes) the criterion is selected. The works by Oliver et al. [6] and Roberts et al. [7] describe several criteria for model-order selection, as well as make an evaluation of its performance. In this works, for each number of components analysed several random initializations of the GMM

---

0 Set initial mixture model Φ
1 Iterate until convergence
    1.1 **Expectation Step**: For each component i compute
$$E_i(j) = p(i|x_j) = \frac{p(x_j|i)P(i)}{\sum_{k=1}^{M} p(x_j|k)P(k)}$$
    1.2 **Maximization Step**: For each component i compute
$$P(i) = \frac{\sum_{j=1}^{N} E_i(j)}{N}$$
$$\mu_i = \frac{\sum_{j=1}^{N} E_i(j)x_j}{\sum_{j=1}^{N} E_i(j)}$$
$$\Sigma_i = \frac{\sum_{j=1}^{N} E_i(j)(x_j-\mu_i)(x_j-\mu_i)^T}{\sum_{j=1}^{N} E_i(j)}$$

Fig. 1. The Expectation Maximization Algorithm

are checked, trying to avoid in that way local minima convergences of the EM algorithm.

Instead of initialise GMM randomly, other works take advantage of classical clustering techniques to do this. Fraley and Raftery [8] obtain good results by applying the Ward's method to cluster the data for different number of components considered, generating in that way the set of GMM to be evaluated. Bregler and Omohundro [9] use the K-means algorithm to determine the GMM initial parameters, and even its number of components, but as long as this algorithm presupposes spherical clusters, poor data models are obtained.

More recent approaches propose to search for the optimal GMM by means of Markov Chain Monte Carlo methods. Richardson and Green [10] present a Bayesian hierarchical model for mixtures, where they detail an assumed prior distribution for the parameters of a univariated GMM. Then, they propose the Reversible Jump Sampling Algorithm, which refines an initial guess of the GMM by updating the component parameters, splitting/merging components, or adding/deleting components, exploring with this process the space of GMM of variable order defined in the Bayesian priors. Roberts [11] applies a variation of this technique to several clustering problems. In their practical application, Roberts notes that their proposal can get stuck in suboptimal solutions. However, the main problem of this techniques is that demand too much computation to be used in practical applications.

In this paper we describe a method that models accurately data distributions using GMM, avoiding an exhaustive search in the space of feasible GMM and the definition of explicit priors of the GMM parameters. Our proposal makes uses of the EM algorithm to fit GMM to data, determining their number of components and its parameters by means of an iterative procedure. Although our method is sustained in heuristic reasoning, our experiments show that their results are comparable to the ones obtained by exhaustive search methods, but requiring far less computation.

3   Adaptive Gaussian Mixture Modelling

In the modelling of data distributions by GMM, there is the implicit assumption that data can be grouped in normal distributed clusters. Starting from that idea, our proposal try to incorporate the concept of GMM inside a classical hierarchical clustering technique.

3.1   Classical Cluster Analysis

Very popular methods used in Cluster Analysis are the Hierarchical Clustering Algorithms (HCA). This algorithms group data from the computation of its dendrogram (a branching diagram representing a hierarchy based on the degree of similarity between elements in a data set). Among this algorithms, exist two different philosophies: Agglomerative HCAs and Divisive HCAs. The formers construct a dendrogram by establishing initially a cluster in every element in the data set, and fusing them iteratively until a unique cluster is obtained. The result obtained has been proved useful in the initialization step of the EM algorithm. Figure 2 show an example of Agglomerative HCA.

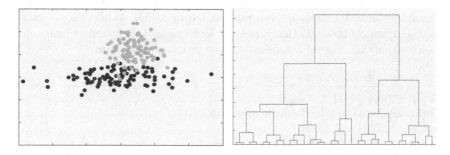

Fig. 2. Data set and its associated dendrogram. *Left*: Data from two gaussian distributions. *Right*: Dendrogram applying the Ward's Method. Although it suggests the presence of several clusters, Fraley and Raftery[8] determine the optimal GMM by evaluating a range of *feasible* number of clusters

Divisive HCA propose to analyse hierarchically the data but in the opposite direction: Setting out from a cluster grouping the whole data set, this one is iteratively subdivided such that the objects in one subgroup are far from the objects in the other groups. When a given number of subclusters is obtained, the algorithm stops. This approach has one major problem: there is no splitting criteria that assures a good partition of data, so incorrect groups are propagated along the cluster hierarchy. We have found that this problem can be avoided if the splitting decision does not mean establishing definitive clusters in the data set, but the verification that the actual clustering give a poor description of the data set. From this idea, we propose to embed the parameterisation of GMM inside the basic procedure of divisive HCA.

3.2   Our Proposal

The simplest GMM to describe a data set is the one with only one component, which is defined by the mean and covariance of the data to be modelled. So being $X = (x_1, \cdots, x_N)$ the data set, a GMM is defined by $\Phi = \{(P(1) = 1, \mu_1 = \mu_X, \Sigma_1 = \Sigma_X)\}$. If this representation describes precisely the real data distribution, there is no need to explain it using more components. Otherwise, more components should be considered. So a criteria to measure the *fitness* of the GMM with respect to data is needed. We define this criteria simply by requiring that the components of a GMM represent normally distributed data clusters. In the first GMM considered, this means to apply a *Test of Multivariate Normality* to X . If it fails, the Gaussian is split in two, and the EM algorithm is applied to make converge the new defined GMM.

When the GMM has more than one component, X is subdivided into clusters by assigning each data element x_k to the component which provides the maximum conditional probability $p(i|x_k)$. Then, the normality of each cluster is checked in decreasing order of its $P(i)$ (so analysing first the components that support more strongly X). When a cluster fails the test, its corresponding component is split in two, the EM is applied to the resultant new GMM, and the overall process is repeated again. We add in this process an stop condition for situations where X cannot be well represented by GMM. With this we want to avoid splitting components that represent *underpopulated* clusters, which appear in such situations. Figure 3 summarises the proposed procedure

---

0 **set** $\Phi \leftarrow \{\Phi_1\} \leftarrow \{(1, \mu_X, \Sigma_X)\}$
1 Sort components in Φ in decreasing order of $P(i)$
2 **set** $i \leftarrow 1, Split \leftarrow FALSE$
3 **while** $i \leq$ NumComp.(Φ) and $Split = FALSE$
    if NumElements$(\Phi_i) > Threshold$ and NormalityTest$(\Phi_i) = FALSE$
    $Split \leftarrow TRUE$
    else $i \leftarrow i + 1$
4 **if** $Split = TRUE$
    $(\Phi_a, \Phi_b) \leftarrow$ SplitComponent(Φ_i)
    set $\Phi \leftarrow \Phi \backslash \{\Phi_i\}$.
    set $\Phi \leftarrow \Phi \cup \{\Phi_a\} \cup \{\Phi_b\}$
    $\Phi \leftarrow$ EM(Φ)
    goto 1.

Fig. 3. Our proposed Adaptive Gaussian Mixture Model Fitting Algorithm

Normality Test. To perform this test we have used the multivariate generalisation of the Wald-Wolfowitz Two-sample test proposed by Friedman and Rafsky [12]. This test determines if two sample sets X and Y are drawn from the same distribution, by evaluating if both are very mixed-up. In the case of multivariate data, this can be discerned by constructing the Minimal Spanning Tree (MST) of the joined data set, and counting the links T that join elements from X to Y.

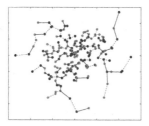

Fig. 4. Minimal Spanning Tree of two data sets corresponding to the same distribution. *Solid lines* correspond to X-to-Y edges

From the observed MST topology the following statistic can be defined

$$W = \frac{T - E[T]}{\sqrt{Var[T]}} \;,\qquad\qquad (3)$$

which it is shown to approach an standard normal distribution for large sample sets. So given a data cluster X, a data set Y can be generated from the cluster mean and covariance (μ_X, Σ_X), and a one-sided test can be performed on the corresponding value of W computed. An evaluation of the performance of this test concerning finite sample sets, as well as a Monte Carlo version of the hypothesis test can be found in [13].

Component Splitting. In the splitting of a component, there is no criterion that is guaranteed to be the correct one (i.e. the one that best describes data).So we put forward subdividing the component into two partially-overlapped new ones, which added recover approximately the divided one. The objective of that is suggesting the necessity of a division, more than establishing one. So we replace a component with parameters $(P(i), \mu_i, \Sigma_i)$ by $(P(i)_a, \mu_{i_a}, \Sigma_{i_a}, P(i)_b, \mu_{i_b}, \Sigma_{i_b})$, where

$$P(i)_a = P(i)_b = \frac{1}{2}P(i) \;,$$

$$\mu_{i_a} = \mu_i + \frac{\sigma}{3}v \;,$$

$$\mu_{i_b} = \mu_i - \frac{\sigma}{3}v \;,$$

$$\Sigma_{i_a} = \Sigma_{i_b} = \Sigma_i \;.$$

v is the eigenvector of Σ_i with the biggest associated eigenvalue, and σ is the square root of the biggest eigenvalue. Figure 5 shows a one-dimensional example of this splitting process.

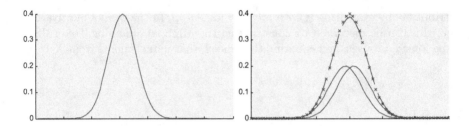

Fig. 5. *Left*: Initial distribution. *Right*: Mixture resulting of the splitting process (*solid line*). Sum of the elements in the mixture (*dashed line*). Initial distribution (*crosses*)

Splitting the component in that way, we make just a weak assumption of how its associated data is really distributed. So we simply separate slightly both gaussians along their principal axe, and we rely on the EM to refine this artificial data partition.

4   Experiments

4.1   Synthetic Data

We have tested the effectiveness of the proposed method by applying it to data drawn from randomly generated GMM. The resultant GMM obtained have been evaluated using the Bayesian Information Criterion (BIC) [14]. This criterion is equivalent to he Minimum Description Length criterion used in information/coding theory. We have chosen the BIC because gives a mathematical formulation of the principle of parsimony in model building, so penalises models that with more mixture components give only a little improvement in their fitting to data. Moreover, the BIC is the most commonly used model selection criterion, and is reported in [7] to have a good performance. Being $X = (x_1, \cdots, x_N)$ a set of samples, and K the amount of parameters of the GMM, the BIC coefficient is computed by the following expression:

$$\mathrm{BIC}(X) = \sum_{i=1}^{N} \log p(x_i) - \frac{1}{2}K \log(N) \ . \tag{4}$$

We have compared the value of the BIC of the solutions obtained, with the one corresponding to the GMM used to generate each data set. Results are provided testing our method, a variation of our method which uses the Ward's clustering algorithm in the splitting of components, and the Fraley and Raftery method[8] (an exhaustive search method that establishes EM initializations using the Ward's clustering technique).

Figure 6 shows the box-and-whisker plots of the results obtained by the different methods. In the graphics, the boxes has lines at the lower quartile, median, and upper quartile values. The lines extending from each end of the

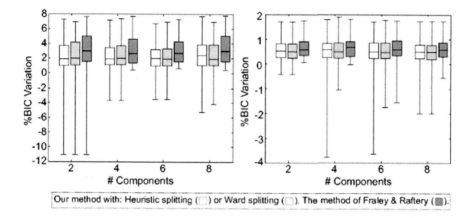

Fig. 6. Percentage of variation between the BIC of the real mixture model, and the converged mixture model. *Left*: Sets of 100 samples. *Right*: Sets of 400 samples

boxes (the whiskers), show the extent of the rest of the data. The test have been done using mixture models with different amount of components, analysing samplings of 100 arbitrary models in each case.

The results manifest that in some cases the different methods have a *better* (i.e. lower) BIC coefficient than the real mixture model, as reveal the negative variations percentages in the graphics. This is due to the fact that some solutions are able to explain a data distribution with less components than the GMM that have generated it. This happens for example when the original GMM has two nearly identical components very close, and the data set does not have enough samples to reveal this. In that case, a single component explains well the data set.

The results also reveal that our method slightly outperform the Fraley and Raftery Method, and that the heuristical splitting rule behaves properly, which discourages the use of more complex heuristic methods. Moreover, if the computational time needed by each algorithm is considered, we find that our proposal is considerably faster than the Fraley and Raftery method (approximately 2.5 times faster for sets of 400 samples), although it has the added cost of a normality test (see Figure 7).

We have also checked our algorithm against data distributions not generated by gaussian mixture models. Figure 8 shows convergences obtained in three-dimensional data sets. As can be seen, our proposal captures reliably the distribution of data sets with a reduced number of components. However, in Figure 8-b) one could argue that the mixture model obtained have more components than the feasible minimum (note the presence of the small tiny component in the top of the data set). However this problem is worthless in most practical applications.

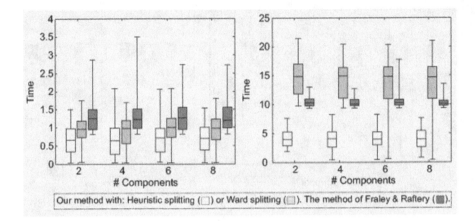

Fig. 7. Time in seconds to converge to the solutions. *Left*: Sets of 100 samples. *Right*: Sets of 400 samples

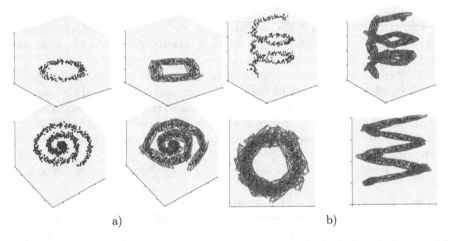

Fig. 8. a) Convergences of the algorithm to a circle and spiral-shaped data set. b) Convergences of the algorithm to a spring-shaped data set

4.2 Automatic Shape Modelling

We have applied our method in the automatic generation of shape models. Shape models are widely used in tracking applications, and they are usually generated from a training set of valid shapes. The shape model have to generate shapes similar to ones contained in the training set, generalising them. Many proposals try to attain this modelling the distribution of the training set [15,16]. By fitting a GMM to the training set, *frontiers* can be established that delimit between valid and invalid shapes. We have applied our method in the context of generating a shape model for a pedestrian tracking application. The training set is formed by vectors containing the coefficients of B-spline curves, which define the outline of a walking pedestrian seen from a lateral point of view. As can be seen in Figure 9, our method extracts the essential information in the data set. Intuitivelly, each one of the GMM components corresponds to the the basic pictures that one may use to describe a walking cycle.

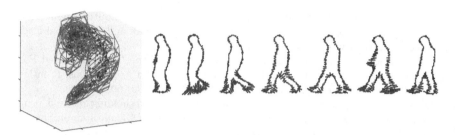

Fig. 9. *Left*: The GMM of 7 components modelling the training set distribution. *Right*: Shapes associated to each component, where the pedestrian contour is drawn from its mean, and its variance becomes apparent in the *lines* across the pedestrian contour

5   Summary and Discussion

In this paper, we have proposed a methodology for learning GMM from data, which is able to select its number of components in an unsupervised way. Our proposal obtains near-to-optimal data models, requiring far less computational time than other proposals in the bibliography. This makes it appealing to be used in practical problems. Our algorithm refines iteratively an initial GMM constituted by only one gaussian, augmenting its order incrementally until a good model is obtained. In our proposal, a good model is identified when the data samples associated to each GMM component follows its respective normal distribution. To check it up, we have applied a normality test to the data associated to each mixture component. If this test fails for a component, this one is split in two, and consequently the order of the GMM is increased. The EM algorithm is then applied to make converge the GMM parameters. This way of proceed implies the assumption that when a GMM fits poorly to the data set, the reason is that too few components have been considered. In general, this can not be took for certain, as depending of the initial state of the GMM the EM algorithm can converge to local maxima solutions. So from this point of view, it seems that our proposal claims to explain data distribution with more components than the really needed. However, the experiments carried out show that our proposal is not affected by this problem, more than other approaches. This can be explained by the method used to add new components to the GMM, which does not induce strong partitions of the data associated to the split component. In practical application, like the unsupervised generation of shape models, our method has proved to be useful, generating compact and coherent generalisations of training sets.

Acknowledgments. This work has been partially supported by TIC2000-0382, Spain.

References

1. Cootes, T., Taylor, C.: Statistical models of appearance for computer vision. Technical report, Wolfson Image Analysis Unit. Imaging Science and Biomedical Engineering, University of Manchester (2000)
2. D.Ponsa, Solé, A., A.López, Cañero, C., Radeva, P., Vitrià, J.: Regularized EM. In Torres, M., Sanfeliu, A., eds.: Pattern Recognition and Applications. Frontiers in Artificial Intelligence and Applications. IOS Press (2000) 69–77
3. Sekita, I., Kurita, T., Otsu, N., Abdelmalek, N.: A thresholding method using the mixture of normal density functions. In: International Symposium on Speech, Image Processing and Neural Networks, Hong Kong (1994) 304–307
4. Bishop, C.M.: Neural Networks for Pattern Recognition. Oxford University Press, Oxford (1995)
5. Dempster, A.P. Laird, N.M., Rubin, D.: Maximum likelihood from incomplete data via the EM algorithm. J. R. Statist. Soc. B **39** (1977) 185–197
6. Oliver, J., R.A., B., C.S., W.: Unsupervised Learning using MML. In: Machine Learning: Proceedings of the Thirteenth International Conference (ICML 96), Morgan Kaufmann Publishers, San Francisco, CA (1996) 364–372
7. Roberts, S., Husmeier, D., Rezek, I., Penny, W.: Bayesian Approaches To Gaussian Mixture Modelling. IEEE Transaction on Pattern Analysis and Machine Intelligence **20** (1998) 1133–1142
8. Fraley, C., Raftery, A.: How many clusters? which clustering method? answers via model-based cluster analysis. Computer Journal **41** (1998) 578–588
9. Bregler, C., Omohundro, S.M.: Surface learning with applications to lipreading. In Cowan, J.D., Tesauro, G., Alspector, J., eds.: Advances in Neural Information Processing Systems. Volume 6., Morgan Kaufmann Publishers, Inc. (1994) 43–50
10. Richardson, S., Green, P.: On Bayesian analysis of mixtures with an unknown number of components. Journal of the Royal Statistical Society (Series B) **59** (1997) 731–758
11. Roberts, S., Holmes, C., Denison, D.: Minimum entropy data partitioning using Reversible Jump Markov Chain Monte Carlo. IEEE Transactions on Pattern Analysis and Machine Intelligence **23** (2001) 909–915
12. Friedman, J.H., Rafsky, L.C.: Multivariate generalizations of the Wald-Wolfowitz and Smirnov two-sample tests. Annals of Statistics **7** (1979) 697–717
13. Smith, S.P., Jain, A.K.: A test to determine the multivariate normality of a data set. IEEE Transactions on Pattern Analysis and Machine Intelligence **10** (1988) 757–761
14. Schwarz, G.: Estimating the dimension of a model. Annals of Statistics **6** (1978) 461–464
15. Heap, T., Hogg, D.: Wormholes in shape space: Tracking through discontinuous changes in shape. In: Sixth International Conference on Computer Vision. (1998) 344–349
16. Cootes, T., Taylor, C.: A mixture model for representing shape variation. Image and Vision Computing **17** (1999) 567–574

Bayesian Classification for Inspection of Industrial Products

Petia Radeva, Marco Bressan, A. Tovar, and Jordi Vitrià

Computer Vision Center, Depart. Informatica, Universitat Autònoma de Barcelona,
Ed. O Campus UAB, 08190 Cerdanyola (Barcelona), Spain
{petia,marco,atobar,jordi}@cvc.uab.es

Abstract. In this paper, a real time application for visual inspection
and classification of cork stoppers is presented. Each cork stopper is represented by a high dimensional set of characteristics corresponding to
relevant visual features. We have applied a set of non-parametric and
parametric methods in order to compare and evaluate their performance
for this real problem. The best results have been achieved using Bayesian
classification through probabilistic modeling in a high dimensional space.
In this context, it is well known that high dimensionality does not allow precision in the density estimation. We propose a Class-Conditional
Independent Component Analysis (CC-ICA) representation of the data
that even in low dimensions, performs comparably to standard classification techniques. The method has achieved a success of 98% of correct
classification. Our prototype is able to inspect the cork stoppers and
classify in 5 quality groups with a speed of 3 objects per second.

1 Introduction

Cork inspection is the least automated task in the production cycle of the cork
stopper. Due to the inspection difficulty of the natural cork material and the
high production rates even the most experienced quality inspection operators
frequently make mistakes. In addition, it is increasingly difficult to find labor
willing and able to do a job that is at the same time both skilled and highly
repetitive. On the other hand, human inspection leads to a lack of objectivity and
uniform rules applied by different people at different time. As a result, there is
a urgent need to modernize the cork industry in this direction. In this paper, we
consider a real industrial computer vision application of classification of natural
(cork) products. Cork products in the manufacture are inspected for different
faults like small holes due to insect attacks, channels due to imprecise stopper
cutting, stopper breaking, cracks and woody surfaces (see fig. 1). Although it
does not seem difficult for human beings to detect different faults in the cork
material, it turns out difficult to precisely formulate the features of the cork
faults due to the porosity of the natural material. It is difficult even for the cork
quality experts to exactly define all cork features that they take into account in
the process of stopper inspection, the feature values and ranges in order to define
whether there is a fault in the cork stopper or the stopper is of poor quality.

M.T. Escrig Monferrer and F. Toledo Lobo (Eds.): CCIA 2002, LNAI 2504, pp. 399–407, 2002.

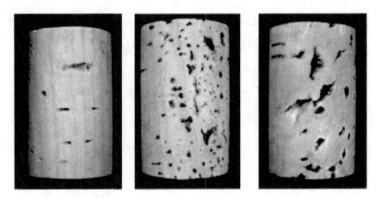

Fig. 1. Cork stopper without fault, woody stopper and a stopper with a crack.

There have been different attempts to develop vision cork inspection systems in the manufacture where the people working in the manufacture should define the values and ranges of the image features and elaborate the decision rules in the process of the stopper inspection. Given that people in the manufacture work with rather qualitative than quantitative information to classify the quality of a stopper, managing such vision cork inspection systems represent a tedious and time-consuming task. The problem of the classification of the cork product in different (in this case, five) quality groups additionally difficult the problem. This fact prevents cork stopper industry from defining and assuring the quality of the products in front of the providers. In order to cope with the problem of subjectivity in the process of cork inspection and quality classification, we study different techniques from the fields of Computer Vision and Pattern Recognition. We propose to apply statistic algorithms in order to analyze a set of 43 different features of the cork (e.g. number of cork holes, average stopper gray level, average holes gray level, holes gray level deviation, length of largest cork hole, etc), that are considered by the operators during the cork analysis.

The problem of high dimensional data classification is presented in section 2, where our approach is exposed. Section 3 describes the visual features used on the characterization of cork stoppers. Section 4 introduces our approach to high dimensional data classification: Class-Conditional Independent Component Analysis. Results and comparisons to other methods are presented in section 5. Finally, in section 6 we expose our conclusions.

2   Classification of High Dimensional Data

High dimensional data appears in many pattern recognition problems such as remote sensing, appearance-based object recognition, text categorization, etc. A stochastic approach for the classification of high dimensional data is always a delicate issue. For linear or quadratic classifiers the number of training samples depends linearly or quadratically on the data dimensionality subset of features, an exhaustive sequential feature selection procedure is required, so the size of the problem grows combinatorially on the dimension. Furthermore, the training sample size needs to increase exponentially in order to effectively estimate the multivariate densities needed to perform nonparametric classification. To avoid the problem of dimensionality, the most common approach is the implementation of feature extraction or dimensionality reduction algorithms. Principal Component Analysis (PCA) [5] is widely used due to its noise reduction properties. PCA treats the data as if they belong to a single distribution, so it has nothing to do with discriminative features optimal for classification. Linear Discriminant Analysis (LDA) [1] can be used to derive a discriminative transformation that is optimal for certain cases. LDA makes use of only second-order statistical information and this causes that if the difference in the class mean vectors is small, the features chosen will not be reliable. More importantly, LDA can not produce more features than the number of classes involved. Feature Subset Selection [6] is yet another perspective on feature extraction. This problem considers a subset of all linear combinations of the original feature set, according to a certain criterion. In order to produce an optimal subset of features, an exhaustive sequential feature selection procedure is required, so the size of the problem grows combinatorially on the dimension.

The approach proposed on this paper does not seek dimensionality reduction followed by the implementation of parametric or nonparametric techniques for density estimation. Instead, it focuses on the higher level statistical properties of the data, which is transformed in such a way that density estimation in the transformed space is simplified and more accurate. For this purpose, we consider an Independent Component Analysis (ICA) [2] representation for each class. This representation projects our data into a space where the components have maximized statistical independence, and in many real problems, sparse distributions. Independence turns an M-dimensional density estimation into M one-dimensional estimations.

3   Cork Stopper Feature Extraction

Our objective is to construct robust algorithms to classify cork stoppers in 5 quality groups (see fig. 2). To this purpose the operators have provided training examples. In order to classify the cork stoppers we extract 43 image features. A blob analysis is done and blob features are considered as follows: stopper area, number of blobs, average blob area, average blob elongation, average blob grey-level, average compactness, average roughness, features of the blob with largest area (area, length, perimeter, convex perimeter, compactness, roughness, elongation, length, width, average blob gray-level, position with respect to the center of the stopper), features of the longest blob, etc.

4   Cork Stopper Feature Classification

The classification problem of cork material is stated as follows: given a set of cork stoppers, each one represented by its image features $H = (h_1, ..., h_L)$, labeled by an operator (the learning set) and a unlabeled set of feature representations

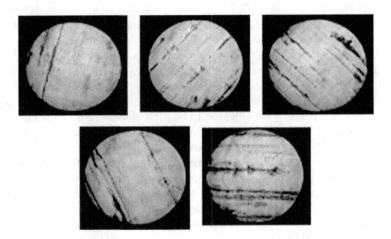

Fig. 2. Cork stoppers of 5 quality groups ordered from best to worst quality (from left to right and from top to down).

from the same group of stoppers (the test set), identify each stopper in the test image set. Under a Bayesian framework, we wish to assign a sample object H_t to a particular class using the probability of misclassification as an error measure. It can be seen that the solution to this problem is to assign H_t to the class that maximizes the *posterior probability*. This is called the Maximum a Posteriori or MAP solution. Using the Bayes rule we can formulate the posterior probability in terms of quantities which are easier to estimate, and the MAP solution takes the form:

$$C_{MAP} = \arg_{k=1,\ldots,K} \max\{P(H_t/C_k)P(C_k)\}$$

where $P(C_k)$ is usually called the *prior* probability, $P(H_t/C_k)$ is referred to as the *class-conditional probability* or, when seen as a function of the parameters, the *likelihood*. In practice, the class-conditional probabilities can be modeled parametrically or non-parametrically from our training set. The priors, as their name indicate, are estimated from our prior knowledge of the problem, and if such knowledge is not available, equiprobable priors are usually assumed.

In our problem, the test object H_t is represented by its feature vector $h_1, \ldots h_L$. If we additionally assume conditional independence in the occurrence of a particular value for the feature vector, the MAP solution takes a new form commonly known as the naive Bayes rule,

$$C_{Naive} = \arg_{k=1,\ldots K} \max \prod_{l=1}^{L} P(h_l/C_k)$$

We still have to model the class-conditional probabilities for the feature vectors. A first approach can be done using the Gaussian Kernel Estimator. The likelihood $P(h_l/C_k)$ is estimated by summing the contribution from a mixture of N Gaussians:

$$P(h_l/C_k) = \sum_{n=1}^{N} \omega_n G(h_l - \mu_n; \Sigma_n/C_k)$$

and a Kernel method is used for parameter selection. (the Kernel method positions a Gaussian on each sample of the distribution).

The precision in the estimation of the class-conditional probabilities $P(H_t/C_k)$ is decisive on the performance of the classifier. This precision is not easy to attain, specially in the case of high dimensional data. In the next subsection we introduce an alternative representation for the data and show how this representation both simplifies and improves the density estimation.

4.1 Class-Conditional ICA for Bayesian Estimation

We choose to represent the data from each class using the transform provided by Independent Component Análisis (ICA) [2]. This linear transform represents our data in a space where the statistical dependence between the components is minimized. After introducing the ICA model, we show how the assumption of independence simplifies density estimation for high dimensional data and analyze the consequences in Bayesian Decision.

The ICA of a D dimensional random vector is a linear transform that minimizes the statistical dependence between its components. This representation in terms of independence proves useful in an important number of applications such as data analysis and compression, blind source separation, blind deconvolution, denoising, etc. Assuming the random vector we wish to represent through ICA has no noise and is zero-centered, the ICA Model can be expressed as,

$$W h = s$$

where h is the random vector representing our data, s is the random vector of *independent components* with dimension $M \leq D$, and W is called the *filter* or *projection matrix*. To avoid ambiguities the filter matrix is chosen such that the independent components have unit variance (they already are zero-centered). The pseudoinverse of W which we will represent as A is called the *mixture matrix*, and it provides an alternative representation of the ICA Model. Given K classes $C - 1, ...C_k$ in a D dimensional space, the ICA model is estimated from the training set for each class. If W_k and s_k are the projection matrix and the independent components for class C_k with dimensions $M_k \times D$ and M_k respectively, then:

$$s_k = W_k(h - \bar{h}^k)$$

Where $h \in C_k$ and $\bar{h}^k$ is the mean of the class, estimated from the training set. We use the following notation for the density distribution of the independent components: $P^k(s)$. The density distribution of the projected data can be rewritten using the independence assumption for the independent components:

$$P^k(s) = \prod_{m=1}^{M_k} P^k(s_m)$$

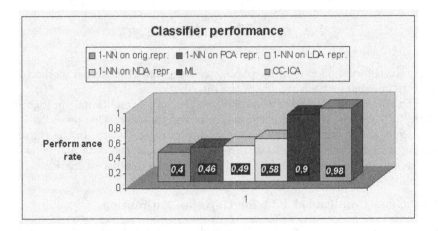

Fig. 3. Classifier Performance.

If H_l is a feature vector from a test object, we can project it into the ICA model learnt for class C_k and obtain the independent components s_l^k. The likelihood of the representative feature vector is obtained from the easier to calculate likelihood of the transformed feature. Using the log-likelihood to turn the products into sums, the Naive Bayes rule can be rewritten as,

$$C_{Naive} = \arg_{k=1,\ldots K} \max \sum_{l=1}^{L} (\sum_{m=1}^{M_k} \log P^k(s_{l_m}))$$

5 Results

In order to compare our approach and to assess which is its performance for the problem of cork stopper classification, we have implemented and tested the following methods:

- The most simple classification technique, the Nearest Neighbor classifier (NN) [3], which classifies each cork representation -on the original space- to the class of the nearest representation of a stopper from the learning set;
- Principal Component Analysis (PCA) of the data for dimensionality reduction, followed by NN classification [3];
- Linear Discriminant Analysis (LDA), as described in [1], followed by NN classification;
- Nonparametric Discriminant Analysis (NDA), as described in [4];
- Maximum Likelihood Classification (ML) using a Gaussian distribution [3];
- Class-Conditional ICA, as described in section 4.

Fig.3 shows the performance of these methods, measured from test data using cross-validation. It can be observed that for this problem, parametric methods are clearly superior to the nonparametric ones. Class-Conditional ICA gets the maximum score.

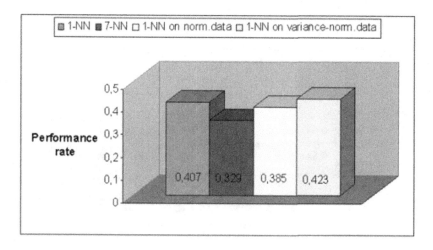

Fig. 4. Dependence of k-NN classifier on representation of data.

In fig.4 the results corresponding to various implementations of the nearest neighbor approach are shown: a) 1-NN classification on original data, b) 7-NN classification on original data, c) 1-NN on linearly normalized data, e) 1-NN on data normalized on variance. Performance of the method is not greatly affected by this fact.

Fig. 5 shows the dependence of the methods on the data representations. Different tests have been run on original data, normalized data and representation on reduced feature spaces by PCA and LDA. Different classifiers have been tested on original and normalized data. The figure shows the final results of applying Nonparametric Discriminant Analysis that gave a success rate of 52% and 58%. After reducing the feature space by PCA to different dimensions the final results were quite similar e.g. classifying a reduced space of 42 and 11 dimensions the success rate was 40% and 46%, respectively. When LDA has been applied to obtain an optimal subspace for class discrimination (the space has been reduced to R4) applying two different training sets, the results achieved 50% of success. Summarizing, the results show that the classification did not depend significantly on the data representation.

The results differed meaningfully when parametric classifiers are applied (see fig. 6). If the mean result of classification success was about 45% with non-parametric classifiers, parametric classifiers doubled the success rate achieving performance rate up to 98%. Furthermore, the results on the graphics show that keeping the full dimensionality of data is important for the classification performance. Maximum likelihood classification of original data got 90% of success while Naive Bayes classification on CC-ICA got 98%. The results from CC-ICA can be explained by a better estimate of the probability density function of the different classes of cork stoppers thanks to complexity reduction when we transform the estimate of an N-dimensional density function to N estimates of 1-dimensional density functions.

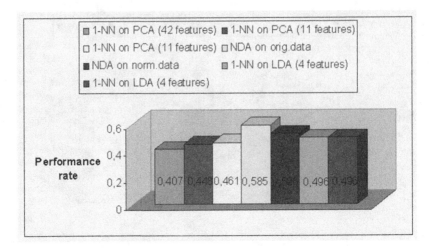

Fig. 5. Dependence on data representation.

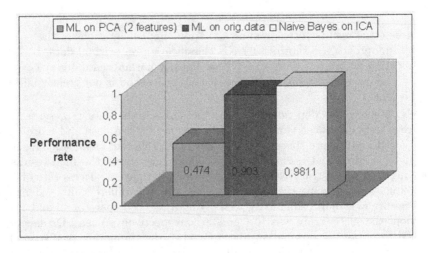

Fig. 6. Results of parametric classification.

6   Conclusions

We have tested the prototype in more than 2000 cork stoppers applying a set of parametric and non-parametric classifiers. Special attention has been paid to data representation. As a result, we have obtained that data representation of feature space of cork stoppers is important to the purposes of the correct classification. In particular, standard techniques for reducing feature space (in terms of blob characteristics of cork stoppers) like PCA and LDA hide the danger of loosing important information for the following process of classification. Our conclusion is that a sufficient representation of the probability density function of full dimensional cork data is the best approach. When faced with this problem, the CC-ICA method proved its advantages as a robust estimate of this function. After testing an extensive set of classifier methods, we concluded that non-parametric group of classifiers showed a low performance rate (mean of 45% of success). In contrast, Bayesian classification achieved high performance rate (mean 94%) in different tests. Although the computational complexity of the selected method of CC-ICA during the learning phase can be high, the process of classification of new examples can be implemented in real-time achieving the best performance rate.

Acknowledgements. This work was supported by IST project IST-1999-20188-CORKINSPECT sponsored by the European Comission. This project was also partially supported by "Ministerio de Ciencia y Tecnologia" grants TIC2000-1635-C04-04 and TIC2000-0399-C02-01. The work developed by M. Bressan has been supported by the Secretaría de Estado de Educación y Universidades of the Ministerio de Educación, Cultura y Deportes de España.

References

1. P. Belhumer, J. Hespanha, and D. Kriegman. Eigenfaces vs. fisherfaces: Recognition using class specific linear projection. *IEEE Transactions on PAMI*, 19(7):711–720, 1997.
2. P. Comon. Independent component analysis - a new concept? *Signal Processing*, 36:287–314, 1994.
3. R. Duda, P. Hart, and D. Stork. *Pattern Classification (2nd Ed)*. Wiley, New York,, 2000.
4. K. Fukunaga and J.M. Mantock. Nonparametric discriminant analysis. *IEEE Transactions on PAMI*, 5(6):671–678, November 1983.
5. I.T. Jolliffe. *Principal Component Analysis*. The MIT Press, 1986.
6. R. Kohavi and G. John. Wrappers for feature subset selection. *Artificial Intelligence Journal, Special Issue On Relevance*, 97(1):273–324, 1995.

Internal and External Coronary Vessel Images Registration

D. Rotger[1], Petia Radeva[1], Josefina Mauri[2], and E. Fernandez-Nofrerias[2]

[1] University Autonoma of Barcelona, Computer Vision Center, Bellaterra
[2] Hospital Universitari Germans Trias i Pujol, Badalona

Abstract. The growing appreciation of the pathophysiological and prognostic importance of arterial morphology has led to the realization that angiograms are inherently limited in defining the distribution and extension of coronary wall disease. By Intravascular Ultrasound images physicians have a picture of the composition of vessel in detail. However, observing an intravascular ultrasound stack of images, it is difficult to figure out the image position and extension with regard to the vessel parts and ramifications, and misclassification or misdiagnosis of lesions is possible. The objective of this work is to develop a computer vision technique to fuse the information from angiograms and intravascular ultrasound images defining the correspondence of every ultrasound image with a corresponding point of the vessel in the angiograms.

Keywords: coronary vessels, lesion detection, angiograms, IVUS, multimodal image fusion, deformable models

1   Introduction

According to the American Heart Association coronary heart disease (CHD) caused 459,841 deaths in the United States in 1998 (1 of every 5 deaths) and in 1999 they estimated 61,800,000 Americans have one or more forms of cardiovascular disease (CVD) [2]. This figure is easy to extrapolate to the most of the developed countries along the western world.

IntraVascular UltraSound (IVUS) images have allowed deepening in the knowledge of the true extension of the coronary vessel illness [6,8,7,4]. It is a tomographic image that provides a unique 2D *in vivo* vision of the internal vessel walls (figure 1(a)), determining the extension, distribution and treatment of the atherosclerotic, fibrotic plaques and thrombus, and their possible repercussion on the internal arterial lumen. Angiography images provide an external vision of the vessel shape and tortuosity (figure 1(b)). The main difference between the ultrasound and the angiography images, as the most used image modalities for vessel diagnosis, deals with the fact that the most of the visible plaque lesions with IVUS are not evident with angiogram.

Studies on intravascular ecography have shown that the reference vessel segment has the 35-40% of its sectional area occluded because of the plaque, although it appears as normal in the angiography. Besides its capacity of demonstrating the plaque extension and distribution inside the vessels, IVUS offer

M.T. Escrig Monferrer and F. Toledo Lobo (Eds.): CCIA 2002, LNAI 2504, pp. 408–418, 2002.

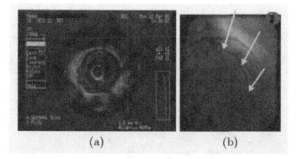

Fig. 1. (a) IVUS image. (b) Corresponding angiography.

information about the composition of the internal lesion; in particular, about calcium deposits as the most important isolated predictors to evaluate if a particular lesion will respond to a catheter treatment.

The studies about stents[1] carried out with IVUS show that the appearance in the angiography of a good stent deployment can hide two possible problems: the incomplete apposition (a portion of the stent is not making pressure on the vessel wall) and the incomplete expansion (a portion of the stent remains closed although the expansion of the rest of the stent areas). Both problems are very significant since they can be worse than the problem they are trying to solve.

Both methods (IVUS and angiogram) provide a lot of information about the internal and the external shape of the coronary vessels, respectively, as well as about vessel therapy (e.g. stent, etc.). The fusion of all this information will allow the physicians to interact with the real extension and distribution of the disease in the space, making easier the arduous task of having to imagine it.

One of the problems of dealing with IVUS is the fact that the images represent a 2D plane perpendicular to the catheter without any depth information. This IVUS property hides the real disease's extension and represents a very unnatural way of conceptualization. The foremost limitation of IVUS on the pre- and post-treatment studies is the need of correlating lesion images in serial studies. This limitation is due to the lack of third dimension that gives much more global information about the internal and external vessel structure. This problem can be solved by using the information given by the angiographies. Using two projections in fixed angles and taking into account the calibration parameters, we are able to create a curve in the space representing the catheter tortuosity. It allows to place IVUS images and define exact correspondence between data coming from both image modalities.

The article is organized as follows: section 2 is devoted to the 3D reconstruction of the catheter from multiple views of angiograms. Section 3 discusses the process of locating IVUS images in space. Section 4 explains the validation process and the article finishes with conclusions.

---

[1] Spiral metallic mesh implanted inside a coronary vessel to save the stenosis effect

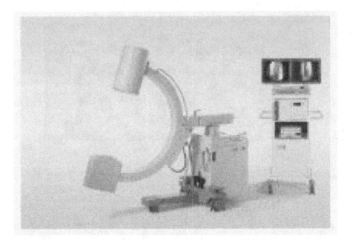

Fig. 2. Siemens C-Arm angiocardiographic system.

2   3D Reconstruction of IVUS Catheter from Angiograms

Intravascular ultrasound images are acquired during a pullback of catheter through the vessel. Using an angiogram-guided process, the catheter is introduced in the vessel to diagnose, and positioned after the vessel lesion. Afterwards, a pullback with constant speed is performed acquiring the IVUS images. Therefore, the obtained stack/sequence of images define a spatio-temporal data that allow to scan the morphology of the vessel lesion in space.

In order to locate IVUS images in space we need an 3D reconstruction of the catheter trajectory. To this purpose, we need to register the catheter in two views of angiograms before and after the pullback of the IVUS catheter. Moreover, to assure precise 3D reconstruction of the catheter from both X-ray views, minimal spatial displacement of the catheter should occur during the process of acquisition of multiple views of X-ray images. A biplane X-ray system provides two views of the catheter at the same time that yield better conditions for a precise 3D reconstruction of the catheter. However, today many hospital environments are equipped with mono-plane X-ray devices (figure 2). Considering the general case, given a mono-plane X-ray image system, we use ECG-gated X-ray images and the patient is asked to keep its breathing during an instant X-ray image acquisition in order to keep minimal spatial displacement of the catheter.

At this stage, our aim is to create a model of the catheter recovering its tortuosity in the space from its projections in both X-ray images. Given that X-ray images are characterized with low signal-to-noise rate, an image enhancement step is necessary in order to improve the visualization and the performance of the following processing algorithms. We perform a histogram-based local image enhancement (see fig. 3) of X-ray images defined as follows:

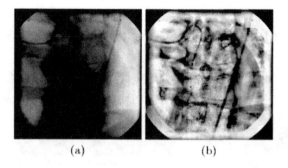

(a)   (b)

Fig. 3. (a) Original X-ray image and (b) after applying local enhancement.

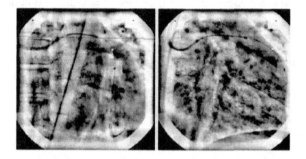

Fig. 4. Localization of catheter head before and after IVUS pullback.

$$I(x, y) = (I(x, y) - a)/(b - a),$$

$$a = min_{x' \in N, y' \in N} I(x', y')$$

$$b = max_{x' \in N, y' \in N} I(x', y')$$

where $N(x, y)$ is a neighborhood of pixel (x, y) of fixed size.

At this stage, the physician is asked to locate the end of the catheter before and after the pullback in both views of angiograms and two 3D points are reconstructed. Note that these points represent the center of first and last IVUS images (see fig.4). A short review of the spatial reconstruction process of an 3D point from its projections is given in the Appendix. For more details, one can consult the reference [1].

The reconstruction of the whole trajectory of the catheter contains 2 steps: a) detection of the catheter projection from both views, and b) reconstruction of its trajectory in space. The process of catheter projection consists of applying the fast marching algorithm that allows to find a path with minimal geodesic distance between two points of an image [5]. The fast marching algorithm is a segmentation algorithm that is based on the level set theory. A surface of minimal action (SMA) is constructed as a level set of curves L where the level corresponds to the geodesic distance $C\{L\}$ from an initial point A. Thus, each

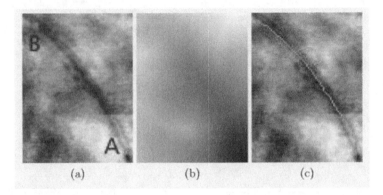

          (a)   (b)   (c)

Fig. 5. (a) Preprocessed X-ray image, (b) surface of minimal action and (c) geodesic path between points A and B.

point, p from the SMA, U has a value $U(p)$ equal to the integral minimal energy of the geodesic path P starting from the initial point A and ending at point p:

$$U(p) = inf_{C\{L\}=p} \int \tilde{P} ds$$

It can be shown that the path of minimal geodesic distance from point B to A can be constructed by following the normal direction of the level sets beginning from this passing through point B (see fig. 5).

Once both projections of the catheter have been obtained, M equidistant points from one of the projections are chosen. It is easy to show that their corresponding points are the intersections of the corresponding epipolar lines and the detected catheter projection in the other X-ray view (see fig. 6). Once defined the corresponding points from both angiograms, their 3D points are reconstructed and interpolated by a spatial B-spline curve [3] that represents the 3D reconstruction of the catheter path done between the beginning and the end of the pullback (see fig. 5). Note that this spatial curve represents the trace of the centers of the IVUS images.

As a result, considering two projections with the catheter stopped before the pullback begins and another two at the end, we create a curve model of the pullback situating one model's extreme at the position of the IVUS catheter before the pullback begins and, using the projections taken at the end of the pullback, situate the ending extreme of the model coinciding with the last position of the catheter during its pullback.

3   Locating IVUS Images on the 3D Catheter Model

Our next goal is to place each IVUS plane in space in order to allow later reconstruction of vessel tortuosity. The position of each IVUS image is determined by IVUS catheter trajectory. Most IVUS acquisition systems grab and save image

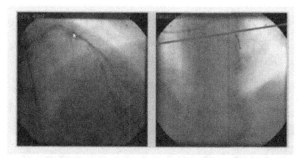

Fig. 6. Each point on the catheter projection defines its corresponding point by the epipolar line on the other X-ray view.

sequence in an S-VHS videotape, some of them assuring constant speed of the catheter movement (0.5mm/sec or 1mm/sec). To analyse IVUS information and fuse it with angiograms, a digitalization of IVUS images is necessary (we used a frame grabber to digitize images at 25 frames per second).

The task of registering IVUS data with angiogram information transforms to situating the IVUS images along the 3D curve. Although using an automatic catheter pullback of constant speed (0.5mm/s), we detected different phases of the catheter movement once the pullback has been switched on: Delay Before pullback (DB), Positive Acceleration phase (PA), phase of Constant Movement (CM) of the catheter and Negative Acceleration phase (NA). Taking into account these characteristics of the catheter movement and the backprojection of the 3D catheter trajectory, we can precisely determine the exact correspondence of IVUS data with the vessel from the angiograms.

We start positioning the last IVUS image at the curve's extreme, corresponding to the ending of the pullback, perpendicular to the curve and go on situating the other images along the curve at a distance given by the pullback speed and the images discretization. To this purpose, we have to calculate the normals and binormals of the 3D curve. Given that we are using B-Splines, we can analytically calculate the Frenet triangle (t, n, b), where t is the curve tangent, n is the curve normal and b is the curve binormal of the B-spline catheter model. We take into account that the IVUS image plane is perpendicular to the catheter that means that coincides with the normal plane defined by the normal and binormal of the catheter model. Thus, taking into account the distance the catheter head has moved from the end point of the catheter model (computed from IVUS data) and the 3D length of the catheter model (computed from the angiograms data), we can locate the IVUS plane in space.

It can be shown that using the triangle of Frenet creates an artificial rotational effect of IVUS planes around the tangent direction of the catheter. In order to minimize the rotational transformation between two consecutive planes, we project the normal and binormal vectors of the previous IVUS plane to the actual one, applying the following formulae:

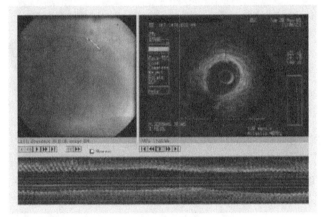

Fig. 7. Registration of angiogram and IVUS data: the red point in the angiogram (top on the left) corresponds to IVUS transversal plane (top on the right) and to the blue line in the longitudinal view of IVUS data (bottom)

$$n_i = n_{i-1} - t_i * (n_{i-1} \cdot t_{i-1})$$

$$b_i = t_i \times n_i$$

Once placed all IVUS images along the 3D curve of the catheter model that is described during the catheter pullback, we can determine the correspondence between IVUS and angiogram data (see fig.7). This fact allows to the user to define corresponding data between angiograms and IVUS data. Note that this fact is very important since angiograms give information about the external view of the vessels, distance to ramifications, lesions, stents and other anatomic parts of the hearts, while IVUS images provide information about the internal shape of the vessel e.g. its morphological structure, vessel wall thickness and composition, plaque, calcium deposits, etc.

4   Results and Validation

Given that the different cycles of the catheter motion depend on the catheter mechanical properties, we estimated them on a phantom provided by Boston Sci (see fig.8). We performed 13 pullback image acquisition on a phantom and estimated the mean and standard deviation of measurements. The mean velocity of the catheter is shown in fig.9 and the estimates of the different phases are given in table 1.

Coupling both information from multimodal images permits to know where IVUS images are in space as well as to show the IVUS image corresponding to given point of the angiography. The user has to select a point on the angiography. Then, automatically its corresponding point on the other X-ray image is determined using the epipolar line. Doing a back-propagation of the given point, the 3D point is reconstructed in the space. From the position of the desired

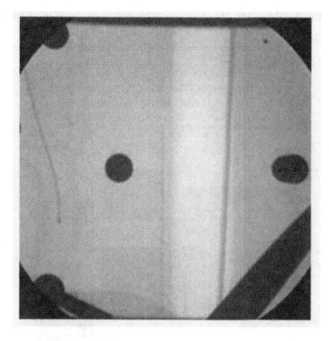

Fig. 8. Phantom used to estimate catheter movement.

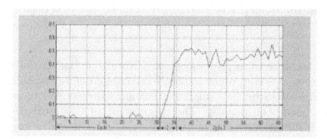

Fig. 9. Average movement speed of the catheter measured on a phantom.

point on the 3D model of the pullback, the nearest IVUS image to the point is determined. Moreover, its position in the longitudinal IVUS images is visualized. Analogously, given a short-axis IVUS image, its position in the IVUS stack is visualized in the longitudinal IVUS data and the corresponding 3D point and its projection on the X-ray image is displayed to the physician (see fig.7).

In order to validate the proposed approach we proceeded with two groups of tests: *in-vivo* and *in-vitro*. The first group of tests had as a purpose to validate the approach avoiding the artifacts coming from the vessel motion. We used 7 IVUS pullbacks on a phantom (see fig. 10) provided by Boston Scientific with a calcium deposit (CD). Once reconstructed the catheter path in space and detected the CD on the IVUS image, we estimated its position in space and

Table 1. Mean and std of different phases of catheter movement.

Phase	mean	std.
DB	$5.2353s(2.6177mm)$	$0.2712s(0.1356mm)$
PA	$0.2749s(0.1375mm)$	$0.1942s(0.0971mm)$
CM	$0.9934s(0.4967mm)$	$0.2031s(0.1015mm)$
NA	$0.0218s(0,0109mm)$	$0.6243(0.3121mm)$

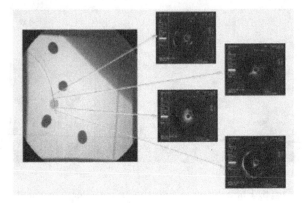

Fig. 10. Validation of localizing calcium deposit by a phantom.

tested its appearance from the angiograms. Note that the second IVUS images in fig. 10 corresponds to a point in the X-ray image before the calcium deposit, while the third IVUS image visualizing calcium corresponds to a point in the X-ray image inside the deposit. The mean error of CD estimate was $0.3mm$ with standard deviation $\sigma = 0.42mm$. We explain the localization error by the human voice annotation of the pullback start and end as well as the impossibility of recording images with precision higher than a second in the current IVUS acquisition systems.

We have also tested the system with 3 real cases of patients in the Hospital Universitari "Germans Trias i Pujol" of Badalona. Patients with vessels lesion that contain calcium deposits have been chosen and again the procedure of validating the registration between angiograms and IVUS images was performed. The results showed a mean error of $\mu_{error} = 1.027mm$ with standard deviation of $\sigma_{error} = 1.2154mm$. The localization error increases due to the vessel motion that leads to less precise 3D reconstruction of the catheter trajectory. Nevertheless, this error is confirmed by the physician team as acceptable to the purposes of lesion localization.

5   Conclusions

Fusing IVUS and angiogram data is of high clinical interest to help the physicians locate in IVUS data and decide which lesion is observed, how long it is, how far from a bifurcation or another lesions stays, etc. In this study, we developed tools to estimate and show the correspondence between IVUS images and vessels in angiograms and have validated it on an IVUS phantom and patient data.

References

1. J.J. Gerbrands A.C.M. Dumay, J.H.C. Reiber. Determination of optimal angiographic viewing angles: Basis principles and evaluation study. *IEEE Medical Imaging*, 13:13–23, 1994.
2. American Heart Association. 2001 heart and stroke statistical update. 2000. Dallas, Texas: American Heart Association, http://www.americanheart.org/.
3. J.C.Beatty B.A.Barsky, R.H.Bartels. *An Introduction to Splines for use in Computer Graphics and Geometry Modeling*. Morgan Kaufmann Publishers INC, 1987.
4. C. Von Birgelen, C. Slager, C. Di Mario, P.J. de Feyter, and W. Serruys. Volumetric intracoronary ultrasound a new maximum progression-regression of atherosclerosis. *Atherosclerosis 118 Suppl*, 1995.
5. Laurent D. Cohen and Ron Kimmel. Global minimum for active contour models: A minimal path approach. *International Journal of Computer Vision*, 24(1):57–78, August 1997.
6. P. Kearney, I. Starkey, and G. Sutherland. Intracoronary ultrasound: Current state of the art. *British Heart Journal (Supplement 2)*, 73:16–25, 1995.
7. M. Sonka, X. Zhang, M. Siebes, and M. Bissing. Segmentation of intravascular ultrasound images: A knowledge-based approach. *IEEE Transactions on Medical Imaging*, 14:719–732, 1995.
8. X. Zhang, C.R. McKay, and M. Sonka. Image segmentation and tissue characterization in intravascular ultrasound. *IEEE Medical Imaging*, 17:880–899, 1998.

Appendix

The projection axes of both systems intersect in the *isocenter* [1]. The acquisition parameters (distances from the X-Ray sources to the image intensifiers, angles of rotation and angulation) are predetermined before the image acquisition process.

The angles by which a left-right movement of a system, with respect to the patient, can be defined determine the rotational angles. The angles by which a movement of a system can be defined towards the head of the patient (Cranial (CR) direction) or the feet (Caudal (CA) direction) determine the angulation angles. With the imaging equipment, the heart can be displayed under X-Ray exposure from Left Anterior Oblique (LAO) view to a Right Anterior Oblique (RAO) view, with either a cranial or caudal angulation. Rotational angles are denoted by α and angulation angles by β. For the frontal and lateral rotation angles $\alpha > 0$ represent LAO views, $\alpha < 0$ represent RAO views; angulation angles $\beta > 0$ represent caudal views and $\beta < 0$ represent cranial views.

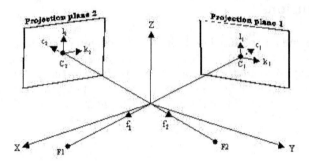

Fig. 11. Global reference system (x,y,z) with the projection planes and their local systems.

For a three-dimensional reconstruction of the catheter, we define a global reference system with origin in the isocenter. We also define a local reference system on the image plane to allow the conversion from an image point to the global reference system (figure 11).

The equations to calculate the local reference system are:

$$k = (0, -\cos\alpha, \sin\alpha)^T$$

$$c = (\sin\beta, \sin\alpha\cos\beta, \cos\alpha\cos\beta)^T$$

$$l = k \times c$$

A data point in the image matrix with coordinate pair (x, y) is transformed into a pair of real coordinates (x_k, y_k) in the projection plane by:

$$x_k = c_{cal}x \text{ and } y_l = c'_{cal}y$$

Here, c_{cal} is the calibration factor and c'_{cal} is the calibration factor corrected for the pixel aspect ratio. We are now able to identify a given point in one image plane in the other image by projecting the epipolar line corresponding to that point in the other projection plane. The epipolar line in the second projection plane of a point d_1 in the first projection plane is computed from:

$$\nu f_1 f_2 + \mu f_1 d_1 + F_1 = x_k k_2 + y_l l_2 + C_2$$

The line $y_l(x_k)$ is represented in the image matrix as y(x) by applying the inverse transform of (1).

The spatial location of a 3D point can be computed from both projections of this point (back-projection). The spatial position of this point is computed by a simple intersection of the lines with vector representation:

$$F_1 + \tau f_1 d_1 \text{ and } F_2 + \sigma f_2 d_2$$

Both parameters τ and σ are solved from any two of the three equations of the vector components by elimination of the other parameter [1].

Textual Descriptors for Browsing People by Visual Appearance

Francesc Tous, Agnés Borràs, Robert Benavente,
Ramon Baldrich, Maria Vanrell, and Josep Lladós

Computer Vision Center, Dept. Informàtica.
Universitat Autònoma de Barcelona,
08193 Bellaterra (Barcelona), Spain
{ftous,agnesba,robert,ramon,maria,josep}@cvc.uab.es

Abstract. This paper presents a first approach to build colour and structural descriptors for information retrieval on a people database. Queries are formulated in terms of their appearance that allows to seek people wearing specific clothes of a given colour name or texture. Descriptors are automatically computed by following three essential steps. A colour naming labelling from pixel properties. A region segmentation step based on colour properties of pixels combined with edge information. And a high level step that models the region arrangements in order to build clothes structure. Results are tested on large set of images from real scenes taken at the entrance desk of a building.

Keywords: Image retrieval, textual descriptors, colour naming, colour normalization, graph matching.

1 Introduction

This work presents a people description module that is a part of a general surveillance system. Images of people entering a building are processed while they are checking-in. Textual descriptors based on people appearance are extracted from these images. This information is saved in a global database where the security personnel of the building can make queries. This might be useful if they can see in a camera inside the building someone who is causing problems, and they want the information that identifies this person. Here is where our module acquires importance, because in our database there is information about the appearance of the people who have entered the building and that has been automatically extracted. With this purpose, the system allows the user to make queries formulated in terms of textual descriptors, to retrieve those images from the database agreeing with the descriptors. Queries are formulated in terms of colour, texture and structural properties of clothes that people is wearing. The system will automatically build an appearance feature vector from an image acquired while people is checking-in in front of the desk.

Retrieving images from large databases using image content as a key is a largely studied problem in Computer Vision. Two major approaches can be

M.T. Escrig Monferrer and F. Toledo Lobo (Eds.): CCIA 2002, LNAI 2504, pp. 419–429, 2002.

stated. First, similarity retrieval consists in looking for images in a database using a reference image as query. The second approach concerns browsing applications and consists in retrieving images by pictorial content, i.e. using symbolic descriptors as indices. Concerning to features used as the basis to formulate queries, usually early visual primitives such as colour and texture are used. Sometimes, structure of objects in the image is also important. A number of works combine low level visual cues as color and texture with higher level information such as structure (e.g. [4,11,15]). Our work follows this approach. Queries are formulated in terms of textual descriptors like 'we are looking for a man in a red shirt' that are compared with descriptions stored in the database that were previously extracted from the input images.

The approach we present in this paper focus on a computational descriptor of clothes features that is based on a three-step process. Firstly, a colour feature vector of pixels is computed, this colour naming step will be the basis of the further analysis. After, a first region initialisation and considering colour properties of pixels plus edges information, a merging process is proposed, it will allow to model any image region. Finally, a high level interpretation of the image regions allows to model an structural description on the clothes that people are wearing. Some examples of content-based queries are shown, they help to illustrate how the proposed descriptor can behave on the system presented.

The paper is organised as follows: section 2 presents how colour has been modelled to provide with a discrete labelling of image pixels, afterwards, in section 3 a region modelling step is done towards to build in section 4 an structural interpretation of people clothes; and sections 5 and 6 briefly present some examples on how the descriptor behaves and a short discussion on them.

2   Colour Modelling

As we have already introduced in the previous section, the final aim of this work is to build with a browsing application based on textual descriptors. One of the most usual ways to describe people appearance is by using colour names for clothes. Therefore, it is quite common to add colour adjectives to clothing articles in order to better specify a visual description.

The association of a colour term or category to a colour perception is a common activity that humans do. The complexity of this process has confronted researchers from visual science to anthropological linguistics for the last twenty years since the book of B. Berlin and P. Kay was firstly published [2]. An excellent compendium of all these research studies can be found in [6], where colour naming can be seen a multi-disciplinary and huge issue.

In this work, we use a statistical colour naming model to build high-level descriptions of scenes. From an engineering point of view we need a colour-naming module that automatically assign colour terms to image regions fulfilling two important requirements: colour categorisation of the model has to correlate with human perceptual judgements and it has to demonstrate invariance to colour and intensity illuminant changes.

To this end, we have based our model on perceptual data we have collected from a psychophysical experiment explained in [1]. In this experiment we have assumed that colour categories can be represented as fuzzy sets and therefore a colour is defined by the membership degrees to the basic colour terms as has been proposed in [8].

To consider the colour constancy problem, that is, we need to assure that colour naming process will be invariant lighting changing conditions of a real-world scene. We will remove this dependency by using the comprehensive colour normalization proposed in [3], and adapted to this problem in [16] since certain constancy on background content can be assumed. Comprehensive normalisation provides a chromatic image representation that present good colour constancy properties. Because, the intensity of image regions is needed on for some specific colours, it will be also normalised and used separately.

Our model will allow to distinguish eight different chromaticities: grey, blue, green, yellow, orange, red, pink, purple. Some of them will be divided in different colour names depending on a normalised intensity value. Thus, grey will provide three different colours: black, grey and white; and within orange chromaticities we will distinguish: dark brown, orange and light brown, which are usual colours when describing clothes. A thresholding process on the normalised intensity space can provide up to twelve distinct colour names, however only chromaticities will be modeled and intensity will be used in the region growing step we present in the following section.

After colour normalisation has been performed the RGB representation will be projected on the 2-D space, we will call **u-v** space, that contains the plane of the chromaticity coordinates. Its origin is located at $(0,0,1)$ and the axis directions are given by the vectors $(1,0,-1)$ and $(-\frac{1}{2},1,-\frac{1}{2})$. It is the space where we fit our colour gaussian model.

Our model of colour naming is inspired by the gaussian model of Lammens [9], that is applied to a 3D chromatic space. We use a multivariant gaussian model that is better adapted to our 2D normalised space. The main idea of the model is to work out the parameters of a multivariant gaussian function for each chromaticity, **x**, and is given by

$$G_{\mu,\Sigma}(\mathbf{x}) = \frac{1}{\sqrt{(2\pi)^d}\sqrt{\|\Sigma\|}} e^{-\frac{1}{2}(\mathbf{x}-\mu)^T \Sigma^{-1}(\mathbf{x}-\mu)} \tag{1}$$

where μ is the vector (μ_1, μ_2) and Σ is a symmetrical matrix given by

$$\Sigma = \begin{pmatrix} \sigma_0 & \sigma_1 \\ \sigma_1 & \sigma_2 \end{pmatrix} \tag{2}$$

Estimation of μ and Σ is achieved by minimizing a similar expresion as the one proposed by Lammens in [9], that considers the set of points in the convex hull of each colour, the center of the current colour and the centers of the rest of the colours. The fitting process is done on a sample of 248 labelled colour points. The obtained parameters are given in table 1.

Table 1. Estimated parameters, μ and Σ.

Colour	CId	μ_1	μ_2	σ_0	σ_1	σ_2
Grey	1	0.447963	0.657606	0.004601	-0.000544	0.000862
Blue	2	0.366035	0.689680	0.001789	-0.000701	0.001396
Green	3	0.383917	0.577454	0.008190	0.003398	0.006287
Yellow	4	0.568662	0.595679	0.008864	-0.001249	0.001595
Orange	5	0.571394	0.675418	0.007354	0.001578	0.003556
Red	6	0.572352	0.758278	0.008407	0.005216	0.004064
Pink	7	0.474046	0.720353	0.002485	0.001841	0.002460
Purple	8	0.419032	0.715220	0.000389	-0.000038	0.001498
Skin	9	0.8641	0.3961	0.004703	-0.000601	0.000792

Due to the specific character of the application in which this work is framed, we will add the skin colour model. It is used in the structure interpretation step, and it will be indispensable in further extensions of the clothes interpretation. Thus, skin color model has been estimated from a set of 11250 samples of skin image regions. The skin colour sample is mapped in the **u-v** space in figure 1.(a), and in figure 1.(b) we can see the guassian distribution of this skin sample, that validates the model used.

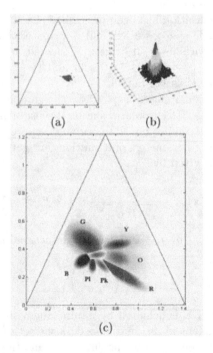

Fig. 1. Colour modelling. (a) Skin samples on **u-v** space, (b) 2D histogram of the skin sample. (c) Adjusted colour gaussian model.

Once, the colour models have been adjusted we can build a complete colour descriptor, C, for any pixel, $I_{x,y}$, of an image I, by

$$C(I_{x,y}) = (p_{x,y}^1, ..., p_{x,y}^9) \tag{3}$$

where $p_{x,y}^i = G_{\mu,\Sigma}(x,y)$, being the parameters μ and Σ of the colour identified by i in table 1.

3   Region Modelling and Segmentation

Colour is an early visual primitive that is used as a coarse indexing cue to retrieve images from the database. This would allow to look for people wearing clothes of a certain colour. In a finer indexing mechanism we look for region structure in the image. With this purpose, once pixels have been colour labeled, they are hierarchically clustered in order to describe the image in terms of a region relational structure. The segmentation of these regions is formulated in terms of colour and texture homogeneity. This relational description of images in terms of regions labeled by basic colour terms would allow to convert textual description queries to a bi-level indexing formulation, namely, colour and structure for browsing images agreeing with the description.

Thus, we define a *region relational graph* $G = (R, E, L_R, L_E)$ where R is a set of image regions obtained after a segmentation process, E is a set of graph edges representing region relationships, and L_R and L_E are two labeling funtions for graph nodes (image regions) and edges respectively defined as follows. Given an image region, $r \in R$, the region labeling function is defined as $L_R(r) = [T(r), BB(r), P(r), A(r), C(r), Z(r)]$. Where the former attributes represent, respectively, type, bounding box, position, area, colour and zone of the region, r. Among the attributes that characterize a region, let us further describe *Type*, *Colour* and *Zone*. $T(r)$ identifies wether a region is textured or filled by an homogeneous color (referred as plain region in this paper). $C(r)$ is a vector attribute that represents a color of a region as it has been defined in Eq. 3 for an image pixel. Finally, $Z(r) = \{face|hair|hands|clothing\}$ classifies a region as belonging to one of the four classes in which the image is presegmented using information of skin colour and region position. The edge labeling function L_E stores information about region adjacency,

Once we have described the attributed graph model that represents an image in terms of its regions and drives the retrieval, let us describe the segmentation process that computes such graph from an input image. Informally speaking, the process can be described as a region growing in which at each iteration those neighbouring regions having a similar color are clustered in a new region. Actually, the region growing is organized in two stages: first, a presegmentation step performs an initial construction of a region adjacency graph in which colour and texture homogeneity is used as a cue to extract the regions. The second step is a graph clustering procedure that iteratively merges graph regions in terms of the similarity of their attributes defined by L_R.

Image Presegmentation

The presegmentation process is mainly focused on the discrimination between textured and plain regions. Following the idea given by Karu et al. [7], we define a pixel to be candidate to belong to a textured region if there exists a spatially uniform distribution of local gray-value variations around it. We state this variations in terms of the density of contour pixels in a certain region of interest. Thus, we use the boundary information to come apart textured regions from the plain ones. Specifically we apply the Canny edge detector to distinct between contour pixels and non contour pixels. A pixel will be candidate to belong to a textured region if we can not find any area of K non contour pixels adjacent to it, being the threshold K preset in terms of the desired allowable density of the texture. Once textured regions have been discriminated, a colour quantization is applied to the remaining pixels to initialize plain regions. We use the Prosise's method [13] that is based on the Gervautz algorithm [5] for colour quantization. The presegmentation process is illustrated in Fig. 2.

Fig. 2. Original image, contour image, quantization, initial regions.

Construction of the Region Relational Graph

The presegmented image is structured in a region relational graph G according to the definition given above. Two issues must be further described at this point, namely, given a graph region r, how the region attributes $C(r)$ and $Z(r)$ are computed. Given a region r, $C(r)$ is computed by the average of the probabilities of the pixels of the region of being i-labeled. Equivalently to image pixels (see eq. 3), we can see the colour of a region as a vector of probabilities of length N where in each position we have the probability of the region of being i-labelled, i.e. $C(r) = c = [P_1, ...P_N]$. The attribute $Z(r)$ classifies a region as belonging to one of the four parts of the person. We use the information of the colour and the position of the region. Concerning to colour, we discriminate between skin-labeled or not skin-labeled regions. We say that a region is skin labeled when the maximum probability in the vector $C(r)$ is associated to the skin label. We decide if a region is located in the lower part of the image or in the upper depending on the position of the center of $BB(r)$ regarding to the center of the bounding box that comprises all the image regions. Thus, given a region r, we decide $Z(r)$ depending on its skin label and the position with regard to the upper-lower part of the image.

Graph-Based Region Growing

The analysis of the colour distribution is one of the main methods to segment an image. However in some cases the colour information is not complete enough and is combined with edge information. Depending on when contours are combined with colour we can distinguish between embedded segmentation or post-processing segmentation [12]. Our region segmentation process belongs to the first class.

At this point we have a set of segmented regions organized in a graph. A graph clustering algorithm is then applied by iteratively merging neighbouring regions. Informally speaking the region growing process can be described as a graph contraction iterative procedure such that, at each iteration, two neighbouring regions (graph nodes) are merged according to a similarity criterion formulated in terms of colour similarity and the significance of image contours between regions.

Let G^0 be a region graph obtained after the presegmentation step described above. Formally, the region growing can be described as a graph hierarchy $G^0 \subset \ldots \subset G^n$ such that at iteration i two regions $r_a, r_b \in R^i$ are merged in a new region $r_c \in R^{i+1}$ if their distance $D(r_a, r_b)$ is under a given threshold T. The distance D is formulated combining information about colour and contours as follows:

$$D(r_a, r_b) = w_1 D_1(r_a, r_b) + w_2 D_2(r_a, r_b)$$

where D_1 is the colour distance, D_2 is the boundary distance, and w_1 and w_2 are two weighting factors empirically set. The colour distance is defined in terms of the distance between the colour probability vectors as follows:

$$D_1(r_a, r_b) = \sum_{k=1}^{N} |(C(r_a) - C(r_b)|$$

Concerning to the second merging criterion, in order to decide to join two candidate regions we also analyse the presence of contours in their common boundary. Then we establish a measure that relates the amount of contours between the two regions with regard to the length of this boundary. We define the common boundary between regions r_a and r_b as the set of pixels $\in r_a$ that have at least one adjacent pixel $\in r_b$. Let us denote as $LCB(r_a, r_b)$ as the cardinality of the set $CB(r_a, r_b)$. On the other hand, let B be the contour pixels of the image provided by the Canny edge detector (but now using more relaxed values of the parameters than the values we have used to detect textured regions). Let $LCBB(r_a, r_b)$ be the number of contour pixels at the boundary between r_a and r_b, i.e. the cardinality of the set $CB(r_a, r_b) \cap B$. Then, D_2 is defined as follows:

$$D_2(r_a, r_b) = \frac{LCBB(r_a, r_b)}{LCB}$$

We must notice that either textured and plain regions are merged according to the former criteria.

When the two criteria allow to merge two neighbouring nodes, a new instance of the graph is generated at level $i + 1$ such that regions r_a and r_b have been joined in a new region r_c. The new graph node representing r_c is connected by new graph edges in E^{i+1} to those nodes of R^i such that r_a and r_b were connected. The region attributes $L_R^{i+1}(r_c)$ are computed as the combination of the attributes $L_R^i(r_a)$ and $L_R^i(r_b)$. Particularly, the computation of the colour attribute of the new region is computed as follows:

$$C(r_c) = C(r_a)\frac{A(r_a)}{A(r_a) + A(r_b)} + C(r_b)\frac{A(r_b)}{A(r_a) + A(r_b)}$$

The region growing steps are illustrated in Fig. 3.

Fig. 3. Final regions, zones (hair, face, clothing), labelled image, average RGB.

4   Structure Interpretation

The region-based information encoded in the graph obtained after segmentation is used to match known clothing configuration models. These clothing configuration is the basis for the formulation of queries. The interpretation of the region structure as the description of the clothing must adjust to several predefined models or classes. These classes are formulated in terms of the number or garments, their position and their size. We understand the garments like ordered layers from the most extern to the most internal. For example we describe a person wearing a black jacket and a blue shirt like a structure of two layers, the first black and the second blue. In terms of regions, this can be seen as two black outer regions and one blue inner region.

When images are encoded using a spatial information on regions, indexing is well performed using approaches based on 2D-strings for pictorial description [10]. Shearer et al. [14] recently proposed a variation formulated in terms of inexact isomorphism detection between region graphs representing two images. Our method is inspired by that one. Thus, the clothing configuration models are formulated in terms of ideal position of regions and the corresponding region graph. Graph matching algorithms are time consuming, this is a drawback when retrieval represents browsing of a large database and, thus, compare a given graph with a number of candidate ones. For the sake of increasing the speed in the indexing process, we simplify the matching by defining each model in terms of a grid that divides the body of a person in four zones of interest in relation to the face that we have located before. So we distinct two zones vertically aligned

under the face, another on the left and another on the right. This zoning model
can be seen in Fig. 4. Each model is described in terms of the presence of regions
with certain features in each zone. For example, the model corresponding to three
clothing layers like a jacked, a buttoned up shirt with a tee-shirt underneath, is
stated in terms of regions like two regions of similar colour label covering outer
zones, one region in the bottom central zone and, finally, a small region in the
top central zone. Thus, given a segmented image, it is assigned to a class with a
distance D_w that is computed in terms of the overlapping area of input regions
to each zone. The strategy to assign images to a clothing class is driven by a
decision tree. The process of retrieving images from the database similar to a
given description consists in looking for the class model corresponding to the
query and compute its similarity regarding to the region graphs representing the
database images. In the example of Fig. 4, since there is a region that covers
zones A, B and D, and another small region in zone C, the interpretation result
in terms of clothing configuration is "outer garnet coloured clothe and inner
black coloured clothe".

Fig. 4. Image interpretation in terms of the structure of regions.

5   Results

To test the algorithms a ground truth has been constructed with 1000 images of
people acquired in a reception desk of a real environment. For security purposes,
sometimes a person must be identified by making a query into the database
in terms of a description. In the ground truth, we also store the reference description of each image made by a human operator. This allows to evaluate the
performance of our algorithms. In order to asses how the system works, Fig. 5
illustrates the ten most similar images to the query "people who wears a clothing
structure consisting in two layers". For each image we show the original one and
the colour labeled. If we refine this query adding colour information "people who
wears a clothing structure consisting in two layers and colour of the second layer
= White" the system provide us only the images (a), (b) and (c).

6   Conclusions

In this paper we have proposed an algorithm for people retrieval from a database
in terms of descriptors based on colour, texture and structural properties of

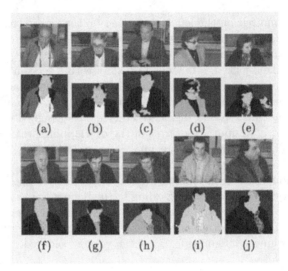

Fig. 5. Results of a simple query.

clothes that people is wearing. This algorithm is used in a real environment by surveillance staff to identify people that has been registered in a check-in desk. The key issues of the system are first, the use of a colour naming process that, considering the colour constancy problem, labels the image pixels with usual colour names of natural language. Secondly, the image segmentation in terms of colour and texture information obtaining an attributed graph structure. Region structure and colour labels are then mapped to people clothing descriptions that form database queries. The use of probability characterizing colour labels and a distance measure between region graphs allow the system to retrieve ranked images in terms of a confidence factor.

The system has been tested using a comprehensive set of images taken in a real environment. Although the results are just preliminary, the overall success of retrieving the desired image within the top ten given a query can be rated near a 70%. A further study on such ratio gives a 81% of success in the colour labeling step and a 75% in the description of structure in terms of clothing configuration. Errors in colour labeling often arise due to subjectiveness in the perception of colours. For example, regions labeled as dark blue can be perceived as black by the human operator that formulates the query. On the other hand, the right identification of clothing configuration is sensitive to occlusions or non frontal position of the people in the image.

From the point of view of the application, since it is not required that the system retrieves just one image after a query but a set of similar ones, the ratio of error is near acceptable levels. Issues to further study and that would contribute to significantly improve the retrieval are: first the inclusion of skin labeled regions in the structural matching. This would allow to identify in the same structure face hands and arms, allowing additional descriptors of clothes such as short/long-sleeved. Secondly, hair is currently segmented using regions located on top of the face region, however the hair colour model should be better learned from examples. Finally, although region interpretation tolerates distortions, important variations in the ideal frontal position of people can make the system misclassify the image. The inclusion of symmetry cue with the skin colour identification would strengthen the recognition of clothing configurations.

Acknowledgments. This work has been partially supported by projects CI-CYT TIC2000-0382 and Inverama S.A.

References

1. Robert Benavente and Maria Vanrell. A color naming experiment.Technical Report 56,Computer Vision Center,2001.
2. B. Berlin and P. Kay. *Basic Color Terms: Their Universality and Evolution.* University of California Press, Berkeley 1969.
3. G.D. Finlayson, B. Schiele, and J.L. Crowley. Comprehensive colour image normalization. In *Proceedings of 5th ECCV'98* pages 475–490, 1998.
4. J. Forsyth, D.A. and Malik, M.M. Fleck, H. Greenspan, T.K. Leung, S. Belongie, C. Carson, and C. Bregler. Finding pictures of objects in large collections of images. *Object Representation in Computer Vision,* pages 335–360, 1996.
5. M. Gervautz and W. Purgathofer. A simple method for color quantization: Octree quantization. *Graphics Gems I,* pages 287–293, 1990.
6. C.L. Hardin and L. Maffi *Color categories in thought and language.* Cambridge University Press,Cambridge,1997.
7. K.Karu, A.K. Jain, and R.M. Bolle. Is there any texture in the image? In *Proceedings of 13th.* ICPR pages 770–774, August 1996. Viena, Austria.
8. P. Kay and C.K. McDaniel. The linguistic significance of the meaning of basic color terms. *Language* 3(54):610–646, 1978.
9. J.M. Lammens. A somewhat fuzzy color categorization model. In *Proceedings of ICCV-95,* 1995.
10. S.Y. Lee and F.J. Hsu. 2D C-string: A new spatial knowledge representation for image database systems. *Pattern Recognition,* 23(10):1077–1087, 1990.
11. P. Lipson, E. Grimson, and P. Sinha. Configuration based scene classification and image indexing. *Computer Vision and Pattern Recognition,* 1997.
12. X. Muñoz. *Image Segmentation Integrating Color,* Texture and Boundary Information. PhD thesis, Universitat de Girona, 2001.
13. J.Prosise. Wicked code. *MSJ* October 1997.
14. K. Shearer, H. Bunke, and S. Venkatesh. Video indexing and similarity retrieval by largest common subgraph detection using decision trees. *Pattern Recognition,* 34(5): 1077–1091, 2001.
15. M. Stricker and A. Dimai. Color indexing with weak spatial constraints. *Storage and Retrieval for Image and Video Databases,* 2670:29–40, 1996.
16. M. Vanrell, F. Lumbreras, A. Pujol, R. Baldrich, J. Lladós, and J.J. Villanueva. Colour normalisation based on background information.In *Proceedings of the 8th ICIP,* volume 1, pages 874–877, October 2001. Thessaloniki, Greece.

Author Index

Lecture Notes in Artificial Intelligence (LNAI)

Lecture Notes in Computer Science